A
Bigger
Picture

To Lucy

MALCOLM TURNBULL

A
Bigger
Picture

BOOKS

Published in 2020 by Hardie Grant Books,
an imprint of Hardie Grant Publishing

Hardie Grant Books (Melbourne)
Building 1, 658 Church Street
Richmond, Victoria 3121

Hardie Grant Books (London)
5th & 6th Floors
52–54 Southwark Street
London SE1 1UN

hardiegrantbooks.com

 A catalogue record for this
book is available from the
NATIONAL LIBRARY OF AUSTRALIA National Library of Australia

A Bigger Picture
ISBN 978 1 74379 563 7

10 9 8 7 6 5 4 3 2 1

Cover and text design by John Canty
Typeset in Adobe Caslon Pro by Cannon Typesetting
Cover photographs by Peter Brew-Bevan
Printed by McPherson's Printing Group, Maryborough, Victoria

The paper this book is printed on is certified against the
Forest Stewardship Council® Standards. FSC® promotes
environmentally responsible, socially beneficial and
economically viable management of the world's forests.

Contents

CONTENTS

I

Beginnings

(1954–82)

CHAPTER 1

Coral and Bruce

What are my first memories of my parents? The earliest are almost all of Mum. Tall, dramatic and eloquent, Coral Magnolia Lansbury was a writer – of radio serials, of plays, of poetry and, in her later years, of novels. When I was small, her writing was confined to radio serials – each episode 15 minutes long and all involving lengthy and complex romances. The longest running one was *Portia Faces Life*, and then there was *The Reverend Matthew*, among others. I didn't listen to them on the radio but often heard them as they were being written. Mum usually banged them out on an old Remington typewriter, sitting at her desk in the living room of our flat at 119 New South Head Road, Vaucluse. But when she was selling more serials than usual, an old lady (who was probably in her 40s!) would be enlisted to type at Mum's dictation. Some weeks she'd write half-a-dozen 15-minute episodes.

I'd sit under the desk watching my mother, one long leg flung over the armchair, head swung back as she became transported in the drama of her imagination. She'd act out every part:

> George [*deep voice, on the verge of tears*]: Forgive me, Maria, forgive me. [*He sobs*]
>
> Maria [*cool and deadly*]: This is the end, George. [*Sound of revolver being cocked*]
>
> George [*sensing his doom*]: No, Maria, remember our love, remember … [*gunshot*]
>
> Maria [*screaming*]: What have I done?

All this was dutifully transcribed by the typist without any sign of emotional recognition. Not sobs, screams or the loud BANG of the gunshot caused her to turn a hair.

Portia ran for nearly 20 years and over 3500 15-minute episodes, of which Coral wrote many. *Reverend Matthew* went for years too, and over a thousand episodes.

Mum's parents started their family late. May Lansbury was eight years older than her husband, Oscar, and gave birth to Mum's only sibling, also named Oscar, when she was 39. Coral was born seven years later.

My uncle Oscar was a keen sailor and, according to Mum, ran away to sea to join the merchant navy. He finished his working days as the harbourmaster in Port Adelaide.

Coral was a brilliant student, both at North Sydney Girls High School and at Sydney University. She won prizes in history as well as the Henry Lawson Prize for Poetry in 1948 for a verse play about an Aboriginal maiden called 'Krubi of the Illawarra'. She was both delighted and appalled when I won the same prize in 1974 for a hundred lines of rhyming doggerel I'd put together as a speech for a Union Night Debate, with the characteristically frivolous topic of 'A woman's just a woman, but a good cigar is a smoke'.

My maternal grandparents were both actors. They'd come out to Australia from England in the early 1920s as part of the cast of *The Vagabond King*. Oscar, a baritone, had a wonderfully rich and beautiful voice. He spoke in perfect unaccented English. He didn't sound posh or grand, nor did he ever acquire an Australian twang.

Oscar's father, Arthur Lansbury, was a dentist who immigrated to Australia in 1884. After stints in Sydney, Newcastle and Brisbane – where Oscar was born in 1892 – Arthur established his practice in Roma. In his advertisements in *The Western Star and Roma Advertiser*, he claimed to be 'the only qualified dentist west of Brisbane'. He returned to England with his family in 1901.

Arthur's brother, George Lansbury, had also immigrated to Australia in 1884 but stayed only a year and returned to England to immerse himself in radical politics. He helped found – and later led – the British Labour Party. George Lansbury was best known for championing women's right to vote, hence his nickname 'Petticoat George'. He was also a Christian socialist, a pacifist and a passionate believer in unilateral disarmament, an idealistic position that became increasingly unrealistic as the dictators rearmed in the 1930s.

George's son Edgar, also a Labour politician, married an Irish actress, Moyna Macgill. Their daughter, the actress Angela Lansbury, came out to Sydney in 1958 for the filming of *Summer of the Seventeenth Doll*, based on Ray Lawler's 1957 play about the lives and loves of Queensland cane cutters. A sign of the times: none of the four leads were Australians – but Angela certainly did a better Australian accent than Ernest Borgnine!

Meeting Aunty Angela and playing with her (somewhat older) children is among my first memories. More than 50 years later we met again when she was in Australia appearing in the stage version of *Driving Miss Daisy*. Angela and Mum shared a distinctively Lansbury look.

Oscar was a star of radio, first as a singer and then as a master of sound effects. He'd performed in music hall as well as opera, and he taught me several music-hall numbers, including 'The Man Who Broke the Bank at Monte Carlo'. Every number had its own 'patter', a line of chat that went before, during and at the end of the song as part of the entertainment.

As a child, I loved visiting Pop Lansbury's studio at 2GB, an Aladdin's cave of delights. The radio serials were produced live in the studio and so, at the appropriate moment, Oscar might have to fire a gun, bang a drum, drop something in a barrel of water, close a door, break a window, simulate the wind through the trees or not too quietly creep up a gravel path.

It was probably because of this connection with radio drama that Mum began writing radio plays at 16. An early one was a Gothic romance called *Ringarra*, which involved a fierce, giant pig ravaging the Australian countryside (*Hound of the Baskervilles Goes Down Under*, you could say). She later turned that into a novel. There were many others, all dramatic, all romantic, with handsome heroes and swooning but plucky heroines. While studying English and history at Sydney University, Coral supported herself by writing.

Two of her university friends I remember coming to dinner when I was very young were Neville Wran and Lionel Murphy. The former would go on to be premier of New South Wales and the latter a senator for New South Wales, attorney-general in the Whitlam government and finally a High Court judge. Neville and Lionel were firm friends at university. Where Neville was as handsome as any movie actor, Lionel was quite the reverse. His red and bulbous nose later became a cartoonist's delight. Murphy's career was colourful and controversial, but even his harshest critics (and he had many of them) would concede that he was remarkably charming. He could make the dullest dinner companion feel that he or she was the most fascinating person he'd ever met. I brought that up with him once, and he replied, 'While men are seduced through their eyes, women are seduced through their ears.'

At university, Mum and Lionel had dated briefly. But I know very little about her romantic life prior to my birth. On 20 February 1953, Coral made a most improbable marriage to George Edwards, a 67-year-old radio actor and producer. He was known as 'the man of a thousand voices' for the way he used to write, produce and then act all the parts in his own radio plays. But not long after the wedding (Edwards's fourth) the groom fell ill, and he died on 28 August that year. Decades later, Mum claimed that her fearsome mother had bullied her into this match. It can't have been for financial benefit as very little of Edwards's modest fortune found its way to his young widow, despite the best efforts of her lawyer, Neville Wran.

However, the young widow wasn't entirely bereft of companionship. Her marital home was a comfortable apartment at 14 Longworth Avenue, Point Piper, overlooking Lady Martins Beach. In the back basement of the rather more modest block of flats next door at number 12, then called Kenilworth, there lived an impecunious but devilishly handsome young salesman called Bruce Turnbull.

According to Mum, Bruce won her over by swimming up and down the beach pretending to be a porpoise. This may seem an improbable mode of seduction and at odds with Murphy's theory. But, in any event, I am proof that the seduction was successful. I was born on 24 October 1954, though my parents didn't marry until the following year. I hope this fact makes the thousands of people who've called me a bastard feel vindicated.

When he and Coral met, Bruce didn't have a bean and Coral was not yet established as a scriptwriter. It wasn't long before the widow was chucked out of the Edwards beachside apartment and the pair found themselves living in a series of small flats in the eastern suburbs. The first one I remember was the flat at 119 New South Head Road.

Coral and Bruce were an unlikely couple. She was a university graduate, a writer and prodigious reader of novels, poetry, history; never happier than in a library. Her friends were mostly writers and actors like herself, although she was a keenly competitive squash player. Bruce's parents were both schoolteachers. He was born in Tumut, but spent most of his childhood in the coalfields of the Hunter Valley, playing rugby for Maitland. At 16 he left Cessnock High and worked as an apprentice electrician in the coalmines. After the war he went into sales. By the mid-50s, he'd become a hotel broker. Bruce wasn't an intellectual; he wasn't a reader. He regretted not having finished high school or having gone to university. The fact that both of his parents were better educated than he was seemed to prey on him.

His father, Fred Turnbull, had been born on the family farm at Euroka, in the Mid North Coast of New South Wales. He started work cutting timber on the Comboyne Plateau and then took up school teaching before volunteering to fight with the Australian Imperial Force in 1915. Despite being gassed in the First World War, he re-enlisted to service in the Second as a captain. I still have his sword.

Like many bushmen of his era, Fred was extremely well read. He knew off by heart the works of Henry Lawson, William Ogilvie and Banjo Paterson, and most of Shakespeare as well. Fred and my grandmother, Mary, or 'Top', retired to a fibro cottage at Wangi Wangi on Lake Macquarie and I often stayed with them: days filled with fishing on the lake for flathead, building steps down to the beach where Fred kept his boat or pottering about in his workshop. I'm not sure that reciting bush ballads helped our fishing expeditions, but I loved listening to him.

Fred's erudition at full flight did have its embarrassing moments. Occasionally, we'd go into Newcastle on some retail expedition or other and generally found our way to the large co-op known as The Store. One day, when I was about seven or eight, Fred was having no luck getting served. The sales assistant gave my grandfather a pretty rude brush-off, and so the old man drew himself up to his full height and delivered Coriolanus's contemptuous denunciation of Rome:

> You common cry of curs! whose breath I hate
> As reek o' the rotten fens, whose loves I prize
> As the dead carcasses of unburied men
> That do corrupt mine air.

And concluding, as he strode out (me following, mystified, in his wake):

> Despising, for you, the city, thus I turn my back:
> There is a world elsewhere.[1]

The Turnbull side of the family had settled in Australia in 1802 in the shape of John Turnbull and his wife, Ann Warr, and four children. They were Presbyterian Scots, and they'd made an epic sea voyage of 121 days on the *Coromandel*. As free settlers they were given land on the Hawkesbury River, where they helped build, in 1809, the Ebenezer Chapel, the oldest church building in Australia.

John Turnbull was 51 when he arrived at Sydney Cove. Family legend has it that Governor King, who went down to welcome the colony's newcomers, greeted my forebear with the words, 'What are you doing here, old man, at the end of the earth, with one foot in the grave and the other out of it?' John outlived the governor, was one of the first customers of the Bank of New South Wales when it was founded in 1817, and died in 1834, aged 83. He was a remarkable man – when he was 70 he was attacked by a bushranger on the Parramatta Road near where Sydney University is today. He held off his assailant until help arrived.

The Turnbulls and the other Hawkesbury River settlers were dismayed by the corrupt military clique of the New South Wales Corps that monopolised the supply of rum to the infant colony as well as engaging in other corrupt activity. They were delighted when from 1806 Governor Bligh sought to bring the Rum Corps' leader, John Macarthur, to book, and appalled when Bligh was overthrown in a military coup in 1808. They were in no position to directly oppose the military but sent a number of petitions to London complaining about the mutiny and extolling Bligh's virtues. New South Wales offered them the chance to own and farm some land, build a chapel and worship as they saw fit.

So admiring of Bligh were the Hawkesbury River settlers that many of the older families called their children after the governor, including John and Ann Turnbull, who named their youngest son William Bligh Turnbull. Happily, my forebears kept up the tradition and so I am Malcolm Bligh Turnbull. This news will disappoint those who assume that I am either directly descended from the notoriously cruel William Bligh of the *Bounty*, or that my parents, anticipating my brutal character, named me accordingly.

Now, it is rather ironic that John Turnbull came to a penal colony in search of freedom, but that's precisely what he and the other Scottish settlers on the *Coromandel* were seeking. In England at that time, there was considerable discrimination against any faith other than that of the Church of England – non-conformist Protestants like the Turnbulls were second-class citizens, as were Catholics and Jews. New South Wales offered them the chance to own some land, farm it as they saw fit, build a chapel, and worship as they saw fit. And they took great risks embarking on their tiny ship to have that freedom.

I am also descended from another of John's sons, Ralph, who married Grace Cavanough in 1813 on the Hawkesbury. Grace was one of the first people to be born on the hitherto uninhabited Norfolk Island – in 1794. She was the daughter of Owen Cavanough and his convict wife, Margaret Darnell. Owen had been a sailor on the *Sirius* and, so the legend goes, was the first sailor to land at Sydney Cove in 1788: he'd held the longboat steady as the officers stepped ashore.

It may have been that Bruce's lack of literary accomplishment was a reaction against his father's reading and reciting, but in any event he was highly intelligent, and above all he was incredibly charming. Dad had a disarming smile and style that could win over anyone – ideal for a salesman. In fact, one of his anxieties about me was that I was too serious and 'heavy'. 'Lighten up, Malcolm,' he'd say, despairing when I'd get myself into long and, to his mind, turgid discussions about politics and history with people we met in the pub.

Bruce was also very athletic. He was good at rugby, swimming, surfing and running. He ran marathons, was a pretty good campdrafter and a reasonable boxer. In some ways he was an idealised Aussie male of his era – street smart, handsome, sporty and funny.

So, my first memories of family were of an amazingly beautiful and brilliant mother who doted on me, and an overshadowed father who was in the background except for when we escaped to the beach, when we entered into an all-male world that was entirely Dad's. Having observed their miserable relationship first-hand, I can only assume that I was conceived in a moment of raw passion, and my arrival caused them to stick together and marry. Other than me, I cannot think of anything they had in common.

Mum made a number of fatal errors in 'husband management'. She patronised Bruce and regularly reminded him of his lack of education. She also reminded him of how broke he was and how our slender family fortunes depended on her income as a scriptwriter (which was probably true). A good lesson learned at a young age: don't belittle people (least of all your spouse).

As a baby I'd been sick with pneumonia, leading to what appeared to be chronic asthma. I was also pigeon toed. The doctors prescribed surgical boots to correct my feet and lots of rest and coddling to deal with my asthma. Any parent with a child choking for breath knows how terrifying asthma can be – imagine what it was like before Ventolin.

Dad was sceptical of the medical professionals, however. He knew a bloke who'd been knock kneed and pigeon toed and, apparently, generally sickly of demeanour. Somehow or other this invalid had secured a job as a beach inspector and Dad observed that after some months of walking up and down Bondi Beach, the man was restored to good health. Walking in the soft sand fixed his posture, and the exercise and salt air cured the rest.

The upshot was that Bruce took me down to Bondi Beach every morning. We'd walk and then, when I got older, run up and down the beach in the soft sand. I became a strong swimmer and, before too long, I was no longer tripping over my feet, and my asthma was at least manageable.

Bondi was most definitely not a fashionable place in those days. The saying, 'You can take the boy out of Bondi, but you can't take the Bondi out of the boy', wasn't a compliment. There were hardly any cafes, no restaurants, and the blocks of flats on the Ben Buckler headland, whose apartments now sell for millions of dollars apiece, were known as 'cockroach castles'.

Bruce was a member of the North Bondi Surf Club, where we always went to change and shower. Consequently, I grew up in a world where the whole colourful diversity of the eastern suburbs would stand around in the change rooms gossiping and joking. There'd be a Supreme Court judge having a shower next to a garbo, a police superintendent next to one of gambling tsar Joe Taylor's enforcers, a hilarious Jewish crowd in the rag trade ... take your pick, they were all there.

It was an ideal place to learn important lessons. No matter how rich or educated you might be, everyone looks the same with their gear off. Respect everybody but defer to nobody. And, above all, just relax, be yourself, and you can get along with anyone.

While I was doing blokey things with Dad at the surf club, Mum was busy ensuring that I loved books and learning. She read to me for hours and hours and I became her 'little bookworm'. The first proper book I can remember her reading me was Tolkien's *The Hobbit* and then the entire 'Lord of the Rings' series. For years after she left us, I'd read 'Lord of the Rings', all three volumes, several times a year. Looking back, I can see that I was trying to recapture those happy days when she read me those stories about dwarves and dragons, hobbits and elves. I don't think I could have been any closer to Coral, nor do I think she could have been a better or more attentive mother.

It's probably not correct to describe Coral as religious, but she was certainly spiritually interested. This may have been hereditary. Her parents had been theosophists, followers of the teachings of the famous Madame Blavatsky and indeed Arthur Conan Doyle. My maternal grandmother was keen on séances. Coral never tried to get me interested in theosophy but I do remember her having a Seventh Day Adventist period (there used to be a reading room in Rose Bay) and, more troublingly, a Christian Scientist period. She said later that her dalliance with Christian Science was because she thought it would be a comfort to me, as a sick child, to know that prayer can heal you. However, I had a little friend at school whose parents were Christian Scientists. According to local gossip, when his mother became ill, she refused any medical assistance, preferring to rely on Mary Baker Eddy's teachings to cure her. Not surprisingly, they didn't. I cannot recall how old I was, but from an early age this convinced me that God helps those who help themselves.

I can only dimly recall my parents sleeping in the same bed. For most of the time we lived together, Bruce slept in a single bed in a tiny room at the back of the kitchen. They seemed to lead separate lives. When Coral had dinner parties, Bruce rarely attended. But like many unhappily married couples, they stayed together for my sake and I wasn't old enough to be troubled by their lack of affection.

At this stage we lived in Flat 2, 119 New South Head Road, Vaucluse. It was a small, rather dark flat of two bedrooms, or three if you included the back room where Dad usually slept. We rented it from a frightening old man called Clarrie Ball, who lived next door in Flat 1 with a snappy dog that didn't like me or the series of Persian cats Mum owned.

Why Mum liked cats so much I can't say. Her own mother had bred Yorkshire terriers, and when I was born she owned a boxer dog called Sheba. But by the time I could remember these things, our animal world was that of majestic, disdainful cats. First, a pure white Persian I called Ribbons, and then the most characterful of all cats, Figaro, a large smoke-grey Persian, who made friends with all the old ladies in the flats up and down New South Head Road. This enabled him to eat five or six times every day.

Most of my friends at Vaucluse Public School lived in houses with big backyards and dogs. I didn't envy their real estate but would have liked to own a dog. They seemed much more useful than cats – they would catch things, follow you down to the shops and come when you called.

The good thing about living at 119 New South Head Road was that there was a park across the street where we local kids built cubbyhouses and forts in the bushes. And a bus ride took me down to Watsons Bay and Camp Cove, where a university friend of my mother, Rhonda Williams, lived in a cottage on the beach with her children, Lisa and Mark. The two university friends had given birth to baby boys within a few days of each other and a family myth (I hope it was a myth) was that the two little brown babies were so alike that one day Coral took the wrong one home. Summer after summer, we were inseparable.

Back then, Camp Cove and Watsons Bay weren't the impossibly expensive suburbs they are today, and many of the old fishermen's cottages were still occupied by fishermen. There were even some sheep living at Nielsen Park in Vaucluse. The beaches, the rocky headlands, even the old fortifications around South Head were my playground with Mark and our other friends. In short, all the best things in my childhood were free. The children of millionaires and struggling salesmen alike were catching the same waves at Bondi, digging the same holes in the sand at Camp Cove. It sounds perfectly unbelievable, even absurd, to many people, but the eastern suburbs of Sydney and the area's beach and sporting culture were thoroughly egalitarian.

Life changed markedly when I went to boarding school at age eight, to the Sydney Grammar Preparatory School at St Ives. I'm not sure why my parents chose Sydney Grammar. Perhaps it was because Uncle Oscar had gone there (before he ran away to sea). I'm sure Dad would have preferred to have me at home, but between his wife's increasing absences and his own – he was often away for days at a time, going around the countryside selling pubs – it wasn't practicable.

Boarding school was the prelude to the end of the marriage. By 1964, Coral was spending most of her time with John Salmon, a professor of history at the University of New South Wales (UNSW), and when he accepted a post in New Zealand she left with him.

None of this was explained to me at the time. Dad started to play a bigger role in my life. He was often the only parent there on weekends when I was home from boarding school. At first, I was told that Mum was in New Zealand studying for another degree (she did in fact obtain a PhD from Victoria University in Wellington). Bruce was determined that I not know, or have reason to suspect, my mother had left us. So, her absence crept up on me, like a slow chill around the heart.

I hated boarding school more than I could ever describe. The Sydney Grammar boarding house at St Ives was a brutal, badly managed place. Bullying was rife and I was particularly unpopular. This was no doubt initially because I wet my bed. The other boys taunted and mocked me, all of which made me more miserable, more anxious and more likely to wet the sheets.

The matron at St Ives made me get up early and take my sheets to the laundry. Alone I'd wash them and then hang them up on the line, where everyone could see Turnbull's sheets drying – a flapping white reminder of my incontinence. Later, a kinder matron appeared, who dispensed with this daily humiliation. No doubt she recognised that adding to my anxiety was hardly going to be a cure.

Both my parents kept the letters I wrote to them from boarding school. They alternated between bogus pluckiness – 'We had a great game of cricket today, Dad' – to heart-rending pleas to take me home.

I went over to visit Mum in New Zealand when I was 10. The visit was the subject of extensive negotiation between my parents. After their deaths, I read the correspondence in which Bruce reluctantly agreed to my going but on the condition that John Salmon wasn't to be living in the house while I was there. He insisted that the pretence that my mother was simply temporarily absent and living alone must be maintained. Coral agreed to all of this.

When I arrived at the airport in Auckland I was greeted by my mother and her friend Professor Salmon, as I always called him. She welcomed me with the words, 'Darling, Professor Salmon and I are getting married.' At that stage I didn't even know my parents were planning to divorce. Worse still, John Salmon had children of his own, who now seemed to feature in Mum's life.

It's striking that I didn't bitterly resent Mum for leaving me. The only explanation I can give is that Dad was relentless in praising her and reassuring me constantly that my mother loved me more than anything else on earth. He literally never spoke an ill word about her.

Reading the reproachful letters he wrote Coral at the time, I still find it hard to believe that he could put down his pen, seal up the aerogramme and then turn to his son and tell him the object of his recrimination was the most brilliant, beautiful and adoring mother in the whole world. As we all know, many, if not most, divorces result in the parents freely expressing their reservations about each other to the children, which no doubt results in the kids thinking less of both parents on the basis that some, at least, of the criticism must be true. So, Bruce's self-discipline was remarkable, especially since Coral's departure resulted in us losing almost all our furniture (she had it shipped over to New Zealand) and then our flat. A few years before they split up, Coral and Bruce had banded together with the other tenants to buy the building from our landlord, Mr Ball, but Coral had put up almost all the cash, and so when the flat was sold she took the proceeds as well as all the furniture, except for my bed.

Financially, we'd never been carefree. Coral had earned good money when she was writing several radio serials at the same time, but by the early 1960s, radio was being overtaken by television, and Coral didn't adapt to the new medium. Instead she returned to academia, writing a slim but important volume on the evocation of Australia as an Arcadian paradise in 19th-century English literature. I should note that her other enduring academic interest was the history of the Australian Workers' Union (AWU). Together with Bede Nairn, she co-authored the *Australian Dictionary of Biography* entry on William Guthrie Spence, the AWU founder, and she wrote several papers on the shearers' strike and the early years of trade unionism in Australia.

Coral loved to say how I startled some of her friends one day. They asked what I wanted to be when I grew up. 'The general secretary of the Australian Workers' Union,' I replied. I have no idea whether this is true – Coral was a fabulous fabulist.

By the time she left Australia, Coral was no longer earning the big money she had as a scriptwriter. Her income as a university tutor was modest, although she supplemented that from time to time with television appearances with Eric Baume on *Beauty and the Beast*. As the occasional grumpy letter from the school bursar indicates, Bruce often struggled to pay my boarding-school fees.

Dad and I moved to a smaller rented flat in 13 Gladswood Gardens, Double Bay, where we lived like two bachelors. We had no furniture in our lounge room until I returned from school one weekend and encountered two enormous white fibreglass armchairs, each on a swivel and looking like something out of *The Jetsons*. A dentist friend of Bruce had decided to refurbish his waiting room (good move, I thought) and had given him the chairs. A childhood dominated by a bookish mother was replaced by one with a father whose interests were largely athletic.

Our relationship was more like that of a big brother and a little brother than father and son. Bruce taught me how to cook (simply), wash and iron shirts. If he had work to do in the country when I was home, he'd take me with him. A stocktake was always required when a hotel was sold and so I'd pitch in counting beer glasses and drip trays and checking them off the inventory. We spent more time at the beach and at the football. I led two lives, a bookish, academic one at school, and then a thoroughly blokey life with Bruce.

By the mid-60s, I was regularly running with Bruce, first up and down Bondi Beach and soon, in what was regarded then as a big effort, from North Bondi to Bronte and back – about 8 kilometres!

Dad and I did much of our jogging together in Centennial Park and the crowd was the same eclectic mix I used to see at the surf club (most of them were members). Our regular running crew included 'Paddington' Jack Florentino, a garbo; Billy Bridges, a real estate agent; Henric Nicholas, an up-and-coming barrister; and Ernie Boyd and Ted Helliar, who, like Dad, were in the pub business.

The leader of all the Centennial Park joggers was the terrifying George Daldry, who ran the gym at City Tattersalls Club and at different times trained our international rugby teams, rowing crews – you name it. George was Mr Fitness. He was also as tough as they come. As a boy soldier in the Second World War, he was captured by the Japanese and exhibited in a cage, half starved, as an example of the scrawny youths the Australians were sending into war.

George survived the war, so he said, because he obtained the stainless-steel dixie of a dead British soldier; they were easier to keep clean than the cast-iron Australian ones. He became fanatical about cleanliness and after the war almost always dressed immaculately in white.

Running round the park, many of the men competed with tales of their romantic adventures. Dad, like the lawyers, made no admissions. He placed a high value on discretion, and most of the other joggers' stories were as mundane as they were implausible.

But there was one raconteur who was in a league of his own. Bruce Gyngell was one of the world's most successful television executives and was always a great friend and mentor to me. At different times he ran

Nine, Seven and SBS. In the UK he ran ATV for Sir Lew Grade and later (as a result of my suggestion) TV AM. He was tall, slim and always elegant – my father used to say Gyngo was like a tailor's dummy: anything you threw on him looked smart. After all the local larrikins had told their tales of bonking in Bondi Junction and other not so romantic locations, it was Gyngell's turn.

'I was flying on the Concorde from New York to London when I noticed that the exquisitely beautiful stewardess was staring at me. I went back to reading my papers and then when I looked up she was staring at me again. "Mr Gyngell," she said, "you are so handsome, I cannot take my eyes off you."'

'Jeez,' said one of the other joggers. 'What did you do then, mate?'

'I squeezed her hand gently and discreetly, I did not want to make a scene, and quietly said to her, "Ask the captain to radio the Dorchester and reserve the Terrace Suite."'

'And then what happened when you got to London?' they asked Gyngell.

'Three days and nights of indescribable passion. She wrote me a sonnet of appreciation.'

Well, I thought, jogging along in the early morning. This was at least a better class of bullshit.

CHAPTER 2

Books, bananas and Jack Lang: school and university

Alastair Mackerras, the master of the Lower School, welcomed me to Sydney Grammar School in 1967. His office was at the southern end of the old sandstone school building on College Street. Next door was the classroom where he taught 1A – the brightest of the new boys, including me. Alastair looked like a rumpled bear. A classicist and mathematician, he was a natural bachelor who preferred the company of children to adults. He used to invite groups of boys to stay with him in his house at Kiama on the South Coast over the holidays. Nowadays it'd be unheard of, but there was never any hint of impropriety.

His understudy was another bachelor classicist, John Sheldon. Alastair and John were two of the most charismatic teachers I ever had. Between them they could make Latin and Greek interesting for 12- and 13-year-old boys. Both were eccentric, and thoroughly Australian in an Anglophile way that was common with academics of that era. As I recalled in a speech in 2012, long before you saw Sheldon you knew he was there. Hanging like a smoky whisper in the cool air of the morning, the unmistakably sweet smell of his tobacco left a trail through the panelled corridors. No one else smoked Balkan Sobranie, a blend of tobacco from Virginia, Macedonia and Syria.

John Sheldon, like his tobacco, was a blend of the conventional and the exotic. He was entranced by the ancient world. In aid of Latin, Greek or indeed Sanskrit, he made no claims of utility or relevance – although many could be made. But you couldn't help feeling that without a more than fleeting acquaintance with the classics, John Sheldon wouldn't regard you as, well, adequately educated. He radiated a love of learning that was, for me at least, quite irresistible.

Sydney Grammar School students felt a strong sense of cultural continuity. As we trudged through *Kennedy's Revised Latin Primer* or Hillard & Botting, we knew we were treading a well-worn path. Some of our textbooks had been printed in the 1890s. One of the Latin masters, Mr Swan, invariably addressed boys by their father's name if he'd taught them – it was unclear whether this was because he actually thought we were still in the late 1940s or because when you're considering Caesar's suppression of the Gauls, a generation here or there is easy to overlook.

John taught us Greek in Second Year, in 1968, and I did fairly well. We had another teacher the next year; I was underwhelmed by the experience and in my exam I scored 6 per cent – presumably for writing my name, and that in English. I resolved to give up the subject, but John persuaded me to continue and I did so only because he was taking Greek the following year. In that year, with John Sheldon as my teacher, I finished third in our class and fourth in the state. While Sheldon did teach me a little Greek and Latin, he taught me something much more valuable and that is the profound – the central – importance of the charismatic teacher.

I continued boarding, now at the boarding house at 43 St Marks Road, Randwick; there were only about 70 of us (out of a school of over 1100) and we'd get the 339 bus in and out of the city. Like the boarding house at St Ives, the one at Randwick was badly run. Bullying was unchecked, and inappropriate, creepy conduct by masters wasn't uncommon. One master was especially sleazy. When I was 14, my friend Ted Marr and I went to see Alastair Mackerras to complain about him. Alastair was an unworldly man, an innocent in many ways, and he couldn't understand what our concern was. I told him that if he didn't move the master out of the boarding school, I'd walk across the park to see the chairman of trustees, whom I knew to be the very grand Sir Norman Cowper, senior partner of Allen Allen & Hemsley. When Ted audibly gasped, I realised that I might have been testing Mackerras's patience. He didn't complain, simply assured us that wouldn't be necessary, and by the next term the master in question was no longer at the boarding house.

I continued to hate boarding. The only redeeming aspect was that because Grammar was a non-denominational school, the boys went to the church of their own affiliation on Sundays. Being under the misapprehension that I'd been baptised and as a Presbyterian, I went to the Randwick Presbyterian Church and joined the fellowship, which included quite a few of the Sydney Girls High students I used to chat with on the 339 bus.

The housemaster lived in an old villa, a relic of Randwick's late 19th-century magnificence. The boarding house closed in 1976, the dormitory blocks were demolished and sold to developers, but the mansion, Rothesay, remained. It was rather eerie to visit it a few years back when its new owner, Professor Michael Feneley, was the Liberal candidate for Kingsford Smith in the 2016 election.

Bruce was an ideal father but wasn't suited for matrimony. He always had a complicated love life, with several girlfriends on the go at any time; he relished the intrigue and occasional drama. As his weekend and school holidays flatmate, I not only witnessed this but received a running commentary of advice – useful had I wanted to have three or four girlfriends at the same time without any of them finding out about the others!

Yet to my immense surprise, in 1968 Bruce told me he'd married Judy Womersley. I knew Judy reasonably well – she used to come around on Sundays when I was home from boarding school and cook dinner for us – but I hadn't expected Bruce to marry her or anyone else. I was 14 by then, so didn't have the resentment a younger child might have, and I wished them well. Soon after that, Bruce kicked a few goals in his business and we were able to move out of the small rented flat in Double Bay into what seemed an enormous apartment – in Longworth Avenue, Point Piper. Happily, when I was 16, my years of boarding school ended; I moved home and into a more conventional domestic existence.

Judy used to describe herself as the 'WSM', or wicked stepmother; she was anything but. She'd have liked children of her own; I was a bit old to mother, but she was good to me. Sadly, the marriage ended in divorce 12 years later. Bruce's fault entirely – monogamy wasn't his thing. Still, we all stayed friends.

As Dad's business continued to thrive, it became easier for him to pay the fees. But I never forgot how hard he worked to send me to Grammar and resolved to prove his investment was worthwhile. From an academic point of view I was a strong performer, especially in the humanities, and very engaged politically, joining Ted Marr in the Moratorium demonstrations against the Vietnam War. I loved history, often embarking on my own independent research on topics as diverse as 'Who Are the Imperialists?' in which I compared British, US and Soviet imperialism, through to 'The Life and Times of Cosimo de' Medici'. I was thrilled years later when my daughter, Daisy, majored in Renaissance history at Sydney University.

Grammar had an extensive library, but I discovered a back room full of books deemed out of date by the librarians. I loved rummaging through the old bookshelves, and developed a keen interest not just in history, but how history was perceived at different times – I probably didn't know the word for it then, but it was the start of a lifelong interest in historiography and, of course, the first real historian in the Western tradition, Thucydides.

I was a mediocre mathematician. In that respect my son, Alex, is a good example of what I should have done. Alex was, like me, a pretty ordinary mathematician at school but he worked and worked at his maths after he went to Harvard and emerged highly numerate. An example of evolution, perhaps?

Even though Grammar's reputation was largely academic, and we were all acutely aware that it had produced two prime ministers, many leading lights in law and medicine and a swag of Rhodes Scholars, private boys' schools of the day were overwhelmingly sporty. Thespians, debaters and intellectuals were suspect; the heroes were all footballers or cricketers. But especially after Mackerras became the headmaster in 1969, the tone of Grammar became more sympathetic to the arts. Music (for which I had no talent) thrived, but I was able to throw myself into debating and acting.

John Sheldon ensured we were well drilled in debating in the Lower School. My debating partners included David Gonski, who was in the year ahead of me. In my final year, with Kim Swan and Steve Scholem, our team won the GPS Debating Competition and I won the Lawrence Campbell Oratory Competition – both rare achievements for Grammar in those days when the debating prizes were dominated by the Jesuits' Riverview. John O'Sullivan led the St Joseph's College team and, as with David, we have remained lifelong friends, our paths crossing frequently in business and then in politics.

However, while I enjoyed debating, it was the Globe Players, Grammar's drama society, that really engaged me. Of course, I relished the showmanship of being on stage, the centre of attention, and, I should add, the co-productions with girls' schools – Abbotsleigh in the first few years and then SCEGGS Darlinghurst.

But it was the poetry of Shakespeare that entranced me the most, and I loved the big long parts: Edgar in *King Lear*, Iago in *Othello*, Bottom in *A Midsummer Night's Dream* and then, in my last year, Prospero in *The Tempest*. Our drama teacher, Tony Gallagher, was also often our English master. He adored Shakespeare so much he couldn't bear to cut the plays, so we did *King Lear* uncut – nearly four hours of it, and in the Great Hall of Sydney University, not known for its comfortable seats!

The Great Hall wasn't designed for theatrical performances and there were no wings, so the cast had to enter from a side door which let out onto Science Road. I was waiting to go on as Edgar in his guise as Mad Tom on the opening night – I'd been made up in body paint that, together with a white loincloth, made me look more like a large, deeply tanned baby than a wild woodland maniac. So, I decided to roll around in the bushes and cover myself with sticks and dirt. As I was doing that, a young man was slowly cruising past in a smart MG, roof down, left arm around his beautiful companion. I couldn't resist bursting out of the bushes to surprise them. I've never seen a car accelerate as fast and if that was the end of the affair … well, forgive me.

I didn't neglect rugby, however, and was a mediocre but enthusiastic front-row forward, encouraged by Dad, who felt that sport and exercise would offset my thespian interests.

Once, displeased that I'd missed some of my patrols at North Bondi Surf Club (guilty as charged), he was up-front with his concerns: 'Son, your problem is you spend too much time hanging around with sheilas and not enough time at the surf club. Keep going on that way and people will think you're a poofter!'

'Really, Dad?' I said. 'So, the way to ensure people don't think I'm a poofter is to spend more time at the surf club having showers with lots of blokes!'

To which he burst out laughing, gave me a hug and said, 'You're right, Bozo, but just don't miss the patrols!'

One of the more idiosyncratic but useful things I learned at Grammar was how to splice rope. It was compulsory for boys in Years 9 and 10 to be in the cadet corps, and enthusiasts could continue on for Years 11 and 12 if they chose. I did a year in the army cadets and then escaped to the naval cadets, presided over by a wonderful history teacher, rugby coach and navy veteran named Clyde Slatyer. We had excursions to naval bases and ships, but by far the best fun was camping on tiny Snapper Island, located near the Iron Cove Bridge in Sydney Harbour. This was more rocky reef than island. An eccentric old sailor called Len Forsythe had leased it from the navy in 1930 for use as a sea cadet training depot and he was still on the scene, although very much the ancient mariner, when I was visiting nearly 50 years ago.

The training depot had been built with bits and pieces scrounged from naval stores and decommissioned ships, and it was a paradise for me. Len had a fleet of 27-foot Montagu whalers, immensely heavy clinker-built boats used in the Royal Australian Navy (RAN) until the 1950s – mostly for training. We used to row them around the harbour and sail them when there was a brisk breeze. We never tipped one over, which was just as well because it would have gone straight to the bottom – I don't recall any buoyancy compartments!

I finished my time at Grammar as the senior prefect, and shared with Tim Murray the role of captain of the school, which, in Grammar's eccentric way, was for the top boy in humanities. The duxes of the school were Jim Colebatch and John Watson, both of whom went on to become neurologists, following their fathers into the medical profession (even more hereditary than law, in my experience). I left Grammar filled with confidence, ambition but above all curiosity. Our Welsh history teacher, Alf Pickard, had encouraged wide reading and research and hadn't minded too much when we occasionally invented imaginary references to see if he was paying attention. And between the English and Classics departments I'd developed a love of words and etymology.

One of the first things my friend John Watson and I did after leaving school was to enrol in a typing course at the Bondi Evening College. Clattering away on old Remingtons in a classroom full of teenage girls, we were the only males, but it was probably the most practical course of instruction either of us ever undertook – touch typing has stood me in good stead ever since.

I was always anxious to be financially independent and so as soon as I was old enough, I had part-time jobs – a bit of labouring and gardening mostly, while I was at school, and then in the long summer before I started university, I found a job at the Sydney Fruit and Vegetable Markets, which in those days were in the centre of Chinatown, in Haymarket.

'Les Walters, Banana Merchants' was my first employer, and my job was to load boxes of bananas into and out of ripening rooms (where they were gassed with carbon dioxide) and onto trucks. It was an early start, around 4 am, and I was finished by midday. I had an offsider but after a few weeks I noticed he wasn't working with us any more and I was doing a lot more lifting and carrying. So, I asked my boss for a raise; what one could tactfully describe as an industrial dispute followed. Out of the banana trade, I was relegated to working on the watermelons, which was the hardest physical work I'd ever done – passing watermelons on and off trucks all day.

However, I reckoned my old boss owed me some money. My polite request was met with a pretty abrupt refusal, so I decided to see if the massed ranks of Australia's labour movement would spring to my defence. There wasn't any union coverage at the markets, as far as I could see, and so after knocking off my eight-hour shift at midday, I walked up Sussex Street to the NSW Labor Council. John Ducker, who was the president, looked me up and down and said, 'I know who you should see – come and meet Bob Carr.' Ducker led me into a small side office, where a young, thin man in a white shirt, tie and with big black glasses was pounding away at a typewriter.

I was in football shorts, a T-shirt, boots and covered in sweat. I'd been working in a hot shed since four in the morning. After I told Bob my story, he thought for a minute and said, 'I've just finished a fantastic book about the politics of Eastern Europe. Do you want to borrow it?' I was taken aback – this seemed a long way from my struggles for wage justice in the city markets – and I told Bob, 'No, I just want you to help me get my money back.' It quickly became pretty obvious that Bob wasn't going to be much help there, and once I accepted that, we became good friends and in due course, Labor premier of New South Wales and Liberal prime minister of Australia respectively.

After that summer, in March 1973, I started at Sydney University doing a combined arts and law degree. I especially enjoyed medieval history; it added the next chapter to my studies of ancient history at school and left me with a lifelong interest in the history of medieval Spain in the time of el Cid.

I hadn't studied French at school beyond fourth form so shouldn't have been able to study French at university. But over the summer, while working in the markets, I'd become friends with a girl visiting Sydney from Marseilles. She spoke no English and so by the time I got to university I thought I was pretty good. As he agreed to admit me, Professor Ross Chambers said, 'You are quite fluent, but your grammar is appalling, you have a gangster's accent and quite a bit of your vocabulary is, in fact, Italian.'

Between reading *El Cantar del Mio Cid* and Camus's *La Peste*, I started writing for the university newspaper, *Honi Soit*, and then, after failing to be elected editor in a contest with two members of the Communist Party, I started writing as a freelancer for the *Nation Review*, a leftish weekly newspaper owned by Gordon Barton. Its editor was George Munster, a Jewish refugee who escaped Europe with his parents before the Holocaust, and an intense chain smoker who seemed as old as time to me then (he was only 50).

The *Nation Review*'s Sydney office was a dingy set of rooms on George Street, near Railway Square, happily above the Malaya Restaurant, where I developed a taste for spicy foods, especially laksa, which I found to be the perfect cure for a heavy cold.

The *Nation Review*'s publisher was Richard Walsh, whom I rarely saw, and it was run on the smell of an oily rag. Well, that's how they justified paying me the distinctly unprincely sum of $30 per thousand words for my deathless prose.

Mostly I wrote about politics, and especially NSW state politics. At university I read a lot about labour history, the foundation of the AWU, the efforts to create 'one big union', the clashes with the communists that finally led to the split in the 1950s. It was the 1920s and '30s that most fascinated me, and particularly Jack Lang, the giant figure of Labor politics in that era.

Twice premier of New South Wales – in 1925–27 and 1930–32 – Lang was a radical, the subject of a personality cult that has no counterpart in Australian politics, thank heavens. 'Lang is greater than Lenin' was the slogan on the posters and 'Lang is Right' buttons were everywhere as he battled with the banks and conservative opposition–controlled Legislative Council. A populist, closer to Mussolini than to Lenin, he spoke to enormous rallies in The Domain, furiously denouncing the banks, the communists and the big end of town – all with an unhealthy dose of xenophobia as he railed against Jewish bankers and defended the White Australia Policy.

He'd parted ways with the federal Australian Labor Party (ALP) government in 1931 – at the height of the Great Depression – over the payment of interest on English loans to the state government. Lang wanted to postpone payment and spend the money on public works in Australia; the federal government insisted on paying the interest as a priority. In the financial crisis that followed, Lang was dismissed as premier in 1932 by the English governor of New South Wales, Air Vice-Marshal Sir Philip Game. It prefigured the sacking of Whitlam in 1975, which occurred just six weeks after Lang's death.

Lang was 98 when he died. He was a giant man with a huge head and intimidating even in the unsteady frailty of advanced old age. For the last few years of his life I often visited him in his old office in Nithsdale Street, south of Hyde Park. He was still editing his newspaper, the *Century*, by then only 16 pages, and wrote most of the articles himself. I wanted to talk about the politics of the 1920s and '30s, and Lang obliged me, denouncing his enemies, all long dead, as though their treacheries were only hours old. Writing his obituary for the *Nation Review* in 1975, I observed: 'Lang knew how to hate. He destroyed or attempted to destroy anyone who came in his way. He was convinced of his own rectitude and regarded anyone who disagreed with him as a saboteur.'[1] But then he would turn to the here and now and hold forth about Whitlam and Fraser and all the political issues of the day.

His successor as NSW Labor leader, later premier and governor-general, was Bill McKell and he too was still alive and happy to be interviewed by me. So, I had a wonderful insight into the history of those times, especially since each of them, Lang in his late 90s and McKell in his 80s, despised the other.

With my tape recorder and notebook I'd shuttle between those old men. As though in a time machine, they'd relive the struggles of a half-century before. It was quite a privilege; they were the only ones left of that era and they loved to talk. My lecturers were most impressed as one essay after another was filled not with references on the reading list but quotes from the great men themselves.

Lang had split off the NSW Labor Party from the federal ALP in the 1930s. After being replaced by McKell in 1939, he was finally expelled in 1942 and started his own party. He'd ended his parliamentary career as an independent 'Lang Labor' MP in the federal parliament for one term, a thorn in the side of the Chifley Labor government. In large part due to a young Paul Keating's efforts, all was forgiven in 1971 and he was readmitted to the ALP.

Lang was bemused by my Liberal Party membership but didn't seek to persuade me to switch to Labor, although he did tell me a story that I never forgot.

'The Liberals have no loyalty or generosity – and no gratitude. The Labor Party is at least sentimental. Take Bertram Stevens, Sir Bertram Stevens …' He almost licked his lips over the 'sir'. 'Well, Stevens was the man who led the United Australia Party[2] into government after I was sacked. He helped remove "Lang the Monster"! He defeated me in three elections! And yet, do you know, he died a pauper in the Lewisham Old Men's Hospital – they had no gratitude for their hero and he died without a penny or a friend.'

Which begs the question why I joined the Liberal and not the Labor Party. Mum wasn't just a Labor historian but a supporter as well. I don't recall Dad being particularly partisan, so there was no strong Liberal impetus from home. But as I reflected on the two parties, while I admired the romance and history of the Labor movement, I always felt I was a natural liberal, drawn to the entrepreneurial and enterprising. Of course, small-l liberals exist in both the major parties, but their natural home should be the Liberal Party and in those days I think it still was.

Around this time I came to know Bob Ellis, who'd go on to become a Labor speechwriter and political commentator. For a while we worked together on a script for a musical about Jack Lang. I lost it long ago and wish I hadn't. Bob and his composer partner, Patrick Flynn, had done well with a political musical about the life of an even earlier Labor politician, King O'Malley, and Jack Lang was, if anything, a more interesting and colourful character.

Ellis was inspired by the writing style of US novelist Norman Mailer, where the journalist is right there in the centre of the story. I found that attractive as well and did my own series of 'road trip' stories for *Nation Review* when I travelled overseas for the first time in 1974. Armed with nothing more than infinite confidence and a dodgy business card, I talked my way into Richard Nixon's hideaway in San Clemente and interviewed his ghostwriter, and also talked my way into the Alabama State Capitol, where I interviewed the governor and former presidential candidate George C. Wallace himself. Wallace was professing he was no longer a racist segregationist, as he had most assuredly been in the 1960s. But I wasn't convinced. I couldn't help but notice that the Confederate star and bars flew everywhere in Montgomery; I only saw the stars and stripes on one building while I was there and that was the US Post Office. I kept these thoughts to myself after he produced a magnificent certificate and appointed me an honorary aide-de-camp and lieutenant colonel in the Alabama State Militia! I was a long way from home after all.

I came home through the UK and Europe, rushing through the great sights at the breakneck pace of millions of other young Australians. But I managed to squeeze in a train trip up to Walsall, the old industrial town near Birmingham whose Labour MP, John Stonehouse, had recently got into financial troubles, faked his own death then escaped to Australia – where he'd been arrested. I wrote that his constituents weren't surprised he'd fled Down Under, one of them observing under their leaden sky, 'I mean, it's very sunny there now … in't?'[3]

Back in Australia, to augment my meagre earnings from the *Nation Review* I used my sketchy journalistic credentials to get access to the NSW parliamentary press gallery. After noticing that neither Channel Nine nor Radio 2SM had a full-time state parliamentary roundsman, I cold-called their management and persuaded them I could provide a cheap and cheerful voice from Macquarie Street. It was piecework – $12 per radio story that went to air for 2SM and $40 per story that went to air for Channel Nine.

Soon I'd completed my arts degree and had two years to go to finish law. It was an exciting time in state politics to be a law student reporting in print, radio and TV. I was covering the 1976 election when Neville Wran brought 11 years of Liberal government to an end. In those days, most of the parliament buildings were temporary timber structures, almost all of which were fire traps, and I was able to find my own cubbyhole in the press gallery and a quiet desk in the parliamentary library (rarely frequented by the honourable members) to pursue my law studies.

Paul Mullins was a legendary reporter for the Ten Network who, like most of his colleagues, was highly sceptical of the young stringer for Nine, and when I impertinently suggested he'd gone soft on the premier, Eric Willis, he king-hit me. A scuffle ensued, which concluded with me sitting on top of Paul in front of the enthralled parliamentary press gallery – most of whom were no doubt taking bets on who would prevail.

'Okay, Paul,' I said, 'I'm really sorry. I shouldn't have said that. Now if I get off you, can we just put all the furniture back before the police arrive?'

'Sure, mate,' said Paul. 'Apology accepted.'

Relieved, I stood up. So did Paul. And hit me again.

Well, we finally got sick of wrestling and someone said there were police on the way, so we quickly tidied things up and could pronounce, when the law did arrive, those immortal words, 'Nothing to see here.'

Working at the state parliament reacquainted me with my mother's old friend, Neville Wran. However, Neville's press secretary, Brian Dale, was a master of media management and rightly suspected I was unlikely to be a reliable conveyor of the government line. Consequently, I was treated with caution and was never an intimate or an insider as some of the other journalists became.

I did, however, make friends with some of the younger MPs, including Paul Landa and Laurie Brereton. Brereton was 30 when Wran was elected and was disappointed not to be in the ministry. I took him to lunch at the Hyde Park Hotel.

'Mate, do you know most of these blokes Neville has put in cabinet are half dead – in their fifties,' and he leant forward to make the point, 'even in their sixties?'

Being 21 years of age, I could see his point. But then Laurie bucked up and raised his glass for a toast. 'Well, comrade, I console myself with this: where there's death there's hope!' Laurie and his wife, Trish, like Bob and Helena Carr, became good friends.

As if my workload wasn't enough, I found another job – as a copywriter for John Singleton's advertising agency, operating then from an old building in Darlinghurst across the road from the Tradesman's Arms Hotel. Singleton specialised in direct hard-sell retail advertisements, and I wrote ads for Best & Less – 'Where do you get it? Can of baked beans 87 cents' – as well as more refined copy for *The Bulletin* and other clients.

It was while working for Singleton that I first met Kerry Packer. Singleton had asked us both out for dinner, along with a rather elegant Irish-born radio announcer called Claire Dunn. When one of Singleton's mates arrived, bringing with him his girlfriend and two 'friends' of hers, fairly obviously escorts, Claire turned up her nose at dining with them and departed. The evening ended almost as soon as it began as Kerry obviously thought better of it too. 'Do you like Chinese, son?' he asked me. Leaving Singleton with the professionals, I climbed into the back of a Mercedes bearing Kerry's dad's FP plates, drove to a Chinese restaurant in Double Bay, picked up takeaway and repaired to his pile at 76 Victoria Road, Bellevue Hill.

'That was a narrow escape,' Kerry chuckled as he tucked into sweet and sour pork. By the time we'd polished off the food I think each of us was somewhat warily intrigued by the other and remained that way for many years.

Singleton and I had our ups and downs – it was a pattern in just about all his friendships – but he treated me well. It always amused him to overhear me in my copywriting den filing stories for 2SM and signing off, 'Malcolm Turnbull, Parliament House'.

None of these jobs would have been possible had it not been for the Marist Brothers, for it was they who'd ensured my old debating rival John O'Sullivan had perfectly legible handwriting. I attended hardly any lectures at law school but for $30 a week, Jos, my fellow student, would take a carbon copy of his own notes for me. Not only were they better notes than I'd have taken, they were legible; my handwriting was scrappy. This practice wasn't unheard of: legend has it that Jim Spigelman, university medallist in law and later chief justice of New South Wales, attended next to no lectures. It was a more relaxed environment than that which law students face today.

Whether it was Singleton or the politicians or the guys in the press gallery, I found myself then, as I did for many years, working with people older than me. Occasionally, a little voice in the back of my brain would ask, 'Why are these grown-ups listening to *me*?' I'd rented a flat in Elizabeth Bay – with so many jobs, I was making reasonable money, even saving a bit – and remarkably, my grades were holding up thanks to Jos's notes. I'd dropped out of the Liberal Party – better for a journalist to be a member of no party – but I was starting to develop firmer political ambitions. Sitting in the press gallery, watching the politicians clash in the parliament below, I thought, I could do better than that.

CHAPTER 3

Journalism, Oxford, marriage and the Bar

Helped by Jos's notes I managed a few Distinctions in my legal studies and my multi-platform news career was humming along pretty well. Over the 1976–77 break, I returned to the UK. I wrote a few pieces for the *Nation Review*, including an interview with the Conservative MP Enoch Powell, a ferocious old man who in some respects reminded me of Jack Lang. I also interviewed Quintin Hogg, later Lord Hailsham. I remember him, perhaps suspecting I was dozing off with jet lag, emphasising a point by slamming his walking stick on his desk.

Fellow Sydney University debater Tony Renshaw and I went together to the Cambridge Union. The debates there, and at Oxford, are in a parliamentary style. The president, then Karan Thapar (matched by Benazir Bhutto at Oxford), sits in the speaker's chair and speakers line up on either side of the chamber to debate the topic of the day. There are several featured, or 'paper', speakers on each side – a couple of prominent public figures matched with senior student debaters. After they've spoken the floor is open to speakers from what one might call the backbench, although the back bar is probably a more apt description.

On this night, Harold Evans was speaking. Now for me, as a young journalist, Harold Evans was a god. He edited *The Sunday Times* and had pioneered the investigative journalism that had exposed the thalidomide scandal and many others. The paper was enormously profitable and most reporters, of any age, would do anything to work there.

Later in the debate I got the call from the president and, no doubt assisted by a few pints in the bar, made a stirring contribution about the importance of a free press. Not long after, I was passed a note from Harold Evans himself, on *Sunday Times* notepaper. 'Good speech!

Come and see me in the Gray's Inn Road.' So, thrilled by the summons and clutching the note, I turned up at the offices of *The Sunday Times* the next day.

I'd never met anyone like Harry before. He was built like a jockey but filled the room with his energy and infectious enthusiasm. He loved journalism and newspapers. He'd written a series of books about every aspect of the craft; he gave me the full set and signed them for me. He spoke about journalism with a romantic passion that was almost impossible to resist. And before too long, he'd offered me a job on *The Sunday Times*. But there was at least one practical brain cell operating, and I said I had to go back to Australia to finish my law degree.

'Law!' said Harry. 'That's the worst possible idea. Don't study law. Because if you do, you'll become a lawyer! The most boring job in the world, and where does it lead? Become a judge? Even more boring! Or –' and at this point his voice dropped to underscore the gravity of what he had to say, 'you could become a politician.' He shook his head – a fate worse than death.

Not entirely sure I hadn't made the biggest mistake of my young life, I stuck to my guns but arranged to stay in touch. I explained that I could keep my options open by continuing my journalism while I finished my law studies. After all, only a few days before a telegram had arrived from Trevor Kennedy offering me a full-time job back in Sydney.

Trevor was the editor of *The Bulletin*, a venerable Australian news magazine nearly a hundred years old that he was reviving for its owner, Kerry Packer. While I could continue covering state parliament for Channel Nine, which Packer also owned, my days at the *Nation Review* and 2SM were over.

I flew back to Australia via New York, where Rupert Murdoch was making waves. He'd moved there in 1974 and in late 1976 purchased the *New York Post* from its 73-year-old publisher, Dorothy Schiff. In January 1977, after a contentious takeover battle, he acquired *New York Magazine* and *The Village Voice*. The 17 January 1977 cover of *Time* summed up the media establishment's horror when it portrayed Rupert as King Kong bestriding the twin towers of the World Trade Center with the headline 'Aussie Press Lord Terrifies Gotham'.

I couldn't help but admire Murdoch in those days. He was Australian, he was politically progressive, he was shaking up the old order, taking on the world.

So, once in New York, I persuaded the team at Channel Nine that I'd do a story on Murdoch's New York triumphs. The only problem was that with litigation going on over the *New York Magazine* takeover, he wasn't giving any interviews – not to anybody, not even to the big US networks.

With the help of Ray Martin, the ABC's New York correspondent, I found a freelance cameraman and sound recordist and started to put the story together. At one point, I was doing a piece to camera in Greenwich Village in front of a newsstand and out of the corner of my eye spotted the well-known Australian art critic and writer Robert Hughes. I only knew him by reputation and I had no premonition that in a few years I would fall in love with his niece Lucy, but I raced up and promptly interviewed him about Murdoch. He was terrific talent and complained, with a wry smile, that Murdoch had sacked him as a cartoonist on Sydney's *Daily Mirror* years before.

The story was falling into place, but one element was missing: Rupert. My contacts, such as they were, couldn't help. Nothing worked. One evening I started ringing every extension at the *New York Post*. Dozens and dozens of dead ends. But then, after I dialled yet another random number, I heard a familiarly Australian voice. It was Rupert, working late in the green-wallpapered boudoir of an office that had been Dolly Schiff's.

'Rupert, I mean Mr Murdoch, it's Malcolm Turnbull here. I'm trying to put a story together for Channel Nine, *A Current Affair*, and it's all about you and the *New York Post* and *New York Magazine*. But unless I get an interview with you, I haven't got a story. So, could you please do me a favour and give me a few minutes?'

Silence … but no click. He hadn't hung up.

'Okay, why not. Come down to the *Post* now and we'll do it. Call me when you're here and I'll come out and we can do it across the road. I don't want anyone seeing you – the networks will go wild if they know I'm giving an interview to anyone else.'

Our motley crew leapt into a cab and flew down to the East River. Rupert came out on a freezing night wearing a pullover and we did the interview. It was a minor miracle that neither of us came down with pneumonia. But just before we wrapped up, I asked him about Robert Hughes. Why had he sacked him? A pause, then a smile as wry as Bob's.

'I recall a dispute over the ownership of a case of champagne.'

• • •

Back in Australia, I threw myself into my new role at *The Bulletin*. Its acerbic deputy editor, Patricia Rolfe, used to call it the 'New Hellas School of Journalism' after the nearby Greek restaurant we used to frequent. Compared to my frenetic existence as a freelancer, life at *The Bulletin* was comparatively tranquil. I was so anxious not to be fired for under-production that I wrote more articles than Trevor could fit into the paper – filing once a week seemed shamefully idle.

In the age of the 60-second news cycle, with news reported online literally as it happens, the stately schedule of *The Bulletin* bears some reflection. We hit the newsstands on Wednesday morning, but the magazine had to be all but complete by the previous Friday evening. We could, with immense difficulty, just manage to get a big story into the magazine by 11 am on the Monday. All this meant that if we wanted to break a story, we needed to keep it under wraps for days. After filing a story on Friday, I used to anxiously wait for each morning's newspapers to see if my exclusive had become old news before our magazine had even been published.

In my ongoing attempts to ensure I didn't get fired (I don't know why I was so concerned but I was), I persuaded Trevor to let me write a weekly column about the law. In that more deferential era, it was disrespectful to the eminent men of the law – they were all men, too. At one point, I wrote a piece about the failings of the Family Court, and the chief judge accused me of contempt! I was so excited, but the attorney-general, Bob Ellicott, wasn't. I caught him striding through the corridors of the High Court and asked him if he was going to prosecute me. He stopped, glared at me with a chilly disdain, and said, 'If you think I'm going to make a martyr of you, Malcolm Turnbull, think again.' And, gown billowing, swept off.

Even though he'd been no help with my industrial problems at the city markets, Bob Carr and I had kept in touch. I knew that he'd left the ABC to work at the Labor Council on the promise of a Senate seat only to be dudded by the party machine. Bob introduced me to his friend Paul Keating and assures me that I asked him, 'If Lang is greater than Lenin, does that mean Keating is greater than Kerensky?'

I persuaded Trevor we should have a correspondent to write about unions and Labor with the insight of an insider, and that Bob was the one to do it.

Naturally, we had to seal the deal at lunch – we were journalists – and so Bob, Trevor and I repaired to another nearby Greek restaurant, the

Ithaca. I'd worded Bob up: 'Ask for twenty-five thousand dollars, Trevor will offer twenty-two, settle for twenty-four.'

Plates taken away, Trevor leaned across to Bob. 'So, Bob, what do you reckon you're worth?'

Bob almost stuttered. 'I don't know, what do you think?' Good grief, I thought, no wonder he wasn't much help in the markets.

'I reckon twenty thousand is good money for you, Bob, getting started with us.'

Before I could tip the table over or start a fire, Bob replied, 'Thank you, that's fine.' Trevor beamed and on the way back to the office congratulated himself on how much money he'd saved.

Bob did well at *The Bulletin* and went on to become the longest-serving premier of NSW, but his passion had always been foreign policy, and so I was pleased for his sake that long after leaving state politics he became a senator and Foreign minister for Julia Gillard. As is the way with politics, partisanship often got in the way when our paths crossed over the years, but he did perform one invaluable service for me in those *Bulletin* days.

Although lawyers rarely spoke to the media in those more taciturn days, I'd persuaded Tom Hughes QC (with a little help from his client Kerry Packer) to do an interview for *The Bulletin*. This was a coup. The Honourable Thomas Eyre Forrest Hughes was the nation's most sought-after barrister. A former attorney-general in the Gorton government, he commanded the incredible fee of $1000 a day. The cover picture was strong; the story was okay – Tom was brief and to the point. His nickname, after all, was 'Frosty'.

But if the father left me a little chilled, that wasn't the case with 19-year-old Lucy Hughes, who was in his office earning some money noting up law reports as I waited to see her father. I would have gladly waited forever. By the time I sat down with the great man, I was madly in love with his daughter.

But would she come out with me if I asked her? Bob and Helena Carr were about the only married couple I knew well and they were kind to provide the cover for our first date – at the Sorrento fish cafe at Circular Quay, as I recall.

To my surprise, a few months before meeting Lucy, I had won a Rhodes Scholarship. Previously I'd applied without success and so I hadn't been optimistic about my chances. My hotel-broker father was out at the North St Mary's Hotel in Western Sydney and I called him as soon as I knew. Dad put down the phone and, bursting with pride, told the publican the good news, who replied, 'That's great, Bruce. I've got a cousin who's high up in the Department of Main Roads – we should get them together.'

The Rhodes Scholarships were Cecil Rhodes's imperial fantasy. With his vast fortune made from diamonds, the founder of Rhodesia wanted to recruit young achievers who'd reinforce the best of British stock in the halls of Oxford and go on to rule the world together. Naturally, they'd all be white, and men, and so were drawn from the old settler dominions such as South Africa, Canada, Australia, New Zealand, the United States and, of course, Germany.

In the late 1970s there were about 60 Rhodes Scholars 'coming up' to Oxford each year, about half of whom were from the United States. They were no longer all white or even all men, with women admitted for the first time in 1977. The Rhodes Scholars from Australia typically did postgraduate degrees, as I did, whereas the Americans would do an Oxford three-year undergraduate degree in two years. The Americans stuck together and when I spent time with them, I concluded they all planned to be president one day. But so far Bill Clinton is the only Rhodes Scholar to be president. Australia has had three scholars become PM so far: Bob Hawke, Tony Abbott and myself.

The news of my selection brought me back to the attention of Kerry Packer. Everyone at Packer's Consolidated Press was thrilled. Even Ita Buttrose, editor-in-chief of *The Australian Women's Weekly*, spoke to me.

Kerry asked me to work as an assistant to his deputy chairman, Harry Chester, who'd been the right-hand man and chief financial officer for Kerry's father, Frank. Harry was a wise and steadying influence on 39-year-old Kerry. So, I spent the nine months or so before I went up to Oxford not just learning about the publishing business but actually doing deals, including spending a few weeks in Chicago negotiating an Australian licence for *Playboy* magazine and signing up the West Indies cricket team in Barbados for World Series Cricket.

Finally, in September 1978, I arrived at Oxford. I'd been accepted into Brasenose College, which sits on the southern side of Radcliffe Square, one of the most beautiful in Europe – especially on a chill night when the mist swirls around the confident neo-classicism of the Radcliffe Camera in the centre, framed by the austerely anxious gothic spires of the university church.

I started doing a business degree. After concluding the course was too much management speak and not enough finance, I returned to the law and enrolled in the Bachelor of Civil Law. The BCL is a tough black-letter law Master's degree by coursework, with the entire assessment based on six exams at the end of two years. This encouraged me to neglect my studies for the first year, a near-fatal mistake.

University life at Oxford was dominated by the undergraduates, who were generally three or four years my junior: I was an ancient 24. Nevertheless, I threw myself into plenty of university activities, even sport. I'd been a mediocre third-grade rugby player in Sydney, and I had no pretensions to an Oxford Blue, but I enjoyed playing for my college. It was almost a pleasure being tackled, as the English pitches were so soft compared to the hard, dry football fields of Australia.

Debating at the Oxford Union was a delight, although not always decorous. Among the guest speakers was Lucy's father, Tom, who came up while in the UK on a Privy Council appeal. Another was Richard Nixon. On one memorable night, future British PM Theresa Brasier and I argued over professionalism in sport with soccer legend Bobby Charlton in a debate presided over by Theresa's soon-to-be fiancé, Phil May.

I'd never been a full-time student and I didn't start at Oxford. Instead, I continued with my journalism, writing for Australian newspapers and magazines, and even contributing a few pieces to the *Chicago Tribune*. It wasn't all news reporting – I rewrote the text for a Time-Life book about Sydney for a flat fee of a thousand quid.

During the years since we'd met at Cambridge, I'd stayed in touch with Harry Evans and he again offered me a job on *The Sunday Times*, which I reckoned I could handle while supposedly studying at Oxford. However, all was not well at Times Newspapers Ltd. Just as I was hired, a long-running industrial battle with the printing unions resulted in the management locking the printers out. Stop the presses indeed!

The journalists union did a deal with management and the reporters remained on the payroll. The papers remained shut for a year. If everybody had known that was going to be the case, they could have gone on long holidays or written books (and a few did) but, as it happened, every few weeks there was news that a settlement was imminent, and we all set out researching and writing stories to fill the paper. Every month, I wrote thousands of words of copy, including a few investigations, that never saw the light of day.

The industrial dispute was over agreements with the printing unions that were completely absurd. And even the printers thought it was ridiculous, laughing in the bar of the Blue Lion pub, on the other side of the Gray's Inn Road, about all the fake names on the printers' payroll, the people who were paid but didn't show up. One archaic rule in particular always tickled me – that on the press floor there was a man with a rake and another with a broom. Why was that, I asked the shop steward.

'Well, the man with the broom is to sweep up the metal filings and the man with the rake is to collect the paper.'

'Why doesn't the guy with the broom just sweep up both?'

He looked at me as though I was a complete idiot and ordered another pint.

So, without much distraction from journalism or my legal studies, I turned my mind back to business and worked up a plan to publish the papers without the print unions. Packer was intrigued by it and I arranged a meeting between him and Harry Evans in Harry's little house in Pimlico. I say little only because it felt that way when Kerry walked in and occupied most of a three-seater couch. Also there was Harry's girlfriend, Tina Brown, who'd just started editing *Tatler*.

Kerry could see the opportunity. Because he didn't own anything else in the UK, the unions couldn't retaliate by boycotting other profitable businesses, as they could have done with the Thomson family, who owned Times Newspapers.

We called in the law firm Linklaters to advise us on all the complex legal implications of my wild scheme and had a meeting with them in Kerry's favourite suite at the Dorchester. Kerry was getting bored with the recital of so many laws and regulations we had to work around. Finally, he said, 'So, let's say I'm driving a truck full of papers out of the basement. There are picketers blocking the way. I lean out of the cab and say, very politely, "Get out of the way! Piss off!" I keep driving, very, very slowly. But they don't get out of the way, and,' he paused to have a drag on his cigarette, 'I run a few of them over. What law applies to me then?'

By this stage the Linklaters partner was white as a sheet, shaking as he nursed his briefcase on his knees. 'The ... the ... the law of murder, Mr Packer.'

We started talking with the Thomsons about a sale, but they opted to stick it out. It was a pity Kerry didn't buy it, as the plan we had was essentially the same as Murdoch later put in place at Wapping when he took on the print unions and brought the London newspaper business into the 20th century.

Packer introduced me to his friend Sir James Goldsmith, another colourful billionaire. Desperate to become a media mogul, he'd started a news magazine called *NOW!* I pitched to Goldsmith that he and Packer should do a new women's magazine in the UK. Ultimately, Packer decided against it, but Goldsmith was enthusiastic. We often met at his grand house in Richmond, where I'd sit in his study while Jimmy strode around the room chewing an impressively long cigar and addressing me like a public meeting. The only problem was that when he was gesticulating, it required enormous concentration to avoid being hit by sodden bits of tobacco flying off the end of the cigar.

For Lucy and me, absence did make the heart grow fonder, and whenever I could get back to Australia on Packer business, I did. She came to see me at the airport once and was so excited and happy she was prancing and bouncing up and down and then we both were jumping and hugging all at once. On all the hundreds of times I've passed through arrivals at Sydney Airport, I recall that moment – the prouncing Lucy in big boots, a long skirt and long blonde hair.

So, the best news I had that year was that Lucy, who was diligently studying law in Sydney, was coming over to stay with me in the Christmas holidays. I'd bought an old Fiat 126 for £100 and we decided to drive it through France to Naples and back. Luigi, for that was the car's name, used to struggle on the hills, and Lucy, who spoke Italian fluently in those days, composed a song of encouragement. '*Luigi il gialo, bravo e bello*', it began.

Ancient history and archaeology have always fascinated me, and I was entranced by the ruins at Pompeii. Perhaps too much. I was down in a hole inspecting the design of a Roman sewer when Lucy decided enough was enough. Hands on hips, in a pair of red overalls, her magnificent blonde mane blowing in the wind, she gave a speech worthy of the futurist Marinetti. 'I've had enough of all these ruins, all these old rocks and graves. This is yesterday, I want to be in today. I want to be where there's steel and glass. Let's go to Milan!' I was mesmerised.

Those weeks together, more than 40 years ago, were when we went from being friends and lovers to something much more. We hugged and cried at Heathrow when Lucy went back to Australia. It was 20 January 1979. I asked Lucy to marry me, and she laughed and said, 'Let's wait until we grow up,' but I think we knew then, tears streaming down our faces, that each of us was holding the love of their life.

My Fleet Street career in London caught up with me eventually. It dawned on some of the Brasenose dons that I was spending most of the week in London and rarely attended classes. Peter Birks was the senior law professor at Brasenose College and the leading authority on the law of restitution, something he expected me to discuss in the six essays I had to write for him. If they weren't up to scratch I'd be out – 'sent down'.

That was the wake-up call. I did the essays and they passed muster. I told Harry I had to put my head down and complete my degree. *The Sunday Times* was still shut, and I was bitterly disappointed to have worked for them for almost a year, writing screeds of copy and seeing none of it in print.

Lucy returned at the end of 1979 and I persuaded her to stay. I'd been living in a flat in North Oxford with Chris Hall, a friend from Brasenose. Lucy and I searched for a place to ourselves and found a tiny cottage, a doll's house really, covered with roses, at Cumnor, a village a little west of Oxford.

My powers of persuasion obviously worked because Lucy did agree to marry me, even if we hadn't both grown up. 'Well, you have,' I assured her. We decided to get married in the local church, but when we visited the vicar, Noel Durand, he told us he wasn't going to assist. I was, after all, a Presbyterian and Lucy a Catholic. 'Have you thought of the Registry Office?' he helpfully suggested.

'So, Vicar,' I said, 'the Church of England is an established church?'

'Yes,' he said.

'So you, therefore, are like a public servant.'

'Yes,' he replied, but with less conviction.

'So, wouldn't you agree that you have a duty to prevent and discourage fornication in your parish? Isn't that your job? And, let me tell you, Vicar, while Miss Hughes and I are not about to make any admissions, we are young, in good health and sorely tempted. You can ensure Long Leys Cottage is free of fornication by marrying us!'

He laughed long and loud. 'Of course I will marry you. Let's set the date.'

And so we did, on 22 March 1980. Geoffrey Robertson stood in for Lucy's dad, and while we had discouraged relatives from going to the expense of attending, my father, Bruce, showed up.

'I've only got one son,' he said when he knocked at the door of the cottage. 'And I'm not going to miss his wedding!'

'Very reassuring,' I laughed.

It was a blissful time to start our married life. Our cottage was surrounded by fields and we could walk along country paths to the River Thames or across the fields to pubs in Cumnor or Appleton. I was so happy to be with Lucy forever.

Encouraged by Lucy, I put in a huge effort to make up for my inattention in the first year of my course and managed to get a respectable '2:1' second-class honours degree. I was furious with myself for only answering four of the five questions in the Evidence exam, but it was probably karma. I was lucky to still be there!

Before returning to Sydney, Lucy and I spent our honeymoon in Sicily in the European summer of 1980, unconventionally bringing my best man, John Glover, along with us for the first week. John was a Rhodes Scholar from Victoria and Melbourne University law medallist. Rather shy and taciturn, he was wickedly funny, although Lucy perhaps shouldn't have taught him so many Italian swear words which, representing almost his entire Italian vocabulary, he had a habit of using at the worst possible moment.

Sicily was a memorable interlude for Lucy and me, and not only because it was our honeymoon. The island's history had included periods of tolerance and respect, which we both found inspiring. We've always been repelled by intolerance and discrimination of any kind. At Sydney University, I'd been captivated by the medieval history of Spain and of Sicily, where for centuries Christians, Muslims and Jews lived together in relative harmony – in what was known as *La Convivencia*, or The Coexistence. What struck us – and still does – was that around the world, with all our modern technology and sophistication, we see less tolerance and respect for other faiths than we did centuries ago.

Take the cathedral at Monreale, built by a Latin Catholic, King Ruggiero II. He covered the walls from shoulder height with mosaic scenes of the gospels and the Old Testament and a huge, haunting image of Christ Pantocrator above the apse. Those mosaicists were from Constantinople. They were Greek Orthodox, like many of his Sicilian subjects among whom were also many Muslims. My recollection is that we were told Muslim mosaicists, bound not to portray living creatures, added patterned designs to the floors and lower walls. Whether that was true or not, the cathedral formed a symbol in my imagination of a time and place where three religions – Catholic, Orthodox and Muslim – so often killing each other, had worked together to create a building, a jewel, of the most sublime beauty.

Back in Australia, Kerry Packer was keen for me to resume my work for him, but I was now committed to proving myself as an advocate. It may be that I wanted to prove myself to Lucy or her dad, Tom, who'd become like a second father to me. I'd acquired other mentors in the law who urged me to go to the Bar. These included Lucy's godfather, Tony Larkins, an extraordinarily generous and charming old judge, who'd been one of Frank Packer's closest friends. Laurence Street, the chief justice, also encouraged me to go to the Bar, speaking of the law with the same passionate affection with which Harry Evans used to speak about journalism.

'The barrister has the best of life,' he told me. 'A brief comes in, filled with challenges. You work them out, present your case, match your wit with your opponents. Perhaps you win, or not. But either way, the case is over, tie the ribbon round the brief and send it back to your instructing solicitor together with a polite request to be paid.'

I had a good start at the Bar. Tom included me in a couple of cases and Packer sent me a few briefs. No longer a journalist, I rejoined the Liberal Party. Not long after, the member for Wentworth, Bob Ellicott, resigned from parliament to go on to the Federal Court.

Though I was just 26 and had only been back in Australia for six months, I decided to have a go at the preselection. I had no reasonable prospect of success, but I thought there were probably going to be quite a few solicitors on the preselection panel and if I impressed them, perhaps they might send me a brief!

Well, that's how I convinced Lucy, who, wise woman that she is, was concerned that I might actually win the preselection. Lucy knew first-hand what it was like having a father in parliament and she wasn't keen at all on becoming a political wife bringing up children with her husband away in Canberra.

Still, she got swept up in the contest and before too long it looked like I might get a respectable number of votes, or even, incredibly, win. Not a chance, I assured her.

It was a huge field of 20 candidates. In the final count, I was beaten by eight votes by the former NSW opposition leader Peter Coleman, who'd lost his seat in the Wranslide of 1978.

Evidently Prime Minister Malcolm Fraser had intervened to support Coleman, phoning preselectors on his behalf. Fraser didn't know me from Adam; some people told me he'd been concerned I'd be an agent of Packer. Sir John Atwill, a towering grandee of the Sydney business establishment and the Liberal Party president, was a preselector, as was his wife, Susan. When John got the call from the PM, he told his wife they must both vote for Coleman. 'Don't be ridiculous,' said Susie. 'I'm voting for young Turnbull.' And she made a habit of it, supporting me in 2004 when I ran in, and won, the Wentworth preselection.

Truth be told, Fraser did me, and Lucy, a favour. After the preselection he rang and asked if I'd work for him as his media adviser 'to do for me what Brian Dale has done for Neville Wran'. Brian, Neville's press secretary, was outstanding in that role, but I was bemused that the chilly and aloof Fraser imagined that an adviser could cloak him with the natural warmth of the gregarious Neville Wran. Fraser's senior adviser, David Kemp, met me to discuss the idea further, but I politely declined. It was time to focus on the law and strive for the top of the Bar.

I enjoyed the Bar, if not all the barristers, many of whom were conservative and stuffy. Among my mentors I counted John Sackar, with whom I read, Henric Nicholas as well as Michael McHugh, who astounded me with his photographic memory: he could recall not only a reference in a law report but the precise place on the page where it was to be found.

Lucy and I bought a terrace in Brougham Street, Woolloomooloo. It was just below Victoria Street, Potts Point, and next to Kings Cross. We used to get to the Cross by walking through the Piccadilly Hotel, whose back door opened into a lane behind our house. They had a lot of live music there. Occasionally, coming back with our groceries from Woolworths, we stopped and listened to Chrissy Amphlett and the Divinyls – this was before they were famous, when they still played in pubs.

We loved living there; it was a quick walk into the city or across to the Andrew 'Boy' Charlton swimming pool on the western side of Woolloomooloo Bay. Lucy swam there daily for most of her pregnancy with our first child, Alex, who was born in August 1982. Outside of the public housing in Woolloomooloo, there were very few families in the area. When Lucy took Alex to the Kings Cross Baby Health Centre, the nurses used to joke about him being their only 'middle-class baby'. Things have since changed; now the inner city is full of families of all ages, the only drawback being the fashionable monster prams that clutter the sidewalk outside the cafes!

Things were going well in every respect by the end of 1982 – my better-than-expected performance in the Wentworth preselection had indeed raised my profile, and my practice, especially in media and broadcasting law, was flourishing. Under the cloak of pseudonymity, given the sensibilities of the Bar, Lucy and I were co-authoring the *Bulletin* law column, now called 'The Officious Bystander', and baby Alex was in rude, and often loud, good health. Our daughter, Daisy, would follow in 1985.

But then disaster. It was Remembrance Day, 11 November 1982, and I was at home having lunch with Lucy and her father and stepmother, Chrissie, when my clerk, Les O'Brien, called. He told me my father was dead, killed in a light-plane crash.

I refused to believe it. Bruce had told me so many times, 'Don't smoke, don't ride motorcycles and don't fly in single-engine aircraft.' He was semi-retired by this stage, living on a beautiful property he'd bought the year before outside Scone in the Hunter Valley. He loved the country and was a keen and very capable horseman, so it was perfect for him. But he was still doing some hotel broking with a Newcastle broker called Des Curran, and he and Des and two other men had been flying to the country town of Casino to complete the sale of a pub.

The pilot wasn't instrument rated, got disoriented in cloud over the Barrington Tops, went into a spin, tore a wing off the plane and crashed in a park in the town of Gloucester. The pilot and his four passengers knew they were in trouble for some time before the crash, and to this day I shudder when I think about those long, terrifying minutes before the final impact.

Until I met Lucy, Bruce was the closest person to me in the world. We had a very different relationship to most fathers and sons; it was less formal, but in some ways more intense. We were more like brothers. When we went to the pub together, Bruce, planning to chat up girls, would often say, 'Don't call me Dad; it makes me look old.' But then we knew each other so well, we could almost read each other's minds. Of course we argued and I often bristled at his constant stream of advice – but looking back, I have to say he was almost always right.

He'd just turned 56 when he was killed and was super fit. Lean and athletic, he was running marathons and, given the genes he inherited from those old Hawkesbury River Turnbulls, he'd have likely lived into his 90s. I miss him every single day. Alex wasn't even three months old when Bruce died, but at least they met. He was very excited about being a grandfather. 'I'll take him to the park,' he said. 'Kids are great for starting up a conversation with the young mothers ... better than dogs I reckon.' Parks aside, he would have been the best grandfather. Every time I took the kids out riding, I could feel him so keenly – as if he was about to ride up beside us.

That was why I buried Dad on his farm, which we kept and expanded. Every paddock, every tree and every rock reminded me of him. I kept all his possessions, even his clothes. They were too small for me but I gave them to Alex when he was older, and he still wears some of his grandfather's boots: Bruce was fastidious about his appearance, a bit of a dandy, and some of his riding boots were handmade for him by a saddler in Kempsey.

The week before Bruce was killed, Kerry Packer had asked me to leave the Bar to work for him and manage all his legal affairs. His long-term general counsel, John Kitto, was retiring and Packer was fed up with the cost of his law firm, Sydney's largest, Allen Allen & Hemsley.

Looking back, it's quite absurd that a man with a vast media empire would put all his legal affairs into the hands of a 28-year-old barrister who'd only been admitted two years earlier. That didn't occur to me at the time; I was pretty confident.

But, while flattering, it was the last thing I wanted to do. I was going well at the Bar and my ambition was to get to the top of the profession and equal, if not excel, Lucy's father. Although I promised Kerry I'd think about it seriously, I left him with the impression I wasn't likely to accept. I wanted to maintain a good relationship with him, as he was a growing source of work as my media practice grew.

Bruce hadn't enjoyed much financial success until he was in his mid-40s, but in the decade or so before his death he'd acquired a few minority shares in hotels as well as some property in Sydney. After serious contemplation, I decided a quiet year in the corporate sector with Kerry would give me time to wind up Bruce's affairs. So, I told Kerry I'd take him up on his offer, for a year, and rented my chambers out with a view to returning in 12 months. That wasn't quite how things would pan out.

2

Law, Business and the Republic

(1983–2003)

CHAPTER 4

Packer:
defending the Goanna

Not long after I started as his general counsel, I had a spirited argument with Kerry Packer about some unorthodox, probably unlawful, transaction he was hatching. He was furious with me – he hated being told he couldn't get his way.

'Kerry, this is a very bizarre way to run a public company.'

Tantrum forgotten, he paused, smiled, folded his hands across his belly and replied in a benign, solicitous tone. 'Ah, Malcolm, of course. But what you overlook is that I am a very bizarre person.'

And so he was; one contradiction piled on top of another.

Kerry had inherited the Consolidated Press television and magazine empire in 1974 from his father, Sir Frank. He wasn't intended to be the heir – that was meant to be his elder brother, Clyde, but Clyde had fallen out with his father. After the old man died, Kerry bought Clyde's share. But years of belittling criticism from his father had left Kerry plagued by self-doubt, despite him being wholly in control.

By 1983, Kerry's confidence had received a boost. He'd set up World Series Cricket in 1977 as a rival international competition to the test matches run by the Australian Cricket Board and their international counterparts. I'd played a tiny role in this, travelling to Barbados in 1978 to sign up the West Indies team. Ultimately, Kerry triumphed, peace was restored, cricket was modernised in many ways and the players were better paid. Best of all for Kerry, his Nine Network got the television rights – the denial of which had started the rebellion in the first place.

The first big deal I worked on was Kerry's 1983 privatisation of Consolidated Press Holdings. He borrowed $350 million to do that, a staggering sum in those days. At the same time, Kerry's gambling addiction got worse and worse. With so much debt, he was struggling to find the cash to pay his growing gambling debts. All of this attracted him to 'clever' investment schemes that promised quick returns for him personally. John Singleton had introduced him to his friend Brian Ray, a charismatic Queensland property developer who always had some great deals promising big and quick profits.

In 1980, Prime Minister Malcolm Fraser set up a Royal Commission to investigate the activities of a particularly corrupt trade union, the Ship Painters and Dockers Union. Its members and officials had been involved in many areas of organised crime, including tax evasion. This led the commissioner, Frank Costigan, and his counsel assisting, Douglas Meagher, to some transactions from the late 1970s involving Kerry Packer and Brian Ray. The commission came visiting.

Kerry used to keep millions in cash in a safe in his office – he told the Costigan Royal Commission this was due to his 'squirrel mentality', but the reality was he wanted to be able to settle with bookmakers in cash. Was it to avoid paying tax? Partly, I think it was, but he was ashamed of his gambling, too.

Tax minimisation schemes of enormous artificiality were being dreamed up by leading law and accounting firms and blessed by the top QCs. They were taking the lead from a very lenient High Court under Chief Justice Sir Garfield Barwick.

I hadn't specialised in tax law, but from the outset I thought most of these schemes would end in tears and I stayed out of them. Lucy and I didn't even set up a family trust. Our view was that it was better to pay the tax and sleep at night so that, refreshed the next day, you could focus on making money rather than scheming up ways to dud the tax man.

When Costigan first took an interest in Packer's tax affairs and dealings with Brian Ray, I assumed we'd find a way through it – likely involving an expensive settlement with the Australian Tax Office (ATO). But the Costigan Commission didn't stop at investigating Packer's tax activities; Costigan and Meagher became convinced that Packer was a criminal mastermind.

Meanwhile, worried about being prosecuted, Kerry started spending a lot of time abroad, and even asked me to investigate getting him citizenship in a country that didn't have an extradition treaty with Australia. For months, he shuttled between the Terrace Suite at the Dorchester or a spa in Carlsbad, California.

Nothing baffled me about Kerry more than his gambling. He'd often go to his friend John Aspinall's casino in London. On a rare evening when I joined him, he lost over $3 million. It seemed completely mad.

'Ah, you don't understand gambling, do you?' he said as I looked on aghast. 'There's no fun unless the amount you can lose is big enough to hurt. So three thousand dollars? Well, it's a tip. But three million, that hurts.'

The public learned of Costigan's wider suspicions about Packer in September 1984 with the appearance in *The National Times*, a weekly Fairfax newspaper, of leaked 'case summaries' from the Royal Commission. The central figure was a person codenamed 'Goanna', who was suspected of the 1982 murder of former bank manager Ian Coote, among other crimes. Coote had been working for Brian Ray. Costigan's theory was that he had been murdered to stop him disclosing the extensive criminal activities of Ray and his partner, Packer.

The Goanna codename didn't fool anyone. It was obvious it referred to Packer; it was obvious the commission had leaked the material to *The National Times*; and it was obvious (at least to me) that Costigan and Meagher had jumped the shark – the entire aquarium in fact.

But knowing your accusers have over-reached is scant consolation if your fortune is tied up in television and radio licences, all of which depend on your remaining 'a fit and proper person', or indeed if your American bankers are getting nervous and asking for their money back.

Kerry's depression worsened; he could see his whole empire crumbling around him. The empire his father had left him, the empire he'd have lost due, ultimately, to his own weakness, his addiction to gambling. He was drowning in a sea of self-doubt and self-loathing.

His fears of being charged peaked. He was convinced he could never get a fair trial. At one point, he sent his Portuguese valet, Manuel, to get his shotgun so he could blow his brains out. With the callowness of youth, I didn't think he was ever likely to take his own life but now, having been through dark periods of my own, I can see I should have been more empathetic.

His senior executives were deeply pessimistic, so perhaps it was as well that at that time his closest adviser was 29 and fearless. As Nine Network CEO Sam Chisholm used to say, 'Malcolm, one thing we have in common is we're both often wrong, but never in doubt.'

So, what was to be done?

A group assembled in the boardroom on the third floor of 54 Park Street, Sydney, on Friday 28 September 1984. Kerry was, as usual, at the head of the table smoking furiously. My father-in-law, Tom Hughes QC, was there, as was Alec Shand QC. They'd been acting for the Packers for decades; ditto Jock Harper, the senior partner of Allens. The three senior lawyers were all of the same mind – Kerry should sue *The National Times* for libel.

But to me, it wasn't a legal issue any more. It was political. 'We have to destroy Costigan's credibility right now,' I said.

'Alright, son, how are you going to do that?' Kerry asked.

I handed out copies of my 6000-word statement describing how Costigan had denied Kerry natural justice. I'd already taken Kerry through it. Now the lawyers had to read it.

'Kerry, Malcolm's written a powerful polemic,' said Tom. 'But it's very defamatory of Costigan and would be in contempt of the Royal Commission.'

'Is that right?' Kerry said. 'So, how long would I get for contempt?'

The lawyers conferred.

'Well, the maximum penalty is three months' imprisonment. You wouldn't get that, of course,' Shand observed.

'Okay, fair enough. I can serve the three months for contempt concurrently with the life sentence for murder. Fuck 'em, Malcolm's right. We're going to fight.'

And with that the meeting was over. Kerry got up and we walked out of the room across to the reception desk on the floor. There sat one of Kerry's oldest employees, Edith, who was in charge of the telex machine.

The 6000-word counterblast had been typed up by Edith earlier and she had a long ribbon which, once fed into her machine, would send the message out simultaneously to telex machines in every newsroom and political office around the country.

Kerry looked balefully at the tape. Even for a gambler like him, this was a big call.

'Righto, Edith, let's roll the dice.'

She fed the tape into the machine. It coughed a couple of times and then started to clatter, slowly at first and then with a steady speed, as the words of the statement began printing out on long rolls of telex paper in dozens of newsrooms across the country.

It was stern stuff, describing *The National Times*'s publication of the case summaries as 'but another step in a malicious and disgusting campaign of vilification' by Packer's commercial rivals and Costigan's conduct of the Royal Commission as 'outrageously unjust'. Among the things I highlighted was that Costigan's refusal to give Packer any details of adverse findings he might make was completely at odds with all the conventional principles of natural justice:

> The commission has proceeded to hear evidence from persons concerning my affairs in secret. I have not only been denied the right to be represented at these secret hearings, but I have been denied access to the transcripts of the evidence. Accordingly, I have been left consistently in the dark by the Royal commission. This extraordinary practice of holding secret sessions is reminiscent of the procedure of the star chamber and, to give a more recent analogy, of the secret trials conducted by the KGB in the Soviet Union.

I'm not sure how strongly Kerry espoused the principles I was putting into his mouth but, for my part, the values I was setting out 35 years ago were sincerely held. Over the years that followed I always sought to uphold them.

> House burglars and car thieves are every day accorded rights which I have been denied. They may not be accused of any crime other than in the context of a fair trial where they can face their accusers and state their case before an impartial tribunal.
>
> I do not ask for any more rights than that house burglar, but I do not expect to be accorded any less. I simply expect a fair go and that is precisely what I have been denied.
>
> The Australian tradition of disrespect for 'the tall poppies' is an important antidote to humbug. But it should not degenerate into an orgy of suspicion, allegation and innuendo at the end of which anyone who has achieved anything in his life will be presumed a crook. We must not forget the greatest Australian tradition, that of fair play.[1]

The impact was electric, and every newspaper in Australia printed the statement in full. It probably could have been shorter, but the comprehensive nature of the response had a purpose. I wanted to demonstrate in great detail why Kerry was wrongly accused: you shouldn't have to prove your innocence, but to stay in business Kerry had no choice.

Remarkably, there was an upsurge of sympathy for Packer both in the media and in the public. Yes, he was a big, rough, rich bastard, but Australians do have a deep-rooted sense of a fair go. Many started to look askance at the Costigan witch hunt, which we'd characterised as a 'new McCarthyism'.

The statement – a ferocious attack on the credibility and integrity of the Royal Commission coupled with a detailed defence – gave us breathing space.

Around this time I got a call from a detective sergeant in the Australian Federal Police (AFP). Brian Brinkler had been working with the Royal Commission and had become increasingly concerned about its direction. He told me that not only had Meagher been aware the case summaries had been leaked to *The National Times* but he and the editor, Brian Toohey, had met to discuss them in a Chinese restaurant in Bank Place, Melbourne. He added that Meagher had reported on the meeting to Costigan, but that neither of them took any step to seek an injunction to stop these highly confidential and defamatory materials being published.

Brinkler professed to be outraged by Meagher's conduct, but obviously didn't want his identity as our informant to be known.

Brian Toohey later claimed the case summaries had been 'widely circulated within Government'.[2] I wasn't convinced: Royal Commissions generally don't circulate their conclusions to governments in draft form – they present the full report, which is then usually tabled in parliament.

But in any event, if Meagher and Costigan knew Toohey had a copy of the case summaries and did nothing to stop them being published, then they were complicit in their publication, even if they hadn't actually handed them over. Years later, both Meagher and Costigan confirmed to journalist Paul Barry they'd had advance knowledge of the leak of the case summaries to *The National Times*.[3]

I wanted to keep up the attack on the Royal Commission. As I said to Packer, 'We have to destroy Costigan's credibility, so that whatever he says in the final report is discredited.'

Fired up, I put out a statement in which I said, 'Meagher and Costigan have conducted themselves most reprehensibly in failing to stop an unauthorised and illegal leak of information which was inevitably going to do immense or irreparable damage to the reputation of Kerry Packer.'[4] And I challenged them both to sue me.

Nothing of the sort happened. Next I hit on the plan of Packer suing Meagher for libel, alleging he'd published the case summaries to *The National Times* to enable us to subpoena the AFP records. Unfortunately,

Justice David Hunt (an early Turnbull hater) was presiding at the preliminary hearing and effectively demanded we provide the evidence to support our allegation. We couldn't do that without revealing Brinkler's identity so we had to drop the case.

Hunt was scathing, calling the case an abuse of process and my statements about Meagher an attempt 'to poison the fountain of justice'.[5]

'Don't worry, son,' Kerry said. 'Badge of fucking honour.'

The Royal Commission's final report was presented to the government on 1 November and most of its volumes were published after being tabled in parliament. Three volumes dealing with Packer were kept confidential – the ones containing the allegations of tax evasion, drug trafficking and, worst of all, murder.

But it was clear from the published material alone that Costigan believed Packer was responsible for Ian Coote's murder. That was but one of many more specific allegations that Kerry had never had an opportunity to answer. I drafted another point-by-point refutation protesting the denial of natural justice.

Costigan had recommended his findings both in the public and confidential volumes be sent off to the police and the new National Crime Authority (NCA) to investigate. That could take years. How could we strike another blow against Costigan's credibility, but quickly?

The most damaging allegation was that of murder. Coote was working for Brian Ray as an accountant when the Bank of New South Wales's internal fraud unit began investigating him for some transactions he'd approved while a bank manager years before. Coote became depressed, and he was found dead beside a road in Loganholme on 16 December 1982. The Queensland Police recorded it as a suicide; no inquest was held.

Central to Costigan's conclusion that the suicide had been faked was that the entry wound was 7 centimetres by 8 centimetres. Costigan had obtained expert ballistic evidence to say that, accordingly, the small-bore .410 calibre shotgun had to have been at least 2 metres away and, therefore, couldn't have been held by Coote. Mind you, none of this had been put to Packer during the commission's secret hearings.

So, I figured if I could prove Costigan had got the murder allegation wrong, that would undercut the credibility of everything else he said.

I phoned the wily old National Party politician Sir Joh Bjelke-Petersen, then in his 16th year as Queensland premier. I'd got to know Joh, aged 73, through Brian Ray and he seemed to like me.

'Sir Joh,' I said after explaining the background. 'The only way I can clear Kerry's name is if we have an inquest into Coote's death. Then we can get all the evidence out in the open.'

Initially, Joh had reservations. 'Look here, young Malcolm, I can't go round wasting public money on inquests where there's no need to have one.'

'Please, Sir Joh, it's life and death here for Kerry ...'

'You see, it's very obvious the poor soul took his own life. No need for an inquest.'

'Well, that didn't impress Mr Costigan,' I pointed out.

'Now, young Malcolm, what do you know about shotguns?'

I told Joh I owned a couple at our farm, and the conversation drifted off onto guns until I got him back to the point.

'You see, Malcolm, shotgun pellets go out in a widening cone, so the smaller the wound is, the closer the barrel must have been to the target or, in this case, poor Mr Coote.'

'Yes?'

'And I have in front of me some very clear photographs of poor Mr Coote when the police found him. Sir Terence was very kind to send them up to me. Do you know Sir Terence?'

Then followed a discussion about the qualities of the police commissioner, and finally we got back to the subject.

'And what I can see is that the entry wound is tiny, not much bigger than the button on his shirt. The poor man was clearly leaning over the gun with the barrel pressed up against his chest.'

My heart jumped. This was it, evidence that for whatever reason Costigan had ignored or missed.

'So, Sir Joh, now I really, really need to have this inquest. This will clear Kerry's name.'

Sir Joh relented, the inquest was held on 6 December in Brisbane and it was a humiliating defeat for the Costigan Royal Commission.

It turned out that the 7×8-centimetre wound was from well inside Coote's chest, as measured by the police pathologists; it wasn't the entry wound at all. For reasons never explained, the photographs sent to Sir Joh hadn't been referenced by the Royal Commission.

Added to that incredible sloppiness, there was irrefutable evidence of malice. On 20 June 1984, Detective Senior Constable Gary Wilkinson, the police officer who'd reported on Coote's death, had been called to give evidence in one of Costigan's secret hearings. I put him in the box at the inquest and asked him whether he'd had any discussions with Douglas Meagher prior to giving evidence.

He said he had. Meagher had told him that Mr Packer was 'involved in organised crime in Australia'. I asked him if he could recall the exact words the counsel assisting the Royal Commission used. Wilkinson replied, 'I don't remember the entire words. But one was "he is a prominent criminal and myself and the Commissioner intend to destroy him".'

The coroner, Bob Bougure, concluded there was a complete lack of evidence to support a finding of murder and no basis for suggesting Brian Ray or Kerry Packer had anything to do with Coote's death.

Flushed with success, I gave a stirring address from the steps of the courthouse, asserting that the decision meant you couldn't give credit to any of Costigan's claims. After all, if you're slipshod with an allegation of murder, why would you be trusted with allegations of lesser offences?

This line was taken up by much of the media and it coloured public opinion. From then on, the Costigan Commission was thoroughly discredited.

The rest of the allegations were left to the NCA to investigate. One way and another, I spent much of 1985 in hearings before the NCA, all held in secret, but at least in accordance with the rules of natural justice.

My original plan to return to the Bar after a year as Packer's general counsel had gone by the wayside. When the Costigan drama broke, about nine months into my time with Kerry, I'd resolved to see it through, believing firmly that nobody was better able to get him out of the mess than me.

Early on, I'd recruited Bruce McWilliam from Allen Allen & Hemsley, and between us we were handling all the legal work of Kerry's sprawling media empire. Bruce is the most brilliant commercial lawyer with whom I've ever worked. He combined great technical skills with considerable charm and had a knack for making deals happen. My assumption, or hope, had been that after I departed Consolidated Press, he'd repay my patronage with lots of lucrative briefs and retainers as I advanced my career as an advocate.

Careerwise, I wasn't where I wanted to be. Working for Kerry was terrifying; his lack of respect for the law or good corporate governance meant disaster was never far off. And while he was more open with me than anyone else, he was never fully transparent.

Once, when I was trying to get to the bottom of some murky transaction or other and pressing him for more details, I said, 'Kerry, you may as well tell me. I already know more about you than anyone else.'

He cast me a suspicious look, and then taking a long drag on his cigarette said, 'Yeah, you might be right, but I know more about you than you know about me.'

Packer made sure his closest executives were locked in with company cars, company loans on their houses, even payment of their kids' school fees. In the days before fringe benefits tax, most of the real value of an executive's compensation was outside of their salary. Wary of that kind of dependence, I'd insisted all of my compensation was in my salary. Frankly, I wasn't comfortable as an employee of anyone, let alone the owner of a family business. Being a lifelong Packer family retainer, no matter how well paid, had no appeal.

Dad had drilled into me the importance of working for yourself, of being your own man. I enjoyed being part of a team but sensed I was better suited to partnership than employment. Plus, if I was out on my own, that meant Lucy could work with me and we'd both be able to better manage our hours. We wanted family time with Alex and Daisy, who had arrived on 5 January 1985. So flexibility was absolutely key.

In the course of 1985, I persuaded Kerry that Bruce McWilliam and I should set up our own law firm. We'd do all his legal work for $850,000 a year – about what we reckoned our in-house operation was already costing him. I'd do all the advocacy required, but he'd foot the bill if he wanted to hire a QC.

It was a great deal for Kerry, saving him many millions compared to using a big law firm. It incentivised Bruce and me to get the job done and not run up hundreds of billable hours as most law firms do.

Bruce and I bought four floors of a small building, 60 Park Street, next to Consolidated Press. For Packer, there wasn't much difference in terms of our availability. But crucially for us, we could start taking on other clients.

CHAPTER 5

Spycatcher:
taking on Number 10

Turnbull McWilliam, as Bruce and I named our new firm, started business on 1 January 1986 with Packer as our first and foundation client. It looked like the NCA would recommend to the director of public prosecutions (DPP) that Packer had a case to answer on tax fraud. Late in 1986, however, the DPP advised us he wasn't going to prosecute Packer, and in March 1987, Attorney-General Lionel Bowen said Packer was 'entitled to be regarded by his fellow citizens as unsullied by allegations and insinuations which have been made against him'.[1]

Our plan was to seek clients beyond the Packer empire but the first was an unlikely one. Only a few weeks into a hot Sydney January, London solicitor David Hooper paid me a visit. David acted for Heinemann, the UK publisher. They had a contract to publish the memoirs of ex-MI5 agent Peter Wright, now living in Tasmania. Wright had served as a scientific officer for the Royal Navy during the Second World War. From 1951 until he retired in 1976, he worked for MI5 – Britain's security service. These were the paranoid days of the Cold War, of British traitors Kim Philby, Guy Burgess and Donald Maclean. Wright's job was hunting for Russian moles and he'd conducted an investigation into whether Roger Hollis, head of MI5 from 1956 to 1965, had been a Russian agent.

In his book *Spycatcher*, Wright recalled his time in MI5 and laid out his case against Hollis, who he believed shouldn't have been cleared. Hooper told me the book was a rehash of Cold War tales others had already told and contained nothing new. The British government had obtained a preliminary injunction preventing publication a few months before. From my work with Packer, I knew that it was settled law in Australia that the

British government would have to first prove the matters they wanted to keep secret were, in fact, still confidential. Then they'd have to prove that there would be some real detriment to the public interest if publication were to proceed. I knew most of the lawyers who'd advised Heinemann they would lose, and they included some of Australia's leading QCs, but, in this instance, I thought they were wrong, and so did Hooper. By now, however, his client had run up costs in excess of $200,000; he was turning to me as the lawyer of last resort.

'I can't retain you now,' Hooper said. 'The clients are still very depressed about it all. They want to throw in the towel. Will you write me an advice and give me a firm and very low quote to do the case? I may be able to persuade them to fight on if they're satisfied it won't cost them very much.'

I certainly met the market on price, agreeing to do the case for $20,000 as a flat fee with an additional sum if the trial went for more than two weeks! The upshot was that the first new clients of Turnbull McWilliam were Heinemann publishers and Peter Wright, whom I visited in the shack south of Hobart that he and his wife, Lois, called home. The fences were falling down, and the few horses looked as miserable as their owners. Peter and Lois were broke.

Peter was 74, frail yet with an intensity about him, almost a fanaticism, that must have been unnerving for all those traitors and suspected traitors he'd interrogated during the dark days of the Cold War.

My efforts to settle the case out of court – both formally and through intermediaries like my friend Tory MP Jonathan Aitken – went nowhere. The Thatcher government responded sternly to our invitation to nominate the passages in the manuscript they wanted to cut out. Their position was that every single line in the book was objectionable. Civil servants were bound by the Official Secrets Act not to ever publish anything about their work, whether it was in the public domain or not. Mrs Thatcher assigned Sir Robert Armstrong, her cabinet secretary and the head of the UK Civil Service, to give the evidence for the British government.

While in the UK in April 1986 doing some work for Packer, I took the opportunity to try again for a settlement. Hooper and I called on the Treasury solicitor, John Bailey. We were making no progress and got up to leave. Bailey said to me, 'Your client, Mr Wright, he's a very sick man, isn't he?' I nodded. He had a serious heart condition, I said; it was one of the reasons I wanted to settle the case as quickly as possible.

Bailey, who was helping me with my raincoat, gripped my arm hard and said, 'Well, you tell him from me that he'd better seek some medical advice before he comes to court. He'll get no quarter in the witness box on account of his ill health.'

'Well, you tell Armstrong from me, Mr Bailey, that whatever happens to Wright, *he* will be politically ruined by this case,' I retorted.

I regretted that arrogant remark as soon as I'd uttered it, not least because it so delighted Bailey. He'd got under my skin. Smiling with satisfaction, he patted me on the back. 'Well, well, young man, we'll see what you are like on your feet, won't we?'

Many lawyers who take on cases like this expect to lose and aspire to a glorious defeat. Lucy and I had no interest in losing. To that end, we put in hard, detailed research and interlocutory work, demanding answers and documents from the British through interrogatories and discovery.

The British fought every step of the way, refusing to produce documents or answer questions on oath. After the trial judge, Philip Powell, ruled against them, they took us up to the Court of Appeal. They had one of Australia's largest law firms acting for them plus several top barristers, three QCs and their own UK legal team. Our legal team was me, Lucy and David Hooper with help from some of the (even) younger lawyers in our office including Colin Winter and Deborah Huber. Bruce, thankfully, kept our commercial practice going.

Part of our case was that the book had no confidential information in it at all. Paul Greengrass, the investigative journalist who'd ghostwritten *Spycatcher*, came to stay with us for eight weeks during the trial. He and Lucy painstakingly produced the 'consolidated particulars of public domain', a huge tome that demonstrated *Spycatcher* was a load of old cobblers.

As we worked through the preliminary hearings and evidence, a story of conspiracy and intrigue emerged, as fascinating as any story in *Spycatcher* itself.

Wright, the son of a radio technician, had followed in his father's footsteps. He hadn't attended a posh school or gone to university, somewhat unusually in the establishment milieu of MI5. However, if Wright wasn't quite 'top drawer', his friend Lord Victor Rothschild certainly was. A member of the great financial dynasty and director of his family's bank, he'd worked in MI5 during the war and stayed close to the intelligence community throughout his life.

The extent to which MI5 and MI6 had been penetrated by Soviet agents was a scandal. Author Andrew Boyle's 1979 book, *The Climate of Treason*, all but named Sir Anthony Blunt as the fourth member of the Cambridge ring of Russian spies after Philby, Burgess and Maclean. Thatcher was forced to confirm Blunt's treachery in a statement in the House of Commons.

It was a very British tale. Blunt was a leading art historian and had been since 1945 the surveyor of the Queen's pictures, essentially the head curator of her immense collection. He'd been knighted in 1956 and held many other distinguished academic posts, including director of the Courtauld Institute – despite suspicions that, like his friend Burgess, he was passing secrets to the Soviets. Finally, he confessed to spying in 1964 and was given immunity from prosecution in return for his informing on other members of the Cambridge spy ring. He retained all his positions until his public exposure in 1979, when he lost them all, including his knighthood.

The hypocrisy of the Blunt case seems breathtaking. Here's a man who was not only suspected of but has confessed to espionage. And yet, because he's part of the establishment and close to the royal family, he keeps his position. And everything is hushed up. Until it isn't, and then he gets sacked and buried under a mountain of public condemnation.

Blunt, like Guy Burgess, was a close friend of Victor Rothschild. Victor knew everyone and everything, including Wright's conviction that Roger Hollis had been a Soviet agent. Wright had written up a dossier about Hollis and asked Victor to pass it on to Mrs Thatcher. Instead, Victor introduced Wright to Chapman Pincher, a leading journalist who specialised in the intelligence world. Pincher was known to be used by MI5 and MI6 as a trusted conduit to whom to leak material they wanted to see published. Wright gave his dossier to Pincher, who proposed to turn it into a book. Wright would brief Pincher on the Hollis investigation and much more besides. The three agreed Wright would get half the royalties; Rothschild would ensure they went to Wright via a Swiss bank account so that Wright wouldn't be exposed as Pincher's source.

It was a conspiracy between Pincher, Rothschild and Wright to breach the Official Secrets Act. Lord Rothschild, pillar of the establishment, was the ringmaster and the paymaster. It was the stuff of a le Carré novel.

The information Wright gave Pincher was genuinely confidential. *Their Trade is Treachery* was the outcome, and its publication in 1981 was a bombshell. Margaret Thatcher had to acknowledge to the House of Commons there'd been an investigation into whether Hollis had been a Soviet agent but, she said, the conclusion was he hadn't been, and all the security breaches of which he was suspected could have been the work of Blunt or Philby.

Plainly, our claim that the *Spycatcher* material had previously been published wouldn't assist us if, as was the case, the prior publication had been the work of Peter Wright himself. He'd be seeking to benefit from his own wrongdoing. However, what if the prior publication had been okayed by the British government?

When we scrutinised all the recent books about intelligence, it was obvious that a number had been seen by MI5 before being printed. One that stood out – released in 1982 – was *A Matter of Trust* by Nigel West, a pseudonym for future MP Rupert Allason. The government had secured an interim injunction to restrain publication, then negotiated on some deletions before waving it through. Why would they not do the same for *Spycatcher*, and why did they not try to stop Pincher's book, *Their Trade is Treachery*, being published in the same year?

Armstrong had sworn the main affidavit for the UK government in the case and, prompted by our interrogatories, stated that the West book had been allowed to be published once the government was satisfied information 'in breach of a duty of confidentiality to the Crown had been removed'.[2] This didn't stack up to me; plenty of never-before-released material remained in the book. And it was well known West had been talking to former MI5 officers, notably Wright's friend Arthur Martin.

But then Armstrong gave us an even more incredible answer about Pincher's book. He confirmed that the government had had copies of the manuscript prior to printing and said the reason no action had been taken to stop its publication was that the government had been 'advised that it had no basis to restrain the publication of the said book'.[3]

That was staggering. Pincher's book was full of new revelations – and boasts that they'd come from highly placed intelligence officers. It would have taken five minutes to get an injunction to stop it being published. This was the lie that brought the British government's case undone.

Armstrong came out to Australia to give evidence in the trial, which began on 17 November. He was used to the deference of an English courtroom and quickly found that in Australia he would be treated like any other witness. I cross-examined him for eight days. In London, it must have seemed like a world gone mad: Whitehall's most important civil servant being grilled in an Australian court by a bumptious 32-year-old lawyer who wasn't even wearing a wig and gown!

And to make matters worse, it seemed like a family affair on our side of the court. Our kids often came into the rather cosy courtroom 8B to see what Mum and Dad were up to. Daisy wasn't yet two, but Alex, a big four-year-old, used to insist on wearing a plastic London policeman's hat someone had given him, which everyone, even Sir Robert, found amusing. My mother was visiting Australia at the time and, together with Tony Larkins, watched most of the trial. I always suspected Coral had put Alex up to it!

We'd established that the government had been well aware of Pincher's book prior to publication – they'd admitted that. But we came across a letter Armstrong had written to the publisher. He noted the book had been reviewed in the *Daily Mail* and sweetly asked if the PM could have a copy of the book so that when she was asked to make a public statement she could be fully informed.

I pressed Armstrong to admit that the letter was calculated to mislead the publisher into believing the government didn't have a copy of the book when, in fact, it did. Armstrong conceded the point yet insisted his creation of a misleading impression hadn't amounted to lying.

Q: What is the difference between a misleading impression and a lie?
A: A lie is a straight untruth.
Q: What is a misleading impression – a sort of bent untruth?
A: As one person said, it is perhaps being economical with the truth.[4]

And then he laughed at his own little joke, only to stop when he realised nobody else was laughing, and especially not the judge. Our entire case was that the British were being hypocritical and cynical, that they'd allowed – if not encouraged – others to publish intelligence matters but for some reason weren't allowing Wright. And now, in one cynical jest, Armstrong had summed up all the hypocrisy of Whitehall.

But we had to drive that home, and the key was the plaintiff himself, the UK attorney-general, Sir Michael Havers. It was perfectly obvious that Armstrong's evidence about *Trade is Treachery* was false. An experienced lawyer like Sir Michael Havers couldn't possibly have advised the government that they were unable to stop the publication of a book that boasted of being full of intelligence secrets.

I pressed Armstrong again and again on this, but he stuck to his guns, declaring that he was 'resigned' to the attorney-general's advice and, 'It is not for me to query the attorney-general's view of what action he should take within the law.'[5]

When I challenged Armstrong that he had connived to ensure the Hollis affair 'would come out in the open through the pen of a safely conservative writer, rather than some ugly journalist on the left', the cabinet secretary brushed it aside: 'A very ingenious conspiracy theory, Mr Turnbull … totally untrue.'[6]

My theory wasn't just ingenious, it was right. Thatcher was directly responsible for encouraging Pincher to write a book about Hollis. Armstrong was lying, as he has subsequently confirmed to Mrs Thatcher's authorised biographer, Charles Moore, who writes in the third volume, published in 2019, 'Armstrong was fortunate that Turnbull had not had sight of his written advice for Mrs Thatcher of 10 June 1980 in which he had explicitly proposed briefing Pincher.'[7]

Working with what we knew then, we had to pressure Havers. Fortuitously, the House of Commons was sitting while the trial was going on. With some help from *The Observer*'s David Leigh, I got onto Neil Kinnock, the leader of the opposition.

'Are you sure that Havers couldn't have simply been rather muddled,' he said to me, intimating that he wasn't the brightest of attorneys-general.

'Nobody's that thick,' I replied. 'Neil, Armstrong isn't telling the truth, and you should nail him. You have to accuse Havers of legal incompetence until his friends in the Temple are laughing at him. No matter how mediocre a lawyer he may really be, he is the first law officer and he must have some pride.'

Kinnock sounded quite alarmed. 'But the real villain is the PM, not Havers. He's sick, you know. So's Rothschild for that matter. They're both old men. This business could kill them.'

Callow youth that I was, I made a joke of it.

'Oh well, comrade, everyone has to make sacrifices for the revolution. Why not start with Havers and Rothschild.'

Once Kinnock grasped that I wasn't backing down, he agreed to have a go. The next day, he asked Mrs Thatcher about the curious decision not to seek an injunction to stop *Trade is Treachery* being published. 'Is it not obvious,' he asked the PM, 'that any government who had fore-knowledge that information prejudicial to national security was to be published would have absolutely no difficulty obtaining an injunction against its publication?'[8]

Thatcher elected to make no response on the basis there were legal proceedings underway in Australia. But the media were all over the issue now. It was pretty simple: if Armstrong was telling the truth, then Havers must be either a fool who didn't know his law or a knave who was prepared to misrepresent it.

Even Justice Powell was puzzled, wondering aloud in court the next day why no one had obtained an order to impound every copy of the book and the manuscript: 'I would find myself pushed further and further towards the view that the Government knew exactly what was being done and it was not going to take a step to stop it and, if that be so, it is no great step towards saying that the Government authorised the book to be published.'[9]

Well, precisely! The next day Havers was asked the same question in the House of Commons and, like Thatcher, declined to give an answer.

Back in Sydney, Armstrong was showing signs of stress. The supremely confident master of Whitehall had shrunk in the witness box. What a disaster it was for him, at the peak of his career, to be looking like a harried, shifty liar in a court at the other end of the world.

By chance, days later I found myself alone with Armstrong in an elevator riding up to the eighth floor of the courts building. 'I hope you don't feel any of this is personal, Sir Robert. It's all part of the job, you know,' I feebly observed.

The doors of the elevator opened. Armstrong smiled thinly. 'Don't worry about me, Mr Turnbull. I'm just the fall guy.'

Thatcher's frazzled press office issued a release highlighting that Wright had received half of the royalties from *Their Trade is Treachery*, something Wright had never hidden. It was designed to make Peter look like a greedy old man rather than the sincere, if possibly misguided, patriot we were representing him to be.

My plan had been for Wright to tell his whole story, in context, in his evidence in the court, but this required a quick response. Peter had been extremely reluctant to say anything publicly about Rothschild, but I persuaded him he now had no choice. The old man thought about it as he played with a glass of whisky. He raised the glass and drained it, and putting the glass down with an emphatic thud gravely intoned, 'Oh well, poor dear Victor. Throw him to the wolves.'

And so, I suppose, he did.

We called a press conference and Peter revealed for the first time all the details of the arrangement with Rothschild and Pincher. Wright concluded his statement, 'All I know about Lord Rothschild and the ease with which *Their Trade is Treachery* was published leads me to the inescapable conclusion that the powers that be approved of the book.'[10]

Back in London, Havers was feeling the heat. He went to Thatcher and told her he wasn't going to carry the can any longer. And so, when Kinnock on 27 November asked the PM directly whether Havers was 'a fool or a fall guy', Thatcher had to reply, 'The decisions are decisions of the government and not of particular ministers.'[11]

The following day was the nadir for Armstrong. Having insisted for weeks that the decision not to stop *Their Trade is Treachery* was that of the attorney-general, he now had to apologise for misleading the court and confirmed the decision hadn't in fact been referred to the attorney-general at all. It was a disaster for Armstrong, much as I'd predicted in the Treasury solicitor's office in April. As one of Mrs Thatcher's junior ministers summed it up, he was 'a wally among the wallabies'.[12]

We'd proved not only that the *Spycatcher* material had previously been published but that it was published with the acquiescence of the British government. So, how could they possibly sue to stop it being published again?

In summing up our case I addressed the argument that there was no public interest in repeating the allegations about Hollis.

> The public interest in free speech is not just in truthful speech, in correct speech, in fair speech, in speech one point at a time and never to be repeated. The interest is in the debate. You see, every person who has ever changed the course of history has started off being unpopular. When the Australian Workers Union was founded under a tree in the bush, when unionists were not permitted to even go on to squatters' properties, there were plenty of people and, I am afraid to say, plenty of judges, in those far-off days who supported the establishment against those people. They spoke out, and they spoke again and again, and they said the same thing a great deal more than once and finally they changed history and there are few people today that would say the struggle of the labour movement in this country ... was not in the public interest, because ultimately, these ideas are tested in debate and it is that debate in which there is a public interest, not in having a say once and once only.[13]

Justice Powell ruled in our favour, handing down his reasons on 13 March 1987. He didn't accept my argument that Armstrong had lied, but agreed that the British government's failure to act to prevent the publication of *Trade is Treachery* and several other similar books 'cannot be categorised as other than an acquiescence in the publication, or televising, and, thus as a surrender of any claim to the confidentiality of that information'.[14]

The British appealed, of course, and the case was first heard in the NSW Court of Appeal in July 1987. The judges gave their decision in September and we won again, Justices Kirby and McHugh ruling for us, with Chief Justice Sir Laurence Street against us.

The British then appealed to the High Court of Australia, our final court of appeal, and the case was heard in March 1988.

The seven judges of the High Court sit in a vast soaring courtroom in a brutalist concrete monolith in Canberra. The chief justice was Sir Anthony Mason, who years before had written the opinion in Commonwealth v Fairfax that established the limits on a government's ability to restrain the publication of confidential information.

And we won there too: 7–nil. My confidence about the High Court, based on Mason's strong views on freedom of speech, had been vindicated. Curiously, Thatcher's advice had always been the complete reverse: Bob Alexander QC – then the leader of the London Bar, who occasionally appeared in Canberra – had told her they'd definitely win in the High Court.

But in many ways the best thing about the decision in the High Court was that the judges' decision was based on the rather academic argument Lucy had worked up several years before: that the whole case was an impermissible effort by the UK government to enforce in Australia a public law of the United Kingdom, the Official Secrets Act. It had the added benefit for their honours that they didn't need to consider any of the evidence, let alone my submission that the cabinet secretary of the United Kingdom had been, if not a perjurer, at least a proxy for it. So, the right side won, but no more offence was given to our friends in London.

And there was the final irony of the case I'd fought – for a bargain-basement fee. The only reason the book ultimately sold well over two million copies was that Margaret Thatcher had tried to ban it. Otherwise, it would have done well to sell 50,000 copies.

CHAPTER 6

Moguls, madness
and the media

The *Spycatcher* trial changed my life. To many lawyers, my efforts in representing Packer had smacked more of politics and PR than of real litigation. But here, with Lucy by my side, I'd taken on the UK government and its army of top lawyers, fought a case through a trial and two appeals and won. What appalled many of my former colleagues at the Bar was that not only was I absurdly young, at 32, but that I hadn't appeared as a barrister, but unrobed as a solicitor. Surreally, the case was much bigger news in London than in Australia. I was being encouraged to capitalise on my international notoriety – move to the Bar in London or New York; head-spinning really.

The victory had deeper significances. I no longer felt I needed to prove anything to Lucy's father. I'd won the highest-profile Australian case at the time; in terms of international coverage probably of all time. But on the other hand, whatever cases I did in the years ahead would be an anticlimax after spies, politics, a cabinet secretary bailed up in the witness box, a prime minister discomfited in the House of Commons.

That begged the question: what did I really want to do? The desire to be my own man remained paramount. But, as Kerry Packer had pointed out when I was negotiating my departure from his employment and the establishment of Turnbull McWilliam, that came at a cost. 'Independence is very attractive, Malcolm,' he growled. 'But it's expensive.' Financial independence was definitely important to me; it always had been.

Quietly, I started looking around to see how I could get into the investment banking business. I was reasonably numerate but had never studied finance and my short legal career had been mostly litigation rather than big commercial deals like Bruce McWilliam's.

While these ideas percolated, my work for Packer kept drawing me into corporate finance. A possible merger of Packer's publishing assets with The Herald & Weekly Times group, an independent listed company controlling newspapers in every capital city except Sydney, was on the boil. Jim Wolfensohn, the Australian investment banker who'd become a star of New York's financial and cultural scene, came out to help. The deal didn't eventuate, more's the pity, but Jim passed on some wisdom about becoming an investment banker.

'The key is a relationship with the chief executive,' Jim said. 'Don't go to see him with a pile of pitch books or financial reports. CEOs don't have time to read that crap. Just have one good idea, or an interesting one. It might be something you read in the paper that morning. Get a conversation started and pitch the idea. It's easy.' Well, it's easy if you are as charming as Jim.

Meanwhile, thanks to changes in media ownership laws, that land-scape started changing. It was now permissible to own more than two television stations. The best performers were the biggest in Sydney and Melbourne, TCN-9 and GTV-9 respectively. Both belonged to Kerry Packer. Around Christmas 1986, while I was relaxing at Palm Beach with the family after the *Spycatcher* trial, Packer rang, whispering with a breathless excitement. 'Come round to the house, son. I've been talking to Bond. He wants to buy the network.'

Compared to Packer, a third-generation media mogul, Alan Bond, the former sign painter born in London's East End, was an upstart. He'd been riding a property and mining boom in Western Australia for years. It helped that Paul Keating, treasurer in the Hawke ALP government, had deregulated the banking sector and foreign lenders had poured in; debt was plentiful and the stock market was just as enthusiastic. When his consortium won the America's Cup in 1983, Bond became a national hero. He was also a leading light of 'WA Inc', shorthand for the dubious culture of deals, alliances and feuds between Brian Burke's ALP state government and Bond, Robert Holmes à Court (the legendary corporate raider and owner of West Australian Newspapers) and the other 'four on the floor entrepreneurs', as Burke liked to call them.

Now Bond wanted to become a media mogul too. He'd acquired the Nine Network stations in Brisbane and Perth. When the media owner-ship laws relaxed, Packer expressed interest in buying them to consolidate his Nine Network. Bond immediately turned the tables: *he* wanted to buy

Kerry's stations. So, Kerry nominated a staggering asking price: $1 billion, at least double what the stations were worth. Astonishingly, Bond had accepted, on the basis that Packer left $200 million in as preference shares. Kerry was cock-a-hoop.

I went round to Packer's sprawling beach house and we reviewed the deal. They were crazy times. It was the year before the '87 stock-market crash. Bond, for some reason or other, was fancied by the National Australia Bank (NAB), which had agreed to lend him the money.

Lucy was bemused. 'This is becoming a pattern,' she said. 'Isn't January meant to be the quiet month where everyone goes to the beach? Last year we decided to take on the British government and this year you're selling our biggest client to Alan Bond!'

Without a breath of the deal getting out to the market or the media, Bruce and I negotiated the sale of the network with Bond's lieutenants. Not only did we take the total price to $805 million in cash, $50 million for some options and $200 million in preference shares, but we made that contract watertight. With so much debt, Bond's grand plan could easily end in tears. If that happened, he'd be looking for every legal angle to get out of redeeming Packer's preference shares.

We were driving such a hard bargain that Bond's chief executive, Peter Beckwith, complained to his boss, who rang Kerry; Beckwith and I then presented ourselves at Kerry's office. Something new caught my eye: a large colour photograph of Sir Frank Packer (whom Kerry loathed). Before Beckwith could get started, Kerry announced he was having second thoughts about selling the stations.

'They've been part of my life, all my life. What will I do without them? Who will I be?' There was a faint snuffling, a hint of tears, more melancholy monologue. Finally, he pointed to his father's picture. 'I just don't think I can do it to Dad.'

Beckwith could see the deal slipping away, Alan's dream of moguldom ending before it began. He assured Kerry everything was humming along well.

'You and Malcolm getting on alright?' Kerry asked.

'Oh, sure, sure. Best friends,' said Beckwith without much conviction. Then, after a few pleasantries, he left us.

Kerry beamed. 'So, how did I do, son?' But before I could get out the words, 'You deserve an Oscar', the grin vanished and Kerry stepped very close. 'You know, I like a tough lawyer,' he said in a low voice. Then, gripping the lapels of my jacket and pulling my face right up to his, he added, 'But don't fuck it up.'

He deserved an Oscar, that's for sure. The NAB gave Alan the money, Kerry got his billion dollars and we didn't warrant much in the contracts. So, I didn't fuck it up, either.

Neville Wran was completing his 10th year as NSW premier in the course of 1986, and I was curious about his plans. When Neville told me he was contemplating going into business with his old friend and contemporary Peter Valkenberg, I said he should go into business with me instead. He was 60, I was 32; he was experienced, I was full of energy; he was Labor, I was a Liberal. All very complementary!

Neville warmed to that idea and began working as a consultant to our law firm. But we had grander ambitions. Why not set up an investment banking business? The only missing element was that neither of us knew anything about banking!

'What about talking to Nick Whitlam, Gough's son?' Neville suggested. He was the chief executive of the State Bank of New South Wales, and at just 42 already had nearly 20 years of international investment banking experience with J.P. Morgan, American Express and Paribas. And we seemed to hit it off. I found Nick erudite and grandly arrogant although, like his father, not without the ability to laugh at himself.

In short order, we'd set up Whitlam Turnbull & Co. Nick and I each had 40 per cent of the partnership and Neville had 20 per cent. Kerry Packer, flush with cash from the sale of the Nine Network, agreed to contribute $25 million in capital, as did Larry Adler, whose company FAI Insurance was a buccaneering dealmaker and stock-market darling.

Bruce stayed in the law, as did defamation specialist Mark O'Brien, but the rest of Turnbull McWilliam, including Justin Shmith and Deborah Huber, moved across to Whitlam Turnbull. Lucy had completed an MBA while she was pregnant with Daisy and recruited her finance professor, Peter Dodd, who was joined by Kerry Schott, Gary Weiss and Roger Casey, among other finance types. It was a good mix of skills.

Lucy split her time between the investment bank and the law firm, which we kept going with Justin's help so we could complete the *Spycatcher* appeals among other cases. We worked together on most of our big assignments whether commercial or legal or a bit of both until in 1994, she decided to write a history of Sydney.[1] That led her into running for the Sydney City Council in 1999 when she became deputy lord mayor and then the first female lord mayor in 2003, a hundred years after her great-grandfather Sir Thomas Hughes had been the city's first lord mayor. Ever since she has had an abiding passion for cities, design, planning and sustainability. From 2015 she's been the chief commissioner of the Greater Sydney Commission (GSC), the city's peak planning authority.

We kicked off the new venture on 1 July 1987. Fortunately, our capital was in cash when the stock markets crashed on 19 October and the Dow plunged 22.6 per cent in one day. By the end of the month the US market had fallen 23 per cent, but Australia was down over 40 per cent. It was a meltdown.

Packer was cashed up from the sale to Bond and sitting pretty, but Adler was under the pump: FAI's market capitalisation had halved. Both would've preferred to have their cash back, not to mention their presence on our board was hindering our attempts to get advisory work. We refunded the $50 million and instead brought in British & Commonwealth Holdings PLC (B&C) as an outside shareholder. B&C was then a large UK financial services company headed by the energetic John Gunn.

But before returning the $50 million, we did put it to good use!

A few months before the October 1987 stock-market crash, 27-year-old Warwick Fairfax made a successful takeover bid for the family empire – John Fairfax & Sons Ltd, the 140-year-old publisher of the most profitable broadsheet newspapers in Australia, the *Sydney Morning Herald* and Melbourne's *Age*, plus the leading financial daily, the *Australian Financial Review*, and many other regional newspapers. His $2 billion bid was financed by the ANZ Bank, and his financial adviser was another Perth buccaneer, Laurie Connell, whose investment bank, Rothwells Ltd, promptly collapsed, courtesy of depositor and creditor anxiety. It was a terrible mess.

Rothwells had engaged Whitlam Turnbull to sell the $100 million fee agreement it had negotiated with Warwick's takeover vehicle, Tryart Pty Ltd. In the end, Connell sold it himself for $70 million to Bond Media Limited, purchaser of Packer's television stations. For us, the real excitement started on 6 January 1988 (another case of losing the summer holidays to business).

Knowing Fairfax was in strife, I went down to its offices on spec: perhaps Whitlam Turnbull & Co could help. The deeply religious Warwick and I were in mid-conversation about the Book of Job when a worried Ron Cotton, Fairfax's managing director, appeared. He said that the merchant bank First National had called on a $13 million loan; the ANZ wouldn't help. Unless Fairfax repaid it by noon the next day, their takeover could become a liquidation.

Quickly, I called Nick, who agreed we should make the short-term $13 million loan. Importantly, in doing so we secured the right to organise a longer term $500 million bank facility and the right to dispose of the many assets Warwick needed to sell to get his debt down to a manageable level. It was a task of considerable complexity and involved a cast of colourful characters. They included Rupert Murdoch, Kerry Packer, Robert Holmes à Court and, most colourful of all, Fleet Street press baron Robert Maxwell.

I negotiated to sell Fairfax's stake in Australian Associated Press to Murdoch and their share in Australian Newsprint Mills to Fletcher Challenge. Holmes à Court held around 8 per cent in both companies. His corporate empire had been hard hit in the '87 crash, so he was desperate to sell his stake. He wanted to close the deal himself, directly with Murdoch, but Rupert wouldn't take his call. Robert asked me to help, so I rang Rupert and explained the situation. After a thoughtful silence, Murdoch replied, 'I didn't like talking to that bastard when he had money. Now that he's broke, he can get fucked.'

Wow, I thought, these billionaires are just so nice to each other. Anyway, Murdoch did finally take the call and the assets were sold.

By March we'd reduced Warwick's debt to around $1.4 billion, which was still too high to be sustainable. He said to us that if he could end up owning just the *Sydney Morning Herald* he'd be happy and agreed to sell *The Age*. The would-be purchaser with the most money was Robert Maxwell, owner of the UK's *Daily Mirror*. He had won a Military Cross in the Second World War, was a passionate Zionist – reputed to be a Mossad agent – and was about as flamboyant and transparently roguish a mogul as I'd ever met. Inexplicably, we got on like a house on fire.

The deal-making took place at the Ritz Hotel in Paris. A large group assembled in the opulent drawing room of the Suite Imperiale, among them Maxwell's son Kevin, the Mirror Group lawyers and a team from

Bankers Trust, whose London head repeatedly assured us Maxwell had no problem paying the price. But what was the price to be?

'Now,' boomed Maxwell, waving two sheets of Ritz notepaper, 'I propose that I will write the highest price I will pay on a piece of paper. And you, Mr Turnbull, will write the lowest price your client will accept on another. And then we will exchange them. If your price is lower than mine, we will settle at the midpoint. If it is higher than mine, then there is no deal.'

Not prepared to play parlour games with *The Age*, I invited Maxwell to step away from the crowd. 'Let's get down to business,' I said. 'Our guy isn't a keen seller, but you have a deal at $850 million.'

We haggled for a while and then Maxwell said, 'My bankers say I shouldn't pay more than $750, but for you I can go to $805 million – that's a little more than halfway.'

But it was to no avail, even when we got him up to $850 million. Lady Mary Fairfax had introduced her son to William E. Simon, the former Nixon-era Treasury secretary. Simon convinced Warwick to refinance with high-yield, or junk, bonds, which Mike Milken's Drexel Burnham Lambert arranged. It was crazy, and I told Warwick so. He wasn't listening. Sadly, nor were his banks, ANZ and Citibank.

Nick Whitlam became unhappy; Neville and I never understood why. It can't have been dissatisfaction with our business performance. On the contrary, in the late '80s and early '90s, the ownership of almost all the major media assets in Australia changed hands – apart from Murdoch's News Corporation – and our firm was at the centre of most of those deals. Nick sought the support of Neville and B&C to depose me as joint managing director; that wasn't forthcoming, as I was bringing in most of the business. And so, in February 1990, he left and we paid out his interest. I'd enjoyed our association and was sorry it came to an end in the way it did.

From then on the firm became known as Turnbull & Partners Ltd, with Neville as chairman and me as managing director. A few years later B&C sold their shares back to us at a discount when they went into receivership, and we traded very successfully until 1997, when Goldman Sachs effectively bought us out and hired our whole team, and I became the head of their Australian business and the following year a partner of the global firm.

If Packer buying back the Nine Network for less than half what he'd sold it for was the deal of his life, it was a deal that nearly never happened. By 1989 Packer had received $855 million in cash. Bond Media was struggling and Packer still held $200 million in preference shares. While revenues had remained strong, Bond had allowed programming expenses to blow out and profits were under pressure. The preference shares were due for redemption after three years – in March 1990 – but couldn't be redeemed other than out of profits or a new share issue. And there remained of course another $500 million of bank debt in Bond Media.

For his part, Kerry wasn't particularly interested in getting back into television and was discussing a sale of the preference shares back to Bond at a discount.

While Kerry saw the preference shares as a dud investment, I saw it as a lever to get the company back on the cheap, but he wasn't showing any interest, until one weekend in May 1989. Lucy and I were at our farm near Scone with Alex, then six, his friend Charlie Garber, and Daisy, aged four.

Kerry was also in the Hunter at Ellerston, on the other side of the valley and about 90 minutes' drive away from us. Flush with Bond's millions, he'd not only taken up polo but had spent a fortune building a new house and an expanse of polo fields and stables. But the season was over and the players were gone. Kerry was all alone and bored. So, he called and asked me to come over to talk about Bond Media. 'I might have been a bit hasty knocking your idea back, son,' he said.

I told Kerry that I had a house full of kids and it was a long drive to Ellerston and back, instead suggesting we meet in Sydney on Monday. 'Okay, son, I'll send the chopper. Bring the kids and Lucy.'

Half an hour later a huge helicopter landed in our front paddock. The door opened and at the top of the stairs appeared Brian the butler, complete with stripy pants and black jacket. We all piled in and flew back across the valley to Ellerston. Once there, Lucy and I were ushered into Kerry's study, where we went through the deal on our laptops, which, thankfully, we'd taken to the country.

Every now and then we heard the thunder of little feet running down the corridor outside the study, but when we started to get up, Kerry said, 'Don't worry, they'll be fine. Brian is great with kids.'

And that was true, until we heard Brian call out, 'Boys, boys, don't climb up the curtains!' Then we did intervene and put the kids to bed.

By the end of the night, Kerry was convinced and we were hired.

Packer demanded the shares be redeemed in full, and when they weren't, made a low-ball takeover bid followed by a move to wind up Bond Media. There were many twists and turns in a characteristically complex deal, which saw my friends Sam Chisholm and Bruce McWilliam desperately trying to refinance Bond Media while Lucy and I did our best to put it into bankruptcy. By July 1990, our plan had worked and Packer's preference shares were converted into around 60 per cent of the company. All up, he was back in charge for about a third of what he'd sold the network for.

Much of the churn in the media space had been generated by another aspect of the changes to media ownership laws: owning newspaper and television assets in the same market was banned. This had prompted Fairfax to sell the Seven Network to the Queensland property tycoon Christopher Skase. Murdoch, who'd expanded his newspaper empire by buying The Herald & Weekly Times Group, sold the Ten Network to Frank Lowy's Westfield Group. Quickly, it became an ultra-competitive market with Nine, Seven and Ten racing to outspend each other at a time when revenues were sliding. In 1989, despairing of ever being able to make a go of the Ten Network and resolving to stick to real estate, Frank Lowy sold his interest in Ten to an emerging new media entrepreneur and former ABC journalist, Steve Cosser, and financier Charles Curran. They in turn split the network: Curran took the Adelaide, Perth and Canberra stations and Cosser retained Sydney, Melbourne and Brisbane. Despite Cosser's valiant efforts to restructure, the business got worse and worse. By August 1990, Ten was losing $2 million a week – before interest on its $450 million of bank debt, most of which was owed to Westpac.

And that's where Turnbull & Partners Ltd came in. Westpac had retained us as their advisers. Since 1989, the best media industry analyst in town, Cass O'Connor, had been working for our firm. Cass and I had persuaded Westpac to put the company into receivership and then radically cut costs: the goal was to be the most profitable television station, not the top rating one. Cass, Lucy and I enlisted Gary Rice to advise us. He was a former CEO of GTV-9, Packer's Melbourne station. Together we went through every cost element in the business, laid out on big sheets of butcher's paper on our kitchen table. We worked on the assumption that we'd just got the licences, had no money (that was accurate) and had to run the stations in accordance with the law at the lowest possible cost.

Businesses always carry a lot of legacy costs and practices. Yet too often, I've seen cost-cutting target the expenses that are easiest to trim without first asking fundamental questions about what resources you absolutely need to deliver a particular product or service. For this exercise, we carefully studied the operations of SBS. This multicultural government network, founded in Malcolm Fraser's day with Bruce Gyngell as its first CEO, had always run off the smell of an oily rag and we shamelessly copied some of their practices.

Cosser fought a furious rearguard action, accusing me of being an agent of Kerry Packer. After the receiver was appointed in September, the Trade Practices Commission (TPC) threatened to take legal action if I was involved in the management of Ten. This gave rise to an interesting meeting with the chairman, Robert Baxt. Neville Wran, Lucy and I attended, and on the way Lucy stopped off to buy a tape recorder. At the meeting, Baxt was flanked by some eager young men with pens and notebooks poised. He asked, 'Nobody minds if we keep a record of the meeting?'

'Not at all,' said Lucy as she produced her tape recorder and turned it on.

The meeting went well enough and Baxt's concerns were largely allayed. At the end, Neville was wrapping up and said, 'Well, Bob, all we're seeking from you is a fair go and justice.'

Baxt smirked and replied, 'Come on, Neville, you know you won't get any justice here.' He started to laugh and then glanced at Lucy's tape recorder – it was still on.

The problems with the TPC seemed to evaporate after that. Somehow, I don't think that little quip would have found its way onto the notepads of Bob's young scribes.

The receiver appointed Rice to run the Ten Network. He implemented our no-frills plan and, in due course, Ten became extremely profitable, although always running third in the ratings.

Rather than take yet another writedown, Westpac turned its debt into equity and took ownership of Ten, on the clear understanding from the Reserve Bank that as soon as it could recover its book value of around $230 million, it would sell. In 1992, still acting for Westpac, we arranged the sale of Ten to the Canadian television company CanWest Global. Their proprietor was a flamboyant former politician called Izzy Asper, whose chain smoking and whisky drinking made him appear a lot older than his 60 years. Westpac warily accepted Asper; he was the only potential buyer not insisting the bank take a writedown on their investment, and he still got the asset at a bargain price.

By late 1990, Fairfax was on our radar once again. Young Warwick was realising he should have sold *The Age* back in 1988 and pruned his debt. His senior bankers, owed around $1.2 billion, were pressing his management to restructure and either sell assets or raise equity. The banks held security over all the Fairfax Group assets; the vulnerable creditors were the junk-bond holders, ranking behind the banks – collectively owed about $500 million. They were all American institutions, many already in stages of bankruptcy or official administration as a result of the savings and loan crisis.

An American friend, Larry Strenger, put us in touch with the chairman of the bondholders' committee, Steve Ezzes, and we were among several advisers who pitched to be retained by them. Cass, Lucy and I wrote the presentation, full of detailed financials, legals and industry analysis. Apparently, it was by far the best presentation in the beauty contest. And the big idea was on the first page: 'There has never been a worse time to sell Fairfax, and perhaps never a better time to buy it. Skilfully represented, debenture holders can secure a substantial share of Fairfax, which can be reconstructed with a sustainable level of senior debt.'[2]

The Fairfax management and their advisers were softening up the bondholders with bleak financial forecasts, offering the senior bondholders 2 cents in the dollar and the junior bondholders 1 cent. They told the bondholders they were prepared to pay for their Australian financial advice, so long as it wasn't Turnbull & Partners. A folder of unflattering press clippings about me was circulated, prepared by Macquarie Bank, who'd been retained by Fairfax. Ezzes's comment was, 'They told us you were a mean, ruthless fighter who'd stop at nothing to win. So, we hired you.'

The banks employed investment banker Mark Burrows as their adviser, and from the outset he treated me and the bondholders with disdain. Our clients were professional investors and they knew all about bankruptcies and reconstructions. So, we prepared several reconstruction strategies, all of which were straightforward. There was nothing about the creditors putting the company into receivership; it involved the junk-bond holders exchanging some of their debt for equity and new management being hired, all with the view of the company trading through the economic downturn. Earnings, after all, remained strong and were more than enough to cover the interest payments on the senior debt.

These perfectly rational conventional work-out approaches were rebuffed. In what I've always regarded as an act of wanton value destruction, the banks – ANZ and Citibank for the most part – put Fairfax in receivership and commissioned Burrows to sell the company. In other words, they exercised their power as senior secured lenders to try to recover their money without regard for the consequences for any other class of creditor, let alone the shareholder, Warwick Fairfax.

The bondholders were aghast. This simply could never happen in the United States, where a court would use its powers under Chapter 11 of the Bankruptcy Code to impose a managed scheme of arrangement. Years later, as prime minister, I made changes to our own insolvency rules to emulate the effect of Chapter 11 and ensure directors of insolvent companies got the breathing space to restructure their businesses outside of receivership.

We'd tried peace but were left with no option but war. The bondholders sued Fairfax, claiming that the company had misled them about its financial prospects when it issued the bonds back in 1989. What's more, the receiver couldn't sell the Fairfax company itself without cutting a deal with the bondholders. Of course, he could sell all the assets over which the banks had security but the stamp duty costs alone would have been enormous. This gave the bondholders real leverage – the only question was, what was it worth?

A buyer was required. Kerry Packer was most interested in the future of Fairfax, but there were issues. With his now restored television interests, he couldn't legally own more than 15 per cent of the company; other buyers were needed. Additionally, any involvement by him would draw political controversy and attention. Plus, I figured, while he'd recognise the strategic value of the bondholders, he'd want to pay as little as possible.

A far better potential partner was Tony O'Reilly, managing director of the colossal US food company HJ Heinz and, in his private capacity, owner of extensive media assets in Ireland and Australia. A few years before, he'd bought a chain of regional Australian newspapers from Murdoch. But Burrows managed to persuade O'Reilly's Australian advisers, Bankers Trust, not to deal with the bondholders because 'they have no leverage' – quite the reverse of the truth, as events were to amply demonstrate. Burrows wanted to run an auction; he knew whoever the bondholders teamed up with would have the inside running, so he discouraged every bidder from talking with us. My attempts to persuade O'Reilly to deal with us were all in vain. Had we joined forces he would have owned Fairfax.

With O'Reilly out of contention, and still needing a credible media player as a partner, we turned to Conrad Black, the Canadian owner of London's *Daily Telegraph*. Kerry had been talking to Black, and in June a meeting took place at the Savoy Hotel in London, where Packer was spending the summer. Black was there, Ezzes was there. And Kerry invited Brian Powers, of the San Francisco hedge fund Hellman & Friedman. Ezzes and I secured the bondholders a share of the deal in return for their bonds and so the Tourang consortium was born.

Reflecting on the big egos in the room, I'd taken immense care in the drafting of the exclusivity agreement between the investors: Packer, Black and Hellman & Friedman on the one hand and the bondholders and Turnbull & Partners on the other. There was already a lot of action in the United States to try to split the bondholders away from me – standard divide and conquer tactics undertaken mostly by Morgan Stanley on behalf of the Fairfax receivers. In truth, I didn't trust any of our new partners, so I ensured that Turnbull & Partners wasn't merely a party to the exclusivity agreement but that it would be impossible to complete an acquisition without my sign-off and without my success fee being paid – in full.

That may seem churlish. But Kerry Packer's famous words, 'You only get one Alan Bond in your life,' had come with a lesson for me. Packer and I had agreed a flat success fee of $3.5 million, superb value given he had won back the Nine Network for a third of what he had sold it for. So, when he settled the invoice with a cheque of $3.4 million, I called Trevor Kennedy, his managing director.

'He just wanted to give you a little haircut,' said Kennedy.

'But, after such a great job, why would he do it?'

'Because he can,' said Trevor.

I didn't want another haircut.

The exclusivity agreement meant the bondholders couldn't deal with anyone else until the end of January 1992. So, time was of the essence. My strategy was fairly simple. Make a tough offer to the banks on a 'take it or leave it' basis. It didn't matter how long they thrashed around; so long as the exclusivity agreement was in force, they couldn't practically sell to anyone else.

Packer was dazzled by Powers, a bright but highly strung, hyperactive investment banker, and put him in charge of the deal. Black, and his lawyer Danny Colson, deferred to Powers. It was a bad choice.

Instead of letting the banks sweat on our offer, Powers kept talking to Burrows, who managed to keep the pretence of an auction proceeding even though there was only one viable bidder – us. As a result, in my view, Tourang paid several hundred million dollars more than it should have, but it was still a fantastic deal and the higher purchase price enabled me to secure a larger payout for the bondholders. Most ended up with about 30 cents in the dollar if they took the cash on the close of the acquisition or much more if they kept the shares. They were issued at $1 and before long were trading at well over $3.

The Tourang takeover was complex and exciting – how could it not have been with all those larger-than-life personalities? And we made a a lot of money in fees and even more on the shareholding we acquired at the time of the takeover. At one stage, I was the largest individual shareholder in Fairfax. But, sadly, it brought to an end my friendship with Kerry Packer.

Politics has no monopoly on madness, and there was plenty of it around in the last stages of the Tourang deal. From the outset, we'd agreed that Packer's managing director and long-time newspaper and magazine editor, Trevor Kennedy, would be the CEO of Tourang and, in due course, of Fairfax. He was the ideal candidate and had the perfect combination of belligerence and bonhomie to run an Australian newspaper company. Those opposing Tourang complained that he was a Packer stooge and that through him Kerry was going to control Fairfax despite only having 15 per cent of the shares. Kennedy was more than able to see all that off, but Powers and Colson used that complaint as a pretext to push him out. The truth was that, from their point of view, Kennedy was too much his own man.

Packer summoned me to his office in Park Street to tell me he'd decided to get rid of Trevor. I was stunned. And the way Kerry was talking about him was weird. 'He drinks a lot at lunch,' said Kerry at one point.

'Are you kidding?' I replied. 'You're telling me that a newspaper editor drinks at lunchtime? And is this the first time in, say, 20 years you've noticed it? And despite all of that, until a few months ago he was your top executive?'

Packer didn't back down, and Trevor was forced out of Tourang. Within weeks, they moved on me too. According to Trevor, Packer had become paranoid that by force of personality alone I would control the Fairfax board. At the Savoy, it had been agreed that I'd be a non-executive director – effectively as a representative of the bondholders, who'd end up with a large shareholding. The directorship was no big deal. When we'd agreed on it at the Savoy, it was uncontroversial – why wouldn't the bondholders have a seat on the board and why wouldn't it be their local adviser?

The Australian Broadcasting Tribunal (ABT) had been looking at the deal and considering whether to hold an inquiry into whether, despite his ebullient evidence to a parliamentary committee, Packer did have effective control over Tourang. With Kennedy thrown overboard, then me, the tribunal started to investigate. Anxious to avoid the ABT inquiry – at which both Trevor and I would have had no reason to be anything other than expansively candid on the relations between Packer and, for example, the notionally independent Hellman & Friedman – Packer exited the deal himself, foregoing a potentially very big profit.

That made him sore for years. Packer blamed me and Trevor, but he had only himself to blame. His treachery had disappointed me, given how supportive of him I'd been in his darkest hour. He'd forgotten that loyalty is a two-way street. Packer was so furious and bitter that he wouldn't acknowledge me on social occasions. It says a lot about the character of his wife, Ros, and children, James and Gretel, that despite this, they'd greet me and Lucy with great warmth. They hadn't forgotten the bleak days of the Costigan inquiry, even if their father had.

Finally, about five or six years later, we arranged to meet. It was in Beppi's restaurant in Darlinghurst. We met in a small wine-lined private room, more like a little cave, in the back of the restaurant. 'You fucked me over, you really did. You cost me hundreds of millions of dollars,' Kerry said with half a snarl.

'Well, you fucked me over first. What did you expect?' I replied, as deadpan as I could manage.

He considered my words for what seemed to be a very long time. 'Yes, I suppose we are a bit alike.'

It was never the same as it had been, but at least we were back on speaking terms and we did a couple of smaller deals in the years ahead.

After the spilling of so much blood, it's a tribute to the potency of the bondholders' agreement that Tourang nonetheless succeeded and bought Fairfax.

One of the sweetest moments in my corporate life was appearing in the boardroom at Mallesons at the settlement of the Tourang takeover of Fairfax, surrounded by people who had, one way or another, spent much of the last year trying to do me in. Delighted I'd made my signature and receipt of fees a condition of the closing, I picked up my bank cheque and turned to leave. The room seemed very quiet. Apart from the soft sound of the grinding of teeth.

CHAPTER 7

From Siberia to
Silicon Valley

1994, my 40th year. Turnbull & Partners had been very successful. Together Lucy and I had achieved the financial independence we'd always sought. Our children, Alex 11 and Daisy 9, were in good health and great company. They still are!

I had not only been able to retain Dad's property 'East Rossgole' but expand it to a scale that made it a commercial operation, not a hobby farm. Our first manager, Libby McIntyre, had moved on but Guy Thomas had taken over and with his wife, Trish, was looking after what for me was part investment, part family retreat and, most of all, part shrine. Every rock, tree and fence reminded me of Bruce and over all the weekends and holidays we spent there with the kids their memories too became part of the landscape.

Wherever I walk there is a family memory; fixing fences, chasing sheep, catching yabbies. But perhaps in these drought years I think most of the time 30 years or so ago when I took the kids, in pouring rain, in their hats and Driza-Bones and walked from the top of the property showing them how the water ran through one contour bank after another into the dams and then shone a light into the bottom of the well to show the water flowing beneath our feet.

Dad had always told me that the ultimate home would be a Sydney Harbour waterfront, and it was in 1994 that we bought our Wunulla Road home in Point Piper on Felix Bay. We have lived there ever since, across the road from the block of flats where Bruce and I had lived 25 years before and just up the beach from where my parents met and I, presumably, was conceived.

While our advisory work had been very lucrative, my ambition was to be more of a principal and Turnbull & Partners were regularly investing our own capital in deals. We made it a selling point to clients – we would never recommend a deal that we were not prepared to invest in ourselves.

The most exciting, and hair-raising, investment we had was in Siberian gold. Back in the 1960s, the Soviets had proved up two huge gold resources – Sukhoi Log in the frozen north and Muruntau in Uzbekistan. They decided to develop only Muruntau, which became one of the world's biggest gold mines. But when the Soviet Union broke up in 1991, Muruntau wasn't in Russia, but in an independent country. There was renewed interest in Sukhoi Log, the largest undeveloped gold resource in the world, with, the Russians claimed, up to 80 million ounces of reserves. For the best part of a century there'd been alluvial gold-mining operations on Siberia's Lena River. In 1992, the principal state-owned gold-mining business there became a joint stock company, Lena Gold, aka Lenzoloto. It secured (so it believed) the right to develop the Sukhoi Log resource.

An enterprising Australian mining entrepreneur, Ian MacNee, had talks with them and through his company, Star Technology, bought 37.5 per cent of Lenzoloto for US$250 million – funds he didn't have – to finance the further exploration and development of Sukhoi Log. In 1993, MacNee sold Star Technology to the Australian Stock Exchange (ASX)–listed Central Mining NL, subsequently renamed Star Mining NL, which he continued to run. We met him through one of our directors, John Mitchell. Over the next two years, together with County NatWest, Turnbull & Partners helped raise over $50 million for Star, and I was frequently in Moscow and Irkutsk trying to get Star's interests authoritatively confirmed.

Despite the bleak winter, I was excited when I arrived in Moscow for the first time in November 1993. It was impossible not to be caught up in the wave of optimism. Surely, with so much in the way of resources, all you needed to do was 'add freedom' to create new fortunes for the swift and prosperity for all.

We secured one legal approval after another. Learned jurists confirmed Star and Lenzoloto's entitlements under Russian law. But as we surmounted one obstacle, new ones kept being thrown up.

Our issues, ultimately, were political, and in Russia in 1994 it was hard to know who was in charge. We needed a resolution passed in the State Duma, Russia's lower house. Our friends there, on the liberal side of the chamber, wouldn't even speak to their opponents. And so I found myself walking the corridors organising votes from old communists on the one hand and right-wing nationalists like Vladimir Zhirinovsky on the other.

Zhirinovsky was a big name in those days. 'When I am president,' he told me, 'I will have Yeltsin shot!'

'Vladimir Volfovitch,' I replied, 'that's not a good idea. The more you say that, the more he'll make sure he shoots you first. Why not say that when you're president, Yeltsin will have a big pension and a beautiful dacha on the Black Sea. That's how you do it in the West. You have to make it comfortable for people when they lose office.'

He thought and then nodded. 'Yes, I'm being too old-fashioned.'

If Moscow was political, in a dark and complex way, Siberia was a different world entirely. One time, we took a party of investors up to Bodaybo, the little mining town where Lena Gold was operating. The mayor entertained us to dinner and there was a bottle of vodka in front of each guest. A brilliant young Australian diplomat, Glenn Waller, had come along with us and he offered to translate.

The mayor's speech was at first grandiloquent but inoffensive: Australia and Siberia were brothers, filled with resources, strong men, beautiful women, born in chains but now free ... and so on. Toast followed toast. And then I noticed he was talking about '*judaiski i kitaiski*'.

'Glenn,' I said under my breath. 'What's he saying about Jews and Chinese?'

Whispering back, Glenn said, 'He's saying another thing we have in common is that we both kept the Jews and the Chinese out.'

'Can you fix it?' I asked him.

'Watch this,' said Glenn.

And so, when the mayor stopped for another drink and it was Glenn's turn to translate, our diplomat rose to his feet and said, 'And as His Excellency has reminded us, another thing Australia and Siberia have in common is our deep commitment to multiculturalism, and in particular our strong bonds with our Jewish and Chinese brothers and sisters.'

At the heart of our political problems was an arm wrestle between the central government in Moscow and the provincial government of Irkutsk Oblast, led by one Yuri Abramovich Noshikov. As his name indicates, his father was Jewish; his mother was Chinese. It was an unlikely combination for a successful politician in Siberia, I thought. Later, when I knew him better, I asked Noshikov how someone from that background could get to the top in a place where they had no love for either the Jews or the Chinese. 'It's simple,' he said. 'Someone has to run the country for the Russians when they're drunk.'

By 1995, with Star's only asset in Russia and most of the mining capital in London, it made sense for the company to move to the UK. Rudolf Agnew, the former CEO and chairman of Consolidated Goldfields, took over as chairman and Neville and I retired from the board. Star continued to work on the Sukhoi Log project until it was double-crossed by the Russians: in 1997, the licences were effectively cancelled without compensation.

Remarkably, more than two decades on, the Sukhoi Log project remains undeveloped. A Russian gold miner, Polyus, is still conducting exploration. With gold at record highs, it says a lot about the dysfunction of Russia that such a valuable resource has been unexploited for so long.

The Star adventure had been rewarding, both financially and in the insights it provided into Russia, its history and its people, then transitioning from one world to another. Their black humour in the face of catastrophe was as amusing as it was disturbing. One time, deep in Siberia in a hot *banya*, several of us were discussing the deteriorating state of affairs, the criminals threatening us, the law and order vacuum. It was decidedly pessimistic. Then a friend from the Ministry of Atomic Energy calmly observed, 'We should not be concerned. This is just the gangster stage of capitalism. It is like America in the days of the Wild West. The rule of law comes later.' He was right about 'later'.

The lessons of Russia and Star Mining would serve me well. In developing countries, you have to get the deals right at the beginning; you cannot rely on the law to help you. When I went looking for mining projects in China soon after, I was fastidious about securing the support and participation of every possible stakeholder before we proceeded.

Through my partners Alan Doyle and Christian Turner, I was introduced to Axiom Forest Resources, a Hong Kong–listed company. In 1991, Axiom, led by Fijian businessman Joe Hill, had acquired several companies with logging concessions in the Solomons and were working with local landowners. One was Anglican bishop Sir Dudley Tuti, who was the paramount chief of Santa Isabel Island. He wanted to transition from unsustainable clear-felling logging practices into plantation forestry, which benefited his people. Accordingly, Axiom had retained one of the world's leading foresters, the Australian Robert Newman, as an adviser and a director of the company.

However, Axiom's good intentions weren't matched by financial skills and after six months, the company was delisted. When the major shareholders asked us to help, we acquired a 16 per cent stake in the company, I became chairman and we got to work sorting out the mess.

It was a real joy to work with Robert Newman. He taught me a lot about forestry and how, around the world, clear-felling of rainforests was not only devastating local environments but adding to greenhouse gas emissions and global warming. Unfortunately, our association was short-lived. In July 1992, now with its listing restored, Axiom was taken over.

As it turned out, the new owners didn't share our environmental goals, and evidence of bad logging practices by Axiom years after I'd left the company were regularly used against me when I went into politics. My critics overlooked the fact that our goal was to end clear-felling and create a sustainable local forestry industry.

But working with Bob Newman sparked in me a lifelong interest in timber and forestry. Well managed, it's the ultimate renewable resource and remains an enormous opportunity in the Pacific, where high rainfall and rich volcanic soils enable the most valuable hardwoods to be grown relatively quickly. As I learned from Sir Dudley, the key is ensuring the local landowners enjoy a regular annual income while the plantation is growing and not just when it is harvested. Otherwise, they have a common interest with the loggers to cut down the old-growth forest and replace it with annual cash crops like copra or palm oil.

But of all the Turnbull & Partners deals and projects in the '90s, and there were many, the biggest and best was undoubtedly OzEmail.

Sean Howard was one of the real pioneers of the internet in Australia. He almost finished a medical degree but became fascinated with personal computers in the early 1980s, publishing what became the leading PC magazine, *Australian Personal Computer*. I met him when Kerry Packer bought a share of the magazine; in 1992, Packer bought Sean out entirely. That left him with a couple of research projects, one of which was a proprietary corporate electronic mail service called Microtex.

Sean Howard was a complex guy, a geek, engrossed in writing code and the intricacies of servers, routers and switches. Sometimes he'd be the saddest person you'd ever meet – Eeyore on downers. And then he could be the wildest party animal. But he was always mischievous. From Sean, I learned a powerful lesson. 'Malcolm,' he'd say, 'there's no shortage of technology – we have that in abundance. What's scarce is having the technological imagination that enables you to work out what to do with it.'

The internet was just starting to become commercial in 1994. Sean had renamed his company OzEmail but to grow he needed to keep spending on marketing – carpet bombing Australia with CDs of his dial-up software – not to speak of investing in his own network hardware. So, he approached Trevor Kennedy, who'd effectively been his boss at Consolidated Press. Trevor then approached me and we invested $500,000 each to acquire half the company between us.

OzEmail swiftly became Australia's largest internet service provider (ISP), and they were heady days. OzEmail was adding thousands of subscribers a week; everything was bursting at the seams, and it felt as though the show was being held together with duct tape. In some respects, that was literally true. Sean was a visionary and an entrepreneur, and so we quickly hired a tough manager in David Spence to run the business. At the same time, we looked around for more capital.

Trevor and I were both back on speaking terms with Kerry Packer, so we sounded him out. Kerry doubted the internet would catch on. 'They'll only use it for porn and gambling,' he opined, adding for good measure: 'and your valuation is ridiculous.'

Several larger ISPs tried to buy us, including Steve Case's AOL and Bill Schrader's PSINet as well as some big telcos like Telstra and Optus. Sean and I used to have a quiet bet before we met these behemoths about how long it would take before the gun went on the table. Not literally, of course. But the meetings all followed a similar pattern. Charming chitchat, then down to price; we had a big number, they had a really low number; and then they'd say, 'And if you don't take it, we'll bury you and you won't be worth anything.' That was the gun moment.

In those days, the ASX had little or no interest in technology stocks and investors' risk appetite was being met with the mining exploration sector. Sean used to say to me, 'How can you float a gold tenement in Siberia but we can't float a real live telecom business, with real live customers paying real live money, growing at 15 per cent a month, right here in Australia?'

All good points, but we couldn't waste time dwelling on that. Guns aside, we were at genuine risk from the telcos, who were bound to become ISPs themselves and swallow our market. The big worry was Telstra, from whom we had to buy bandwidth. In a sign of how much bandwidth has exploded, in 1996 OzEmail leased from Telstra, as our main link to the United States, an exclusive 2 Mbps connection![1]

Our best prospects for a listing were in the United States. With help from Steve Ezzes, we secured two underwriters – Montgomery Securities and C.E. Unterberg, Towbin & Co. By mid-May 1996, Sean was about to fly to the USA for the customary two-week investor roadshow prior to listing on the NASDAQ exchange. Ours was the first Australian technology firm to do so, and we were all nervous. I was worried about the state of the markets – looking good, but how long would it last? We were a small Australian ISP, a marginal proposition on the American market.

Agonisingly for poor Sean, his mother fell gravely ill; there was no way he could leave her side. Lucy was characteristically emphatic. At an emergency meeting at our home, she declared that I'd have to go. 'If you miss this moment, it may not come again,' she said.

Our chief technology officer, Andy Kent, gave me the fastest course in the design and operation of packet-switched networks and, armed with the most superficial understanding imaginable, I set off with Spence for the roadshow. By the time I'd made the same pitch three or four or more times a day travelling from the West Coast, through the Midwest, then to Boston and New York without my lack of real technical knowledge being found out, I started breathing easier.

As we pulled up outside a building in mid-town New York – Sean had joined us by then – the limo driver warned us that the fund manager we were about to meet was tough. 'The last guys I took to see her came out crying,' he said. We were ushered into a room to await the terrifying one. Noticing a hole in the table for a power cord, Sean dived under to plug a cord in. Just as he did, in she came, so I introduced myself and David Spence. 'Our CEO and founder, Sean Howard, is also here,' I added, 'but he's been told you're really scary and he's hiding under the table.'

She shot me a quizzical look. Then Sean poked his head out and said, 'But I will come out if you promise not to be mean!' Fortunately, she laughed, gave us a good hearing and later bought a big chunk of the issue.

With the $45 million we raised, OzEmail was able to keep growing and more than doubled customer numbers every year. Nevertheless, still more capital was needed. Meanwhile, Sean identified a number of new ventures: a search engine optimised for Australia and New Zealand called ANZWERS; a long-distance internet fax service, using OzEmail proprietary hardware; and the first global commercial voice-over-the-internet business, OzEmail Interline, using proprietary technology developed by Rick Spielrein. Interline allowed customers to call a local number in Australia and then have their call switched over the internet to an OzEmail server in the location they were calling. We even persuaded Paul Keating, just defeated in the 1996 election, to launch the service.

The most exciting new business we started, however – also in 1996 – was an ad-serving and targeting business we called Web Wide Media (WWM), and we entered into a joint venture to expand the business with BSkyB, then controlled by Murdoch and run by our old mate Sam Chisholm. The partnership had great potential, and Elisabeth Murdoch and I were named as co-chairs of the new venture. Anthony Bertini was the CEO. However, as Rupert started to feud with Chisholm, he decided to renege on the WWM deal. It was obvious to me that ad serving was starting to boom and if we stuck with it, being one of the first players, we couldn't fail to succeed. Although I was furious, and made my feelings plain, suing Rupert wasn't an option as we lacked the time and resources. To my dismay, WWM was sold to Softbank and in a series of subsequent transactions basically vanished from sight. Doubleclick, which was started around the same time and with the same concept, was listed in 1998 and ultimately acquired by Google for $3.1 billion in 2007.

By late 1998, OzEmail was still growing rapidly, and we were preparing to raise another $250 million to build more of our own fibre networks. A few years before, we'd had talks with John Sidgmore. He ran the big American ISP UUNet, which had since been acquired by US telco WorldCom. In 1997, its $37 billion merger with MCI Communications was the largest in US history.

Sidgmore came back to us at the end of 1998 with a cash offer too good to refuse and in December, OzEmail was taken over in a $520 million deal. Turnbull & Partners' $500,000 investment in 1994 was now worth nearly $60 million. Did we sell at the top of the market? Maybe. I was becoming sceptical about the renewed tech and telecom bubble in the United States and insisted we sell for cash. Just as well! Three years later, WorldCom collapsed in a morass of accounting fraud culminating in the biggest bankruptcy in US history.

And I nearly blew it. I was negotiating the offer price with Sidgmore on my cell phone. We were a dollar apart. He was at $21.50 a share, and I was at $22.50. 'This is no time to nickel and dime, John,' I told him.

Trevor and Sean were watching with growing anxiety. Trevor took the phone away from me and handed it to Sean, quietly but firmly adding, 'And that applies to you too, Malcolm.' When he gave back the phone, I quickly split the difference and the bid was agreed at $22!

Turnbull & Partners wasn't a conventional investment bank. We were more like Winston Wolf in *Pulp Fiction* – the people you call when you have a really bad problem. From Fairfax bondholders to gold mines in Siberia, I never shied from a challenge or the chance to learn more. We were even hired by the WA Labor government in 1989 to sort out the mess created by all the WA Inc deals done by Premier Brian Burke with entrepreneurs like Alan Bond and Robert Holmes à Court. Colourful times, like when I told Alan Bond we were going to wind him up and, under huge pressure, he indignantly replied in a cockney accent – the stress had taken him back to his childhood voice. And of course it was during that assignment I first got to know Julie Bishop, then working at the government's lawyers, Robinson Cox.

However, working on our own account was even more rewarding than advising others. By 1997, the year before we sold OzEmail, I was spending most of my business time on the firm's own principal investments and was well on the way to raising our own private equity fund, with a focus on technology.

But then, a wholly different opportunity arose. What kicked it off was an interesting meeting back in 1996. I was in New York, as was Sam Chisholm. We caught up at the Carlyle Hotel. Sam was always at home in a bar, and the Carlyle Hotel's is one of the best. He also invited John L. Thornton, the chairman of Goldman Sachs Asia.

Thornton was the classic urbane investment banker. His charm and erudition brought to mind Jim Wolfensohn and, like Jim, his elegant demeanour barely concealed a sharp and ruthless business brain. I found Thornton to be a thoughtful globalist with a fascination for China and its history. He sat on Murdoch's board of directors, so we also shared a keen interest in the media industry. He too was observing the growing impact of the internet. By early 1997, Thornton and I were in serious discussions about me and my small corporate finance team joining Goldman Sachs. Perhaps it seems like a straightforward move, but I agonised over giving up my independence and wasn't sure I'd be entirely comfortable in the big Wall Street partnership. Over many months, I met more of John's partners, including the chairman, Jon Corzine. Their overtures were flattering and the opportunity potentially lucrative, so in August 1997 Turnbull & Partners closed its doors at 1 Chifley Square and moved down the road to Goldman Sachs Australia.

There was adjustment all round. For our new colleagues, I was a controversial choice; I found the politics within Goldman surprisingly intense. But for the most part I was warmly welcomed and a number of the partners, including Thornton, Tim Dattels, Carlos Cordeiro and Phil Murphy (now the governor of New Jersey), have been good friends ever since.

At times, I felt like a yokel from the colonies. One of the first things that struck me about Goldman wasn't how profitable the firm was, and it was certainly that, but the scale of its expenses. Everything was lavish: its offices, its entertainment. By contrast, at Turnbull & Partners we'd adhered to the cracked-linoleum school of office decoration and constantly strived to keep our overheads as low as possible. The Goldman CFO, John Thain, told me to relax and focus on the top line, the revenue, and let the costs take care of themselves.

More troubling was the workaholism whereby bankers, especially the younger ones, felt they had to stay at the office until midnight or later and then, after barely enough sleep, turn up again first thing in the morning. I guess because Lucy and I had worked together for years with the aim of spending as much time with the kids as we could, we'd never expected people to work such long hours. My only interest was in what people produced. The hours they worked or where they worked them were of not much relevance to me.

I remember one young man at Goldman who used to work all day and night. He was married and had a baby. Noticing his hours hadn't changed, I asked him to come into my office. I encouraged him to spend less time at the office and more time with his family. I wasn't making any headway so, never fond of losing an argument, I tried another tack.

'Why are you working at Goldman Sachs?' I asked him.

He pondered for a moment and said, 'Because I like helping people.'

'Really?' I replied. 'Couldn't get a job at the Red Cross? Come on, you're here because you want to make a lot of money.'

He squirmed a little but agreed, 'Well, there's that too.'

'Okay,' I said, 'this is what's going to happen. You're going to work here night and day, become a partner and make an absolutely indecent amount of money. You'll be so rich.' His eyes gleamed. I had his attention. 'But your wife will become lonelier and more unhappy because you're never there. And so she'll divorce you. And take most of that money you made by neglecting her.'

He sat bolt upright, as though he'd been electrocuted. 'I never thought about it like that.'

A good lesson for politics: the hip-pocket nerve is always the most sensitive. And he did spend some more time at home after that.

On another occasion I attended a meeting of the firm's diversity committee and we discussed why so many brilliant young women recruited after university left in their late 20s and early 30s. I thought the question was a trick, so I held back, and then couldn't help myself. 'Well, isn't it obvious we've created a work lifestyle that makes it almost impossible for anyone to spend time with their family, and that works against women in particular?' There wasn't a lot of sympathy for my point of view at that time, but the experience at Goldman crystallised my strong lifelong commitment to making workplaces flexible and family friendly.

Years later, Annabel Crabb described the problem brilliantly in her book *The Wife Drought*, which highlighted that many roles in our society were designed for men whose families were looked after by stay-at-home wives. The short point is that if we want a society where men and women have equal employment opportunities, we need to ensure that workplaces allow parents the flexibility, which technology amply enables, to combine work and family.

CHAPTER 8

An Australian republic

All my life I've believed Australians have created something unique here. We are by nature self-critical, and cynical about boasters and boosters, but we too often fail to appreciate the exceptionalism of our achievement. Australia will never be a flag-waving, jingoistic country, but we should be proud of what we've made, lest by neglect or complacency we lose it.

We are an immigration nation, multicultural, as new as the baby receiving her citizenship in the arms of her migrant mother. And we are as old as our First Australians' 60,000 years of continuous civilisation here in their ancestral land, which we all share and call Australia. In the complex weave of our national fabric there are the threads of every culture, race and religion. There's no comparable nation as diverse as ours, with nearly 30 per cent of our people born overseas and more than half with a foreign-born parent. And yet in a world where intolerance and fear seem more threatening than ever, here in Australia we live together in relative harmony.

And at the heart of the success of the Australian project is that we don't define our nation by reference to one religion or race or cultural tradition. Every face, and every faith, can be Australian. What defines us, and unites us, is our commitment to common political values, more innate and better felt than they are defined. The foundation of those values is respect for each other, and that enables us genuinely to uphold the freedom of our parliamentary democracy and the rule of law that applies to both government and governed, that constrains the powerful and protects the powerless.

My Australian vision has always been a positive one. It's been about the values we are for, about enlarging our opportunities and our understanding of the world. Outward-looking, optimistic and curious – always seeking to learn something new. Determined to get to the front of the pack, but making sure none of us fall behind.

There are times in history when a nation pauses to reflect. One such time was when we celebrated our bicentenary or, better put, 200 years of European settlement. It was 26 January 1988 – Australia Day. I was providing some television commentary from the top of the InterContinental Hotel, overlooking the harbour, the Opera House and Sydney Cove, where 200 years before, Arthur Phillip had landed to proclaim a British colony. The sun was shining, the harbour was sparkling blue and covered in ships and boats of every kind all decked with flags. It was deliriously festive.

And our prime minister, Bob Hawke, was there. But not to give the main address as the leader of France or the United States would have done. Here in Australia, on our national day, the prime minister's speech was but the warm-up, the introduction, to the main event: a stirring message from Her Majesty the Queen, delivered by her son and heir, Prince Charles.

So when, bursting with national pride, we dressed up our most magnificent arena, decked it with flags and invited the world to look at what we've achieved, we showed them not a great Australian leader or hero, not our First Australians, whose 60,000 years of history were barely recognised – but the Prince of Wales, who to his enduring credit, seemed somewhat puzzled as to why he was there.

And that was the moment I resolved to do whatever I could to ensure Australia would have an Australian as head of state. I didn't then, and don't now, have an ounce of anti-British sentiment. My republicanism is the necessary consequence of my patriotism. I am an Australian republican because I am an Australian. I love this country, our country, too much to share our head of state with another nation.

The foundation in 1990 of the Australian Republican Movement (ARM) gave the republican cause the momentum it had previously lacked. Neville Wran and I were founding members and the author Thomas Keneally was our first chairman. Tom later wrote that the idea for establishing the ARM had emerged from a long boozy lunch with Neville over several bottles of chardonnay.[1]

When the British colonies federated in 1901, Australia wasn't an independent nation at all, but rather a largely self-governing dominion of the British Empire. Our constitution is a thoroughly colonial document, anything but the so-called birth certificate of a nation. Indeed, it still includes provisions that would allow the monarch (in those days acting on the advice of the British government) to disallow an Australian law that had been enacted in the previous year.

I was fascinated to read what Menzies wrote in 1948 – 'the boundaries of Britain are not on the Kentish coast but at Invercargill [New Zealand] and Cape York'[2] – and said in the House of Representatives in 1953 – 'the Crown … will always be the sign and proof that wherever we may be in the world, we are one people'.[3] One British people, that is.

The truth is that our independence and separate identity as Australians, rather than British, evolved both legally and culturally. It's still not possible to point to a day when Australia went from colony to independent nation.

While the text of the Australian constitution has hardly changed (only eight of 44 attempts to amend it have succeeded), its practical meaning and import have been transformed. In 1901 and until 1930, the governor-general was appointed by the queen or king on the advice of the British government that they represented. The UK didn't have a high commissioner to Australia until 1936. And since 1930, with respect to Australian matters, the queen or king acts solely on the advice of their Australian ministers.

The ARM was established more as a ginger group than as a political movement or party. Neville and I provided the ARM with some office space at Turnbull & Partners and, over the years, most of its funding – close to $5 million by 1999. Neville was adamant we needed to win the support of people on both sides of politics. And we did. From early on we had strong support from Labor Party leaders and members plus prominent Liberals like Nick Greiner and John Fahey, both premiers of New South Wales, Victoria's Jeff Kennett and South Australia's John Olsen. In 1993, even the Young Liberal Movement resolved, in the words of their president John Brogden, that 'our nation's future is as a republic'.[4]

The debate was largely conducted between the ARM and the Australians for Constitutional Monarchy (ACM). Its inaugural chair was Lloyd Waddy, a charming and good-humoured barrister. His great love was presiding at the annual Victoriana music-hall dinner at St Paul's, a high-profile Sydney Uni residential college, where the highpoint of the evening is waving sparklers while singing 'Land of Hope and Glory'.

Lloyd and I got on well and often debated each other. One evening, we were set to debate each other at another Sydney institution, the University & Schools Club.[5] Many in the audience seemed to be quite drunk so we decided to abandon serious argument and Lloyd gave a humorous speech for the republic and I for the monarchy. It said a lot about the state of the diners that nobody could subsequently remember what either of us had said! Which was just as well.

However, the geniality of the ACM came to an end when they recruited Tony Abbott as their executive director; he brought a toughness to their campaigning. The two of us had many debates – our first encounters. I doubt either of us imagined we'd become successive Liberal prime ministers.

Paul Keating had become prime minister in 1991 after deposing Bob Hawke. The republican cause hadn't featured in Keating's speeches in years past, but he almost stumbled onto it after the opposition, led by John Hewson, rather clumsily attacked him for showing insufficient respect to the Queen. After his re-election in 1993, he appointed me as chairman of a Republic Advisory Committee to examine the different models for an Australian republic and recommend accordingly.

The committee, a good one that included Nick Greiner and Susan Ryan, a former Labor federal minister, travelled around the country holding public meetings – 22 in all – and received hundreds of submissions. Most of the drafting was done by me and another committee member, constitutional law expert Professor George Winterton.

There were then, as there are today, two big questions. What should the powers of the president be? How should the president be elected?

We encountered almost no support for a US-style president who has executive head-of-government powers. Most people agreed the president should have the same role, powers and responsibilities as the governor-general. It is, however, not entirely clear what these are. Not even the Queen's powers are clear-cut. The constitution isn't helpful – it doesn't even mention the prime minister; a literal reading would suggest the governor-general runs the country!

In practice, the governor-general's powers are defined by 'conventions' – unwritten traditions of responsible parliamentary government. These generally require the governor-general to act in accordance with the advice of the prime minister, whose office, in turn, depends on him or her retaining the confidence of a majority of the House of Representatives.

But there've been hard cases, such as Sir John Kerr's dismissal of Prime Minister Whitlam in 1975. And in my own time as prime minister, as I describe elsewhere in this book, I came very close to uncertain territory as to the respective responsibilities of myself as prime minister and Sir Peter Cosgrove as governor-general.

Currently, the governor-general is appointed – and would be removed – by the Queen on the advice of the Australian prime minister. Few people argued that a president should be appointed and removed solely on the say-so of the prime minister. In practical terms, the two main options coalesced as appointment by a bipartisan two-thirds majority of a joint sitting of both houses of parliament or direct election by the people.

Nobody would seriously contemplate leaving the powers of a directly elected president in the undefined, and thus potentially uncertain, world of convention. And so, George Winterton and I drafted examples of how the constitution might be amended to spell out, or codify, the president's powers. The alternatives were to effectively abolish the reserve powers or provide that the constitutional conventions that previously applied to the office of governor-general would apply to the office of the president.

Either way, as I set out in my book *The Reluctant Republic*, my belief was that all the powers should be spelled out, and not solely because clear ground rules make for stable government. 'As we have seen our Constitution is a quite misleading document, giving the impression that the governor-general is an all-powerful ruler who appoints and dismisses ministers at his pleasure. Australians should be able to pick up their Constitution and find in it an accurate description of how their democracy works.'[6]

The Republic Advisory Committee's report was a solid piece of work, with a lot of valuable research into the experience of other Commonwealth countries that had made the transition to a republic. But despite his enthusiasm for the republic, Keating had more pressing matters on his prime ministerial agenda. While we kept the issue bubbling along, we had to press him for a formal response and an indication of how he'd take the issue forward.

Keating gave his answer in June 1995. He adopted a model for electing the president very close to that of the ARM – a president with the same powers as the governor-general appointed by two-thirds of a joint sitting of parliament. He expressly rejected a directly elected president.

It should be recognised that a Head of State, whose powers derived from a general election, would be the only person in the political system so elected. His or her powers would be nominally much greater than those of all other Commonwealth office holders, including the Prime Minister and the Cabinet, who are, without exception, indirectly elected via large elected parties. With a popularly elected President, potential would exist for the representative and democratically elected parliamentary chambers, the repositories of the diffuse power of Australian democracy, to be gradually diminished, while the embodiment of the nation and great powers were vested in one person. That would constitute a very dramatic – and undesirable – change to a system which all of us agree has served us well.[7]

Keating promised that if he were re-elected in 1996, he'd hold a plebiscite on the threshold question of whether Australia should be a republic, and that if that vote was carried, parliament would be tasked to settle the details of the model for the referendum.

Back in 1994, Liberal opposition leader Alexander Downer had proposed a constitutional convention to consider the issue. Half the delegates would be elected and half appointed. When John Howard became opposition leader in 1995, he retained Downer's policy and so after he won government in 1996, I found myself in his office in Sydney.

Howard's interest was in keeping the monarchy, although he'd occasionally suggest he was open to change at some point in the future. Importantly for him, the branch membership of his party were overwhelmingly monarchists too. However, Howard and I both agreed that while a president appointed by parliament wouldn't unsettle our parliamentary democracy, a directly elected president would constitute a substantial change: it would mean that our head of state would become a politician, in all likelihood the endorsed candidate of one or other of the big parties. And Howard and I weren't alone; it was hard to find anyone with experience in government or politics who didn't think a directly elected president was a bad idea. After all, if the job description of the president is a non-political ceremonial head of state and occasional impartial constitutional umpire, then a rowdy political contest is hardly the best way to choose them.

But in the wake of his 1996 election win Howard showed no sign of actually wanting to hold the constitutional convention. At one point, his minister Senator Nick Minchin declared the promise was a non-core promise – this being a promise that the government's polling indicated the public didn't remember having been made!

The ARM launched a campaign to demand either a plebiscite or a completely elected convention. The highlight was a big rally in the Sydney Town Hall on 3 December 1996. Lucy's uncle Robert Hughes was the lead speaker. He began his address to a packed house with the salutation, 'Chardonnay-swilling elitists …'

The parliament finally passed the legislation to establish the convention in August 1997. Its stated purpose was to discuss whether Australia should become a republic and if so resolve what kind of republic we should have. It was a thoroughly unsatisfactory design – 152 delegates from all round Australia, half appointed by the government and half elected by way of a voluntary postal ballot. Myriad groups contested the postal vote, with the ARM and the ACM by far the two largest. For the first time I saw the way in which the reactionary right of politics would target me personally. Abbott ran the ACM's campaign and in one of his strategy documents for them wrote, 'As their public face Turnbull is arrogant, rude and obnoxious – a filthy rich merchant banker, out of touch with real Australians, he is the Gordon Gekko of Australian politics.'[8]

The ARM won the most elected delegates, 26 out of 76; 19 were won by other republicans. The ACM and other monarchists won 27 seats collectively and there were four delegates whose positions were too unclear to categorise.

Normally a staid place, Canberra was buzzing for the two weeks of the convention, which took place at Old Parliament House in February 1998. It was an extraordinary gathering of Australians from all walks of life: the great, the good, the garrulous. For the bemused Australian public watching the TV news coverage every evening, it may have seemed like an expensive and elaborate party. However, the ARM weren't there to socialise. Our delegates were well prepared and disciplined and we worked effectively. Apart from Neville and myself, there was Hazel Hawke, Janet Holmes à Court, Eddie McGuire, Steve Vizard and Lindsay Fox. Tim Costello, brother of Liberal treasurer Peter, was there on a 'Real Republic' direct-election platform. All of the premiers and state opposition leaders were out in force, as were many of John Howard and Kim Beazley's respective frontbenchers. Howard had made an interesting range of appointments, including two prominent lawyers from Perth, Professor Greg Craven and solicitor Julie Bishop, whom I had got to know when I was helping unravel the chaotic mess of WA Inc in the late 1980s. Howard also appointed two archbishops – Peter Hollingsworth of the Anglican Church and the Catholics' George Pell.

The appointed delegates also included Richard McGarvie, a former judge and Victorian state governor. McGarvie's model for a republic, which he modestly described as 'the McGarvie Model', basically involved the president being appointed in much the same way as the governor-general is today but included a council of elders who'd advise the prime minister on the appropriate choice. There were a number of delegates elected on direct-election platforms, including Clem Jones, a former Labor mayor of Brisbane, and former independent MPs Ted Mack and Phil Cleary. Clem had come with a detailed model, based it appeared on the French system with both an executive president and a prime minister.

Since 1990, the ARM had consistently worked at our goal to build the broadest body of support from both sides of politics for having our own Australian head of state; we'd thoroughly vetted all the options and backed the parliamentary appointment model. The soundness of our position had attracted many conservatives, including eventually Peter Costello, whom we all confidently expected would succeed John Howard as prime minister within a few years. Andrew Robb, who'd been the Liberal campaign director in 1996, had established a republic group called Conservatives for an Australian Head of State. But, as is so often the case in politics, as we were building up our base on one side of politics, support started to fall away on the other.

Peter Beattie, Geoff Gallop and Mike Rann were the Labor opposition leaders of Queensland, Western Australia and South Australia respectively. Without any forewarning, they announced themselves supporters of direct election and gave that cause substantial additional credibility. They were contradicted by NSW Labor Premier Bob Carr and Victoria's Labor opposition leader John Brumby, but the damage was done.

Far from being inflexible, the ARM team compromised. Working with Jason Yat-sen Li, who'd come on a direct-election ticket, we developed a model that would win the support of the convention, formulating a public nomination process of the candidates to then be considered by parliament. We took on board the concerns of conservative republicans who felt a president that could only be removed by a two-thirds majority would be effectively unsackable and agreed that the House of Representatives could remove a president by simple majority provided the president would be replaced in the interim by whoever was the senior state governor.

Neville and I spent a lot of time with John Howard, and he continued to listen carefully to our argument that Australia had outgrown the monarchy. At some stage, we would become a republic, we said. Here was a chance for him to put his own stamp on it, to ensure it was done safely and conservatively. That didn't move him and neither did the vision I painted of a future Labor government proposing a blatantly populist direct-election model.

The convention ultimately endorsed the parliamentary appointment model and Howard undertook to put it to the vote in a constitutional referendum. There was hope, and plenty of it, but we had work to do.

The referendum was scheduled for 6 November 1999 and I was campaigning for a 'yes' vote for almost all of 1999. It was a surreal existence: flying to Melbourne, going to the ANZ Bank to advise their board on their takeover defences, then slipping out to a pub to speak at a republican fundraiser or into a radio studio to debate one of the monarchists. Goldman Sachs were remarkably forbearing.

The campaign was certainly a good foretaste of what a political career would be like – endless events giving much the same speech, taking the train around the suburbs of our big cities to address audiences large and small, shrugging off personal attacks from the media and (occasionally) anonymous backbiting from 'senior colleagues'.

Part-way through, a devastating personal accident brought my campaigning to a temporary halt. Lucy's uncle and my dear friend Robert Hughes was badly injured in a head-on collision near Broome in Western Australia in May 1999. The entire right side of his body was smashed and he was brought barely alive to the Royal Perth Hospital. Lucy and I rushed over to be with him. That he recovered at all speaks volumes both for his determination and the skill of the medical team at Royal Perth. It was a bleak time; it's harrowing to see someone you love in a shattered state, barely alive in intensive care.

But there were some typically Bob moments – such as when, by now conscious but unable to speak, he signalled to a nurse to bring him something to write on. His message was in a language unknown to the nurse, but eventually someone recognised it as being in Catalan, the language of Barcelona, where Bob's history of that city had made him a hero. It read, 'Please call me a taxi, I wish to go to a good hotel!'

Three months later, we were able to bring him back to Sydney. Some quick renovations were undertaken so Bob could convalesce at our place. Everything got back on track, slowly but surely.

By 4 August, when we hosted a 40th birthday dinner for our friend Sean Howard, Bob was much better. Paul and Annita Keating joined us, and Bob and I had a long talk with Paul about the referendum. Kim Beazley had previously commented, 'Comrade, the fate of the republic is in the hands of its greatest enemy,' and Keating's view was the same. He couldn't see how we could win with the prime minister against us.

It was sobering, but we maintained our determination, Bob Hughes style. As is typical of political campaigns, our polling waxed and waned. One moment, it would seem we were utterly doomed, with our vote heading down into the 30s; at others our hopes rose.

In a classic case of allowing the perfect to be the enemy of the good, the direct-electionist republicans joined the monarchists to campaign for a 'no' vote, claiming all the while that if the referendum were defeated, we'd have another vote on a direct-election model in a few years' time. One of the great political lies of our time.

When the votes were counted, despite our forebodings, almost all – but not enough – republicans had rallied around the Yes campaign. Ultimately, however, we fell short. The national vote was a little over 45 per cent for 'yes'; we came very close to winning in Victoria, where the 'yes' vote was over 49 per cent, but only the Australian Capital Territory voted 'yes'.

We were left with the grim emptiness of defeat and the certain knowledge that I wasn't exaggerating when I warned, 'If we vote "no", it means "no" for a very long time.'

After the defeat, the direct electionists faded away, never lifting a finger to promote a second vote. The ARM has soldiered on regardless, but the republican cause is still fractured by the question of how to elect the president.

This account has been brief, as I have written two books already about the republic campaign. Over the 20 years that have passed, I've remained of the view that we won't have enough political interest or momentum to win a referendum until after the end of the Queen's reign. That will be the next big watershed. And before we have a referendum, we should have a plebiscite that offers a choice between direct election and parliamentary appointment and allows that issue to be thrashed out over months of debate and resolved. With that done, the constitutional amendment proposed would incorporate the mode of election chosen in the plebiscite. That's our best chance of ensuring our head of state is, at last, one of us.

CHAPTER 9

Second time lucky: member for Wentworth

While I threw myself into traditional corporate advisory work at Goldman, my heart lay in investing as a principal. Thornton recognised that and in 2000 I started working on a new business called GS Ventures, designed to invest in 'fintech' – new technologies and applications in the financial services sector.

It was headed by a Goldman and Wall Street legend, Mike Mortara, who in days past had effectively founded the mortgage-backed securities business. My US Goldman colleague Pete Briger and I were his two deputies; I had responsibility for Asia and Japan. Sadly, Mike died suddenly in November 2000 and I was invited to move to New York and co-head the business with Briger. It was tempting but Lucy and I were reluctant to move Daisy, then 15, out of her high school, and Lucy was deputy lord mayor of Sydney.

Passing on that opportunity concentrated my thinking. I'd become a Goldman partner in 1998. Clearly, if I wanted to progress in the firm, I needed to move away from Australia. But it just wasn't the right time, and so I made plans to retire from Goldman at the end of 2001.

I'd enjoyed Goldman's collaborative culture – most businesses in those days had two and sometimes three co-heads; it was very much a partnership. And we did some big deals – selling OzEmail was close to my heart, but we also sold Grindlays Bank for the ANZ, advised the Commonwealth on the second stage of the Telstra privatisation, and in a memorable transaction I managed to buy Montana Wines in New Zealand for Philip Bowman's Allied Domecq. I also started the negotiations that led to the merger of Goldman's Australian business with the JBWere stockbroking firm – itself also a partnership.

Whenever I anticipated a move away from corporate life I'd consider all the possibilities that might be open to me. The pull was always to politics, public service. I hadn't dwelt on the defeat of the republican referendum or grown bitter about the pointedly personal abuse I'd received. I am above all a very positive person; I've never defined or motivated myself by what or whom I am against – I'm not a hater, as so many people in politics are.

All the time that I'd chaired the ARM and while I'd been chairman of Goldman Sachs Australia, it hadn't been appropriate for me to be active in any political party. Now I felt ready to return to the political fray, led by the essentially liberal Australian values that had inspired my republicanism. I was 47 and had made as much money as I needed or wanted. The financial independence I'd worked hard for was achieved. Shouldn't I try to do my bit to make Australia a better, fairer nation, a place where more people could have the opportunities I had?

Over the years, many people in the Liberal Party had sought to woo me back into the fold. Friends in the Labor Party had tried to recruit me, too. I'd seen Keating regularly during my work on the Republic Advisory Committee in 1993. On one occasion, at Kirribilli House, Paul made an approach: Graham Richardson was about to retire from the Senate. It was flattering, but I doubted I'd be comfortable in the ALP; neither would it be comfortable with me. At Paul's insistence, I had a chat with Richardson. It turned out he and I were of entirely the same mind – that it wasn't a good idea or a good fit. Subsequently, Richardson has falsely claimed I sought his support to join the ALP; not that anyone would readily believe a man who in his memoir boasts of his skill at lying. If I had ever needed a mentor to join the ALP, I would have turned to my closest friend and business partner, Neville Wran.

The Liberals had a reactionary right-wing element, embodied by my monarchist foe Tony Abbott, but at the heart of the party, I believed, was a philosophy of freedom, of real liberalism. I believed I could help keep the Liberal Party true to its liberal foundations, steer it towards the centre and in so doing better maintain the political values on which it had been founded.

So, in December 2000, I'd walked across Phillip Street to the prime minister's Sydney office to discuss my political future with him. Howard was delighted, or appeared to be. Before long I was chairing the Liberal Party's think tank, the Menzies Research Centre (MRC), and was the honorary federal treasurer – meaning the chief fundraiser. I threw myself into both roles. To reinvigorate the MRC, I initiated a series of research papers on matters such as housing affordability and school education.

I nurtured my interest in demography, and learned a lot from Professor Peter McDonald of the Australian National University (ANU). I pored over one fact he taught me: that the population of a country with a total fertility rate of 1.3 and no net migration will shrink by 75 per cent over a century. It clicked: sustainable replacement fertility rates occur in developed countries where women have opportunities to combine work and family. It's the more patriarchal and traditional developed societies, such as Italy and Japan, that have low birth rates. Affordable childcare and flexible workplaces matter. And flexible jobs, such as part-time work, go hand in hand with urban design whereby work and education are readily accessible – not at the end of a long commute from a dormitory suburb.

Although I'd looked forward to having more free time after leaving Goldman Sachs, it wasn't to be. Instead, I was drawn into the fallout of Australia's largest-ever corporate collapse. When HIH Insurance, Australia's second-largest general insurance company, went into administration in 2001, thousands of families and businesses no longer had insurance cover and no assurance of claims being met.

On 23 September 1998, HIH had made a takeover bid for a much smaller insurance company, FAI Insurance, then controlled by Rodney Adler. HIH had made the bid without seeking any due diligence, although it no doubt believed it understood FAI's business well. There'd been talks about this acquisition for some years. Rodney Adler contacted me as soon as the bid appeared and Goldman Sachs Australia was engaged to advise FAI on the takeover offer, which was completed early in 1999. Our attempts to find a higher alternative bidder were unsuccessful. Adler accepted the offer for the remainder of his shares (having sold a portion of them on market to HIH at the time they announced their offer).

I'd known Rodney for years, and my Goldman Sachs colleague, later business partner, Russel Pillemer and I had also discussed some strategic options with him in late 1997. One of them was the possibility of his taking FAI private with a financial partner; some preliminary consideration was done both by the team in Sydney and some of our colleagues in New York. The discussions were held at FAI's offices during business hours and I advised Adler to keep his chairman, John

Landerer, appraised of his discussions. He assured me he had, copying correspondence to me about the project to Landerer. Goldman decided not to pursue the transaction. Within a few weeks of saying that to Adler, the HIH offer, which was unsolicited, was made and Adler, who'd been discussing what his next steps might be with us, formally retained Goldman to advise on the offer.

It would be fair to say that FAI didn't cause HIH's collapse, which would have almost certainly occurred given the scale of its own problems. However, it's also fair to say that FAI turned out to be a costly acquisition largely because it had, on a much smaller scale, similar problems to HIH in that it had inadequate reserves to meet its insurance liabilities. This, of course, underlined the recklessness of HIH in making a takeover offer for another insurance company without doing due diligence.

In May 2001, the Howard government set up a Royal Commission headed by Justice Neville Owen to investigate the collapse. While Owen was unerringly polite and businesslike, one of the counsel assisting, Norman O'Bryan, set out to target me and Goldman Sachs as being responsible for the FAI acquisition, which he argued was to HIH what the Trojan Horse had been to Troy! He prosecuted this case aggressively both by briefing the media and in his submissions in the commission.

The Australian media, who love the spectacle of a high-flyer being brought down, joined in the hunt. Lucy and the children were devastated. Only a few years before that, they'd wept at the defeat of the republic referendum and tactfully not responded as their father was slammed every day in the press. Now, I was being accused of being a crook. I felt I was re-enacting the Costigan Royal Commission, except this time I was the target. I couldn't sue O'Bryan for libel for what he said in the commission as he was protected by privilege, but I did make it clear I was prepared to hold him to account for what he was saying to the media, and after that his briefing quietened down.

The HIH Royal Commission was excruciatingly embarrassing for me. I could see my own reputation being trashed – just as Packer's had been. An adverse finding would have completely wrecked any of my political plans. Our lawyers, principally Robert Mangioni and Tom Jucovic QC, did an outstanding job, although both observed (they weren't the first to do so) that I wasn't the ideal client, having very strong views of my own. They did remind me, as politely as they could, that the lawyer who acts for himself has a fool for a client!

I was questioned why, when Goldman was retained to advise FAI in response to the takeover, we didn't formally disclose to the board of FAI our previous work with Adler. The answer was that not only did the two executives on the FAI board, CEO Rodney Adler and CFO Tim Mainprize, know all about our prior work, but we'd been assured by Adler that the chairman, John Landerer, had been fully informed. Owen accepted our evidence on all these points.

Ultimately, Justice Owen realised the pursuit of me and Goldman Sachs was wasting the commission's time. Despite the many days dedicated to us, only nine pages of the 1500-page report referred to Goldman Sachs or me at all. No adverse findings were made against us.

Even so, the liquidator of HIH included Goldman, myself and Russel Pillemer as defendants in his mammoth legal proceedings against virtually every possible party with any conceivable connection to the collapse of HIH. The principal targets were the large reinsurance companies who, it was alleged, had connived in covering up HIH and FAI's financial problems.

Our legal advice was that the case against us was utterly without merit and Goldman came close to getting most of it struck out. In the end, the liquidator made a confidential settlement with all the defendants, including Goldman. Given that the overall settlement was less than the liquidators had been offered several years before, I could only assume that, as is so often the case, the biggest winners were the lawyers, rather than the creditors.

Happily, Russel Pillemer and I had more to collaborate on than witness statements for the HIH Royal Commission. I had a non-compete with Goldman, so couldn't get back into the investment banking business, but they agreed I could re-establish Turnbull & Partners as a private equity investor. Russel, who'd returned from New York with his young family, also left Goldman and joined forces with me.

We set up our office in the Australia Square building on George Street. It was one of architect Harry Seidler's most famous edifices and it was perfectly round. Fortunately, we inherited a fit-out from a previous tenant that was carefully designed to suit the space, so that the board table, for example, was shaped like a slice of pie – widest at the window's edge.

Over two years, often working with Russel's brothers Johnny and Michael, we established a series of new businesses in asset management, private wealth advice, life insurance and leasing. The leasing business wasn't a success, but the other three were – it was a good track record, especially when so much of my time was spent on the HIH Royal Commission.

As the Liberal Party treasurer I became friends with the federal director, Lynton Crosby, and our pollster, Mark Textor, who worked for Wirthlin, an American research company. Each of them was thinking about new opportunities and I encouraged them to go into business together. Their firm, Crosby Textor, would become one of the world's leading political consultants. I declined their invitation to invest and become chairman as I felt there was too much potential for conflict, and Robert de Crespigny did so instead.

But between policy work, fundraising and deal making, I was also keeping my eye out for an avenue to get into parliament.

Andrew Thomson had won the seat of Wentworth in 1995 after John Hewson retired. He was the son of the famous golfer Peter Thomson, a lawyer and spoke fluent Japanese and Chinese. Thomson was quickly promoted by Howard after the 1996 election and served as minister for Sport and Tourism until 1998, when he was dropped to the backbench. By late 2001, there was a lot of speculation that he would be challenged for preselection, and likely lose.

I'd only been back in the party for a few months, but a number of my early backers, including Bill Heffernan and the party president, Shane Stone, suggested I seriously consider running in the preselection scheduled for 2001. I made some enquiries, but it was obvious the moderate faction in New South Wales had the numbers in the local conference and that Peter King, a former state president of the Liberal Party and local councillor, would almost certainly win.

King, it was generally acknowledged, was a pretty underwhelming prospect – not much better than Thomson. Ron Phillips was a former state MP and minister for Health and the leader of the moderates faction at the time. 'I know they say Peter's a mediocrity,' he told me. 'But if he is, he's our mediocrity.'

So, I didn't nominate for the preselection in 2001; however, the speculation about my going into parliament provoked some interesting encounters, including my first with Scott Morrison.

Scott had become the NSW Liberal Party's state director in 2000, the year after Labor had won a second term in a landslide. The Liberal leader, Kerry Chikarovski, had performed poorly in the campaign, where there was a 7 per cent swing to the Carr government. A few people had speculated that I should move into state politics – this was particularly attractive to federal politicians who didn't welcome my joining them in Canberra.

Scott hatched an ingenious idea in 2001 that involved a Liberal member of the Legislative Council retiring, my taking up the casual vacancy and then becoming leader of the opposition, running for a seat in the lower house at the next election, due in 2003.

'That's a great idea, Scott,' I said tongue in cheek. 'I'd be like Lord Salisbury, who was prime minister, sitting in the House of Lords!'

We were sitting on the terrace at home – the location of many intense political discussions over the years that followed.

'But, Scott, seriously, why do you think I'd be an attractive leader for the Liberal Party? Wouldn't Labor simply go after me for being wealthy – an out-of-touch plutocrat?'

'Well, I thought you'd raise that,' Scott replied as he bent down to pull out a bundle of spreadsheets. 'We've been throwing your name into our polling in Western Sydney. And you know what? The battlers like you. They admire your success; they reckon you're self-made – it's all about aspiration. Australians don't want class wars.'

Scott thought Chikarovski could be persuaded to step aside to make the transition easier. She knew she'd get rolled sooner or later and preferred her replacement wasn't one of her colleagues.

The 'Malcolm for Macquarie Street' idea didn't come to anything. If any Turnbull was to go into state politics, it should have been Lucy with her interest in urban planning. Almost all of my policy interests were in the federal arena. And in March 2002, John Brogden successfully challenged Chikarovski.

I had another curious political interview on our terrace around that time. Bill Heffernan was a senator, an assistant minister and a former party president. But more importantly, the craggy old farmer from Junee was also one of John Howard's closest confidants.

'Malcolm,' Bill said, 'the best thing about you is that there has never been a breath of scandal.'

I looked at him. He seemed to be quite serious.

'That's very kind, Bill, but I don't think you could have followed my career very closely.'

'Oh no,' said Bill. 'Not that kind of scandal. I mean –' he dropped his voice, 'no funny business.'

That's a relief, I thought. Bill had a weakness for conspiracy theories, but as long as we steered away from them he was great company and shrewd politically and commercially. I told him once the most sophisticated thing about him was his flawless impersonation of a country bumpkin.

As I looked around at the various options to go into parliament, I kept coming back to Wentworth. It was where we'd always lived and the one place where nobody could call me a carpetbagger. I was at least a local.

I'd joined the Point Piper branch of the Liberal Party and had got to know its president, Jason Falinski, and his friends Alex Calvo and Adam Schofield. They all agreed the best place for me to run was where I lived. But that would mean a fight.

The preselection committee would be composed of 160 people – 48 from the state executive and the state council. We had no control over who they'd be. The balance were elected by the local branches based on their respective memberships.

There were about 750 members in the Wentworth branches, so we decided to recruit as many as we could into the Point Piper branch. And so, starting in the middle of 2003, began the great Wentworth branch-stacking drama. By the time it was finished, we'd recruited over 1500 new members; in response, Peter King had signed up nearly as many. At $95 for a married couple, it wasn't a cheap way to participate in what became something akin to a US primary. Normally, this kind of thing is done by word of mouth, and that was how we started – with friends of friends. Russel Pillemer, Gary Perlstein and other members of the South African Jewish community in Wentworth were especially active on my behalf.

We had to be fastidious in our record keeping and make sure that everybody paid their own membership fee themselves. Liberal Party activist Scott Briggs came and worked with me full-time on the recruitment drive from our offices in Australia Square. Daisy was also an enthusiastic recruiter.

On one occasion, Daisy and her friend Melissa Chan were on a street corner in Rose Bay recruiting passers-by to join the Point Piper branch when they encountered Peter King's wife, Fiona Sinclair, there to sign up supporters for her husband's Rose Bay branch. Realising Sinclair was trying to blacken my reputation, Daisy sprang to my defence. It was hand-to-hand politics.

King naturally called on his parliamentary colleagues to back him and most of them did, especially Tony Abbott and Bronwyn Bishop, both fellow monarchists. Meanwhile, my references included one from Shane Stone, as well as Joe Hockey, Lynton Crosby, Bruce McWilliam and Chris Corrigan. Lady Nancy Gorton, the widow of Sir John Gorton, and Lady Susan Atwill, widow of Sir John Atwill, had both supported me in the 1981 preselection and did so again.

Across all the references, there were consistent themes: my backers believed I wasn't going to be a time server, wasn't afraid of stepping on toes to get things done and, in Wendy Spry's words, 'He is a natural leader, always seeing the bigger picture.'[1]

Another referee and long-time Point Piper resident, Max Raine, recalled a meeting in the 1950s when Menzies campaigned for Les Bury saying, 'It is the duty and indeed privilege of those in Wentworth to put forward only candidates of cabinet timber for Canberra.'[2]

The campaign run against me featured derogatory letters and brochures flying around the electorate. The negative refrain was that I was really a Labor Party person (that remained a favourite of the right throughout my political career) and that I was a corporate villain.

Anxious that I not get into parliament, several Labor figures, including Graham Richardson, Nick Bolkus and Kim Beazley, claimed that I'd sought their support to get a Labor seat in parliament. As previously explained, at various times, Labor people had sought to recruit me (most notably Keating himself) and I'd always declined. Never rudely; perhaps I should have been less chatty.

Another attack was that I was a republican (guilty as charged was all I could say there). King was strongly supported by the monarchists, who routinely referred to me as 'President Turnbull'. Lastly, there was the smear that I was a corporate crook as shown by my involvement with FAI. The Royal Commission's failure to make any adverse findings against me blunted that line of attack.

The recruiting went well beyond the usual low-key word of mouth approach. As we got closer to the 19 October deadline, we felt King's membership drive catching up with us, and we even advertised on radio to find new members. In its frenzy, this preselection contest was utterly without precedent.

Scott Morrison was enjoying all the money coming in from the new membership fees, but had to spend at least some of it on legal advice when I successfully challenged some of King's new members on the basis that inadequate notice had been given for several branch meetings. Another appeal of ours didn't succeed, but the outcome was that we finished ahead of King in terms of the membership drive.

Ripples from the Wentworth branch-stacking war reached Canberra. Prime Minister John Howard opted to stay well out of it. Tony Nutt, John's principal private secretary, called me and said, 'The PM isn't going to help you or King. So, you'll have to catch and kill your own.'

A month later, as the number of new recruits approached 3000, Nutt called me in a panic and asked what was going on and when was it going to stop. 'You told me to catch and kill my own,' I protested.

'I did, but we didn't expect you to catch and kill so many!' Tony replied.

Once the numbers were settled and the preselectors named, the schmoozing began in earnest. Elaborate brochures were prepared and sent to each preselector. We held dinners at home and parties at Michael Carr's art gallery to win the preselectors over. Deborah Hutton and former Hockeyroo Danni Roche were among our many helpers.

Lucy by then was lord mayor of Sydney. Her career in politics came about after she'd written her magnificent book about the history of Sydney, and in the process of writing it, she'd got to know Frank Sartor, the independent lord mayor. After Frank persuaded her to run on his ticket in the council elections in 1999, not only was she elected but she became deputy lord mayor. Then, in 2003, she succeeded Frank after he went into state parliament.

Lucy was the first woman to be lord mayor of Sydney and the family was so proud of her. Her father, Tom, was thrilled. His grandfather Sir Thomas Hughes had been the first lord mayor of Sydney in 1903. Tom hadn't marched on ANZAC Day for many years, but on 25 April 2003, aged 79, he marched with his old squadron and as they passed Sydney Town Hall, he was almost leaping as he waved with pride to the lord mayor as she reviewed the parade from the balcony.

Lucy is as knowledgeable as she is passionate about urbanism in general and Sydney in particular. Her time as lord mayor was too short. Frank Sartor had been an independent lord mayor but joined the Labor Party to get a seat in the NSW parliament, where he subsequently became a minister in the Carr government. While Labor regarded Frank as a friendly independent, they didn't see Lucy in that light. And Labor wanted to get control of the city council, no doubt because of the influence it would give them over planning and zoning decisions – extremely helpful if you want to raise campaign finance from the property developers.

In October 2003, the Labor Party state secretary, Eric Roozendaal, asked Lucy to join the ALP. She declined, saying she wanted to stay an independent.

Because I was active in the Liberal Party and likely to go into parliament, the Labor government concluded they had to do everything in their power to ensure Lucy couldn't get re-elected. They announced they'd be running a star candidate of their own and, to help their cause, included in the Sydney council area the inner-city suburbs of Kings Cross and Potts Point in the east of the city and Glebe in the west. But Lucy moved quickly to improve council services in those areas and much to Labor's chagrin her popularity rose, especially when she explained that while I was in the Liberal Party, she was not and would campaign as an independent.

In early 2004, the state Labor government sacked the Sydney City Council and merged it with South Sydney Council, which had a much larger residential population, most of whom had never heard of Lucy and were rusted-on Labor voters. Lucy anguished about what to do – I encouraged her to run and believed she could still win, but she decided not to run again. Labor was delighted; they thought this meant they'd easily get control of the town hall.

However, Lucy knew Clover Moore, then an independent South Sydney councillor and member of the NSW parliament. Recognising Clover as the one potential independent who had high name recognition and support in the South Sydney Council areas, Lucy persuaded her to run. She won and has been lord mayor of Sydney ever since.

Lucy's truncated career as lord mayor was just an early taste of how my own family and friends would pay a price for my political career.

The preselection was held on 28 February 2004 at the Swiss Grand Hotel on Bondi Beach. After a series of roundtables where the two candidates would meet individually with a small group of preselectors, there were speeches to the full preselection committee. We had gone through the numbers very carefully. Our Point Piper branch had 1305 members (out of a total conference of 3633), which translated to 40 out of the 112 local preselectors. A few weeks out, we figured we had overall 81 solid votes, King 67, and there were 12 in play.

King was confident of his numbers too, but I'd noticed he tended to push people to tell him whether they'd vote for him or not. It turned out that the only person whose stated voting intentions you can rely on is the one who says, 'I'd rather cut off my right arm than vote for you, you bastard!' The better approach, I find, is not to ask the question: if people volunteer, they're more likely to tell you the truth, and often you can work it out by listening to them, reading their body language and so on. The best numbers people can sometimes make mistakes, but bullies always get their numbers wrong.

By the morning of the preselection, we were confident we had the numbers, estimating our support at 87 votes. We were wrong in the best way: it turned out to be 88, and with King at 70 that was a substantial margin of victory in a tight contest. But it was a fraught day, although it ended with a dry jest.

When the result was announced, one of King's supporters leapt to her feet and said, 'This is a disgrace, I'll resign from the party. Look, I'm tearing up my membership card.' And then as she struggled to do precisely that, Shane Stone, in his best Northern Territory drawl, quipped, 'Yes, love, now you know why we laminate them.' That brought the house down.

The preselection contest had engaged the whole electorate and Peter King's supporters were naturally bitterly disappointed that a 'radical republican' had won the Liberal Party's crown jewel. On the other hand, many saw me as a fresh voice of progressive liberalism, and the media were overwhelmingly positive about my win, as an example of Liberal Party renewal.

My campaign as the Liberal candidate began the day after the preselection. My critics had predicted I'd have no patience with grass-roots politics, and to be frank I wasn't sure how much I'd enjoy it myself. But I found it one of the best parts of being in politics. People interest me, and one of the privileges of being a candidate for parliament is that you can walk up to a complete stranger, introduce yourself and start up a conversation. You can go round knocking on doors, bailing people up on the street or on the train – in other words, it's a licence to be a complete and utter pest, yet most people appreciate your interest!

It was just as well I got going quickly. We set up an office in Bondi Junction and Scott Briggs continued as the campaign manager, with Bev Martin and Samantha Hughes taking over from him when he went overseas. Daisy was active on the campaign, and Sally Betts, who was the conference president and had fought hard for King, campaigned just as hard for me. There were hundreds of people working on the campaign – leafleting, holding street stalls, knocking on doors.

Bill Heffernan, like a latter-day Clancy of the Overflow, came down to lend a hand with the campaigning and, at Scott Morrison's suggestion, stayed with us at home for three or four weeks. Best house guest – never left a mess in the kitchen and always made his bed, complete with hospital corners! 'The complete opposite of Uncle Bob,' Lucy observed.

Doorknocking is a rite of passage for political candidates, but it wasn't terribly effective in Wentworth because most people lived in apartments and it was hard to get into the buildings. One time Heffo and I were doorknocking a street of houses in Randwick. Most people weren't at home, but finally a door opened. Standing there was a young woman, bleary-eyed from lack of sleep; in one arm she was cradling a newborn baby and we could hear another crying inside the house. She wasn't listening as I introduced myself. 'Thank God. Adults!' she said as her gaze focused. 'Come in and talk to me!' We were there for an hour, chatted about everything except politics, and if Bill had had his way we'd have stayed for dinner.

The Daily Telegraph had said after the preselection that I was left with the 'less-than-arduous job of winning the blue-ribbon seat of Wentworth'.[3] That task proved to be more arduous than expected when in September Peter King decided to run as an independent. I knew this wasn't as quixotic a venture as it appeared; if King could finish ahead of Labor and the Greens on primary votes, then their preferences would quite likely put him ahead of me on a two-party preferred basis.

The months leading up to the 9 October election were anxious ones for the Liberal Party. The Labor Party had elected Mark Latham as their leader in December 2003 and for most of 2004, Labor was ahead in the polls.

At the same time, King wasn't directing preferences to the Liberal Party and some of our polling was very bad, indicating we'd lose the seat to Labor. I felt terrible: was Wentworth going to be the seat that lost the Liberal Party government? I called Howard and offered to pull out. 'John, if you think the only way to hold the seat is for me to step aside so you can re-endorse King, then do so.'

Howard was quite relaxed. 'Don't worry, Malcolm, you'll be fine. If we lose government, and we won't, it won't be because we lose Wentworth.'

Alex was overseas at college, but Lucy, Daisy and I threw ourselves into the local campaign and I ran with any local issue I could find. We campaigned against a crematorium at Waverley Cemetery and for a leash-free dog park at Vaucluse. No issue was too small or too local. I was meeting hundreds of people every week on the streets of the electorate and I could see that the issues that concerned them the most were local ones. So, if someone complained about a cracked pavement, I rang the council and persuaded them to fix it. Over the months of campaigning, people started to realise that in addition to having 'cabinet timber' I could also be a good local member.

Latham had an air of simmering anger about him, as though he was about to explode, but it wasn't apparent at first. I was campaigning on the streets every day, and it was women who woke up to him first. A typical comment was, 'I just don't like him; he reminds me of a boyfriend my sister had,' followed by a grimace. And then about a month or more later, men started to go off him as well.

At the election, not only did Howard win, but with a swing to the government. In Wentworth, King polled 18 per cent, well behind Labor's 26.3 per cent and my own primary of 41.8 per cent. King had handed out how-to-votes preferencing Labor in left-leaning booths, but most of his votes had come back to me as preferences. With 55.5 per cent of the two-party preferred vote, the swing in Wentworth against the Liberal Party amounted to only 2.4 per cent.

I was as relieved as I was elated: it had been a wild ride, starting with the preselection and the world's biggest branch-stacking competition, and ending with the election. I felt very good about the win and not just because I love new adventures and the opportunity to learn new things. This was coming at the right moment for me and for the family. Lucy was taking over most of my business responsibilities. The kids were grown up: Alex was 22 and three years into his undergraduate degree at Harvard, and Daisy was 19 and in her second year at university. If ever there was a good time to go into parliament, this was it.

3

Parliament

(2004–13)

CHAPTER 10

On the backbench

Before the 41st parliament officially assembled on 16 November 2004, the new MPs had a few days of instruction on how to navigate Parliament House. The Parliamentary Library impressed me. It doesn't have a huge collection, by the standards of the state or national libraries, but its researchers are superb. Any backbencher wanting material for a speech will get a detailed brief within days, if not hours.

The library's head of research, Dr June Verrier, was appropriately austere and wore her hair pinned in a tight grey bun. 'So, in conclusion, our job is to make you' – she paused and balefully surveyed the class of 2004 – 'look intelligent.' And then she sighed, as though this might have been a goal beyond reach.

A parliament is a place for the people's elected representatives to discuss laws, form governments and hold them to account. It's also a place for the public to meet their MPs and senators – from chief executives to community organisations to school groups. It's truly the people's house. But the form of Parliament House seems to frustrate, rather than follow, its function. It's immense, has 4700 rooms, and members routinely walk several kilometres a day. And because it's so spread out, the corridors almost always seem empty, even on a sitting day when there must be several thousand people in the building. Sitting in their self-contained offices, MPs and senators can easily become isolated. There isn't the natural collision space of Old Parliament House, where to get anywhere you had to pass through King's Hall. Consequently, friendships between MPs in different parties are fewer than they were in the old building. The vast monument, in truth, works against the whole purpose of a parliament, which is to bring together people with different views in the hope that through discussion and debate they can reach common ground.

Surprisingly, everyone in Parliament House was very friendly to me; the papers had been saying my public profile and wealth would make my colleagues resent me. When I mentioned the warm reception to veteran journalist Michelle Grattan, she dryly observed, 'Oh well, it's early days, and Christmas is almost upon us.'

I was allotted a seat between two old hands. One was Wilson 'Ironbar' Tuckey, the member for O'Connor in Western Australia. Wilson was 70, had been in parliament for 25 years, and had just been sacked from the ministry by Howard. Fiercely conservative, he wasn't going to be an ally of mine. The other was Russell Broadbent, the member for McMillan, now Monash. Russell, four years my elder, epitomised political resilience. He'd been elected in 1990 and lost his seat in 1993, was elected again in 1996 and tossed out in 1998. His 2004 election win had given him his third entry to the House, and he was determined to stay there. He'd seen a lot. To this day, Russell is a liberal Liberal. He and some other moderates, including Judi Moylan, Petro Georgiou and Bruce Baird, were regularly putting pressure on Howard to treat asylum seekers with more compassion and they succeeded in getting all children out of migration detention.

The main event of every parliamentary day is question time at 2 pm; it seemed absurd to me. The questions were either sycophantic so-called Dorothy Dixers from the government – 'Would the minister advise the House of how splendidly successful his latest endeavours have been?' – or allegations from the opposition – 'When will the minister admit to his shameful culpability and resign?' I exaggerate for emphasis but not much.

'Why,' I asked Russell, 'do the ministers hardly ever give a straight answer to the question?'

Wearily, Russell replied, 'It's called question time, Malcolm, not answer time.'

For my maiden speech, on 29 November, four hundred of my supporters came to Canberra by bus, packing out all the public galleries. I spoke of the natural beauty of Wentworth, whose 'green hills and golden beaches are strung like jewels between the harbour and the sea', and the egalitarianism of the community in which I'd grown up, the surf club 'no respecter of rank or privilege' and rubbing shoulders there with 'judges and garbos, teachers and policemen and businessmen of all types – from shmattas in Surry Hills to high finance in Martin Place'.[1] It was a love letter to my home, to that part of the world which I'd adored all my life. Corny, I suppose, but heartfelt.

Family should always feature in a maiden speech and after I'd thanked my supporters, I turned to Lucy, Alex and Daisy: 'Their love gave me the strength to run, their charisma made up for my many shortcomings and their advocacy was as compelling as it was sincere.' All so true. Alex had been away at college for most of the campaign, but his mother and sister had been indefatigable. Lucy had written to the whole electorate to tell them I wasn't the monster they'd read about in the media, and Daisy was everywhere, especially persuasive when accompanied – like the Roman goddess Diana with her hounds – by our three dogs wearing little jumpers that read, 'Fetching votes for Turnbull'.

In words I was to repeat frequently, I observed, 'Our immigration programme is essentially a recruiting exercise conducted in the national interest of Australia. It is a competitive world and we want as many of the world's enterprising and energetic to join and strengthen our Australian family.' Curiously, I spoke only briefly about climate change – in the context of water scarcity. That wasn't self-censorship; for whatever reason, in 2004, I hadn't fully grasped the significance of global warming.

With my political career launched, the media commenced speculation about how soon I'd became a cabinet minister, if not leader. My focus, however, was on getting up to speed on public policy issues I hadn't had time to explore in my business life. I joined a host of committees, but the most interesting and influential of these was the Standing Committee on Environment and Heritage chaired by WA Liberal Dr Mal Washer, a wise, thoughtful and humane politician. During the committee's inquiry into 'Sustainable Cities' I became persuaded that the climate was becoming hotter and drier and that a wholly different approach to water management would be required in our cities.

While researching the technologies and economics of recycling waste water and desalinating sea water, I visited Israel and saw first-hand how that very dry country makes every drop count. Soon I was reflecting on the bore and well at our farm in the Hunter Valley that I'd operated for many years without a proper understanding of ground water. It appeared that Australia had made a mistake in how we designed water management in our cities: all of our storm-water management was designed to collect water in gutters and drains and quickly send it out of town, generally into a river or ocean. But we should be finding ways to slow it down so that it can permeate the ground and replenish the ground water. I started to realise that in a hot, dry climate like ours, the best place to store water was under the ground.

In the final report, completed in November 2005, we also pointed out that modern cities need a combination of transport modes – walking, cycling, light rail, metros, heavy rail, buses and private cars. And that these need to be integrated. For years, Coalition governments had been resolutely opposed to supporting mass transit infrastructure, preferring to channel federal dollars into roads. Plainly, the consequences of this policy direction would be worsening congestion. And with that, increasing social disadvantage: 'It is self-evident that suburbs which are car dependent discriminate against those who cannot afford to drive (or park) a car or who by reason of age or disability are not able to drive.'[2]

Over the following decade, I continued to develop my thinking on urban issues, culminating in my government's Cities Agenda in 2016, which in a first for any federal, let alone Coalition, government funded the development of urban rail in every major city in the nation.

Another burgeoning interest was tax policy. I hadn't specialised in tax when I was a lawyer. From experts in the field, including John Freebairn from Melbourne University and Neil Warren from UNSW among others, I gathered there was broad consensus that our marginal rates were too high. Our top rate – of 47 per cent plus the Medicare levy, then at 1.5 per cent – also cut in at a low level. Inflation had resulted in bracket creep: in the 1960s, the threshold for the top rate was nine times average earnings; by 2003 it was only 1.3 times. Even after Treasurer Peter Costello increased the thresholds in the 2005 budget, the threshold was 2.4 times average earnings.

In concert with a doctoral student at the ANU, Jeromey Temple, I looked into a range of tax reform possibilities, costing each of them and projecting the likely increases in employment and economic activity that would come from the lower rates. We also set out the way in which different reforms would impact on the share of tax paid by different income groups.[3]

It was pretty academic stuff, to be honest, and its ripples wouldn't have gone much beyond the tax policy crowd but for the reaction of Peter Costello. As well as ridiculing the report publicly, he told me directly how unhappy he was, and bluntly suggested I needed to know my place as I was no match 'for the full weight of the Treasury'.

John Howard was bemused by Costello's reaction. At the same time as he counselled me to tread carefully, he did wonder aloud why Costello hadn't just said, 'Thanks for the paper. Looks interesting; will put it on my pile of books to read.'

The Costello contretemps aside, the work left me with a clearer understanding of our tax system and persuaded me of the wisdom of reducing tax thresholds and flattening the tax system. These incentivise work and investment.

Besides swotting up on policy, I enjoyed disproving the general expectation that I'd be a hopeless local member. Whether it was going to a school, or meeting people on the bus, I was always energised by and interested in the people I met. And the best way to do that is not in some formal political setting, but just hanging out, being yourself. Lucy and I had always taken lots of walks around the area and she started calling them 'light campaigning'. Every weekend on our strolls we'd have casual chats with dozens of locals, and hundreds of others would see us out and about. I particularly enjoyed schmoozing with the Jewish community in all its diversity. An occasional dip into the Talmud and its commentators like Maimonides might ensue; it was always stimulating.

I also established a regular email list and, before long, it was going to about 20 per cent of the electorate, and many thousands outside it. In those days, I read all my emails. Often, I'd engage with a disgruntled correspondent and try to win them over. The funniest exchange was after the 2006 budget. A constituent from Bondi observed that she was a childless, 58-year-old lesbian poet and science teacher and 'there is nothing in the Budget for me'. She offered some unflattering appraisals of my character as well. I replied that she was 'correct that the Budget did not target childless, 58-year-old lesbian poets and science teachers, but you are better off nonetheless', and proceeded to explain why.

She forwarded my email to Sam Maiden at *The Daily Telegraph*. I don't think she ever voted for me but she certainly knew her local MP was listening.

My website included regular policy blogs, which Daisy insisted were dull. Why couldn't our dogs have a blog? Soon they did, mostly courtesy of Daisy. I started adding links to these on my email newsletters. It turned out that a blog 'by' Rusty, our red cattle dog, would generally get four or five times as many clicks as any of my learned speeches on tax reform – a practical political lesson. Dogs are far more interesting than fiscal drag.

CHAPTER 11

First rung on the ladder: parliamentary secretary

By 24 January 2006, I was no longer on the backbench: John Howard appointed me his parliamentary secretary. Now I was in that middle bench zone of an assistant minister – not able to answer questions in the House, but part of the executive and expected to help manage government business through the parliament.

Eastern Australia had been in drought for most of the last five years, and 2006 looked as though it would be hot and dry, too. Not only were the farmers suffering, but water storages for cities large and small were running low. Impressed by my recent work on water recycling, Howard gave me responsibility for national water policy. Consequently, I saw more of 'the boss' than I had before. My contact was mostly through Arthur Sinodinos, Howard's chief of staff (CoS), and a senior adviser, Helen Georgopoulos, who handled environmental policies in his office.

Historically, water management had been exclusively the responsibility of the states and territories. In the '90s, the federal government and the states had agreed on a National Water Initiative and $2 billion was set aside to spend on water-saving infrastructure. Trading in water entitlements (licences) began in the Murray–Darling Basin with the intent of ensuring that water found its way to its highest and best use. That all made sense, but it didn't address the growing sense of crisis about water scarcity.

Everyone in the water business, from academics to irrigators to engineers at big urban water utilities, was happy to talk to me. I was in my element, constantly learning. Among the leading lights were John Pigram at the University of New England and hydrogeologist Rick Evans, the latter also sharing his findings about Northern China's dwindling water reserves.

I was never going to be one of those politicians who skimmed along the surface, leaving the detail and technicalities to others. If I didn't have an in-depth understanding of a problem, I felt frustrated and insecure; I didn't want to be answering questions with slogans and inanities. Mindful that if you become immersed in the minutiae of any topic you can lose sight of the big picture, I would dive deep into the detail as I expanded my knowledge and then surface to reflect on how it all fitted together, trying to identify the key factors driving our water challenges.

There's our flatness: only 7 per cent of Australia is above 600 metres, as compared with 45 per cent of the United States. Another factor is our volatile and capricious climate. Droughts are often followed by equally destructive floods. There's the extreme variability of our rivers. The ratio between the maximum and minimum annual flows of the Rhine and the Yangtze is 2:1; for the Murray it is 30:1 and for the Darling, 10,000:1![1] And all of this was being made progressively worse by global warming and the drier and hotter climate it caused.

Our big cities, I realised, had little or no ability to build new dams, and even if they did, the declines in streamflow meant they couldn't be relied on to be adequately filled all the time. As far as urban water was concerned, my passion became recycling waste water as well as capturing storm water and directing it into ground water. That wasn't possible everywhere, but I enthusiastically promoted and helped fund schemes to do that in Adelaide. I used the not especially lofty platform of an assistant minister as a way of informing the public debate on water.

The city of Toowoomba, perched on the Great Dividing Range, was known for its gardens and cooler climate – a relief from steamy Brisbane. It was running out of water; its largest dam, 457 metres down the range, was nearly empty. Being far from the sea, desalination wasn't an option. The council, led by its formidable mayor, Di Thorley, resolved to recycle waste water and pump it back into the town's dam.

As with sea-water desalination, the waste water would pass through a series of filters and screens and finally through very fine membranes that would admit nothing other than the water molecules. This was completely safe. The recycled product would be pure, distilled water. And the process would require less energy than desalination of sea water, so was cheaper.

Several cities were using recycled water for watering parks and so on, typically conveyed in a purple pipe. And any city on a river is using water previously used by the cities upstream. Given the safety of the treatment, dual pipes were deemed to be an unnecessary expense. Toowoomba's thoroughly clean recycled water was to be returned to the main system from which water for personal use is drawn. The Toowoomba council, the Queensland government and the city's local federal member, Ian Macfarlane, Howard's Energy minister, were all in favour.

The government was set to offer a substantial federal grant to complete the project when local councillor Lyle Shelton,[2] supported by retired politician and property developer Clive Berghofer, started to campaign against it. Before long the 'toilet to tap' plan was being slammed. Claims were made that it would result in male genitals shrinking and fish in the local streams changing sex. Worse, their fair city would become known as 'Poowoomba'!

It was nuts, but it started to work, and Ian Macfarlane asked me if we'd make our federal grant conditional on a local referendum. Thanks to the scare campaign, the July vote was overwhelmingly negative. I concluded the only way to get people to accept augmenting drinking water supplies with recycled water was very indirectly – by recharging aquifers and hoping the public would accept that years of gurgling through sediment would make the difference.

As the drought worsened, more regional inland towns, like Goulburn in New South Wales, started to run out of water. Whether it was an emergency pipeline or water tankers, we cooperated with the states to deliver immediate solutions to maintain water security for essential use. But then it looked like some of our capital cities could run dry. Perth was the only city that had built a desalination plant at that stage – they knew their water availability was plummeting, thanks to climate change, and to their credit they addressed the challenge in a timely and pragmatic manner.

It appeared that for years the water utilities in Australia's cities had been treated as cash cows by their state government owners. Sydney's population, for example, had doubled without any augmentation to its water supplies. In South East Queensland, new dams had been planned and then cancelled. And Adelaide just assumed the Murray would flow indefinitely.

By the middle of 2006, there were signs that the big dams at the head of the Murray River would actually run dry. With Adelaide's water supply under stress, Howard asked me to speak to South Australia's ALP premier, Mike Rann, and offer to help fund a desalination plant. Rann said, 'If we build a desalination plant and it rains, everyone will laugh at me.'

'They will, Mike, they will,' I replied. 'But if you don't build the desalination plant and it doesn't rain, they'll lynch you.'

Fortunately for Rann and for the people of his state, they made it through the Millennium Drought, but it was a close-run thing. Adelaide's desalination plant opened in 2012.

Nothing keeps me happier than solving complex problems and learning about new things at the same time. I'd come to parliament to serve the nation, and what could be more important than water security. However, policy isn't the long suit of the press gallery and they – and many of my colleagues – were instead absorbed with the perennial questions about leadership.

Howard passed his 10-year anniversary as PM in March 2006. Although the media would often write me up as a rival to Peter Costello, it was obvious to me that there was only one viable successor to Howard – and that was Costello. He had a barrister's ebullient confidence, and by the time I got into parliament he was well entrenched as treasurer and certainly knew his economic brief. He was, I thought, a class act.

After serving John as deputy for 10 years, he had every right in the world to want to step up and take the top job. 'It's my turn' isn't especially persuasive but it is very human. Costello had a small group of supporters, probably no more than 25 per cent of the party room at any time. Some of them, like Christopher Pyne and George Brandis, actively disliked Howard; others just wanted him gone so that their friend could be leader and, no doubt, promote them.

But the Howard–Costello narrative was uncannily familiar. Labor's Paul Keating had also been treasurer, deputy and would-be leader. Keating had asked Hawke to resign and claimed he had an agreement that he'd do so. Hawke declined and so Keating resigned and challenged. When he was unsuccessful, he went to the backbench until he challenged again and won, becoming PM at the end of 1991. Costello was living in Keating's shadow.

One evening, Costello and I attended a Liberal Party fundraiser at the Royal Motor Yacht Club in Point Piper, so Peter stayed the night at our place. Before turning in, we sat up and talked. While he argued that Howard was too old, had run out of ideas and should go, when it came to himself, he said nothing to me about why he, Peter Costello, would be a good prime minister. He offered no vision or policy of any kind apart from saying he'd ratify Kyoto and apologise to the Stolen Generations. These, though important, were crazy political corners into which Howard had painted himself.

Rather than making a case for himself, he proceeded to argue that nobody else was qualified to succeed Howard. He told me I was too rich, Downer was a proven failure as leader, Abbott was crazy and more Democratic Labor Party (DLP) than Liberal, and Brendan Nelson was really a Labor person and a lightweight, and so on. It was very underwhelming and left me less convinced about Costello's leadership capacity.

I interrupted this demolition of every leading figure in the government to ask, 'If you want to be leader, why don't you just say to John that he should resign? It's time – ten years is a great innings – and you want to have a go at the top job.'

Peter dismissed this idea. He said Howard would never hand over the leadership.

Soon after that evening, a story surfaced that in 1994, on the verge of winning back the Liberal leadership, Howard had agreed with Costello that he'd serve only two terms as PM and then hand over to him. This commitment was apparently recorded in a note by the only witness, Ian McLachlan, later Howard's Defence minister. McLachlan confirmed the note; Howard denied making the commitment. If it was an attempt to pressure Howard to retire, it backfired. Howard wrote in his memoir that before the McLachlan note incident, he'd been planning to go at the end of 2006, but subsequently felt he couldn't do so.[3]

Knowing Howard reasonably well, I believe he would have stepped down at the end of 2006 – and definitely would have if Costello had approached him in a straightforward way.

But succession has to be managed. Had Howard relinquished the leadership in 2006, he'd have done so still on top after 10 years in office (as Wran had done in 1986). His successor, Costello, would have had a year to establish himself as PM before an election. While Costello did handle it badly, weirdly even, that misses the point. It was John's responsibility to manage his succession and he failed to do so both to his own cost and to that of the Liberal Party.

CHAPTER 12

Water is for fighting over

As the drought worsened through 2006 and into 2007, community anxiety about water increased. So too did concern about global warming: rising levels of atmospheric CO_2 were hard to understand, but water restrictions, parched paddocks and dead sheep were all too clear.

If somehow there was always a way to ensure cities had enough water, that wasn't the case in the bush. The effects of more erratic and lighter rainfall were devastating for unirrigated farming operations, whether they were growing wheat and other crops or running sheep and cattle, as Lucy and I have been doing in the Hunter Valley since 1982.

When we took over the farm on Dad's death, we were going through a bad drought and sold most of the cattle. After the drought broke it cost a lot of money to restock, so in the droughts that followed, I chose to hand-feed our stock and keep our breeding herd together. These things are always a gamble: if you sell the stock and it rains, you kick yourself; if you hand-feed and it doesn't rain, you lose a fortune and still have to sell. During this Millennium Drought, we had cattle in the 'long paddock', the travelling stock routes established when cattle and sheep were moved around by drovers – celebrated in Banjo Paterson and Henry Lawson's bush poems. Modern drovers will take a mob of cattle or sheep, moving, as the law requires, at least 6 miles (10 kilometres) a day, eating their way along if there's grass to be had.

Farmers who have irrigated country get through droughts better. Water is licensed according to an estimate of reliability. A horticulturalist will want high-security water that can be relied on: fruit trees need water every year; if they don't get it, millions of dollars and years of investment are lost. A cotton or wheat farmer, by contrast, always has the option of not planting a crop in a very dry year.

Over the years, the states had issued far too many water licences, especially in New South Wales and Queensland. Scant regard had been paid to the needs of the environment. Our river systems run through flat country and the ecology relies on the rivers flooding. In the course of the last century, and with increasing pace, those rivers and ground water systems have become regulated or industrialised, with more water being diverted to agriculture and industry. The environment has suffered – the river rarely floods to water the red gums because it's being stored up in dams and diverted to grow food and fibre.

Getting the balance right between the environment and agriculture is hard – both technically and scientifically on the one hand and politically on the other. The Murray–Darling Basin contains most of Australia's irrigated agriculture, a vast connected system of surface and ground water covering large parts of Queensland, New South Wales, Victoria and South Australia. Historically, the upstream states sought to ensure as much of the water as possible was used in their state and as little as possible went downstream. The big loser was South Australia, sitting at the end of the river.

Back in the 1890s when our constitution was being negotiated between the six British colonies, the South Australians argued that inter-state rivers, like the Murray and the Darling, should be under federal jurisdiction. Needless to say, the bigger and more powerful colonies of New South Wales and Victoria disagreed. As I travelled around the Murray–Darling Basin and began to understand the complex water story, it was obvious the South Australians had been right. In a time of scarcer resources, it made no sense to have one rule about water use on one side of a river and a different rule on the other.

Bill Heffernan had come to the same conclusion long ago. With his support, in the second half of 2006 I'd started work on a radical water reform agenda – to reverse the mistakes in the 1890s of the founding fathers and put the management of the Murray–Darling Basin under federal control. There were plenty of obstacles – the Nationals for starters. They'd resist any reduction in water allocation to agriculture. We also had to get around the constitution. Section 100 stated, 'The Commonwealth shall not, by any law or regulation of trade or commerce, abridge the right of a State or of the residents therein to the reasonable use of the waters of rivers for conservation or irrigation.'

Howard was unpersuaded until he realised that the public were deeply concerned and wanted action on water. He asked me how could we do it legally. Water was totally in the jurisdiction of the states, who'd been accustomed to getting money from the feds without any corresponding obligations.

'Well,' I said, 'you've just succeeded in using a broad interpretation of the corporations power to take over workplace relations.' This was a reference to the government's WorkChoices reforms – heroic in every sense; as far reaching as they were politically dangerous, giving the union movement something to fight for in a way they hadn't had for generations.

'So, here we use the external affairs power. Over the years, the Commonwealth has entered into numerous international environmental agreements – protecting rivers and wetlands and so on. The High Court decided in the dams case that the Commonwealth can legislate to fulfil its obligations under the treaties, and section 109 says Commonwealth laws will trump state legislation.'

John sat back in his Chesterfield chair and pondered for a minute. 'Or,' he said, 'we could get the states to refer their powers to the Commonwealth. They know they can't solve the problem themselves. If we offer enough money, they won't be able to resist.'

I doubted the states would refer their powers: they were all Labor states; we were in the lead-up to an election; they were unlikely to help us with such an historic reform. Nonetheless, we began in earnest on what became known as the National Plan for Water Security. If the big idea of a federal takeover of water was my contribution, Howard's (appropriately perhaps) was the money – he felt $10 billion over 10 years sounded right! It did have a ring to it.

We planned to replumb our irrigation systems so we could make more food and fibre with less water and use the water saved to restore the environment. This would take up $6 billion and involve everything from piping or lining irrigation channels to reduce evaporation and seepage, to replacing flood irrigation with computer-controlled drippers and sprays.

We allocated $3 billion to fund both the purchase of water and the support of communities where water licences had been acquired and, consequently, economic activity reduced. Water purchases were intended to be made strategically. If part of an irrigation area we were co-investing in was a long way from the river, had poor soils or for whatever reason didn't justify the investment, we'd buy those specific water entitlements and, in a just fashion, support the upgrading of the whole irrigation area.

The balance of the money was to be used for research and monitoring – we still know far too little about our waters, especially ground water. Most of Australia's rainfall is in the north, and efforts to exploit these massive water resources have been disappointing. Wanting to look at this again, we also established a Northern Australia Taskforce, headed by Bill Heffernan, to examine the water resources of our north and the opportunities for sustainably using them.

On 25 January 2007, Howard announced the water plan and also appointed me minister for Environment and Water Resources. This put me into the cabinet for the first time and, significantly, took water out of the National Party–controlled Department of Agriculture.

The water plan was well received. On the Labor side, former PMs Whitlam, Hawke and Keating all rang to congratulate me. Both Gough and Paul said they'd have done the same thing if they'd had more time. Malcolm Fraser called to say well done and was curious to know how I'd persuaded Howard to do something so progressive!

For somebody whose farming experience was limited to dryland grazing, I'd learned an enormous amount about irrigation and irrigators, discussing the water plan with one irrigation community after another. There are too many to name, but Laurie Arthur, president of the National Farmers' Federation (NFF), was helpful, as was specialist water lawyer Jenni Mattila. We rewrote more than a few sections of the bill ourselves. And I had highly knowledgeable water experts in my office in James Baird and Bruce Male.

What attracted the irrigators and their communities was that our recovery of water for the environment was going to be off the back of infrastructure upgrades. These enabled them to have at least as much useable water as they did before. In many cases, 30 per cent and more of water was being lost from leaky channels and outdated irrigation methods.

Meanwhile, there were protests from the Treasury that we should simply buy water back – it was cheaper than saving it through better infrastructure. But large-scale water purchases coupled with the trading of water in the market to more productive uses (from dairy to almonds, for example) would mean that some communities would lose most of their water. That was fine for the farmers who took the cash and moved to a cottage on the coast, but all of the people and businesses in the town who depended on those farmers would lose out, and there was no compensation for them.

While I finetuned the plan and began what seemed endless negotiations with irrigators and environmentalists alike, Howard spoke with the states. To my astonishment, he enlisted the support of New South Wales and Queensland. South Australia was always going to be in the bag – anything that increased river flow would win their support. But Victoria effectively vetoed a referral of power, demanding its own special deal. So, we then moved quickly to introduce what became the Water Act 2007, relying exclusively, as I'd originally intended, on the Commonwealth's own powers.

Introducing it on 8 August I said, 'Our scientists tell us that we can expect throughout southern Australia a hotter and drier future. We must learn to do more with less water, we must make every drop count and to do that, we need a new approach where our greatest system of waters is managed in the national interest.'[1]

The Water Act became law on 3 September 2007, a few months before the Howard government was defeated at the polls by Labor's Kevin Rudd. It remains the legal basis for the management of the Murray–Darling Basin by the Murray–Darling Basin Authority (MDBA), which went on, as required, to establish a Basin Plan with sustainable diversion limits to get the balance right between the environment and irrigation. Rudd reached a deal with the states, who referred some of their powers to the Commonwealth. But the changeover in Commonwealth leadership had unfortunate consequences, including extending the timetable for finalising the Basin Plan. And even more damaging than Labor's changes to the governance of the MDBA was that the Rudd and Gillard governments lost interest in the irrigation efficiency agenda and, instead of spending money on water-saving projects, simply went into the market and bought water. Confidence in the water plan was badly dented.

When Tony Burke succeeded Labor's first Water minister, Penny Wong, this provided an opportunity for bipartisanship: he and I had worked together briefly on the ARM. During a chat, he asked me, 'Why are farmers always so angry at the meetings I go to?' He was a city boy.

'Tony, if you lived thirty kilometres out of town on a dirt road, would you really get into the truck and drive into town just to tell the minister he's doing a good job?' He learned quickly. Astutely, Tony recruited the former NSW Water minister Craig Knowles to assist him and settled the irrigation sector and the states.

Despite the controversies, the Water Act 2007 is one of the most enduring reforms of the Howard government. As water gets scarcer, the pressure from irrigators and their communities to reduce the allocation to the environment will only become more intense. Our reform set a scientifically determined and ecologically sustainable amount of water that can be taken for agriculture and other human needs, with the balance to be used for the environment. The legislation established the Commonwealth Environmental Water Holder, who has the responsibility of using the water acquired by the government to return the system to health. A century of environmental degradation isn't easily or quickly reversed but already there are good results, even in drought.

As I write, there's less water than there was in 2007. The current drought's severity, not the Basin Plan, is the root cause of the scarcity of water in our rivers and dams. New dams aren't the answer: they can help buffer water supply in dry times but only rain can increase the size of the water resource.

With no rain in sight and low prices for milk solids, many dairy farmers are selling their entitlements to producers of higher-value crops like almonds or olives. It's all hitting irrigation communities hard. The natural action of water markets facilitates competition – sometimes brutal – between different agricultural commodities and sectors: those getting good returns can afford the high temporary water allocation prices that come with low water availability in dry times.

Global warming means for most of Australia a hotter and drier future. Water is the source of life, but also of civilisation, which began in irrigation societies because they required a high level of social cooperation and common purpose.

Confronted by the Millennium Drought, our common purpose resulted in the Water Act and the Basin Plan. Facing an even worse drought and the prospect of more to come, we'll have to be smarter and more cooperative than ever before.

The immediate impacts of climate change, fires, floods and droughts bring out the best in Australians. We must maintain that common purpose as we adapt to its long-term consequences and sustain, as best we can and while we can, the environment our folly has so endangered.

CHAPTER 13

Surviving 2007

In December 2006, Kevin Rudd replaced Kim Beazley as opposition leader and Labor shot ahead of us in the polls, sometimes by huge margins. Throughout 2007, defeat seemed inevitable. I wanted to get as much done as I could. If I could reset the government's environmental image, maybe we could defy the odds and win the election or, at least, not lose it as badly as it seemed we might.

The technology for cutting emissions in the energy sector was costly and time-consuming in 2007. But quickly turning around deforestation had been done in North America and Europe, formerly among the world's top carbon emitters from deforestation. Within 30 years, their forests had become net absorbers of carbon – carbon sinks – as a result of tree planting and natural regeneration.[1]

Globally, the most immediate opportunity to reduce emissions was to reduce deforestation, especially in tropical countries, the two largest of which are Indonesia and Brazil. The similarities to the situation I'd faced in the Solomon Islands years before – trying to persuade landowners to replace clear-felling with sustainable management of their forests – were striking. Providing a means of paying communities to leave their forests unlogged remained key.

Howard liked my idea of a 'Global Initiative on Forests and Climate' and we agreed to provide $200 million to support action to reduce deforestation in developing countries with our focus primarily on Indonesia.

In a lightning trip over Easter 2007, Lucy and I travelled to Washington and Jakarta to secure support and I convened a global conference on forests and climate in Sydney in July. Over 60 countries were represented and the initiative was reflected in the Asia-Pacific Economic Cooperation (APEC) communiqué made in Sydney in September.

While our water reform policy survived the Labor years, the forest and climate initiative wouldn't. It was to be rebranded by Kevin Rudd and then abandoned by Gillard. Since then the devastation of our forests, the lungs of the earth, has continued. The pace of deforestation has slowed somewhat in Indonesia but accelerated in the Amazon in Brazil. If we'd stop destroying our rainforests and start reforesting areas that have been cleared, we could make a dramatic difference to the climate crisis.

My Indonesian counterpart, Rachmat Witoelar, and I held a press conference in Jakarta after our agreement to work together to reduce deforestation in the peatlands of Kalimantan. The media in Jakarta, especially the Australians, are notoriously cynical and homed in on our contribution of – as well as money – satellite and radar capabilities to enable the Indonesian authorities to detect illegal logging and so on. The minister was asked why he couldn't see this was simply another opportunity for Australia to spy on Indonesia.

The room fell silent and my heart sank. This great plan of mine was going to explode before my eyes. I was about to be responsible for another breakdown in Indonesia–Australia relations. Rachmat smiled. 'Oh, no, that's no worry. You can go onto Google Earth anytime and see me in my swimming pool! We have nothing to hide!'

Everyone laughed. Occasionally in politics, a flash of terror is quickly followed by exhilarating relief. That was one such moment. Disaster narrowly avoided.

The sense of racing against the clock mounted. On 15 August, I addressed parliament. 'This bill is the first major step in establishing the Australian emissions trading scheme,' I said, introducing the National Greenhouse and Energy Reporting Bill. Four weeks before, Howard had announced we'd introduce an ETS, to commence no later than 2012. 'This,' I added, 'will be the most comprehensive emissions trading scheme in the world, broader in coverage than any scheme currently operating anywhere.'[2]

In the last term of the Howard government we were running big surpluses as tax revenues surged in response to a commodities boom, plentiful credit and a global economy firing on all cylinders. We missed a huge opportunity to create a new sovereign wealth fund. The cyclical boom-time peaks in revenue were being treated as structural, and unsustainable welfare benefits or tax concessions were legislated. Later I was to spend a lot of time, and grief, on winding some of these back.

I also tried to encourage our investing in infrastructure, in partnership with the states, rather than just writing them cheques as grants.

For example, rather than give half a billion dollars to Queensland to build a water recycling scheme, I argued, we should invest and own half the scheme ourselves.

Nobody liked that idea either. I recall Warren Truss, then the Trade minister, telling us, 'If you own the infrastructure, then you have to manage it, appoint a board to oversee it and so on. Better to kick the money out the door.'

I had to wait until I was prime minister to change the grant culture to an investment one.

It's to John Howard's credit that in his fourth term as PM, he was still driving a dynamic reform agenda, of which water policy and an ETS were just two examples. Another, the radical industrial relations reform WorkChoices, fired up the union movement to get behind Rudd, who was way ahead in the polls, including as preferred prime minister.

Howard and I discussed the polls and his leadership on several occasions. He struggled to understand why he was so well received in the electorate but was polling so badly. 'When Keating was this far behind,' he said, 'he was hated in the electorate; people wanted to throw him out with a vengeance. I just don't sense that.'

Even though I wasn't enthusiastic about a Costello prime ministership – he had no love for me at all – I encouraged Howard, to whom I'd become much closer, to hand over to his long-time deputy. Why not get out now. Costello's age – 49, same as Rudd – might make the difference if the problem was, as Howard himself described it, 'the anno domini problem'.

Since Costello's bizarre leadership non-challenge the year before, he'd seemed deflated and kept a low profile. He mused one night over dinner that when we lost the election he'd exit politics altogether. I thought that seemed theatrically gloomy. Surely, if we lost, he'd take over as party leader and opposition leader and with all of his experience be more than a match for Rudd.

Leadership issues were far from my mind when the APEC summit took place in Sydney in September 2007. I'd met George W. Bush before, but it was the first time I met Vladimir Putin. Howard had a bilateral meeting with him and invited a couple of his ministers to join him. When he introduced me he said, 'In his business career Mr Turnbull spent some time working in Siberia.'

A thin smile crossed Putin's lips, and he leant forward to me, asking in a soft voice, 'Really? What crimes did you commit?'

Hundreds of ministers, business leaders and officials from all the APEC countries gathered in the overseas passenger terminal on Circular Quay for a glamorous reception. Foreign Affairs Minister Alex Downer sidled up and whispered, 'The PM has asked me to get the cabinet together in my hotel room tonight. He wants to know whether we think he should resign.'

Astonished, I pulled him away from the other guests. 'Are you both crazy? If we all go to your hotel room the media will find out and then we'll be completely finished.'

Alex was unmoved. 'We're finished anyway. But make sure you're there and if you see any other cabinet ministers, can you ask them to come?'

We did assemble at Alex's hotel, on the other side of the Quay, and the media didn't ambush us. Costello wasn't there; nor was Abbott. Downer explained that Howard wanted to know if the rest of us thought he should hand over to Costello. Apart from Philip Ruddock, everyone agreed he should do so. But although Downer took this news to Howard the next day, he obviously had second thoughts. Most cabinet members then told him in person that he should resign.

Parliament resumed the following week. Costello phoned both Downer and me and asked us to move for a spill in the party room. Each of us said that if he wanted to be leader, he should front Howard and ask him to hand over; then, if he didn't, move the spill himself. But Costello wouldn't do it. Next, Howard made matters worse by promising to hand over to Costello some time in the next term. Between Costello's lack of courage and Howard's reluctance to step down, we were left with the worst of both worlds.

By now, the government was irretrievable and my top priority was to hold my own seat. A redistribution had meant my majority was down to 52.5 per cent – it was the most marginal Liberal seat in New South Wales.

Labor ran a local councillor, Jewish community leader and refugee lawyer George Newhouse – pretty much the candidate from central casting.

The redistribution had added to Wentworth the inner-city suburbs of Darlinghurst, Potts Point and Kings Cross. Historically, the Liberal vote there had been around 30 per cent. The environment was the biggest issue: a massive campaign against a proposed Tasmanian pulp mill I'd conditionally approved was raging. Although it was obvious to my constituents that I took environmental issues, including global warming, seriously, Howard's refusal to ratify the Kyoto Protocol (even though we were well on track to meet our Kyoto targets) was very damaging.

Wentworth was the smallest electorate, about 26 square kilometres, and we divided it into three parts. We waged a traditional Liberal campaign on lower taxes and national security in the blue-ribbon suburbs like Vaucluse, Dover Heights and Bellevue Hill. In the Greens-leaning beach suburbs like Bondi, Waverley and Bronte, we campaigned on environmental issues. My posters didn't include the Liberal logo and were coloured green. In the new inner-city suburbs, we emphasised my support for the LGBTIQ community and ending discrimination against same-sex couples. The only posters of me and Howard were put up by the Labor Party and we managed, tactfully, to dissuade him from campaigning in the electorate.

The local Wentworth Liberal Party conference still had the largest membership in New South Wales in 2007 and an army of local volunteers, many of whom were young professionals who'd joined a political party for the first time to support me. Despite a huge Labor effort to win the seat, our blue 'Malcolm Turnbull' T-shirts well outnumbered the white 'Kevin 07' ones on polling day.

My opponent's campaign struck problems. A former girlfriend, Danielle Ecuyer, also ran as a candidate, and he feuded with journalist Caroline Overington, who slapped his face at a polling booth on election day. In a harbinger of dramas to come, it emerged that Newhouse may not have resigned from a state government tribunal before nominating and so could be ineligible to run under section 44 of the constitution. I made sure everyone knew about that with a full-page ad in the *Sydney Morning Herald* on polling day.

Despite the 5.85 per cent swing against the government in New South Wales, I retained Wentworth with a 1.3 per cent swing to me. Howard, as we expected, lost his seat to Labor's Maxine McKew with a swing of just under 6 per cent. The 11-year Howard era was over.

Our celebration, more relieved than exultant, was bittersweet. Yes, we'd held Wentworth against the tide. I'd demonstrated that far from being the out-of-touch toff, I could run a sophisticated grassroots campaign and hold the most marginal seat in the state. But we were cast into opposition.

Labor had run an entirely presidential campaign. Rudd bestrode Australian politics like an invincible colossus. 'He's looking good now,' I said to Lucy, 'but he won't be able to match Costello in the House.'

Often in politics, just when you think things can't get any worse, they do precisely that. At 12.45 pm on Sunday 25 November 2007, Peter Costello convened a press conference and announced he wouldn't contest the Liberal Party leadership and would retire from parliament during the coming term.

Like many Liberals, I was shocked and disappointed. Peter had only himself to blame for not becoming leader while we were in government. He hadn't had the courage to stand up to Howard, let alone challenge him. And now, when he could take the leadership with unanimous acclamation, he was walking away. Why would someone of his age and experience not rise to the challenge of leadership when it was available?

More importantly, who would lead us now? At 50, Peter was three years younger than me. I assumed that whoever became leader would be younger than both of us. I thought Andrew Robb, then 56, made a lot of sense when he said, 'I think we got into parliament at the wrong time, Malcolm. By the time we get back into government, we'll be old men, well into our 60s.'

On reflection, however, with Costello out of the running, I felt I had the best chance of rebuilding the party in opposition and moving it back into the centre of Australian politics – putting the liberal back into Liberal Party. I was the first to announce I'd stand as leader, followed by Brendan Nelson, who'd been Defence minister. Tony Abbott thought aloud about it but recognised he had no support and didn't stand. He'd had a shocking election campaign and, as we learned later from our pollsters, had made a material contribution to our loss.

While Brendan and I weren't close, I knew that, like me, he believed Howard had made a mistake in not saying sorry to the Stolen Generations and in not ratifying Kyoto. As I rang around colleagues to seek their support, I gleaned that Brendan was telling moderates he supported 'Sorry' but was telling conservatives, like Concetta Fierravanti-Wells, that he opposed it. In other words, he was telling people what they wanted to hear.

I wasn't prepared to do that. Plus, when I was interviewed on Radio National the day before the ballot, I set out my own views on both 'Sorry' and Kyoto. This candour apparently lost me enough votes to ensure Nelson narrowly won the ballot – 45 votes to 42.

The result tormented me. I was infuriated that Nelson could have won so disingenuously. I was so naive. Further, Costello – who chaired the meeting – allowed members of the House of Representatives whose seats were in doubt to vote and one of Nelson's supporters, Dave Tollner, was later found to lose his seat. Costello also pushed on with the meeting even though two senators were running late and missed the vote; at least one, Judith Troeth, was certain to vote for me.

Nelson didn't perform well as leader. He struggled to make an impact against Rudd, and the press gallery had written him off as weak within a few months. When his protectors on the right of the party, led by Nick Minchin, started trying to walk away from taking action on climate change, Nelson obviously saw some security shifting in their direction. However, in July 2008, plenty in our party room shuddered at the prospect of being seen to be 'browner than Howard' and after a dust-up in the shadow cabinet I managed to persuade Nelson and my colleagues to stick with our policy to support an ETS.

Costello, who still hadn't resigned from parliament, declared himself a protector of Nelson against any challenge from me – not that I was threatening one. I'd reconciled myself to the situation and was neither advocating a change of leader nor counting numbers. But the media assumed it was only a matter of time, given Nelson's bad polls. In the first Newspoll in March 2008, for example, Labor was ahead 63:37, and on preferred prime minister, Rudd was ahead of Nelson 70:7. By August, Labor was ahead 57:43 and Rudd was ahead on the preferred PM measure 68:12.

Naturally, people inside and outside the Liberal Party wanted Peter Costello to step up and take over as leader. Costello revelled in the speculation and did nothing to discourage it. Yet by neither taking the job, which Nelson would have gladly handed to him, nor resigning from parliament, he made Nelson's problems far worse. Many made this point at the time; perhaps the most brutal was Barnaby Joyce, who told a journalist that Costello was 'a disloyal hypocrite who had undermined Dr Nelson with his self promotion'.[3]

Lucy had been appointed commissioner of the Australian pavilion at the Venice Architecture Biennale. It was a delight to escape with her to Venice for a week in September and be her consort. She'd rented an apartment in a very old house on the Grand Canal where, legend had it, Othello's Desdemona had lived. We had some wonderful parties at the Ca' Desdemona, the most dramatic of which was interrupted by a violent thunderstorm just as Amanda Vanstone, our ambassador to Italy, was arriving by boat. I was dispatched to receive Amanda and her police detail. With a surfable swell rolling down the Grand Canal, a furious wind and driving rain, we came close to toppling off the narrow jetty into the water.

Still jet-lagged, I got back to Canberra on the morning of 15 September. An unremarkable parliamentary day followed until 5.45 pm: Nelson called a party room meeting for 6.30 pm and announced he was going to spill the leadership at a party meeting at nine the next morning. He gave a strong speech, and said that if he was successful, there'd be major changes in the shadow ministry and he'd take a tougher line on the ETS. Back me or sack me, was his message. The implication for me was clear: if I either didn't run or ran and lost, I'd be dropped from the frontbench.

It hadn't been a last-minute decision. Nelson knew I was overseas and he knew I wasn't counting heads. He'd even organised for Joanna Gash, who'd been representing Australia at the United Nations, to come back from New York to vote for him.

I felt I didn't have much choice but to run, although quite a few colleagues urged me not to. 'He'll implode anyway; give him more time,' Ian Macfarlane said. On reflection, Ian was probably right.

My supporters included Andrew Robb, Steve Ciobo, Michael Keenan, Michael Ronaldson and Christopher Pyne.

After a long night and early morning on the phones, I went into the meeting reasonably confident I was a few votes ahead. That turned out to be right – I won 45–41.

Brendan had had the worst job at the worst time – opposition leader straight after losing government. He'd never looked like he could succeed. While he'd later point the finger at me, the truth is that if I hadn't been there, the party would have looked to someone else.

I became leader of the opposition on 16 September 2008, a day after Lehman Brothers collapsed, which was when the global financial crisis (GFC) was seen to begin in earnest.

CHAPTER 14

Leader of the opposition

The GFC began in the United States, where a long period of low interest rates coupled with imprudent lending practices resulted in a large percentage of home loans being made to people with poor credit histories. There was little prospect of them repaying the loans. These 'sub-prime' loans were made on the expectation that property prices would keep rising. The asset bubble inevitably burst and by the end of 2008, house prices in the United States had fallen dramatically – by more than 20 per cent on average overall, and in some areas by 50 per cent or more.

The loans had been securitised – sliced and diced and sold as complex securities and derivatives that were difficult, almost impossible, to reliably analyse. As the US housing market fell, the value of these securities also fell; their complexity made them hard to value and the fact that they were widely held across the banking world made banks distrust each other; confidence collapsed and banks were reluctant to lend to each other. US and European banks asked themselves, was the institution they were dealing with today going to be the next Bear Stearns or Lehman Brothers or Washington Mutual – all venerable financial institutions that collapsed.

Brendan's chief of staff, Peter Hendy, had decided to move on and Peta Credlin, a former adviser to Helen Coonan, became my acting CoS. At Alex Downer's suggestion, I recruited journalist Chris Kenny to replace her as my CoS and Peta continued as deputy CoS. Kenny suppressed his climate scepticism while he worked for me! Sally Cray was a key part of the team, as were two economists, Paul Lindwall and Alex Robson, who had worked for me while I was shadow treasurer. Tony Parkinson, Downer's former press secretary, also joined my office.

Newly minted as opposition leader, I saw scope for bipartisanship: surely we could assist the government in its response to the financial crisis. Rudd, however, showed no interest in working with us at all. He wouldn't meet with me to discuss the crisis and when I tried to engage him at public events, he'd cut me off.

Labor's consistent refrain was that we should get out of the way. Rudd's scornful rejection of our proposals suited the bulk of my colleagues: it invited partisanship. One of the tensions for an opposition leader, I was learning, is that the party room wants you to fight and slam the other side day in day out. Yet the public want to see constructive solutions and cooperation. That's why the ferocious denunciation of your opponent in the House will get the backbench cheering and banging their desks but cause people at home to switch to another channel.

Rudd appeared reluctant to sully the prestige of his role by mixing with the wannabes on the other side of the chamber. However, at a time of real crisis, the greatest power of incumbency is to convene, to bring the whole nation together. Rudd seemed to be thinking more like an opposition leader than as a prime minister. He certainly misread me. Despite having been in many political punch-ups and never being shy of confrontation, my instinct is always to be constructive and to find a solution. I'm a builder not a wrecker and in that sense the antithesis of politicians like Abbott.

Together with my shadow treasurer, Julie Bishop, we made a number of practical suggestions to the government, all of which were initially indignantly rejected and then later taken up. These included having a limited guarantee of bank deposits to ensure retail deposits in smaller banks didn't flee to the larger banks, and Treasury investing in residential mortgage-backed securities to maintain liquidity in that market.

When the government announced it was considering providing guarantees to support the banks' borrowing in the wholesale markets, I was surprised that Treasury, then led by Ken Henry, was not advising an appropriation act be passed to authorise payment under the guarantee, if called on.

Helpfully, I offered to ensure an appropriation bill was rapidly enacted, but was again scornfully rebuffed until the ratings agencies indicated government guarantees had to be utterly unconditional. The appropriation bill was passed through both houses in the last sitting week of the year. Had it not been, there could have been catastrophic consequences for Australian banks.

This incident was instructive. First, I was now aware the advice Treasury was giving was quite uncommercial. Why would you not take the opportunity to give absolute belt and braces security to the guarantee? Second, the lack of anyone in the Labor cabinet with real-world commercial experience to offset the unworldliness of Canberra was very apparent.

I was to enlarge on this in a speech to the National Press Club on 24 November 2008:

> But recognising Mr Rudd is in unfamiliar territory when it comes to economics and business, nonetheless when a policy is shown to be mistaken it should be swiftly corrected. And yet we see an extraordinary reluctance to change tack not for fear of demonstrating the Opposition has been right, but rather that the Prime Minister has been wrong.
>
> Running through all of these errors is the relentless desire of the Prime Minister to show that he is right and above all much cleverer than anyone else.[1]

We supported Rudd's first stimulus in November 2008 – $10 billion of one-off pension and welfare payments, even though he'd offered no evidence this was the right amount. We'd argued that a tax cut would be seen as more permanent and would likely encourage more spending and investment.

Research showed that, as we'd predicted, most of the cash splash stimulus wasn't spent, as I observed on 3 February. 'As an economic stimulus it was not effective because, in times of uncertainty, one-off payments are largely saved or used to reduce debt, which of course is a very prudent thing to do in the context of a household.'[2]

Over the summer Rudd wrote a long paper on the economic crisis, which he attributed to unbridled capitalism and the neo-liberalism personified in the Coalition and in particular its leader – me. The answer, he said, was to put government at the centre of the economy!

His analysis was quite wrong, as I often pointed out. One of the causes of the collapse in the US housing market (which triggered the GFC) was that, unlike Australia, the government was at the centre of the housing economy. Far from the free market being allowed to rip, the US government underwrote two-thirds of the national mortgage book through Fannie Mae, Freddie Mac and other government-guaranteed funds. Added to that, governments, especially President Clinton's, had mandated and encouraged banks to increase their sub-prime lending.

In Australia, by contrast, apart from the appropriate financial and prudential regulation, there was no government interference with banks' lending policies.

In America there was a banking crisis; in Australia we had none.

When parliament resumed in February 2009, Rudd presented a massive, $42 billion stimulus package and demanded it be passed by parliament in 48 hours. Not to acquiesce, he declared, would be to do *nothing*.

I responded as calmly as I could. 'We have said from the outset that we are prepared to, and indeed seek to, sit down and work cooperatively with the government on the appropriate response to the financial crisis. There is no suggestion that the government should do nothing. Governments are acting all over the world. The question is: is the right decision being taken? Is the policy that is being undertaken correct?'[3]

The $42 billion package was both too big and poorly composed. It contained yet more cash handouts – most people got another $950 – but no tax cuts. A third of the package was a program to build school halls and libraries, mostly in primary schools, and around a quarter of the package was to pay for subsidised roof insulation and solar hot-water systems.

A number of my colleagues, including some of the self-styled conservatives, like Kevin Andrews and Eric Abetz, argued we should simply wave the second stimulus through. I didn't agree. If the Liberal Party stood for anything it should be responsible economic management and I persuaded my colleagues that we should oppose Rudd's package. When added to the first stimulus, it amounted to nearly 6.5 per cent of gross domestic product (GDP) and was larger than most other countries were undertaking at the time.

'Why,' I asked the House on 12 February, 'would the government of a country whose economy remains strong, where employment, while falling, remains nonetheless relatively high compared to other countries, spend more on fiscal stimulus than nations that are much worse situated? … The answer is that here we have a government which has been in a blind panic since the crisis began and is more interested in the grand sweeping gesture than making sound and measured policy decisions.'[4]

We proposed a smaller stimulus of between $15 and $20 billion. For example, rather than throwing $14 billion at the states to spend on school halls (whether they were needed or not), we proposed spending $3 billion in a continuation of an existing and proven school building program.

The stand we took for fiscal prudence was unpopular in the community. The news from overseas coupled with Rudd's over-the-top rhetoric fed into a sense of panic, the salve for which was, apparently, massive government spending.

Whereas our support for the first stimulus had given us a tick up in the polls, our principled opposition to the second one sent them south again – although they were dire in any event. However, opposing Rudd's extravagance enabled the Coalition for years to come to credibly attack the Labor deficits that followed as well as criticise the variously mismanaged stimulus programs – whether school halls or pink batts – and even the National Broadband Network (NBN). The votes on the second stimulus were held on 12 February and went late into the night. As is so often the case in Canberra, many of the members were drinking heavily and none more so than Tony Abbott. He staggered back to his room and passed out and was so soundly asleep the opposition chief whip, Alex Somlyay, and his henchmen could not rouse him to come in to vote. Opposition is a dark time.

By the time of the budget in May 2009, Rudd's spendathon was in full swing and far from the surplus predicted the previous year, there was a $57 billion deficit. As I'd also done in February, I provided a measured alternative approach to the Labor government's budget that involved spending and borrowing less. As I told the House, 'Our plan for recovery will be based on four key principles: the protection and creation of jobs for all Australians; government should not incur one dollar more in debt than absolutely necessary; spending should be targeted at creating jobs and building economic infrastructure; and private enterprise and small business must be supported because they are the drivers of economic growth.'[5]

Most alternative policies in the opposition leader's budget reply vanish into the ether, never to be heard of again. But two of mine turned out to have legs. I proposed the establishment of a Parliamentary Budget Office, modelled on the Congressional Budget Office in the USA, to provide 'independent, objective analysis of fiscal policy, including long-term projections of the impact of various measures on the economy –

employment, real interest rates and debt levels'. This was adopted at the insistence of the crossbench in the 43rd parliament after 2010 and has been operating effectively ever since.

I also proposed, as I had in 2008, a change to our corporate insolvency laws to better encourage business continuity in the way Chapter 11 does in the United States. I'd seen too many good businesses destroyed by secured creditors. This would have to await my time as prime minister and the reforms in the 2015 National Innovation and Science Agenda.

A burnt-out shell of a car. Nothing left apart from the steel; the glass in the windows had melted, spread out over the dashboard and the floor, and become solid once more. Likewise, the aluminium from the wheels had melted and run away from the car in what was now a frozen stream. A family had tried to escape the fire in that car, but there was no trace of them. They'd been vaporised.

One of the responsibilities and privileges of leadership is to provide comfort to the victims of natural disaster. On 7 February 2009, a terrible bushfire, travelling at 120 kilometres an hour, roared through the Yarra Valley, taking 173 lives and destroying communities including Kinglake, Marysville and Narbethong.

I visited the fireground two days later with the local member, Fran Bailey, and met Phil – or 'Smiley', as he's known. I spoke about Smiley's experience in a speech in the House that day:

> His neighbours were one minute behind him. Later he saw their burnt out car. He does not know for sure whether or not they escaped alive. One minute – was that the difference between life and death, between life and a holocaust of fire and wind of 120 kilometres an hour? Smiley has lost all his possessions but I could see in his eyes, as in those of so many others today, a sense of amazement and wonder: 'How did I make it and why did I make it when so many of my friends did not?'[6]

Over the years that followed, I saw the devastation from many other fires, cleaned up after floods and cyclones, and helped farmers battling drought. And I saw again and again that when nature is at its most cruel, Australians are at their best. The firefighters, almost all volunteers, risk their lives to protect other people's lives and property.

But it was the burnt-out car from Kinglake that remained most fixed in my mind. The sheer intensity of the fire: how do you fight a 1000-degree fury coming at you at 120 kilometres an hour? And as we walked across that blackened landscape, we knew that 2000 kilometres to the north, floods were sweeping across Queensland.

And I understood then, as the decade that followed confirmed, that the fires, floods and droughts were getting worse and more frequent. And we knew why. It was precisely what the scientists had foretold would be the consequences of global warming.

How many fires, how many deaths, how many droughts and floods would we need to have, I wondered, before the climate deniers would admit they were wrong? I thought then, in early 2009, that there'd soon be a wake-up call, a tipping point when the evidence was irrefutable. But as the natural disasters built up, the denialism became more entrenched.

Julie Bishop was struggling as shadow treasurer. During February I spoke to Peter Costello to seek his view. He told me she was ineffectual and should go; then, perversely, he told Julie she should keep at it. His presence hung over my leadership like a looming menace. It was incongruous that, as the GFC worsened, the person who'd been an effective treasurer of Australia for nearly 12 years continued to sit quietly on the backbench. Nobody in public life could match his experience or credibility. When I'd asked him if he wanted to come back on the frontbench, he said no. Somehow, the content of our discussion found its way into the media. I felt he was playing childish political games, right at the time his experience was most needed.

Julie decided to resign as shadow treasurer. Helen Coonan graciously agreed to make way for Julie to become shadow Foreign minister, a role she held in opposition and government for the next decade. It was the right call – Julie turned out to be widely, and justly, recognised as our best Foreign minister.

I made Joe Hockey shadow treasurer. Julie believed, not without good reason, that Joe had enlisted some of his supporters to anonymously brief against her in the media. As is often the case in politics, this created a rift between the two that never healed.

From my perspective, however, the switch worked. I'd known Hockey through the Republican Movement long before I came into parliament. He's always been as happy as he is well upholstered and is a gifted salesman. Years later, I appointed him ambassador to Washington, a role for which he was perfectly cast and carried out very well.

Hockey was never a detail person, which later counted against him when he was treasurer under Abbott, but he had a natural commercial sense. He was one of those people who if given a desk and a phone would make money. 'I'm part Arab and Armenian,' he'd explain.

And belied by his jolly giant demeanour, Joe was a highly experienced factional player in the NSW Liberal Party, the leading figure on the moderate side. Philosophically, he and I were generally completely aligned – economically rational and socially liberal. That meant we were both out of step with the right wing of the Liberal Party, which was and still is socially conservative and increasingly – like the National Party – in favour of more regulation and bigger government.

Despite being well behind Rudd, I was feeling a lot better about our position by the time parliament got back after the budget. I was recovering from the hit in the polls I'd taken for opposing the second stimulus and our criticism of Rudd's economic management was starting to get some real traction.

But then disaster struck.

In 2008, I'd been introduced to a Treasury official named Godwin Grech. Several of my parliamentary colleagues and advisers were friendly with him; he was generally well known and well liked in Coalition circles. Godwin liked to be helpful and had a reputation for being fiercely intelligent. From time to time, he'd give us tips about what the Treasury was working on as well as his own suggestions for what Coalition policies should be.

My first mistake was to have anything to do with him at all. Canberra is a city where leaks and private briefings are commonplace, especially to members of parliament. We deplore it when we're in government but in opposition lap it up as much as the press gallery does. Especially once I became leader of the opposition, I should have stayed clear of him and let somebody else manage the relationship.

But I liked Godwin. He had a chronic bowel condition and was painfully thin. I admired both the way he bore his disability and his almost monastic dedication to his job. And above all, I trusted him. He was a bit zany and was clearly fascinated by the intrigue of politics, but he struck me, as he did my colleagues, as honest and fastidiously precise – the sort of person who'd give you a number to the 10th decimal point.

Grech was working on a program called OzCar, which was set up to provide government-backed alternative funding for the car dealers. Their main sources of finance had started to quit the market following the GFC, as they couldn't access finance at competitive terms.

Grech told us that Andrew Charlton, an adviser in Rudd's office, had written to Grech on 19 February asking if the OzCar financing plan could be available to assist John Grant, a dealer in Queensland. Then the following day, an official in Wayne Swan's office asked Grech to follow up on the John Grant issue. He said he called Grant, who told him he knew 'Kevin and Wayne' well and that 'Wayne and Kevin want this fixed'. Grech then went back and forth with Swan's office as he sought to find alternative financing for John Grant.

John Grant wasn't only a friend of Rudd and Swan; he'd also provided Rudd with a ute for use in election campaigns. From the suspicious viewpoint of an opposition, it looked like Rudd and Swan were giving a mate special treatment.

Grech proposed to us that the best way to get this matter out in the open was by his appearing before a Senate committee. He requested a meeting with myself and Senator Eric Abetz, the leader of the opposition in the Senate. We held the meeting at Lucy's office in Sydney on 12 June; it was at that meeting that Grech showed us the email from Andrew Charlton to himself.

Grech briefed the journalist Steve Lewis about the email and gave evidence about it before a Senate committee on Friday 19 June. Rudd had previously denied any approach from his office had been made. Thinking I might be on the verge of at least shaking Rudd's hitherto unassailable lead, I called on him to resign unless he could demonstrate he hadn't misled the parliament.

Rudd, meanwhile, checked his records, confirmed no such email had been sent from his office, and started saying the email must be a fake. On the Monday, the AFP raided Grech's home and established that the email was a fake created by Grech on his own computer.

Enquiries followed, and by 4 August, Grech admitted publicly that he'd faked the email and that he'd shown it to me and Abetz. One of the advantages of almost all our communication being by email was that it was obvious that we'd been thoroughly misled by Grech, who'd drawn us into his own political conspiracy.

I suffered the largest single drop in approval in any Newspoll. The debacle smashed my public standing and undermined immensely my authority as leader of the Liberal Party. Costello phoned and told me bluntly I should resign. I asked him if he wanted the job; he said he didn't. 'Get out now,' he said. 'Abbott and Hockey just want you to lose the election for them.'[7]

But if the public impact of what became known as 'Utegate' was devastating, its private impact was much worse. I was mortified and deeply ashamed that I'd made a false accusation against the prime minister, that I'd been associated, however innocently, with a forged email and that I'd been so stupid as to have anything to do with Grech.

As soon as it was clear what had happened, I wanted to walk into the House and apologise to Rudd. My advisers urged me not to do so. As did Abbott and Hockey. They argued, rightly, that Rudd had made appalling false allegations about Howard and Downer at different times, accusing them of corruption, and had never apologised, even when he'd had to abandon his claims.

The Labor attack on me in the House was ferocious, especially in the week the fake email was revealed. Pyne was overseas and Abbott stood in for him as manager of opposition business and did an outstanding job defending me. In some respects, I think that week revived his spirits, which had been very low following the 2007 election loss.

Grech was a physically frail and often very sick man. That we knew. What we didn't know about was his struggle with depression and anxiety. But I still cannot understand why somebody who professed to be such a supporter of mine and the Liberal Party would forge an email and then deliberately set out to encourage me to rely upon it. Surely he must have realised that what he was doing was wrong and in any event the forgery would be found out. And that when it was, the people he wanted to help would be dreadfully damaged, as would he.

Albeit shaken, I battled on as leader. Rudd reigned supreme; he was miles ahead in the polls and nobody doubted for a second that he'd be re-elected, probably with an increased majority.

In the immediate aftermath of Utegate, I lost faith in my own political judgement. I didn't apologise to Rudd, other than to say I would do so if he apologised for accusing me of forging the email. My advisers did have a point – if the roles had been reversed, Kevin wouldn't have felt a moment of remorse.

The hubbub receded slightly and I returned to my economic critique of the Rudd government. Some of Rudd's loopier stimulus programs were already starting to disappoint. As I'd predicted in my May budget reply speech, the $14 billion school halls program was proving to be beyond the capacity of state governments to manage. Already we had an example of one primary school in Sydney where $2.5 million was being spent to demolish three perfectly functional classrooms and replace them with three perfectly functional classrooms.

Significantly, I'd pointed out that Rudd was spending too much and I'd urged him to spend less. I'd reminded him that the parliament wasn't closed. If he needed more, he had only to come back and ask for it. My concern was that much of that largesse was likely to be misspent. Should the economy perform better than Rudd had been leading the nation to expect – with his hyperbolic talk earlier in the year about 'a rolling national security crisis' and 'staring into the abyss' – the stimulus spending that was intended to be counter-cyclical (offsetting a downturn) could turn out to be pro-cyclical (adding to already growing demand). And that was precisely what happened as the China-fuelled resource construction boom took off from 2009. In reality, the stimulus that did most for Australia wasn't from our government but from China's.

CHAPTER 15

Climate, denial
and downfall

Imagine a time when both the Labor Party and the Liberal Party were strongly committed to reducing Australia's greenhouse gas emissions. When Prime Minister John Howard would say, 'The Government is moving to implement the emissions trading system', which will be 'one of the most important economic decisions that this country will take in the next decade'.[1] And when Rupert Murdoch counselled, 'The planet deserves the benefit of the doubt.'[2]

It seems fantastical now, but that was how things were in 2007, the year I first became intensely involved in climate change policy. And in every meeting I had as minister for Environment and Water Resources, there was an elephant in the room: the Kyoto Protocol.

In 1997, not long into Howard's government, world leaders had gathered in Japan to tackle climate change. Foreign Minister Alex Downer and Environment Minister Robert Hill had attended this UN Framework Convention on Climate Change Conference of the Parties in Kyoto and had succeeded in negotiating a highly achievable target for Australia to reduce the growth in its emissions. But while Bill Clinton's administration had been prepared to ratify it, the US Congress was not – because commitments hadn't been forthcoming from China and other large developing countries to reduce their emissions. Howard agreed with President George W. Bush that Australia wouldn't ratify Kyoto, a show of solidarity to his friend and ally. That proved to be a major political mistake.

For all of his political brilliance, and four election wins on the trot takes more than luck, Howard handed the opposition a hugely impactful symbolic issue. ('Sorry' ranked alongside it.) 'Kyoto' gradually became a one-word symbol. Failing to ratify it sent one message: I don't care about climate change.

Yet, when the Shergold report[3] recommended Australia establish an ETS and argued it should do so ahead of a global agreement, Howard adopted all its recommendations. Journalist Paul Kelly described this as the biggest policy reversal and switch of belief in Howard's whole 11 years as prime minister.[4] But his timing was off: his opponent, Kevin Rudd, had already framed climate change as the greatest moral challenge of our times.

While rhetoric like that always gets panned in Australia, it was a fair comment. We take action today to reduce emissions, at some cost or inconvenience, in order to stop global warming, the most adverse consequences of which may not be felt until long after we're dead. Conversely, not taking action today means we're creating a world of pain for our children and grandchildren. Some Australians say, 'Oh, we're responsible for only 1.3 per cent of the world's emissions, it doesn't matter what we do.' Well it does matter. As a rich nation already facing the dry and fiery consequences of a warmer climate, we have a moral duty to act and a vested interest in the world doing so. How can we expect other nations to cut their emissions if we do not?

Rudd had outplayed us on climate change. We'd been right in substantive policy terms by committing to an ETS but too late to the party. The same team Howard had set up to design the ETS, headed by senior public servant Martin Parkinson, kept working on it under Rudd. This provided remarkable policy development continuity, given there'd been a change of government.

Along with most of my Liberal colleagues, I felt the right approach was to support the new government in ratifying Kyoto, and to help ensure that the ETS was well designed and didn't unfairly disadvantage Australian exporters when competing against countries that hadn't and probably wouldn't put a price on carbon anytime soon. This group became known as the emissions-intensive trade-exposed industries (EITEIs) and they included obvious high-emission sectors like aluminium, steel, cement and liquefied natural gas production as well as agriculture itself.

Rudd was determined the ETS should start in 2010. Dismayingly, consultation and analysis with affected industries was rushed. An uneasiness developed as to whether Rudd and his team had the skill set to competently manage the introduction of such a big reform.

When I took over as opposition leader, I needed to reaffirm our climate change policy. Brendan Nelson's political opportunism had opened the way for vested interests in the fossil fuel and manufacturing sectors to mobilise against an ETS on economic grounds. Climate deniers and sceptics were also gaining strength: no coincidence there. Just as the tobacco industry in the '60s and '70s funded 'research' to discredit evidence that smoking caused lung cancer, the resources sector – people like the Koch brothers in the United States, Gina Rinehart in Australia – was supporting sceptical scientists like Ian Plimer, Bob Carter and Jennifer Marohasy. The right-wing (mostly Murdoch) media, both in Australia and the United States, started to become climate denialists, and voices like Andrew Bolt at News Corporation and Alan Jones on Radio 2GB became louder as they recycled the growing flood of anti-climate-action propaganda.

While this didn't materially shift public opinion overall, it had a polarising effect on my colleagues. The more conservative members of the Liberal Party, and most of the Nationals, were all for abandoning the Howard policy of establishing an ETS.

Rudd picked up on the growing split in the Coalition. From the moment I became leader, he did everything he could to draw attention to it. He made my downfall his priority where, assuming he really wanted to legislate an ETS, he should have done everything he could to make it easier for me to win over my own party.

It was easy for Rudd to drive a wedge into the Liberals. Many on the conservative wing didn't trust me at all. Already politics was being defined by 'values' issues rather than economic ones. Here I was, a 'warmist' who believed in taking action to reduce greenhouse gas emissions, a republican and a supporter of equal rights for same-sex couples.

Needing to balance that, I gave Andrew Robb shadow ministry responsibility for assisting me on ETS design. I figured that if we could get to a negotiated point with Andrew's seal of approval, the former Liberal Party federal director's credibility would get the conservatives across the line. The other two key ministers were Ian Macfarlane, the Energy shadow minister, and Greg Hunt, who had Environment. We all believed we should negotiate with Labor and put the ETS issue to bed.

An election was due in 2010. If the ETS was sorted out, the remaining issues were all promising for us. I'd warned Rudd not to weaken Howard's border protection policies, but he'd done so, arguing that it was the 'push factors' of international events that drove the rate of illegal migration, not the 'pull factors' of Australian border policies. This ignored the fact that, around the world, about 60 million people could plausibly claim refugee status in Australia. Our domestic policies are like a gate valve; any moderation to them results in more arrivals.

That grim prediction would prove correct. Rudd was hugely embarrassed by a group of asylum seekers picked up by the Australian Customs vessel *Oceanic Viking*. They refused to disembark in Indonesia and the local authorities wouldn't allow them to be removed forcibly. The month-long stand-off was highly damaging, and demonstrated Rudd's loss of control over our borders.

To colleagues who didn't have convictions on climate change either way, I argued that with a sensibly framed ETS in place, we could make in-roads not just on border security but on familiar Coalition territory: debt, deficit and economic management.

Anxiety caused by the GFC was now driving community concern about energy costs. Businesses and families worried about what an ETS would do to their electricity bills. Yet a key attraction of an ETS is its cost-effectiveness. An ETS puts a price on carbon emissions across the economy. A number of permits are given or sold to the emitters covered by the scheme. These broadly approximate what they're emitting today. Over time, the number of permits declines, which encourages them to reduce their emissions. They might then switch from brown to black coal, or from black coal to gas, or to wind or solar. Or a manufacturer might buy some new plant that uses less energy overall. People who can create carbon offsets, or credits – typically by planting trees – can sell them to emitters. A well-functioning ETS should mean there's no need to subsidise one form of technology over another. The government lets the market find the cheapest path to emissions abatement and stops trying to pick winners.

Along with an ETS, Rudd also announced a large increase in the Howard-era Renewable Energy Target (RET). The energy sector was to acquire 41,000 gigawatt hours of its electricity per annum from renewables by 2020, or around 20 per cent of the total amount of forecast 2020 generation.

The policy argument for the RET was that it would give renewables support during the early years of an ETS. Subsidising renewable energy would encourage technological advances; consequently, their cost would decline. That was debatable. Rudd's real reason for increasing the RET was that it was popular. His government needed to be seen to be *doing something* about climate change.

By mid-2009, there was open hostility within the Liberal Party to the very concept of climate change. Right-wingers like Senate leader Nick Minchin were describing global warming as a hoax by left-wingers who'd adopted environmentalism as their new ideology after the collapse of communism. Their goal, he argued, was to deindustrialise and destroy Western society. And Barnaby Joyce, among others, was calling the ETS a great big electricity tax.

Christopher Pyne used to say, 'The right want us to be browner than Howard.' He was correct. Indeed, the consensus was developing among the more conservative members, like Minchin, and most of the National Party, led by Warren Truss, that Howard was never sincere in proposing an ETS, that he'd been panicked by bad polls, a bad drought and former US presidential candidate Al Gore, whose 2006 feature film *An Inconvenient Truth* had brought the issue of climate change into people's living rooms the world over.[5]

The damage to my leadership standing thanks to the Utegate fiasco made it difficult to assert my authority over the energy debate. The Liberal Party was at a tipping point on climate change policy. When I lost the leadership, what would happen next? Would whoever succeeded me be seen to take climate change seriously and be a sincerely constructive partner with Labor? An ETS wasn't a Labor Party idea; it was John Howard's policy. I had to fight on.

In order to hold the party together, I'd argued that the design of the ETS shouldn't be finalised until we'd seen the result of the United Nations Copenhagen Summit in December 2009 and the final outcome of the Waxman-Markey legislation, which had passed the US House of Representatives and was before their Senate. Hopes were high that with Barack Obama in the White House, Americans would embrace an ETS.

Rudd's rushed ETS – now known as the Carbon Pollution Reduction Scheme (CPRS) – was full of flaws. I highlighted gaps like the failure to provide for offsetting industrial emissions of CO_2 by improving the level of soil carbon, let alone giving credit for capturing and generating energy from fugitive methane emissions from coalmines. But I wanted the bill to progress.

In this endeavour, Kevin Rudd was one of the biggest obstacles. Rudd refused to meet with me to negotiate or discuss the terms of the CPRS, just as he'd refused to meet to discuss the response to the GFC the previous year. In the Senate, the Greens were highly unlikely to support Rudd's CPRS because it wasn't aggressive enough, and so he'd need our support to get the bill through. But he gave every impression that he wanted the Coalition to block the bill in the Senate twice so he could trigger a double-dissolution election. We could have refused to vote for the CPRS before the Copenhagen Summit regardless of what amendments we could secure from Rudd. But then, we believed, Rudd would just go to a double-dissolution election. The last thing we could afford was an election against a first-term government: I was still recovering from the Utegate debacle and Rudd remained well ahead of us in the polls. While public concern about climate change had moderated since the high point in 2007, there was still more than ample support to enable him to win enough seats in the House and the Senate to have a majority in the joint sitting, in which case he could frame the CPRS as he wished and get it passed – without any amendments of the kind we were proposing. That was why business was so keen for us to cut a deal.

There were also ominous signs that Copenhagen would disappoint. If it did, what then? Inside the Coalition, opposition to the CPRS would strengthen. In an election campaign, the nuance in 'yes, but' is lost; it would be hard to run on a platform that argued for a range of amendments to the CPRS – the Coalition would obviously end up having to campaign to stop the 'electricity tax'. That would be seen for what it was – denying the need to act on climate change. This was our last best chance to achieve bipartisanship in climate policy. As of 24 July, the shadow cabinet had agreed we'd support an ETS in 2009 if it was amended to meet nine specified areas of concern.[6] In a nutshell, we wanted to ensure that an Australian ETS offered no less protection for Australian industry, agriculture and business than the Waxman-Markey bill, that EITEIs weren't disadvantaged and agricultural emissions were excluded (as was proposed in the United States), as were fugitive emissions from coal mining for the same reason.

Andrew Robb and I, together with Nick Xenophon, commissioned Danny Price's firm, Frontier Economics, to undertake a review of the

Rudd CPRS and recommend changes; these were published on 11 August. Price proposed the scheme be reoriented to a baseline and credit model, where power generators were allocated emissions up to a specific baseline, as opposed to buying them. I brought Price to the Coalition party room to discuss his proposals and the ETS generally and the party room approved our continuing negotiations with the government.

However, my opponents on this issue continued to gather strength. For a time Tony Abbott was an ally, arguing in a front-page story in *The Australian* on 24 July that we should just get on with it and pass the Rudd CPRS,[7] but this was just one of the positions he took before finally landing in opposition to putting a price on carbon at all.

Abbott and I occasionally rode our bikes around Lake Burley Griffin. He didn't try to persuade me that the science on climate change was wrong but rather argued that my principal duty was to keep the party together, which meant giving in to the minority who wanted to vote down the CPRS a second time. I accepted his advice as well intentioned, but it underlined the way the right of the Liberal Party play by different rules. They threaten to blow the place up if they don't get their way and are utterly reckless in their destabilisation of any leader or policies they don't like. So 'keeping the party together' means giving in to them. This pattern, which became painfully clear in my first time as party leader, was to continue for the next decade and is likely to remain entrenched into the future. It is how a determined minority terrorises a majority into submission and then, over time, becomes the majority as more moderate or genuinely liberal members peel off.

The CPRS legislation was first debated in August, with very little opportunity for debate or amendment. It was presented on a 'take it or leave it' basis and we voted it down in the Senate. Rudd and Wong promised to bring it back after three months with a view to triggering a double dissolution.

Wong wanted to work constructively with us, and it was thanks to her practical approach that in August we succeeded in separating from the CPRS the legislation establishing the new RET so that it could be legislated. We voted to support the expanded RET on the basis that it included some additional protections for energy-intensive industries.

As I said to an energy industry group in the Hunter Valley on 1 September, 'A lot of people in industry, including industries in this room, have been saying to us, for heaven's sake seek to amend the legislation, try to limit the damage it is doing to us.'[8]

Shortly after that talk – while I was in the UK meeting my British counterpart, David Cameron, and his colleagues William Hague and George Osborne – the internal opposition to negotiating with Rudd coalesced and a bloc was formed. Robb and Macfarlane both maintained it was a small group. They said there were 10, including Joyce, chief among the Nats' climate deniers, as well as Minchin, Abbott and Cory Bernardi.

Returning from the UK on 29 September, I found the media obsessed with the leadership story. For example, the ABC's *Four Corners* program on 9 November, 'Malcolm and the Malcontents', was effectively an advertorial for the insurgents and further sapped my authority. Climate change was becoming a political battlefield. After securing shadow cabinet backing, Macfarlane, Robb and I took our proposed amendments back to the Coalition party room on 18 October. With their support we pushed on with negotiations with the government: principally to exclude agriculture from the scheme; give higher compensation both to generators whose assets would be reduced in value and to EITEIs like liquefied natural gas (LNG), aluminium and cement; and better compensate small businesses affected by higher electricity prices.

Ian Macfarlane had taken over the CPRS negotiations from Andrew Robb, who'd taken leave on 19 September to seek treatment for his depression. But both Ian and I remained in the closest contact with Robb, whose staff continued to help with the negotiations.

Negotiations were still going on when the CPRS bill came back to the House of Representatives and, accordingly, we voted against it on 28 October. I flagged our intention to reach agreement on amendments.

By 24 November, with the CPRS bill still before the Senate, we'd secured the government's agreement to almost all of our amendments. There was general surprise that the government had conceded so much and it was marked up by the press gallery as a win for the Coalition.

Macfarlane and I took them to a shadow cabinet meeting that morning, which endorsed them. Next, we held a joint party meeting at 10 am on 24 November that ran for four and a half hours. Just about everyone spoke for or against the deal. It was a chaotic and bitter debate. Given the Nationals had indicated they wouldn't support an ETS in any form, I should have gone with my instincts and just held a Liberal Party meeting, where there remained a majority, albeit slim. But I was talked out of it by some senior colleagues, including Macfarlane.

Robb had returned from leave to attend the meeting and spoke early. In what Macfarlane later described as the worst act of treachery he'd ever seen, Robb savagely denounced the deal and urged the party room not to support the shadow cabinet's recommendations. Robb had been intimately involved in every step of the negotiations and had given no indication of unhappiness or reservation about the deal that was finally agreed between Macfarlane and Wong. Likewise, he gave me no notice he was about to attack the deal.

Many people have subsequently sought to excuse Robb on the grounds of ill health, but that doesn't explain the deliberateness of his actions. Had he told me and Macfarlane he didn't agree with the deal, we would likely have done it differently – maybe not at all. We wouldn't have let the matter come to a head in the party room. He knew all that. It was an ambush and all the more despicable, given the support I'd given him during his illness.

More pressing, however, was my opponents' assertion that most of the party room had opposed the deal, which showed I'd lost my colleagues' support. Events moved quickly from that Tuesday. Kevin Andrews called for a vote to spill the leadership, which was defeated on 25 November. On Thursday 26 November, Abbott announced his resignation from the shadow cabinet, as did Eric Abetz and Sophie Mirabella, joining Fifield, Cormann and Brett Mason, who'd resigned the previous day. Concetta Fierravanti-Wells and Guy Barnett also resigned. On Friday 27 November, when I was back in Sydney, Scott Morrison arranged to see me at my office in Edgecliff; amazingly, the media arrived at the same time as he did and were well briefed on his withdrawal of support. That afternoon, I received a letter from Abbott and nine other Liberals asking for another meeting to consider a spill of the leadership. I agreed to hold it the following Tuesday, 1 December.

I couldn't see any possibility of surviving the challenge. The Coalition looked a smoking wreck.

The press gallery were now in full flight, smelling blood, and doing everything they could to heighten the drama, tension and likelihood of a leadership change. This is one of the consequences of politics as reality television. Policy is boring; personalities, betrayals, the rise and fall of leaders – that's what rates, and so that's what the media encourage. It's not limited to Australia, of course, and with Trump in the White House it has reached its apotheosis.

At a press conference on Thursday 26 November, I'd set out my position as calmly as I could. I reminded the media of their fulsome praise for the concessions we'd achieved from the government to make the CPRS more environmentally effective and save tens of thousands of jobs.

> This has now become a question not simply of the environmental responsibility of the Liberal Party but of its integrity. We agreed with the government on this deal. We must retain our credibility of taking action on climate change. We cannot be seen as a party of climate sceptics, of do-nothings on climate change. That is absolutely fatal. And we also must be seen as men and women of our word. We entered into a bargain. There was offer and there was acceptance.

It was cold comfort at the time, but the strong stand I took was winning support in the media and the electorate. Brisbane's *Courier-Mail* wrote, 'Australians will give Mr Turnbull credit for sticking to his beliefs and convictions. Although it was somewhat lost in the noise of the week, Mr Turnbull's statement that Australians want political parties to have credible positions on climate change is a basic truth.'[9]

The *Sydney Morning Herald* was equally supportive, although with a twist: 'If the federal Liberal Party eventually decides it does not want Turnbull as leader, NSW will gladly take him as our next premier.'[10]

By-elections were under way in Bradfield and Higgins to replace the retiring Brendan Nelson and Peter Costello. Our pollster, Mark Textor, told me that my numbers and the party's improved markedly when I stood my ground against Minchin and co. 'The punters like leaders who are principled,' Textor concluded.

I was interviewed by Laurie Oakes on Sunday 29 October and let rip. Oakes counselled me against the stand I was making, but I was unmoved. 'The vast majority of Australians want to see action on climate change; they are horrified that a major political party would turn its back on this great challenge and say, as Nick Minchin has said, it's all rubbish, it's just a left-wing conspiracy, we don't need to do anything about it.'[11]

Not for the last time, the public may have yearned for a sensible, centrist approach to climate policy, and so many other issues. But, as Oakes also pointed out, too many of my colleagues did not.

Back in Canberra on the Monday, it was deathly quiet in my office. You can always tell when your number's up in politics: the phone stops ringing and you're alone. Because the caravan has moved on. In politics, that happens to everyone eventually, but being rolled by your own colleagues is one of the nastier ways to go.

Lucy was with me, and we decided to go back to our apartment. On the way out of the building a pack of cameramen and reporters chased us down a stairway, pushing cameras in our faces and shoving Lucy to the point where she was nearly knocked down a flight of stairs. Familiar press gallery faces were barely recognisable: flushed with excitement, eyes blazing, yelling and shouting, like a pack of wild dogs closing in on the kill.

Joe Hockey had indicated he was prepared to nominate as leader and he and I met. He'd always supported my approach to the CPRS and said he'd stand only on the basis that the bill be referred to a committee and then, after Copenhagen, be the subject of a free vote. At a press conference afterwards, I said, 'You can ask Mr Hockey about his intentions: I am standing tomorrow. I am the leader and I will be standing tomorrow.'[12] When I nominated after the spill motion was carried the next day, Hockey claimed I'd given him an undertaking not to run. That is simply not true. In the first ballot, against Hockey and Abbott, I expected to get half-a-dozen votes, but the numbers were 35 for Abbott, 26 for me and 23 for Hockey. Abbott defeated me in the next ballot by one vote, 42:41.

It had been very close but the repercussions of the leadership change confirmed my worst fears. The Liberal party room promptly fell in behind the new leader and voted 2:1 to oppose the deal with Rudd on the CPRS. Two brave Liberal senators, Sue Boyce and Judith Troeth, crossed the floor and voted for the CPRS, but it was to no avail. To their eternal shame, the Greens, whose votes could have carried the day, voted down Rudd's CPRS. Had they not done so, the CPRS would have been passed and become as mundane a part of our tax system as the goods and services tax (GST). This was the moment, when a so-called environmental party slammed the sliding door on our best chance to secure an economy-wide price on carbon and the emissions reduction that would follow.

Over the summer of 2009–10, Abbott and Greg Hunt cobbled together a direct action policy that involved the government paying business to reduce emissions and, especially, farmers to plant trees and improve soil carbon as a means of offsetting greenhouse gas emissions by industry.

This was no more than a short-term fig leaf designed to get the Coalition to the double-dissolution election it expected to lose. Unfortunately, it became entrenched as Coalition policy for years thereafter.

Rudd missed the opportunity to take the CPRS to a double-dissolution election in early 2010, then walked away from the whole scheme, sacrificing his moral authority and political capital in one stroke. By June he'd been deposed by Julia Gillard. She managed to enact an ETS with the Clean Energy Act 2011; the permits under the scheme had a fixed price of $23 for the first two years. However, following Abbott's election in 2013, the Gillard 'carbon tax' was repealed from 1 July 2014 and hasn't been reinstated. Abbott next proceeded to wind back the RET. All these events I describe elsewhere.

By 2015, we no longer had an ETS or a carbon tax but had reconfirmed a massive continuing subsidy for renewable energy both at a large utility scale and, with no limit, on a small scale for households. In other words, we'd stopped directly targeting the reduction of emissions and opted instead, by retaining and reconfirming the RET, simply to provide a subsidy for the installation of wind and solar generation.

If I'd prevailed in the party room on Tuesday 1 December 2009, the CPRS would have been passed and we wouldn't have embarked on a decade of climate wars and destructive indecision about energy policy. But for the sake of my sanity, I had to push from my mind thoughts of what might have been. I'd come into politics to make a difference. If I wanted to do so, I'd have to learn to be more pragmatic, more compromising and keep repeating to myself that politics is the art of the possible.

CHAPTER 16

A dark aftermath

Lucy wisely got me out of the country as soon after the leadership change as she could. We escaped to South America, which I'd never visited, spending one week in Buenos Aires and then another in Peru. What better place to contemplate the ruins of your own political career than amidst the ruins of Machu Picchu?

But all holidays must come to an end and when we returned to Australia in January 2010, I visited Kevin Rudd at Kirribilli House. I apologised to him in person for repeating Grech's false allegations against him. One of the first things I'd done after I ceased to be leader of the opposition in December 2009 was to phone Rudd and, belatedly, apologise. As he'd done then, he accepted my apology and was most understanding. But he seemed puzzled as to why I was so cut up about it.

Returning to Canberra for the autumn sitting period was gruesome: every step, every face reminded me of the ghastly events of the previous year. Rudd introduced the emissions trading legislation to the House for a third time. I spoke in favour of the bills and on 11 February 2010, for the first and only time in my parliamentary career, crossed the floor and voted against my own party.

> All of us here are accountable not just to our constituents but also to the generations that will come after them and after us. It is our job as members of parliament to legislate with an eye to the long-term future, to look over the horizon beyond the next election and ensure that, as far as we can, what we do today will make Australia a better place, a safer place for future generations to live in.
>
> Climate change is the ultimate long-term problem. We have to make decisions today, bear costs today so that adverse consequences

are avoided, dangerous consequences are avoided many decades into the future.[1]

I pointed out that the scheme proposed owed as much to John Howard as it did to Kevin Rudd and reminded the House of Peter Shergold's observation in his report that, 'Waiting until a truly global response emerges before imposing an emissions cap will place costs on Australia by increasing business uncertainty and delaying or losing investment.'[2]

Crossing the floor earned me a barrage of criticism from my own side and the right-wing media, but I felt I had no other option; the legislation was in line with the deal I'd done, as leader, with the government. The opposition could renege on that, dishonourably in my view, but I would not. All my life, my word had been my bond and I wasn't about to change now.

To some extent I was running on a depleted reservoir of adrenaline and then, after that speech, was done in. I remained in a torment of indecision as to whether to stay in parliament or not and, without realising it, I slipped into a deeper depression.

I'd never given any thought to my mental health before – mental illness was something others had to worry about. And while I'd had periods of real gloom, especially after the defeat of the republic referendum, what I felt enveloping me now was much more serious. For the first time in my life, suicidal thoughts started to enter my mind, unbidden and unwanted.

My family could see all this and were horrified. They associated my misery with politics and encouraged me to say I wouldn't run again at the next election. I'd earlier said publicly I wouldn't resign and create a by-election, but it would have been far better for my mental health if I had done so. The indecision was so corrosive.

From being constantly busy as leader, surrounded by lots of staff and with people always going in and out of the office, suddenly I was alone. Very few of my old colleagues in parliament made contact; Joe Hockey was an exception, as was Labor's Greg Combet. I recalled the advice given to me long before by Laurie and Trish Brereton: keep hold of your friends when you go into politics; you won't make any in parliament.

I was also worried we wouldn't hold Wentworth if I didn't run again. Abbott was unpopular generally but particularly in my electorate. I'd held the seat in 2007 on the basis of my personal following. What hope would the party have of holding it against the still popular Kevin Rudd?

Abbott and I needed a discreet place to talk, so I invited him to dinner at home on Sunday 21 March; Lucy was overseas. I cooked and we sat out on the terrace and discussed the future. Senator Minchin had let it be known he was going to resign at the next election, so the position of shadow Finance minister would be available. Abbott made it clear that there was no scope for that, given my position on climate change. He left me in no doubt he'd prefer me gone and asked if I'd thought of state politics.

In the weeks that followed I sank further and further into depression. I was prescribed antidepressants. None seemed to help and one in particular made me much worse. At my wit's end, I announced on 6 April 2010 that I wouldn't recontest the election:

> This is a very tough business, politics. It's easy to get resentful or full of bitterness, but I took a different approach. I think hatred hurts the hater more than the hated. So I'm looking back on my time positively.
>
> Having got to the top of my own party, having become the leader, and then that having come to an end in some fairly trying circumstances, I think the best thing is to move on. I'm 56 in October, if I was 46 I may well have made a different decision.[3]

I told the *Sydney Morning Herald*, 'The last five and a half years have been a wild ride, filled with achievements and disappointments. Losing the leadership was heartbreaking, but while political leaders will come and go, the threat of global warming will not.'[4]

I said that Lucy and I would return to investing in technology start-ups and innovation, and then concluded, from the heart, 'People often say politics is a thankless business. Certainly this politician owes a debt of thanks to so many – my family, the members of the Liberal Party, especially here in Wentworth, my parliamentary colleagues, as well as thousands of Australians with whom I have met and corresponded and who have shared and helped to inspire my vision for Australia.'

Rudd called and wished me well, as did Abbott. It was the end of my career.

But it wasn't the end of the depression. Within hours I felt sure, surer than anything, that I'd made the wrong decision.

Thousands of messages and emails poured in urging me not to quit. That was heartbreaking. Now I felt I'd let the party down with my blunders with Grech and, in the chaos that followed – the fight over the ETS and the leadership challenge – we'd ended up with Abbott as leader. Sure, I'd made a stand on principle, and an important one, but Tony Abbott was the leader. Didn't I have a responsibility to stay and at least try to moderate the sharp turn to the right Abbott was going to embark on and which, I was convinced, wasn't just wrong for Australia but would be electorally disastrous?

John Howard had earlier urged me not to quit. He was pretty pragmatic about it, saying, 'Malcolm, I don't think they'll ever come back to you – not for a long time anyway. But what else are you going to do? You've got enough money. You're too young to retire. Anyway, you don't even play golf.'

He was right about the golf at least.

Arthur Sinodinos, John's former chief of staff, came round on 13 April and encouraged me to change my mind. 'What have you got to lose? You never know your luck in the big city.'

At least a dozen would-be Liberal candidates for Wentworth started lining up for the preselection. The show was moving on; I was yesterday's news and yesterday's man.

The depression got worse and worse.

Lucy and I went to Turkey to attend the Anzac Day service at Gallipoli and it was in Istanbul that my times were darkest and my thoughts of self-destruction the most intense. I hadn't kept a diary for many years but started again, in a series of entries I simply headed 'Darkness' and then filed away locked with a password I couldn't recall – until, just as I was researching this book, it came back to me.

On 20 April I wrote:

I feel at present like a complete and utter failure. I blame myself for losing the leadership, a job which by the time I lost it had become one of excruciating pain and daily humiliation. The Grech affair had me despise myself for allowing myself to be connected, no matter how innocently, with something as vile as a forged email. Then having lost the leadership I sank deeper and deeper into depression, couldn't make up my mind whether to stay or go and was finally persuaded to say I would go when it was obvious I should stay. Now I have engineered a rapidly closing window of opportunity where I could backflip and run again and stay in parliament. But for what? More humiliation? A rebirth? Unlikely. The answer is the pain will end at some point – suicide is a permanent solution to a temporary (we hope) problem. But frankly I am thinking about dying all the time.

The dawn service at Gallipoli was profoundly moving. Being surrounded by reminders of death probably wasn't the best environment for someone in my bleak frame of mind, but it did serve to remind me that my misfortunes were trifles compared to the misery and slaughter of 1915.

John Key, New Zealand's PM, was also there. Three of his servicemen had died in a helicopter accident that day and Lucy and I offered our sympathy. He encouraged me to stick with politics, putting up a similar argument to Howard's, but added, 'It's a crazy business; you might make a comeback.' I doubted that.

After the Gallipoli ceremony, Lucy and I explored some of the old Greek cities in Asia Minor. As my diary entry for Pergamon reveals, my depression hadn't entirely robbed me of my sense of humour:

> *The Asclepion was very interesting. Apparently (a/c to our v good guide), it specialised in mental illnesses. I should check in. Thoughts of suicide flit in and out of my mind, but not as pressingly as they did some time ago. The big qn remains whether to run or not.*[5]

And then, incredibly, Rudd walked away from the ETS; far from going to a double-dissolution election on climate change, he was abandoning it altogether. I was totally stunned by his backflip. Surely that would be the death knell for his leadership.

All the way back from Turkey, I tossed up whether there was any sense in making a comeback. Would I be able to redeem myself? Would I be out of place now in the party room?

Although I was still experiencing anxiety, I realised I'd never do anything as desperate as take my life and devastate Lucy and the kids:

> *Look where my last (political) suicide got me. Self-destructive conduct has to end from now. So qn arises is running again self-destructive or not? Don't know the answer to that one. What if I lost the seat? The credibility problem is my leadership was blown over a policy not even the Labor party supports anymore. What a fool!!! Am I the only person left in the parliament who believes in putting a price on carbon? No wonder I think about pulling the pin on it all.*[6]

Back home, I followed my instinct and announced to the state division of the Liberal Party that I would, after all, run again. They'd undertaken some polling that suggested we'd lose the seat 45:55 if I didn't run, but win it 55:45 if I did, and reinstated my earlier endorsement, even though the preselection process for my successor was underway.

Back on the hustings on 1 May, I reiterated my support for an ETS and was scathing on Rudd's backflip. 'The Prime Minister's abandonment of the central element in his climate change policy, measures which he said were necessary to combat the greatest moral challenge of our times, constitutes an extraordinary act of political cowardice,' I told the assembled media.[7]

Wayne Swan's observation, 'I'd reckon that Tony Abbott wouldn't be popping any champagne corks tonight,'[8] was probably the most astute.

Over the months that followed, my battle with depression continued. At least the indecision was over and I was running again. I went back to doing my regular media rounds and was consistent in my support for putting a price on carbon as the most effective market-based method to reduce emissions. Lucy, my kids and my staff, especially Sally Cray, were helping me get back on my feet. Nobody in the media or the public generally seemed to suspect I was unwell. Fake it 'til you make it, had to be my motto.

I was determined to get off the antidepressants. I weaned myself off, tapering the dose over weeks until I was completely drug free. It was a relief.

They say that what doesn't kill you makes you stronger; my experience with depression certainly made me wiser and calmer. I realised that I had to be as aware of my mental health as I was of my physical health and that I had a vulnerability to depression. So I learned to recognise the early warning signs of the spiral beginning and how to pull out of it. Exercise and sunlight were always important but also simply counting your blessings, which in my case were too many to number.

And while I'd felt at times as though I was literally clawing myself out of the deepest pit, I also recognised that my depression had been preying on the self-absorbed side of my character. Nobody is selfless, and politicians least of all. You simply cannot do the job without strong self-belief. But there are limits, and the boundary between healthy self-confidence and narcissistic egomania can be a fine one.

In the midst of that self-absorption, it's easy to forget how many other lives depend on yours. Assume there's no heaven or hell and death is just like switching off a light: is death really the end of pain? Maybe – for the person who takes their own life. But what about all the others left with the pain and the loss, the guilt, real or imagined?

So yes, I did emerge from this time a stronger person, but also a better person. Less self-absorbed, perhaps less ambitious, certainly more forgiving of others and of myself. Glad to be alive. More determined than ever to serve, to advance Australia. And humbler too, I believe, not least because I realised that there are mysteries and emotions within your own mind that you don't fully understand and struggle to control.

My old friend Dr Mal Washer represented the Western Australian electorate of Moore from 1998 to 2013 and was the unofficial parliamentary doctor. He never billed his patients or Medicare, but over the years hundreds of MPs and senators called on him.

Mal reckoned far too many of the MPs and senators were suffering from unacknowledged depression and, all too often, self-medicating with alcohol. Politics is a highly stressful job and the isolation from home and family makes it worse.

Subsequently, throughout my time in parliament, and especially as prime minister, I made mental health a key priority, whether it was with increased funding for programs like Headspace or, at a local level, securing the money from the Gillard government to improve the fencing, surveillance and landscaping at The Gap at Sydney's Watsons Bay, where far, far too many people choose to leap to their deaths on the rocks below.

Only my family, my doctors and a few very close friends were aware of how sick I'd been. They all know who they are and I thank them for the love and trust that enabled me to pull through it.

CHAPTER 17

Back from the edge and back on the frontbench

Rudd's abandonment of his ETS was a fatal error, and wholly unforced. There wasn't a movement against it within his own party. Indeed, in crass political terms, it was the perfect political issue: it united his side of politics and divided his opponents. And he'd ramped up the moral rhetoric as high as he could – climate change was the greatest moral challenge of our times, and his weapon to deal with it was the ETS, which he summarily dumped.

His polling numbers fell off a cliff. But it was a high cliff and Labor was behind on only a few Newspolls – and then not far behind at 48:52.[1]

Kevin was panicking, I thought. He always looked harried – not sleeping didn't help – but he became more frenetic than ever, darting around the country trying to stitch up a new hospital funding deal that nobody could understand, Western Australia wouldn't agree to and even the Labor states would not embrace unreservedly.

On 2 May 2010, he produced the Henry Tax Review, which had been delivered to government before Christmas in 2009. Holding this off was a classic handling mistake, as Abbott discovered when he delayed releasing the Commission of Audit in 2014. If you receive a report and publish it on receipt, you can plausibly say, 'It's a very interesting piece of work; we'll read it carefully, consider the reaction from the public and determine our response in due course.' However, if you sit on a report for months, it isn't credible to release it without a response. Rudd hedged his bets: responding to some recommendations, leaving others open for consideration and ruling a few out.

Plus Rudd made a bad call. The Henry Review had recommended the introduction of a Resource Super Profits Tax (RSPT). It was thoroughly impractical and prompted a ferocious reaction from the mining industry and from state governments, who feared it would cannibalise their income from minerals royalties. Yet it was the centrepiece announcement from the review. Rudd and Swan stood side by side when they finally released the report and the top priority was announcing what would be dubbed the 'mining tax'.

To their mind, the RSPT would be applied to profits made from resources, with the proceeds used to invest largely in infrastructure. They contended that Australia belonged to all its citizens, so what was in the ground had to be shared. Rudd believed the tax would deliver $700 million in 2012–13 and eventually raise $5.6 billion over the decade.

Of course, it would do nothing of the sort.

While none of this was a good look, Rudd's cause was far from lost. He was well ahead of Abbott as preferred prime minister and whatever mistakes he was making in 2010, he could lay claim to having saved Australia from the GFC in 2008–09. As I've already said, this was spurious. Nonetheless, we dodged a recession while he was the PM, so he had the bragging rights.

But then, out of the blue, Julia Gillard secured the numbers to replace him as prime minister. Everyone was stunned. Gillard said, 'A good government was losing its way,'[2] which wasn't much of an excuse. No policy disagreements were evident, or none of any consequence. Apparently, Kevin was difficult to work with. His control-freakery and temper were well known, but couldn't they have been addressed in a frank discussion between colleagues? The Australian public never accepted the legitimacy of Rudd's removal, and it haunted Gillard for the rest of her political career.

To this day, I don't believe the evidence put forward was enough to warrant Rudd's removal. A more sensible option would have been an intervention about the way he was running the government. As I wrote in an op-ed, it was hard to watch him stumble and cry through his last speech in the prime minister's courtyard:

All I could think was: 'Someone should give the poor bastard a hug.'

Was he unjustly treated? Well, I don't think the former Labor leader Kim Beazley would think so. Politicians live and die by the sword. But all of them, all of us, are human beings and those who pretend these disasters leave them unperturbed are doing just that, pretending.

… Rudd's downfall came like the thunderclap in a summer's storm – one minute he was the master of all he surveyed, packing his bags to hang out with Barack Obama at the G20, and then the assassins struck and he was gone.

… Unlike her deadpan husband, Thérèse Rein's face spoke volumes – the horror and the pain and the sheer black screaming injustice of it all. How could they do this to my husband? How could they do this to him after all he had done for them, after all we had done for them?

And watching her, stoical and strong, I thought of my wife Lucy and how she had stood by me when it was my turn to be battered and bashed by this grim and brutal business of politics.[3]

To my surprise, Gillard enjoyed a bounce in the polls, and on 17 July 2010 she called the election for 21 August.

As campaigning started, I was still fragile but I was off the anti-depressants and threw myself into my campaign. As in 2007, it almost looked like I was running as an independent in a by-election. It was a 'Malcolm Turnbull' campaign with only slight traces of 'Liberal Party'.

If the party wasn't popular in Wentworth in 2007, now with Abbott as leader it was even less so. While not ever denying or hiding the fact that I was the Liberal candidate, it was smart politics to focus on me. It certainly worked, and I achieved a swing of over 10 per cent, making my very marginal seat a safe one.

On top of my own campaigning, I helped some colleagues in marginal seats with fundraising and a few events. But, by and large, I kept to my own patch throughout the five-week lead-up to the election.

Everyone expected Gillard to win the election with a reduced majority; that was certainly what the polls were indicating. She was also well ahead of Abbott as preferred prime minister. While Queensland voters didn't seem to find her appealing, she had strong support in the southern states of South Australia, Tasmania and her home state of Victoria.

But her campaign was rocked on 27 and 28 July when Laurie Oakes of the Nine Network and Peter Hartcher at Fairfax published claims that, in the Rudd cabinet, Gillard had opposed increasing the age pension and introducing a paid parental leave (PPL) scheme. These policies were core parts of Labor's platform. On the hustings, Gillard was talking them up every day and now it appeared she didn't believe in them at all.

Hartcher's piece was particularly damaging. Allegedly, during the cabinet debate, Gillard had said that 'old people never vote for us' and the parental leave scheme was being proposed because it was 'politically correct'.[4]

When she was confronted with this by Oakes at the National Press Club, he confirmed that the source of the leaks was Labor colleagues. Instantly, every finger was pointed at Kevin Rudd, but it was Gillard's reputation that mattered. From that point on, the polls switched and it looked like Labor could lose. An awkward patch-up meeting with Rudd only made things worse. And then, in my view worst of all, Gillard announced she was going to take personal charge of the campaign and proclaimed that she'd ensure people saw the 'real Julia'[5] – which of course implied the Julia we had been seeing hitherto was a 'fake Julia'.

It was something from which she never really recovered.

Abbott had been regarded as unelectable by both the media and by many of his colleagues. However, an election campaign is like a football match. It's all relative. You may think your team is hopeless, but if their opponents are even more hopeless, your team will still win.

Labor suffered a 5.4 per cent swing on primary votes and 2.6 per cent on the two-party preferred vote, finishing narrowly ahead of the Coalition on the national vote.

Queensland swung hard against Labor, with seven seats switching to the Liberal National Party (LNP). We picked up two seats in New South Wales, including John Howard's old seat of Bennelong, won by John Alexander from Maxine McKew, and one in Western Australia. Gillard was popular in Victoria, where Labor won two seats from the Liberals. An independent National Party member, Tony Crook, won Wilson Tuckey's old seat of O'Connor in Western Australia from the Liberal Party, and the left-leaning independent Andrew Wilkie won the Tasmanian seat of Denison from Labor. The Greens' Adam Bandt won the seat of Melbourne from Labor.

That left Labor down 11 seats to 72 in the House. Depending on how you accounted for Crook, the Coalition was at 72 or 73, up seven or eight. To form a majority government, you need 76 seats out of the 150 in the House.

Assuming Crook and the former Nationals MP and now independent for Kennedy, Bob Katter, were going to support the Coalition, Abbott was on 74. The outcome would hang on the four seats unaccounted for.

Adam Bandt, the Green, was a safe bet to stick with Labor, as was independent Andrew Wilkie in Denison. By 2 September, Gillard had stitched up deals with both of them.

During the campaign, rattled by Abbott's assault on the now-abandoned ETS, Gillard had made the fateful pledge, 'There will be no carbon tax under any government I lead.'[6] This came as no surprise to me. Gillard had apparently encouraged Rudd to drop it earlier in the year.

But in her deal with the Greens, she committed to putting a price on carbon and generally, without saying so explicitly, gave the Greens so much influence over her government that the slogan 'Labor–Greens government' went from being Coalition rhetoric to a fair description. She did a deal with Wilkie that involved additional funding for the Hobart hospital – standard crossbench pork-barrelling – but also promised to limit poker machine gambling. Later, that would come back to haunt her too.

With Bandt and Wilkie put away, Gillard could count on 74.

She needed two more, but Rob Oakeshott in Lyne on the NSW North Coast and Tony Windsor in New England, both former members of the National Party, held traditionally conservative seats. Surely they'd go with the Coalition and give Abbott government.

But they did not. A 33-page agreement was hammered out with Gillard, enshrining their commitment to a three-year parliament. It promised billions of dollars of extra spending in their electorates. They both knew that if they'd supported Abbott, he'd have gone to an election as soon as possible and likely won a majority, whereupon their crossbench leverage would evaporate.

Oakeshott and Windsor both claimed that Labor's election promise to build a better NBN to deliver better health services in rural areas, among other things, was a big factor in their consideration.

Abbott had come so close to being prime minister and now it had been denied him. It stung that Gillard was being maintained in office by two renegade Nationals from conservative electorates.

He came to believe the broadband issue had cost him the election and, given the fine margins involved, he may have been right. Labor's grand plan to build a national fibre-to-the-home network to 93 per cent of Australian households was certainly inspiring – albeit, at that stage, very short on detail. But, with me gone, there was nobody in Abbott's shadow cabinet able to mount an effective opposition to Labor's plan and, more importantly, present a viable, affordable alternative.

The Coalition's alternative broadband plan had been announced at Parliament House late in the election campaign by an obviously nervous Tony Smith and Andrew Robb. Smith had tried to release it much earlier so he could explain it but was held back by Abbott, who then didn't attend the launch.

It looked rushed and second-rate compared to Labor's plan. On 10 August, belatedly trying to back it in on *The 7.30 Report*, Abbott too looked awkward and uninformed, at one point protesting to Kerry O'Brien, 'I don't claim to be any kind of tech head.'

In the days after the election, nobody – on our side, at least – thought the 43rd parliament would go for a full three years. Abbott's strategy was to shake the minority government hard in the hope of forcing a fresh election, and as soon as possible. He needed a new broadband spokesperson to both create a credible alternative broadband policy and knock the paint off the shiny new Labor plan.

So, I wasn't surprised when Abbott asked me to be the shadow minister for Broadband and Communications. I felt sorry for Tony Smith, who was dropped, but appreciated the opportunity to immerse myself in something I actually understood. And the opportunity was in its own way a lifeline, a distraction from politics, a technical and commercial problem of the kind I had dealt with all my life.

Things were starting to look up again and 2010, for all of the dark periods, ended on a high note with Daisy marrying James Brown on 4 December. They were married in the chapel at Lucy and Daisy's old school, Kincoppal Rose Bay. The school had been established by the Sacre Coeur nuns, whom Lucy's great-great-grandfather John Hughes had brought out to Australia. Several of John's daughters became nuns and are buried in the little graveyard at the bottom of the school grounds.

We held the reception at home in our garden. At the end of a bleak and troubled year, the wedding was a reminder of what was really important – love and family.

CHAPTER 18

The NBN

Even with the benefit of some distance in time and diminishing partisanship, frankly, Rudd's NBN was crazy. He'd identified something everybody wanted – ubiquitous high-speed broadband – but he couldn't have gone about it in a worse way.

To be fair, technology has changed enormously since then. If we go back 25 years or so, to when we founded OzEmail, a typical dial-up connection to the internet would enable the customer to download data at the rate of 14.4 Kbps. I've just checked my mobile phone's 4G connection, which shows an unremarkable download rate of 34.3 Mbps – 2400 times faster.

By the early 2000s, dial-up was being replaced by digital subscriber line (DSL) technologies, which offered consumers continuous connection to the internet. A fierce struggle was ensuing between new entrants – including our old company OzEmail – and Telstra, still partly government-owned. Telstra owned all the exchanges and the linear infrastructure of pits, pipes and copper wires. The new entrants needed to access the Telstra infrastructure cost-effectively to deliver their services. They claimed Telstra was overcharging them or obstructing them or both, arguing it had a conflict of interest being both the owner of the ubiquitous network and a retailer of broadband services. It was a fair point.

Telstra had become the sole provider of fixed-line services thanks to a series of public policy blunders over more than a decade. Then again, it wasn't practical for anyone to build a rival fixed-line 'last mile' network that extended – as Telstra's did – to every home and business in the country. And as a part shareholder of Telstra, the government had a vested interest in maintaining the value of its investment.

In the 1990s, the Hawke government announced an end to government monopoly, paving the way for Optus to become a second carrier. It also merged Telecom, the domestic monopoly telephone company, with OTC, which owned interests in the international cables connecting Australia to the rest of the world, to form Telstra. If only the network business of Telecom – the exchanges and the wires – had been split off into a separate wholesale utility then. A 'last mile' monopoly should never belong to a retail telco.

Around then, cable television was coming to Australia. It was another opportunity for competition; common carrier access would be essential to all players. I recall Chris Corrigan and I paying a visit to the treasurer, Paul Keating, to propose setting up an independent, wholesale-only cable company, a regulated monopoly funded by the private sector but with an obligation to run cable to households in all the accessible areas of Australia. Paul rejected our idea, saying he preferred to have a competitive cable roll-out. In the event, Telstra and Optus each built a cable network. Workmen would appear in a suburban street to roll out the Optus Vision network and Telstra would turn up virtually the same day to overbuild it with its own cable network. Cost overruns and a patchy roll-out resulted. In most countries, incumbent telephone companies weren't permitted to build cable networks. Not in Australia!

As internet usage grew, retail ISPs demanded more and cheaper access to Telstra's network. Telstra didn't want to invest billions in upgrading its fixed-line networks to allow higher-speed broadband if it was going to be obliged to give access to its retail competitors; it fought every access claim by third-party retailers. Hundreds of millions of dollars were spent on experts, lawyers, lobbyists and economic analysts. Telstra behaved like a First World War general who, forced to retreat, does so as slowly and with as much cost to the enemy as possible.

While DSL technologies were improving broadband access over the twisted copper pairs of the old telephone lines, another technology – DOCSIS[1] – was achieving rapid data rates over the HFC[2] cables used by the cable TV services of Optus and Foxtel, owned by Telstra and News Corporation. However, the coverage had gaps. By the early 2000s, both pay TV companies were using satellite delivery as well.

For years, certainly for the last two terms of the Howard government, what prevented all Australians having access to high-speed broadband – and at an affordable price – was geography. In rural and outer-urban areas, it's not economic to provide access without some form of subsidy. Yet once a government subsidy is provided to construct telecom infrastructure, the case for making it available to competitive retail telcos is overwhelming.

When Labor originally announced their $4.7 billion investment in a national high-speed broadband fibre-to-the-node (FTTN) network, they said it'd be delivered in partnership with the private sector. Effectively, that meant Telstra. In April 2008, Rudd's Broadband minister, Stephen Conroy, called for proposals to partner with the government. His specifications included: minimum download speeds of 12 Mbps to 98 per cent of the population, delivered over five years; open-access arrangements so all service providers could use the network at uniform and affordable retail prices; and a return for the government on its investment. A tall order! Telstra lodged a non-conforming tender and was then excluded from the process.

Then, on 7 April 2009, Kevin Rudd thoroughly jumped the shark, terminating the previous tender process and announcing a new government-owned company would be established to build and operate an NBN. This was NBN Co.

No longer was this going to be a $4.7 billion investment to support the private sector. Instead, $43 billion (a figure plucked out of the air) would be invested to put the private sector, namely Telstra, out of business. Now the objective was to connect 90 per cent of Australian households and businesses with fibre to the premises (FTTP), delivering speeds of up to 100 Mbps. The government would hold a majority stake, but it was going to be such a good deal, Rudd assured us, that significant private sector investment was anticipated. The government stake would be sold down five years after the network was completed, which would take eight years.

No business plan or financial analysis preceded this stupendous announcement, which appeared to have been worked up between Rudd and Conroy on the back of a beer coaster on the prime minister's plane between Sydney and Brisbane. I could see no prospect of commercial viability and said so. The assertions of commercial returns were unsupported by any evidence. (Incidentally, another of Rudd's 2007 election commitments was that all major infrastructure projects should be subject to a rigorous cost–benefit analysis overseen by the new agency Infrastructure Australia. But no such analysis was done on the NBN until 2014, when the Coalition was back in government.)

Rudd thought he was muscling up to Telstra. On the contrary, this placed the government in Telstra's hands. Telstra's existing fixed-line network was still essential. Telstra would always be able to undercut NBN Co on price.

Coincidentally, across the Tasman, a newly elected centre-right National government, under John Key, was seeking to achieve the same objective of ubiquitous broadband.

Key had been elected in 2008. Like Rudd, he came into office with a broadband plan. Key was a former investment banker with Merrill Lynch and his Communications minister, Stephen Joyce, had made his fortune in commercial radio. Using their business sense, they produced a simple, affordable broadband policy. They offered subsidies for the provision of high-speed broadband and started a competitive process. As long as each player was credible and met the government's requirements, the one asking for the least amount of subsidy won.

But there was a special proviso: no tenderer could be owned by, or part of, a retail telco. In other words, you had to be a wholesaler, a common carrier.

The Telstra equivalent in New Zealand was Telecom New Zealand (TCNZ). It had been privatised, like Telstra, and had the same government ownership history, national telephone network and associated infrastructure. Being an integrated telco, it couldn't tender. It solved this by splitting into two companies: a stand-alone network business called Chorus (whose shares were offered to TCNZ shareholders) and a separate listed retail telco called Spark (which would, like all other retailers, have to buy wholesale access from Chorus).

Chorus was able to tender. With the advantages of its incumbent network, it was able to secure the government subsidy for most of the zones in New Zealand. It has become the dominant wholesale broadband provider.

The great virtue of this approach was that the new broadband network was rolled out and upgraded by a company that owned and controlled the entire network infrastructure and was responsible for the continuity of service and experienced in managing telecom networks. They'd been doing it for more than a century, after all.

Back in Australia, in the wake of Rudd's latest bold move, there followed the usual conga line of consultants, most notably McKinsey, who undertook an implementation study in May 2010. Remarkably, they concluded the Rudd policy was a terrific idea that augured a rosy future for Australians. Most joyous of all, it forecast that the government could expect a return on its investment to fully cover the cost of funds.

Labor set up NBN Co and employed a former Alcatel executive, Mike Quigley, as the CEO. While familiar with the industry generally, Quigley was a first-time CEO and had never built nor operated a telecom network. The board was also relatively under-qualified.

NBN Co agreed to pay Telstra billions to decommission its copper and HFC networks as the NBN overbuilt them so as to ensure there was an NBN monopoly. Telstra must have been thinking, 'You only get one Stephen Conroy in your lifetime.'

On assuming the shadow portfolio, I immersed myself in the nitty-gritty of broadband technologies. Over the next three years I visited, at my own expense, New Zealand, South Korea, Hong Kong, Malaysia, Singapore, Canada, France, Germany, the USA and the UK to learn how they were upgrading their networks. On a shoestring budget, I was doing the kind of detailed due diligence and practical market research the government should have done. Not for the first time, I was astounded by how little attention Australian policy-makers paid to how other countries were dealing with comparable policy problems.

Ably assisted by Jon Dart and Stephen Ellis, both economists and former journalists, I developed a detailed alternative broadband policy to take to the 2013 election. Former Turnbull & Partners colleague and Telstra executive JB Rousselot also helped with our policy research, as did Mike Galvin from BT and Robert Kenny from Oxford.

Among the insights we gained was that customers ultimately will pay for the cheapest speed that delivers them the service they want. In South Korea, for example, customers were churning from a 100 Mbps service to a 50 Mbps one in order to save a few dollars a month. Most customers could stream all the content they wanted at 50 Mbps, so why pay more? Indeed, the very high speeds some telcos advertise are just marketing. At a broadband conference in Malaysia in 2012, Jon and I asked some executives from NTT West in Japan why they were offering a 2 Gbps product. They looked at us as though we were idiots. 'Two gigs,' they said, holding up two fingers, 'is twice as good as one gig!' Well, I guess if you don't charge any more for two than you do for one, it doesn't really matter.

The NBN's business plan was all premised on customers being prepared to pay substantial premiums to move up to speed tiers of 100 Mbps and beyond. This was a fantasy, and in due course NBN Co had to reduce the price of its 50 Mbps product substantially to both drive uptake and reduce congestion.

We also quickly learned that the costliest component of any network upgrade was in the civil works. Moore's law doesn't apply to digging holes. Telcos were finding ways to minimise construction costs by using as much of the existing networks as possible. Because the ducts or pipes between the exchange and the street cabinets were reasonably large, it was fairly easy to pull fibre to a node and then connect to the existing copper connections to people's homes. This FTTN approach was faster and cheaper to deploy and could still deliver 50 Mbps for 90 per cent or more of the population. Which is why it's being used around the world.

By the end of June 2013, in the lead-up to the election, Labor's NBN project was failing. In the four years since its launch, it had missed nearly every public target it committed to and only around 33,000 households were connected to its fixed-line network. The NBN had imposed tough terms on its construction partners and, in Western Australia and Tasmania, work had ground to a halt. None of the contractors were making money. Furthermore, NBN Co couldn't even say how much it was costing to connect premises with FTTP.

While I had nothing against Siobhan McKenna, who'd recently replaced Mike Quigley as NBN Co chair, I sensed a completely new team was needed. Immediately following the election that brought the Coalition to government, we replaced all of the board except for corporate lawyer Alison Lansley and the well-regarded economist and adviser to government Dr Kerry Schott, who had considerable infrastructure experience, including running Sydney Water for some years. As she'd also worked with me at Whitlam Turnbull years before, I knew her to be highly effective.

I appointed the former Telstra CEO Dr Ziggy Switkowski as chairman and interim CEO as well as Justin Milne, formerly head of Telstra BigPond, and Patrick Flannagan, who possessed years of experience building linear infrastructure and had, for a period, worked at NBN Co. In addition, we brought onto the executive team JB Rousselot as well as Greg Adcock, also from Telstra. Earlier in 2013, JB had, at his own expense, met with a number of the European telcos to get first-hand insights, as I had, into how they were managing their broadband upgrades. In other words, I made sure the board and much of the senior executive team had relevant experience. Greg had to quickly recut all the deals with the contractors so that they could profitably get back to work.

Our team was considerably reinforced by Abbott's appointment of Paul Fletcher, at my request, as assistant minister for Communications. In the '90s, Paul had been an adviser to Communications Minister Richard Alston, and had then worked for Optus and written an excellent book on the broadband policy disasters.[3] It was a rare combination to have two ministers with relevant real-world experience.

We then commissioned a strategic review of the existing approach to see what could be changed to complete the network sooner and at less cost. The strategic review, which was done by NBN Co assisted by Deloitte, Boston Consulting Group and KordaMentha, recommended a shift to a multi-technology approach, where the company could use whatever combination of technologies would most effectively deliver the outcome of ubiquitous high-speed broadband. This was consistent with the approach in practically every other comparable market we'd studied.

In the end, we opted for FTTP for all greenfield developments, upgraded the HFC-cabled areas – to deliver initially 100 Mbps and in due course 1000 Mbps – and, in the rest of the fixed-line footprint roll-out, FTTN as well as FTTC, where the fibre is taken to the curb outside the customer's home at much lower cost than FTTP but with speeds of 250 Mbps plus. That left 4 per cent to be serviced by fixed wireless and the last 3 per cent to be served by satellite (both as before). It was estimated this approach saved up to $30 billion in cost and brought forward completion by six to eight years.

Assisted by John O'Sullivan and Emma-Jane Newton, we'd tried to persuade Telstra to split their network business off (as TCNZ had done) and merge it with the NBN assets with a view to creating an Australian version of New Zealand's Chorus. However, Telstra believed the multi-billion-dollar deal they'd done with Labor to give NBN access to their pits and pipes was too good to forego.

But we were able to secure, without additional payment, the transfer to NBN Co of Telstra's copper and HFC network assets as NBN Co overbuilt them. And, most importantly, the relationship with Telstra changed from bitter animosity to collaborative partnership.

At the time, based on the analysis contained in the strategic review, I believed that up to $20 billion of value had been destroyed by the shambolic way the Labor Party had approached the project. We couldn't get that money back.

In many speeches, I likened my predicament with the NBN to the man who gets lost driving around Ireland. He walks into a pub and asks for directions to Dublin only to be told, 'If I were you, I wouldn't be starting from here.'

We hired Bill Morrow as the new CEO. Bill had a track record of turning around failing telecom companies. He did an outstanding job on the operations side, but also in transforming what had been a toxic corporate culture. No doubt because the Labor government wanted to keep putting out good news about the roll-out, employees had been discouraged from reporting real outcomes.

By the time I became prime minister in September 2015, the course of the turnaround strategy was set. Mitch Fifield took my place as Communications minister and worked well with the management and board. The project continued to meet every corporate roll-out target for the first three years straight, until there was a pause in construction of the HFC part of the network to deal with some unanticipated technical problems.

When JB Rousselot and the new management took over the construction roll-out in October 2013, NBN Co was connecting 8000 premises a week. Two years later, it was connecting 8000 a day.[4] Under Labor, it was never clear what progress was being made. We fixed that by publishing every week a spreadsheet showing how many premises had been passed by the network, how many could be connected and how many were connected. The project is on track to be completed, as we promised in the 2013 Strategic Review into the NBN, by 2020. As of 14 February 2020 it is more than 90 per cent complete.

As of the week ended 14 February 2020, there are 10.6 million premises ready to connect and, of them, 6.5 million are activated. At 30 June 2013, a few months before the election, those numbers were 179,075 and 70,100 respectively.[5]

In terms of peak funding, the first ever corporate plan by the new management in 2014 identified a range of $46 billion to $54 billion. Five years later, the total funding requirement of the project remains on track and well within this range, with $29.5 billion of equity and another $21.5 billion of debt for a total peak funding requirement of $51 billion.

One troubling thing that's remained constant throughout the project is the cost of connection. As of September 2019, connecting existing premises to FTTP costs on average around $4400. FTTN was $2313, HFC, $2658 and FTTC, $3198.

All through the project, the average revenue per residential customer on FTTP has never exceeded $2 per month more than the revenue gained from a customer on FTTN, or $1 a month on HFC.

The picture on usage shows by far the majority of customers choosing speeds of 50 Mbps or less: FTTP, 87 per cent; FTTN, 95 per cent; and HFC, 89 per cent. The average speed ordered on FTTN is 42 Mbps and on FTTP and HFC, 46 Mbps.[6]

Once complete, over 90 per cent of Australians will have access to broadband speeds at or over 50 Mbps. No comparable developed country of Australia's size and diversity of settlement can match that.

The NBN Co turnaround was, for me, familiar territory. We recruited executives of proven capability, responsible to a board with relevant experience. We prepared a realistic business plan based on a pragmatic analysis of what needed to be done to get the desired outcome: ubiquitous, affordable, high-speed broadband.

I made many political speeches about the NBN and had fun on occasion mocking Stephen Conroy's increasingly outlandish attempts to cover up the project's failure under his leadership. But, in truth, the substance of the work I did to restructure the project was non-political and thoroughly technocratic.

The shift to a multi-technology mix was no more than common sense: focus on the customer and get them the bandwidth they need – and will pay for – as quickly and as affordably as possible. The technology is merely the means to that end. The conspiracy theory that the move away from near-universal FTTP was to protect Murdoch's Foxtel subscription TV business is ridiculous. Subscription TV, whether via satellite or cable, has been disrupted by streaming services, like Netflix, enabled by ubiquitous broadband. Streaming doesn't require 1 Gbps, or even 100 Mbps. In fact, a Netflix HD stream needs about 5 Mbps. Under the NBN, which enables 90 per cent or more of Australians to get 50 Mbps or better, the environment is ideal for streaming. Our approach meant this was achieved earlier and more affordably. Streaming was always going to smash the subscription TV model; thanks to our NBN, that day came much sooner.

I never established a personal rapport with Julia Gillard but one time in 2012, as she was leaving the chamber after question time, she asked me, 'Do you really believe what you're saying about the NBN?' I assured her I did and had I been in my old avocation of investment banking, I'd probably be charging her a handsome fee for that advice. She looked me in the eye: 'Is that right?' And nodded. She probably knew the project was out of control. Soon after, Kerry Schott was appointed to the board. But by then it was too late for Labor to fix the NBN or anything else much.

From a political viewpoint, governments don't get thanked for delivering broadband any more than they're thanked for keeping the lights on. It's expected. The team at NBN Co knew not to expect many bouquets from the public – indeed the only people who get in touch are experiencing problems. But they have the satisfaction of knowing they turned a smouldering trainwreck of a project into a success story and in doing so built the largest single piece of infrastructure in Australia's history.

CHAPTER 19

The 43rd parliament

The 43rd parliament was predicted to be a short one, but it raged chaotically for three full years from 2010 to 2013.

Abbott was furious he wasn't prime minister. He regarded Gillard as lacking legitimacy and was resentful that two former Nationals representing conservative electorates had enabled her to form minority government. He unleashed all of his natural aggression and negativity against her.

Had there been a by-election in Rudd's Brisbane electorate, Gillard would have lost – and in so doing lost government. Consequently, she'd included Rudd in her cabinet as Foreign minister. She didn't have a lot of choice. However, Kevin was as relentless in his efforts to undermine Gillard after the election as he had been beforehand. And poll after poll indicated that he was far more popular than Gillard, reminding the Labor Party of the mistake they had made in dumping him.

The public saw Gillard as a backstabber who'd betrayed her boss and stolen his job. This impression of untrustworthiness was reinforced when she introduced legislation for an ETS. It was an evolution of the ETS that had been Howard and Rudd's policy, but to ensure some initial stability it had a fixed price of $23 a tonne for two years, as opposed to one year under Rudd's design. Gillard's problem was semantics: pressed in an interview, she said that yes, her ETS was 'a carbon tax'. One of her closest Labor colleagues told me she did this to differentiate it from Rudd's CPRS. This may well have been her second-biggest mistake in politics (after rolling Rudd). Again and again we saw the clip of her promising 'no carbon tax under any government I lead' and then her concession that she was in fact doing just that.

Meanwhile, we were consistently ahead in the polls, but Abbott was more unpopular than Gillard. He was consumed with only two issues: the carbon tax and border protection. Abbott's mantra was to 'axe the tax' and 'stop the boats', and he spoke about precious little else.

Polls kept showing I was the preferred opposition leader – sometimes by two to one. Bob Hawke spoke for many Labor people when in 2012 he called Abbott 'Labor's best asset'. I was in the audience at that event, so he added, 'Sorry Malcolm.'[1]

In 2010, after deciding to stay in parliament, I was convinced I'd never lead the Liberal Party again and was determined not to be seen to be undermining Abbott.

After Rudd was dumped, I contacted him, concerned he'd be sinking into the same pit of depression as I had, probably even worse. Kevin said he was fine but we developed a sardonic rapport, sometimes addressing each other as 'fellow pariah'. He seemed miserable, wounded by the betrayal of 2010 and determined to exact revenge on Gillard and vindicate himself by making a comeback.

So, throughout the 43rd parliament you had two opposing leaders, Gillard and Abbott, each of whom was the other's best asset. In the wings, on each side, you had two former leaders, myself and Rudd, each of whom enjoyed much higher public support but were bitterly opposed by sections of their respective parties. The difference was that while Kevin was busy undermining Julia, I was being very Zen.

The fight about Gillard's misnamed 'carbon tax' was excruciating. In February 2011, the shadow cabinet committed, against my and Hockey's advice, to repealing the carbon tax if it were passed. I'd encouraged Abbott to emulate Labor's response to the GST – rail against it if you must, but once it's enacted accept it; take the revenue. Business would prefer the issue is settled, I told him. 'Nobody wants a perpetual war about climate change.' But Abbott did, and he ensured we got one and it rages on today – a decade later.

At one point just 18 months before, he'd supported us voting for the CPRS; now Abbott wanted me to publicly say market-based mechanisms for pricing carbon were wrong and direct action was best – 'That was then, this is now.' I was prepared, at most, to say that while I personally supported a market-based mechanism, the party had resolved on direct action and as part of the shadow cabinet I'd support the consensus position.

I reminded him that I did not demand such 'discipline' from him when I was leader. I expect he will sack me shortly, but his request is absurd – demanding that I disavow all that I have said and stood for before … I was simply not going to start telling lies for him or anyone else.[2]

Even my friend Ian Macfarlane, who insisted I'd be the only alternative when Abbott inevitably fell over, took Abbott's line. 'Say, "After Copenhagen, everything changed. That's why I oppose a carbon price and support direct action,"' he suggested. When I mildly protested he said with characteristic Queensland bluntness: 'I had to eat that shit sandwich and so should you.'[3]

Within Abbott's team, our modest emissions reduction goals were now mocked. Egged on by his brazen climate-change-denialist supporters, Abbott barely paid lip service to the issue. For his political advancement, he'd weaponised climate change.

I am concerned that I am slipping back into a depressed state – the whole carbon debate is churning me up, I feel so uncomfortable being part of Abbott's Liberal Party. … It is obvious that he does not believe in the climate science and has no intention of effecting any cut in emissions. He said yesterday he did not want to reduce the burning of brown coal for heaven's sake. God will not and should not forgive this selfish generation for its failure to take action on climate change, and I doubt that our grandchildren will either.[4]

Abbott was part of what was becoming a war on science, the intensity of which has only increased over the years since. Daniel Patrick Moynihan may have said, 'Everyone is entitled to his own opinion, but not to his own facts,' but in the age of 'alternative facts', people can readily find support for almost any prejudice.

Around that time Maurice Newman, who was still chairman of the ABC, having been appointed by Howard, upbraided me for being sucked in by the 'global warming hoax'. I asked him why he took that view and he sent me some crackpot material he had downloaded off the internet. I referred it to one of our leading scientists at the ANU, Will Steffen, who patiently described why Newman's 'authority' was wrong. Newman's response was, 'The ANU are just a pack of lefties, worse than the CSIRO and the UN!'

The day after my gloomy July diary entry, I entreated Liberals to support the science in a speech about the future of the Great Barrier Reef. I likened the rejection of climate science to 'ignoring the advice of your doctor to give up smoking and lose 10 kilos on the basis that somebody down the pub told you their uncle Ernie ate three pies and smoked a packet of cigarettes a day and lived to 95.' I said we couldn't allow the science to become a partisan issue, and added, 'To achieve the necessary cuts in emissions by mid-century, all or almost all of our stationary energy – and when I say our, I mean the world's – will need to be generated from zero or near zero emission sources.'[5]

When chastised for this speech and similar statements, I reminded my critics I was stating Liberal Party policy. While the party had abandoned an ETS, officially it remained committed to emissions reduction and making a response to climate change. I had to hang onto that: if I didn't, the party would follow Abbott off into avowed climate denialism.

Disappointingly, Gillard was as confused and incoherent in defending her ETS as Abbott was clear and simplistic in trying to demolish this 'great big electricity tax'. One of her closest supporters despairingly lamented to me that she couldn't get her head around it. Perhaps that's why the *Financial Review* ruefully observed, after the Great Barrier Reef speech, 'It says a lot about the federal government's difficulty in promoting its carbon change policy that its best advocate is staring across the parliamentary chamber taunting Labor's ministers, as well as his own side, with his periodic bouts of truth in marketing.'[6]

Barely a week passed in the 43rd parliament without a rumour that Gillard was about to be overthrown by Rudd. I took care to ensure that kind of leadership speculation got no traction on our side.

But, thanks to growing despair about Gillard's ineptitude on the one hand and Abbott's furious negativity on the other, I received some unusual entreaties.

Quite a lot of people, including several captains of industry, some of them extremely close to Rudd, urged me to do a deal with Rudd: join the Labor Party and form a dream team of Kevin as PM and me as treasurer.[7] More like a nightmare than a dream, I thought, although I surmised that some of the Labor Party would find me easier to stomach than Kevin. As Yuval Rotem, the Israeli ambassador, said to me in 2012, 'Some of these Labor people talk about Kevin Rudd the way Israelis talk about [Iran's leader] Ahmadinejad.'[8]

The attacks on Gillard steadily intensified. Tony Windsor and Rob Oakeshott asked me, if they were prepared to support the Coalition 'in a baton change', would I be able to become leader because they wouldn't have a bar of Abbott.[9]

The wildest idea came from Clive Palmer. A self-described billionaire, he'd made his fortune in property development and mining – largely by selling a Western Australian iron-ore project to a Chinese company for way too much money. Then a life member of the LNP, Clive had worked in his youth for Queensland Premier Sir Joh Bjelke-Petersen and was generous to Coalition candidates.

On 21 June, Clive met Abbott: he wanted the Liberal Party's federal council to rule that lobbyists shouldn't be senior office-bearers of the party. In Clive's sights was fellow Queenslander Santo Santoro, a Howard-era minister who'd resigned over undisclosed share trading, now influential on the right wing of the LNP – and an Abbott ally. According to Clive, Abbott flew into a rage, called him several obscene epithets and threatened to throw him out of the party. That was something, I thought: throwing around someone of Clive's dimensions would take a huge effort.[10]

Abbott resisted Clive's proposal and the motion was defeated at the federal council.[11] By November Clive had reserved the name United Australia Party (UAP).[12]

On 20 November, Clive spent two and a half hours with Lucy and me at home. He had $20 million in funding for the UAP, which he wanted me to lead! Clive's main focus was state government: he claimed that 20 LNP members would defect to the UAP in Queensland and that Barnaby's friend Brendon Grylls in Western Australia was also a starter. In my diary entry for that day, I wrote, 'He is utterly self-obsessed. He doesn't want me to be PM – he wants to be PM and probably president of the world too.' I also noted how smart he was.

> But when it comes to politics he is bonkers. Anyway, I told him dozens of ways why the new party wasn't for me. By 5 pm he reluctantly gave up on that and after a long discussion about his plan to rebuild the Titanic, in which he took me through every single element in the launch party, the music, the food, the bands, the guests etc, he headed off. Phew.

Bonkers or not, Clive started his party, ran in the 2013 election and won himself a seat in the House of Representatives and three seats in the Senate.

As sliding door moments go, it's worth wondering how events may have unfolded if Tony Abbott had agreed with Clive's eminently reasonable suggestion back in 2012. Was Scott Morrison the ultimate beneficiary in 2019?

If Abbott wasn't raging about the carbon tax, he was raging about boats – or, rather, stopping them. Gillard was living with the consequences of Rudd's foolish decision to abandon elements of John Howard's border protection policies. Every month saw more boat arrivals; the people smugglers were back in business. The Labor government had lost control of the borders.

In May 2011, Gillard announced a deal whereby the next 800 unlawful arrivals would be removed to Malaysia. In return, Australia would take 4000 UNHCR[13]–approved refugees currently in Malaysia. While the 5:1 ratio in the people swap seemed inequitable, the concept of the deal was strong. People weren't going to pay up to get on a boat to go to Australia, take all the attendant risks of the ocean passage, if they thought they were going to wind up back where they started.

When the High Court issued injunctions to prevent Australia sending asylum seekers to Malaysia, Gillard sought the opposition's support for legislation to get around the ruling. But Abbott vehemently opposed the 'Malaysia Solution': he knew it might work and, for him, the more boats the better.

It was a sore point in the shadow cabinet. Philip Ruddock wanted us to support the amendments. He believed sending people to Nauru wouldn't work because the people smugglers would assume they'd end up in Australia anyway. He opposed turning boats back too.[14] Many of us agreed. Shadow Immigration Minister Scott Morrison told me he'd privately urged Abbott to support the Malaysia Solution but nothing would induce him to help Gillard stem the flow of boats. Various hypocritical arguments were mounted about not wanting to send people to Malaysia because it wasn't a signatory to the UN Refugee Convention.

Eventually, Abbott agreed to allow the removal of asylum seekers to Nauru only. By August, legislation to restart offshore processing of asylum seekers was passed. But the episode had reinforced the perception that the Abbott Coalition was as ruthless as it was cynical in its effort to defeat Gillard.

• • •

Opposition is thoroughly frustrating at the best of times. The bitter antagonisms of the 43rd parliament only made it tougher. It's ironic therefore that it was during that bleak period I was able to make another consequential contribution to the Australian media industry.

I was beginning to despair about the state of Australian journalism. I wasn't especially concerned about the political slant of one outlet or another, but more about the fact that newsrooms were shrinking and editorial standards were dropping to the loopy standards of the twittersphere. Gina Rinehart was threatening to buy Fairfax – no doubt so that its newspapers could emulate her own ultra-right-wing views.

In June 2012, I suggested to Alan Rusbridger, editor of the UK's *Guardian*, that he should establish an Australian edition. For a modest cost, he could start a digital-only edition. That would provide a good base from which to build. Alan was interested. We exchanged some rough numbers and he concluded he'd need $20 million of underwriting for three years – if it couldn't get to break-even in that time, it never would.[15]

Given my political role, I could hardly participate myself, but I thought I knew someone who would. Graeme Wood had made hundreds of millions of dollars from an online travel booking business called Wotif. He was on the political left and had been generous in the past to the Greens. He'd also recently funded a progressive free online newspaper called *The Global Mail*. It wasn't going to make it. So, I suggested to Graeme he drop *The Global Mail* and instead use his fortune to bankroll an Australian edition of *The Guardian*. Its progressive politics suited him plus it was one of the greatest newspapers in the English language, nearly 200 years old and, unusually, wasn't controlled by any media mogul but rather an independent trust dedicated to 'quality, independent liberal journalism'.[16]

Once Graeme Wood was on board, I introduced Rusbridger to two seasoned Canberra political writers, Lenore Taylor and Katharine Murphy (aka murpharoo). He sent his deputy, Kath Viner, to Australia to be the first editor. The (digital) paper exceeded expectations, broke even after a few years and Wood got all his money back. Clearly, my deal-making skills remained intact.

The Guardian rarely endorsed my or my government's policies, but under Kath Viner and now Lenore Taylor's editorship, the paper has maintained high editorial standards. It's a paper avowedly of the left, but facts and professional journalism still matter, and that's becoming all too rare in our deteriorating media landscape.

Love, life and family go on despite the roars and tribulations of politics. I began 2012 in a reflective mood, writing in our boatshed:

> *This is a very beautiful place, we are so lucky. I said to Lucy yesterday that notwithstanding a few disappointments along the way, we are so blessed – happy marriage, financial security, wonderful children, good health (touch wood), beautiful home and lives that while they might have achieved more had things gone better or we had taken different decisions, nonetheless were more momentous than the vast bulk of humanity.*[17]

And it was a momentous year for our family as well. Alex was married to Yvonne Wang, whom he'd met in Hong Kong where he was now working in finance. She was as elegant as she was erudite and spoke both Chinese and English better than her husband.

Yvonne's parents lived in Beijing in a traditional courtyard house. We spent time there with them before the wedding; it was very special. Her dad, already 90 years of age, was a scholar and expert in Chinese history and foreign policy.

I was present when he solemnly addressed his future son-in-law. We were in his library. 'Alex,' he said, 'when you are married you must have a big house.'

Alex looked across to Yvonne for help. 'Is that for all the babies I'm going to have?' she asked.

'No,' the old man replied with just a hint of a smile. 'For all my books and paintings.'

But, for the family, there was sadness that year as well. Lucy's uncle Robert Hughes died in New York on 7 August, a rich, large life ended. We had an apartment in the city and had been visiting Bob. We last saw him on 28 July, his 74th birthday; we took him a cake and tried to cheer him up. But he was fading fast and knew it. And we knew how desperately he wanted to be home in Australia.

I'll be forever grateful that Julia Gillard agreed to there being a condolence motion in the House of Representatives for Bob on 14 August. Lucy's father, Tom, came down to Canberra for it. I had the privilege of eulogising not just the great man of letters but the Bob our children called 'WU' – for Wicked Uncle – a title he loved. Recalling his time as our colourful guest, I described how Lucy, especially, always gave Bob free rein, granting him 'a leave pass denied to all the other men in her life'.[18]

It wasn't a gloomy speech: there was so much to celebrate. But in an unscripted moment Tony Abbott became my straight man. I recounted how, during a republican debate, a calipered Bob – recovering from his 1999 car crash – had a swing at Abbott.

Tony Abbott: He missed!
Malcolm Turnbull: Yes, he missed! What a loss for the nation it would
 have been had he connected.

On 22 February, Kevin Rudd resigned as Foreign minister; Gillard said she'd spill the leadership at a party meeting on the 27th and renominate.

Rudd claimed Gillard couldn't beat Abbott; were he leader, he could give the party a fighting chance to hold government. But at the ballot Rudd was decisively beaten, 71 votes to 31, and pledged not to make another challenge. He didn't rule out being drafted – a circumstance he then set about doing all he could to procure.

Gillard had appointed an LNP member, Peter Slipper, as speaker of the House. Slipper was coming to the end of his parliamentary career. He wouldn't have been many people's choice for that role, but desperate people do desperate things. Gillard was pleased to peel off an LNP member; she calculated Slipper's move to the speaker's chair made her hold on government that little bit more secure.

But suddenly Slipper was facing allegations of misusing travel entitlements and sexually harassing a young man on his staff – James Ashby, who'd later become Pauline Hanson's political svengali. As the lewd text messages to Ashby circulated in the media and police investigations got underway, Abbott moved a motion of no confidence in the speaker on 9 October. Now Gillard saw red.

Gillard had heaped on her more indignities than any prime minister before or since. Alan Jones had called for her to be put in a chaff bag and dumped in the ocean; Abbott had stood in front of signs calling to 'ditch the witch'; overweight, middle-aged male politicians and journalists regularly mocked her pear-shaped figure and choice of jackets; and even feminist trailblazer Germaine Greer made comments about the size of her bottom.[19]

Defending Slipper – the worst possible cause – Gillard delivered her finest ever speech. It was as though all of her indignation was boiled up and refined into one deadly fusillade aimed at Abbott.

'I will not be lectured about sexism and misogyny by this man. I will not ... if he wants to know what misogyny looks like in modern Australia, he does not need a motion in the House of Representatives, he needs a mirror.'[20]

Slipper resigned and was later charged and convicted of misusing his Cabcharge account. On appeal his conviction was set aside.

Gillard was certainly a fighter and her government wasn't without achievement. She did succeed in establishing an ETS but of course the Coalition was sworn to repeal it and did so. The revised mining tax was a shambles and raised very little. When it was subsequently repealed, it wasn't even mourned by the bean counters at the Treasury.

She did establish the National Disability Insurance Scheme (NDIS), for which she had the Coalition's support, although grossly underfunded it. Her Gonski education reforms, which I describe in another chapter, were a patchwork of special deals providing federal funding that was neither consistent nor needs-based.

Despite all the chaos, the polls at the end of 2012 showed Gillard well ahead of Abbott as preferred prime minister and the party vote was often 50:50 or 49:51, with the government just behind.

The complaints about Abbott's leadership grew, and by November Scott Morrison was sounding me out, at first through a mutual friend and then directly, about whether I'd be prepared to challenge Abbott if, as Scott believed, it became clear in the new year that he couldn't win. In January 2013, as we kayaked together at Port Hacking, he shared his view that Abbott was in a psychological bunker of anxiety, listening only to Peta Credlin and her husband, Liberal Party Federal Director Brian Loughnane. If we won with Abbott, Scott asked, what kind of government would he lead?[21]

I listened carefully to Morrison. He should have been part of the Abbott inner circle: after all, our highest-profile policy challenge was to 'stop the boats' and Scott was the responsible shadow minister. He'd always been a highly pragmatic political professional. Apart from moral issues like same-sex marriage, which he resolutely opposed, it would be hard to find any political issue on which he appeared to have a deep or principled conviction. Scott above all believes in winning elections, and so I knew his concerns about Abbott were untainted by any sentiment, emotion or animosity.

Scott wasn't alone in these concerns, but I didn't encourage or take advantage of them. As Arthur Sinodinos advised in December 2012, if

Abbott looked like he'd lose, the party would likely dump him: 'Stay cool, as you have been, and await events.'[22] And so I did.

In February, I had a long discussion with Abbott about how his government would run. I told him straight: there was anxiety it'd become an Abbott–Credlin dictatorship; the electorate needed to see not just a change of leader but a change in the culture of government. He gave me a commitment he'd lead a traditional cabinet government and not try to run the government out of the prime minister's office (PMO). At a shadow cabinet shortly afterwards, he repeated everything we'd discussed, without attribution to me. Privately, everyone chuckled at his promise not to be erratic or wilful, but it was appreciated. Abbott and I spoke to Paul Kelly on the same theme. Dutifully, he reported on the harmony between us and the pending return to conventional cabinet processes, adding a clear message to Abbott not to let Credlin take over. At a press conference that day, Abbott repeated his undertaking to run a consultative cabinet government.[23]

My fears remained. It wasn't in his nature and it wasn't in Credlin's to be collegiate. Uneasiness dogged me in the lead-up to the 2013 election. Still, I was determined to give it my best shot.

On Thursday 21 March, in one of the more unhinged episodes in politics, cabinet minister and former ALP leader Simon Crean called for a leadership spill and was sacked by Gillard, who then called a meeting at which nothing occurred – because Kevin Rudd announced he wasn't going to stand against her. That evening, the Labor people in the airport lounge looked like wrecks. Nicola Roxon, whom I barely knew, chatted with me rather than her colleagues – they were so miserable. My friend Greg Combet despaired that the agendas of too many of Labor's leading lights were about personal ambition and nothing more.[24]

In the days after Crean's sacking, more resignations followed and Gillard reshuffled her ministry. The government's only purpose, it seemed, was to preserve Gillard.

The idea of the party switching to me that Morrison and others had floated earlier in the year had no legs. The public mightn't like Abbott, but they were going to vote for anyone to get rid of Labor. But I was deeply unsettled about the future.

I feel bad that Abbott will be leader, not for what it deprives me of, but rather for what it will do to the country. There I am uneasy. He knows he has to tack

to the centre and stay there to become and remain PM. So I am less concerned
about him doing mad rightwing things than I was. But I am concerned about
his not being consultative, doing more things like the paid parental leave
without running it through cabinet. He has said all the right things recently
about cabinet government, not being a president etc, but I remain concerned.
It's one of the things that keeps me in parliament actually, to ensure the next
govt is a good one.[25]

When parliament wasn't sitting, I travelled constantly, campaigning in marginal seats. Occasionally, I came across Labor people. Sometimes we'd have a laugh. Penny Wong told me she'd tried unsuccessfully to get on the Ellen DeGeneres show, then shooting in Sydney. 'What's the point of being a lesbian,' she said, 'if you can't get on TV with America's most famous lesbian?'[26]

Cooking was another way to distract from the general horror of Chateau Despair, as Rudd used to describe Parliament House. Our flat in Kingston, which we'd purchased in 2007, had a big terrace overlooking the lake, perfect for dinner parties with amusing colleagues and, sometimes, journalists. The dinners were best when Lucy was there, and Christopher Pyne and Julie Bishop always made for an entertaining night.

And another delight of 2013 was catching up with Mum's cousin Angela Lansbury when she was in Australia for a few months playing *Driving Miss Daisy* with James Earl Jones. She was 88 then and now, in her mid-90s, is still working. Whenever I saw her she reminded me of Mum – that rather square Lansbury face is very distinctive. (Despite Angela being a rock-solid Labour supporter, I encouraged my friend David Cameron, then PM of the United Kingdom, to make her a dame – like so many of the other great actresses of her vintage.)

Abbott and I joined forces to launch our broadband policy on 9 April and started doing more events together. He and the Liberal Party had worked out I wasn't seeking to overthrow him (as Rudd was Gillard) and that the more we were seen to be working together, the more of a contrast it was with a bitterly divided Labor Party. Abbott, thrilled, sent me a congratulatory SMS: 'Mate, what a good week. You have consummately outplayed them.'[27]

The polling trends firmed. By June, Gillard and Abbott's stocks sank further relative to Rudd's and mine. Rudd was leading Gillard by 26 points and I was leading Abbott by 30 as preferred leader of our parties.

More importantly, the polls showed Labor would be wiped out under Gillard but if Rudd returned they could save up to 30 seats.[28]

On 18 June, I bumped into Rudd, who was with his daughter, Jess, in the parliamentary dining room. Kevin was proudly nursing Jess's baby. 'Darling, this is Uncle Malcolm. The Australian people love Grandpa and Malcolm but their parties hate them.'[29] We both laughed, and I wondered how much closer to the abyss Labor had to get before survival trumped hatred.

We didn't have long to wait. On 26 June 2013, Kevin Rudd made the comeback most of us had thought would have happened at least a year before. More ministers resigned, including Wayne Swan, Craig Emerson, Greg Combet and Stephen Conroy.

The first polls saw Rudd pull well ahead of Abbott as preferred PM and Labor's party vote improved markedly as well, with their primary vote up six to 35 and ours down five to 43. We were still ahead on the two-party preferred but only just, at 51:49.[30]

Our pollster Mark Textor messaged that it was going to be a very tight election. Several polls put Labor ahead, but the Newspoll on 9 July showed the vote tied at 50:50 and Rudd as preferred PM over Abbott 53:31. The Fairfax Nielsen poll on 15 July was also 50:50.

I had lunch with Morrison at Beppi's the same day. While he said it wasn't clear Abbott couldn't win, he was very worried that he wouldn't and that there would be no time to switch to me, which he said was the only option. He thought Rudd would go to the polls next week so parliament didn't come back and we had no chance to switch. He urged me to be ready to move. I told him I'd keep my head down – it was all too late; we had to do the best we could with Abbott.[31]

The media was full of leadership speculation and polls comparing me with Abbott. It was crazy stuff, but anxiety among our supporters and colleagues mounted as they thought what should be an assured Coalition victory could be lost because of Abbott. The Newspoll on 23 July showed us ahead of Labor again on 52:48, which calmed some nerves, but Morgan showed Labor ahead and Galaxy had us at 50:50. Every poll suggested we'd win easily if I were leader rather than Abbott.[32] Every meeting I had, especially with business, people were asking me when I'd replace Abbott. I hated it, and could only imagine Abbott's anxiety as he contemplated the inevitable victory being snatched away by Rudd's last-minute return.

Finally on 4 August Rudd called the election. I was relieved.

Rudd says the election question is 'Who do you trust?' Abbott says it is who is fair dinkum. Suspect most will say 'neither'. Good thing now people will stop asking me to overthrow Abbott. It is now clearly too late.[33]

And so it was … Elections are like hangings: they concentrate the mind. When it boiled down to taking a punt on the Coalition led by a disliked Abbott or signing up for three more years of Labor chaos, Australians went for the Coalition. While the only poll that matters is the one on polling day, you could see in the published polls throughout the campaign how the Rudd bubble was deflating.

As we celebrated the national election win for the Coalition, and another strong local result in Wentworth, where my vote was over 67 per cent, I knew that I'd done everything I could to support the team and, with all my misgivings, its leader. Despite many encouragements to do so, I hadn't undermined Abbott – as he acknowledged.

In my diary, I mused about whether the result might have been better had I been leader.

… certainly yes. But more importantly, would we have got there, and there I have my doubts. I am not sure I have the mental toughness of Abbott. He is something of a robot, a political Dalek, he has a simple single-minded focus on his own personal success. He does not have much interest in policy and when he embarks on it his judgement is often way out, like the paid parental leave policy … but I am not grinding my teeth about not being PM, indeed I am excited about getting stuck into this new portfolio …[34]

4

Abbott
Government

(2013–15)

CHAPTER 20

Tony and Peta

Abbott was no sooner elected than his inadequacies as a leader became even more apparent. His natural pugnacity had suited opposition – he could get up every morning and go out with 'axe the tax' and 'stop the boats' – but government required a positive agenda.

Dominating him was his CoS, Peta Credlin. In all my life, I've never known a leader more dominated by another than Abbott was by Credlin. Peta has always strongly denied that she and Tony were lovers. But if they were, that would have been the most unremarkable aspect of their friendship.

From my observation, the relationship was completely asymmetrical. He worshipped and feared her; she, on the other hand, treated him with disdain. I recalled from when I was opposition leader, Credlin (and her husband, Brian Loughnane) had always been scathing about Abbott – about his lack of discipline and his drunkenness, in particular. Then he became leader; she became his CoS; he nearly won the 2010 election and, of course, won in 2013. And she believed that without her, he couldn't have done it. She'd remade him. She'd turned him into a prime minister – he was her creation.

And Abbott acknowledged it, publicly and privately. When Peta was upset, Abbott rushed to calm her. She could do no wrong and no matter how tyrannical or vindictive she became, he wouldn't hear a word against her. He believed that without her he couldn't do his job – maybe he was right; she certainly thought so.

This dependence on Credlin, and downright fear of her, was at odds with Abbott's carefully cultivated image as the hairy-chested, bike-riding, weight-lifting, fire-fighting alpha male – complete with a swagger that would put a sailor to shame.

More than just about anyone I've encountered, Abbott is primarily driven by hatreds, fears, prejudice – anything negative. It's as though he's defined himself by what he's against, without much thought for what he's for. Right from the outset, the government lacked a coherent economic narrative: apart from repealing the carbon tax and the mining tax, what else did we have to say? Budget repair? But was it all to be about cutting expenditure? What was to be done to encourage investment and economic growth?

Neither Abbott nor Credlin were prepared to work within a conventional cabinet system where matters were discussed candidly in private, decisions were taken collectively and then announced. Instead, everything was geared to whether it would make a headline. Decisions were impetuous and more often than not briefed out to the media, typically *The Daily Telegraph* or *The Australian*, before being discussed with cabinet colleagues.

Credlin would humiliate ministers she didn't like. Julie Bishop was a prime target. Her travel requests were often denied or held up until literally the last minute – all to make sure Julie (whose popularity outstripped Abbott's) knew her place.

I had a number of invitations from technology and telecom companies in the USA and asked for approval to travel there in January 2014. This was denied. I felt it was sufficiently worthwhile to go at my own expense. This leave was grudgingly approved, but at Credlin's direction the secretary of Prime Minister and Cabinet (PM&C), Ian Watt, instructed our missions in the United States to offer me no assistance in lining up meetings and so on. To his credit, our ambassador in Washington, Kim Beazley, ignored the directive.

Returning from New York in January, I reflected on my situation. Lucy and I were now grandparents to little Jack. We had never been happier. Lucy was expecting me not to run for parliament again and to retire in 2016; her only reservation was the chance I might sink into another slough of despond. I mulled it all over in my diary:

Truthfully, if I am not leader, it is hard to see why I would go around again. The NBN will be sorted out by then and there isn't really another portfolio I am keen to do … Julie has asked me if I would take the Ambassador role in

Washington, but that doesn't appeal, although I can see why Abbott would like me out of the way … As [a former Howard government minister] was saying to me last night, the government looks very unsettled, unstable and in large part because Abbott does not appear to be in charge, the country is being run by Credlin. And that makes people disrespect Abbott, despise him in some quarters in fact. So, we shall see. But for the time being all is well.[1]

At our first cabinet meeting in 2014, Abbott accused the ABC of being 'on everybody's side but Australia's'. They'd run (rather uncritically I thought) a story about RAN personnel holding asylum seekers' hands on hot pipes and burning them while turning boats back.

However, he seemed at least to recognise the emerging problems with his office and said, 'I want ministers to run their portfolios. I don't have the slightest desire to micromanage portfolios.'

The cabinet meeting of 10 February was a good example of how Abbott and Credlin's wilful disregard for due process was creating tensions within the government. George Brandis, the attorney-general, brought in a submission for a Royal Commission into union corruption to be headed by Dyson Heydon. This wasn't news to the cabinet – it had been extensively previewed by Samantha Maiden in *The Sunday Telegraph*, much to the annoyance of many cabinet members. George assured me the leak had come from the PMO.

About a week later, on 18 February, I was having a quiet dinner with Lucy at Cipri in Paddington when journalist Simon Benson called me to say *The Daily Telegraph* was going with a front-page splash accusing me of attempting to interfere with an AFP investigation. Earlier in the day, the Seven Network had been raided by the AFP looking for evidence of Seven paying Schapelle Corby for an interview. My friend Bruce McWilliam, who worked at Seven, had rung me to complain. I'd done no more than pass on the fact of his complaint to Attorney-General George Brandis and suggest to Bruce that he call George if he wanted to take it further. I told Benson, and later his editor, Paul Whittaker, that the allegation was false and highly defamatory. They said several times they'd received the information from 'the heart of the government', which I naturally took to mean the PMO, and were going to publish. They claimed I'd tried to get Brandis to call off the raid and that he'd slapped me down.

Brandis wasn't available until after 9 pm. He phoned Whittaker to tell him the story was rubbish, and it was toned down, much to Whittaker's annoyance, as he had to redo the front page. 'It cost me $250k,' he later complained to me. A *Telegraph* photographer was waiting outside the restaurant to get one of those late-night pictures calculated to make you look guilty.

Brandis told me that the only person he had mentioned our discussion to was Credlin. She denied briefing Benson, of course. I had no doubt she, or someone with her authority, had done so. The gravity of the allegation and the reckless malice with which it had been made left me in no doubt I was a marked man.

The right wing of the Liberal Party has generally shown little interest in economics. Like Abbott, many of them are more DLP than Liberal and their economic instincts are invariably populist and interventionist. What gets them going are 'values issues'. In the Abbott years, the two most prominent ones were same-sex marriage (they were furiously against it) and the reform of section 18C of the Racial Discrimination Act.

Ever since Andrew Bolt, the right-wing columnist, had been found to have breached the act because of some offensive remarks he made about several Indigenous leaders, there'd been a campaign to 'amend 18C'. The proponents of change were either champions of free speech (according to News Corp) or advocates of hate speech (according to the left and the multicultural lobby). Brandis didn't help things when, trying to channel Voltaire, he justified the reform proposal with the immortal line, 'Everyone is entitled to be a bigot,' in response to a question from Indigenous senator Nova Peris.

Section 18C prohibits acts that are 'reasonably likely, in all the circumstances, to offend, insult, humiliate or intimidate another person or a group of people' where that act is done because of the person's race, colour or ethnic origin. There'd developed a consensus, at least on the side of the reformers, that the best amendment would be to replace the words 'offend, insult, humiliate' with a stronger term, such as 'vilify'.

However, on 24 March, a few hours before cabinet was due to meet, a set of sweeping proposed changes to 18C was circulated. They made the 'vilify' change but went much further. Once again, proper process was being bypassed; this was designed to railroad a proposal through the cabinet without ministers having the opportunity to fully consider it.

As soon as I saw it and recognised the problems, I wrote to George and copied Abbott. One of the proposed changes had the effect, I pointed out, 'that promoting hatred against a group of people, Jews for example, will no longer be prohibited unless a particular Jew can satisfy a court that hatred has been incited towards him'.[2] This would effectively license hate speech so long as it wasn't directed at a particular individual.

However, there was worse. As I also said, the current exemption for public commentary and opinion applied so long as it was done 'reasonably and in good faith'. Brandis, no doubt on instructions from Abbott, was proposing to remove that provision.

I noted that these amendments:

> ... are designed to ensure that a person CAN vilify or intimidate somebody else on the basis of race etc so long as it is expressed in the form of an opinion or belief and that opinion or belief can be unreasonable, motivated by malice, unfair and/or inaccurate.
>
> This will be seen by many as a licence for racial hate speech. It will undoubtedly permit holocaust denial, not to speak of the expression of views about the inferiority and/or depravity of particular races.

The cabinet debate was ferocious. Brandis defended his position and Abbott appeared to back him to the hilt. I took them through my letter and one by one ministers agreed with me. Even Kevin Andrews! The proposal was rewritten in the room. To cap it off, the cabinet required that the amendments be published as an exposure draft only – so not even as a concluded proposal from government.

I observed to Pyne, it was one of those occasions I was glad I'd stayed in politics. 'Very good of you; if you'd let it go through unamended he'd be even more unpopular,' he replied.[3]

And if the turmoil over 18C wasn't enough, the next day Abbott announced he was going to reinstate knights and dames in the Order of Australia. I was able to have a little fun with it in a blog pointing out that many republics, including Peru, Argentina and Guatemala, all have orders of knighthood.

My diary on 31 March read, 'The shrewd, like Penny Wong, saw this as subtly seditious. Others said it was craven, but there is no point in allowing this to become another rift story.'

And it wasn't. Abbott texted me on Wednesday morning, 'That was an elegant blog, thanks.' I replied, 'No worries.'

'But,' I added, 'just for the record, if you had consulted me I would have counselled against it – seductive though the example of Guatemalan knighthoods may be, I am not a fan!'

The knights and dames announcement was widely panned. Brian Loughnane said to me that it was 'an indulgent folly'.[4]

I kept hearing bad news from the PMO at this time, all centred around Credlin and her domination of Abbott. On 5 April, Arthur Sinodinos described to me how Abbott felt he was being stalked by Hockey now and was trying to promote Morrison as a rival to him. My diary note on 5 April was, '[Sinodinos] is interesting on Credlin, describing one incident after another in which she yells at Abbott, treats him with contempt, walks out of meetings and sulks and Abbott has to beg her to return.'

Within days, however, Abbott was in Japan announcing a trade deal. With positive announcements there came some relatively clear air for the government. At such times, I'd find myself wondering what might have been. I was still haunted by the feeling I'd let people down.

> I cannot help think that if I hadn't fucked up my time as opposition leader with Grech and then over climate (although I still think I made the right moves for the right reasons given the circumstances) then maybe I would be doing it – not because I crave the limelight etc but because I know I would be a better, more contemporary, more liberal PM than he is.[5]

I was sure I was never going to get a second chance.

By the eve of the budget in late April, I was fully occupied with the restructuring of the NBN. Although I'd spent much of my investment banking career sorting out corporate messes, none had involved as much wasted money as the NBN.

Julie Bishop summed up most of the party room's view of the NBN later in the year when she said, 'Whenever the NBN comes up with our colleagues, they say first, "Thank God I'm not the Communications minister," and then, "I hope Malcolm knows what he's talking about, because I don't understand a word of it."'[6]

There was more on my plate than the NBN. Just before the election, Abbott had promised not to make any cuts to the ABC or SBS. This surprised both me and Joe Hockey. We'd discussed undertaking a rigorous efficiency review of the ABC and making savings where we could without diminishing the quality of services.

For many of my Liberal Party colleagues, the ABC was a nest of dangerous, mung bean–munching, latte-sipping lefties out of touch with the world beyond their inner-city elitist enclaves. The Nationals (and some rural Libs) generally had a more nuanced view. They recognised the ABC did an outstanding job in its coverage of rural and regional Australia. To them there were good programs (*Landline*) and bad ones (*Q&A*, *The 7.30 Report* … pretty much everything that wasn't hosted by people wearing akubras).

Personally, I was thoroughly pro-ABC. In an age where social media had smashed the advertising business model of the mainstream media of newspapers, television and radio, the ABC had a crucial role to play. But it needed to improve its journalism so it was genuinely accurate and impartial. This was harder than ever of course, not because of left-wing bias but because the rest of the media had, by and large, become debased to the level of social media: light on facts, dripping with bias, full of fake news and outrage.

Recalling how effective it had been, 20 years before, when Lucy and I conducted a thorough analysis of the Ten Network, I knew what I wanted. I engaged Peter Lewis (just retired as the CFO of the Seven Network) to assist my department with a similar review of the ABC. As expected, it showed that plenty of expense could be saved, either for return to the budget as a saving or to be redeployed for better use within the ABC.

My ministerial responsibilities kept me happily busy, though for the government overall, it was heavy sledding. Abbott had commissioned the Business Council of Australia (BCA) president, Tony Shepherd, to head up a Commission of Audit shortly after the election, and the report was delivered in February with recommendations for reforms to the public sector and, most controversially, cuts to welfare and a $15 Medicare co-payment.

I dined with Shepherd on 24 February, after he'd delivered the report. He said frustratedly, 'Abbott is sitting on it too scared to publish it and too scared to implement most of its recommendations.'[7] Hockey was similarly fed up. I repeatedly reminded the cabinet of Rudd's mistake in sitting on the Henry Tax Review and the general rule that it's always better to put out a report when you receive it. Then, when people ask you to rule things in or out, you can say you haven't yet read it and look forward to the public discussion.

As a consequence of this timidity, we had the worst of all worlds; the Commission of Audit hung over the government like a dark cloud, not assisted by bits and pieces being selectively leaked to the media.

This constant feeding of cabinet material to the News Corporation newspapers was corroding the trust between cabinet members – Abbott's plan to impose a 2 per cent surcharge on the top marginal rate of income tax (taking it from 45 to 47 per cent) was leaked before cabinet ever discussed it, apparently a last-minute even-up to offset all the cuts (and broken promises) in the budget. When we asked if he could reconcile this with his 'no new taxes' pledge, Abbott said, with a perfectly straight face, that it was a levy and not a tax.

Meanwhile, Abbott's paid parental leave policy was languishing in the Senate; apart from Tony, not one member of the cabinet wanted it to pass. His PPL had been a captain's call when we were in opposition, allegedly a thought bubble of Peta Credlin, who was concerned professional women weren't having enough children. It basically meant that for 26 weeks after the baby was born, the government would pay the mother her salary up to a cap of $150,000 a year. This was to be funded by increasing company tax by 1.5 per cent for the 3000 largest companies. It was a unique idea – a means-tested benefit where the people with the most means got the most benefit. A nurse or a teacher on $75,000 per annum married to a cop on $100,000 got half the benefit of a lawyer on $150,000 married to a banker on $250,000. Whenever we challenged Abbott on this inequitable and poisonously unpopular policy, he'd say his daughters thought it was a good idea.

People often say the 2014 budget wrecked the Abbott government, but it has to be said the polls were bad leading up to it. The floating of the so-called deficit levy and an increase in the pension age to 70 were going down like lead balloons.

I was in Geneva, so I participated in the pre-budget cabinet meeting of 7 May from our embassy. Joe Hockey complained about how hard he was working: 'HIH sent me grey, this budget has sent me blind.' He then went on to complain about Peter Costello who, like most Liberals, was astonished by the proposal to raise the top marginal rate of income tax. Hadn't we gone to the election and promised no new taxes? Joe was almost Churchillian in his truculent rejection of criticism: 'We cannot cower in the face of criticism, otherwise we'll be like Rudd backing down over the ETS.'

I agreed that Rudd's ETS backdown was walking away from a promise, but pointed out that so was jacking up the top marginal rate.

The budget was seen as mean, unfair and dishonest. What made it worse was Abbott's white line fever–induced promise shortly before polling day: 'No cuts to health, schools, ABC or SBS.' The budget broke all those promises and the hike in the top marginal rate (for three years only) did nothing to assuage the public's anguish.

On 19 May I wrote in my diary:

> Nielsen has us behind 44–56, Newspoll 45–55. Budget worst received ever, Abbott unpopularity comparable to Whitlam in loans affair or Gillard after breaking her no carbon tax promise. Shorten 11 points ahead as preferred PM. This is very bad news for Abbott and for us. Later today Morgan comes out with the vote with Labor ahead 57.5/42.5. So there is no doubt things look grim.

A few days later, I had my regular post-budget meeting with the Liberals of Wentworth when the Point Piper branch met at the Royal Prince Edward Yacht Club, surrounded by Australia's most expensive real estate. They were scathing about Abbott and Hockey and hated the budget – thought it was unfair to the poor. 'God knows,' I reflected, 'what they're saying about us in Penrith if this is the attitude here.'

When I reported on the view from Point Piper at the next cabinet meeting, Hockey and Abbott dismissed it. 'The problem with your constituents, Malcolm,' Hockey observed, 'is that they spend too much time watching the ABC and reading the Sydney Morning Herald.'

His view was at odds with the assessment of the 2014 budget given in a 2015 qualitative research report by Crosby Textor.

> Voters believe the budget last year was 'confusing' and 'cruel' and the ensuing public backlash from the surprise hits on Australia's most vulnerable (pensioners, low income workers, etc) was fierce. The lasting takeout for voters of that budget was that the Government was prepared to look only at the numbers when trying to fix the budget and

reduce debt, without thinking about the real, practical consequences of their decisions. Essentially to voters this is the definition of being 'out of touch'.[8]

Even as the government was getting whacked for making (take your pick) tough *or* unfair decisions, Abbott's displays of weirdness continued. When a woman called in to a talkback show to say she was so hard up she was working on a sex line, he responded with a lewd wink. Then, while he was cutting money Labor had promised for schools (money that, by the way, they had no plan to fund), it appeared his daughter had won a scholarship worth $60,000 at a design school. But there was no competition, no scholarship program: it was only made public when *The Guardian* found out about it. That week, for the first time, I noted people were saying Abbott was terminal.

TV host Karl Stefanovic earned a withering blast from Peta Credlin in the same week by daring to ask Abbott if his leadership was safe in light of the bad polls. The question was predictable and would normally have passed unnoticed. The massive overreaction from Credlin ensured that it was very carefully noted.

CHAPTER 21

'Not like you do, Alan'

On the evening of Wednesday 28 May, I was planning an early bedtime preceded by some spicy soup at Wild Duck – at that time the Kingston waterfront's only restaurant. As I was leaving Parliament House, I bumped into Martin Parkinson, whom I invited to dinner, and also Tom Harley, the Liberals' federal vice-president. On the way there, Tom invited Julie Bishop and Clive Palmer. Julie couldn't make it but Clive joined us. As the concluding course of a convivial banquet that would make an emperor blush, Clive consumed a giant plate of deep-fried ice cream. He was in good form, laughing about his unlikely election to parliament and recalling my warning him not to run 'as you might get elected'.[1]

A *Telegraph* photographer snapped us on the way out of the restaurant, and so our 'secret dinner' became the latest tabloid beat-up. On his TV program, Andrew Bolt asked Abbott whether my dinner with Clive meant I was after Abbott's job. Bolt followed this up on the Monday with a similarly crazed column, linking my dinner with Clive and attendance at the launch of 'Parliamentary Friends of the ABC' as evidence I was planning a move against Abbott.

Fed up with this, I called it out for what it was – 'quite unhinged'.[2] This merely resulted in more attacks from Bolt. Meanwhile, the polls remained dire. Newspoll had us 46:54 and Abbott 10 points behind Bill Shorten as preferred PM. Preferred Liberal leader polls were being run and generally they confirmed I was twice as popular as Abbott.[3]

These bad polls made Abbott's media backers go in harder. After days of demented denunciations from Alan Jones, I agreed to go on his program. On 4 June, the night before the interview, at 5.59 pm, I called him up. We spoke (mostly he spoke) for 31 minutes. I wrote in my diary that night:

> *I tried to persuade him to stop this mad jihad against me on the basis that it was (a) utterly baseless and (b) very damaging to the Government, creating issues of leadership all at a time when we were behind in the polls and thus vulnerable.*
>
> *Jones was totally hysterical, screaming (literally) at me. He kept on accusing me of being 'a traitor, a treacherous schemer'. He said again and again, 'I love Tony Abbott and I will stand between him and anyone who tries to undermine him and that means you Malcolm Turnbull … You don't love Tony Abbott.'*
>
> *'Well,' I said, 'I am quite fond of him –'*
>
> *'But you don't love him, like I do,' screamed Jones.*
>
> *'Not like you do, Alan, that's true,' I replied.*
>
> *At one point, he started screaming, 'Don't you know, everybody hates you, they hate you, everybody, everybody hates you …' At another point he said, 'Why aren't you out there every day selling the Medicare Co-payment?' I said that it might be because I wasn't the Health minister. 'That's just an excuse!' said Jones.*

Jones wasn't quite as mad the next morning, but when he tried to get me to repeat after him a statement of support for the budget, I put him back in his place. 'Alan, I am not going to take dictation from you. I am a cabinet minister.'[4]

By the end of the interview, I was exhausted but I could tell I'd won it. I'd stood up to Jones: few politicians do that. I told him he was doing the Labor Party's work and was a bomb-thrower. He hated that. And if I needed any confirmation how weird he was, this is the text message he sent me after the interview: 'Malcolm. Thank you for your time today. Now that all that stuff is out in the open everyone can get on with the job. I look forward to being able to support you in the future. Alan.'

Unbelievable. Had he asked Julia Gillard out for a beer after he said she should be dropped into the sea in a chaff bag? Consensus was I'd put him back in his box.[5] He wouldn't stay there for long.

In what was to become a standard modus operandi, the attacks by Bolt and Jones were dovetailed with a campaign against me in *The Australian* – loudly complaining that I wasn't doing enough to sell the budget! The editorials on 3 and 6 June denounced me, echoing and endorsing Bolt and Jones.[6] I wrote to Lachlan Murdoch on 6 June to remind him I was doing as much media as the PMO would allow me to do. And just in case anyone imagines the Murdochs don't influence the editorial line of their papers, following my email an editorial of 7 June took a different line, urging Abbott to 'make better use of his government's best-credentialled and, in theory, most persuasive advocate'.[7]

At the end of that mad week, *Insiders* presented a graphic showing the response to the question about who was the best leader of the Liberal Party. The rankings were: Malcolm Turnbull, 31 per cent; don't know, 21 per cent; someone else, 19 per cent; and in fourth place, Tony Abbott on 18 per cent.[8]

After the cabinet meeting on 23 June, I noted in my diary: 'Abbott's political summary was as usual delusional. Everything is going very well he says: we are not as unpopular as he thought we would be.'

The bad polls kept coming. By 30 June, Newspoll had us 45:55, Morgan 43:57 and Abbott well behind Shorten as preferred PM. And to think it was only nine months since we'd been elected – a reminder perhaps of the grim truth that Labor lost in 2013; we won despite, not because of, Abbott. Gallows humour alternates with dire consolation. Julie Bishop just said, 'Oh well, three years as Foreign minister isn't too bad.'[9]

On Thursday 17 July, a Malaysian Airlines plane, MH17, was shot down over Ukraine – presumably by Russian-backed separatists. Of the 298 passengers and crew most were Dutch, but 27 were Australians and the nation was simultaneously shocked, grieving and outraged. Abbott responded strongly, condemning Putin for providing the separatists with a surface-to-air missile system, and at the same time dispatching Julie to the United Nations Security Council (UNSC), where she spoke powerfully, securing their condemnation of the crime and support for a thorough investigation. Australian police were dispatched to Ukraine to assist with victim recovery and identification.

This type of crisis energised Abbott; it lifted him from the intractable wrestling with Clive Palmer and the Senate over domestic policy. But while ministers praised his leadership publicly, privately they had concerns. His promise to 'shirt-front Putin'[10] looked anything but prime ministerial. Abbott held National Security Committee (NSC) meetings almost continuously for the days that followed and was determined that Australian commandos would be sent to Ukraine to secure the crash site as the bodies and the wreckage were recovered. The military resisted this – the separatists were heavily armed; why inflame tensions – but it took American intervention to finally talk him out of it. Sanity prevailed and we sent unarmed AFP personnel.

Abbott's original idea was so obviously risky. An Australian armed contingent would be overwhelmed and captured; we'd then be begging Putin to help us get them released for years. And, as I pointed out in the subsequent cabinet meeting, while we mourned all those killed – including Sister Philomene Tiernan, who'd taught Lucy and Daisy – why would we put more young Australians into harm's way?

The week beginning Monday 4 August was a shocker for the Abbott government and everything that went wrong was entirely the PM's own doing. This time, it concerned my portfolio area. A front-page story in *The Daily Telegraph* revealed that the NSC had resolved to introduce new metadata retention laws, and that this was to be presented in cabinet. When reporters asked me about this, it was news to me.

Ministers were furious, and that included those on the NSC because it was obvious, given the deadlines involved, that *The Daily Telegraph* had been briefed before the NSC had concluded its meeting.

This was all part of a strategy Loughnane had canvassed with us a few weeks back, of seeking to exploit people's anxiety about terrorism. With a failed budget and a disheartened treasurer in Joe Hockey, Abbott was hoping national security would rescue his fortunes. He started doing more press conferences with uniformed police and military – and flags. The flags kept multiplying until at one point he had eight – four on each side.

In years past, telephone companies had captured details of phone calls for billing purposes. This was metadata in the analogue era. With the internet, an enormous amount of additional digital metadata arose, much of which was retained by telcos. It included the IP address assigned to your device when it connected to the internet and, in some cases, the IP addresses you visited. While its retention was no longer needed for billing, the Australian Security Intelligence Organisation (ASIO) and the police had argued that telcos should be obliged to retain it for a period. It could be invaluable in certain types of investigation.

Credlin and Abbott grabbed this longstanding request, dressed it up as a counter-terrorist measure and rushed it out into the media – ahead of the cabinet meeting that was meant to discuss it.

This bold strike against the forces of evil became a humiliating shambles. The cabinet meeting on Tuesday 5 August was bad enough, with ministers furious that yet again their discussions had been pre-empted by a PMO leak. But then it became clear in the meeting that neither Abbott nor Brandis knew what metadata was or what was actually supposed to be retained. How, I asked, could they brief to the media a security measure that not only hadn't gone to cabinet but that neither understood? 'We are all concerned about terrorism but surely we ought to get these matters properly defined and designed, discuss them in private and only make an announcement when we have actually made a final decision,' I said.

Worse still, George did a train wreck of an interview on Sky News with David Speers in which he took his confusion public. In particular, he suggested ISPs would be obliged to retain the IP addresses to which a customer connected, but not the names of the websites: a distinction without a difference. He'd failed to recognise that retaining a customer's destination IP addresses would mean retaining details of every website, every chatroom, every online service a person visited or connected to.

By the following day, the damage was worsening by the hour. Abbott's own interviews weren't much better than George's. He said that the policy would capture 'the sites you are visiting' and then subsequently his office said that wasn't the case.[11]

I wrote in my diary on 6 August:

> *At 3:17 pm I received this text from Dennis Shanahan:*
> *'Hi Malcolm, I'm doing a story for the Oz tomorrow based on what I have been told about yesterday's cabinet meeting and the metadata decision. I've been told of the tenor of some of your remarks – disappointment about not being included in NSC meetings as relevant minister and finding out about it in the Tele – from a sympathetic viewpoint and some concern about Cabinet process. I want you to know what I'm writing and would like to talk but understand if you don't want to participate. Cheers Dennis'*
> *I spoke to Shanahan and told him I couldn't discuss what happened in cabinet and didn't. I did say that I did not lose my temper in cabinet (a question of degree). He was very critical of Abbott's mishandling of this.*

I called Abbott and tried to get some clarity into what the government was doing. He flew into a rage and started to threaten me: 'Don't you come between me and national security.'

I'd talked Abbott through the chaos of the day, highlighting the folly of doing policy on the run. He and the attorney-general had been contradicting themselves. Now the telcos were confused and the public was confused.

Rather than let the chaos continue, on the Thursday evening I convened a meeting at my office in Sydney with Brandis and representatives of the Australian Signals Directorate (ASD), ASIO, the AFP as well as my own department.

ASIO's representative left us in no doubt they wanted to get as much metadata retained as possible and they certainly had destination IP addresses on their wishlist. The political implications of that were terrible, the practicality of actually doing it not much better. However, we were lucky to have with us Andrew Colvin, who at that stage was deputy commissioner of the AFP. He was by far the clearest thinker among the officials.

We resolved that we'd seek to have retained for two years the traditional telephone call records and only the customer IP address – not the IP addresses of sites or services visited by the customer.[12]

The next morning, I proceeded to clean up the mess, providing reassurance that Australians' web surfing wouldn't be monitored by the government and that there was at least one minister who had a reasonable understanding of how the internet worked.

Two consistent themes had developed around Abbott and his government. The polls were bad enough, but the growing dysfunctionality of the government – the lack of proper process, the leaks from the PMO, the domination by Credlin – all fed into a growing sense of crisis. While some, like Scott Morrison, were starting to sniff out interest in removing Abbott, most had no appetite for such a change. For myself, I was staying very quiet on that score – making no outgoing calls; when it came to leadership issues, I was determined to be on receive, not transmit.

Abbott's supporters looked to find others to blame and Treasurer Joe Hockey was first in line, despite the fact that the most disastrous elements in the 2014 budget were the work of Abbott and Credlin. But Joe was, at least nominally, the author and his efforts to sell it subsequently were pretty feeble. Defending an increase in the fuel excise, Joe said that poor people wouldn't be affected because they didn't drive cars. He was jumped on as out of touch – an image assisted by his being snapped smoking cigars with Mathias Cormann just before the budget in May.

Mind you, it wasn't an easy bill of goods to sell, consisting as it did of one broken promise after another. Abbott didn't help his treasurer. He refused to admit that there were any broken promises. When colleagues like Craig Laundy or Wyatt Roy suggested he 'do a Peter Beattie' and simply admit he'd broken promises but that the state of the public finances gave him no choice, his response was so aggressive that many described it as psychopathic.

Many parts of the media, including Abbott's staunchest allies at News Corporation, started urging him to replace Hockey with me, as did many colleagues. This would, so they hoped, give the government a new economic credibility. Abbott, notwithstanding his economics degree, showed no interest in finance or business and in all the years I knew him seemed to border on the innumerate.

I was careful to play no part in this. Abbott would never move me to treasurer. And I felt I was being used as a stalking horse by others, especially Scott Morrison, to position themselves.

Not only was the budget unpopular and a breach of many promises, the key savings measures couldn't get through the Senate. This rather underlined the absurdity of Abbott's media mates attacking me for dining with Clive Palmer, whose votes we'd need to pass anything.

A good example of how colleagues were feeling is in my diary of 9 September after a cabinet meeting.

Cabinet went well – nothing notable. The appointment of Peter Lewis to the ABC Board was approved as was the cabsub [cabinet submission] revised on children's e-safety. Only other matter of note was the industry and innovation paper, which was pretty mundane but did include reversing Labor's 2009 changes to the taxation of employee options, but not shares. Joe was not able to explain why not shares and was pretty hopeless generally in a discussion about the economy and then in base erosion and profit shifting by multinationals. Discussing it with Macca [Ian Macfarlane] later he said it was perfectly obvious that Joe was way, way out of his depth in the Treasury role. Julie took me aside and said how worried she was about the government's performance in the polls – her explanation for the continued poor performance was that we were failing in what should be our core competence – economic management, a failing she attributes to Joe's inability to frame and sell the budget.

They were gloomy times in Canberra as the year went on, but there were some lighter moments.

Nothing eventful at parliament today but a hilarious dinner at the flat in the evening. The party was me and Lucy, Daisy and James, Sussan Ley, Scott Morrison, Sen James McGrath, Christopher Pyne and Robert Hill. All very jolly and we had lamb pasta, Daisy's favourite, but Pyne was on fire. He is one of the most outrageous and funny dinner guests you could ever have. He described how [his wife] Caroline had just got a degree from Adelaide Uni and had asked him not to come to the graduation because the students would all demonstrate.

'So, I said to her that I would come in disguise. Cyrano de Bergerac with a huuugge nose,' he squealed.

I suggested some other disguises.

Christopher's eyes lit up; a natural thespian, he was excited by the thought of dressing up.

As he described one improbable costume after another, everyone was laughing so hard most were weeping. Even Scott Morrison, who thoroughly disapproves of Pyne, was laughing too.[13]

I was relieved to escape on an Italian holiday with Lucy in October – our plan was to celebrate my 60th birthday in some of our favourite places. Alex and Yvonne joined us in Venice and we had a blissful week there, staying once again in Ca' Desdemona, where we'd been in 2008 shortly before I became opposition leader.

It was a good time and place for reflection. Once again I turned my mind to retiring from politics. On 12 October I wrote:

I have been mulling away a lot here – what am I still doing in politics? Lucy is very, very keen that I retire at the next election and I think I probably should. At 62 I will be young enough to do some other things. But I am reminded always of what Howard said to me back in 2010 when I retired and then changed my mind: 'What else would you do that would be more interesting than politics?' A good question, so I think the reason for getting out would be to have more freedom, spend more time with family, but would a more sedate life appeal? That's the big question. Spending time here makes me think it would, but as I learned in 2010 when I became so depressed I feared I was going to harm myself, the mind, my mind, is a very complex thing, unfathomable even to its owner.

It wasn't long after I returned to Australia that Gough Whitlam died, at the grand old age of 98. Fairfax journalist Mark Kenny and others in the gallery kindly reviewed my speech in the condolence motion. But in a sense, while I was praising Gough I was lamenting the meanness into which our politics had descended.

> We know Gough Whitlam's government was not unmarked by error
> ... The truth is that nobody on our side or on the Labor side would
> agree with Gough's economic agenda. We would not agree with Billy
> McMahon's economic agenda. Life has moved on ... What is that
> thread, that narrative that emerges from history out of the humdrum
> daily grind of political argument? What is it? It is an enormous
> optimism and all of us admire that, whether we voted for him in the
> '70s or our parents voted for him, or whether we approved of what
> [Governor-General] John Kerr did or not, all of that recedes. What
> people remember of Gough Whitlam is a bigness, generosity, an
> enormous optimism and ambition for Australia. That is something we
> can all subscribe to.[14]

CHAPTER 22

Arise, Sir Phil the Greek

Just as many people were urging Abbott to dump Hockey – the papers regularly ran polls to show how unpopular he was – as were urging Abbott to 'do something' about Credlin. John Howard was most concerned. While they couldn't persuade Abbott to part company with his 'dear Peta', he agreed, at John's suggestion, to replace the low-key and compliant secretary of PM&C, Ian Watt, with Michael Thawley. Formerly a senior adviser to John Howard, and for a time our ambassador in Washington, Thawley became a strong and considered counterbalance to Credlin, whose influence and control he believed was excessive.[1]

The international stage should always be a strength for a prime minister: unlike on the floor of the House, the opposition leader cannot compete with you. But it never really worked for Abbott. The strong intervention over MH17 was spoilt by his desire to send armed troops into Ukraine. Our support for the anti-ISIL (Islamic State of Iraq and the Levant) mission in Iraq and Syria was accompanied by his unsettling enthusiasm for conflict. Even when he hosted the G20 in Brisbane, he managed to be off-key by trying to keep climate change off the agenda and then giving a bizarre opening speech at the conference in which he whined about his difficulties in getting things through the Senate, including the $7 Medicare co-payment – about as popular as Ebola, as I noted in my diary at the time.

The year continued in fairly chaotic fashion. I'd finalised cuts to the ABC to be funded through the efficiency measures identified by Peter Lewis. But Abbott didn't want to call them 'cuts' and referred to them as an efficiency dividend. I wasn't going to tell lies for him, especially in the House, and so said that while the amount of the savings was similar to what a traditional efficiency dividend would achieve, this wasn't in fact an efficiency dividend. And around and around we went as he refused to admit he'd broken a promise.

And then the $7 Medicare co-payment issue became as confused as it was toxic. The PMO's press office briefed Mark Kenny it was to be dropped but failed to let Hockey and Dutton know; they promptly disowned the idea. All in all, as Abbott acknowledged himself, it was a ragged way to end 2014.

On 5 December, I attended the PM's Christmas party at Kirribilli House: 'Usual grisly crew of right-wing nut jobs, ministers, senior civil servants and supporters.'[2] To avoid the traffic and amuse myself, I took a water taxi there and surprised everyone by emerging through the garden.

The year was ending about as badly as it could – the polls all showed us behind by 10 points, and the News Corp papers were continually polling on Hockey. The Galaxy Poll on 7 December, for example, asked who was the better treasurer out of me and Hockey – only 22 per cent nominated Joe, 41 per cent me and 37 per cent were undecided.[3]

Joe, always anxious, was rattled by this campaign. He correctly recognised I had no hand in it, but identified Morrison as his main detractor.[4]

I had dinner with Morrison down in his electorate on 10 December. It was the first time he laid out, fairly comprehensively, his thinking on Abbott, who he felt would have to go by the middle of 2015 if his performance didn't improve. He said Hockey should go now and he was making the case to Abbott to replace him with me. He was closely in touch with the key figures at News, he told me, and said they were getting ready to dump Abbott. And he made it clear he saw himself as the successor.

There was considerable criticism of Credlin in the media at this time, all designed to pressure Abbott to fire her. Abbott called me on Saturday 13 December and I wrote later that day:

We discussed Credlin. I said I didn't think he needed to sack her but she did need to improve her interpersonal skills, and stop micromanaging ministers' work. I said re Julie that she was not a plotter, a Lady Macbeth or Julia Gillard but that she was sick of being treated contemptuously by Peta. Tony agreed (to my surprise), didn't defend Credlin at all, conceded she had been too high-handed and that ministers had to be given more latitude.

We discussed Joe. I said I was not urging him to sack Joe. He said repeatedly how much he appreciated my loyalty and the fact that I had not been briefing against him or colleagues, including Joe. I said that I wanted to find a means to contribute more to the economic debate, to make our case. He agreed I should do that, said I was one of the best political communicators and that I should get out there and talk about economic issues.

By the following evening, however, I was writing in my diary about how Credlin was paying me back for my comments:

Late this evening Sally [Cray] sent me a page from the first edition of the Tele, which accused me and Julie and various others, including Morrison and Kelly O'Dwyer, of being malcontents undermining Credlin. Sally sent it on to Julie's CoS, who got it to Julie in PNG, who then rang Benson and ripped into him. She called me and we canvassed where it came from. Possibilities: Abbott's crazy office or possibly Hockey, but I think likely Abbott's people. This was confirmed when Abbott texted me to say it wasn't his office!!

> *'Mate, I gather there's a Tele story about people going Peta. As far as I am concerned the story is dead wrong and the journo made no attempt to contact anyone in this office. Cheers Tony.'*[5]

After Julie's blast to Benson, the *Tele* amended the story and took all the names out.

The following day, 15 December, the Martin Place siege began. The gunman, an Iranian self-styled imam called Man Monis, had been on and off the ASIO radar for a long time. He entered the Lindt Café in Martin Place at 8.33 am and held hostage 18 customers and staff, proclaiming as he did his loyalty to ISIL. He had a history of violence, especially against women. He was out on bail, and shouldn't have been.

The siege was ended at 2 am on 16 December and two people were killed. The manager, Tori Johnson, was shot by Monis, and a young barrister, Katrina Dawson, was killed by bullets ricocheting across the cafe. It was a tragedy, but despite the efforts of some to use the siege as a means of whipping up hatred towards Muslims, overall the city responded with love. Lucy and I went to a mass that afternoon at St Mary's and when I was doorstopped outside the cathedral I said:

I was on a train this morning, and you could feel the numbness in the carriage. Everyone was thinking the same thoughts: shock, horror, imagining how those people suffered during that terrible night. Thinking about the courage of the two young people that were killed. And yet I feel that everyone was also filled with love ... a determined love; a recognition that it's love for each other, it's love for our country which binds us together and makes us the most successful, harmonious society in the world.

I felt that there was, as the train rattled across the Harbour Bridge, a quiet determination that we weren't going to be intimidated by such hatred.[6]

The polls continued to be bad as the year was ending and I started getting calls from backbenchers urging me to challenge Abbott. One, with whom I wasn't close at all, was Don Randall from Western Australia. I listened carefully but didn't say anything that could be construed as disloyalty. If Abbott was going to fall over, I had no interest in pushing him.

There was a reshuffle at this time, notionally triggered by Arthur Sinodinos's forced resignation as assistant treasurer. He'd been involved in some Independent Commission Against Corruption (ICAC) hearings in New South Wales and was furious about being pushed out by Abbott. Arthur was Liberal Party royalty, as Howard's former CoS.

Notably, Morrison was moved out of Immigration, where he'd 'stopped the boats', and into Social Services. He too was furious and saw this as a demotion. It moved him out of the NSC. Dutton was moved out of Health, where he'd failed utterly, and was shifted to replace Morrison in Immigration. I welcomed Sussan Ley's promotion to cabinet as Health minister – that meant we now had two women in cabinet.

Morrison had been muttering to me about Abbott for a while, but this was the first time I recall him saying, 'We will need to remove him before the budget.'[7] Ten days later, Morrison returned to this theme, ringing me while I was in the Hunter with Lucy, to complain about Abbott, his office, the paid parental leave policy (well, we all hated that).

I wrote in my diary about the ominous note he struck:

He does not believe we can afford to have a second failed budget and that consequently either Abbott and Hockey will have to do an amazing turnaround before the budget OR they will both have to go before the budget. I am not so sure about this, it seems to me that the party room would not expect to remove Abbott before the Budget, but I may be wrong. I am assiduously not making calls and when others ring me I don't encourage them.[8]

So, 2014 ended uneasily. The government, barely a year old, was eight points behind in the polls; Shorten was preferred PM; and the general sense among ministers and colleagues was that Abbott's office was dysfunctionally led by Peta Credlin. While Scott Morrison was evidently limbering up to tip Abbott out, most other ministers (like Julie, who joined us at home for New Year's Eve) were looking to other changes, chiefly replacing Joe with me as treasurer. Julie told me that when she raised this with Abbott, he acknowledged it would lift our numbers but would result in added leadership stress – whatever that meant.[9]

The first polls for 2015 were all bad and the preferred Liberal leader polls were, for the first time, showing both me and Julie ahead of Abbott. Even his close supporters in the business community were abandoning him. A good example was Servcorp founder Alf Moufarrige, a long-time Liberal Party donor who, so he said, had always been generous to Abbott. He told me on 16 January he was urging Abbott to dump Credlin, whom he described as 'an evil influence', and also to dump Joe. He told me the only way to stop a Labor government was for Abbott to resign or be removed.[10]

Scott Morrison had asked me for a private meeting with him and Scott Briggs, our mutual friend and political ally. Briggs, who'd helped me on the Wentworth preselection contest, was both a friend and neighbour of Morrison.

We met for dinner at my place on 19 January. To my surprise, Morrison was advanced in his planning to overthrow Abbott and said the change should happen before the Easter break. He produced a list of names of those he believed would vote to roll Abbott and said they needed to agitate for a change of leader without getting behind anyone in particular. Some on the list were surprises to me, but I agreed most seemed credible.

He was concerned about Julie's ambitions. I tried to assure him she had no interest in playing Lady Macbeth and, in my opinion, she wasn't convinced she should run for leader at all. Morrison said he thought he should succeed Abbott but didn't want to be seen to challenge him. He felt the right-wing commentators (by whom he meant Alan Jones and Ray Hadley) would never support me. Briggs disagreed because while the so-called right-wing base mightn't like me, they'd vote for me rather than Labor. Our experience in Wentworth – and every poll – showed that.

Morrison was pressing – almost urgent in his entreaties – for me to get on the 'roll Abbott' bandwagon. He wanted to commission Mark Textor to do some qualitative research to identify the issues we'd need to address on a change of leadership. I counselled him against this, as I recorded in my diary that evening.

> We have been very careful not to do anything that could be seen as disloyal to Abbott and to date have been essentially talking about what happens if and when Abbott falls over. Now Morrison has decided he wants to push him over and I am uncomfortable about that. Plan for the contingency yes, but do not have a hand in bringing it about.

From my point of view, these were dangerous times. Colleagues were becoming more and more anxious. A few days later two Queenslanders, Wyatt Roy and Mal Brough, both dropped in to my Sydney office to share their concerns. Both felt Abbott had to go. What Wyatt said was troubling. There was a state election going on and he'd been doorknocking. He reported that not only did the voters hate Abbott and Campbell Newman (the LNP premier) but they were warming to Shorten, seeing him as 'prime ministerial, electable and a safe pair of hands'.[11] That was bad news.

There was a strong southerly blowing early on Australia Day, and as I was leaving for the United States later in the morning, I got up early and paddled out to South Head. Once I'd put my kayak back on its rack, I checked my phone and saw a text message from Craig Laundy saying that Abbott had knighted Prince Philip. 'Very funny,' I texted back.

Craig called. 'No, mate, it's serious. Check the *Herald* website!' Which I duly did and to my astonishment it was true.

'Good grief. This guy is becoming a weird caricature of himself,' I wrote in my diary. My reaction was pretty typical.

While I was flying across the Pacific to officiate at 'G'day USA' events on the West Coast, my parliamentary colleagues were going to one Australia Day function after another and by the end of the day most of them were punch-drunk as their constituents berated them for the sheer craziness of our leader. Reinstating knights and dames was wacky enough, but Prince Philip? Hadn't Abbott pledged that knighthoods and damehoods would be reserved for 'pre-eminent Australians'?

Queenslanders were particularly horrified. Premier Campbell Newman was struggling in the pre-election polls but still tipped to hold on to government. To have this only days out from polling day was too much. Brisbane's *Courier-Mail* summed up the mood with a scathing front page depicting Abbott dressed as a court jester and the punchline, 'Jester PM's palace pleaser the act of a political fool, furious Libs declare.'[12]

Laundy reported to me that Steve Irons had told him Western Australia was shifting away from Abbott, but not to Julie. Morrison was working them up, apparently. That came as no surprise. Laundy and others, like Mal Brough and Wyatt Roy, all reported widespread unhappiness. The Prince Philip knighthood had been a tipping point. They reported that while Morrison was pushing his own barrow, most felt the best combination for a new team was me as PM, Scott as treasurer and Julie remaining deputy and Foreign minister. As Wyatt observed, Scott would be seen as too conservative, and not enough of a change from Abbott to make a difference. As for Julie, I knew that many colleagues, rightly or wrongly, doubted her ability to handle the economic agenda.[13]

While I was busy promoting Australia to the Californians, driving a Tesla for the first time, giving speeches about the geopolitics of the Asia Pacific region and catching Auntie Angela Lansbury onstage in *Blithe Spirit* at the Golden Gate Theatre in San Francisco, Julie Bishop was over on the East Coast doing the other half of the 'G'day USA' promotion. She had been in touch with Abbott about the growing storm and told me he was contrite about the knighthood but was determined to get on with business as usual. He was preparing a Press Club speech that would reveal new directions, he told her.

Abbott's Press Club speech was scheduled for Monday 2 February. In the week prior, his office was briefing out that he planned to do a backflip on the paid parental leave policy. This, coupled with knighting Prince Philip and the backflip on the Medicare co-payment, presented a federal government in disarray. Then to top it all off, on Saturday 31 January at the state election in Queensland, the one-term Campbell Newman LNP government was completely smashed with a swing to Labor of over 14 per cent and the loss of 36 seats.

That day, I wrote:

> *Everyone is blaming it in large measure on Abbott and with some justification. James McGrath observed to me during the week the LNP asked Abbott not to say or do anything that would put the feds back on the front page – so*

we had the Medicare backflip, followed by Sir Phil the Greek, followed by the foreshadowed PPL backflip.[14]

The downside of being in California while all this was going on was that I got little sleep: my evenings were taken up with increasingly anxious phone calls from Australia. Apart from that, I had time to listen, think and make notes.

This is how I saw the state of play over the weekend of the Queensland election disaster.

The mood in the party is pretty grim, based on my conversations today this is what is happening:

Julie Bishop – spoke to her at length. She is of a mind to be the leader, but only on the basis that I would do the Treasury. Problem is that while I would do that, and support her unreservedly as I told her on a true partnership basis, I just am not sure that it would work. … We discussed it at great length. … Her theory is that I will cover her for all the domestic economic stuff, and while I would do so to the best of my ability, my concern is that a minister cannot cover for the PM on issues that are so central to the debate and the public interest. Julie argues, while acknowledging she has misgivings, that the party membership would prefer her and that she was able to manage a domestic policy portfolio in Education with success.

Morrison; had several discussions with him. He is a little all over the shop and talks about being PM himself but seems to recognise it's too soon for him. He is very keen to engage Pyne and seems to think he has a lot of numbers, something I doubt. Christopher who has told me he thinks Abbott is completely terminal has, according to Morrison, floated a Morrison/Pyne ticket! Ye gods, that would really work.

The problem with Morrison it seems to me is that he wants to marginalise Julie. Now, I agree she is a risk as PM, but it is absurd as I point out to him to take her deputy role. Morrison thinks that the Right will demand as their price that he at least be deputy … but as I point out to him, the optics of doing Julie over are horrific and if he is Treasurer he is effectively the no. 2 anyway. Morrison makes one powerful point about Julie – she has been part of the leadership group for all of this period of political error. Now, the answer to that charge of course is that Abbott has ignored her and treated her with contempt. But what does that say about Julie? If she couldn't stand up to Peta Credlin and Tony Abbott, how is she going to go with the much greater pressures of the PM's office?

Later in the evening, spoke with Scott Briggs, who strongly agrees with me that Julie should not be marginalised. It is interesting how many of the men in the party really resent her. But the point about her numbers is fairly made. Where are they? The West Australians would not support her, at least most of them wouldn't. Cormann loathes her and both Ken Wyatt and Randall for example have assured me of their support. Christian Porter would go with Cormann, as would Simpkins, I imagine, although he is very right-wing and would probably prefer Abbott were it not for the polls.

Many colleagues called but the message was the same – Abbott should go. The hesitation about me was the one Morrison had raised – that the right-wing base, especially in the media, wouldn't accept me.

My diary helped me get my thoughts straight.

I should note that when people raise Julie with me, I consistently say that if the party room did want her to lead, and if she asked me to be Treasurer, which I am sure she would, I would do the job gladly, support her resolutely etc etc. JB's stated idea is that we would work as partners, something that could work with her and me as we get on very well.

Heffo in the midst of all this has called Lucy and told her that John Howard is very strongly of the view that I am the only alternative to Abbott …

There is a savage Miranda Devine piece about Credlin which does not miss. About as tough as it could be calling on her to resign. This is the last desperate throw of the Abbott lovers, demanding he throw Credlin out of the sleigh to slow down the approaching wolves … A few people – Scott, Greg Hunt, Macca – have raised the ETS question. I have said to them that in my view we should not change our climate policy at this time. Not that I think it is a good one, but that there has just been too much chopping and changing and we need things to settle. Let direct action work … Pity it ever got through the Senate but now that it's there, and it was a very prominent election promise we have to stick with it for a few years anyway.[15]

Having completed the official duties in Los Angeles, I returned to Australia on Monday 2 February. I summed up my thinking on the plane.

Abbott's position is untenable. He is so loathed in the community, his judgement so flawed and frankly crazy, he has to go. The public want him to go. Apparently the Ipsos poll shows only 30% think he will make it to the election, there was a similar figure from Essential recently, which means that if he is rolled while it is not pretty, it is not like Gillard ambushing Rudd which was a shock to everyone. The mood seems today more like, 'What are you lot waiting for?'

The new leadership team it is generally accepted is me, Julie and Scott. Scott's vaulting ambition aside, I don't think there is any material support for him as leader and I don't think it would work for us either. The real issue is who is PM between me and Jules. I don't think there are many people who don't believe I would be the better choice in terms of doing the job, but it may be the politics demand Julie lead. I am relaxed about that and would back her to the hilt.

The big question is mechanism. Julie told me before we left LA that she was going into a meeting with Abbott at 5 pm on Sunday night to tell him he should resign.[16]

Abbott's speech at the Press Club didn't resolve anything, although it did allow him formally to dump the PPL scheme – a disastrous captain's call of a policy and one that united all sides in opposition. We had a cabinet strategy meeting the following day. Beforehand, I met with Abbott to ask him what his plan was to get out of the hole we so plainly were in. He seemed completely un-self-aware and simply gave me the summary of his Press Club speech.

While most people felt that Abbott was finished and could lead us only to defeat, there was only a handful of members actively working on organising a spill. They were principally from the west and were all right-wingers – no fans of mine, or Julie for that matter.

All of the media attention was focused on me and Julie as potential successors to Abbott, although both of us disowned any plans to challenge. Morrison was vocal in his support for Abbott and publicly denied discussing leadership issues with me.[17] Of course, he'd done so on many occasions, and every indication was that he'd encouraged, if not masterminded, the spill itself.

The frenzy that followed was intense and, at times, hilarious. On Thursday 5 February, I was due to make a visit to the Central Coast to inspect the progress of the NBN with the member for Dobell, Karen McNamara, and after that hold a 'politics in the pub' at The Dam Hotel at North Wyong.

I've always preferred public transport wherever feasible, and the train ride up to the Central Coast is one of the best – snaking along the Hawkesbury River with sandstone ridges on either side. Imagine my surprise as I was taking in the view to learn that Ben Fordham on 2GB was announcing that Julie Bishop and I had held a secret meeting at my home in Point Piper. She'd arrived by water taxi at 11.30 that morning, he revealed. He was very confident of his facts. When my office denied the claim, he tweeted that I wouldn't deny it, and neither would Julie.

Then I had great fun tweeting pictures of myself on the train, select scenic views of the river and finally a triumphant arrival shot at Tuggerah station. Julie, who was in Penrith with Lindsay MP Fiona Scott, likewise tweeted pictures of herself not meeting with me! It became a rather weird Twitter war, which I ended with this tweet:'@BenFordham, you have to let this go. No I have not met @JulieBishopMP today and won't unless she comes to The Dam Hotel North Wyong tonight.'

Momentum began to build in the media. Like clockwork, Jeff Kennett went on air to say that Abbott's leadership was 'terminal'; Peter Costello published an op-ed that was deeply critical of the Prince Philip decision and the government generally; more backbenchers came out either calling for a spill, like Warren Entsch and Mal Brough, or for a major change in direction, like Luke Howarth and Arthur Sinodinos. Andrew Robb, the senior Victorian cabinet minister, reflected the concerns of his state's division over Abbott's leadership by stressing that his support for him was conditional on performance.

The next day Luke Simpkins, the member for Cowan, a big, gruff ex-military policeman, lodged a notice with the whip calling for a spill of the positions of leader and deputy leader of the Liberal Party. It was seconded by Don Randall, a veteran MP for Canning, and again another right-winger. They were strongly supported by Dennis Jensen, member for Tangney and another right-winger, and Steve Irons, member for Swan and a very close friend and supporter of Morrison. Jensen and Randall had been prominent in the move against me in 2009 and were very vocal climate change deniers – Jensen, who was a scientist, particularly so.

Simpkins's email calling for the spill of the leadership underlined where he and his seconder stood on climate change: 'The last time this outpouring of concern happened was when we were being led to support the Rudd Government's ETS and faced with this erosion of our base support we acted.'

A number of other members were active in promoting support for the spill, including Wyatt Roy, Mal Brough and Warren Entsch from Queensland and Arthur Sinodinos and Craig Laundy from New South Wales.

The usual polls were done, all showing how unpopular Abbott was and what a positive difference a change to me as leader would make. A Seven News ReachTEL poll showed us behind 45:55 under Abbott but ahead 54:46 under me as leader. The media frenzy continued. Rupert Murdoch tweeted in support of Abbott, while over at *The Sunday Telegraph* 'a new 11th hour deal' was floated to install me as treasurer to head off the spill.[18] That was news to me, but in the feverish environment of leadership spill rumours, kite-flying – wild speculation – abounds and every story is too good to check.

The media were staking out our home over the weekend before the spill and rather than walk into a wall of cameras I made a seaborne escape on my kayak over to Darling Point, where I met with Sally Cray, David Bold and Jon Dart to discuss the week ahead. It was fun watching breathless TV reporters standing in front of our house and saying, 'Malcolm Turnbull has not left his Point Piper mansion ...'

Julie and I were both due to attend a fundraiser for the Bellevue Hill branch of the Liberal Party in the gardens of a grand residence in Woollahra on Sunday 8 February and we had to struggle through a press pack to get in. Abbott had just announced that he'd bring forward the date of the spill from Tuesday to 9 o'clock Monday morning and a number of colleagues, including Arthur Sinodinos, panned him for it. He clearly didn't want the spillites to have any time to build up any more momentum.

After chatting with the local Liberals and their supporters, Julie and I adjourned to a private room in the mansion for a chat. Neither Julie nor Morrison trusted each other, so I was finding myself a clearing house for discussions between them. Tired of that, I rang Scott and the three of us had a discussion. Each of us assured the others we planned to vote against the spill, as cabinet ministers should, but then canvassed what would happen if the spill was carried or if Abbott, for some reason or other, decided to declare his position vacant. Morrison and, to a lesser extent, Julie were keen that I should publicly state that if the spill was carried I'd stand as leader. They both thought that would encourage waverers to vote for the spill.

I asked them what they would do. Morrison by this stage was on board with the team being me as PM, Julie deputy and Foreign minister and himself as treasurer. Julie was too, but played her cards close to her chest with Morrison on the phone; she didn't trust him at all.

I told them that if the leadership was vacant, I would nominate, that I doubted whether anyone imagined I wouldn't do so, but going public about it would be effectively making this a leadership challenge by me against Abbott. I reminded Scott that the spill was being called by his friends, not mine, and reminded Julie that this appeared to emanate from her state, not mine.

Early on the morning of the spill, 9 February, I wrote:

> *If the spill succeeds and I win the consequent ballot, which I believe I would, then I don't have blood on my hands. On the other hand, if it does not succeed and Abbott limps on for a few more weeks or months, or perhaps only days, there would be no question of me going to the backbench or being somehow or other tainted with stalking etc.*
>
> *Many colleagues and wise heads have counselled me to be low key in this way. The universal consensus is that he is utterly finished and that is why some people have argued against the spill's timing on the basis that Abbott should be allowed to 'burn down to the water line' so that they 'are begging to have you as leader'.*

The News Corp papers that morning were interesting – staunchly defending Abbott, with Benson on the front page of *The Daily Telegraph* predicting a 'voter revolt' if Abbott was dumped. Yet the Newspoll was showing me far ahead as preferred Liberal leader over Abbott 64:25 and, most ominously, the government behind Labor 43:57 and Abbott behind Shorten as preferred PM 30:48.

The spill was defeated 61 votes to 39. This was much worse than Abbott had anticipated. His office had been briefing the press gallery there were only 15 likely votes for a spill (out of a party room of 102).

The cabinet met that evening and Abbott tried to get on with the agenda without any political discussion. I insisted that we have one, and the advisers were asked to leave. Everyone was very direct. I reminded the cabinet that we were now worse off than Gillard because, given the state of the Senate, we couldn't legislate and people were already writing us off.

Abbott plaintively said repeatedly, 'I just need time to prove that I can recover.'

The mood around the table was about as bleak as it could be. Dutton was particularly blunt. 'Tony, you can't expect us to go over the cliff with you. Malcolm is the only alternative and if you can't improve, then we expect you to make an orderly transition.' You could have heard a pin drop. But as the meeting wore on, it was plain that was the sentiment of the room.

Everyone then turned to get back to work, in the hope, but not expectation, that things would improve.

CHAPTER 23

A very dangerous
prime minister

The weekend after the failed spill motion, there were a number of serious leaks from both the National Security Committee and the Expenditure Review Committee (ERC) of cabinet. I was not a member of either. However, the most troubling leak was that Abbott had proposed sending 3500 ground combat troops to Iraq in support of the anti-ISIL mission.

This was at a time when President Obama wasn't sending ground troops and when ISIL were posting increasingly brutal videos of cruel executions. It was presumably designed to show that Abbott had a muscular foreign policy in contrast to what he regarded as the flabbiness of Obama's. Credlin, who more often than not spoke for Abbott, had described Obama as the lamest of lame ducks to a group of journalists the previous year.[1]

Fortunately, senior Defence people managed to head this wild idea off, just as they'd headed off Abbott's plan to send armed troops to Ukraine to guard the MH17 crash site. But it reinforced the suspicion that our problem with Abbott wasn't simply electoral unpopularity – he was crazy. And was that surprising? He had, after all, been nicknamed the 'Mad Monk' at university.

The anti-Credlin campaign began to revive. Increasingly, it was being driven by conservatives who felt that the only way to avoid my becoming leader again was to 'save' Abbott from the domination of Peta Credlin. Of course, there was probably no minister who had less insight into the Abbott office than I did. I rarely spoke with Abbott, less frequently with Credlin, saw him in his office only on a few occasions during his time as PM.

Abbott continued to double down on national security, doing his utmost to whip up anxiety and fear about terrorism all the while stoking anti-Muslim prejudice. His speech on 23 February on security was almost hysterical: 'We have seen the beheadings, the mass executions, the crucifixions and the sexual slavery in the name of religion ... it is the demand to submit – or die. We have seen our fellow Australians ... succumb to the lure of this death cult.' He went on to chastise Muslim leaders: 'I've often heard Western leaders describe Islam as "a religion of peace". I wish more Muslim leaders would say that more often, and mean it.'[2]

If the object of terrorism is to terrify the population, Abbott's speech, like so many of his public statements on security, was certainly assisting. And by targeting Muslims in the way he did, he was similarly helping the terrorists; after all, their pitch to young Muslims was, 'They hate you; they will never accept you; you aren't really Australian; join us and strike back against the infidels who hate you and your religion.'

While stoking up fear on the security front was Abbott's positive agenda, if you can call it that, the so-called conservative commentators in the media now renewed their campaign against me. I called Ray Hadley on 3 March and asked him why he was attacking me so intensely. I pointed out that the leaks against Abbott were all from places like the NSC and the ERC, to which I had no access. Hadley's response was, 'But you want to be PM. Why don't you pledge never to run for PM?'

Their strategy was pretty plain – they saw me as the most viable alternative to Abbott and so in the absence of having much good they could say about him, better to pre-emptively destroy my public standing. It was the same tactic they'd used in 2014.

I went up to Queensland for an extended visit and gave a speech on 'Responsible Economic Leadership' at The Brisbane Club on 11 March. Without parting company with any government policies, I set out a distinctly different, positive and optimistic approach to the economy and the budget. I talked about how Australia, thanks to progressive income taxes and means-testing of social payments, among other things, is a much more equal society than countries like the USA or the UK. But like many other developed nations around the world, we were under pressure to reduce budget deficits, to compete effectively with emerging market rivals and to manage ageing workforces.

I talked about how we'd secure our future prosperity by embracing the future, not running from it. Whereas Abbott and Hockey were full of budgetary gloom and national security doom, scaring the pants off people, I wanted to project a vision of opportunity for Australia, the 12th-largest economy in the world.[3] We were creative, innovative and thought globally, which put us in a strong position to succeed in an era of such rapid change.

The decade-long boom came to an end with a slump in coal prices in 2013 and iron ore in 2014 – but as the cyclical rise in tax revenues receded, the permanent spending commitments and tax concessions made in the boom years continued, leaving us with a structural deficit, according to the International Monetary Fund (IMF), of about 3 per cent of GDP.

Government spending was growing faster than revenues and, as I explained to the audience, that's why the 2014 budget had been one of austerity. Loyally, if implausibly, I argued the budget was not so much a failure as unfulfilled, because the savings measures hadn't been able to get through the Senate, and I tagged Labor with the responsibility for this. However, I acknowledged that it was the Coalition's failure to explain the need for cuts in spending that was at the heart of the political problem.

It was time for an alternative and positive approach to economic reform. 'At the heart of this issue is confidence,' I said. 'It is critical that the public have confidence economic management is in safe and competent hands. That means policies need to be carefully thought through, painstakingly explained and be robust enough to withstand rigorous policy debate.'

The time for spin and slogans was over. The Australian people wanted all of us in public life to respect them by laying out the challenges we face clearly and accurately, not insulting them with exaggeration or oversimplification.

Meanwhile, Abbott was hitting the headlines with yet more weird behaviour in Tasmania (eating a raw onion with its skin on) and Hockey was suing Fairfax for defamation and having a hard time in the witness box.

The mood on the backbench was getting bleaker and bleaker, both about Abbott and Hockey, and several of my supporters were encouraging me to formally challenge Abbott before the budget and the NSW election. Mike Baird, while still favourite to win, was being weighed down by Abbott and the consequent brand damage to the Liberal Party.

The two leading younger figures on the right were Dutton and Cormann and I checked in with both of them. Dutton told me he believed I was the only alternative to Abbott. He completely dismissed Julie (they loathed each other), and told me that both Abbott and Hockey should go – Hockey to be replaced by Morrison. Dutton said I needed to work to win over more of his colleagues in the hard right. On timing, he said they would need to suffer more from Abbott's ineptitude and I shouldn't challenge until June. Cormann, on the other hand, while of the same opinion on leadership, was more open to a pre-budget challenge. He felt it would help Mike Baird, who could lock into the relief rally that would follow Abbott's removal.[4]

As it happened there was an improvement in Newspoll for Abbott in the week of the state election, a Baird bounce some speculated, and I resisted those urging me to challenge.

Over the Easter break, Lucy and I spent a week in New York with Daisy, James and 18-month-old Jack, who definitely won the good baby prize for his cheerful calm on the long flight from Sydney.

The New York visit turned out to be a precious family holiday, a time of calm before an even more intense political storm. I wrote in my diary on 12 April:

> *Very sad today as it is my last one in NY. Jack I should note has taken to calling me not just Baba, but now 'Happy Baba'. We are not sure why and speculate he relates it to Happy Birthday. But Daisy gave me the biggest hug yesterday and said, 'I love it when Jack calls you Happy Baba because I remember when you were sad Baba and I don't want you ever to be sad again.'*
>
> *Jack's vocabulary gets better and better – but I will always treasure some of his first words. In particular 'wow', which he says often, and 'oh no', which he says as a sort of commentary and not just when things go wrong, and of course 'hooray', which he normally says accompanied by throwing his arms up in the air – he was doing lots of 'hoorays' when we were watching the seals at the zoo in Central Park. He also picks up our words. He likes saying 'hang on', which he says is what Baba says a lot, and when you ask him what Gaga says he replies, 'I wuv oo', which is very sweet.*[5]

The 2015 budget went down fairly well; at least, much better than its predecessor. Whereas 69 per cent of people thought the 2014 budget left them worse off, that number was only 30 per cent with the 2015 budget.[6] The dumping of the PPL was a plus, but its replacement was designed to ensure that women who received paid parental leave from their employer did not also receive the government paid parental leave based on the minimum wage. Hockey and Abbott described women who did so as double dipping and rorters, which produced the inevitable, and deserved, outrage. Overall, the government's polling went backwards after the budget, although not by much. But the government was drifting, lacking an agenda. As Arthur Sinodinos said to me, 'Everything is just about getting the prime minister through another week.'[7]

When Abbott gave his terrifying speech about terrorism back in February, he'd foreshadowed taking action to strip citizenship from terrorists, but no detailed proposals had seen the light of day. Then, at the end of a fairly routine cabinet meeting on 25 May, Abbott said he proposed to introduce legislation that would not only give the Immigration minister the power to remove the Australian citizenship of dual nationals who fight for terrorist groups but to further give the minister the power to remove the Australian citizenship of people who 'could' become a citizen of another country. No papers were presented to the cabinet to support this. In the course of what became a stormy debate, it transpired that a discussion paper dealing with these proposals had been prepared but shared only with Dutton, Abbott and Brandis – and George wasn't comfortable with its content. Nobody else had seen it, not even Julie – who, as Foreign minister and a member of the NSC, should have been centrally involved in anything that involved stripping people of their Australian citizenship.

After the meeting, I noted in my diary:

> A telling exchange was when Barnaby said to Dutton, 'If we don't have enough evidence to charge someone with terrorism, how can we have enough evidence to cancel their citizenship?' Dutton replied, 'That's the whole point. We don't need as much evidence; it's an administrative decision and we don't have to justify it.'[8]

Everything about this proposal underlined the dysfunction of the Abbott government. Removing an Australian's citizenship was a momentous matter. Proposing that a minister, without any judicial process or oversight, could of his own motion strip someone of their citizenship – their most fundamental civic identity – well, surely that deserved a fully informed cabinet discussion. And yet, here we were almost as an afterthought, being asked to sign off on an idea with which the attorney-general didn't agree and was apparently the subject of a discussion paper which only three members of the cabinet had actually seen.

I asked Abbott if this matter had been briefed out to *The Daily Telegraph* – Abbott said of course it hadn't. But the following morning (26 May) Neil Doorley and Simon Benson, the latter Abbott and Credlin's preferred mouthpiece at News Corporation, had an exclusive that read:

> Prime Minister Tony Abbott will announce today, after cabinet last night approved the policy, that a bill will be introduced before the end of June that would strip dual national terrorist sympathisers of their Australian citizenship.
>
> Included in the bill, yet to be drafted, will be controversial measures based on the UK model to also strip nationality from Australians who hold sole Australian citizenship but only if they have legal access to citizenship of another country – getting around international law preventing countries from making people stateless.[9]

Of course, that turned out to be wrong. The proposal didn't go into a bill because cabinet deferred a decision. But crucially, Benson had been briefed *before* the meeting even started at 7 pm, and by the time it ended without the outcome Abbott wanted, it was too late to change the story.

Then the substance of the cabinet discussion was immediately briefed out to Credlin's favoured journalists to paint me and Julie in particular as soft on terrorism. Samantha Maiden's column on 30 May lampooned my concern about 'the rule of law' and highlighted Abbott's strong stand on revoking the citizenship of terrorists as a sign of how he was winning back support in the party room.

Indeed, the mover of the February spill, Luke Simpkins, was the lead author (with 37 signatures) of a letter from the backbench demanding that Abbott not give into the petty, legalistic concerns raised by me and Julie – one of the letter signers was anonymously quoted by Simon Benson (naturally) in *The Daily Telegraph*: 'Malcolm and Julie have found themselves isolated now. They have guaranteed that Tony will lead the Government to the election.'[10]

This was at the core of the dysfunction of the Abbott cabinet. Abbott's own office, largely through Credlin, shared cabinet discussions and cabinet papers with the media, principally *The Daily Telegraph* and *The Australian*. If the PMO was leaking from cabinet, why would other ministers feel constrained?

But from Abbott's point of view, the cabinet row was working perfectly for him. He figured there was only electoral upside in being as tough on terror as he could be – even if it meant dispensing with technical niceties like the rule of law. And putting his two leadership rivals on the 'over-educated lawyers soft on terrorism' side of the debate was perfect.

Neither Julie nor I backed away from our principles on this. Indeed, on the Wednesday of that week, 3 June, I was pressed on the issue by the media while campaigning in Queanbeyan. I decided to take Abbott's attempt to wedge us head-on:

> Some people like to suggest that they are tougher on terrorism or tougher on national security than others. Honest people, knowledgeable people, can have very different views about what the right measures are on national security, and the right balance between, say, citizenship and national security … it is not good enough that laws simply be tough, this is not a sort of bravado issue, it is that they have got to be the right laws.[11]

At the end of the week, Dutton revealed to David Speers on Sky News that he intended to strip the citizenship of dual-national Australian citizens resident in Australia whom he, the minister, suspected of being involved in terrorism.

The next morning, I spoke with Brandis. He agreed with me that Dutton's plan was crazy and said the High Court would strain every sinew to knock it out as being unconstitutional. 'Dutton is a Queensland cop who has always found the third limb of government – the judiciary – an inconvenience,' George said. 'This is an opportunity for him to avoid it altogether.'[12] We agreed he should urgently get advice from the solicitor-general.

Dutton was freelancing, no doubt with Abbott and Credlin's authority, but what he was canvassing wasn't just unconstitutional but hadn't been approved by the cabinet. Because of the shambolic manner in which this policy initiative had been floated, a fundamental constitutional requirement was overlooked. Our constitution decrees in chapter III that the judicial power of the Commonwealth is vested in the courts, and the courts alone. It means that the executive branch cannot impose penalties or fines. Plainly, depriving an Australian citizen of their birthright is a very severe penalty, and what Dutton was proposing would have meant the minister had the power, entirely at his own discretion, to exile an Australian citizen who may well have been born here. It was almost unthinkable – but Abbott saw it as his lifeline.

I summed up my thoughts of the week and the issue in my diary on Friday 5 June: 'I am coming to the conclusion that Abbott is stripping us of freedoms which we should be fighting to retain, and his wedge politics are only about one thing – keeping his job.'

But, as I'd done on other issues, while trying to restrain Abbott from bad policy, I also offered a solution. Section 35 of the Citizenship Act, I pointed out, already provided that an Australian citizen, also a citizen of another country, who took up arms against Australia in armed conflict lost their Australian citizenship automatically. So, I explained, if an Australian soldier who was a dual national had deserted in the Korean War and fought for North Korea, he'd have ceased to be an Australian citizen from the moment he took up arms for the DPRK. It wouldn't be too much of a stretch to extend that section to people who take up arms with ISIL. That would certainly cover the circumstances of most Australians fighting for ISIL in the Middle East and ensure they couldn't ever come back to Australia.

A series of tense encounters followed with Dutton, his secretary of the Department of Immigration and Border Protection, Mike Pezzullo, and Abbott's national security adviser, Andrew Shearer. All insisted that the citizenship revocation plan was supported by advice from the solicitor-general in August the previous year.

Dutton and Pezzullo were dripping with contempt, almost sneering at me, as Dutton replied, 'Why should we take your advice, Malcolm, when we have rolled gold advice from the Solicitor-General?'[13]

Immediately after this brush-off, Brandis showed me fresh advice he'd just received from the solicitor-general, Justin Gleeson. It confirmed what I'd told Abbott: the revocation of citizenship by a minister is a very heavy penalty – exile in fact – and cannot be constitutionally imposed other than by a court. Gleeson also said that the advice he'd given on a citizenship revocation proposal of Scott Morrison's in 2014 had been premised on the person being first convicted by a court of a serious terrorism offence.

So Dutton, Shearer and Pezzullo had all either lied to me or, more likely, didn't understand the advice they'd received – they didn't have 'strong legal advice' that their proposal was constitutional at all.

I wrote again to Abbott asking that the matter come back to cabinet, pointing out that we now had advice from the solicitor-general that the proposal would be struck down in the High Court.

Abbott and Dutton's scant regard for the rule of law, or due process, underlined the extent to which neither of them could reasonably be described as conservatives. A conservative values and seeks to defend established institutions – and none are more important than the courts. Their rationale was, just as Brandis had observed, that requiring evidence to be proved in courts was too much trouble.

Finally, common sense (and the constitution) prevailed, and the citizenship revocation law proceeded as I'd proposed by way of amending the existing provision in section 35. The press gallery wrote this up as 'a win' for me over Abbott – a pathetic reminder of how much the news media are part of the political problem where personalities are more important than policies and every political debate or issue is reported on like a football match or a horse race.

Arthur and I reflected on it all on 21 June when he dropped around in the evening and we chatted for about an hour. I wrote in my diary that night:

> Arthur, like me, believes Abbott is a dangerous prime minister, a threat to the nation and its security. The question is how and when can we move him on? Not yet, but we need a change. We talked about Morrison and his relentless ambition, Arthur thinks Morrison has been anointed by Abbott as his successor and is likely to try to protect Abbott from any threats for the time being. I said I thought that unlikely, given Morrison had been the prime mover behind the spill in February. Anyway, bleak times ahead.

When I spoke to Pyne the following day, he recounted how Abbott had rung around the cabinet to persuade them not to agree to my call for the citizenship matter to come back to cabinet.

There was a series of terrorist attacks overseas at this time – in France and Tunisia among other places. Abbott took the opportunity to once again ramp up his rhetoric, this time claiming in front of 10 Australian flags that ISIL were 'coming after us'. At every turn he sought to heighten fear and anxiety. It seemed to work for him; the polls improved. It had the added benefit that I appeared to be on the 'soft' or 'wet' lawyers' side of the argument, worrying about trivial issues like the constitution and the rule of law.

• • •

On 7 July, I spoke at the Sydney Institute on the 800th anniversary of Magna Carta about the rule of law in the digital age. It gave me the opportunity to set out a considered, authentically Liberal response to the challenge of terrorism, one which rejected, without breaking into open conflict, Abbott's multi-flagged terror hysteria.

> The genius of liberal democracy is that the rule of law, which empowers the majority, also constrains it. A society where the majority can trample over the rights of the minority is nothing more than a tyranny. We often hear claims that in times of threat, security trumps liberty, or as Cicero put it, 'In the midst of arms, the laws are silent.'
>
> In Menzies' day, our democratic way of life was threatened by two totalitarian ideologies – Soviet Communism and fascism. One was defeated in battle in 1945, the other expired, largely from its own contradictions, 25 years ago. China, the last nominally communist superpower, does not seek to export its way of government.
>
> But Da'esh is not Hitler's Germany, Tojo's Japan or Stalin's Russia. Its leaders dream that they, like the Arab armies of the seventh and eighth century, will sweep across the Middle East into Europe itself.
>
> They predict that before long they will be stabling their horses in the Vatican.
>
> Well, Idi Amin wasn't the King of Scotland either.
>
> We should be careful not to say or do things which can be seen to add credibility to those delusions …
>
> In 1939 Robert Menzies, Prime Minister, was leading Australia into a war against Adolf Hitler, a foe whose march across Europe must have seemed nearly irresistible. This was an existential threat. And Menzies introduced a National Security Bill that gave extensive powers to the government to control the economy and much of Australia's daily life in what was to become a total war effort.
>
> His warning to the House of Representatives should resonate down the years to all of us, especially those in the party he founded …
>
> 'The greatest tragedy that could overcome a country would be for it to fight a successful war in defence of liberty and to lose its own liberty in the process.'

CHAPTER 24

'It was all a bit of a shock': leader again

Abbott was weirdly upbeat at the cabinet meeting of 14 July, and urged us all to be careful not to become complacent!

> *Pyne pointed out that complacency wasn't the problem, anyone who thought we were doing well couldn't read or count. He noted that unemployment was 8% in SA, and that the blame was all being placed on the feds. Morrison made similar points – we are behind somewhere between 4 and 6 points and that's with the opposition leader in terrible trouble [in the Hayden Royal Commission into Trade Union Governance and Corruption], so what's to be complacent about??*[1]

In my diary, I noted the characteristically droll text exchange I had with Christopher the following day:

Christopher Pyne: Do you think the rest of the cabinet pretended that the political climate was going so well on Tuesday because they are nervous about a reshuffle at the end of the year? Or is this level of delusion just easier for people than facing the reality?

Malcolm Turnbull: I have no idea. I felt like I had missed the pre party and quite a lot of booze. Unbelievable delusions. We must not fall victim to complacency!!!! I would have thought clinical depression was more of a threat.

Christopher Pyne: I felt totally disconnected from the government. I was wondering if maybe I am unsuited to this nonsense. It is like a meeting of the Chinese Politburo during the Great Leap Forward or Cultural Revolution, where in spite of the obvious catastrophe of both, the meetings all ended with communiques in praise of Mao Zedong Thought and more of the same. I'm quite depressed actually.[2]

Pyne's wicked message wasn't the only black humour of 15 July. The Department of Finance's report on members' entitlements revealed that Speaker Bronwyn Bishop had chartered a helicopter to go from Melbourne to Geelong so she could attend a Liberal Party fundraiser. Bronwyn, naturally, defended herself and truculently asserted that this was fully within her entitlements.

Bronwyn's self-importance and vanity was, even by political standards, off the charts and so initially everyone doubled up laughing at the absurdity of Madame Speaker descending out of the sky like a Valkyrie to entertain a gaggle of Liberal Party supporters at a Geelong golf course. But as she dug in to defend her 'entitlement' and as Abbott rushed to her defence, the helicopter trip came to represent everything people disliked about Canberra – wasteful and out of touch.

More examples of her extravagant use of entitlements came out over the weeks that followed. Abbott – initially rock-solid in his support of her – started to back away, at one point saying that she was now on probation. Bronwyn saw this as the ultimate treachery. After all, hadn't Tony described himself as the political love child of John Howard and Bronwyn Bishop?

I travelled out to South Geelong myself on 29 July to visit Sarah Henderson, the member for Corangamite, and (as I always did) took the train there from Melbourne. Cross-examined by the media, I assured them that 'there was no aerial component' in my travel, which had cost $8.26.

I also chronicled my journey on Twitter: 'Trains and trams are fun. Meet new people. See new sights. Avoid road rage. A conductor checked my myki to confirm I had tapped on. So flattered he thought I was fit enough to have been able to leap over the barrier.'

The next day I received a rather terse message from Abbott: 'Mate, I think it would be best if no-one said anything about Bronwyn today. She obviously made a serious error of judgement but has sought to make amends by repaying the money with a penalty.'

Julie, then in New York, messaged to say Abbott wanted to know if I would take the Washington post she had raised with me. I replied, 'Regarding the Washington job – have thought about it and discussed with Lucy but we must decline. Very kind to think of us of course.'[3]

Despite Shorten's bad few weeks in the witness box, the polls, and the mood in the electorate, started to turn against Abbott once more.

Craig Laundy called me on the 20th to report that the mood among the backbench was back to where it had been in February.

The next day we were all rocked by the sudden and unexpected death of Don Randall, the member for Canning. His funeral was 10 days later, on the 31st, and I flew over to Perth to attend it. Don's friends were mostly from the conservative wing of the party and their gloom was palpable. Craig was right: in terms of sentiment, they were back to February, and Abbott's inability to cut Bronwyn loose was being seen as yet another failure of leadership and judgement. As I wrote in my diary: 'Almost every day brings a new revelation of another expenses rort – the latest being to charter a plane to fly to Nowra to do a fundraiser for Ann Sudmalis.'[4]

Finally, after three weeks of bleeding, and with Coalition MPs threatening to vote against Bishop on a no-confidence motion, Abbott prevailed on her to resign as speaker on 2 August. Abbott tried to suggest that it was the system (which he proposed to review) that had failed, not her – nonsense that I couldn't parrot when I was asked about it: 'Well, I think there are some areas of ambiguity in the entitlements system, but the fundamental principle is one of common sense ... it was Bronwyn's decision. The helicopter was her call, right? She didn't have to get a helicopter to Geelong.'[5]

Warren Entsch, and others, had been preparing a private members' bill to legalise same-sex marriage, on the basis that he expected there'd be a free vote on the matter. Warren brought it up at the Liberal Party meeting of Tuesday 11 August. There was insufficient time to conclude the discussion and Abbott announced the issue would now go back to cabinet, which would bring a proposed course of action to the party room. However, within hours Abbott called a joint party room meeting for later in the day, to begin at 3.15. With one short break to hear Jo Lindgren's maiden speech in the Senate, the meeting went for six hours.

It was probably the most shambolic example of policy on the run any of us had ever seen. It began with Pyne accusing Abbott of the equivalent of branch stacking by including the Nationals in the meeting: whether an issue is a free vote or not is a matter for each party under the Coalition Agreement. So, the only forum to debate this issue, if it was to be debated at all, was the Liberal Party room. But Abbott knew the Nats were overwhelmingly against same-sex marriage and could be relied upon to block a free vote, so they stayed.

Like many others, I argued that we should have a free vote in accordance with our tradition as a party – indeed, every other controversial amendment to family legislation (including the Family Law Act itself in 1975) had been a free vote. However, the conservatives definitely had the numbers and it was obvious most of the room didn't favour a free vote. But, as I pointed out, this undermined the whole concept of a free vote, which was to allow those in the minority to vote contrary to the majority on issues that particularly touched on faith or morals.

Several speakers proposed that the question be referred to the people in a plebiscite. Of course, the politics of the plebiscite was simply to allow us to kick the issue beyond the next election and to be able to campaign at the election on the basis that 'everyone will have their say'. The conservatives also genuinely believed that they could run a successful scare campaign against same-sex marriage in a popular vote.

Some, including Joe Hockey and Scott Morrison, argued for a constitutional amendment, presumably because they saw that the requirement for a double majority – of voters nationally and of states – would make it even harder to achieve marriage equality. Scott explained to me a few days later, 'I don't want gay marriage. And because referendums are almost always defeated, I think that's a good way to ensure it never happens.'

It wasn't clear at all what the room thought of these ideas. The observations were so contradictory, with speakers often changing their minds in mid-speech, that drawing a consensus out of the meeting was impossible.

Late in the evening, after the meeting, Abbott decreed that there'd be no free vote in this parliament. However, in the next parliament – after the next election – members wouldn't be bound by the party position on the matter and the issue would be put to the people in a popular vote.

As more polling results poured in showing we were way behind Labor and that I was way ahead of Abbott as preferred Liberal leader, my supporters became more anxious that we get on, make the challenge and set a new course. Morrison's position was intriguing. A year ago, he'd been the most anxious of all to move on Abbott but now he was being more circumspect. Many of us thought he was hoping that Abbott would fall over and anoint him, a fellow social conservative, as his successor.

After I spoke with him the following week, on 17 August, I made this note in my diary:

Had a long chat with Scott Morrison after QT; broadly speaking, he says that TA cannot possibly lead us to victory, but that he feels he cannot challenge him. At one point, with hypocrisy dripping from every syllable, he said, 'I cannot raise my hand against the Lord's anointed.' This from the guy who basically set up the February spill. He concludes by saying that while he would not help a challenge, he would not hinder one, but was evasive about what he meant by that. He is clearly playing his cards close to his chest on this, but I suspect he will want to sit on the fence.

The cabinet meeting that evening had been particularly colourful when after a little political discussion, the subject of same-sex marriage came up. Whether for or against same-sex marriage, everyone was appalled by the chaotic evening in the party room and the absence of any cabinet deliberation.

Abbott contended the problems of last week had been the result of ministerial ill-discipline. I responded by saying that he had single-handedly created last week's horror by dispensing with cabinet government. I noted our meeting of 7 July [in his Sydney office], where we discussed the issue and had agreed we did NOT want it to be an issue at the next election. I said that this is obviously a difficult issue for political handling which should have been discussed in cabinet. I said that this sidelining of cabinet, poor process, inadequate discussion had resulted in the citizenship fiasco and now he was doing it again. I noted that in the Liberal Party meeting last Tuesday, he had said the issue would come to the leadership group, the cabinet and THEN back to the party room and then he had called a sudden joint party meeting without the knowledge of most of the cabinet and indeed leadership group. Abbott got angrier and angrier and at one point said, 'If you don't like the way I run the cabinet –' I interjected and said, 'You aren't running the cabinet at all. You are ignoring it, suspending it.'

'Well, if you don't like it then why don't you ...'

'Yes?' I asked. To my disappointment he didn't invite me to resign or sack me.

Pyne supported me, and while I had been calm Abbott became quite heated. At that point the discussion was brought to an end because the back-bench committee chairs were waiting to join us. The conclusion of the cabinet

(it was the only practical outcome) was that members would not be bound to
the existing policy after this parliament and that it would be put to the people
in the course of the next parliament, terms and details to follow.[6]

The same-sex marriage debacle was the last straw for many senior members of the government. Andrew Robb asked to see me on 20 August, the final sitting day of that week, and told me that Abbott was finished, he had to go, and that I was the only viable candidate. 'I shored him up in February, but won't do so again,' he said.[7]

Michael Kroger, the president of the Liberal Party in Victoria, phoned to encourage me to challenge Abbott. I was surprised to get his call; he was from the right of the party. He told me that they were polling 41:59 in Victoria and that with Abbott as PM the party would be wiped out. He said I was the only alternative. I summarised the conversation in a message to James McGrath, who was helping me as I considered whether, and when, to move:

> Spoke to Kroger today. Very hot to oust Abbott. I was v discreet and did not tell him how I thought anyone was leaning. He assumes [Senator Scott] Ryan is for Abbott for example. I didn't disabuse him. He says he can help with [Michael] Sukkar, Josh [Frydenberg] and some others. His support is pragmatic and real but he is very chatty. He thinks Morrison is up and running – the Abbott people are obviously talking this up but as you know Scomo has given me some undertakings to the effect that he will not run but will not prop up Abbott, as has Robb. Anyway just FYI – he canvassed the idea that [Matthew] Guy[8] and [Stephen] Marshall[9] jointly call for Abbott to go, thinks that would help them both. I am not sure. FYI Tom Harley said to me you had told him Kroger leaning to Scomo. As it happens, Kroger being pragmatic thinks Scomo would not help them in Victoria one iota hence his enthusiasm for a switch to me.[10]

A by-election had been called in Don Randall's old seat of Canning and a young former Special Air Services (SAS) officer, Andrew Hastie, had been selected as the Liberal candidate. While time would prove my trust in him was misplaced, he presented as an ideal candidate. The Abbott factor, however, was weighing heavily on the seat. Randall had held it with a 62 per cent majority in the last election, but the first polls were showing it as neck and neck, with the Liberal Party just behind in some polls and just ahead in others. On leadership, the Canning voters were pretty much in line with the rest of Australia, strongly favouring me as a better PM over Tony Abbott, Julie Bishop or Scott Morrison.

While I was heading over to WA to campaign in Canning, the Sunday papers contained a story by Samantha Maiden that Abbott was planning to replace Hockey with Morrison in a bid to stave off another spill.[11]

Barnaby had his own theory on this story. After the cabinet meeting on 1 September, he 'ventured the opinion Credlin is trying to get on the Scott Morrison bandwagon so she can be his chief of staff after Abbott is dumped'.[12] I thought it was a bit wild, but who was I to argue with Barnaby; after all, he was in the inner circle and I wasn't.

I spent most of this week in Queensland on NBN business. Yet even in the midst of telecommunications minutiae, the weirdness of Abbott intruded: he confided in Alan Jones that ISIL – who boasted about their atrocities – were worse than the Nazis, 'who had sufficient sense of shame to try and hide it'.[13] So, it was to the Nazis' credit that they tried to conceal the concentration camps?

By this stage, the only senior member of the cabinet unsure what to do was Julie Bishop. Our numerous discussions about the leadership invariably became circular. She loathed Abbott and wanted him gone. But she felt she should stand. 'Okay,' I'd say, 'I will support you.'

But Julie would then say, 'If you don't stand, Morrison could come through the middle and win. And he is almost as bad as Abbott.'

'Okay,' I'd respond, 'you don't stand and I will.'

'But then if I don't stand, I'll be like Peter Costello and never have a go. But if I do stand, I look like Julia Gillard.' And around and around it went.

Julie had, and has, no greater supporter in politics than me and I understood her dilemma. I think the truth is that while she'd have liked to be leader, she knew she didn't have the support she deserved.

All of these discussions were taking place under the tightest secrecy. I was keeping my intentions to myself, receiving not transmitting. The other question was timing and, more specifically, whether a challenge should occur before or after the Canning by-election. It was put to me by a number of my supporters that even though a change of leader before Canning would improve our position, and certainly help us retain the seat, there would nonetheless be a swing against the government – it was a by-election after all. Not an ideal way to start a new government.

> *Ian Macfarlane was on board, as were the moderates. Pyne double-checked with Morrison, who assured me he wouldn't stand in my way, and as for timing believed I should move when I wanted to. Some of the moderates were worried that if we won Canning, even by a whisker, Abbott would talk it up as a great victory and we'd lose momentum for the change.*[14]

David Petraeus was visiting Australia and came to lunch on Sunday 6 September. Astute as always, he asked me how the political situation was developing. 'I think I am approaching the up or out stage of my career, General,' I replied.

A good example of sentiment at the time was a fundraising dinner I did in Melbourne on 10 September with some of Josh Frydenberg's wealthy supporters. Their message to Josh couldn't have been stronger – Malcolm must replace Abbott. Needless to say, I was discreet, but Josh (who nonetheless did ultimately vote for Abbott) could see that his base had moved on.

By this stage Morrison was no longer on the fence and was now working actively to assist me. We collaborated closely on the challenge, mostly through our mutual friend Scott Briggs. Morrison's public position, of course, was that he supported Abbott, but few insiders were taken in by that. His modus operandi was well known from February.[15]

The last planning meeting was at Peter Hendy's house just out of Canberra on Sunday 13 September. Peter's wife, Bronwyn, cooked a light supper for us and a core group of supporters went through the final numbers and timing. Abbott was in Adelaide on Monday morning and came back not long before question time. Julie went to see him and, according to her, told him that he no longer had the numbers and should consider resigning. As I wrote in my diary:

> *At the same time, Morrison was firming up his people to vote for a change – we mostly communicated via Scott Briggs either on the phone or by confide – and it worked well. Morrison was playing an audaciously duplicitous game, protesting publicly that he supported Abbott while busily working to bring him down.*
>
> *I had resolved to see Abbott after question time and walked with him out of the chamber. I said to him, 'We need to have a chat about a very important matter.'*

'Oh yes?' he said and then we walked silently to his office. Once there, I told him I intended to challenge him, that he had no prospect of winning the next election, that he had been given a second chance but we were worse off than before. I added that he had all but abandoned cabinet government and, for good measure, that he was a bad PM and a threat to national security. I told him that his wild captain's calls were frightening people – it was the antithesis of orderly government.

Abbott reacted with anger and incredulity. He kept on saying again and again, 'You are going to blow up the government! In the week of Canning. In the week of Canning!' I replied that if we changed leader, our vote would improve in Canning [that proved to be right]. He went on to say that I was committing suicide, I had lost my mind, that I was by reason of character and temperament utterly unsuited to be leader, my first time as leader had been a disaster.

He then went on to say that he would assume we had never had this conversation and that I would go back to my office and get back to work. I told him that was a rash assumption, that I was resigning as Communications minister and that I would now go and make a public statement. I asked him if he would agree to a spill. He said he would not agree and then he said he would think about it. I said we had a number of members ready to sign a motion so we would do that.

On that note I left, went back to my office briefly and then, at about 4 pm, went out into the Senate courtyard and explained why I was challenging him.[16]

I was so calm, almost still, as I walked out to the Senate courtyard. I felt like a great weight was being lifted off my shoulders. Serving in Abbott's government had been painful, humiliating, embarrassing all at once. Cleaning up the messes created by his lack of discipline, trying to rationalise or temper his latest weirdnesses … I felt like I needed to take a shower some days just to wash off the indignity and taint of being part of such a shambles.

But now, one way or another, it was going to be over. Either we rolled him and I became prime minister or we didn't, in which case I would resign from parliament.

And I was uplifted too. Here was the chance to provide the leadership the country deserved: positive, modern, rational, appealing to people's hopes rather than their fears.

I told the press pack that Abbott hadn't provided the economic leadership and confidence the nation needed.

> We are living as Australians in the most exciting time. The big economic changes that we're living through here and around the world offer enormous challenges and enormous opportunities.
>
> And we need a different style of leadership. We need a style of leadership that explains those challenges and opportunities, explains the challenges and how to seize the opportunities. A style of leadership that respects the people's intelligence, that explains these complex issues and then sets out the course of action we believe we should take and makes a case for it. We need advocacy, not slogans. We need to respect the intelligence of the Australian people.

I talked about the values of the Liberal Party – of freedom and individual initiative – and why they were the right values for 2015. But they needed to be translated into a policy and a vision for the future.

> We also need a new style of leadership in the way we deal with others, whether it is our fellow members of parliament, whether it is the Australian people. We need to restore traditional cabinet government. There must be an end to policy on the run and captain's calls. We need to be truly consultative with colleagues, members of parliament, senators and the wider public.
>
> We need an open government, an open government that recognises that there is an enormous sum of wisdom both within our colleagues in this building and, of course, further afield.
>
> But above all we have to remember that we have a great example of good cabinet government. John Howard's government most of us served in and yet few would say that the cabinet government of Mr Abbott bears any similarity to the style of Mr Howard.[17]

But it was the most mundane observation that I came to regret. 'We have lost 30 Newspolls in a row. It is clear that the people have made up their mind about Mr Abbott's leadership.'

Those who see politics as no more than a stage for the pursuit of personal ambition won't have much difficulty explaining why I challenged Abbott: yearning to be prime minister all my life, I wanted to seize the moment to take the top job.

But that's far from the truth. I'd stayed in politics after losing the leadership in 2009 without any expectation that I'd become leader again. Staying in politics enabled me to regain my mental equilibrium and pull back from the brink of a very dark abyss. The task of sorting out the NBN was challenging and satisfying – in many ways, a return to the kind of work I'd done for years in business. So, I planned to get the job done on the NBN and then retire at the 2016 election.

But then Abbott was so much worse than I expected and not simply unpopular. Howard's government had been unpopular, markedly so after Rudd became Labor leader. But Howard, no matter how bleak the polls,[18] kept governing, legislating, reforming, while the Abbott government was a bad government and in some respects was barely governing at all. There were a few moments of panic under Howard, but they were the exception. With Abbott, whether you called it panic or frenzy or just madness, there was no remission.

The published polls were bleak enough but as I learned much later, the Liberal Party's own private polling was even worse. The last Federal Track done under Abbott (from 28–31 August 2015) showed the party's vote and Abbott's favourability continuing to deteriorate (as it had through the year) to the point we were facing a complete annihilation.[19]

Back to the office and we hit the phones; all of our key people had call sheets to chase up the last votes. I called as many as I could, now that I could openly ask people for their vote.

I was surprised Abbott didn't respond to the challenge until 6.30 pm and then that he called the meeting at 9.15 pm. He would have known that Michael Ronaldson and Dean Smith (both supporters of mine) wouldn't be at the meeting so perhaps he wanted to exclude those votes. I suspect, however, that he knew the morning papers on the Tuesday would be overwhelmingly in favour of the change and thus time was not his friend.

> Anyway when the votes were counted the whips came in with faces like death, especially Scott Buchholz. I won 54:44 – a huge margin for a challenger – and so once again, nearly six years later, I was leader of the parliamentary Liberal Party.
>
> It was all a bit of a shock.[20]

On New Year's Eve, I summed it up in my diary.

I am sitting on the balcony reading about the Middle East and surveying the harbour filling up with ships to watch the fireworks. This time last year I was doing much the same except I was the Communications minister! What a year it has been.

So how do I review it? I guess things went spectacularly wrong for Abbott in February. I was wise then to hold my fire and not to put my head above the parapet as Morrison and Scott Briggs were so strongly urging me to do – Julie too. The vote in February was a little lower than I thought, but it was always going to be hard to call as it had come on so fast, people were shocked, didn't know what to think and I imagine quite a few flinched from the act of voting him out at the last minute. The 'zen approach' worked. The government under Abbott got worse and worse and worse. To the point where … Cabinet was barely functioning – after the debacle over citizenship it never recovered and the bypassing of it over gay marriage only underlined the fact that Abbott was not prepared to argue the case for anything to his cabinet colleagues. He had become a besieged would-be tyrant, always prepared to resort to a right-wing pack in the party room to support him when he knew his most senior colleagues wouldn't.

The best thing about the coup, when it came, was that it was so elegant. Security was tight. The numbers were kept by me on Google sheets and only [James] McGrath and Sally [Cray] could access them, but they couldn't share them or download them or print them. So, nobody had a copy on their computer. I probably gave the best speech of my career when I challenged Abbott, that five minutes in the courtyard. I need to do that more often – I am too wordy and I need to think carefully about the points I want to make and distil them. Doesn't take long, but it needs some discipline.

I challenged Abbott because I believed he was misgoverning Australia, making us less safe and less prosperous, cramping and constraining our future rather than creating new opportunities. And so, this couldn't be a case of a 'good government losing its way', as Gillard so feebly said about Rudd – it had to be much more than a change of leader. I needed to create a new government with a new agenda.

5

Turnbull Government

(2015–18)

CHAPTER 25

'We did it, Baba!':
prime minister

It was the flag that did it, flapping madly on the bonnet of the white BMW. We were speeding down the long avenue from Government House, racing to get back to parliament for question time. The pace of events hadn't allowed a moment of reflection, but it had happened: Lucy and I were sitting in C1. I was the prime minister.

Long into the previous night, there'd been a drunken wake in the cabinet rooms after the ballot, so rowdy that one of Abbott's supporters, Jamie Briggs, tore an ACL ligament leaping off a table. First thing that morning, while Abbott nursed his wounds and his hangover, the Nationals had visited me to set out the terms on which they were prepared to continue the Coalition Agreement. I didn't have a lot of leverage or time: I needed to be sworn in and at the despatch box for question time at 2 pm.

The Nationals were led by Warren Truss, calm and quiet for a politician, the antithesis of a populist, with a Lutheran dourness that was absent in his rowdy successor, Barnaby Joyce. Warren told me the Nationals were anxious about the change. They wanted reassurance on key issues – same-sex marriage and climate policy in particular. He added that he was under internal pressure from Joyce and Matt Canavan, who were urging him to muscle up to me – and the Liberals – and extract more concessions.

I agreed we'd stick with the policy to have a plebiscite on same-sex marriage and wouldn't change our existing climate change policy before the election. I didn't want to have an internal fight on either of those issues. At Barnaby's insistence Warren Truss also pushed for the Water portfolio to move from the Environment minister to Agriculture, where it had been prior to 2007 when Howard gave me Water in addition to

Environment. I managed, however, to keep the Environment Protection and Biodiversity Conservation Act water trigger within Environment. With tensions high and the clock ticking, I had little choice. Plus there were more than a few angry people in both parties who were prepared to burn the house down. It was a timely reminder of the constraints of leadership.

All morning, we'd been waiting for Abbott to formally resign as prime minister. Now that I had the letter of support from the Nationals, we could get on with the swearing in. Julie Bishop came out, as did Lucy's father, Tom Hughes QC, and his wife, Chrissie. Daisy and James and little Jack, not yet two, joined us as well – running into the grand reception room clutching a toy train and announcing, 'We did it, Baba. We did it!'

Like the morning, the ceremony was swift and a bit of a blur. And as we left Government House by the side entrance reserved for prime ministers, we thought: that's the easy part over.

As coups go this one wasn't just swift and elegant, it was also popular. It didn't have the surprise or shock of the Rudd coup: the public had been expecting it for months. Most people didn't think it was unfair either: Abbott had been put on notice in February and since then, things had got worse.

But I couldn't count on much goodwill from inside the Liberal Party – the right, who'd stuck with Abbott, would never forgive me or, truth be told, accept me. Increasingly, they were developing the theory that only people with their reactionary views were 'real Liberals'.

Abbott, of course, was anything but a 'real Liberal'. Years earlier, Peter Costello was on the money when he described him as Australia's first DLP prime minister. But reality wasn't especially relevant: the group Miranda Devine aptly dubbed 'delcons', or deluded conservatives, could tell themselves whatever they liked and have it confirmed every hour of the day in one accommodating echo chamber after another in the right-wing media.

The Canberra press gallery cover politics as though it was sport – all that matters is who's ahead, who's in the team, who's the captain. Policy is of secondary importance, and so leadership change, any leadership change, will always be viewed by them through the prism of polls. And I reinforced that by mentioning 30 Newspolls in my speech on the 14th.

However, the challenge for me now was to present not just as a new leader, the winner of the latest Canberra coup, but as the leader of a new government with a new agenda, one that was different in both substance and in tone. People had to almost feel like there'd been an election and a new government had been installed. The public had emphatically made up their mind about Abbott and the Liberal Party – I needed to give them the reason to have a fresh look at our side of politics.

At the same time, I had to hold the show together and that meant careful management of both personalities and policies so that the bulk of the conservatives could feel they were being listened to, that they had a place at the table.

And I knew that there was a significant cultural difference between the moderates and the conservatives. Keating used to say, 'In the great race of life, always back self-interest because you know it's trying.' And so it had always been reasonable to work on the assumption that most members of the party room, regardless of their factional or philosophical disposition, would act in their own best interest and, personal ambitions aside, wouldn't consciously act in a way that would bring down their own government.

After all, the only purpose of a political party is to win and hold government because you cannot achieve anything in opposition.

However, over the years, I'd seen more and more of the right of the party acting like terrorists – not with guns or bombs, I hasten to add, but rather regularly threatening to blow the show up unless they got what they wanted. And the third-rail issues, like same-sex marriage and climate change, were the ones over which they were most prepared to pull the pin. The moderates, on the other hand, faced with this type of threat, would invariably buckle and compromise in order to keep the show together, no matter how tenuously.

So the bottom line was I had to expect I'd be fighting on two fronts – a reminder of Churchill's apocryphal advice to a young man who asked whether the 'enemy' was over on the Labour benches. 'No,' the great man gravely observed, 'that's the opposition; the enemy is behind us.' And so it was going to be for me.

I needed to switch the economic narrative from a gloomy one of 'debt and deficit' and 'budget emergency' to one of optimism, growth and above all innovation. My speech in Brisbane back in March had basically set out the framework. How were we going to ensure we remained a high-wage, First World economy with a generous social welfare safety net? Only through stronger economic growth, more investment, higher productivity, more trade, more innovation.

Most importantly, not only was this the economic leadership the country needed, it was completely authentic to me; in fact, my life had been one of enterprise, risk taking, having a go and – if it didn't work – dusting myself off and having another go. So, I wasn't just another professional politician mouthing talking-point platitudes. I could turn my business background, my financial success – always seen by my critics as a liability – into a real asset.

Border protection was a definite strength for the Coalition. To their great credit, Abbott and Immigration minister Scott Morrison had 'stopped the boats' and while praise for that would diminish over time, this represented a sharp political difference with Labor.

National security more generally was also a Coalition strength, but it wasn't as clear-cut. Nobody seriously thought the Labor Party were ISIL sympathisers or about to sell the country out to the Chinese or the Russians, but overall our side of politics was seen as a steadier, safer pair of hands when it came to defence and security.

However, Australians aren't mugs, and as Abbott's rhetoric of 'death cults' that were 'coming to get us' had become more and more shrill, as the flags and generals and police commissioners multiplied at his press conferences, they could see he was whipping up fear and anxiety to restore his political fortunes.

Now, that was bad enough; worse was that this frightening rhetoric was actually making us less safe – and for all the reasons I'd pointed out in my speech to the Sydney Institute in July. The advice I received from the security chiefs in the days after I became PM confirmed this assessment.

We needed a clear-eyed approach to national security. We couldn't stop the media from whipping up hysteria – it helped them sell newspapers. But the government had to show confidence, competence and, above all, calm so that people knew their safety was being looked after by grown-ups.

On 15 September, on the drive back from Government House, my immediate problem was getting through to the end of the week. There's a reason leadership coups are usually timed for a Thursday – the end of a sitting week; it gives the new management time to reshuffle the cabinet, recruit or move advisers and generally straighten things up before the blowtorch of question time.

It took days for Abbott and Credlin to vacate the PMO and in the interim we were running the government from my ministerial office with 11 staff. Every journalist in the building and many outside were on the phone to David Bold and Pete Anstee while I was doing my best to heal the wounds that are left after any leadership change – and, of course, handling the long line of aspirants for a spot in the inevitable reshuffle.

We needed a wise political head to handle the transition and nobody was better qualified than Tony Nutt. Large and somewhat stooped, always self-deprecating, Nutt was the quintessential political professional. He'd been John Howard's principal private secretary, then his chief of staff and had held pretty much every organisational job in the Liberal Party except federal director, a post I appointed him to in late 2015 after Brian Loughnane retired.

Tony was the NSW state director and then NSW Premier Mike Baird kindly agreed to allow him to come to Canberra. Together with Sally Cray, he helped us recruit the additional staff we'd need for the PMO. In the meantime, after a slow start, PM&C seconded advisers to help us: Lynette Wood on foreign policy, who went on to be an outstanding ambassador to Germany, and Katrina di Marco, a brilliant economist with superb budget experience, who stayed with me throughout my time as PM and made an indelible contribution to our economic policy success.

Apart from Abbott, the cabinet continued all in place until the reshuffle I foreshadowed for the weekend. Even those most likely for the high jump, like Abetz and Andrews, were reasonably compliant for a few days, hoping that they wouldn't be dropped or would have a soft landing somewhere else.

My first three question times went as well as could be expected. Labor didn't yet have a clear line of attack against me – so they settled for 'Malcolm is Tony in a better suit' (unkind to Abbott's tailor, I thought) and pointed to my committing to stick with the existing policies on climate and on the same-sex marriage plebiscite.

But all this demonstrated that, wherever I could, I needed to make big changes in substance, in tone and style and in process. Accordingly, this was no time for a neat, nip and tuck minimalist reshuffle. I needed to deliver, as I said at the time, a '21st-century government and a ministry for the future'.[1]

As previously agreed, I appointed Scott Morrison as treasurer to replace Joe Hockey. Hockey was angry with me, but he knew Abbott had offered his job to Morrison on the day of the ballot, so he was done for whoever had prevailed. Discussions quickly began about his future.

I appointed five women to the cabinet. Joining Julie Bishop and Sussan Ley, who was Health minister, were Marise Payne, the first woman to be Defence minister; Michaelia Cash, minister for Employment and minister for Women; and Kelly O'Dwyer, assistant treasurer and the first woman to serve in the cabinet in the Treasury portfolio. This was the largest number of women in any Coalition cabinet to date, five out of 21, and Rudd's short-lived 2013 cabinet had only one more. It says a lot about the under-representation of women in Australian politics.

I brought Arthur Sinodinos in as cabinet secretary – his job was to help me restore traditional consultative cabinet government. It had essentially disappeared under my three predecessors, who'd all amply proved you cannot run the entire Commonwealth government from the prime minister's office.

Mitch Fifield came into the cabinet to replace me as Communications minister. I brought in Christian Porter, a former WA attorney-general and treasurer, as minister for Social Services to take over from Morrison, who became treasurer. I also brought Josh Frydenberg into cabinet as minister for Natural Resources and Simon Birmingham in as Education minister. I rewarded a number of my supporters: Mal Brough returned as special minister of state and James McGrath was appointed one of my assistant ministers.

George Brandis took over from Abetz as leader of the government in the Senate, with Mathias Cormann as his deputy.

I had hoped that Bruce Billson, who was Small Business minister with very little responsibility, would be happy to be minister for Cities, a passion of his and mine, in the outer ministry. He chose not to accept, so I appointed Jamie Briggs to that role for what turned out to be a brief stint.

Among the firsts was Ken Wyatt – appointed as an assistant minister for Aged Care and Indigenous Health, and the first Indigenous Australian to be appointed to the executive of a Commonwealth government. That this didn't happen until 2015 speaks volumes.

So, my first cabinet was younger and more reflective of Australia than its predecessors. This, however, came at a cost. In addition to Abbott and Hockey, I dropped Kevin Andrews and Eric Abetz. Each of them had been earmarked by Credlin for replacement already. Those were easy decisions. The tough ones were to drop two of my best friends in the parliament, Ian Macfarlane and Michael Ronaldson. Each of them was capable and loyal, but they'd both had long parliamentary and ministerial careers, and you can't promote the younger women and men unless you're prepared to move on some of the men in their 60s.

Kevin Andrews showed remarkable initiative after I phoned to say he wouldn't be included in the new ministry. On 20 September he quickly moved to appoint one of his staffers, Nick Demiris, inspector general of the Australian Defence Force (ADF) for a term of five years on a salary at that time of $365,000. It was a shocking thing to do on the day you're walking out the door, not least because Demiris was not qualified for the role. Fortunately, Tony Nutt, with his characteristic combination of charm and menace, persuaded Demiris to make himself unavailable.

Former ministers who stay in parliament all too often become fixated on revenge – as we were to see with Abbott. For that reason, I wanted to encourage them to move on.

Kim Beazley's term as our ambassador in Washington was coming to an end and I thought Joe would do an outstanding job in his place. While it's commonplace to denounce 'political appointments', in the ultimate political environment of Washington, an ambassador who has actually served in politics is far better able to win the respect of the Congress and the White House than a career diplomat. Joe resigned from parliament and we comfortably held his seat of North Sydney in a by-election in November. He was succeeded by his former staffer and fellow moderate Trent Zimmerman.

Abbott didn't want a diplomatic job. Within weeks of the leadership change, he was telling his supporters that he'd be back before the next election. His promise of 'no wrecking, no undermining, and no sniping'[2] was broken almost as soon as he gave it. And, of course, this continued for the entire period of my prime ministership.

I didn't meet with Tony until 26 November, when he asked me to appoint Peta Credlin sex discrimination commissioner on the Human Rights Commission and Brian Loughnane as ambassador to the Vatican. I'd already spoken to Brian about it, but it seemed an odd posting for somebody with Brian's commercial and political background. I'd suggested instead several trade positions in Europe or the UK.

The issue of sending Loughnane to the Vatican became a sore point with Abbott. In December, he became menacing and threatened, 'If you don't appoint Brian, I will be very fucking difficult. Very fucking difficult.'

When I wished him a happy Christmas, he told me to fuck off several times and hung up.[3] I never heard back from Loughnane and on the matter of the Vatican got the impression he was only half-hearted about it himself. His lack of interest in any other overseas posting, including ones that would be more suitable, was puzzling.

Over the years that followed Abbott made it clear to me that he wanted to return to the cabinet, ideally as Defence minister, and that if he didn't he'd remain, as he'd promised, 'very fucking difficult'. My view, shared by almost all my colleagues, was that he was so fixated on vengeance that he'd do more damage inside the cabinet than outside it. In fact, apart from Barnaby Joyce and Matt Canavan (both Nationals) – and only faintly – I cannot recall any minister encouraging me to restore Abbott to cabinet. After all, as we recalled too well, Tony's office had leaked from his own cabinet and had briefed against his own ministers – why would he keep the confidences of my cabinet?

While there was no cabinet support for an Abbott return, his friends in the media regularly suggested it, as we noted in November 2016 in a group chat on WhatsApp:

> **Christopher Pyne:** So, listening to Abbott's voice through the words of Cate McGregor today, restoring Abbott to cabinet will help him to control himself. A bit like putting a serial kleptomaniac in control of the petty cash tin to prove they are reformed.
>
> **Scott Morrison:** It's more blunt – put me in cabinet or I'll tear down the govt. There is only one way to respond to that type of approach.
>
> **Christopher Pyne:** He's now down to Cate McGregor, Andrew Bolt, Ross Fitzgerald. And he basically writes all three columns by dictation. It's pathetic, most of his mates have stopped flogging a dead horse.
>
> **Mathias Cormann:** A reshuffle which leaves him on the backbench would surely remove any hope by formally reaffirming that the Party and the Government have moved on and that he is not coming back. Backbench or retirement.[4]

My appointment as prime minister was better received by Australians than any comparable change of leader. In the polls, we moved from trailing the Labor Party to being well ahead and I was also leading Shorten as preferred prime minister: in the last Newspoll of the year, I polled 60 per cent to Shorten's 14 per cent. The Fairfax Ipsos Poll on 18 October showed 67 per cent of Australians preferred me as prime minister compared to just 21 per cent for Shorten. The two-party preferred vote had the government now 53:47 ahead. Our primary was up to 45 and Labor's had dropped from 36 per cent, prior to the leadership change, to just 30 per cent.

Deluded self-belief is a useful prop for leaders, especially when beleaguered. I've always been pretty objective about myself, tending more towards self-criticism. I recognised this surge of support was a relief rally. Cate Blanchett spoke for many when she said to me, being rid of Abbott was like having a weight taken off your chest.

Arthur Sinodinos busied himself re-establishing the traditional cabinet processes for running the government – essentially involving thorough analysis and presentation of policy options, consultation between departments and ministers, confidential discussion within the cabinet and then an announcement only after a collective decision had been taken.

And an important symbol of how the government had changed was to reverse Abbott's widely ridiculed 2014 decision to restore knights and dames to the Order of Australia.

With careful consideration, I set up my own office in a conventional fashion. It was clear to me that both Abbott and Rudd had demonstrated you cannot run the government of Australia from the prime minister's office. An effective government needed to work with, not against, the Australian Public Service (APS) and ensure we got the best of their advice. I also needed to ensure that my ministers were my principal advisers, and that they were empowered to run their own departments. My very strong belief was that if a minister needed constant handholding from the PMO, then they probably shouldn't be a minister at all.

As Communications minister, I'd had an outstanding, but small, team in my office and I brought almost all of them into the PMO. Sally Cray became my principal private secretary and David Bold my press secretary, and Jon Dart was on digital media and communications policy. Darto recruited Sahlan Hayes as our photographer, and Tommy Tudehope returned to manage our social media. Jenelle Frewen stayed to support the new minister, and Richard Windeyer returned to the department. Both continued to do great work in Communications.

No recent governments had matched John Howard's in effectiveness, and for most of his time as PM, the person running his office as CoS had been Arthur Sinodinos. He was first and foremost a Treasury economist, a bureaucrat who understood the public service, was respected by them and knew how to get the best out of them. I was very fortunate that Drew Clarke, the secretary of Communications, agreed to be my chief of staff – on a temporary basis that extended for well over a year. After he retired in April 2017, he was succeeded by Greg Moriarty, whom I later appointed secretary of Defence, and Peter Woolcott, another diplomat, who became the APS commissioner. My last CoS, Clive Mathieson, while not a career public servant, nonetheless brought a very keen policy implementation focus to the role.

Supporting them were two experienced journalists in Brad Burke and Tony Parkinson. Both had worked with me before when I was leader of the opposition, and had long experience before that in the Howard government, which brought wide respect from my colleagues, including those in the more conservative wings of the party.

On economic policy, Katrina di Marco agreed to stay on permanently with Dr Alex Robson, from Griffith University, who'd worked with me before. On foreign policy, I brought in Frances Adamson, our ambassador in Beijing, and whom I later appointed the first female secretary of the Department of Foreign Affairs and Trade (DFAT), supported by another brilliant diplomat, Philippa King. On national security, I brought in Justin Bassi, who had extensive experience in ASIO and the Attorney-General's Department and most recently worked for George Brandis. We also recruited as a social policy adviser Kerry Pinkstone, who'd worked with me when I was opposition leader and had since developed deep connections with Indigenous Australians when she worked for Nicola and Twiggy Forrest's Minderoo Foundation.

In short, my office was chosen on merit and was policy- and delivery-oriented while remaining keenly political. You have to bring the two together: good policy will be lost without effective political communications and management. And, as Rudd and Abbott especially discovered, running a government to meet the demands of the tabloid news cycle can very quickly look like an ineffectual mess.

As soon as possible, I organised briefings on all the major policy areas – deep dives – and ensured that I had the relevant policy experts in the room. Throughout my career, and especially in government, I've always taken care to ensure that I'm talking to the most knowledgeable people I can find – and when I do I take lots of notes. There's a tendency in Canberra for the secretary of the department to want to brief the minister or prime minister, sometimes with a few senior people, but all too often the middle-ranking public servant who's actually done the work is left outside. I pushed back against that and whenever I could find the people who really knew what was going on, I made sure to get them into my office.

There were prosaic changes. Parliament House was designed in the 1970s and the prime minister's office is suitably vast. It traditionally had the large PM's desk down the western end of the room and four bucket armchairs at the other end, apparently for more informal chats. It was a similar set-up in the PM's Sydney office. This wasn't my style. My preference was to have a smaller, private office for working in and small internal meetings and then a separate meeting room for receiving guests and larger meetings.

That wasn't possible so Sue Cox, who'd worked at parliament for nearly 30 years, found a board table and 10 chairs languishing unloved in a back room of the Parliamentary Library and liberated them for my office. It was much more practical but also symbolic of the collaborative approach I took as PM. We made a similar change in Sydney.

Once everything was set up, literally the first decision of my government was to tackle domestic violence. Not all disrespect of women leads to violence against women, but that's where all violence against women begins. Numbered in accordance with convention, MT15/001 was a $101 million women's safety package, which I launched on 24 September with the new minister for Women, Michaelia Cash, who described how I had told 'our very first cabinet meeting that within his government respect for women will be a number one priority'.[5] And an enduring one; I didn't want to make an investment of funds in front-line services, as we did, and then just move on.

We needed to change the culture of our country to one where respect for women is ingrained, second nature, and disrespect is called out. As Lucy had said in 2012 to an International Women's Day event, we need to ensure our sons and grandsons grow up to respect the women in their lives.

Throughout my time as prime minister, I worked to effect that change of culture and did so on all fronts. I supported many organisations that raised awareness of family violence and the disrespect of women that is at its heart. They included Our Watch, of which Lucy was an ambassador, and which was led by our friend and former senator Natasha Stott-Despoja. Promoting women into leadership roles both in cabinet and in the public service was equally important. One very effective advertising campaign, 'Stop it at the Start', was inspired by Lucy's insight and targeted the way parents subconsciously allow their sons to disrespect their sisters. And with Queensland Premier Annastacia Palaszczuk, I hosted a Council of Australian Governments (COAG) in Brisbane focused on family violence.

We're living in times of change unprecedented in all of human history in both its scale and its pace. This had implications for every aspect of policy – whether it was economic policy, including taxation and trade policy, or national security policy relating to terrorism, the rise of China as a global power or the new conflict theatre of the cybersphere.

Right at the heart of it all was the need to be innovative and agile, and above all to change the way in which policy and politics were debated. Just as I wanted to move the culture of government to one that was more consultative and considered, so in the public debate we had to find a way to break out from the blame games and the slogans. Not only was it not working politically – the public hated it – but it wasn't delivering the policy reform the 21st century demanded.

As I said in Melbourne on 5 November:

> We are living in the best times in human history. There has never been a more exciting time to be an Australian. The challenge for our government is to do everything we can, with your help, with all of the ideas and the advice, with all of the consideration and thought that you and so many other Australians can muster, to do all we can to ensure that we enable Australians to do their best, enable them to realise those opportunities, seize that future, confident, optimistic, proud and strong. This is a great era of opportunity. We are a great nation with a great future.[6]

CHAPTER 26

Innovation, trade and a *blusukan* with Jokowi

The first part of the new economic agenda was the National Innovation and Science Agenda (NISA). I'd moved the irrepressible Christopher Pyne from Education to be the minister for Industry, Innovation and Science and supported him with two Queenslanders: Karen Andrews as an assistant minister for Science and Wyatt Roy as assistant minister for Innovation. Wyatt, at 25, was the youngest person ever appointed to the federal executive.

I'd been talking up innovation long before I was PM. One of the advantages of being prime minister is that people pay close attention to what you say – even if you'd been saying it for years!

We consulted widely, including at a successful forum with venture capitalists like Seek's Paul Bassat, Google's Maile Carnegie, Freelancer's Matt Barrie and the new head of the CSIRO, Larry Marshall, joining academics and other experts at the University of Western Sydney's Corporate Centre at Werrington Park.[1] It was a great opportunity to show that innovation and technology weren't just for inner-city hipsters but meant more jobs and better opportunities right across the community. We took the train out from Sydney, with a shocked Christopher complaining the last time he was on a train was 'when Mama and Papa took me on the Orient Express'. I was never entirely sure he was joking.

The NISA was a comprehensive reform, with 24 separate measures including tax breaks for start-ups, insolvency reforms, and greater collaboration between industry and universities. NISA also launched a series of firsts: Australia's first ever national science accelerator, ON; the government's first ever venture capital fund via the CSIRO (now managed by Main Sequence Ventures), which was also the first fund in Australia to specialise in deep tech and science; as well as the establishment of landing pads for Australian start-ups in San Francisco, Berlin, Tel Aviv, Singapore and Shanghai. NISA also provided support for initiatives such as teaching school students, especially girls, how to code; and UNSW Professor Michelle Simmons's quantum computing research. Consistent with my collaborative approach, it was the product of a task force that involved nine government departments and 11 ministers.

I summed up the purpose and the vision at the launch on 7 December 2015:

> This is a century of ideas, this is a time when Australia's growth, when our living standards, when our incomes will be determined by the human capital, the intellectual capital that all of us have. By unleashing our innovation, unleashing our imagination, being prepared to embrace change, we usher in the ideas boom. That is the next boom for Australia and, you know something, unlike a mining boom, it is a boom that can continue for ever. It is limited only by our imagination. I know that Australians believe in themselves, I know that we are a creative and imaginative nation and inspired, led, incentivised, we will have a very long ideas boom in the 21st century.[2]

Whether it was the NISA or simply the fact that I spoke a lot about innovation, the 'ideas boom' I talked about did come to pass. In 2018, a record $1.25 billion was invested in start-ups, almost 10 times the amount invested in 2013. Venture capital investments reached $3.1 billion in 2018, double the amount in 2017 and up from $230 million in 2013. This rapid growth in the innovation ecosystem enabled a massive growth in overall science investment when you combine the public and private sectors. In short, innovation became both a buzzword and a benchmark for governments and businesses – a theme continued throughout my government. We ensured more government data, especially geospatial data, was made publicly available than ever before and set up the Digital Transformation Agency to bring government services into the 21st century, as well as Data61 within the CSIRO, which has become one of the world's leading institutions for big data research. In 2018, in the face of a great deal of official scepticism, I also established the Australian Space Agency, which is leading the growth of the vitally important industries around space, particularly satellite technologies and science.

My enthusiasm for innovation was often parodied in the press and internal opponents liked reminding me, and everyone else, that 'innovation' frightened people. Yet while it may be comforting to be lied to by politicians and assured everything will remain the same, that's like going to the doctor and being told what you want to hear.

Catherine Livingstone, the president of the Business Council of Australia, however, described the impact on national sentiment as 'almost unparalleled', adding, 'You have given us the permission to have conversations about things that matter to people, and helped, through your own example, to make those conversations positive.'[4]

Another important part of my economic policy and another break from the past was a Cities Agenda. Coalition governments had been reluctant investors in urban infrastructure, preferring to kick the money out the door as a grant, without being involved in the projects in any meaningful way.

There was also a marked prejudice against public transport. While ready to make grants for road infrastructure, whether it be vast freeways like WestConnex in Sydney, or the myriad local roads grants made to councils, Coalition governments had never supported urban rail projects.

The explanation, given to me in Howard's day, was that if the feds funded urban rail they'd never get their feet off the sticky paper and be stuck forever subsidising these poorly run, highly unionised state government enterprises. And theoretically, federal funding of roads freed up capital for the states to use on mass transit. However, over the years I'd concluded that by favouring roads at the expense of rail, the Commonwealth was merely ensuring there'd be more freeways built and less mass transit. Essentially, the Commonwealth grant allowed the state to pay as little as 20 per cent of the cost and get, in practical political terms, 100 per cent of the kudos. I'd tried to persuade Howard to take a different approach in years past, but it was a deep-set Coalition prejudice and one that had continued under Tony Abbott.

One of my first announcements, in October 2015, was to agree with Queensland Premier Annastacia Palaszczuk that the Commonwealth would jointly fund a 7.3 kilometre extension of the Gold Coast light rail. While the funding was a $95 million grant, I said we needed 'to look at more innovative approaches where we can partner with state or city governments as shareholders, as investors' and capture some of the value created by the new rail line in adjacent real estate.[5]

Equally, I couldn't understand why the Commonwealth would be so passive in its dealings with the states. Why hand over tens of billions of dollars in grants and have no involvement in the project? A classic case was the freeway from Ipswich to Toowoomba. It was a $1.5 billion project and the Commonwealth in Abbott's day agreed to pay 80 per cent of the cost. However, the Queensland state government, led by the LNP's Campbell Newman, did a public–private partnership to fund the remaining $300 million. The upshot was a toll. Consequently, none of the motorists will give the Commonwealth any credit for the road and assume they're paying for the road themselves through their tolls!

So, right from the outset of my prime ministership I set out a thoroughly new federal Cities Agenda, one in which the Commonwealth would be a partner and an investor rather than just a maker of grants. We'd enter into city deals, where the three levels of government and others would sit down, agree on what we wanted to achieve in a particular city or region and then agree on who'd build what infrastructure and how it'd be paid for. The Commonwealth would be prepared to be an investor in infrastructure and not simply make grants to the states.

Self-evident, it may seem, but it was in fact a revolutionary change. It had plenty of opponents and especially in the Canberra bureaucracy, which I knew from my time in Howard's government had little appetite for hands-on involvement. An exception was Stephen Kennedy, who I appointed to run the Cities Unit in PM&C and later to head the Department of Infrastructure. He got it, as did my cities adviser, Alice Thompson, whom at Lucy's suggestion we recruited from the NSW government.

A case in point was the Western Sydney Airport. Land had been acquired by the Commonwealth at Badgerys Creek more than 30 years before and several governments had announced work on the airport was about to commence – yet nothing had happened.

When Sydney's Kingsford Smith Airport at Mascot was sold under the Howard government in June 2002, the purchaser was given a first and last right of refusal to build the second airport at Badgerys Creek. Presumably, this was thought to enhance the purchase price. But it was dreadful policy – what's the point of having two airports in the one city owned by the same company? Surely the point of having a second airport is to engender some competition? And isn't that what the Liberal Party is all about?

My mother, Coral Lansbury, at 16 – actor, poet and dramatist.

Keen to follow in Mum's writing footsteps from a very early age.

An early family portrait: Dad, Mum, me and our boxer dog, Sheba.

Bruce and I were more like brothers. Below left, in 1975, and below right, with my stepmother, Judy, after I was admitted to the Bar in 1980.

Despite distractions in London, I did get my BCL at Oxford in 1980.

With Lucy at Stonehenge, 1980.

Lucy said, 'Let's wait until we grow up,' when I asked her to marry me. We didn't wait too long: 22 March 1980.

The four of us: Lucy, Daisy, Alex and me at our farm in the Hunter Valley, 1987.

Lucy with Daisy, Alex and Lucy's father, Tom Hughes, 1987.

Going into the Costigan
Royal Commission with
client Kerry Packer in 1983.
The Age

Right, with journalist Paul
Greengrass, publisher
Sandy Grant (obscured) and
solicitor David Hooper at the
Spycatcher trial in 1986, and
below, with David Hooper
and Peter Wright.
Below: Paul Wright / SMH

With Nick Whitlam, Neville Wran and some of the team at the office of Whitlam Turnbull & Co in 1988.

Up at the farm with Lucy's uncle Bob Hughes and our cattle dog, Rusty, in 1995.

Singing along with Eddie McGuire and the National Children's Choir at the launch of the Yes campaign for an Australian republic, 1999. *Jerry Galea / The Age*

At a Yes rally outside the Opera House during the 1999 referendum.

Voting with Lucy at my first election on 9 October 2004.
Rohan Kelly / Newspix

First speech in the House as a cabinet minister – Howard and Costello clearly not entirely convinced! 6 February 2007.
Gary Ramage / Newspix

Talking to students about energy-saving light bulbs as minister for the Environment and Water Resources in February 2007.
Alan Pryke / Newspix

With Lucy and Daisy at Bar Coluzzi, Darlinghurst, in 2008; Lucy and I have been getting coffees there for more than 40 years. *Jacky Ghossein / SMH*

With Daisy after winning the Liberal Party leadership from Brendan Nelson, 16 September 2008. *Andrew Meares / SMH*

An obviously entertaining speech on Labor's broadband policy, 19 November 2013
(L–R: Joe Hockey, Tony Abbott, Warren Truss and Christopher Pyne).
Andrew Meares / SMH

Helping install NBN cables with Paul Fletcher and Peter Hendy, June 2015.
Lukas Coch / AAP Image

Announcing a challenge
for the leadership on
14 September 2015.
David Foote / Auspic / DPS

Walking to the party room
with key supporters to
challenge Abbott for the
leadership (L–R: Wyatt
Roy, Peter Hendy, Arthur
Sinodinos, Mal Brough
and Mitch Fifield).
Andrew Meares / SMH

A kiss from Lucy after my
first press conference as
new Liberal leader.
David Foote / Auspic / DPS

Being sworn in as prime minister by Governor-General Sir Peter Cosgrove, 15 September 2015, and below, with the family afterwards.
Above: Andrew Meares / SMH; below: Ray Strange / Newspix

Walking into the chamber for the first time as prime minister with Christopher Pyne and Julie Bishop on 15 September 2015. *David Foote / Auspic / DPS*

With the women members of the first Turnbull ministry, 21 September (L–R: Marise Payne, Karen Andrews, Sussan Ley, Anne Ruston, Fiona Nash, Julie Bishop, Concetta Fierravanti-Wells, Kelly O'Dwyer – with baby Olivia – and Michaelia Cash). *David Foote / Auspic / DPS*

With President Joko Widodo on a *blusukan* at Tanah Abang Market in Jakarta on 12 November 2015. I was melting in the heat – cool but compassionate Jokowi (right) joined me in taking off our coats and ties, as did Tom Lembong (centre).

Private discussion with Obama after a press conference at APEC in Manila on 17 November.
Sahlan Hayes, official photographer to PM Turnbull

Lucy and I with NZ PM John Key and his wife, Bronagh, (far right) on *Wombat One* from CHOGM in Malta to the Paris climate conference on 29 November.
Sahlan Hayes, official photographer to PM Turnbull

Announcing the National Innovation and Science Agenda on 7 December 2015.
Mick Tsikas / AAP Image

Launching Australia's first Cybersecurity strategy on 21 April 2016.
Sahlan Hayes, official photographer to PM Turnbull

With Treasurer Scott Morrison before the 2016 budget. *Andrew Meares / SMH*

With Governor-General Sir Peter Cosgrove on 8 May 2016, when he accepted my advice to dissolve both houses of parliament and call an election on 2 July.

Sahlan Hayes, official photographer to PM Turnbull

Well, apparently not. Between Infrastructure Minister Warren Truss, Tony Abbott and Joe Hockey, they'd agreed in principle that the owner of Sydney Airport – Sydney Airport Corporation Ltd (SACL) – would be assisted in building the new airport at Badgerys Creek with $2 billion in a very concessional loan, possibly to be enhanced with a grant as well.

I thought this was nuts. So, the Commonwealth was going to subsidise SACL to build a second airport, which it would no doubt do as slowly and as ineffectually as it could, given its massive vested interest was to maintain traffic at its existing airport at Mascot?

The first and last right of refusal held by SACL was designed to make it practically impossible to build the second airport with anyone else. But after carefully reviewing the legal agreements and our lawyers' advice, I recognised that one way we could practically ensure the Western Sydney Airport wasn't owned by SACL was for the Commonwealth government itself to resolve to build it and to fulfil its contractual obligations to SACL by offering it an unsubsidised, and thus unattractive, opportunity to build the airport. SACL duly rejected that, and so the Commonwealth is building the airport, which is at the heart of the Western Sydney City Deal, providing the industrial and economic basis for tens of thousands of jobs into the future.

Better for the Commonwealth to spend its money on building its own airport, I reasoned, than subsidising SACL to very slowly build an airport that would never be able to realise its full competitive potential.

Another priceless example of the way Canberra thinks (or doesn't think) was the way the Department of Defence transferred to Defence Housing Australia a large parcel of land adjacent to the new airport. With some difficulty I got it back and it's now the location of the Western Sydney Aerotropolis, a technology and industry hub being built in partnership with the NSW government that will create thousands of high-paying jobs. Together with city-shaping rail, road and other investments, these developments form the basis of the Western Sydney City Deal, the largest of the city deals we agreed with states and local government during my time as PM.

The media love to beat up the idea of the politician's wife (or husband) being the power behind the throne and often breathlessly reported that Lucy was influential in the counsels of my government. This was always overstated, but as one of Australia's leading urbanists, a former lord mayor of Sydney and the chief commissioner of the Greater Sydney

Commission, I couldn't have had a better source of advice on cities policy than Lucy.

Trade, and especially with our region, was absolutely central to my vision for a more dynamic, prosperous Australia. We were perfectly positioned to take advantage of the rapid economic growth in Asia. Technology had in large part abolished longitudinal distance – and we were in the same time zone as all the major centres. Moreover, with a growing percentage of our community of Asian heritage, we had the background, the cultural understanding and language skills to connect.

I often commented on how our multicultural society and its diversity was a source of strength. I imagine more than a few cynics thought those were just warm words, but they were not only heartfelt but hard-headed. Large global firms generally recruit far more Australians than they can ever use in Australia because growing up in our diverse society we're generally well equipped to work with people from very different cultural backgrounds.

The Abbott government, through its (and later my) Trade minister, Andrew Robb, had secured free trade agreements with Japan, South Korea and, most importantly of all, China. These agreements, especially the Chinese one, were controversial. Real opposition to them was coming from the union movement and, for a time, the Labor Party. One of my government's early legislative wins was finally securing Labor's support for the ratification of the China–Australia Free Trade Agreement (ChAFTA) in November 2015.

As an open economy with very low tariffs, and which generally welcomed foreign investment, free trade deals were always going to be of advantage to us. I believed that wherever we could open a door for Australian exporters or push it a little wider, we should do so.

However, there was a bigger deal in play – the Trans-Pacific Partnership (TPP), which had become President Obama's signature economic policy for the Asia Pacific region. The TPP included 12 economies, among them the USA, Japan, Australia, Canada, Vietnam and Mexico. It offered enormous additional opportunities for Australia in almost every market covered, including the USA, where the TPP would improve access for Australian grains, sugar, beef, cheese and rice.

Obama saw the TPP as a strategic measure, tying key Asia Pacific economies not simply into lower tariffs but also improved labour and environmental standards, as well as enhancing both cybersecurity and protection for intellectual property. Obama's defence secretary, Ash Carter, acknowledging economic security and the growth flowing from it as the bedrock of peace in the region, said that the TPP was 'as important to me as another aircraft carrier'.[6]

I became prime minister just as the negotiation of the TPP was concluding in Atlanta and we came under enormous pressure from the Americans to agree to amendments to patent protection for biologics, a new and increasingly important type of drug created by complex biological, as distinct from chemical, processes. The amendments would benefit the immensely influential US pharma lobby but would inevitably be politically damaging for us as an increase in the cost of some drugs in Australia was a likely outcome. We were only just getting the ChAFTA through the parliament in the teeth of furious opposition from the unions and we simply didn't have the political capital available to have a fight over the TPP too.

President Obama called me to press the case and did so with his characteristic quiet charm. But I couldn't help him; we wouldn't change our law relating to data protection for biologics. It was political kryptonite for us. Barack said that meant the TPP could fall over and we'd be blamed. I took a deep breath and quietly replied, 'Well, Mr President, like you, I think the TPP is vital for our region. But you know, nobody is marching in the streets here saying "Sign the TPP", but they sure will be marching if they think we're going to put up the price of drugs on our Pharmaceutical Benefits Scheme. Those pharma companies hate our PBS because we use our monopoly buying power to force down prices – but that's not my problem. Sorry, no can do.'

Barack Obama entirely understood the politics. And he acknowledged he was an unlikely advocate for big pharma. We just moved on to talking about Syria and other security issues.

I then gave Andrew Robb authority to stonewall on the issue. 'Just say "no" to drugs, Andrew,' I told him.

Our ambassador in Washington, Kim Beazley, reported to me on 3 October that, following my call with the president, Obama's National Security Council trade adviser was trying to elevate the issue to one of national security, and was arguing that our standing our ground wouldn't just put the whole deal but the alliance at risk. We were warned that the atmospherics with the Americans would likely be poisonous if talks collapsed. Peter Varghese, secretary of DFAT, Julie, Andrew and I talked. We resolved that we would not be spooked by the US pressure and concluded the idea that Australia was standing in the way of the US rebalance in the Asia Pacific was self-serving bunkum. The USA was trying to knock us off one by one on biologics, and Australia was by no means the only TPP party that could not accept eight years. We recognised that if we failed in Atlanta it wouldn't be because of Australia. So, concluding our position on biologics was both entirely defensible and in our national interest, I instructed our negotiators to hold firm. [7]

And we did. The deal was signed in Atlanta – only to be abandoned a year later by President Trump. But it was a reminder that, especially when it comes to trade, nations – particularly big ones – will ruthlessly pursue their own interests. It was important that at our first encounter, Obama saw that I was just as committed to Australia's interests as he was to America's.

While Operation Sovereign Borders had succeeded in stopping the boats, we were left with the problem of the several thousand asylum seekers on Nauru (mostly families) and on Manus (single males). They'd been moved there by Kevin Rudd in his brief second period as PM as he tried desperately to reverse Labor's failed border protection policy.

The people-smuggling gangs had become sophisticated criminal businesses and especially adept at using social media to market to would-be passengers. With good cause, we feared that if we brought the people from Nauru and Manus to Australia, the people smugglers would use this as a promotional opportunity and the boats would start again.

The counterargument was that the turn-back and take-back policy would continue. But it overlooked the fragility of boat turn-backs, which depended on the cooperation of our neighbours, including Indonesia, Malaysia, Vietnam and Sri Lanka, who were prepared to accept the return of persons intercepted at sea. What's more, our capacity to intercept the people smugglers was limited by our resources at sea. We simply couldn't cope with a large number of boats at any one time.

Added to this was a pending High Court case, M68, challenging the detention on Manus. Should the outcome go against us, it could result in our being required to bring the detainees to Australia. I quickly sought an assurance from the Department of Immigration that it had the resources and a plan to deal with the inevitable upsurge in boats as the people smugglers sought to take advantage of such a High Court decision.

The news wasn't good. Not only were there no developed contingency plans, but a year earlier one of the two large border protection vessels, the *Ocean Protector*, had been let go – to save $80 million. Quickly, we got the vessel back.[8] As it happened, the High Court decision didn't have the outcome we feared, but all the agencies involved in Operation Sovereign Borders understood my determination to ensure the boats remained stopped. The people smugglers, and their customers, had to know they couldn't get to Australia by boat.

What we needed was somewhere to resettle the 1852 asylum seekers on Nauru and Manus. Morrison, as Immigration minister, had tried to find resettlement options in other countries but to date had only succeeded in a very expensive deal with Cambodia – a country to which only a handful of the asylum seekers wanted to go. New Zealand had a standing offer to take 150 a year, but they didn't want any single men (the bulk of the detainee population), and the advice from our agencies was that resettlement in New Zealand would be exploited by the people smugglers as being the same as settlement in Australia.

Dutton, despite his carefully cultivated reputation as a hard Queensland cop, was genuinely concerned about the situation and in particular the mental health of the detainees if they felt there was no hope of escape. But short of offering increased financial incentives for people to return to their home countries, he didn't have any new ideas – no other developed countries had shown any interest; all had irregular migration issues themselves and took the view this was Australia's problem.

Finding a third country resettlement solution for the asylum seekers on Nauru and Manus was one of my highest priorities and I met regularly with Dutton and Julie Bishop about this in the first few months. As we worked through all the options, it was obvious that our best, and possibly only, realistic option was going to be the United States. So I started to formulate how I'd approach President Obama when I had the opportunity to raise the matter privately.

• • •

New Zealand's John Key wasn't just a friend but a role model. He'd been able to achieve major economic reforms in New Zealand, including substantial cuts in taxation, and by growing the economy faster than government outlays, he'd got the budget back into balance without big reductions in spending.

So, my first overseas visit as prime minister was across the Tasman. Remarkably, the sight of two former investment bankers now PMs was well received, not least because it was obvious both John and I, and our wives, Bronagh and Lucy, got on very well on their return visit to Sydney. They stayed a night at Point Piper, which the press hilariously dubbed 'a pyjama party', and John and I went kayaking the next day.

However, there were a few tensions in the relationship. Our parliament had recently passed a law that allowed for the revocation of the visa of any non-Australian citizen who'd been convicted of an offence carrying a term of more than 12 months' imprisonment. As there were about 600,000 New Zealanders living in Australia, a number were being deported back to New Zealand. Some of them had spent almost all their lives in Australia and there was growing resentment about the deportation policy.

John recognised that, whatever the merits of the policy, it would never be reversed as it was hugely popular in Australia. I offset the upset on that score by later agreeing to make it easier for New Zealanders living in Australia to obtain Australian citizenship.

Over the years, I'd often felt New Zealand handled matters more efficiently than we did, at lower cost and with less red tape. John said that was because, lacking a minerals bonanza, the Kiwis couldn't afford to be as wasteful as we were. Plus it's a smaller country: no state governments, and a single national parliament with only one chamber, so, no Senate!

Australians pay too little attention to our Kiwi cousins, as I said while there. Governments need to look further afield for examples of what works and what doesn't. Everybody is trying to solve the same problems; yet, in a world of global business where firms are watching and learning from every market, most governments are introspective and parochial, paying far too little attention to what's happening around the world – and, in our case with New Zealand, right on our doorstep.

John Key resigned in December 2016 and was succeeded by Finance Minister Bill English, who was widely expected to win the 2017 election in September. However, in August, Labour switched to the charismatic

37-year-old Jacinda Ardern, who went on to win the election and become prime minister 12 weeks later.

Jacinda is genuinely warm and engaging; we got on very well as two leaders and as two couples when she and Clarke joined Lucy and me for dinner at our home in 2018.

When Jacinda and I first met in Sydney after her election, I said that Australia did not want to accept New Zealand's offer to take 150 asylum seekers until after we had completed the US deal. She was later to press me on this but wanted to prioritise taking women and children; as I pointed out, these were the most likely to get offers to go to the USA. There has always been a lot of criticism of Australia's border protection policies from New Zealand, but it is one of those cases where the Kiwis effectively free ride on our security. As at 2017, NZ had taken in 33,000 refugees since the Second World War. Australia took in that many in 2016 and 2017 alone.

Jacinda's response to the 2019 Christchurch mosque shootings was inspiring but not surprising: it was as natural and sincere as she is. And however her political story unfolds in the years ahead, the healing and love she showed will remain an example to leaders everywhere.

Back home, in late 2015, Labor had concluded that their best line of attack was the politics of envy. By their reckoning, I had to be out of touch because I was wealthy and had investments in funds in the Cayman Islands. I pointed out that, from an Australian investor's perspective, the only consequence of investing in a Caymans-registered fund was that none of my income was taxed in the Caymans; it was therefore entirely taxed in Australia.

I didn't try to pretend I wasn't well off, but, after a few days of this line of attack, largely put it to rest with this reply.

> The fact is that Lucy and I have been very fortunate in our lives. We have more wealth than most Australians. That is true; that is absolutely true. We have worked hard, we have paid our taxes, we have given back. I do not believe that my wealth or, frankly, most people's wealth is entirely a function of hard work. Of course, hard work is important, but there are taxi drivers who work harder than I ever have and they do not have much money … There is a lot of luck in life, and that is why all of us should say, when we see somebody less fortunate than ourselves, there but for the grace of God goes me.

So, really, if the honourable member wants to go around wearing a sandwich board saying, 'Malcolm Turnbull's got a lot of money,' feel free. I think people know that. I ask that further questions be placed on the Notice Paper.[9]

The quick visit to New Zealand was the first and easiest of a long schedule of international visits – it was summit season. And while I'd have dearly preferred to stay at home and concentrate on getting our economic policies nailed down, none were avoidable. You can't not turn up to the G20 or the East Asia Summit or APEC.

However, the most important visit wasn't on the annual conference calendar.

Indonesia is our closest neighbour and its population of 270 million is the world's fourth largest. It is also the largest Muslim majority nation in the world. We relied on their goodwill to maintain boat turn-backs, the foundation of our border protection policy. And given their country stretches across our northern approaches, a stable and friendly Indonesia was vital to our own security.

Previous prime ministers had had close relationships with Indonesia's leaders: Keating with Suharto and Howard with Susilo Bambang Yudhoyono are good examples. But latterly the relationship had come under a lot of stress. The Gillard government had banned live cattle exports to Indonesia in 2011, and the public outcry in Australia over the execution in April 2015 of two Australian drug traffickers, Andrew Chan and Myuran Sukumaran, had been widely resented in Indonesia.

I was keen to meet the new president of Indonesia, Joko Widodo. Unlike most of his predecessors and his rival in the 2014 election, he wasn't a general. Jokowi, as he's known, was a self-made businessman who'd gone into local politics, first as mayor of his hometown of Solo and then as governor of Jakarta in 2012.

Lucy accompanied me on the trip to Jakarta and made a big impact on the president, whose main interest was infrastructure and urban planning. Nobody was better able to talk about those subjects than Lucy and together with Ibu Iriana, the president's wife, we got on famously.

At a practical level, efforts to agree on a free trade deal, the Indonesia–Australia Comprehensive Economic Partnership Agreement (IA-CEPA), had languished for years and I asked Jokowi if he'd agree to work with me to get it moving again. He did so, and it was agreed by the end of 2018. (Temporarily, it was put into the freezer following Scott Morrison's 'Jerusalem embassy' decision, of which more later.)

One of Jokowi's trademark practices was the *blusukan*, a surprise visit to some part of the city to meet the people and check on government services. I'm sure they were genuinely impromptu in Solo, but there isn't a lot of room for impromptu performances in a presidential life.

Nonetheless, after our meetings at the palace, we set off in the presidential limo for a fabric market. When we stepped out of the car, it was already sweltering and I figured it would be even hotter inside. 'Shall I take off my coat?' I asked.

'Oh no,' said Jokowi, gently shaking his head. 'You will be fine.'

No, I won't be, I thought, but left the coat on.

The fabric market was hot, steamy and packed. The people loved Jokowi and were kissing his hand as he passed, joyously happy to see him. One little boy was pushed aside in the crush, so I reached out to him and introduced him to Jokowi. He was crying with joy as he met the president.

By this time the sweat was running through my eyes and I could barely see. I looked at Jokowi; there wasn't a bead of sweat on his brow. A cool cat in every respect. Tom Lembong, his Economics minister, at least looked a little warm, so I said, 'Sorry, Mr President, but I'm going to have to take off my coat and tie.' Jokowi smiled and did the same. That was the money shot, the picture on every front page in Jakarta the next day.

As we left in the limo, Jokowi reached over to me. 'I want the people of Indonesia and Australia to see that you and I are this close,' he said, as he hooked his two index fingers together. I was sure that we'd fulfil that promise and over the three years that followed we did so.

Throughout my time as PM, I did everything I could not only to support Jokowi, and Indonesia, but also to encourage him to play a larger role on the global stage.

Jokowi said, 'Malcolm, Indonesia is the proof that Islam, moderation and democracy are compatible. That is why we cannot let the extremists take hold.' He described his three-pronged attack on extremism. First security measures, including lethal force; second religion, making sure that young people understood that Islam in Indonesia is moderate and tolerant – 'That is our tradition,' he said, 'and we must maintain and defend it'; and third he said we needed to combat the extremists on social and cultural grounds and especially online, where ISIL in particular was far too effective.[10]

Muslims are 25 per cent of the world's population; those who think they can fight terrorism by declaring war on Islam are simply doing the terrorists' work. Moderation is the key. But when you look around the Muslim world, there are no leaders who can match Jokowi. A far cry from a severe old general, let alone a mullah or a sheikh, he's young, charismatic, democratically elected, a wizard on social media and a fan of Metallica. In more ways than most realise, he's the hope of the side.

CHAPTER 27

'Can you say that again
in English, PM?'

Most of my travel as PM, domestic and international, was conducted in one of the Royal Australian Air Force's (RAAF) two Boeing Business Jets – 737s that John Howard leased 17 years earlier. Lucy came up with the very appropriate nickname *Wombat One* while we were flying to Paris from Malta with the Keys.

Wombat One was noisy, had limited range and wasn't as comfortable as Qantas. But there was something special about flying with the RAAF, whose stewards were always cheerful, no matter how long the flight. And long trips meant time for in-depth discussions with my advisers.

The last half of November was a taste of the furious pace at which PMs travel in the 21st century. No more Menziean six-week voyages on a steamship to an imperial conference in London (coinciding with a test match naturally).

The itinerary was: 12 November Jakarta; 13 November Berlin, then arrival in Antalya for the G20 on the 14th and departure for Manila and APEC on the 16th. Two days in Manila, then a day out to return to Australia for a visit to Darwin on 20 November. And then off to Kuala Lumpur for the East Asia Summit for the 21st and 22nd; back in Canberra at 6 am for parliament on Monday the 23rd. Four days of parliament, then an evening flight on the 26th for the Commonwealth Heads of Government Meeting (CHOGM) in Malta. Two days there before flying on Sunday the 29th to Paris for the Climate Change Conference, leaving the following night, Monday the 30th, to arrive back in Canberra at 6.15 am on 2 December. Lucky I was good at sleeping on planes!

When we left steamy Jakarta for chilly Berlin, the diplomatic priority was our relationship with Germany and the EU. Mathias Cormann, ably supported by Lucy (who was president of the German Australian

Chamber of Commerce), had led a working group to advance our neglected relationship; with his fluent German, Cormann was raising the profile of Australia in Germany and in doing so enhancing our influence with the EU.

It's hard to think of another city on which history hangs so heavily as it does on Berlin. Whether it's Daniel Libeskind's holocaust memorial, or the triumphant graffiti daubed on the walls of the Reichstag by the Red Army, or the vast Soviet war memorials, let alone the banality of the Wannsee House, where the Final Solution was planned, everywhere there are reminders of the insane inhumanity of the Nazis, their savage defeat in war and the decades of humiliating occupation that followed.

And it's filled with contradictions. 'Advance Australia Fair' is always sweetest at home, but I'd never heard it played more beautifully than by the Bundeswehr band in the chancellor's courtyard; then came the 'Deutschlandlied'. The first verse, which begins, '*Deutschland, Deutschland über alles*', is never sung any more, but nobody can forget it. The anthem was played in Hitler's day, had been written in the 19th century to salute the unification of Germany and was being played this day a few weeks after the 25th anniversary of Germany's reunification.

And in her deceptively maternal calm, Angela Merkel embodies the practical lived experience of it all. She grew up in East Germany and learned Russian as her second language. She and Putin are about the same age and each was there – she a research chemist, he a KGB officer – when the Wall came down and the Soviet Empire collapsed.

It meant liberation for Merkel, who joined the democratic movement and began a political career. For Putin, the end of the Soviet Union was the greatest catastrophe of the 20th century.

No European leader better understands Putin than does Merkel. She sees how, despite its weak economy, he's striving always to restore Russia's greatness. With what seems now like an ominous prescience, Merkel talked about how Putin sought to create divisions in the West, both between and within nations. We discussed the situation in Syria at length, Putin's motives, the West's missteps, how to resolve the most bitter of civil wars. And of course we talked about terrorism and ISIL, their pretensions to a caliphate and the reach of their propaganda beyond the Syrian battlefield.

Little did we know that as we were discussing the threat of terrorism, an ISIL cell was about to execute a series of violent assaults across Paris, including at the Stade de France. Several explosions interrupted a game between Germany and France attended by Foreign Minister Steinmeier – within hours of my meeting him in Berlin.

There were five other attacks, mostly in restaurants, with the most devastating at the Bataclan theatre, where 90 of the 130 killings took place. Three groups of three terrorists acted with ruthless efficiency. The scale and sophistication of their operation was deeply disturbing, especially the ease with which they bypassed the increased security after the *Charlie Hebdo* attack in January.

I hadn't been long asleep when I was woken up with the news. Was this the beginning of a wave of attacks? Was Paris the prologue to a major assault in Turkey for the G20 talks in Antalya? Immediately, I spoke with all our national security chiefs – Duncan Lewis, director general of ASIO; Andrew Colvin, AFP commissioner; Greg Moriarty, counter-terrorism coordinator – and then with Foreign Minister Julie Bishop, acting PM Warren Truss and Attorney-General George Brandis. We didn't know how many had been killed, whether Australians were among the victims (miraculously, they weren't) or what the implications were for other cities, including our own. And then at 5.30 am in Berlin, I stood up to provide the calm reassurance Australians needed to hear from their PM. I described what we knew, affirmed our solidarity with the people of France and confirmed that our security settings, including the terrorism alert level, were appropriate.

But as more news came in from Paris, it cast a tense and unsettling pall over all the discussions ahead of us at the G20. The conference was held in a series of huge resort hotels to the east of Antalya and the security was menacingly tight.

It was my first opportunity to meet so many of the world's leaders, from the newly elected Justin Trudeau to Xi Jinping, Narendra Modi, David Cameron, Shinzo Abe and our host, Turkish President Recep Tayyip Erdoğan. We'd arranged to sit down at length with Barack Obama in Manila at the APEC meeting a few days hence. But one thing was certain – apart from Vladimir Putin, nobody had a clear view about how to resolve the civil war in Syria.

Everyone was agreed on the strategic objective in Iraq – driving ISIL out – but that sending Western armies into the field in Syria would be counterproductive: they could seize ground but the enemy would melt away and return when the foreigners had left – just as they had in Iraq.

There, in a lightning campaign the year before, ISIL had occupied Mosul, Iraq's second-largest city, and then in subsequent campaigns Ramadi, Tikrit and territory right up to the outskirts of Baghdad.

While no Australian ground troops were engaged in fighting, together with the New Zealanders we were training Iraqi soldiers at the Taji base near Baghdad. A smaller group of our Special Forces were providing advice and assistance to Iraq's elite counter-terrorism service. In the years to come, that support would be of vital importance in the retaking of Mosul. Our air force was supporting the campaign against ISIL in both Iraq and in Syria.

But the big question in Syria was: what are we fighting for? From the time the Arab Spring erupted in 2011, leaders in the West had sought to end the murderous tyranny of Bashar al-Assad and provide support and encouragement to his opponents, principally the Free Syrian Army. But his most effective opponents were ISIL, and they were our enemies too. And who would replace Assad? Potential successors had a habit of dying in unpleasant circumstances.

Putin had a naval base in Syria and a longstanding relationship with the Syrian regime. But when I spoke to him in Antalya, he had a simple point to make: 'Why are you and your friends in the West making the same mistake you made in Iraq? Saddam was a monster, sure, but what has come after is much worse. You pushed him over without any idea of what you would replace him with, and then you did the same in Libya – another disaster. And if it had not been for Russia, you would have done the same in Syria.'

Uneasily, I felt he was making too much sense, so I asked Putin how he saw a final settlement in Syria. Would a partition work, as many were suggesting at the time? 'Assad will prevail. It's just a question of time. And then there will need to be some kind of federal solution – power sharing similar to Lebanon perhaps.' He trailed off; perhaps he was as unclear as everyone else.

So why was he there? Was it just to prove that Russia was a global player, as Merkel had told me in Berlin?

As Laurent Fabius, the French Foreign minister, said to me, 'Some [Western] special forces could be deployed, but history has shown anything more would be both inefficient and viewed as an occupation. The international community needs to fight back through Arabs, Syrians and others in the region.'

If the security outlook was gloomy at Antalya, there was still momentum for free trade – this was pre-Trump and pre-Brexit. In my concluding remarks, I'd spoken about how Australia's open economy and floating exchange rate had allowed us to make a soft landing at the end of the mining construction boom. I also talked about 'the potential for distributed renewable energy, especially solar, coupled with storage. The big technological game-changer in energy is efficient cost-effective storage'.[1]

International conferences, like all conferences, have a bad reputation as 'talkfests' but they're extremely valuable because they enable leaders to meet lots of their counterparts both formally – in bilaterals surrounded by officials, in a form of ritual speed dating – but also, and much more valuably, informally. I've had many meetings, for example, with Xi Jinping. Unlike his more relaxed and informal premier, Li Keqiang, Xi has a monumental and predictable formality in large meetings where typically there are a dozen officials down each side of the table and the same again taking notes in seats behind. However, at APEC in 2015 and in 2016, we found ourselves sitting next to each other at a lunch and dinner respectively, in circumstances where it wasn't really possible to talk to anyone else, so we ended up having on each occasion well over an hour of uninterrupted discussion with only his interpreter as our witness. I learned more about him and his priorities in half an hour of those discussions than I did in all the formal bilaterals put together.

At another similarly long APEC event, I found myself in discussion with Prime Minister Hun Sen of Cambodia. We passed the time building some rapport, including by comparing pictures of our grandchildren on our smartphones. Did it result in an outburst of democracy and civil liberties in Cambodia? No, it did not. But it did build a level of trust that enabled us later to come to an agreement that James Ricketson, an Australian charged with espionage in Cambodia, would be sent back to Australia as soon as he was convicted.

At the Manila APEC I had my first good discussion with President Obama. Our differences over biologics and the TPP were forgotten, although I wasn't confident his trade representative, Mike Froman, had entirely forgiven me. It was obvious Obama had no clear view of what a postwar Syria would look like. He lamented the lack of alternatives to Assad, and how anxiety that the Shia backed by Iran would take charge in Syria, as they'd done in Iraq, was driving the Gulf States' support of

Sunni rebels. We talked about my recent discussions with Erdoğan and Putin. Obama correctly identified Erdoğan's pre-eminent goal was to suppress the Kurds, even though they were the most effective allies the West had in the battle against ISIL. There was a real risk, I thought, Erdoğan would in due course resume his friendship with Assad and then combine with a restored Syrian regime, supported by Iran, to finish off the Kurds or at least drive them away from the Turkish border.

If Obama's insights into the Middle East were murky, he had a sharper analysis of Indonesia, where he'd spent much of his boyhood. 'When I was growing up, it was very pluralistic. There was anti-Chinese sentiment at times but, beyond that, different groups lived side by side fairly harmoniously. You rarely saw women with headscarves; it was pretty secular. But then the Saudis started financing Wahhabi schools and that over time has founded an intolerant Islamic tradition, completely at odds with the traditional moderate Indonesian one.'

I asked him, if the Saudis had done so much harm promoting Wahhabism, why had the United States stood by and continued to support the regime. 'Malcolm, one word: oil. Before 9/11, Faisal and the Islamic clergy in Saudi had done a deal where Faisal got to run the country and the business of oil and the clergy had a free rein on matters of religion. And the United States and Saudi had a tacit deal where America agreed not to interfere in return for oil. And by 9/11 it was all too late to unwind, and we are living with the consequences.'

We got on well. Subsequently, the only slightly discordant note was when Obama complained about the decision by the Northern Territory government, taken before I was PM, to lease the Darwin Port to a Chinese company, Landbridge. He complained the US government first heard about it in *The Wall Street Journal*.

Something had gone amiss in the communications there – the fact that the port was up for lease and that Chinese firms were interested had been public knowledge long before the deal was done. The US government's liaison officer in Darwin had been well aware. Our own Defence Department had satisfied themselves it wasn't a security threat. Nonetheless, with the USA stepping up its commitments of Marines to rotate through our army base in Darwin, it wasn't a good look. I did offer to buy the White House a subscription to the *NT News*.

The setting for CHOGM was exceptional. The apparent tranquillity of the island state of Malta belies the frequent violence and war it's seen in its long history. The sandstone fortifications of the knights of Malta kept the Ottoman Turks at bay for centuries, only to fall to Napoleon Bonaparte in 1798. Then came 150 years of British occupation during which, perhaps most heroically of all, the Maltese resisted the onslaught from the Luftwaffe in the Second World War.

It was a poignant location for the Queen and Prince Philip. They spent the first years of their married life in Malta while Prince Philip served in the Royal Navy after the war. And to give the *recherche du temps perdu* an added romantic touch, all of the security for the conference was provided by the Royal Navy's red-coated Royal Marines, who were everywhere. The Maltese prime minister, Joseph Muscat, who radiated good humour and political guile all at once, said, 'For a few days, we have been occupied again!'

At the final dinner, I shared a table with Justin and Sophie Trudeau and the Duke of Edinburgh. Sophie was seated next to Prince Philip and so charmed the legendarily crotchety old sailor that he came to life, regaling us all with tales of Malta in the years during and after the war and much more besides.

At the conclusion of CHOGM, we gave John and Bronagh Key a lift to Paris on *Wombat One*. We'd resolved that on arrival, all of us would go to the Bataclan theatre to lay a wreath in memory of those killed in the terrorist attacks of 13 November. It was a cold, wet and dark evening. Even the large press contingent was quiet at this place where over a hundred people had been murdered only two weeks before.

The people who were waiting for us, journalists and local residents, were almost all French, so I spoke simply in their language: '*Nous sommes ici, les premiers ministres de l'Australie et de la Nouvelle Zélande et nos femmes, et nous vous offrons, le peuple français, le peuple de Paris, nos plus sincères condoléances et notre plus forte solidarité.*'

There was a moment's silence; all I could hear was Lucy sobbing as she stood by my side overcome with grief. But then, for the first and only time in my life, a familiarly Australian voice quietly said, utterly deadpan, 'Could you say that again in English please, PM?'

All the leading players at the Paris climate conference were determined that it not end as rancorously as Copenhagen – the world needed to see some real progress. Not for the first time, as we went from one meeting to another, it struck me how out of step the climate deniers at home were with international opinion.

Greg Hunt was the Environment minister, a portfolio he'd held from the time I'd appointed him shadow Environment minister in 2008. He was knowledgeable and committed and had done well to persuade Abbott, and the cabinet, to agree to Australia taking a commitment to reduce emissions by 26–28 per cent from 2005 levels by 2030. This wasn't the most heroic commitment but, especially on a per capita basis, it was a substantial, realistic and well-received one.

I had no doubt then, as I have none now, that the key to cutting emissions is technology and I wanted to deliver a positive message in Paris, where gloom was in abundance thanks to the menace of terrorism on the one hand and global warming on the other. Our 2030 target would halve our per capita emissions – one of the biggest reductions of any G20 country – while we'd meet and beat our 2020 emissions reduction target.

> From Australia we come with confidence and optimism.
>
> We are not daunted by our challenge.
>
> It inspires us. It energises us.
>
> We do not doubt the implications of the science, or the scale of the challenge.
>
> But above all we do not doubt the capacity of humanity to meet it – with imagination, innovation and the prudence that befits those, like us, who make decisions that will affect not just our own children and grandchildren but generations yet unborn.
>
> Here in Paris Australia supports a new – and truly global – climate agreement.
>
> We firmly believe that it is innovation and technology which will enable us both to drive stronger economic growth and a cleaner environment.
>
> Australia is not daunted by the challenge. With great optimism and faith in humanity's genius for invention, we are confident that with your leadership, Mr President, we will, in common cause, secure our future.[2]

Returning to parliament and its last sittings for the year, all looked well. The leadership change had been better received than anyone could have imagined. The general consensus was that I'd handled myself capably on the international stage. I'd even been described as striking up bromances – with my old mate from New Zealand and with the handsome new PM of Canada, Justin Trudeau.

Abbott and his supporters had attempted to wedge me on national security while I was overseas, calling for more Australian ground troops to be sent in to fight with ISIL. In a national security statement in the House in late November, I made some unequivocal statements of principle, which many saw as marking a clear line of differentiation with my predecessor. 'We must not let grief or anger cloud our judgement. Our response must be as clear-eyed and strategic as it is determined. This is not a time for gestures or machismo.'[3]

ISIL was in a fundamentally weak position, unable to command broad-based legitimacy even in those areas under its direct control. The best way to support the global community's resolve to defeat it was through a combination of air strikes in both Syria and Iraq and support and training for Iraq's army. And our contribution to coalition forces was second only to that of the United States.

I said, 'The government of Iraq believes that large-scale Western troop operations in its country would be counterproductive,' and that the consensus of the leaders I met at the G20, at APEC and at the East Asia Summit was that there was no support currently for a large US-led Western army to attempt to conquer and hold ISIL-controlled areas.

While we couldn't eliminate entirely the risk of terrorism any more than we could eliminate the risk of any serious crime, we could mitigate it. In the wake of Paris, we were receiving updated intelligence on our domestic situation every day, with public safety the highest priority. Our security agencies were constantly vigilant, and this vigilance went hand in hand with the need to limit the spread and influence of violent extremist ideas. I reminded the House, 'The condemnation of ISIL and the promotion of authentic, modern and tolerant Islam by the leaders of big majority Muslim nations – including Indonesia, Turkey and Malaysia – has been especially important.' A strong and trusting relationship between the government and communities was crucial to ensuring the right messages reach the hearts and minds of those who might be vulnerable to the propaganda of terrorist groups.

There were no quick fixes, but we would defeat these terrorists with our strongest weapons – ourselves, our values and our way of life.

I'd reset our national security strategy on what were rational, non-hysterical foundations. Calm, cool and objective was the approach I took – and this set me apart from those who sought to exploit public anxiety both in politics and in the media. It also had the benefit of keeping us safe. The fundamental mistake so many people make is to play into the hands of the terrorists – the more you demonise Muslims, or Islam, the more you're fulfilling ISIL's objective.

Predictably, some of the people ramping up criticism of Islam per se, like Tony Abbott, wanted to use this issue to portray me and what *The Australian* described as my 'soothing language'[4] as being 'soft on terror'. This anti-Islam backlash was of concern to our security chiefs, including ASIO head Duncan Lewis. He and his colleagues were appreciative of the change of tone since I'd become PM. In December, he described this backlash as extremely dangerous, pointing out that any estrangement with the Australian Muslim community would be 'very unfortunate for our operations. It would impact negatively on what we are trying to do. We need to be very temperate and we need to be smart as a community.'[5]

As I said many times, 'Everything I say on this topic is with the benefit of the advice from the heads of ASIO and the AFP and designed to make Australians safer.'[6] Regrettably, a number of my colleagues – led by Abbott and supported by, mostly, the Murdoch newspapers – wanted to keep up their anti-Islam campaign, even to the extent of leaking confidential briefings Duncan Lewis held with MPs as so-called evidence of my using him to silence my colleagues.[7] Of course, their real objective wasn't the reform of Islam or the downfall of ISIL but rather the demise of my own government.[8]

One of the conversations that found its way into the media was between Lewis and Andrew Hastie, the newly elected MP for Canning. Too generously, I put it down to inexperience on his part.

I'd appointed Mal Brough as special minister of state. Mal had been a cabinet minister in the Howard government, had lost his Queensland seat of Longman in the Ruddslide of 2007 but had returned as the member for Fisher, on Queensland's Sunshine Coast, in 2013. Mal was a confident, energetic and capable minister who'd led the Howard government's controversial Intervention in the Northern Territory following the revelation of widespread child abuse in the 'Little Children are Sacred' report. He'd also been a strong supporter of mine in the challenge against Abbott.

However, Brough's association with the Slipper–Ashby saga resurfaced. As previously described, Julia Gillard's speaker – reviled as a Liberal traitor – had resigned after his grubby communications with James Ashby and alleged misuse of travel entitlements were exposed. But Ashby had received assistance from Brough and others and a judge concluded Brough's role had been improper, though this finding was rejected on appeal.

When I appointed Brough, the saga appeared to be over. Brough wrote to me on 25 September, shortly after his appointment, saying the AFP had confirmed he wasn't under investigation. Then it emerged that the AFP were investigating Brough over the claim he'd requested Ashby remove Slipper's diary and disclose extracts – in breach of the Crimes Act. In a *60 Minutes* interview years before, Brough had apparently admitted he'd done so and then made confused responses to opposition questions about it in the House.

It made for a messy finish to the parliamentary year. There's nothing more miserable than a minister in question time walking up to the despatch box again and again to try to bat away allegations of wrongdoing. Brough's position was that there were no new facts from what had been disclosed in earlier proceedings. The only position I could take was to argue that the police should complete their investigations. I told Brough to get proper advice on evidence from a competent lawyer so he, and I, would know where he actually stood. On 29 December, he finally stepped down from his ministerial positions pending the outcome of the AFP inquiry. When it became obvious the inquiry wasn't going to be concluded swiftly, he resigned from the ministry in February.

Brough's problems were unedifying but at least they were old news. That wasn't the case with the next ministerial drama, which related to Jamie Briggs, my minister for Cities and the Built Environment.

Julie Bishop contacted me on 5 December to tell me a young DFAT officer in Hong Kong had made a formal written complaint about the behaviour of Briggs. He and his chief of staff had taken her out for dinner and drinking late at night in various bars in Hong Kong. His behaviour, she said, had been inappropriate.

Jamie had a reputation for being something of a party animal, as his exuberant conduct at Abbott's wake had demonstrated. But I was amazed that a minister, a married man, would be so indiscreet as to go out drinking in the wee hours with a young DFAT officer in a public bar in Hong Kong which, one assumes, he knew was in China. I wondered whether, if there was any dispute about what had happened, the Chinese intelligence agencies would be kind enough to send us the video!

I was furious. I'd contemplated dropping Briggs from the ministry after I took over as PM because of reservations about his judgement; he'd been retained only because Bruce Billson had declined the Cities portfolio. How could Briggs have been so stupid?

The prime minister's adviser on the application of ministerial standards is the secretary of PM&C and so I duly sought Michael Thawley's advice. He asked former APS Commissioner Lynelle Briggs to investigate the matter. She interviewed both Jamie Briggs and the young diplomat. Her conclusion was that he'd breached the ministerial standards and Jamie Briggs's resignation followed.

Regrettably, he shared pictures of the diplomat, and text messages from her, with some of his friends. Her identity found its way into the media and, as too often happens, the complainant became identified. Already upset, she now had to endure an element of public humiliation. The News Limited tabloids lapped this up and began staking out her parents' home in Melbourne, chasing down pictures of her, all so they could expose her identity and, no doubt, challenge the substance of her complaint.

I did my best to protect her, phoning the News chief executive, Peter Tonagh, on New Year's Eve, arguing that publishing her identity would make her 'a double victim'. Moreover, it would send a message to every woman who's the subject of unwanted attention from a boss or superior: don't complain. It would make a mockery of everything their papers had said about respect for women.[9]

Despite these tremors, from a political point of view, overall the year seemed to be ending well. We were now way ahead in the polls, whether it was on the party or preferred PM measures. The celebrated psephologist Malcolm Mackerras predicted I'd win both the 2016 and 2019 elections![10] (Well, that proved to be half-right, which is better than most predictions.)

I should address here the question of whether I should have taken advantage of my electoral honeymoon and gone to an election in late 2015.

There were practical obstacles to an early poll. The Liberal Party was broke: fundraising had dwindled to a trickle as the Abbott government's fortunes declined. Brian Loughnane, the director, was getting ready to go and was certainly not planning to fight another election. When Tony Nutt took over as federal director later in the year, there wasn't enough money to pay his salary. The party organisation was simply not ready for an election.

Andrew Burnes, the honorary treasurer of the party, summed up the situation in his 2016 report:

> When I took over as Federal Treasurer in late June 2015, the party had negative working capital, there were no YTD accounts, no campaign funding was set aside for the 2016 election, no budget for FY16, no Financial Controller and there had been virtually no fundraising at all in the first 6 months of the 2015 calendar year.
>
> Significantly, there was no funding plan for the 2016 election, which at that point was likely to occur in 12–14 months' time.[11]

We could find no evidence of any policy or campaign preparation. Abbott had been surviving day to day, with little time to think ahead to an election. We needed a platform for an election that was forward-looking and gave people a reason to vote for us, not simply a reason not to vote Labor.

Above all, the public is always sceptical about early elections. They expect governments to govern, to get on with the job they've been entrusted with. Theresa May's experience in 2017 with a snap poll that went disastrously wrong is a good example; Julia Gillard's near-fatal experience in 2010 was another. Or, to quote Sir John Carrick's famous phrase, 'You can't fatten the pig on market day.' You need to build a case for re-election. And there's no substitute for a budget to present a fully costed economic platform to campaign on.

There were also several important pieces of housekeeping I needed to get done. One of these was reforming the Senate, which I address in chapter 32.

So, all those considerations meant we were better off getting on with government and going to an election in 2016, recognising that even though my honeymoon had lasted longer than that of any other new leader, it wasn't going to last forever.

CHAPTER 28

Tax reform and other indiscretions

The year 2016 began with the misconduct of Jamie Briggs, a sobering reminder – reinforced by an *SMH* editorial[1] – that I alone was responsible for ensuring my ministers complied with my standards of ministerial conduct. At stake was the public's confidence in them and in the government. It didn't help when Peter Dutton inadvertently sent journalist Sam Maiden a message (intended for Briggs) in which he described her as a 'mad fucking witch'.[2]

But while issues of propriety occupied the tabloids during the January holidays, my attention was on the policy agenda and the election, which was due within months. My weeks were full of the 'deep dive' briefings I commissioned on every policy area, always with the relevant minister and senior officials. I ensured policy experts also joined us, and not just the departmental secretary as was the usual Canberra practice.

Right from the outset I'd signalled that I was leading a new government, not a new marketing effort for an old one. I had to restore a sense of optimism in our economy, to inspire confidence to grow by investing more capital and employing more people. My mission was shamelessly boosterish – to exhort Australians, in businesses large and small, from all walks of life, to strive to get ahead. My message was that we lived in times of rapid change and volatility, so we had to make volatility our friend by being smart, agile and innovative.

There was a worsening culture of complaint in the media, especially social media. Even when things were fine, we were told we should feel bad. Say it enough and you soon will feel bad.

That was disturbing when so much of what we do – as individuals, businesses, nations – depends on confidence. We don't have to delude ourselves with false confidence in Australia – we're so hypercritical of ourselves, so good at knocking, that simply restoring a bit of objective balance can work wonders.

But negative expectations feed into decision-making and downbeat views become a self-fulfilling prophecy. We'd had years of it. There wasn't any positivity in Abbott's economic message. Whether it was 'axe the tax' or austerity to deal with the 'debt and deficit disaster', it was gloomy. He no doubt wanted to hang the budget deficit around Labor's neck, but in my view he overdid it and didn't complement it with a positive agenda. That took a toll. The initial boost to business confidence that the Coalition had enjoyed upon coming to office in 2013 had steadily reversed itself, and business confidence declined rapidly between June and August 2015.[3]

Australians wanted to know how we were going to fix things, create a better life for them and, above all else, how a Liberal government would put more money back in their pockets. They knew Lucy and me well. There was an expectation, with my business background, that I'd deliver both a stronger economy and a balanced budget.

Our 'jobs and growth' slogan had an important message. The 'growth' was good because it delivered more jobs and, importantly, enabled us to afford the generous social-welfare safety net, the infrastructure both social and economic that Australians expected. We needed to reform to stay ahead and by doing so have the means to look after those who might fall behind.

From day one, our economic message was relaunched. More than a few cynics sneered as I said repeatedly that there's 'never been a more exciting time to be an Australian'. But it's true. The growth in technological innovation, the opportunities to grow and expand are limitless. It truly is the most exciting time to be alive!

I was happy with the narrative, and so was the market. But what were the new measures, the reforms we were going to undertake?

We weren't going to be able to cut our way to a budget surplus: that was the lesson of the 2014 budget failure. As John Key had done in New Zealand, we needed to ensure that the economy, and thus tax receipts, grew faster than expenditure.

The most important economic lever of any Commonwealth government is tax. And the problems with our tax system were well known. In theory, it was a field well ploughed; in practice it was full of landmines.

Our tax system had evolved to the point where we discriminated in favour of older people with savings, who often paid little tax, and against younger people trying to get ahead, who paid high rates of personal income tax. Increasingly, by world standards, our company tax was uncompetitively high and we raised too little of our revenue through indirect taxes, like the GST, that are hard to avoid.

The Commission of Audit had made all these points, as had many other tax reviews, and Joe Hockey had sought to pull it all together in a tax discussion paper he released not long before I became prime minister. The most contentious issue, a hoary chestnut if ever there was one, was the GST, a 10 per cent value-added tax levied on most goods and services, collected by the Commonwealth but all paid to the states. It had been part of the big tax reforms undertaken by John Howard and Peter Costello in 2000. The prospect of the GST, we all recalled, had very nearly lost Howard the 1998 election.

The tax reform most widely canvassed was to increase the GST's rate from 10 to 15 per cent, if possible broaden its base so it picked up some of the areas that had been exempted (such as water) and then use that additional revenue for … well, that was where the problem began. Everybody had a different idea of where the money should be spent.

There were many other areas of potential tax reform – unwinding some of the generous superannuation concessions to wealthy retirees was one, reining in or even abolishing negative gearing on residential property was another. But all of them had enormous political risk and sensitivity – which is why an old tax is often described as a good tax, not because of any fiscal merit, but because people are used to it. Any change in tax, unless it's an across-the-board cut, is going to have some losers. And even if they're fewer in number than the winners, they'll scream much louder at what they've lost than the winners will thank you for what they gained.

Put another way, if a government gives somebody an extra dollar, be it a tax break or a benefit, they may reluctantly thank you, but will just as likely say it should have been $1.50 or $2. On the other hand, if you take 10 cents away from somebody, they'll come for your head.

However, unless you're going to slash government spending, which is always somewhere between impossible and politically suicidal, you have to design tax reform on a revenue-neutral basis. The theory is to abolish or reduce inefficient taxes and thereby increase economic growth, and offset the lost revenue by increasing efficient taxes. And what's an efficient tax? Well, one that least hinders economic activity.

Taxes should have as broad a base as possible. Ideally, they'll apply to revenue sources people find hard to reduce or avoid and thus have as small a distorting effect on the economy as possible. That is, unless you actually want to reduce something – 'sin' taxes on alcohol and tobacco do reduce boozing and smoking, just as a carbon tax will reduce high-emission activities.

The problem for federal governments is that almost all the most inefficient taxes are levied by the states. Stamp duty on property transactions is a shocker because it's a brake on trade. If we believe in markets, then we shouldn't discourage trade by taxing it. That's why stamp duty on share transactions was abolished long ago. But the revenues from stamp duty on property transactions are as large as they're alluring to state governments.

Another shocker is payroll tax – the more people you hire, the more tax you pay. And small companies have a payroll-tax exemption, which then creates a disincentive to grow. Tax experts regularly argue that if you can't abolish payroll tax altogether, at least abolish the exemption for small businesses and remove the disincentive to grow above the threshold. Well, that might make fiscal sense in theory, but it would be politically impossible and probably fatal for any government that tried it!

The most inefficient tax the federal government levies is company tax. Capital is mobile; investors can invest anywhere in the world. The higher a country's company tax, the less the return to shareholders and thus the less they'll be inclined to invest. Which is why, over the years, both Labor and Liberal governments have reduced company tax – something treasurers Keating and Costello had in common. And of course, most shareholders pay tax, one way or another, on their dividends.

If lower overall company tax was positive for the economy, what about personal income tax? Well, it's not as much of a disincentive as it might appear – labour is much less mobile than capital.

As I argued back in 2005, the ideal personal income tax system has few deductions or exemptions; it also has the broadest base that enables you to have a low rate.[4] In our system, by world standards we have a high top marginal rate (45 per cent plus 2 per cent for the Medicare levy) and it currently cuts in at $180,000, which at only a little more than twice average full-time earnings, is a relatively low threshold.[5]

Like most countries, our progressive personal income tax system is designed to ensure the rich pay a larger percentage of their income in tax; however, inflation pushes taxpayers into higher tax brackets. This bracket creep means that while you're earning no more in real terms, you're paying more tax, so as a consequence your real income is being reduced.

When you couple this with the tapering off of means-tested family and other benefits as income rises, you exaggerate the disincentive from higher marginal tax rates. In some cases, the combination creates an effective marginal tax rate close to (and sometimes even above) 100 per cent – in other words, all or almost all of an additional dollar earned is lost in a combination of extra tax paid and welfare benefits lost.

Politicians regularly promise to index thresholds to inflation and occasionally actually do it. But in reality, governments love bracket creep because as wages rise with inflation, tax receipts increase at a higher rate and, if and when a threshold adjustment is made, the government of the day can claim credit for cutting taxes.

From an efficiency point of view, the ideal income tax is one with a low rate and few thresholds. We couldn't afford that in 2016 but we got there in 2018. The result of that year's budget was that 94 per cent of Australians would pay a tax rate no higher than 32.5 per cent by 2024, which would apply as an effective flat tax from $41,000 up to $200,000. In the 2019 budget, that rate was reduced to 30 per cent.

Broaden the base, lower the rate – that's the mantra of good tax reform and basically what the GST reform of 2000 was all about. Regrettably, in order to get it through the Senate, the base wasn't as broad as it should have been: fresh food, health, education and water-utility (but curiously not power) bills were exempt. But it was a huge improvement on the tangle of sales taxes it replaced.

So, for many years there's been an argument, the intensity of which ebbs and flows, that the relatively efficient GST should be increased, either by broadening the base and/or raising the rate, and that inefficient taxes should be reduced.

Determined to lead a more optimistic and open government, in the last few months of 2015, I encouraged an open discussion about tax. This may have been unwise because Labor was able to run every conceivable scare campaign – especially around the GST. In such an environment, ministers have to be very disciplined. On the one hand they can acknowledge the government is carefully considering a wide range of possible reforms; on the other hand they must take care not to front-run actual decisions. The goal is to consult widely, confer privately and make an announcement when a decision is made.

And all of our tax discussions were taking place in the context of a tight budget. Not only had Abbott and Hockey been unable to secure passage through the Senate of most of the 2014 budget savings, those savings that had been passed were more than offset by new spending such as the special Syrian refugee intake and the abandonment of revenue measures of which Labor's bank deposit levy was the largest. So, at the same time we were seeking to see how we could afford tax relief, we also needed more revenue and that meant winding back tax concessions of one kind or another.

I encouraged Scott Morrison and the Revenue minister, Kelly O'Dwyer, to reach out – as I was doing – to the widest range of interest groups, including the welfare lobby, like the Australian Council of Social Service, and the Australian Council of Trade Unions. The *AFR* sponsored an economic summit that Craig Emerson organised, and we met with them and benefited from their recommendations and research.

In a speech to the Australian Chamber of Business Leaders in November 2015, I summed up the approach I was taking on tax. Our aim was to ensure our tax system should be the servant of our economy and its people and their businesses, not the other way around. I said, 'Australia is an egalitarian, fair society. So any changes to the tax system must be seen to be fair overall. But we are also a nation of hard workers, innovators and doers. So it is absolutely vital that any changes to our tax system reward enterprise, effort and success.'[6]

I mentioned we'd be examining company tax and personal tax particularly carefully.

We wouldn't be playing the rule in, rule out game. Wayne Swan had taken that approach with the Henry tax paper in 2010 and found that if you salami-slice an issue before you've thoroughly reviewed it, you end up with no options at all.

Media outlets responded by racing each other to tell their readers what the government was going to do. Meanwhile, plenty of people in the business community expressed their views, including the BCA, who wanted to see an increase in the GST offset a cut in company tax. The states said they wanted an increased GST to fund what they forecast were growing demands for investment in hospitals and health care.

To put it another way, everyone was keen on increasing the GST (and getting a share of the proceeds). Only the Commonwealth government would cop the political pain from doing so.

Personally, I was always completely open-minded about increasing the GST rate or broadening the base – but the most important objective was that there had to be a real, demonstrable economic gain in doing so. There was a view among some economic commentators – almost an article of blind faith – that increasing the GST and broadening its base would automatically produce economic gains. But prime ministers don't have the breezy luxury of simply expressing an opinion on economic issues. I needed hard evidence. I was becoming concerned that an increase in the GST was a solution in search of a problem. What precisely was the benefit we'd gain from increasing it, and how did it compare to the downside?

Now, this was early in my time as PM and Scott Morrison's time as treasurer. We developed into a successful partnership, not least because we were friends and had each other's confidence. But we worked in different ways. I like to have as many options as possible on the table, debate them freely and without preconceptions and then arrive at a decision. And this all had to be done in confidence, by which I mean secrecy. Scott, however, liked to start with a firm view of the solution – or, more often, the announcement – then go in search of the problem. Plus he confided in journalists much more than I thought was wise.

During my time as PM, I didn't sense Scott was using the media to damage the government or undermine individual colleagues. He was more a briefer than a leaker – the difference between the two similar concepts is subtle. Most of the time, he wanted to promote a particular policy. This was acceptable if it was coordinated, but risky. He used to describe the practice as 'tilling the soil' in advance of a formal decision.

At least, that's how he justified it. However, there were two other aspects to his serial indiscretions that are less high-minded. Scott, like many other politicians, used leaks to ingratiate himself with journalists and newspapers – especially News Corporation's Simon Benson and editors like Chris Dore and Paul Whittaker. In return for a drip of good political stories, he'd be rewarded with favourable coverage. The other aspect is that he used leaks to front-run government decisions in the hope that by giving them a head of steam in the media, his colleagues couldn't push back.

In the three years we worked closely together, this issue was the only sore point between us.

My philosophy, which eventually I'd persuaded almost all ministers to abide by, was simple. We consult widely, make sure we're fully informed. We confer, canvassing many options and alternatives, but always in total confidence. We make a decision collectively – as a cabinet. And then we announce our decision in a time and manner of our choosing.

This may seem, to the gentle reader, to be common sense. And it is. But it's worlds away from how most politicians and most governments have operated in recent years.

I took a thoroughly practical approach: there was no point in changing the GST if we couldn't show that there was a strong economic benefit. We couldn't use it as a solution if we couldn't be certain there was a problem that needed fixing – and demonstrate that this was the case.

Morrison, though, unfortunately nobbled any chance of GST reform becoming a reality by front-running policy options in the media. Time and time again he'd float ideas on the front page and monitor the public reaction before determining whether it was good policy or bad policy.

The biggest problem with Scott's preferred approach of reverse-engineering economic policy via the front pages of the tabloids was that once an idea was in the public domain, no matter how good or bad it was, you couldn't put the genie back in the bottle. You immediately faced a barrage of questions about it in the media, in the House, and were forced to rule things in or out before you'd done a proper analysis and consultation.

A change to an idea floated was branded a 'backflip' – and a bad reaction to an idea floated gave Labor a scare campaign. Everyone knew tax reform proposals floated in the newspapers had to come from meetings among ministers, so it wasn't credible to brush off an unpopular policy briefed as being 'fake news'. Colleagues, backbenchers and ministers are always unsettled and often frightened by these leaks and briefings, feeling that journalists are in the know but the people on whose support the government relies – them – are left in the dark.

Never was this more apparent than on 1 November 2015 when the News Corp Sunday tabloids had splashed across their front page, '15 per cent GST!'[7] Samantha Maiden described Treasury as canvassing four options for reform, the toughest of which would see the GST increased to 15 per cent and include fresh food, health care and education, which are currently GST-exempt.

It was news to me when I woke up to read the papers. Naturally, it spooked the backbench, had various industry groups up in arms and gave Labor a free hit into the highest-rating news of the week, the 6 pm Sunday-night bulletin. But the story was correct. These were all options we were considering, although we certainly hadn't landed on any of them.

Scott's constant front-running frustrated me and many of my colleagues, especially Mathias Cormann, who regularly wanted to cut Scott out of discussions because he knew they'd wind up in *The Daily Telegraph* days later. 'We have seen this movie before,' Mathias would say when economic proposals wound up in News Corp papers. If we were negotiating the passage of economic legislation through the Senate, Cormann would often swear me to secrecy lest Morrison find out. I didn't always oblige him, but it wasn't easy managing the pair of them as their mutual distrust grew.

Morrison grew bolder with his push for an increase of the GST – a point noted by many in the gallery, who'd begun to write columns suggesting Scott and I weren't on the same page. I understood Scott's desire to do something big while he was treasurer, and he'd persuaded himself that raising the GST and lowering income tax was the big reform. And I was as keen to pull off a big tax reform as he was. We were an ambitious PM and treasurer, but new in our jobs.

There were at least two big problems with Scott's project (and which the economic commentators never bothered to explain).

First, the GST is ultimately a tax on real wages – increasing the GST raises the price of goods and services and reduces workers' purchasing power. Of course, income taxes have a similar effect. So the net economic benefits of a 'tax mix switch' – simultaneously increasing the GST and reducing income taxes – weren't immediately obvious. Wouldn't we just be increasing people's take-home pay by cutting income tax and then funding it by jacking up the price of everything they buy by increasing the GST? We'd have to make that case based on hard evidence.

Second, even if you wanted to cut income taxes, there was never a credible plan to deal with the states and territories (who under existing arrangements received every single dollar of GST revenue). What about compensation for people who didn't pay income tax but would be hit with a higher GST – such as pensioners, welfare recipients and self-funded retirees? It quickly became apparent that the package would require careful consideration of significant changes to our welfare system and to our federation – both huge policy issues in their own right.

I was always mindful that the impacts of any change would be borne unevenly across the community: any reform would have to address that. The Howard–Costello GST reform had a compensation package equivalent to a full percentage point of GDP – \$18 billion in today's dollars. And the reality was that the economics (never mind the politics) of a tax mix switch simply didn't stack up in the absence of a substantial compensation package.

For example, a 5 percentage point increase in the GST (taking it from 10 to 15 per cent) applied entirely to reductions in personal income tax would result in over 90 per cent of those people in the bottom 20 per cent of income earners and nearly 80 per cent of those in the second-bottom quintile being worse off. Even in the third-highest quintile, 40 per cent would be worse off.

By the time everybody on lower incomes was put in a position where they were no worse off – a political necessity – there was less than half of the \$30 billion increase in GST available for personal income tax cuts, company tax cuts, health spending in the states and so on. In short, a straight 'GST up, personal income tax down' tax mix switch didn't work. Too many people were either on low incomes and not paying tax or, like many pensioners and self-funded retirees, benefiting from high-income tax thresholds or exemptions from tax on their superannuation fund income.

By Christmas 2015, I believed we couldn't proceed with reforming the GST unless Scott produced Treasury modelling to show a positive benefit for the economy. Modelling isn't everything but recent experience in Australia indicated that reform would be difficult to sell without solid economic evidence and analysis backing up the case. Labor had made this mistake time and again, with policies like the carbon tax, the mining tax and the NBN.

Eventually, as expected, the modelling showed that from an economic-growth standpoint there was no compelling reason to simultaneously increase the GST and cut income taxes. Or, in the words of the Treasury briefing:

> To achieve major economic gains – that is a shift in the level of GDP – tax reform must lower Australia's reliance on taxes that are most harmful to economic growth. While there are many possible variants, tax reform would only generate significant economic growth if it includes a cut in the company tax rate or state stamp duties – a switch from personal tax to GST alone will not generate significant growth.

As if that wasn't bad enough, the advice went on to say that 'if all groups in the lower-to-middle income range are fully assisted for their average price impacts then the economic gains will be negligible or even negative as there is no extra incentive to work'.[8]

Well, I thought to myself, as I read that, so Treasury says the only way jacking up the GST and reducing income tax will deliver positive economic growth is if we make sure everyone on welfare or low incomes is worse off! That's why economists are often described as knowing the price of everything and the value of nothing!

But when we announced in February 2016 that there'd be no changes to the GST – and released the modelling results to show why – it was painted as a political backdown because Morrison had briefed so hard that we *would* reform the GST. We were hit in the media and in the polls even though it had never been to the ERC or the cabinet, let alone the party room.

By Saturday 20 February, I had even more of a mess on my hands. Morrison had just done a Press Club speech and a whole series of interviews that seemed to have reinforced his impotence. To me he seemed depressed. I wondered if he was out of his depth.

The following day, Sunday 21 February, began badly, with yet another leak of budget planning. This time, plastered across the front pages of the News Corp tabloids were changes to superannuation and negative gearing.[9]

I didn't have long to wait for the first sign that this was hurting us in the polls. We were having a cabinet dinner at The Lodge when the Newspoll figures came through. Our primary vote was down three points and we were now 50:50 on the two-party preferred, having been consistently ahead 53:47 for quite a while. This was very bad. My diary entry that day recorded the terse conversation that ensued.

> *I was very blunt with the cabinet and in remarks clearly directed at Morrison made it plain the lack of discipline and the leaking had to stop. I was very emphatic. I have spoken to Morrison again and again about this and it was important the cabinet see that I am putting my foot down. He has to be, and be seen to be, on notice. He almost offered his resignation to me afterwards but didn't. In my study here at The Lodge we agreed to go forward but strictly on the basis that we agree on matters like this privately and then announce. No more front-running. He claims to have no idea where the leaks to Sam Maiden came from but everything we know and his past track record point to him. As [our mutual friend] said to me later, this has always been his MO … Anyway things will be tough. We agreed to do the Senate [voting] reforms, so that will be the big story this week. Scott did not enjoy the feedback from his dining companions.*

With the GST tax mix switch idea discarded, and for good reason, we looked at other taxes to determine whether there were opportunities for reform.

Capital gains tax (CGT) for individuals was taxed at a concessional rate – only half of the gain was taxed. So for someone on the top marginal rate of 47 per cent, their CGT was 23.5 per cent. Many economists had argued the concession was too generous. I never agreed with that because, in many cases, a person could hold an asset over a long period, see it grow in value at, or even below, the rate of inflation, and then get hit with a tax on what is a purely paper gain.

When Keating introduced CGT in 1985, he taxed capital gains at the taxpayer's marginal rate but indexed for inflation. That at least made sense and was consistent, but Costello abolished it on the basis it was too complex and replaced it with the concessional model we have now.

But the fundamental point is that we should have a concessional rate on investment gains because – wait for it – we want more investment. If you tax long-term investment gains at the same rate or close to the same rate as you tax short-term income, then you reduce the incentive for long-term investment, which is surely something we should be encouraging.

Neither I nor my colleagues supported any change to the CGT discount. We were fortified in that approach by the knowledge that the revenue gains would be a long way off and highly uncertain, so were unlikely to be of much help to the budget over the four years of the forward estimates.

For many years, I'd been concerned about the way in which our tax system was changed to provide more concessions to older people with savings, while the tax rates younger workers paid remained very high. These concessions were particularly generous during John Howard's time as prime minister and reflected both the Coalition's affection for older Australians, who habitually voted Liberal, and the high budget surpluses that enabled such generosity.

Prior to my first budget as PM, the superannuation system was especially generous to the very rich. For example, income from super funds was taxed at 15 per cent and capital gains at 10 per cent, but once a person turned 60, they could move their super fund into the retirement phase. This precluded them making further contributions and also meant the retirement account paid no tax on income or capital gains. Thus, somebody could have tens of millions of dollars in their retirement account, earn millions of dollars of income, and pay not one cent in tax!

Among other reforms, we decided to change the law so that a retiree could contribute only $1.6 million to the tax-free retirement account, and would therefore pay tax at 15 and 10 per cent on income and capital gains respectively on the balance of their super fund.

These changes adversely affected only 4 per cent of those with super accounts and returned money to the budget. This enabled us to increase the 37.5 per cent tax threshold from $80,000 to $87,000, thus preventing half a million middle-income earners from going into the second-top tax bracket. But it also enabled us to ensure the tax rate on low-income earners' super contributions would be reduced, effectively to zero, and helped enable women to catch up on their super contributions after time out of the workforce with small children.

However, the outcry from the wealthy, many of whom were Liberal Party members, was very loud. One person, who had over several hundred million dollars in their retirement account, wrote to the Liberal Party's treasurer saying he'd never make another donation to the party, which had become, so he said, communistic! Needless to say, I was unmoved and we were able to get all our super reforms through the parliament after the 2016 election, with only a few changes.

Another contentious area of tax reform was the treatment of net rental losses, or negative gearing. Australia has always had a comprehensive income-tax system where individuals are able to aggregate all their different sources of income and then deduct from that all of the different expenses incurred to earn that income.

Negative gearing entails people borrowing to buy real estate, renting it out and then offsetting the net rental loss on the property after interest against their salary or professional income. Because of the CGT concessional rate, this meant that a person on the top marginal rate could deduct their net rental loss from their taxable income at 47 per cent but their capital gain on the sale of the property would be taxed at only 23.5 per cent. Add to this the fact that interest rates were low; housing demand was high; values were growing strongly year after year; banks were prepared to lend large amounts against the value of the property, often as much as 90 per cent of valuation; and you had a strong incentive to engage in negative gearing.

As housing prices rose, housing affordability suffered. Many young home buyers found themselves being outbid again and again by (older) investors who, they believed, were benefiting from a tax-system loophole to subsidise their investment.

Many tax reviews over the years had recommended abolishing negative gearing, which practically meant prohibiting a person from offsetting a net rental loss against their personal income, as opposed to other investment income. The Labor Party had announced in February 2016 that they'd abolish negative gearing, a bold move given that most of the 1.3 million negative gearers were on middle incomes. There were many more teachers and police officers with negatively geared properties than there were barristers, surgeons or investment bankers.

And after Keating prohibited negative gearing in 1985, he quickly reversed the reform – in 1987. That was because of the impact it was believed to have had on reducing housing supply and pushing up rents.

On the other hand, most comparable economies, including the UK and the USA, at the time didn't allow negative gearing on residential property, at least to the full extent we had in Australia.

We looked at the issue very carefully in the run-up to the 2016 budget and again, at Scott's insistence, in the run-up to the 2017 budget. I wasn't persuaded that abolishing negative gearing was a good reform. Labor's proposal went further than real estate; it applied to business investments. This seemed to me to be a really bad idea – why shouldn't someone be able to subsidise a new business from their salary income while it was getting going?

Labor's opposition leader, Bill Shorten, would often accuse me of looking after my 'rich Point Piper mates' in my opposition to Labor's policy, but what he overlooked, as I reminded him, is that my rich Point Piper mates all had plenty of investment income, so would have no difficulty being able to negative gear against that. The people Labor's reform hit were those whose main income was from personal exertion – yes, that included some high-flying professionals like barristers and surgeons, but the bulk was middle-of-the-road wage and salary earners.

The only thing that attracted me, at all, to negative-gearing reform was the prospect of additional revenue at a time when we were struggling to meet our budget targets. I was never persuaded by the public policy rationale that you should change negative gearing because house prices were rising. Labor's approach of making a structural, irreversible change to the tax system to address a cyclical issue in the housing market made absolutely no economic sense. If housing was too expensive, the answer was to build more houses and that meant reforms to planning so that supply could respond more readily to demand.

Scott Morrison, however, came at this issue from a very political perspective. He saw housing affordability as one of the hottest of hot political issues, as it was, and recognised that Labor had an advantage over us because they had one simple message: 'ban negative gearing'. He wanted us to get on board and ban it first. He was strongly supported in this by his assistant minister, Michael Sukkar.

We considered many different permutations on negative gearing. Barnaby Joyce, for example, initially favoured the idea of capping the number of properties that could be negatively geared, say to one or two properties. But then he realised that would encourage people to invest in more expensive properties in the city, at the expense of property investment in the regions where housing affordability wasn't an issue. Then we considered capping deductions on net rental losses from properties worth a particular amount, but discarded it as being too complex. We also looked at capping the annual amount of losses that could be offset – say at $10,000 or $20,000 – or the period – say five years – over which losses on any one property could be offset. Scott was particularly keen on the $20,000 limit, which, to my dismay, surfaced in the papers on Sunday 21 February.

If we were to move down this track at all, I didn't want to prevent middle-income wage and salary earners from investing in residential rental property and getting the tax break that negative gearing offered.

Given that you'd have to grandfather any change so that prohibition only applied to properties acquired after a stated date, the budget benefits would be slow in coming. And, of course, any of the refinements we considered would make that benefit to the budget even less.

We didn't make any changes to negative gearing in the 2016 budget but we reconsidered negative gearing reform again in the lead-up to the 2017 budget. I discussed the issue with the governor of the Reserve Bank, Phil Lowe. He was concerned that it would have too big a negative impact on housing prices. Instead, we settled on some tweaks to negative gearing. We abolished the right for landlords to deduct travel expenses (flying to the Gold Coast to inspect the rental property was all too common), among other changes. And the Australian Prudential Regulation Authority (APRA) started to change the rules on how much banks could lend on investment properties and in particular how many interest-only loans they could make. These macroprudential levers are more effective brakes on an over-buoyant housing market because they can be calibrated – dialled up or down, on or off – whereas a tax change is long-term and, in this area, hard to change.

Again though, this was an example of looking with an open mind at all taxes to see whether they could be improved, tweaked or modified.

Prior to the 2016 budget, we were focused on tax reform that would drive economic growth and there was no doubt that if we didn't have the means to abolish stamp duty or payroll tax, the best reform by which to do that was reducing company tax.

This wasn't just Liberal Party orthodoxy; the Hansards are littered with statements from Labor prime ministers and treasurers endorsing that proposition. Bill Shorten said in 2011, 'Cutting the company income tax rate increases domestic productivity and domestic investment. More capital means higher productivity and economic growth and leads to more jobs and higher wages.'[10] Julia Gillard said the following year, 'If you are against cutting company tax, you are against economic growth. If you are against economic growth, then you are against jobs.'[11]

And for good measure, the former Labor treasurer Chris Bowen had advocated cutting company tax in a recent book: 'It's a Labor thing to have the ambition of reducing company tax, because it promotes investment, creates jobs and drives growth.'[12]

Our economic policy had to be, and be seen to be, driving higher economic growth. At its heart was the Enterprise Tax Plan, a long-term reduction of company tax.

We were all in agreement that company tax cuts would deliver economic growth and create more jobs – this was the whole point of our economic-growth agenda. And at this stage, we thought we'd receive bipartisan support, as Labor was also in agreement. Indeed, as late as September 2015, Chris Bowen had argued that the company tax was a tax on workers and urged that it be cut to 25 per cent. And Bowen's economic argument was exactly the same as ours (and Bill Shorten's): reducing the company tax rate would increase the return on investment, leading to higher investment, higher productivity, more jobs and higher wages.

We were also starting to see movements globally in this area – Australia's tax rate was increasingly becoming uncompetitive. A number of nations were considering cutting company tax and we wanted to be ahead of the curve. Things were moving so rapidly that by the end of the debate, we ended up in a situation where we didn't want to fall off the curve! As a high-wage country, we have to compete on other factors: the skills of our workforce, a certain regulatory environment and the tax rate.

As it turned out, Donald Trump would cut company taxes from 35 per cent to 21 per cent, and France – under Emmanuel Macron, himself from the centre left – agreed to cut its rate from 33.3 per cent to 25 per cent. The UK already has a low company tax rate of 19 per cent and had legislated to cut it to 17 per cent this year (a reduction Boris Johnson said last November may be put on hold).

But how did we pay for the tax cut? Notwithstanding the BCA, we knew there was nothing less saleable than jacking up the GST to pay for a cut in company tax. Immediate cuts in company tax provide a windfall gain to investments that were committed when the rate was higher, so we developed a model similar to that used in the UK, where we could phase in company tax cuts over a decade, starting with smaller companies.

I reasoned that if larger companies, whose investment plans are longer term, know that the tax rate in five or seven years will be lower, then that will encourage them to invest now. Smaller companies, often family businesses, have shorter investment horizons, so a near-term tax cut will be effective for them. It would allow us to argue we were the party that put small business first and we could also double-down by continuing the instant asset write-off for small companies. Essentially, by bringing the company tax cuts in over time, we could get the same economic benefit of incentivising more investment as we would with an immediate across-the-board cut but at a lower financial cost to the budget.

The full proposal we took to the election was a 10-year enterprise tax plan that would see all companies by 2026–27 pay a company tax rate of 25 per cent, down from as high as 30 per cent in 2016, when the policy was announced. It would be phased in over several years. Companies with a turnover of $2 million would receive relief first and it would gradually increase.

Lowering taxes would encourage companies to increase investment, expand and employ more people in better-paid jobs. Ultimately, this would grow the economy. Inspiring confidence in our economy, as I promised.

One of the biggest problems in our federation is that almost half of the money the states spend is raised by the federal government. In 2017–18, the states and territories spent $263 billion, of which $120 billion came from Canberra, and $63 billion of that was the proceeds of the GST.[13] This unsatisfactory state of affairs is called 'vertical fiscal imbalance' and it produces a lot of moral hazard. A state premier can complain the feds aren't giving them enough for schools or hospitals or infrastructure, but then if the feds try to find more money by raising taxes, they're pilloried – often by the very same state premier!

The GST is a good example. It's a tax, all of whose proceeds go to the states. But if it were to be increased, all of the political pain would be visited on the federal government.

There's no doubt that in an ideal world, each level of government would raise all of the money it spends. If, for instance, the people of Victoria wanted more money spent on schools, the state government could say, 'Well, we can do that, but it means either we spend less on something else – hospitals perhaps? Or we raise taxes.' But as it stands, the state government can rail against Canberra for not giving them enough money.

Of all our taxes, the best growth tax is personal income tax. And it's the largest, collecting $223 billion in 2018–19 compared to company tax at $94 billion or the GST at $66 billion.[14]

The states, of course, originally levied their own income taxes (as they still do in the USA) but gave their income tax powers to the Commonwealth in 1942.

At different times people have tried to give back to the states a direct share of personal income tax. Malcolm Fraser had a go at it in the mid-70s but the resistance from all the states saw him drop it. As I learned in March 2016, nothing had changed.

Looking for a new tax policy that could deliver real reform, we decided to propose to the state premiers that we'd identify a share of income tax that would be handed over to them and that they'd be able to increase or lower their rate of tax. We'd lower our tax rate to make room for them, so that the total amount of personal income tax collected wouldn't change, but, as for the future, states would be free to raise more or less. Taxpayers would see clearly they were paying so much income tax to the feds, and so much to the state – just as they do in the USA and other federations.

I took the proposal to our cabinet, which approved it, and then asked the secretary of PM&C, Martin Parkinson, to discuss it discreetly with state officials to determine whether it was worth bringing to the Council of Australian Governments meeting scheduled for 1 April.

When I pursued the proposal with the premiers directly and collectively at a dinner at The Lodge on 31 March, the Labor premiers were all outright opposed. Annastacia Palaszczuk said that coming to Canberra for money was too good to pass up. 'It suits us perfectly. We get all the credit for spending the money, and you get all the blame for raising it. And when we can't spend enough, we blame you!'

Mike Baird beat a hasty retreat. Soon only the Western Australian premier, Colin Barnett, remained enthusiastic. I had to abandon the plan within 48 hours of announcing it.

It was a good idea, but sadly there's no room for good ideas like that in the bitterly contentious Australian political environment. Mercifully, unlike the GST front-running, the backlash was quick, passing like a summer's storm, and the proposal was soon forgotten.

I should have realised the only way a reform like this could be effected was if the proposal came from the states to the federal government and in circumstances where Labor and Liberal states were aligned. And even then, it'd be easy to kill off with the 'double tax' sound bite. It wasn't a captain's call by any means, but I should have known better.

On the positive side, it meant that when the states demanded more money I could say to them, 'I offered you the means to raise more money and you knocked it back. So are you only in favour of higher taxes if somebody else has to raise them?' Their unashamed and unhesitating answer to that of course, was 'Yes!'

I was reminded then, as I was on many subsequent occasions, of the wisdom of Christian Porter's observation: 'Complaining about Australia's federation is like complaining about Switzerland's mountains.'

CHAPTER 29

Keeping Australia safe

While domestic political dramas dominate the headlines most of the time, national security is the constant preoccupation of any prime minister. I was very fortunate to have capable, trusted friends as Foreign and Defence ministers in Julie Bishop and Marise Payne, but national security issues always end up on the prime minister's desk, and mine was no exception.

During my prime ministership, Australia faced the most complex range of threats it had ever experienced in peacetime. When I became PM, the most acute, and most existential, was the threat of a nuclear conflict on the Korean Peninsula. Succeeding his father in 2011, Kim Jong Un accelerated North Korea's nuclear test program and missile launches in 2016 and 2017, by which time he had the capacity to launch a nuclear attack on Japan and had either achieved, or was close to achieving, the ability to fire a nuclear-armed ballistic missile to the continental United States.

It's a terrible indictment of past leaders that North Korea was ever allowed to get to this point. It isn't just a tyranny that starves and brutally oppresses its own brainwashed people, but it exports drugs, missiles and other weapons of mass destruction. North Korea is a cyberterrorist as well, spreading malware and ransomware around the world.

The goal of the international community has been to persuade North Korea to stop its nuclear weapons program in return for a lifting of the economic sanctions that have been imposed on the rogue state for many years. Kim Jong Un knows very well that no nuclear armed state has ever been overthrown by force. Gaddafi abandoned his nuclear program and ended up dead in a ditch.

The problem the United States and its allies have faced for many years is that there are no feasible military options. Even if an attack on North Korea managed to neutralise its nuclear capabilities, the close-range artillery attack on Seoul would turn that city into a smoking crater – as one American general colourfully put it to me.

So, the best weapons are economic, and that was why I consistently urged the Chinese government to enforce the UN sanctions and in particular cut off North Korea's supply of oil. While I stressed China wasn't responsible for its rogue neighbour's misconduct, it undoubtedly had the greatest leverage and with that came responsibility. This wasn't welcome, but China did eventually reduce supplies of oil to North Korea. Australia has imposed its own sanctions in addition to those mandated by the UN.

My advice to Trump was that the only hope of a peaceful deal with North Korea would be one where the United States gave an unequivocal security guarantee in return for denuclearisation – much as the Kennedy administration did to Cuba in return for the removal of Soviet missiles. Nearly 60 years later and long after the USSR has faded into history, the United States hasn't sought to invade Cuba.

So, that would be the precedent that could form the basis of a deal. And Trump has had several meetings with Kim Jong Un to try to pursue it. So far, the only beneficiary of those encounters has been Kim. He's achieved what his father and grandfather could not – meeting the United States president as an equal. The kudos he gained from that has won him grand receptions in Beijing, where he wasn't well regarded at all. Trump is proud there hasn't been a war, but so far at least the legacy of his attempts to resolve the problem has been a stronger and more defiant North Korea.

Apart from North Korea's threats of nuclear war, terrorism was the most pressing and high-profile national security issue we were confronting at home, in our region and in the Middle East. Domestically, the federal government's effort was coordinated by Greg Moriarty, formerly our ambassador in Tehran and Jakarta. Abbott had appointed him to the role in 2015 and it was a good choice.

I'd abandoned the furious and divisive 'death cult' rhetoric of Tony Abbott, much to the relief of ASIO and the AFP. My measured tone was also noticed in the Muslim communities, whose cooperation was absolutely vital if our agencies were to remain well informed about the extremists' plans and be able to disrupt terrorist plotting before an attack was launched.

The Murdoch press was obsessed that 'politically correct' politicians weren't calling out the Islamic nature of the ISIL- and Al Qaeda–inspired terrorism. As I said repeatedly, while you couldn't pretend their terrorism had nothing to do with Islam, suggesting that all Muslims or Islam at large were to blame for terrorism was doing what the terrorists wanted and would only lead to more alienation of young Muslims and more recruits for extremists.

Following the murder in October 2015 of NSW Police accountant Curtis Cheng on the steps of the Parramatta police station, I said, 'Australia is the most successful and most harmonious multicultural society in the world. There is no comparable country with as large a percentage of its citizens and residents born from outside its shores with such a diverse cultural mix of peoples. None of us, no one of us can look in the mirror and say, "All Australians look like me." Australians look like every race, like every culture, like every ethnic group in the world.'[1]

Our success was because of the mutual respect that was fundamental to our harmony as a multicultural society, to our future prosperity and our national security. If we wanted our faith and our cultural background to be respected, then we had to respect that of others. Violence began with intolerant, hateful speech, and we had to call it out.

Duncan Lewis, ASIO director general, sent me a text thanking me for my remarks and forwarding positive feedback from Muslim community leaders who applauded my vision 'to protect, promote, celebrate our successful Australian multicultural social cohesion and harmony'. Duncan also liked the firm messages I'd given on people smuggling but concluded, in suitably diplomatic language, 'As a general point I would suggest a shorter press conference, but I recognise these are early days so you want to make your points more fully.'[2]

My persistent mantra was 'no place for set and forget' on national security. At my own initiative and with the support of all the states and territories, we amended the law to keep a terrorist offender detained after the end of their sentence if the court is satisfied they are a continuing terrorism risk. We also agreed to make it much harder for those accused of terrorism offences to get bail.

In July 2016 an ISIL supporter drove a truck down the Promenade des Anglais in Nice, killing over 80 people and injuring many more, including one young Australian woman. Terrorists have always been attracted to crowded public spaces, but the use of ordinary and readily available vehicles raised new issues – a person, like the Nice killer, could be radicalised very quickly online and then simply get behind the wheel and do their worst. Such a deadly attack didn't need bombs to be made or guns to be acquired. Many more of these vehicle attacks followed around the world, including one in Melbourne in January 2017, killing six, and on the London Bridge in June 2017, killing eight, including two Australian women.

Immediately following the Nice attack I asked the counter-terrorism coordinator, Greg Moriarty, to develop a national strategy for crowded places. It was a collaborative effort involving all states, territories, local governments and the private sector, and has produced a set of online tools and guides for both protecting existing public places from attack and incorporating safety features into the design of new or altered places.

The crowded places strategy involved considerable international cooperation as well. I made sure our agencies were working closely with their international counterparts. Just as there should be no set and forget on national security, nobody has a monopoly on wisdom and we should always be looking to learn how other countries keep their people safe.

Our security agencies thwarted several large-scale terrorist plots during my time as prime minister, notably a planned attack at Federation Square in Melbourne at Christmas 2016 and a conspiracy to blow up an airliner in July 2017.

In the latter case, two brothers in Sydney had received a viable explosive concealed in a meat grinder and planned to put it on an Etihad flight to Abu Dhabi in the luggage of a third brother. At the last minute, the bomb wasn't put on the plane. Shortly afterwards, Israeli intelligence advised ASIO about the plot and we realised the bomb was still at large and likely to be placed somewhere else. At the same time, we learned that the conspirators in Sydney had been preparing special explosives to release poisonous gas – fatal inside a confined space like a bus or a train.

Duncan Lewis briefed me within hours of ASIO being tipped off by the Israelis and an anxious day followed as the AFP and NSW Police worked with ASIO to identify the conspirators and the location of the bomb. As a precaution, security at our airports was ramped up.

Fortunately, when the Khayat brothers were arrested the bomb was found, as was the evidence of preparation to make a poison gas explosive.

I was relieved that disaster was averted, but shocked that a viable bomb, big enough to bring down a plane, had simply been sent to Australia through the post. We quickly moved to permanently tighten airport security, especially for air cargo.

Equally troubling to me, however, was that the pair in Sydney had been receiving step-by-step live video guidance on bomb-making from a terrorist in Syria over Telegram, an encrypted end-to-end messaging application. This underlined the need for good intelligence and the closest possible collaboration with international partners.

Our regional counter-terrorist efforts were largely the province of the Australian Secret Intelligence Service. The elegant diplomat and spy Nick Warner was its director until I made him the first director of National Intelligence.

Nick had procured an airborne intelligence-gathering capability that was of critical assistance to several countries in our region in tracking terrorist groups. One was the bloody struggle by the Philippines Armed Forces to retake the southern town of Marawi after it had been occupied by ISIL-linked terrorists. This, I should add, was meant to be something of a secret, but when I visited Manila in 2017, the Philippines army chief openly referred to it as 'the game changer', so our cover was blown!

All of this underlined to me the need to work closely and swiftly with our regional neighbours, especially Indonesia, and to stay at the cutting edge on signals intelligence. The better our capabilities – and they are the best in the region – the more incentive our neighbours have to work with us. Thanks perhaps to Peter Wright, I have always had a deep interest in signals intelligence and all the technologies associated with it. Australia's agencies, especially our Australian Signals Directorate, are world-class, the equal in capability of agencies in countries many times our size.

However, while our counter-terrorist efforts at home and in the region were typically secret, or at least low-profile, the work of our ADF in the Middle East was anything but.

By the time I became PM, our air force was supporting the Coalition effort against ISIL in Iraq and Syria; our army, together with the New Zealanders, were training Iraqi troops and later police at the Taji base outside Baghdad; and a smaller group of special forces were providing closer support and assistance to their Iraqi equivalents, the Counter Terrorism Service.

In Afghanistan, we'd withdrawn from combat operations in Oruzgan Province and our role was largely confined to working with UK and NZ partners in an officers training academy in Kabul. It required a large number of troops to protect our trainers because of the frequency of 'green on blue' attacks, where supposedly friendly Afghan troops turned on their foreign allies.

In mid-January 2016, I left for the Middle East. These visits are always cloaked in secrecy and the media crews who accompany the PM are required not to broadcast any details of the visit until the party is outside of Iraq or Afghanistan. A visiting head of government is a very tempting target, so the less notice or awareness our enemies have the better.

Air Chief Marshal Mark Binskin, the chief of the defence force (CDF), accompanied me on the trip. Somewhere over the Indian Ocean, I asked what we could do to further support our troops in the field. His answer was surprising. Mark described an arcane conflict between Australian and international law. Under international law our pilots, for example, could target ISIL operatives whether they were in active combat roles or providing support, including financial support. Under our domestic law, however, in conflict of this kind, our troops could only target individuals actually engaged in combat. 'So, if they don't have a gun in their hand, our guys are at risk if they target them,' Mark said.

This seemed bizarre to me. Straightaway, with Justin Bassi and Pete Anstee, we started researching the international law of armed conflict, the Australian Crimes Act and other authorities – all uploaded onto our iPads on *Wombat One*'s generally sketchy wifi. We worked out a solution, conferred with the attorney-general, and by the end of 2016, changes were made to enable our troops to target all ISIL personnel. Binskin later told Bassi that outside our huge investment in defence capabilities, this was the most significant practical change during his time as CDF.

In the course of that visit, I met with Mohammed bin Zayed, who is the effective leader of the government of the United Arab Emirates. I found him then and subsequently to have a keen and shrewd strategic perspective.

Like all Sunni Arabs of that region, he is fixated on the threat from Iran and recognises that the consequence of the 2003 Iraq War was to give Iran an influence in Iraq that Saddam had, for decades, denied them. He was right of course: the US-led invasion was, as President Trump acknowledges, one of America's worst foreign policy mistakes.

We took the time to discuss the situation in Syria. He agreed with Putin that trying to bring down Assad was simply making the same mistake the West had made in Iraq and in Libya. You shouldn't overthrow one tyrant unless you can be reasonably confident that what you put in his place will be an improvement.

Like Putin, he believed the solution in Syria should be essentially a federal one with a secular government, like Assad's Ba'athist regime, and with power sharing between Sunni, Shia and Christians agreed along the lines of Lebanon. It seemed then to me to be unrealistic, and subsequent events confirmed that, but I found it interesting that his thinking, despite his close ties to the USA, was more aligned to Putin's than to the idealistic view of the Americans at the time.

He was very opposed to the deal Obama was negotiating with Iran. The US and European nations were on the verge of lifting oil and financial sanctions against Iran in exchange for it dismantling the majority of its nuclear program.

'The message it sends to the Gulf is that this agreement would contain the Iranian regime for 15 years, but after that the Gulf is on its own,' he told me, a criticism identical to that made by Netanyahu. Trump has since disavowed the Iran nuclear deal and ramped up sanctions.

For the next legs of my journey – to Baghdad and Kabul – we flew on a C-17, which had defensive systems *Wombat One* lacked. Once in Iraq we wore body armour almost everywhere and were ferried around in American Blackhawk helicopters, which featured two large M-60 machine guns trained by their fiercely alert gunners out of a window on each side of the passenger compartment.

I was proud to see our troops there, as I was in Kabul and elsewhere in the Gulf. They were mostly younger than my own children and as bright as they were enthusiastic. The team working on cyber operations could have stepped out of the army and started their own technology firm; maybe they have by now.

Iraqi Prime Minister Haider al-Abadi thanked me for the contribution of our forces to his nation's security. The Iraqi security forces had been disbanded after Saddam's overthrow and hadn't yet been effectively reconstituted. Our trainers at Taji were vital to Iraq having a functioning army. Al-Abadi stressed that while he welcomed our trainers and our special forces advisers, he didn't want to see foreign troops on the ground, especially in any of the large population centres like Ramadi or Mosul, where it would be counterproductive.

In the last weeks of the Abbott government, with my strong encouragement, we'd agreed to take 12,000 additional refugees from the Syrian conflict zone with priority given to oppressed minorities like Christians and Yazidis. It's tragic that some of the most ancient Christian communities, which had lived alongside their Muslim neighbours for over a thousand years, were now being driven out, caught between the Shia anvil and the Sunni hammer as each sought to demonstrate their contempt for non-Muslims. ISIL had embarked on a genocidal campaign against the Yazidis and came close to succeeding. Al-Abadi's assessment confirmed my view that the prospects of his Christian communities were bleak. The diverse and multicultural Middle East was coming to an end.

In Kabul, I met with our troops there and with the nation's leader, President Ashraf Ghani. He received me in the old royal palace, much of which he told me, delightedly, had been hauled up over the Khyber Pass on the back of elephants more than a century ago. Ghani is an academic and an unlikely president of a war-torn nation like Afghanistan. He spoke with conviction about advancing the prospects of women in Afghanistan, who've been so wickedly oppressed by the Taliban and, it must be said, the harshly patriarchal Pashtun culture.

In terms of both Iraq–Syria and Afghanistan, I was immensely proud of the service of our ADF personnel and appreciated President Ghani's sincere and grateful acknowledgement of the 41 Australians who'd been killed while serving in his country. Our contribution in both theatres has been substantial compared to many other countries, especially European ones, but is nonetheless modest compared to the immense resources the United States brings to bear.

I get no thrill from military matters and feel uneasy about politicians, generally lifetime civilians, rushing to be pictured in planes and tanks and surrounded by uniforms. I was always conscious – and in that part of the world more so than anywhere – of our responsibility as leaders to seek to resolve conflict by peaceful means. And when we do put our troops in harm's way, to ensure they are well led and well equipped so they have the very best prospect of being able to return safely home once their mission is accomplished.

Our son-in-law, James Brown, had been deployed twice to Iraq and once to Afghanistan. He introduced me to many of his 30-something veteran mates. Australia's troops in Iraq and Afghanistan rarely numbered more than a few thousand at any one time, but the wars had been going on for so long there were now over 40,000 young veterans of those conflicts.

They were sceptical of much of the elaborate sentimentality we attach to our military. 'Australian kids know much more about the diggers at Gallipoli a hundred years ago than they do about our soldiers of today,' James would say; he went on to write a book about the way the Anzac legend, and its adoration, has seen millions spent on memorials to the long dead but not nearly enough on supporting veterans today.[3]

As I met more of the young veterans, I realised we had to do more and I summed it up by saying, 'There is no better way to honour the service of those diggers from a century ago than to support the servicemen and women and veterans of today and their families.'[4] I had good ministers for Veterans Affairs in my time, especially Dan Tehan and Darren Chester. We substantially increased the awareness of and funding for veterans' mental health and in 2017 made mental health services free to all veterans.

But there was a trap in all of this, as I learned at the North Bondi Returned and Services League (RSL) Club one afternoon. The increased attention to veterans' mental health, high rates of post-traumatic stress disorder and suicide didn't encourage businesses to employ them. Equally, our servicemen and women had little guidance as to how to go about getting a job in the private sector. 'How do I fill in my résumé,' a young sergeant asked me, 'when most of my work was classified? How do I explain what I did?'

So, I set up a Prime Minister's Veterans Employment Initiative in 2016 and used my convening power as PM to bring business leaders together to recognise the value of our servicemen and women's unique skills and experience. Some of those business leaders, like banker George Frazis, were veterans themselves and I made sure that both the RSL and newer ex-service organisations like John Bale's Soldier On were engaged. It has been a tremendous success, and as Mark Binskin shrewdly observed more than once, 'We can recruit so many more young people if they think their time in the ADF will set them up for a good job in civilian life.'

After visiting the Middle East, the next stop was the USA – Washington, the imperial capital itself. The founders of the republic built all its great buildings and monuments in a neo-classical style, creating their own Rome on the Potomac. And the inhabitants of this 21st-century Rome were as anxious about their decline, and the rise of rivals, as were their counterparts two thousand years before.

Barack Obama is a warm and keenly intelligent man, one of the most successful politicians of our era. Simply being elected president, twice, as a black man in America was extraordinary enough, but everything about his campaign was contemporary and optimistic. And yet he appeared to lack the weary cynicism of so many politicians: his idealism was only slightly dented, his quiet confidence only a little dimmed by nearly eight years of the world's most demanding job.

Part of the business of running a successful empire is to ensure that visitors are received well and suitably impressed, and we were. I especially enjoyed staying at Blair House, the president's official guesthouse, and exploring the historic rooms, including one where President Harry Truman had been shot at, through the window, by a would-be assassin in the street outside! A far cry from today's overwhelming security around American presidents.

Obama's and my views were well aligned on all the major issues. I spent time both at the White House and at Congress talking about the TPP. Obama was candid about the pushback he was getting from the Republicans over the TPP protections for biologics. They still felt we hadn't given the big pharma companies enough. I assured the president and the senators that our position was settled on the terms agreed last year.

Both at the meeting in the Oval Office and the lunch that followed, we were joined by John Kerry, the secretary of state; Susan Rice, the national security advisor; Mike Froman, the trade advisor; and a number of other senior officials. For my part I was joined by our ambassador, Kim Beazley, as well as senior advisers, including Sally Cray, Frances Adamson, Justin Bassi, Peter Anstee and John Garnaut.

We got onto the subject of refugees. I described the issue of people smugglers encouraging vulnerable and desperate people onto boats to come to Australia and the related unlawful arrivals and drownings at sea. How Kevin Rudd's Labor government had moved several thousand intercepted asylum seekers to Nauru and Manus Island in Papua New Guinea. 'We wanted to close those centres and resettle the detainees,' I explained, 'but we have been unable to find enough resettlement opportunities in countries the detainees would move to. And we believe if we bring them back to Australia, the people smugglers will use that as a marketing ploy and the boats will start up again.'

Obama nodded, and asked me to go on. Emphasising that these people weren't terrorists or criminals, I said, 'And we want to get them off those islands. So, can we do a deal where you offer asylum to them and we do the same with some of the people seeking refuge in the US?'

The president described his nation's challenge: waves of unaccompanied children and youths crossing the border from Guatemala, El Salvador and elsewhere fleeing gang violence. But then he returned to Australia's situation and wanted to know how many people there were and where they were from.

'Mr President, there are about 1800,' I said. 'The largest single group are Iranians but there are many from Afghanistan and other parts of the Middle East and Central Asia. Many of the Iranians won't get refugee status and are essentially economic migrants but cannot be returned to Tehran because Iran doesn't accept involuntary returns.'

As the meeting in the Oval Office wrapped up, I was left alone with Obama for a few minutes. 'I think we can do something there. I want to help those people on Nauru and Manus and I want to help you. And you can help us. We will get working on it,' he said.

Back home, Defence Minister Marise Payne and I were busy completing the Defence white paper. Work on this had begun under Abbott. It set out our strategic environment and described the capabilities we'd need to protect ourselves in the decades ahead. In terms of the content, the changes made by me and Marise to the draft we inherited were important. I put the language about China into my own words and expanded the discussion of cyber capabilities. Disappointed the draft paid so little regard to Indonesia, I also wrote an expanded section on our nearest neighbour.

Marise was a good friend of many years: we'd worked together on the republican campaign two decades before. She'd prepared herself for the role as Defence minister with years on the Joint Standing Committee on Defence and Foreign Affairs. She knew her stuff, and when she spoke – as I often said to her – I always felt safer. She was calm, knowledgeable and considered. But she lacked confidence in her own considerable ability and wouldn't get out enough in the media to promote our Defence Industry Plan, which is why I later appointed Christopher Pyne minister for Defence Industry.

Beyond doubt, our region had become more contested in the last 20 years. The rise of China had brought enormous benefits to its own people but also Australia and the region. However, a wealthier, stronger China was going to have a defence force that matched its economic strength and would naturally compete for influence with the USA. We had no interest in containing China, even if the means to do so existed, but we needed to ensure that together with the USA, Japan and our other regional friends, we could provide a balance to maintain respect for the rule of law and the rights of smaller nations. Whatever warm and soothing words might emanate from Beijing from time to time, in planning the defence strategy of a nation, you have to look at the long term, and hubris, ambition and disregard for the rights of others are all too often regular companions of the unchecked hegemon.

The defence investment we were making was enormous – over $200 billion in new capabilities over the decade. The centrepiece, appropriately for our island nation, was the re-equipment of the navy with 12 new submarines to replace the six *Collins* class submarines as well as three air warfare destroyers, nine new anti-submarine 'future frigates' and 12 new offshore patrol vessels.

When we launched the white paper on 25 February 2016, apart from the three destroyers which were already being completed, we hadn't yet decided on who'd build the ships. But one of the ways I'd shifted the focus of the white paper was in stipulating that, as far as possible, every dollar spent on defence procurement would be spent in Australia. And so, together with the white paper, we released a Defence Integrated Investment Program and a Defence Industry Policy Statement.

Marise and I held the launch at the Australian Defence Academy in front of an audience of cadets and young officers – the men and women who'd be commanding the new navy in the decades ahead. I spoke about the strategic picture and our desire to build on our already strong ties with Indonesia and Japan, and invest in increased engagement with India. To continue to be a constructive and influential player in our region, to have the capacity to defend Australia and to contribute effectively to international coalitions, we had to adequately fund our defence effort. I announced we'd grow defence spending to 2 per cent of GDP by 2020–21 – three years earlier than promised. It was a substantial reinvestment that would promote a long-term and sustainable defence industry in Australia. As well as an historic modernisation of the navy, we'd also considerably strengthen our cyber capability; create a more potent air-combat and air-strike capability, centred around the joint strike fighter; and upgrade our army's equipment and armoured vehicle fleet.[5]

At the time we launched the white paper, the Defence Department and the navy were considering competing proposals to build our new submarines from Japan, Germany and France. In that work, they were assisted by a high-powered expert advisory panel chaired by naval architect and former US Secretary of the Navy Don Winter. Their advice and the whole process was peer-reviewed by two retired US Navy admirals.

So, I was satisfied we were getting the best advice and, most importantly, we were working closely with the Pentagon and the US Navy. President Obama had made it clear to me that the choice of manufacturer was ours to make.

When I became PM, the secretary of the Defence Department was Dennis Richardson, one of the most experienced of all the Canberra mandarins. A former head of ASIO and ambassador to Washington, Dennis had been at Defence since 2012. He was blunt and, as he was at the end of his career, had no problems with telling politicians what they didn't want to hear. Which was exactly how I liked it.

I'd known him for years and can count a few ferocious arguments among our many amiable encounters. He'd often, in the National Security Committee, start off a contrarian observation with, 'PM, as the devil's advocate here, may I say …' One day, temptation overwhelmed me and I replied, 'But, Dennis, isn't that unwise? You know what they say about the lawyer who appears for himself?'

But he was in no mood for banter, satanic or otherwise, when we met in my first week in the job. Dennis came straight to the point. 'PM, you will by now have a copy of the draft Defence white paper. It's a good piece of work. But part of it is complete and utter bullshit.' Well, that got my attention.

'It says,' he continued, 'that the future submarines can start to be delivered in the mid-2020s – so about ten years from now. That's simply not possible. I told your predecessor this and he insisted that the 2020s date should go in and leave the problem for another government.'

I didn't have to think too long about that – so I told Dennis we should include a completion date that matched reality, which was the early 2030s.

A week after we launched the Defence white paper, on 2 March, *The Australian*'s Greg Sheridan, a close friend of Abbott, wrote that he'd obtained a copy of an early draft of the paper as it stood when Abbott was still PM and noted the change in the expected delivery date of the first new submarine. His article included some incendiary criticism from Tony Abbott himself.[6]

Abbott denied leaking the draft to Sheridan and, as usual, an AFP investigation failed to establish who did. But his comments were indication enough that, just as Abbott had sought to make trouble for the government over defence deployments in the Middle East and our response to terrorism, so now he was prepared to do so over our naval shipbuilding program. I refrained from saying publicly what Richardson had told me and after a while the furore subsided.

The submarine tender seemed to be a straightforward procurement process and while I was kept updated on it in general terms, I wasn't involved in the assessment of the bids and let it take its course, being, as it was, in the hands of experts.

However, as I was to learn, the political story of the submarines acquisition was as complex as their engineering.

When the Abbott government was elected in 2013, it inherited some serious problems in terms of naval shipbuilding. The program to build three air warfare destroyers was behind schedule and over budget; the six *Collins* class submarines were rarely available because of technical and maintenance problems. In fact, we were lucky to be able to have two of the six at sea at any time. Plus they were getting old, and nothing had been done to find a replacement.

The Defence Department wanted to have a new submarine designed in partnership with another country with proven submarine expertise (as the *Collins* had been built with Sweden's Kockums) and built in Australia. Tony Abbott felt the need to get new submarines was urgent; he felt the construction of submarines in Australia was high-risk and decided we should buy new submarines based on the Japanese *Soryu* class, to be built entirely in Japan.

He approached Shinzo Abe in April 2014. This wasn't an easy issue for Abe. Japan had legislative restrictions on exporting defence matériel and there was no export culture in their defence industry at all. But after a big effort from Abe, the Japanese system agreed to explore the possibility of building submarines for Australia. The prospect of closer strategic cooperation between Australia, Japan and the USA reinforced this move.

By late 2014, Abbott had concluded the primary focus should be a new submarine designed and built in Japan. This was widely known and there were calls for an open tender. In Senate estimates, naval experts argued the *Soryu*'s capabilities did not suit our requirements. Many others, particularly South Australian MPs and senators, loudly argued that the submarines should be built in Adelaide as had been promised before the election.[7] None of this shook Abbott's resolve to contract to build the new subs in Japan.

However, the 'empty chair' spill of February 2015 changed all that. Senator Sean Edwards and some other South Australian Liberal members traded their votes in return for Abbott agreeing to a competitive tender so that local Commonwealth-owned shipbuilder ASC Ltd could bid for the work.

While the decision to hold the tender was a blatantly political one, from the time I became PM in September 2015 I could see it was being conducted rigorously and with all the appropriate standards of probity.

However, as the process was concluding in April 2016, I became concerned for the first time whether Abbott may have encouraged Abe and his staff to believe that not only was the tender decision a political one, but it had not changed his previous determined intention to build the subs in Japan.

I was troubled as I recalled visiting Shinzo Abe in Tokyo in December 2015, where we discussed the submarines and I dutifully said that we had a competitive process and we'd assess the bids on their merits. Was Shinzo listening to that and thinking, 'Oh well, he just has to say all this for the benefit of the others in the room, but I know we are going to win'? Or had he realised that whatever Abbott's intentions had been, with me as the new PM the process was, as I indicated, rigorously objective and merit-based?

The recommendation from Defence was unequivocal: the French proposal for a conventionally powered version of the latest French nuclear sub design – the *Shortfin Barracuda* – was the best of the three. The independent panel chaired by Don Winter also endorsed the choice of the French subs, as did our other naval experts.

The challenge for me now was to break the bad news to Abe, which I did on 25 April. He was disappointed as both he and his government had put an enormous effort into the Japanese bid. I could tell he felt, with some justification, that they'd been let down by us. I'd just returned from a visit to China and had to reassure him that the decision wasn't the result of any pressure from Beijing, and it certainly wasn't – a point I made publicly.

The political way in which the tender arose always had the potential to create awkward misunderstandings in Japan. There should have been a competitive process from the outset, as there was with the other naval shipbuilding projects undertaken during my time.

It says a great deal about Abe's grace and generosity that he didn't hold it against me or against Australia as our subsequent collaborations demonstrated. He and I were able to work together productively, not least on keeping the TPP alive after Trump pulled out in 2017. Shinzo was always a mensch.

Angela Merkel was thoroughly philosophical about the German bid failing – the Germans were, after all, in the hunt for several other big procurement contracts and subsequently secured the deals to build our 12 offshore patrol vessels and several hundred light tanks, or combat reconnaissance vehicles.

François Hollande was, naturally, ecstatic. This was a $50 billion deal, one of the biggest in the world, and offered the opportunity for a long-term strategic partnership between France and Australia – one I was able to advance considerably under his successor, Emmanuel Macron.

In 2017, in a $4 billion contract, we agreed with the German ship-builder Lüerssen to build 12 *Arafura* class offshore patrol vessels, with the first two being built in Adelaide with ASC Shipbuilding and the rest in Perth with Civmec. And in June 2018 we agreed that Britain's BAE Systems would design nine *Hunter* class frigates in a $35 billion contract and that they would be built by ASC Shipbuilding in Adelaide. The timing of all the contracts was designed to ensure continuous shipbulding for decades into the future.

There was criticism of my determination to build the submarines and other naval vessels in Australia. Abbott had been of the view that we couldn't afford to build all the new vessels in Australia and had essentially resolved to build the frigates and the offshore patrol vessels here but build the submarines overseas in Japan.

I wasn't persuaded by this. Certainly, a foreign yard with current experience in building submarines will build faster and at less cost than an Australian yard would build the first one – but stress 'the first one'. We'll never have a sustainable continuous shipbuilding industry unless we start building ships and do so continuously. And if we want, over the decades to come, to develop an Australian advanced manufacturing sector, there is no industry more likely to provide the 'pull-through' stimulus than defence, and no project more at the cutting edge than submarines – the most complex, sophisticated and lethal vessels in the fleet.

We decided to build the submarines in Adelaide, which was where the *Collins* class submarines had been built and were, for the most part, being maintained. This was portrayed as a thoroughly political exercise designed to help Christopher Pyne keep his seat. However, Adelaide made sense in many dimensions. South Australia had a long manufacturing tradition, which had declined with the closure of the Australian auto industry, and it needed some additional stimulus. With great schools and universities and the beginnings of a defence industry culture, it could become the regional centre for shipbuilding, if we had the ambition to think big and the concentration to execute effectively on that vision.

One of the artists at *The Adelaide Advertiser* told the editor, Sam Weir, 'My son is a natural at mathematics and doing really well at school. And I always assumed he'll never work in South Australia – there just aren't enough high-tech jobs here. These shipbuilding projects mean there will be.'[8]

I heard many observations like that, and they matched my own experience over the years going to Adelaide, meeting with people of roughly my own age and learning, almost without exception, that their children were somewhere else. That's why I said again and again, 'The jobs of the 21st century are not somewhere else; they're here in South Australia.'

It's commonplace to argue that Australia should have a nuclear submarine fleet. A nuclear submarine can stay submerged indefinitely and operate at very high speeds while submerged – over 25 knots, more than twice the speed of a conventional submarine. In fact, a nuclear submarine's time on patrol is only limited by the endurance of the crew.

Conventional submarines, like our *Collins* class subs, are powered by batteries that are in turn charged by diesel engines connected to generators. Because the batteries have limited capacity, a conventional submarine has to come up to the surface, or just below it, in order to run the diesel engines and recharge the batteries. This is called snorting because a mast is put out of the water to suck in the air to run the engines and in turn to emit the exhaust. And snorting makes a conventional submarine more open to detection.

So, if nuclear submarines are faster, have much more endurance and can operate in stealth mode for much longer, what's not to like, and why aren't we building them?

Simplistically, you could describe our future submarine as a nuclear submarine design with a conventional power and propulsion system. One of the advantages of partnering with the French is that if Australia were to move to a nuclear navy in the future, we have both a partner, in France's Naval Group, with nuclear submarine experience and a boat design that could accommodate a switch to nuclear.

There'd be no point in us having a nuclear navy if it wasn't completely sovereign and able to be operated by, and at the direction of, the Australian government. That means the submarines and their nuclear power plants would have to be maintained in Australia. Similarly, the nuclear waste from their reactors would have to be disposed of here.

Some people have suggested Australia could 'lease' several nuclear submarines from the Americans and have them maintained by the US Navy at their base in Guam or in Hawaii. But even assuming the Americans would do that (and they'd be more inclined to oblige Australia than anyone else, I believe), the dependence on the USA for maintenance would mean the submarines weren't, in reality, a sovereign Australian capability. We would, in effect, just be paying for two US submarines.

Our law currently prohibits the construction or operation of nuclear power plants, nuclear enrichment, fuel fabrication or reprocessing facilities.[9] And any change to that would prompt a massive political debate about nuclear power. We've had that debate several times before, most recently when John Howard was prime minister and commissioned Ziggy Switkowski to do a review of nuclear power in Australia in 2006.[10]

And then there's the environmental challenge of nuclear power plants, their operation and the disposal of their waste. Whether in response to the disaster at Chernobyl or more recently Fukushima in Japan, the developed world, for the most part, is moving away from nuclear power. Germany and Japan are committed to decommissioning their nuclear plants. A recent effort by the South Australian Labor government to win support for establishing an industry of storing nuclear waste in a remote, deep, geologically stable bunker failed miserably.

There's no country with a nuclear navy that doesn't also have a civil nuclear industry – the latter supports the former with expertise and, of course, job opportunities for retired nuclear submariners. If we were to move to nuclear submarines, we'd need to have some civil nuclear industry, justified by its support for the navy rather than its offer of cheap electricity. It would need long-term, bipartisan support and well over a decade would be needed to establish the pool of skilled personnel in every field to support it.

There are a couple of other considerations to bear in mind. The United States would almost certainly welcome our having nuclear submarines – it would make us a more useful and capable ally. China, however, would perceive the move as directed at them and use it to justify their own naval expansions. Other powers, like Indonesia, would be tempted to follow suit, but would be unlikely to see the development as targeted at them.

This sounds like I'm putting nuclear submarines in the 'too hard' basket. Well, not quite. Shortly before my time as PM was rudely interrupted, I'd started to investigate the question again. My judgement then, and today, is that this is a debate that will continue, so the government should make sure it's well informed.

A final consideration is that battery technology is progressing rapidly due to the boom in electric vehicles. It may be that, with better battery technology, the range, speed and endurance of conventional submarines will significantly improve. Then the gap between their conventional and nuclear capabilities would be sufficiently diminished that a switch to nuclear submarines, for Australia, isn't justified. By 2030, some experts forecast, lithium ion batteries should enable an Australian *Attack* class submarine to stay submerged for over 30 days. While not being able to match a nuclear submarine for speed, it'd be much quieter. A nuclear power plant cannot be turned off to allow a nuclear submarine to run on batteries alone.[11]

Time will tell. It wasn't the reason for the choice, but accepting the French submarine bid, as opposed to the Japanese or German bids, at least gives us a potential option to move to a nuclear design in the years ahead.

Cybersecurity had featured prominently in the Defence white paper. In it, we had for the first time acknowledged that the Australian Signals Directorate – our equivalent to the US National Security Agency (NSA) and the UK's Government Communications Headquarters (GCHQ) – had an offensive cyber capacity. In other words, it had the ability to use cyber means to disrupt and disable opponents. This wasn't a revelation to the cognoscenti, but it was important for our adversaries to understand that we could hit back and do so effectively and covertly.

The other big national security announcement we needed to make was that of our first Cybersecurity strategy, which I released on 21 April. Because of my background with OzEmail and other tech companies, I'd developed an exaggerated reputation for being 'tech savvy' – Tony Abbott, on one occasion, credited me with having invented the internet; of course, that was Al Gore, I hastened to add, tongue in cheek. But in truth, my technological knowledge only looked good compared to most politicians and senior bureaucrats, who often struggled to work their smartphones and made little effort to understand the networks and applications on which, increasingly, their livelihoods and security depended.

So, the principal object of the Cybersecurity strategy was to put the cybersphere front and centre in the consciousness of leaders in both government and business, to make it an issue for the CEO, and not just the CIO or CTO. As I observed in the strategy document, the threats were often neither software nor hardware, but 'warmware' – human beings who interfered with or stole from their employer's systems. Edward Snowden was the archetype. I often asked CEOs, 'Do you know who your system administrator is? And do you know whether anyone oversees them?' Blank stares were the usual response.

The strategy put additional funds behind cyber research and innovation, including the data science wing of the CSIRO, Data61, and established the Australian Cyber Security Centre with former AFP officer Alastair MacGibbon as its head, and as my Cybersecurity adviser. Alastair had done a terrific job as the eSafety commissioner, a position I'd established in 2015 to promote safety online – initially for children – when I was Communications minister. He combined considerable technical knowledge and practical experience with a very engaging ability to explain the cyberworld to lay audiences. Given the nature of the internet, international cooperation was vitally important and so to strengthen and focus our message we appointed Toby Feakin as our Cyber Affairs ambassador. We also made the ASD an executive agency to give it more independence and a direct reporting line both to me and the Defence minister.

With the Defence white paper and the Cybersecurity strategy completed and released, as well as the decision to proceed with France for the 12 new submarines, we'd put in place the key elements of our national security strategy by the end of April. From then on, all our attention was focused on the budget and the election that was to follow immediately thereafter.

CHAPTER 30

The element of surprise: proroguing the parliament

The Senate in the 44th parliament became almost unworkable for the Abbott government.

Australia's Senate has 76 members – 12 from each of the six states and two from each of the territories. The territorial senators are elected every three years for a three-year term, and the state senators are elected for six-year terms, so half go up every three years.

Although it's possible to have a half-Senate election separate from the election for the House of Representatives, the two are usually held together. While the House is, since 2019, made up of 151 members elected for their respective constituencies, the senators are elected by proportional representation (PR) for their state or territory: they're required to achieve a quota of votes based on the number of vacancies to be filled.[1]

At that time, almost all voters simply placed a '1' in the box next to the party group they favoured and their preferences were then distributed automatically in accordance with complex 'group voting tickets', which the parties had lodged with the Australian Electoral Commission. Elaborate preference-swapping deals were done, managed by expert 'preference whisperers', such as Glenn Druery.

In 2013, the use of PR and the group voting tickets had delivered a large crossbench in the Senate of independents, some of whom had received hardly any primary votes. The best example was Ricky Muir of the Motoring Enthusiast Party, who found himself in the Senate despite only 17,122 people (0.51 per cent of the electorate) having actually voted for him. Nobody was so unkind as to repeat Paul Keating's description of the Senate as 'unrepresentative swill'[2] but the sentiment was widely felt, as was the need for reform.

Abbott had taken a pretty disrespectful approach to the Senate cross-bench, not helped by the fact that his Senate leader was the notoriously abrasive Eric Abetz. Even though, once PM, I secured more support from the crossbench than Abbott had, it had become hard to win the six votes we needed from the eight independents. Two of the original three Palmer United Party (PUP) senators (Glenn Lazarus and Jacqui Lambie) had defected and were broadly supporting Labor. We could generally only rely on two or three of the crossbench: David Leyonhjelm from the Liberal Democrats, Bob Day from Family First and Dio Wang, the sole remaining PUP senator.

A joint committee had recommended reforms to the Senate voting system – specifically, abolishing group voting tickets and providing that only the voter could allocate their preferences. These recommendations had been supported by the Coalition, Labor and the Greens. Abbott had stopped pursuing them, presumably because he didn't want to further alienate the crossbench, but I revived them. I announced on 22 February 2016 that we'd press on with the reforms, even though Labor had now decided they wouldn't support them.

There was another reason for my interest, however.

Where the Senate rejects legislation passed by the House and does so again after an interval of three months, the prime minister can advise the governor-general to dissolve both Houses and hold an election for all of the MPs and all of the senators. After that election, the rejected legislation is presented again. If the newly elected Senate again rejects it, a joint sitting of both Houses can be held to vote on it.

In a joint sitting, there are 76 senators and 151 MPs,[3] so a majority is 114 votes out of a possible 227.

If, for example, we could win back our current 33 Senate spots, we could carry the day in a joint sitting as long as we won 81 seats in the House. Given that we'd won 90 seats in 2013, we could lose nine of those and still command a majority of the votes. And that's without taking into account any support we could get from individuals on the crossbench.

Several bills had been rejected twice and therefore met the double-dissolution trigger rules. But one sought to abolish the Clean Energy Finance Corporation and another sought to abolish the Australian

Renewable Energy Agency. As I wanted to retain both bodies, I couldn't use those triggers. There was only one other bill that could form a trigger and that was one setting up a Registered Organisations Commission to oversee the governance of unions. It imposed similar standards on union officials as applied to company directors.

This was particularly relevant given the Heydon Royal Commission's revelations of systemic corruption in the union movement.

Abbott had set up the Royal Commission in large part for the purpose of getting at Shorten, who'd been secretary of the Australian Workers' Union when a lot of shabby deals had been done with large employers. In some cases unions had traded away workers' penalty rates at the same time as receiving, unbeknown to the workers, fees from the employers for one dubious service or another.

The greatest corruption and criminality had been revealed to exist in the construction industry, and especially by the huge Construction, Forestry, Maritime, Mining and Energy Union (CFMEU), whose construction division was constantly in the courts. Indeed, at the time, over 100 of their officials had been fined on what amounted to over 1000 occasions.

This wasn't a new state of affairs. Back in 2001, Howard had set up a Royal Commission into the Building and Construction Industry, presided over by Justice Terence Cole, who among other things recommended the establishment of an Australian Building and Construction Commission (ABCC) to police the industry. This was finally established in 2004, with considerable benefit to the industry, but was abolished by Labor in 2012.

Abbott had moved to reinstate the ABCC, but after the legislation was rejected by the Senate in 2015 he'd taken no steps to present the bill a second time. When Heydon presented his findings on 28 December 2015, the need for an ABCC was again highlighted. It seemed we should do everything we could to get the ABCC re-established. However, there would be no prospect of the Senate passing the bill on a second attempt with that crossbench. Equally, Labor and the Greens, and the majority of the crossbench who supported them, had no interest in rejecting the bill a second time and giving us a trigger for a double dissolution on the ABCC.

It appeared that the only way to get these industrial relations reforms passed was through a double-dissolution election. Not only would I have to win in the sense of having more than half of the House but I'd also need sufficient senators – a total of 114 in both houses, assuming no independents could be counted on to support us.

To add to this complexity, a double dissolution cannot be called within six months of the expiry of the three-year term of the House. This put the last possible date to call the election at 11 May 2016. The constitution also provides that after a double dissolution, the senators' terms commence on the 1 July prior to the election. In other words, if we called the double dissolution on 9 May, had a conventional five-week campaign and held the election on Saturday 13 June, our new senators' terms would be deemed to have begun on 1 July 2015. This would mean, in turn, that there'd need to be a half-Senate election prior to 1 July 2018, thus giving us only a two-year term.

The upshot of all of this was that if I wanted to elect a new Senate with a new, hopefully more cooperative, crossbench, and if I wanted to establish the ABCC and the Registered Organisations Commission as recommended by Heydon, and if I didn't want to be going back to the polls in early 2018 (as opposed to 2019), then I'd need to dissolve parliament on 9 May and hold the double-dissolution election on Saturday 2 July – an eight-week winter campaign.

This wasn't an appetising prospect but, as is almost always the case in politics, there was no shortage of bad options. The alternative was effectively giving up on both industrial relations reform and the possibility of having a more cooperative Senate.

Abbott and the right of the party were continuing to snipe and undermine, so being seen to take on a core part of our industrial relations agenda that Abbott had given up on wasn't going to do me any harm with the party's more conservative supporters. And I had no reservations about the importance or timeliness of the reforms.

Before going to a double dissolution, we first needed to get the Senate voting reforms passed by the Senate. At a double dissolution where all 12 senators are up for election in each state, the quota for election is $100/(12+1) = 7.69$ per cent, whereas at a regular half-Senate election, it's 14.28 per cent. Potentially, all other things being equal, a double dissolution could see even more independents elected. But the voting reforms would offset that considerably. So yes, we'd likely have more independents than at a half-Senate election but at least they'd be candidates whom the people had voted for and thus, hopefully, more accountable and responsible.

The risk was that Labor would filibuster in the Senate on the voting reform bills. If the Greens then failed to support us in cutting off debate, we mightn't have enough time left before 9 May in the Senate to also consider the ABCC bill a second time and vote to reject it.

Working in utmost secrecy with Brandis and our in-house constitutional expert Don Markwell, we developed a plan. The Greens received a lot of money from the CFMEU and they'd do nothing to assist us in getting a trigger over the ABCC, whose restoration they fiercely opposed. It was important that they believed there wasn't enough sitting time before 9 May for the Senate to pass the voting reform legislation, and consider and debate and finally reject the ABCC bill. In other words, they had to believe we were snookered. And so they did, as did everyone else, especially the press gallery.

On Sunday 13 March 2016, with only three days of sittings left before we rose for the six-week break prior to the budget in May, I reflected on my plan and my state of mind:

Where are we? Well, this coming parliamentary week the only objective apart from avoiding mistakes is to get the Senate voting reforms passed. These will mean that the group-voting tickets are a thing of the past and that voters choose their preferences, not backroom deals. It means that the microparties' and preference whisperers' days will be over. As it happened, when it came to moving on it, Labor reneged. There had always been internal opposition led by Conroy, and so we are moving with the support of the Greens and Xenophon. Labor and the crossbenchers have tried every procedural delay they could and the Greens unfortunately have been unwilling to apply the gag. So we ended up with this coming week dedicated to the reform bill and with a provision to keep sitting until it is dealt with. So we should get it through if the Greens hold.

And therein lies the delicacy. The Greens are under ferocious pressure to break ranks with us, especially from the CFMEU; they can see a DD looming with ABCC on the menu. Robocalling into inner-city seats saying the Greens are in bed with us is all designed to get them to crack. Currently, [Richard] Di Natale is holding firm but part of the arrangement is that we don't deal with ABCC this coming week. We don't have time anyway but it enables him to soothe the CFMEU at least. And for that reason we are being pretty indefinite about DDs, timing etc.

However as soon as the Senate voting is done, the trap will be sprung and this is it. We will ask the GG to prorogue the parliament, i.e. end the current session, and summon both houses back on a date most likely to be 18 April. He will open the session in the Senate chamber with reps attending and say the purpose is for the Senate to consider the ABCC bill and for the House to deal with the Budget, which will be brought forward to 3 May. If the Senate passes ABCC then no DD; if it doesn't and it won't, then we ask the GG for a DD subject to interim supply, which I am sure the Senate will pass and we are off to the polls for July 2. We would then have an election in which the big issues would be for us: economic growth powered by innovation and tax reform, and federation reform and investment, reform of union corruption viz reg orgs bill and ABCC. Our negative against Labor is obviously their failure to support us on the union corruption and lawlessness issue and of course their reckless policies on negative gearing etc etc.

Our current polling slump is, in my view, a combination of an inevitable end to the honeymoon, raggedness on our side with ministers going and the appearance of internal division with Abbott behaving appallingly especially … plus the apparent policy vacuum on tax caused by ScoMo running out and effectively front-running a GST tax mix switch policy, which was neither ready nor agreed. Completely half-arsed. Extraordinary. The solution to that of course is to roll out policy including tax and we can do that but not before we are ready – in the sense of not before the policy is ready, and I am not entirely sure we should not just wait for the Budget. It is, after all, rather weird that we are being criticised in March for not disclosing what is in substance the guts of the Budget due in May!

Position with Abbott is extremely odd. He is angry, depressed, crazy, deluded. The Niki Savva book[4] has been devastating, not just because of what it discloses but there are so many firsthand accounts it is impossible for him to say it is all cruel and unfounded gossip. At the moment he wants to become the CEO of some Paul Ramsay-founded foundation for Western civilisation of which Howard is chair and some of Paul's old mates like Tony Clark are directors. The problem, according to [one of the directors], who I saw on Friday night at a fundraiser at MacBank, is that nobody wants him. They think he is mad and polarising. Fair enough, and they are his friends! So heaven knows what he will do next.

As for my own state of mind – amazingly calm really. I go through periods of anxiety, but generally only when the media are chasing stuff relating to me, such as this weekend the AFR is sniffing around the PlayUp investment, which is all kosher, but it still rattles me and brings back memories of

Godwin Grech, HIH and all the other disasters I have known. Main thing is to keep the exercise up.

Lucy is going well. Very happy in her new role as Chief Commissioner of the Greater Sydney Commission.

As the exhausted senators completed the debate on 18 March and passed the Senate Voting Reform Bill, they knew the Senate was adjourning for seven weeks, as was the House. Parliament wouldn't come back until 10 May for budget week, meaning there was no time at all for the ABCC bill to be considered and rejected before 11 May, the last day I could call a double-dissolution election. So the CFMEU could rest easy … there was no way I could get the ABCC bill passed. We'd run out of time.

Or had we?

I made a few notes in the car on the way to Government House on Monday 21 March:

Very nervous. Butterflies. Most unlike me. This is the day we spring the trap. The Senate has now passed the voting reform legislation under the impression that we have run out of time to deal with the ABCC Bill before the latest date to call a DD. So we will prorogue[5] parliament and call it back on the 18th of April, so the Senators have a full three weeks to debate, and presumably reject ABCC.

The press conference that followed was very satisfying – the journalists were shocked by the announcement. When they pressed me on how long I'd had this in mind, I replied, 'Well, I've been aware of section 5 of the constitution for quite a long time.'

They realised that far from drifting without a plan, I'd had a plan all along, and quite an elaborate one. Moreover, it was kept very tight. The cabinet had only been advised a few minutes before the press conference; an hour earlier, Scott Morrison was saying the budget would be on 10 May, and now I announced it was being moved back to 3 May.

And that of course was one of the lessons. Plan your moves carefully, keep it confidential, don't share it with the indiscreet, and announce it when it suits your purposes – not anyone else's.

It was interesting nobody had even thought we had the option to do this. Indeed, in the pages of commentary over the previous month, it hadn't dawned on anyone else that by proroguing and recalling the parliament in mid-April I could give the Senate more than enough time to debate the bill.

The Sydney Morning Herald's Peter Hartcher summed up the moment, the strategy and its significance, saying:

> Malcolm Turnbull has transformed his prime ministership at one stroke. The picture emerging from his first six months was that he was wasting his time. We now see that he has been biding his time …
>
> From hopeless ditherer to decisive leader in a moment, Turnbull has now staked his government on a challenge and put all the other political parties on the defensive …
>
> Turnbull and the Coalition already have a strong lead in the polls in the public's perception of economic management. His protracted Senate showdown gives him an ideal mechanism to keep the national debate on the government's favoured ground.
>
> Turnbull has yet to prosecute his case with the voters, but he has now taken control of the agenda, wrongfooted the other parties and asserted himself as a decisive leader.
>
> Enjoying the reaction to his bombshell announcement on Monday, Turnbull observed to colleagues that the Canberra press gallery had been wrongfooted into thinking him a hopeless ditherer: 'Just because the press gallery doesn't know what I'm doing doesn't mean that I don't know what I'm doing.'[6]

The parliament duly returned on 18 April. The governor-general arrived, installed himself in the Senate chamber, and the usher of the black rod walked across the Members' Hall to summon the members of the House of Representatives to hear from His Excellency why they'd been recalled. Sir Peter Cosgrove was short and sweet – the parliament had been recalled so that senators could get on with and pass the ABCC and related legislation.

Whether it was because the Labor senators couldn't stomach three weeks of filibustering or that they welcomed the fight, on the 18th they didn't waste any time in voting down the ABCC bill for the second time.

There was a collateral benefit from the early return: it enabled us to abolish the Road Safety Remuneration Tribunal (RSRT), which had been set up by the Labor Party at the behest of the Transport Workers' Union (TWU). It hadn't done much since it was established but on 18 December 2015 it had made an order, to become effective on 4 April 2016, that imposed minimum freight rates on owner-drivers but not on larger companies. This meant that the owner-drivers would be at a huge competitive disadvantage compared to the big trucking companies like Toll and Linfox, whose drivers were, of course, members of the TWU.

Thousands of owner-drivers couldn't comply with the new regulations and I met many Australian families whose whole livelihood was being threatened by the tribunal's order. Initially, we'd thought the best we could do was get the order suspended, but when more of the crossbench came on board, we were able to abolish the RSRT entirely.

Ahead of us now was the budget and then the campaign. The polls were tight, and the campaign would be long and cold. There was plenty that could go wrong. If we won, we should be able to restore the rule of law to the construction sector, and hopefully secure a more cooperative crossbench in the Senate and a productive 45th parliament. There was a lot to play for.

CHAPTER 31

Cities, Kevin and the budget

One by one, I was getting the major policies in place as the clock ran down to the budget on 3 May and the eight-week election campaign that was to follow. Eight weeks!

'Can we afford an eight-week campaign?' I asked Liberal Federal Director Tony Nutt.

'Of course not, PM. But we can't afford a five-week one either.'

Cheery news. Anyway, at least we weren't completely broke, which was where we were a few months before.

With the big national security measures announced, it was time to lay out my vision for Australia's cities. This was a subject especially close to my heart, not least because it was Lucy's life's work. In her role as the chief commissioner of the Greater Sydney Commission, she is responsible for the overall planning of the greater metropolitan Sydney region.

As I said at the launch of our Cities policy in Melbourne on 29 April, historically the federal government had been just an ATM – dispensing cash to state governments for their infrastructure projects, generally on a completely ad-hoc basis. I was determined to change that and ensure that in future all three levels of government worked closely together. So, I announced we'd be establishing City Deals, between the federal, state and local governments, which would set out the agreed outcomes in terms of liveability and economic and social infrastructure.

We committed ourselves to the goal of a 30-minute city, which of course didn't mean you should be able to get from one end of Sydney to the other in 30 minutes but rather that wherever you lived in an Australian city you should be able to find, within a reasonable travelling time, places to work, play and learn. This was at the heart of Lucy's work at the GSC and we were both passionately committed to it.

The other big change in policy was that the Commonwealth would no longer solely dispense grants. Grants had their place, but wherever we could, we would invest in economic infrastructure and own it, or at least a share of it. This was anathema to the traditional thinking of the Department of Infrastructure, but in my time we saw the Commonwealth invest directly in many infrastructure projects. Some were wholly owned, like Snowy 2.0, Western Sydney Airport or the Inland Rail from Melbourne to Brisbane; others were joint-ventured with state governments, like the Melbourne Airport Rail Link or the North South Rail Line linking Penrith to Western Sydney Airport.

Another key element in this approach was to ensure that as much as possible of the cost of new infrastructure was recovered from those who directly benefited from it or, in the case of rail especially, from the owners of neighbouring real estate that increased in value because of the new infrastructure. Value capture has rarely, if ever, been practised in Australia, but it is in fact the way railway companies were financed in the 19th century. The key insight here was to look at new urban rail not as a project in isolation but as part of a city-shaping plan. That meant thinking like a property developer, except the outcomes went beyond the financial; rather, they prioritised improving urban amenity and liveability.

The Department of Infrastructure was most unenthusiastic. I recall a submission that, in commenting on the new policy of making investments as opposed to grants, observed that with investments there was 'a risk' that the Commonwealth wouldn't recover the full amount of the investment. Of course, I responded, there is no risk with a grant – no risk that you will get one cent back! Only in Canberra ...

The new Cities policies I introduced were not only fundamental changes to Commonwealth policy but they have been enduring. There are now City Deals underway in Townsville, Launceston, Western Sydney, Darwin, Hobart, Perth and Geelong (all commenced during my time) as well as Adelaide and South East Queensland under my successor.[1]

A rather dramatic episode in the lead-up to the budget was Kevin Rudd's aspiration to become secretary-general of the United Nations (UNSG).

For some time, and well before I became prime minister, Kevin Rudd had been expressing an interest in becoming UNSG when Ban Ki-moon's term came to end. He and I had discussed it on a few occasions, both in New York and in Australia, including at a lunch at my home in Sydney. I hadn't taken it especially seriously as nobody felt he had any prospects of success but had not sought to encourage or discourage him. At the time I hadn't appreciated he would need to be nominated by Australia – something he should have formally lined up before he began his soundings. Recognising the challenges to his candidacy, Kevin hadn't made a commitment to nominate. Indeed, he'd gone to some lengths to suggest that he wasn't running – not least because, so he said, only an Eastern European would have a chance of success and his name wasn't Ruddovich.[2]

I was PM by the time Rudd finally decided he did want to run and he did need Australia to nominate him. We spoke about it by phone, the day before the budget, on 2 May at about 7 am.

'Kevin, as I told you last year, I would take this to cabinet and I'm happy to do so. However, I don't believe cabinet will support your candidacy and so it would be in everyone's best interests if you didn't ask me to do so,' I said.

Kevin was most indignant and pressed me as to why, so I told him. 'Kevin, the consensus view, and it's my view too, is that you aren't suited to the role because of your poor interpersonal and management skills.' That was about as tactfully as I could put it.

'You little fucking rat, you piece of shit! I'm going to get you for this. I'm going to come down to Australia and campaign against you in every part of the country. I will remind them of Godwin fucking Grech, you …' A torrent of obscenities followed as he went on in this way for quite a few minutes.

'Look, Kevin, calm down. Don't you see this is just confirming what I've said to you. You don't get what you want and immediately you are screaming at me, swearing at me, threatening me. Don't you think this is a bit unedifying you doing this, an ex-PM to the current PM?'

He kept going and didn't appear to draw breath. Finally I had to bring the call to an end.

'Okay, Kevin, now I'm not hanging up, but as you know this is a big job, very busy, lots of meetings, so I have to go,' and then gently I put down the phone with the abuse still echoing through my office.

I reported on the call to the secretary of DFAT, Frances Adamson. She responded in one word: 'Yikes.' Fortunately, Julie Bishop was able to calm Rudd down and the matter went into abeyance until after the election, when he made another application for our support.[3]

My senior colleagues all agreed on two points. Nobody thought he was really suited for the role, and everyone agreed that he had no chance of winning. Julie's view, which was shared by others, was that nominating Kevin would make us look bipartisan; it avoided him being out in the media attacking us and, given he wouldn't win, no harm would be done.

Bill Shorten had the same view. When we later talked about it, I reminded him that a number of his colleagues had described Kevin as a psychopath. Bill just laughed. 'Oh well, I guess at least he's our psychopath.'

The more conservative ministers were, by and large, opposed to nominating Rudd. No doubt partisanship played a part, but central to their thinking, and mine, was, how do you recommend someone for such a big job when their failings as a manager are so notorious? Scott Morrison was right when he said to me, 'Well, Malcolm, if we do nominate him and if, by some bizarre miracle, he were to win – you would own the ensuing catastrophe.' But opinions were pretty evenly divided, as was revealed in the press at the time. Julie's arguments were, as usual, eloquent and pragmatic. But I wasn't persuaded. The moment we nominated Kevin, I'd have to look down the lens of a camera and say why I thought Kevin Rudd was the best-qualified person to be secretary-general of the United Nations, so much so that we were deploying our diplomatic resources around the world to campaign for him. How could I credibly defend that nomination in the face of all of the obvious evidence that he wasn't well suited to the role? So, the government resolved not to nominate him.

Kevin cut up rough and complained bitterly, as expected. But the story had a most unusual twist.

On 16 August, about three weeks after our decision, my national security adviser, Justin Bassi, called me at The Lodge to say that the president of Botswana wanted to speak to me to discuss his nominating Kevin Rudd as UNSG. As it happened, a few cabinet ministers, including Barnaby Joyce and Julie Bishop, were joining me for dinner and when one of the staff came in to say, 'PM, the President of Botswana is calling,' all of them sighed – Julie, because she knew what it was about, and the others, who didn't, because they assumed it was a codename for a late-night call on some sensitive matter.

I left my dining companions and went to the study. Ian Khama congratulated me on my re-election and then came straight to the point. 'I think Kevin Rudd would make a very good secretary-general of the UN, and he tells me you think so too.'

'Really?' I replied.

'Yes, Kevin says you wanted to nominate him but you couldn't because you had done a deal with another political party not to do so.'

'Well, Mr President, that's not quite right. I didn't nominate Kevin because I didn't think he was suited to the job.'

'What would be the view of the Australian government if we were to nominate Kevin?' he asked me.

I told the president that I'd understood he was calling to tell me he was nominating Kevin, but if he wanted our view I was happy to discuss it with my colleagues. I suggested we speak again in an hour.

So I returned to the dining room and consulted Julie Bishop and Barnaby Joyce – the Foreign minister and deputy PM. We agreed we should neither encourage nor discourage Ian Khama, and so when he called back I told him, 'It is entirely a matter for Botswana.'

He told me he hadn't been aware of my reasons for not nominating Kevin and now wanted to think about it. I assured him I hadn't said anything to him that wasn't in the public domain, but it was, I stressed, a matter for Botswana. As it happened no nomination was made by Botswana.[4]

Kevin has been so bent out of shape by this decision that I've reflected on whether I shouldn't have simply gone along with Julie's pragmatic advice to nominate him and assume he couldn't win. I bore him no ill will and knew he was still hurting badly from being dumped as PM in 2010 and losing the election in 2013; I worried I was missing an opportunity to at least cheer him up. But I still think I made the right call. After all, one of the most important roles of a prime minister is hiring and firing, and if you believe someone is the wrong fit for an important job, you shouldn't nominate them unless you can put your hand on your heart and say you believe they can do the job and do it well.

On 5 April, the Australian Securities and Investments Commission (ASIC) announced it was launching legal action against Westpac and other banks, alleging that the banks' officers had rigged the bank bill swap rate (BBSW) that's used as a benchmark for billions of dollars of financial transactions every day. The integrity of that BBSW rate was central to maintaining a fair market; if it was being rigged by banks, for their benefit, then it was not only a crime but it undermined confidence in the whole financial system.

That was bad news enough, but what was worse was that I was due to speak at a big lunch the following day to celebrate the 199th anniversary of Westpac's founding as the Bank of New South Wales in 1817, my forebear John Turnbull being one of the new bank's first customers. Brad Burke's first reaction was that I should pull out of the lunch, but I felt that would look both cowardly and churlish. So, I turned up, but had some tough words for Westpac and the banks generally.

> We expect our bankers to have higher standards, we expect them always, rigorously, to put their customers' interests first – to deal with their depositors and their borrowers, with those they advise and those with whom they transact in precisely the same way they would have them deal with themselves. Banks don't just operate under a banking licence, they operate under a social licence and that is underwritten by public confidence and trust.

During the GFC, the Australian public and Australian government provided the banks with vital support. Had the bankers done enough in return for this support? Had they lived up to the standards we expected, not just the law? I didn't think so.

> Our bankers have not always treated their customers as they should. Some, regrettably as we know, have taken advantage of fellow Australians and the savings they've spent a lifetime accumulating, seeking only dignity and independence in their retirement. Redressing wrongs is important, especially where it is done promptly and generously ...
>
> The singular pursuit of an extra dollar of profit at the expense of those values is not simply wrong but it places at risk the whole social licence, the good name and reputation upon which great institutions depend.[5]

The audience received these blunt words with a mixture of astonishment and horror. It was evident they didn't appreciate how far the public goodwill for the banks had run down. The BBSW scandal had come on top of a series of cases of misconduct in the banking and financial services sector, all of which could be sheeted home to a failure of culture and leadership.

While I'd owned and run an 'investment bank', I'd never worked as a commercial banker advising people on their savings, let alone making loans – whether for buying homes or businesses. However, one of our principles at Turnbull & Partners was that we wouldn't recommend a deal to a client unless we'd be prepared to invest our own money in it.

After I left Goldman in 2001, among the companies I helped set up was a private wealth management business called Centrestone (later Centric), with Rob Keaveney and Russel Pillemer. One of our key points of differentiation from competitors was that we wouldn't take fees, kickbacks or trailing commissions from the funds our clients invested in, and where they couldn't be avoided, they'd be rebated to our client. Centrestone's fee income came from the client, so there could be no conflicts of interest.

As I understood the problem, it was simply this: the banks, and others in the financial services sector, hadn't put their customers first. Like a doctor who recommends unnecessary tests or procedures or a lawyer who runs up hours on fruitless litigation, the banks had all too often put their profits ahead of their clients' interests. This very often involved conflicts of interest – recommending to clients funds and other products that just happened to be managed by the bank itself, or perhaps involved a higher fee to the adviser.

Shorten was no doubt momentarily perplexed by my forthright critique, especially since it was given directly to so many bankers. It was hardly consistent with the caricature of me as the bankers' friend. But, in the manner of most opposition leaders, within 48 hours he responded by going one better and demanded a Royal Commission.

It was an utterly cynical call. After all, only a few years before, in government, Labor had rejected the idea of a Royal Commission into the financial services sector. The cry for a Royal Commission was populism pure and simple, a demand that bankers be publicly shamed: a show trial. Shorten summed it up well when he used to say I wanted to give the banks a tax cut; he'd give them a Royal Commission.

As a cabinet, we took the view that a Royal Commission would be expensive and tell us nothing we didn't already know; it could only hold an inquiry and write a report. The failures in governance and culture at the banks were already well known and documented. As the government, we should get on with the reforms to ensure that the wrongdoing didn't happen again. There was extensive regulation of the banking sector with agencies like ASIC and the prudential regulator APRA that had considerably more power than a Royal Commission. It would be more effective to give them better resources to bring the wrongdoers to account.

But as it later turned out, this was one of those cases where Shorten had the policy wrong but the politics right. Public indignation, amplified in the media – both social and mainstream – turned banks and bankers into arch villains and continued to grow over the course of 2016 and into 2017. In due course, I did establish the Royal Commission in late 2017.

We went into budget week 2016 behind on Newspoll 49:51, and level-pegging on the Ipsos poll – 50:50. I remained well ahead of Shorten as preferred prime minister, but the numbers were a reminder of how much goodwill had been squandered by the *apparent* chopping and changing on tax policy. Only a few months before, at the end of January, we'd been six points ahead, 53:47.

Exhausted, I recorded my thoughts late on budget night.

Some highlights – the party-room meeting, the last of this parliament, perhaps my last ever. Anyway the objective is to ensure crazy people don't start attacking me or Scott about various issues, backpacker tax, pathology etc. I gave them a lecture on discipline and a general rev-up of how good our Budget would be and how bad Labor is, but then given there were so many retiring I thought I would invite each to speak. All but Bruce Billson spoke too long.

Interim Supply is through, so we are all set for the double dissolution. That's great, another piece of deft work by Cormann. He is a highly efficient person.

Scott did well with the Budget, after an enormously complex process and lots of twists and turns we have nailed the politics well – the Budget is fair and pro-growth. We have neutralised in large part hospitals and schools, we have slugged rich superannuants, only the top 4 per cent, and of course the poor old smoker and the anti-avoidance measures aimed at multinationals are draconian. It is being well received.

My duty on Budget night is to go to literally a dozen different events, some large, such as the ones in the Great Hall or the Mural Hall, others smaller, and glad-hand the donors of colleagues – who have been brought down for the night. Exhausted at the end, we had a debrief with Scott and [Tony] Nutt and Tex [Mark Textor] on the phone. Sounds like it has been well received in punter land as well. So good. Off to the polls now, just have to win.[6]

We were still wearing the consequences of the harsh cuts and broken promises of the 2014 budget – that's the type of self-wounding that takes a long time to heal. But as I noted, we'd secured a new hospital-funding agreement with the states that reversed the Abbott cuts and we'd put more money into schools, all while maintaining our trajectory to a balanced budget, which was vital for our economic credibility.

Budget week is a peculiar type of Canberra madness. On the Tuesday, almost all the journalists and dozens of other stakeholders are locked up reading the budget papers, only to be let out just before the treasurer stands up to read his speech at 7.30 pm. The treasurer has the media to himself on budget night, and then the following day the PM joins the treasurer in a full-court press of interviews and speeches promoting the budget. After two days of that, on the Thursday night, the opposition leader gives his reply, which is normally more political than economic.

And so it was in 2016. Shorten had his line and length for the campaign: it was all about fairness. We were for tax cuts for the big end of town; he was for the battlers.

After Shorten's budget in reply speech, the governor-general dissolved both houses of parliament on the Sunday and we were off to the polls.

On Monday 9 May I had a moment to reflect on the week just past and, ever self-critical, my own missteps:

Last week was good and bad. The Budget I thought went very well and we did well on the Wednesday too. On Thursday things went to shit, at least for me. Our tax cuts for companies run out over ten years and everyone gets to 25% by year ten, but the Budget only estimates in detail for four years – the forward estimates – but supplies an overall estimate of the underlying cash balance over ten, but does not break out the line items, no doubt because forecasting over that time frame is so uncertain as to be utterly speculative. Anyway it has become fashionable for people to talk about ten-year costs, complete BS IMHO. Scott was firmly of the view that we should NOT release the Treasury's estimate of the ten-year cost of the tax cuts prior to Shorten's Budget in Reply speech in the hope that he would assume a figure that was wrong …

As he had with the tobacco tax hike. Now this got me into diabolical trouble with a Speers interview in which I was discombobulated, poorly prepared and generally did badly. Worse still, I said the Treasury had not identified the cost of the tax cuts over ten years (meaning in the Budget, as I explained) but this line could be taken out and then matched against what [Secretary of the Treasury] John Fraser said the next day (when I ensured he did reveal the ten-year costs in Senate Estimates) to suggest I was lying. Complete crap but this is what Shorten does. He did the same in his Budget speech, saying I had given tax avoidance my blessing (in a radio interview I had made the point tax avoidance was legal, tax evasion illegal and that was why when you wanted to stop tax avoidance you need to change the law, as opposed to just enforce the existing law) and had urged young people to get wealthy parents to pay for their homes. In fact I had teased the rich [ABC broadcaster] Jon Faine in a radio interview that he should help his kids if they were, as he asserted, locked out of the housing market. All in all very messy.

Polls since the Budget have been mixed but generally on the party vote we are either steady at 50–50 on Reachtel, or 49–51 on Newspoll or up slightly on Morgan and Ipsos on 51–49. So close.

I spent some time with John Howard at home on Saturday, he came around and we discussed the election. John was very comforting and encouraging. He told me that if I just stuck to the economic themes I would win – he was very confident there wasn't a mood to chuck the government out.

On Sunday morning Lucy and I went to Centennial Park to muck around with Jack and Daisy and James at the play area near the cafe to give the media some pix and then I flew down to Canberra. I was getting more and more and more nervous. Very unlike me.

Anyway on a grey day we flew to Canberra and then went straight to The Lodge and on to Government House to secure the GG's assent to the double dissolution. The ABC chopper tracked us all the way to Government House.

CHAPTER 32

The 2016 election

With both houses dissolved by the governor-general, the phony war was over and the election campaign began in earnest. All political life is something of a bubble but an election campaign is the most surreal bubble of all.

For a start, the government goes into what's called 'caretaker' mode, which means no major commitments should be entered into pending the result of the election. Any unavoidable commitments or decisions should be taken in consultation with the opposition. At the same time as the authority of government is somewhat diminished, so does the opposition come into its own. For most of the parliamentary term, the opposition leader is the perennial critic, the dog barking long into the night when everyone wants to go to sleep. But once the starter's gun is fired, no matter what the polls may say, the opposition is in with a chance – it is a two-horse race after all.

Each of the leaders and their entourage gets one of the government's Boeing Business Jets and the press pack splits in two – well almost two: a small contingent follows the leader of the Nationals on their own rural campaign, fondly described as the Wombat Trail.

The days all merge into each other with a tediously monotonous rhythm.

Up at 5 am and an hour's exercise (vital to stay sane), then a phone conference with the campaign HQ team to go through the results of the overnight polling and to discuss an outline of the day. What's working, what's not? Does the polling indicate we should go somewhere different? Has a colleague misspoken (generally that's a yes)? How do we clean it up? Tony Nutt usually opened the discussion and then quickly handed over to our pollster, Mark Textor, for the numbers. It was brisk and businesslike. Apart from Arthur Sinodinos, I was the only politician regularly on that call – the numbers were too sensitive to share widely, given the chattiness of politicians.

Tony Nutt and Tex then joined me for a call at 6.30 am with the leadership group: Barnaby Joyce and Fiona Nash from the Nats; Julie Bishop, Scott Morrison, Arthur Sinodinos, Mathias Cormann, Christopher Pyne, Peter Dutton and Mitch Fifield.

That done, I'd do a couple of radio interviews, normally one national and one local wherever I was, followed in the morning by an event with the key message and pictures to back it up for the evening news.

Generally, I did only one event like that every day. This ran against my workaholic grain. But as Tex pointed out, the evening news only has a few minutes, if that, for whatever we do. So, if you do two or three events with the media pack, you're crowding out your own pictures; best to do it once and get it right. And so we did.

After that, it was typically a fundraising lunch and a speech. The afternoons were taken up with drive-time radio or travel to the next location. In the evenings, we'd usually do another fundraiser with a local candidate or a local community event, like politics in the pub.

Australia is a big country and, even with your own plane, getting around it is both time-consuming and exhausting. But in the first two weeks of the campaign, we went to every state – twice to Queensland and four times to New South Wales. Sundays we tended to spend in Sydney planning, preparing for debates and, most importantly, resting.

And resting was essential. Whether it was because the campaign was over winter or just bad luck, I picked up a flu I couldn't shake for two of the last three weeks. It wasn't a good look and there isn't a lot of sympathy in politics. Labor cut up some vision of me coughing and spluttering and turned it into an ad with the tagline, 'Malcolm Turnbull can afford to pay an extra $20 to see the doctor – can you?'

Taking time off campaigning wasn't an option and the flu unhelpfully was at its worst in time for my appearance on *Q&A* on 20 June. When I got to the Brisbane Powerhouse for the show I could barely speak, so we took an 'all of the above' approach to flu remedies – from Codral to Benadryl to lemon juice, honey and a little whisky. The last mentioned was the most effective, and I managed to get through the hour and a quarter of live television without falling over or going completely hoarse.

If Labor and the media were less than sympathetic to my man-cold, the RAAF were fantastic – Wing Commander Steve Parsons even made sure the jet flew at a lower altitude than usual to relieve the pressure on my blocked sinuses!

We went into the campaign level-pegging with Labor on the public polls.

While our support bounced around over the eight weeks, one consistent figure was the high percentage, around 60 per cent, of voters who expected us to win. This was unhelpful, especially since the actual voting intention was around 50:50 and meant that a considerable number of people would imagine they could record a protest vote for Labor or another party, confident in the knowledge we'd still win.

The other consistent figure was that I led Shorten as preferred prime minister, an advantage I enjoyed throughout my time as PM, even during the worst periods of self-indulgent disruption inside the Coalition. It showed that Labor's biggest weakness was its leader, whereas ours was our own disunity.

One week in, I reflected on the madness of the campaign:

A mad media pack dogs my every move, dozens of cameras everywhere, all desperately anxious to capture some slip or gaffe. That is literally all they are interested in, when you meet people there are so many of the media that they push the public aside and indeed prevent themselves getting the interesting pictures or engagement that you think they would want.

Today was a good example, so before the announcement [about providing free continuous glucose monitors to young people with diabetes] we had a meeting in the park with lots of kids with Diabetes Type 1 and their parents. The media piled in, pushed the kids aside and we had to force the cameras apart to talk to any other than the two or three that had been isolated by the camera pack.

In terms of the debate,[1] the only part I think I could or should have done better was on the banks – bank bashing is very popular, very dangerous and I was too rational, not empathetic enough. The trick is to match Bill for empathy but do better on reason. I thought the audience was very skewed Labor's way – the questions showed that all the focus was on health and education, only one on debt and deficit.

The general feel from colleagues is that there isn't a mood for change – Labor is trying to ramp up the 'out of touch' line on me, ably assisted by

Credlin who earlier in the week after the faux furore about the cancelled
streetwalk in Penrith described me as 'Mr Harbourside Mansion' – she and
Abbott are playing a tag team. He is passive aggressive and she is aggressive
aggressive. Each of them doing their best to undermine the campaign.[2]

The 'cancelled streetwalk' was a good example of the way trivia takes off in election campaigns. I was out in Penrith campaigning with Fiona Scott, the member for Lindsay, on Wednesday 11 May. I had a commitment, a fundraiser as usual, in the city at lunchtime and when we ran out of time in Penrith my team cancelled a streetwalk – apart from the media, nobody would have known it was going to happen, so no offence was given, but it was easily beaten up in the media as an example of my being out of touch with Western Sydney.

The media pack make the whole business of campaigning a complete farce. A politician is supposed to be able to relate to people normally, in a relaxed and empathetic way. Which is one of the reasons I enjoyed taking public transport – meeting new people, and some old friends, in an informal setting.

But in an election campaign, this casual-and-empathetic-man-of-the-people politician is trailed by up to a dozen television cameras and even more journalists, all with their smartphones and recorders trying to catch every word and gesture. Normal people are terrified by this pack and plenty of others who would, in other circumstances, have a perfectly civil conversation, take the opportunity of all the cameras to get some grievance or other off their chest. My program and advance team – including Jacqui Kempler, Janelle Walker, James Hart and Emily Zatschler – had their work cut out scoping out the venues ahead of and during my visit, identifying some shoppers or shopkeepers who'd be happy to engage in casual chit-chat on national television, and keeping an eye out for troublemaking stirrers working, typically, for Labor or the Greens.

And all the time you knew how easily an hour of great footage of superb engagement with admiring, persuaded supporters could be swept off the news, replaced by 10 seconds of irritation, abuse from a passer-by, a dropped coffee cup or, fate worse than death, being filmed in front of an 'Exit' sign or perhaps a 'Reject Shop', as happened once to Tony Abbott.

On one occasion in Adelaide, Lucy slipped away from the frenzy of the trailing media pack to buy a present for Jack. For a moment we were concerned we'd lost her, and then she returned with a little knitted dog! All of which became the election story of the day.

So, while appearing to be calm, happy and relaxed, the candidate has every reason to be utterly terrified that his or her whole campaign is about to implode every time they step out of their car into the clutches of the media pack. For my part, I suppressed the terror, took a couple of imaginary Valiums and, suffused in fatalism, sallied forth day after day, reckoning any outing that didn't end in terminal catastrophe was a win.

The other source of election anxiety is your colleagues. Kim Beazley once wisely observed to me that, for the most part, a leader's colleagues play the role of sceptical spectators, sitting back and observing with a desultory clap when the leader does well and scathing under-the-breath commentary when they don't. However, what's worse is when colleagues in an election campaign decide to go off-piste and run their own lines. Sometimes, like Abbott, they do it deliberately to trip you up. Others, you assume, are just cack-handed.

Dutton was a good case in point at the beginning of the campaign.

National security was a strong suit for us, but voters took it for granted: Labor me-tooed us; it simply didn't have the traction it used to have. We could make use of our superior record on border protection and remind voters of Labor's tragic incompetence but it had to be done calmly, more in sorrow than in anger. It called for sober, nuanced responsibility.

Nuance wasn't Peter Dutton's strong suit. A bullet-headed former Queensland cop, he tried to play the tough guy but, like Abbott, didn't have the strength of character to stand up to the crazy right-wing commentators like Ray Hadley on 2GB or Paul Murray on Sky News, with whom he felt most comfortable. As a result, he often misspoke or over-spoke, no doubt endearing himself to right-wing members of the LNP but alienating everybody else. Although, it may be his remarks were quite deliberate: as they'd say in the LNP, 'throwing red meat to the base'.

About 10 days into the campaign, Dutton went on Sky News (audience maybe 25,000) and proceeded to not only extol our management of border protection and warn about the risk of Labor mismanaging it, as they had before, but added that most refugees were illiterate – not just in English but in their own language – and, at the same time, were a threat to Australians' jobs. How an illiterate, welfare-dependent refugee could simultaneously take an Australian's job wasn't explained. It was a characteristically confused effort and dominated the news cycle for days, even becoming an international story: 'Australian minister Peter Dutton says refugees are illiterate and a drain on welfare'.[3]

Thoughtlessly, Dutton forgot that Australia was full of people, including some of our captains of industry (and generous supporters) like Frank Lowy, who'd come as migrants not speaking English. Indeed, a few days later I found myself with Tasmanian Premier Will Hodgman, talking up our economic policies and our trade deals at the beautiful Josef Chromy vineyard outside of Launceston. Josef's story represented what I stood for – enterprise, small business, multiculturalism. I couldn't have been happier.

First question: 'Mr Turnbull, given that the owner of this winery is an immigrant who arrived with little English and fleeing an impoverished country, were you a bit embarrassed about the previous comments of your Immigration minister?'[4]

I did my best to clean it up, even to the extent of writing op-eds praising our success as a multicultural society and arguing that what Dutton really meant was 'a reminder that having welcomed people to Australia we must ensure they have the support and the training to be able to succeed in our society'.[5]

And if colleagues aren't putting their foot in their mouth, there's always the disaster that springs from left field. Someone at NBN Co had been regularly leaking sensitive commercial material to the Labor opposition and late in 2015 the board, unbeknown to us, had asked the AFP to investigate. For reasons known only to themselves, the AFP chose to execute search warrants on the premises of a number of Labor staffers a week into the election campaign! Labor accused them of doing the government's work; naturally, we rejected that slur against the integrity of the police with all the indignation we could muster, but equally naturally, many people believed it, and everyone was distracted from our economic message, as I noted on 25 May in my diary:

Didn't sleep especially well last night – no doubt because I had a glass of wine and dinner at Becco's[6] with the team or some of them, but an abstemious early night with room service is pretty grim. Anyway up at 5 and did about half an hour in the gym and then on the early call ...

I am feeling very calm (writing this on the plane to Rockhampton) but the pressure is immense. The whole show rests on my shoulders and it is easy to say 'let Malcolm be Malcolm', whatever that is, but it certainly means I have to appear sunny, relaxed, confident, competent and at the same time not drop my guard or screw up.

On the screwing-up front, there has been something of a screw-up yesterday – Morrison and Cormann have claimed Labor has a $67 billion Budget black hole but a big chunk of that assumes Labor will reverse our cuts to overseas aid (which they had last year indicated they would) but over the weekend Plibersek indicated they wouldn't or at least wouldn't for the most part. Anyway, when Morrison and Cormann did their presser today on this, they stuck to the $67 billion and then quickly retreated when confronted with the overseas aid point and were saying the black hole was at least $32 billion – messy, I thought, but at least it is on the economy. Apparently they had thought it all through with Nutt. I just don't have time or bandwidth to micromanage this kind of stuff. But it seems untidy in the prints this morning.

This morning did my first interview with Alan Jones in two years – went well, he is a weirdo but we need to keep him relatively sweet for the next five weeks.

First stop was Punt Road Oval for the announcement with Michael Keenan[7] of a $625,000 grant for the Bachar Houli Academy, which brings young Muslim men into playing AFL and following in Bachar's footsteps. He is a great fellow, very handsome and like so many of the AFL players much slighter than the enormous muscled-up guys who play rugby. Then we drove out to Emerald and got on Puffing Billy with Jason Wood[8] and Richard Colbeck[9] and announced some funding for the railway and a road and a discovery centre – all good tourism stuff, so my theme was as ever jobs and growth in the tourism sector this time.

Doorstop went well and the pictures were great with the steam train – best of the campaign the TV guys said.

A stop at a business in Deakin with Michael Sukkar[10] to say hi, at Daisy's Gardening Supplies, and pix with Tony Smith,[11] Jason Wood, Alan Tudge[12] as well to promote our commitment to the East West Link.

Reflecting:

I am worried about the polls, and that our message of jobs and growth is not cutting through. However not sure what Bill's message is other than spend more on schools and hospitals – there is certainly no big idea there, no narrative I can discern.

I worry that the campaign is so presidential, but there isn't much I can do about that.

Troubled about this black hole 'debacle' as some media outlets are calling it. How could ScoMo and Cormann make such a hash of it?[13]

The so-called black hole debacle was almost impossible to understand, but as I said in my diary, at least it meant we were talking about the economy. It was timely: we'd leaped on Shorten when, in an unguarded attempt at humour, he'd referred to putting 'another million dollars on the spend-o-meter'.[14]

Children are the best part of campaigning – your own and other people's! Our grandchildren made regular appearances throughout the campaign. Daisy's son, Jack, loved a visit to a trucker's rally at Smeaton Grange and getting behind the wheel, and little Isla, Alex's daughter, made her political debut in Chinese–Australian selfie madness at Hurstville in David Coleman's seat of Banks. With their skills as Chinese speakers, Alex and his wife, Yvonne, were particularly helpful in making sure David retained the seat.

But perhaps most special of all was meeting little Lulu at the Sydney Children's Hospital, where we were announcing our funding of the Zero Childhood Cancer Initiative. Lulu's six years had been spent undergoing chemo, surgery and radiation trying to cure one of those childhood cancers. Cheerful and undaunted, she drew me one picture after another. Her optimism was an inspiration. I kept those pictures in my office just as I promised her, and I still have the braided wristband she made for me.

It was looking like a pretty straightforward Liberal vs Labor election with each side relying on their respective strengths – economy and national security for us, health and education for Labor. But then there was Mediscare.

Back in February, Andrew Probyn had written a story in *The West Australian* headlined 'Private Medicare' and with the opening line, 'Medicare, pharmaceutical and aged care benefits would be delivered by the private sector under an extraordinary transformation of health services being secretly considered by the Federal government.'[15]

Stories in *The West Australian* often took some time before they morphed into an issue on the eastern seaboard. Breakfast television on the east coast never monitored the *West Oz*, nor did the radio shock jocks or indeed most of the political operatives in Canberra. But that Tuesday happened to be a sitting day in Canberra so, as the day wore on, gradually people in the building started to look at the story. Shorten opened with it in question time:

> My question is to the Prime Minister. The front page of today's *West Australian* newspaper reveals that the government has a radical plan to privatise Medicare and the Pharmaceutical Benefits Scheme. Will the Prime Minister categorically rule out privatising Medicare or the PBS? Yes or no?

I answered with:

> Let me just reassure the Leader of the Opposition that the government is, as always, totally committed to Medicare. What we are looking at, as we look at in every area, is improving the delivery of government services, looking at ways to take the health and aged-care payment system into the twenty-first century. … the Department of Health is investigating ways, as the minister said today, to digitise its transaction technology for payments to what it describes as a more consumer-friendly format – a modern, contemporary format.[16]

Shadow Health spokeswoman Catherine King followed up with a question relating to the data of Australians being compromised or moved overseas by a foreign company and Labor then quickly changed topics. I had the distinct feeling they didn't know where to go with the issue.

Shorten, like Abbott before him, had no shame. Question time was a vehicle for him to get the most outrageous sound bites onto the 6 pm news. It wasn't hard. Truth be told, oppositions aren't anywhere near as busy as governments, particularly in sitting weeks. They spend most of each morning coming up with the most effective one-liners to make the news.

The problem with TV news is the journalists want to run what *sounds* the best. They have little regard for whether it's factually correct or not. The good journalists will call out the lie in their reporting but will still run the grab, nonetheless. Shorten no doubt knew this and slept untroubled by how misleading or untruthful he had been during the day.

The *Australian Financial Review* slammed the comment in their editorial the following morning, claiming Shorten had 'jumped the shark'. And then went further:

> While young members like Ed Husic and Jason Clare want to embrace an agile and digital economy, the trade union dinosaurs controlling the party want to extend their monopolistic tendencies over new parts of the economy. In denouncing this sensible policy as an attack on 'universal healthcare', Mr Shorten is really just a defender of unions masquerading as a protector of the public interest.[17]

As the days went on, Labor continued to label it a plan to privatise Medicare. Again, the papers attempted to call Shorten to account for telling such a blatant lie. In fact, the *Sydney Morning Herald* devoted their editorial of 15 February to it:

> The ideas boom in government departments began long before Malcolm Turnbull became Prime Minister. It's just taken Labor almost two years to begin a scare campaign over one idea which it claims is a plan to privatise Medicare. The proposal is nothing of the sort ...[18]

Despite being panned in the media, Labor continued with the big lie that we would sell Medicare. My mistake was not to take it more seriously at that time. It was so absurd, embarrassingly so, that we all assumed people would see it for what it was. And more than a few of the Labor members were visibly embarrassed by it too.

However, big lie though it was, it was being sown into fertile soil. The 2014 budget had been, for many voters, the great betrayal. Abbott had promised 'no cuts to health'[19] but instead not only cut hospital funding (which I made right in April 2016) but also proposed a $7 GP co-payment so that everyone would have to pay extra to see the doctor. Even though he'd abandoned the co-payment proposal in March 2015, the damage had undone decades of bridge-building.

Labor had for years claimed you couldn't trust the Liberals on Medicare because the Coalition had opposed universal health care when it was first introduced by Whitlam. But time had mended that: free universal health care, via Medicare, was seen as having bipartisan support. It was part of the furniture. The 2014 budget, the co-payment and the broken promise all shattered that trust.

Meanwhile, Shorten toughed it out. Leigh Sales humiliated him on the ABC's *7.30* by asking him to put his hand on his heart and say he had evidence we would privatise Medicare – of course he couldn't. But he didn't care; he wasn't sending a message to the *7.30* audience but rather to the old, the sick and the poor – anyone who was most likely to be anxious about their health care and likely to believe such a lie.

Shorten had at his disposal a massive advertising budget that we couldn't match, plus the social media platforms of Twitter, Facebook and direct messaging to deploy. The unions and GetUp! got behind it with more videos, and the claims became more blatant that we would 'sell Medicare'.

This type of campaigning is more effective now than ever before because of the decline of the mainstream or curated media. It doesn't matter if newspapers and current affairs programs see through the big lie; the 21st-century politician can bypass all those filters by going direct to the voter through their smartphone – the source for most of their news and information.

The Mediscare lie was at its most deceitful in the 72 hours before polling day, and after the radio and television blackout. The Labor Party sent out millions of text messages, mostly to older voters in low-income areas in marginal seats.

The sender of the text message was 'Medicare' and the message read: 'Mr Turnbull's plans to privatise Medicare will take us down the road of no return. Time is running out to Save Medicare.'

A reader would assume the message was sent to them from Medicare itself and many did. It was an outright fraud.

We later changed the law to prevent it happening again, but the damage was done and the last-minute swing away from us in seats with older, poorer communities was savage. We estimated that Mediscare cost us five or six seats, and because it was targeted at older Australians, who are more likely to vote for the Coalition, it was especially effective.

As I said at our campaign launch:

Labor believes its best hope of being elected is to have trade union officials phone frail and elderly Australians in their homes at night, to scare them into thinking they are about to lose something which has never been at risk.

Bill Shorten put this Medicare lie at the heart of his election campaign. And they boast of how many people they have deceived.

That's not an alternative government; that's an opposition unfit to govern.[20]

The AFP investigated and concluded the law made it illegal to impersonate a Commonwealth *officer*, but not a Commonwealth *agency*, and so decided not to prosecute. A mistaken assessment in my view, I might add. After the election we changed the law to prohibit impersonating a Commonwealth agency and to require that all digital messages, text or voice, had to be clearly authorised like other political advertising.

The triggers for the double-dissolution election were the bills to establish the ABCC and the Registered Organisations Commission – both designed to address the corruption and thuggery identified in the Heydon Royal Commission.

Important though these reforms were, they weren't front of mind for most Australians. Years of slanging matches over industrial relations (IR) had made them cynical about the political or ideological motivations of Liberals attacking unions. While my colleagues and I included IR reforms in all our economic pitches, as part of our national economic plan, we were careful to frame it as a way of ensuring that infrastructure projects were more affordable for the community. Equally, we framed the repeal of the RSRT as a win for small family-owned businesses, rather than simply a battle over union power.

In Victoria, however, one IR issue was front of mind. The state government, headed by Labor Premier Dan Andrews, wanted to put the United Firefighters Union in charge of the Country Fire Authority – overwhelmingly staffed by volunteers. We sided with the volunteers and undertook to change the Fair Work Act to make it harder for Andrews to achieve the takeover. This helped us do better in Victoria, winning one seat from Labor – Chisholm, won by the magnificent Julia Banks, a moderate Liberal, who was subsequently rewarded for her victory by constant undermining and denigration by the right-wing group that controlled the Victorian division and was later to enthusiastically support Peter Dutton in his attempted coup of August 2018.

You'd think that the unpredictable Senate crossbench elected in 2013 would have discouraged people from voting for independents, but far from it. In the 2016 election, Pauline Hanson's One Nation made a serious comeback, campaigning nationally and especially in Queensland. And Senator Nick Xenophon, an idiosyncratic hero to many South Australians, launched the Nick Xenophon Team (NXT). So popular was the new party that it looked like it might not just win a bunch of Senate seats but also seats in the House. The normally safe Liberal seats of Barker, Grey and Sturt appeared vulnerable to NXT. As it happened, Rowan Ramsey hung on in Grey and, despite a 12 per cent swing against him, beat NXT 52:48.

When I became prime minister, I was determined to lead an inclusive government that embraced and promoted Australian multiculturalism and, in particular, didn't demonise Muslims, let alone tag them all with the crimes of a small extremist minority. No PM before me had ever held an *iftar*, the dinner that breaks the fast during the month of Ramadan. The first opportunity to hold an iftar was in June, which was during the last four weeks of the campaign. So, we arranged to hold it on 16 June at Kirribilli House in Sydney.

The guest list was assembled by my department and included leading members of the Islamic community as well as of other religions, including Christianity, Judaism and Buddhism. We also invited Bill Shorten and sent him a copy of the guest list. He accepted, but 48 hours beforehand pulled out of the event without explanation.

Four days earlier, Omar Mateen, an American-born Muslim of Afghan ancestry, had entered a gay nightclub in Orlando and murdered 49 people and wounded another 53. He'd pledged his allegiance to ISIL and claimed the attack was in retaliation for American air strikes in the Middle East. At 4 pm just as the guests were arriving, *The Daily Telegraph* contacted my office to say that one of them, Sheikh Shady Alsuleiman, had some years before given a sermon in which he condemned homo-sexuality as sinful and spreading disease. He had recently been elected president of the Australian Imams Council and had been invited in that capacity.

I was in the study at Kirribilli House when the call came through and my heart sank. It was hardly surprising that an Islamic cleric had denounced homosexuality – plenty of Christian ones had said much the same thing. But this was going to be an opportunity for News Corp to pursue its continuing campaign against Islam and, so far as they could, punish me for daring to reach out to Muslims.

And that's precisely what happened – News Corp journalists cross-examined the guests on their views about Sheikh Shady's sermon as they arrived.

Naturally, I rejected Alsuleiman's views. I was disappointed my department hadn't better researched each guest's previous statements, but to be fair to them, most had been invited because of their official positions. Any number of Christian leaders, let alone politicians, had made equally intolerant statements about gays, not to speak of adulterers, drunkards and other sinners.

I again condemned the Orlando attack and all forms of intolerance and extremist violence in my speech and added, 'The Australian Muslim community is valued and respected – and it is not confined to a narrow security prism – you are an integral part of an Australian family that rests on the essential foundation of mutual respect and understanding. Every one of us is enriched by the cultures and faiths of our friends and neighbours.'[21]

The truth was that News Corporation, like others on the right wing of politics, did want to define Muslims only in terms of national security. But it's equally true that I shouldn't have held that iftar during an election campaign. I underestimated the extent to which my opponents would seek to exploit it. Shorten obviously was tipped off to Sheikh Shady's past statements and may have even collaborated with News Corp to complete the hit. It transpired that he spent the evening at a vigil in memory of the victims of the Orlando massacre, which he no doubt thought was a useful contrast.

The same newspapers that denounced Sheikh Shady's intolerant views about gays were, in 2019, defending rugby player Israel Folau's right to say on Instagram that gays will burn in hell. He, of course, is a Christian, and I don't think Prime Minister Morrison would be criticised by *The Daily Telegraph* for inviting him to dinner.

It may well turn out to be a disaster for Britain, but the Brexit vote on 23 June was a big help for us. The surprising news that 'Leave' had won came through on the Friday morning when I was in Devonport, and I was quick to take advantage of it. On 24 June I reminded the Australian people that in the midst of concern over instability in global markets, falls in currencies and generalised uncertainty, a stable majority Coalition government with a strong economic plan was exactly what was required to set Australia up for a prosperous future.

Flying back to Sydney that afternoon, I spoke with David Cameron and did my best to persuade him not to resign. 'David, you have held the referendum as you promised; now surely you should deliver on the people's decision.' But he was determined and, I fear, compounded the error of holding the referendum with the other one of resigning.

Had the election been held that coming Saturday, we'd have won and won very well. Brexit put the economy back on centrestage and it played perfectly into my core economic message. As I said at the campaign launch on 26 June, five days out from the poll: 'Calm heads, steady hands and a strong economic plan are critical for Australia to withstand any of those negative repercussions.'[22]

Meanwhile, Tony Abbott found himself under threat in his own traditionally safe Liberal electorate of Warringah. A young TV presenter called James Mathison was running as an independent and was starting to get support from traditional Liberal voters who abhorred Abbott's reactionary views on so many issues, including climate and same-sex marriage.

About two weeks out from the election, Abbott called Tony Nutt, the federal director, and told him he was concerned Mathison might pull into second place and win on Labor preferences. He asked Nutt to get some polling done but insisted it not be done by Crosby Textor, whom he didn't trust as he believed they were too close to me.

Nutt commissioned Mike Sexton to do a poll on 22 June and its results were alarming. It showed Abbott was loathed in his own electorate: he had a net favourability of −40 per cent, compared to my having a net favourability of +21 per cent and the Liberal Party itself having a net favourability of +16 per cent. In this staunch Liberal Party seat, Bill Shorten was more liked than Abbott: his net favourability was 'only' −33 per cent.

Sexton's conclusion was that absent drastic remedial action, Abbott would lose the seat to Labor by 57–43 per cent. He'd found that Abbott was at odds with his own electorate on many social issues:

The Mathison vote is basically a protest vote on gay marriage, climate change and offshore processing, but these same voters like Turnbull and need a strong economy and jobs to support their inner urban lifestyles.[23]

Sexton noted that among those proposing to vote for Mathison, Abbott had a −83 per cent net favourability rating, whereas I had a +49 per cent rating and John Howard a +47 per cent rating. Moreover, over 80 per cent of all those voters planning to vote independent preferred me as PM to Shorten (as opposed to 61 per cent for the electorate as a whole).

The solution, according to Sexton, was for John Howard and I to communicate directly to these voters and, basically, ask them to hold their nose and vote for Abbott. And we did precisely as advised. It meant spending several hundred thousand dollars on keeping Abbott in his hitherto safe Liberal seat that could have been better used elsewhere defending some of our marginals. John Howard and I sent a letter to every constituent, as well as doing robocalls in which we were joined by NSW Premier and local state MP Mike Baird. The letter contained a particularly ironic line: '... only a local Liberal vote for my colleague, Tony Abbott, ensures stable majority government, with a clear and detailed economic plan.' Abbott eventually had a 9 per cent swing against him on primary votes, but managed to hold the seat.

Crosby Textor did our polling through the campaign and, with the aura once ascribed to soothsayers and wizards, Mark Textor interpreted the results for us every morning. Our first election track was on 17 May, a week into the campaign, and things were looking good – the economy was the biggest issue and our leadership on that was recognised; we were ahead 53:47 on two-party preferred with a 45 per cent primary vote.

However, a week later our vote had slipped and we were running 50:50. Labor was outspending us on television at least three to one[24] and had a vastly bigger field force. Textor explained the dip in support as 'a lack of clear, unfiltered exposure to the Liberals' campaign, with low advertising and direct media weight'.[25]

With disciplined messaging, we kept attention on the economy as the top issue, ahead of health and education.

We remained very short of money, so much so that Lucy and I contributed $1.75 million to the Liberal campaign. Several of our traditional corporate donors gave less in 2016 – some because they were cross about our super reforms; others because they thought we'd win anyway; and more than a few, I suspect, were free riding, expecting me to pay for the campaign.

Paid advertising was essential to campaigning because the free media weren't interested in the election issues and when they covered the contest focused on gaffes and colour stories. Labor's superior resources enabled them to buy advertising to hammer their messages home night after night on television and through all the direct digital channels as well.[26]

Then Labor's relentless Mediscare campaign started to pay off for them and health moved ahead of the economy as the key issue. On two-party preferred Labor was ahead 51:49. Tex noted that some of our big spending announcements, such as funding a stadium in Townsville, were counterproductive as they undermined our credibility as economic managers. 'Cash splashes' have a habit of rebounding on the splasher: any big spending projects have to be carefully framed as worthwhile and not simply as an election bribe. Despite the rising prominence of health, however, the advice was to stick to the economy.

Labor intensified its negative campaigning and 'saving Medicare' was the main theme of Shorten's launch. By 20 June, our track showed us behind 48:52 – we were heading for a thumping defeat. Tex insisted that we should stay positive and not reply in kind to Labor's attacks. By the Tuesday of the last week of the campaign, 28 June, our track showed us ahead of Labor 51:49 on self-nominated flows, a 2 per cent swing from the 2013 result, and 52:48 on historical preference flows: 66 per cent of Australians expected us to win. I was ahead of Shorten as preferred PM 46:31. Concern about economic management had risen following the surprise vote in favour of Brexit in the UK. Against all that was the Mediscare attack.

Tex concluded that the swing was between zero and two points, indicating we could expect a Liberal win. Remaining positive had worked in our favour, he reported:

> While Labor continues to gain traction on its Medicare attack, this is now appearing more shrill and has downgraded Shorten's relative standing versus a more prime ministerial, positive and focused Turnbull-led team … Labor's negative national focus appears to have downgraded the standing of their local candidates, allowing the Liberals to claw back ground locally.[27]

The last track was on Wednesday 29 June and predicted a narrow win. Our vote had declined over the preceding few days and we were at 50:50 because, Tex advised:

> A media focus on same-sex marriage, Labor's continued focus on health and a broader focus on gaffes and missteps has distracted from the Liberals' core message. We are now getting further and further away from Brexit and the costings release and the economic and financial messages are being diluted. This makes message discipline in the final days all the more important – majority gov, jobs and growth ... While it is tempting to refute Labor's untruths, this should not be our closing focus.[28]

Health remained the dominant issue as it had done for the last weeks of the campaign – reflecting Labor's relentless Mediscare attack. Expectations of a Coalition win were at 65 per cent and 44 per cent of voters preferred a majority Coalition government as opposed to 21 per cent preferring a Labor one.

The same-sex marriage issue had been relatively well confined in the course of the campaign. I supported marriage equality and was quite open that the plebiscite was something I'd inherited from Abbott. At the time, about two-thirds of Australians supported the public vote. And I assured voters that if the plebiscite was carried, as I expected it would be, the legalisation of same-sex marriage would sail through the parliament. As, of course, it eventually did.

However, this equilibrium was thrown out in the last crucial week of the campaign by Scott Morrison, who had been the principal advocate of a plebiscite. During an interview with Leigh Sales on 7.30 on Tuesday 28 June, he refused to say how he'd vote if the plebiscite was carried and this immediately raised concerns about the government's sincerity.

Scott had a very sincerely held and viscerally intense opposition to same-sex marriage and could have said he'd abstain, but I fear his troubled conscience was reserving the right to vote against it. Every other minister was then asked how they'd vote; most sensibly said they'd vote for legalisation if the plebiscite passed. A cautious answer from Julie Bishop was unreasonably portrayed as equivocal. She was a strong supporter of same-sex marriage despite a ferocious anti-same-sex-marriage element in her constituency, led by Margaret Court.

The result was two vital days in the last week talking about same-sex marriage and the government's sincerity as opposed to the economy. It wasn't a vote shifter, in my view or Tex's. But it obscured the messages we wanted to get across, and we lacked the resources to compete with Labor on direct advertising and messaging.

We knew the election was coming down to the wire. My final speech to the National Press Club on the Thursday of the last week was probably my best. I was over the flu, thankfully, and felt a new energy as we rushed to the finishing line. Tex was encouraging us to believe that Mediscare was starting to lose its impact and many of our candidates and front-line campaign workers said they felt the vote was coming back to us. I knew, however, this was just as likely to be wishful thinking.

As I did every election, I spent the closing days of the campaign in my own electorate going from booth to booth thanking the volunteers and delivering some final messages to the media pack that trailed along with us. I thought to myself, 'Will this be my last or second-last campaign?' As always, Lucy was by my side and Daisy and Alex were out at the polling booths as well, as were most of the team from the PMO – Team Turnbull was family and we were now at the end of the longest, most exhausting campaign. I was quietly confident we'd win, but troubled that everyone else was too. This meant that the electorate was focused on us, not on Labor, and were likely to cast protest votes against us, thinking we'd win anyway.

The usual drill for an election night is for the Liberal Party and supporters to gather at the Sofitel Wentworth Hotel in Sydney to watch the results come in. These evenings can either be better than the best party (if you win) or worse than a wake (if you lose). But what's worse than both is when you don't know what's going on at all.

I hadn't taken much interest in the planning of the election-night events, but I found myself with the family at home on the Saturday night, together with Tony Nutt, Sally Cray and our in-house psephologist and all-round savant Al Campbell, a senior adviser in the PMO. The plan was to wait until the result was clear – we were expecting a win – and then to go into the Wentworth to speak to our supporters, and the millions of Australians who were sitting up at home waiting to find out who was going to run the country for the next three years.

Unfortunately, there was no such clarity. In most seats, up to 30 per cent had voted early and the counting of the pre-polls was slow; the election was clearly very close. My natural instinct was to go into the Wentworth and simply say, echoing Bill Clinton, 'The people have spoken but we don't yet know what they have said,' have a few drinks with the supporters, thank them and then go home to bed. However, Tony Nutt was getting reports from the field that suggested we'd get more votes in, which would provide the clarity we needed. And so we waited – too long, as it turned out. By the time I did go in, everyone was over-tired and fed up, and we still didn't know the final outcome.

It was, however, pretty clear that we'd have more seats than Labor and that the outcome would be a Coalition government, most likely a majority government.

I was still outraged by the brazen dishonesty of Mediscare; I said:

> The Labor Party ran some of the most systematic, well-funded lies ever peddled in Australia.
>
> We have seen the massed ranks of the union movement and all of their millions of dollars telling vulnerable Australians that Medicare was going to be privatised or sold, frightening people in their beds. And even today, even as voters went to the polls, as you would have seen in the press, there were text messages being sent to thousands of people across Australia saying that Medicare was about to be privatised by the Liberal Party.
>
> And the SMS message said it came from Medicare. An extraordinary act of dishonesty. No doubt the police will investigate. But this is the scale of the challenge we faced. And regrettably more than a few people were misled.[29]

That last sentence turned out to be an understatement. Our candidate for Chisholm, Julia Banks, recalls one old friend of her parents weeping over how he'd have to vote Labor because he couldn't afford to pay his sick wife's medical bills when the Liberals sold Medicare. The big lie strategy worked in Australia in June 2016, as it did later in the year in the US presidential election, as it had a few weeks before in the Brexit referendum campaign.

We'd gone into the 2016 election with 90 seats in the House of Representatives, but a redistribution in New South Wales had meant three of them had become notionally Labor on the basis of the 2013 election results. These were Paterson in the Hunter Valley, Dobell on the Central Coast and Barton, centred on Kogarah, in Sydney. The longstanding member for Paterson, Bob Baldwin, decided to retire, which meant that seat was definitely gone and for us to hold the others would need a positive swing over 2013, which wasn't going to happen.

Equally, Macarthur in Western Sydney was massively redistributed, going from an 11.3 per cent seat to a 3.3 per cent seat. More ominously, local member Russell Matheson's main area of support – the city of Camden, where he'd been mayor – was moved out of the electorate into the neighbouring seat of Hume, held by Angus Taylor. Russell had wanted to challenge Taylor for Liberal preselection in Hume – not unreasonably, given it now contained much of his old seat – but I persuaded him not to do so and to stay and fight in Macarthur. Taylor, like Abbott, rewarded me for this support by becoming a key supporter of the 2018 Dutton coup.

All up, we lost 16 seats but won back two, a net loss of 14, and finished with 76, with five on the crossbench and 69 for Labor, who picked up a net 14 seats.

Our two wins were Julia Banks, who won Chisholm from Labor with a 2.8 per cent swing, and Ted O'Brien, who recovered the safe LNP seat of Fairfax, which Clive Palmer had held in the previous parliament.

The impact of Mediscare was especially seen in Western Sydney and Tasmania. We lost Macarthur, not surprisingly, but also Lindsay and Macquarie. In Tasmania we were expecting to lose Bass, where the local member, Andrew Nikolic, had become a polarising figure. And we did, with a 10.1 per cent swing against us. But we also lost Braddon and Lyons which, absent Mediscare, we would have held.

Queensland held up reasonably well, but there Pauline Hanson preferenced against our sitting members and there was a concerted campaign against both Wyatt Roy in Longman and Ewen Jones in Herbert. Labor won each seat on One Nation preferences.

There were some heroic performances. Michelle Landry had won Capricornia, centred on Rockhampton, by the slimmest margin in 2013 and Labor expected to win it back. But she managed to hold on, suffering only a 0.1 per cent swing. Hers was the last seat to finalise its count and the one that got us to 76 and a majority in our own right.

Self-styled political analysts, most of whom have never run for parliament, often underestimate the granularity of elections and how each seat and each member will have idiosyncrasies that can count for or against them. I've observed that if a member offends enough of their constituents for long enough, they can lose the safest seat. That's how Sophie Mirabella lost the seat of Indi to independent Cathy McGowan in 2013, and incredibly the Liberal Party ran Mirabella again in 2016 when Cathy, predictably, won with an even bigger majority.

Jamie Briggs was another case in point. His seat of Mayo was a blue-ribbon safe Liberal seat and had been held by Alexander Downer. Jamie was then a fairly entitled, arrogant young man and his unedifying behaviour in Hong Kong and demotion from the ministry all counted against him. He was naturally downcast about that but wanted to run again, and our polling indicated he'd do better against the Nick Xenophon Team candidate than anyone else. I didn't agree with that, but chose not to make an issue of it.

That was a mistake: we lost Mayo to NXT's Rebekha Sharkie. She had formerly worked for Briggs and been the chief of staff to Isobel Redmond when Redmond was Liberal leader in the SA parliament. I suspect she'll hold the seat for as long as she cares to be an MP. Safe Liberal or National seats are particularly vulnerable to independents. If they can run second on primaries, they'll generally win on Labor and/or Green preferences, so long as the Liberal primary vote isn't too close to 50 per cent.

The Senate result saw us lose three seats, leaving us with 30, but overall it was a much better result. Labor ended up with 26, the Greens with nine, and so a total of 35. A majority is 39, so we'd need to find nine votes from the crossbench if Labor and the Greens were voting against us.

Despite all the punditry to the contrary, the combination of the double-dissolution election and the change to the Senate voting rules worked out well for us. Out of the 11 members of the crossbench, most were at least amenable to supporting the government and, broadly speaking, came from the right side of the political spectrum. This ranged from four members from the far-right One Nation through to the three centrist liberals elected for NXT from South Australia. David Leyonhjelm from the Liberal Democrats was a libertarian free-market person and Derryn Hinch was certainly open to persuasion – a sensible small 'l' liberal ready to do business. Bob Day from Family First was a former member of the Liberal Party and could almost always be counted on, which only left Jacqui Lambie, the colourful and unpredictable former PUP senator, now independent, from Tasmania. She was more likely to vote Labor than Liberal on most issues.

Many people have said the size of the crossbench was a consequence of my holding a double-dissolution election. In fact, in the 44th parliament there were eight crossbenchers, six of whom had been elected in 2013. So, if we hadn't reformed the Senate voting rules and simply held a regular half-Senate election on the old Senate election laws in 2016, we'd have reasonably expected at least another six crossbenchers to be elected, for a total of 12: one more than the result from the double dissolution.

However, one thing was certain – we were well short of a 114 majority in a joint sitting. Our 76 MPs and 30 senators amounted to 106, so if we were to get the ABCC as well as the Registered Organisations Commission established, we'd need to secure at least eight of the cross-bench in a joint sitting, or nine if we were to get the bills passed by the Senate sitting alone.

I recall shortly after the election a downcast Josh Frydenberg pronouncing those bills were 'dead in the water'. He shouldn't have been so gloomy: as we will see, both were passed, vindicating the double dissolution.

And above all, we won.

CHAPTER 33

Back in government

When in November 2016 the *Oxford English Dictionary* announced 'post-truth' as the international word of the year, I thought: tell me about it. Labor, supposedly the defender of the poor and the sick and the vulnerable, had in this election with a cynicism as deadly as it was deceitful targeted those very groups and frightened them into voting Labor to 'save Medicare'.

After the election, I'd been exhausted, furious, gutted. It wasn't the result that burned me up so much. It was always on the cards we could lose; after all, we went into the campaign polling 50:50 and at times slipped well behind. But the fact that Labor could do so well with the shocking and outrageous lie that we were planning to sell Medicare shook me to the core.

Then there was Shorten's surreal victory lap in the days that followed – congratulating himself on a victory he hadn't won, with the media applauding the effectiveness of his lies.

I took responsibility for the result, of course, but it said a lot about the culture of Australian politics that few reflected that our win was remarkable given where we'd been before Abbott was deposed. It was bemusing that I was given no credit for our improved electoral prospects after replacing Abbott but was marked down savagely because our majority was reduced in 2016. Nor did many acknowledge that we'd received nearly a million more first-preference votes than Labor and were the first government to be returned with a majority in its own right since 2004.

There was a great deal of criticism that we hadn't spent more time and money attacking Shorten and expressly refuting the Mediscare campaign.

Looking back, and instinctively, I think this is probably right, but the reasons for staying – largely – positive were compelling.

We had very little money – Labor outspent us by many millions and had I not contributed $1.75 million to the campaign myself, we'd have almost certainly lost. In a crowded and confused free media environment – made all the more crazy by the fake news on social media – the only way to be sure of getting your message across is with paid advertising, and that costs a lot of money.

In short, we went into the campaign with a primary vote too low to win and behind in many key seats. We had to get our primary vote up, and we knew from our research Australians were sick and tired of the political slanging match and wanted to see a positive economic plan – and this is what we delivered.

We probably underestimated how much harder it is in the media scene of today to get a positive message across without substantially superior economic resources. And yet, while Shorten's negative campaign was ferocious, it delivered Labor their second-lowest primary vote in their party's history.

Equally, while it would have been satisfying for me – and especially for Lucy – to go after Shorten with a negative campaign (as Labor went after me), we knew Australians already had a negative view of Shorten – he was a drag on the Labor vote. Tex was adamant it would have been a waste of time and resources reinforcing something Australians already knew.[1]

Definitely, when Shorten first ran with Mediscare in the House of Representatives, we should have hit back much harder and made sure it was notorious as a lie long before the election was called. It was then conventional wisdom that, when faced with outrageous lies like that, one should be sparing in the rebuttal for fear of giving credibility, or 'salience', and hence publicity to something that's inherently unbelievable.

That kind of thinking is out of date. In the age of social media, any lie, any message of hate for that matter, can get viral reach. You cannot any longer rely on editors or producers to responsibly set aside palpable lies – their publications and programs are not what most people are watching, or at least not in the overwhelming numbers they were.

However, I didn't have much time for this kind of reflection in July 2016 as I swiftly moved to secure commitments from some of the crossbench that they'd support the government on motions of confidence or supply. Cathy McGowan and Bek Sharkie were quick to give me those assurances, as indeed was Bob Katter – although, shortly after announcing his agreement, he added that he could change his mind at a moment's notice!

In any event, securing government all came down to two narrow wins and one even narrower loss in Queensland. Michelle Landry and Ken O'Dowd hung on in their seats of Capricornia (Rockhampton) and Flynn (Gladstone), but unfortunately Ewen Jones lost Herbert (Townsville) by 37 votes. The final result was that we held 76 seats in the House of 150, which meant that as long as all our people turned up to vote, even with Tony Smith as the speaker, we'd have 75 votes against a combined 74 from the opposition and the crossbench.

Heather Henderson consoled me by saying that her father, Sir Robert Menzies, had always maintained the best majority was a majority of one. Why, I asked. 'He always said to me,' Heather recalled, 'that it's very good for discipline – concentrates the mind of the colleagues.'

It was Sunday 10 July, eight days after the election, and I was carrying Alex's one-year-old, Isla, when the phone rang. 'Hi, Malcolm,' said a familiar voice. 'I guess I better do the formal concession thing: you've won. Congratulations.'

I laughed. 'Well, Bill, despite all the fury and the theatrics, I am holding one of the young people we are doing this for.'

Bill agreed. 'Yes, there has to be some purpose to this madness. It's all about the kids. Give them and Lucy all my love.'

And so, at the end of such a long and bitter campaign and despite all the dreadful lies he'd told about us, we had a perfectly normal chat enquiring about the health of our families, passing on best wishes to our wives. Hostilities would shortly resume, but as the call ended I thought that there was far too little of that kind of warmth in politics today.

Two of my assistant ministers had lost their seats in the election: Wyatt Roy and Peter Hendy. The Nationals had held on to all of their seats and had won Murray, a traditional Liberal seat, in Victoria, when the sitting Liberal member, Sharman Stone, had retired just before the election. As a result, the Nats were entitled to one more seat in the cabinet. Politics, I reminded a press conference, is governed – as John Howard likes to say – by the iron laws of arithmetic.[2]

The most important changes to the ministry related to two of my most industrious colleagues, Christopher Pyne and Josh Frydenberg. I'd appointed Christopher minister for Industry, Innovation and Science when I became PM and he was a suitably enthusiastic advocate for the Innovation and Science Agenda. It was a key element in my economic program, in securing our nation's future prosperity.

But I needed his dynamism in Defence Industry. We had the largest-ever peacetime defence industry investment program underway and unless I was talking about it nobody knew it was happening. Given a lot of the investment related to the naval shipbuilding program in Adelaide, I figured he'd have every incentive to talk it up, and so he did. He was taking over Defence Industry from Marise Payne, who remained Defence minister, and the two were close personal friends and political allies, so I figured that was a plus. As it turned out, the defence industry program got the profile and the energetic political leadership it needed.

Josh Frydenberg wears his ambition, and his prime ministerial destiny, on his sleeve. But unlike many others, his ambition is matched by an extraordinary work ethic. He is by far the most frantically productive politician I've ever known, assuming productivity is measured in media appearances, newspaper articles or WhatsApp messages seeking support for one thing or another.

Originally, I'd put Josh into cabinet as minister for Resources and Northern Australia, and he'd performed well, technically and politically. But in this term, one of the most important and complex priorities was to bring to an end the climate and energy wars with a durable energy policy that would enable us to meet our emissions-reduction commitments while ensuring we had affordable and reliable power. This meant I needed to bring climate and energy policy together, so I appointed Josh minister for the Environment and Energy.

Greg Hunt, who'd been Environment minister, was desperate to get out of that portfolio (he'd held it in opposition and government for nearly a decade) and was pleased to be moved into Industry, Innovation and Science. He's a close friend and contemporary of Frydenberg, though cannot match Josh's warmth and charm.

I wasn't aware of it at this point, but Hunt all too often used abusive and vulgar language towards others, including to his department secretary, Martin Bowles, and on another occasion the 71-year-old mayor of Katherine, Fay Miller.[3] I knew he was also widely distrusted by his colleagues – although he wasn't unique in that regard – but despite those flaws, I'd found Hunt to be an effective technocrat and so was confident he wouldn't drop the innovation ball.

It's worth reflecting on the strengths and weaknesses of our parliamentary system of government. All of the ministers have to come from either the House or the Senate and, of course, in selecting a ministry a prime minister has to take into account the claims of different states, regions versus cities, gender equity and factional allegiances. It's an art, not a science.

But all that aside, the singular feature of our system, unlike that in the USA, is that the talent pool from which we draw ministers is relatively small. For an Australian government, it's around 100 people. In a state parliament it may only be a few dozen. Whereas in the UK, with 650 members of the House of Commons and about 800 in the House of Lords, there's a sizeable pool of potential ministers. With all of the practical political constraints on whom to choose coupled with a small pool from which to choose them, really capable ministers are often hard to find.

As we got ready to go back to parliament on 30 August I worked through my priorities. There were a number of difficult issues we needed to address – barnacles we had to get off the boat. All of them were regularly used by the right wing of the party to destabilise the government and my leadership of it.

The most immediate was same-sex marriage. The best outcome was to hold the plebiscite, win it and legislate for marriage equality. I had hopes at the outset that Shorten would support a plebiscite; he'd actually advocated a public vote on the issue only a few years before, something I'd never done until, despite my best efforts, it became government policy under Abbott.

It turned out he wasn't going to budge. He had two goals. First, he wanted Labor to deliver marriage equality, not the Coalition. Second, he knew that if I walked away from the plebiscite, my party room would blow up. And if it did and I lost the leadership in the process, he believed he'd win the election that followed.

And there was no downside for him being unreasonable. The public expects governments to govern and to make the parliament work, and so when an opposition works with the crossbench in the Senate to frustrate government legislation, it isn't the opposition, let alone the crossbenchers, who are blamed. It's the government. Nothing is more damaging than the appearance of impotence. John Howard had a chat with me when we both attended the National Rugby League grand final on 2 October. 'The only thing that's really hurting you now is the same-sex marriage issue, Malcolm,' he said. 'It's the inability to resolve it; makes you look like you aren't in control. And coupled with a divided party, it's very damaging. Reminds me of how Wik hurt us in '96, because we just couldn't come to a landing.'[4]

We didn't get marriage equality sorted in 2016. The Senate rejected our legislation for a plebiscite but, as I describe in chapter 39, we were finally able to legalise same-sex marriage at the end of 2017. Another barnacle was school funding. Abbott's cuts in the 2014 budget had broken a signature promise. Yet the funding arrangements we'd inherited from Labor were neither equitable nor affordable. I describe in chapter 40 how we addressed this issue and delivered for the first time federal school funding that was genuinely national, consistent and needs-based.

I introduced the legislation to establish the ABCC and the Registered Organisations Commission as soon as parliament resumed at the end of August. These were the two pieces of legislation, twice rejected by the Senate, that had been the trigger for the double dissolution and could never have been passed without it.

We had the numbers to get them through the House but needed nine of the 11 crossbench senators to get them passed by the Senate. The debate in the Senate was long and tortuous, with the corridors filled with union officials doing all they could to pressure the crossbench not to side with the government. Their main targets were Xenophon and Derryn Hinch, and they were in and out of my office with minister Michaelia Cash during the last sitting days of November. But by the end of the year we succeeded in passing both bills, with the support of One Nation's four senators, Nick Xenophon's three plus Derryn Hinch and David Leyonhjelm.

I had much more success with the Senate than either Abbott or I had had in the previous parliament. Flushed with the success of his election win, Abbott had demanded the senators accede to his mandate and support the government's legislation. Whatever merits the mandate argument may have in political science textbooks, it cuts no ice in the red chamber, and the senators became increasingly resentful and, consequently, uncooperative.

In the new parliament, charm and cooperation were to be the order of the day. I instructed ministers in the House of Representatives not to undertake negotiations with the Senate crossbench themselves unless they were doing so with the active involvement of one of the senior government senators. We had many good crossbench whisperers on our side, especially Mathias Cormann, Michaelia Cash, Mitch Fifield and Simon Birmingham. George Brandis, then the Senate leader and attorney-general, was a powerful advocate in the chamber, but often made his lack of patience with lesser minds a little too obvious to be entirely effective.

For my own part, I was patient, attentive and respectful to all the Senate crossbench, no matter how loopy they appeared. They all had a vote. Jacqui Lambie was rarely supportive but I was always ready to see her, even though afterwards it was often difficult to finalise her position. The One Nation senator from WA, Rod Culleton, was invariably incoherent but he always got a cup of tea and an attentive half-hour or so.

Part of the ABCC reform was the establishment of a Commonwealth Building Code with which all building companies would have to comply if they wanted to get work undertaken or funded by the federal government. In order to comply, their enterprise agreements with the unions couldn't have provisions that conflicted with the new legislation, such as those giving unions a veto on which subcontractors are employed or on the number of staff that can be hired. Some transition period was appropriate but we wanted it to be as short as possible. We'd obtained broad agreement with the crossbench to make it nine months from 2 December 2016 when the new laws commenced.

However, during the Senate debates, Derryn Hinch came under enormous pressure not to agree to the legislation from both the CFMEU and several of the large building companies. In a final compromise to secure his vote we agreed, at his insistence, that the transition period would be two years. This was seen by many as taking some of the gloss off our win in the Senate, but I persisted and invited Derryn to our home a few days before Christmas.[5] Over lunch and a bottle of non-alcoholic wine in our boatshed, he agreed to switch and vote to make the transition period nine months after all. We did that in February, when parliament came back in 2017; the whole exercise demonstrated that with patience and respect, you can achieve more than many, if not most, would expect.

• • •

It was 7.17 pm on 9 August 2016 – census day – and Lucy and I had just completed our online census form. The Australian Bureau of Statistics (ABS) were hoping that most of the census would be conducted online and so to encourage others I tweeted that we'd filled in the form: 'v easy to do. And so important for planning better Govt services & investment in the future'.

Just 11 minutes later a distributed denial-of-service (DDoS) attack began on the ABS website. A DDoS attack is a large number of coordinated requests designed to flood a website and prevent it responding. The ABS took the census website offline 41 minutes later.

No online exercise could have been higher profile than the 2016 census. Every Australian household had to respond; tens of thousands of collectors were out in the field collecting forms in the traditional way; millions had already completed the form online. It was a humiliating debacle, especially for a government that was promoting innovation, agility and the promise of the digital era.

Lucy and I were having dinner that night at home with Paul Whittaker, the editor of *The Australian*, and his wife. I managed not to let on to him what was going on while – in between a convivial dinner conversation – I was briefed on the failure and also ensured that Paul Taloni, the director of the Australian Signals Directorate, was all over it trying to find out what had happened, who'd done it and how we could get it back online.

There were meetings and briefings early the next morning and into the following days. While the ABS is ultimately the treasurer's responsibility, Scott Morrison had delegated it to the new minister for Small Business, Michael McCormack, a Nationals MP from New South Wales. I only just managed to stop Michael from going out with a statement, drafted by ABS and its IT contractor IBM, claiming there'd been a massive cyberhack and implying it was the work of a foreign state.

As it turned out, the DDoS attack was nothing special and quite modest in its scale. The ABS website failed simply because IBM, who'd been contracted to deliver the online census, failed to deliver on their clear contractual obligation to provide standard denial-of-service protection. It was a massive failure on the part of IBM as well as the ABS and a reminder of how vulnerable government agencies are when they complacently rely on big-name IT contractors to do all their work and thinking for them. IBM ultimately apologised and paid compensation to the government, which was no doubt galling, but in every practical respect – political and reputational – almost all of the damage was worn by the government. So, those politicians and public servants who think they're getting some insurance by outsourcing are wrong – the buck always stops on the prime minister's desk.

The ASD, on the other hand, demonstrated enormous skill in getting quickly to the bottom of what had happened, and ensuring the site was back up and running in a few days. Without the ASD we very likely would never have known the truth.

I instructed the relevant officials, including Martin Parkinson and Alastair MacGibbon, that we must be 'open and truthful about what occurred. We should work on the basis of full disclosure, subject only of course to legal or national security issues.'[6] This was the approach I took with all national security or disaster events – provide the public with a swift and accurate account of what has happened and if there are details that have to remain confidential, make sure people understand why that is so. Transparency and honesty are the keys to public confidence. Alastair's report into the incident not only laid bare what had gone wrong, but recommended how failures like this could be prevented in the future, including by getting the ASD more involved in projects of this kind.

By the end of 2016, people were starting to see that we could make the parliament work. The negotiations were often extremely complex. But the Australian people had elected the Senate and presumably expected me to work with it. We also managed to secure passage of our reforms to the superannuation taxation regime, with a change to only one of the 12 elements in the reform package in order to secure the support of my own party room.

To reverse the hurt inflicted by Mediscare, I was determined to be seen to guarantee Medicare and do so emphatically. We examined the feasibility of increasing the Medicare levy (currently 2 per cent) to a level that would fund all of the cost of Medicare and the Pharmaceutical Benefits Scheme. It would mean increasing it from 2 per cent to 4 per cent. My idea was to reduce income tax to the same extent. However, the problem was that the Medicare levy is a flat rate so a doubling of the levy would disproportionately impact people on lower incomes. Equally, there are some taxpayers who are exempt from the Medicare levy entirely and so they'd get a windfall from a reduction in income tax.

In the final result, I had to settle for the establishment of a Medicare Guarantee Fund which ensured all of the funds necessary to pay for

Medicare were deposited in a special account that couldn't be used for any other purpose. It was in large measure addressing a problem that didn't exist – Medicare's funding was never threatened – but we needed to be able to say we'd guaranteed Medicare.

Simultaneously, we restored the indexation of the Medicare schedules and delivered a new public hospital funding agreement from 2020 to 2025 that – in line with the deal done in 2016 – funded 45 per cent of the efficient growth in hospital activity with total funding capped at 6.5 per cent per annum. This amounted to an extra $130 billion for the states' hospitals over the five years.

These changes, together with the continued listing of new drugs on the PBS, made it difficult for Labor to continue to maintain a credible scare campaign on health or Medicare.

The combination of our health funding decisions together with the new Gonski 2.0 funding deal on schools meant that by the time of the 2019 election, the traditional Labor complaints about inadequate funding for schools and hospitals lacked credibility.

We were reminded of our narrow majority on the floor of the House early in the new parliament. On Thursdays, the last day of the sitting week, the practice is that at 4.30 pm there's a motion to adjourn the House. Five-minute speeches are then given by MPs, generally on constituency issues and notionally in support of that motion, which is then carried at 5 pm, whereupon everyone goes home.

But with a tight majority, there's always the risk that the opposition will vote against the adjournment and the House will keep sitting. On 1 September, a number of our members, including several ministers, had, without seeking leave from the whip, left early. When the opposition called for a division, we lost. It took hours to get all our members back – Michael Keenan had to fly back from Melbourne – and we narrowly avoided a motion being passed to establish an inquiry into the banks!

I didn't have long to reflect on the precarious state of our majority. Two days after the debacle in the House, I flew to Hangzhou for the G20 meeting, followed by the East Asia Summit in Vientiane, Laos, and then the Pacific Islands Forum in Pohnpei, Micronesia.

I was meeting most of the other world leaders for the second or third time and that, coupled with the election win, gave me an added confidence. I was no more dazzled by the trappings of international meetings than I had been by the wealth of billionaires. Then, as in the past, I was simply focused on the task at hand: as Australia's chief advocate, advancing and defending our interests in every forum.

At the G20, Obama and Xi announced their nations' ratification of the Paris Agreement on climate. It was to be Barack Obama's last G20 and while Trump wasn't regarded as likely to win the US election in November, his protectionist 'America first' rhetoric was biting – as evidenced by Hillary Clinton echoing his commitment to pull out of the TPP.

The Brexit vote in the UK had rattled all the leaders. David Cameron had since resigned after the referendum. Hangzhou was the first time I'd seen Theresa since she'd become prime minister and we assembled for a bilateral meeting – a characteristically intimate gathering with 20 people around the table.

As we began, Theresa asked after Lucy's health and I did the same for Philip, whereupon she said, 'Philip has never forgotten that advice you gave him at Oxford all those years ago,' and smiled.

I had no idea what she was talking about; my mind raced back to the bar at the Oxford Union in 1979 – God knows what I could have said. Best not to enquire, so I briskly replied, 'Well, not much time and lots on the agenda, so shall we proceed?' And then we went back to affairs of state.

I found a quiet moment afterwards to ask Theresa what my apparently memorable advice had been. 'Oh, Malcolm,' she said. 'It's a rather sweet story. You told Philip he should stop being so hesitant and hurry up and propose to me.' Since they'd been married for nearly as long as Lucy and me, I could only conclude Theresa was pleased that Philip had taken my advice!

While in Hangzhou, I made a visit to the Alibaba headquarters to visit founder Jack Ma, who'd studied in Australia in his youth. Jack made the powerful point that the combination of our free trade agreement with China and online platforms like Alibaba had put 'mum and dad' businesses and start-ups on a level playing field with big business in accessing new markets like never before.

Another important element in building public confidence in free trade was making sure multinational companies paid their tax. As I often said, while I believe in lowering taxes, I don't accept a self-help approach to tax reform – tax is compulsory. Australia had passed some of the world's toughest multinational anti-tax avoidance legislation and was adding to that a diverted profits tax that would impose a 40 per cent tax on profits that were artificially shifted offshore.

After flying back to Australia for a week of parliament, I was on the move again to New York for the annual UN General Assembly leaders' week. Australian prime ministers don't attend these events every year, but they are, like all international conferences, a great opportunity for meeting a large number of leaders who don't attend regional forums in the Pacific or the big summits like the G20. In addition to old friends like Bibi Netanyahu, I was particularly interested to meet several Eastern European leaders – including President Grabar-Kitarović of Croatia and her counterparts from Romania, Ukraine and Bulgaria. All of them attributed the Brexit vote in June 2016 to the decision Angela Merkel had made in September 2015 to allow a million asylum seekers from Syria to enter Germany. Their message was unequivocal – nothing is firing up right-wing populism so much as the threat of uncontrolled migration.

And migration and refugees were the key themes of the week, with President Obama holding a special summit on refugees. On 20 September Rachel Noble, the deputy secretary of our Immigration department, signed the refugee resettlement deal with the United States. It was a fair deal: we were resettling people for the Americans, including some complex cases, as they were assisting us. There were no security issues; as I had told Obama, the people on Nauru and Manus were all pre–Syrian conflict and had been thoroughly vetted, many of them simply economic refugees. Obama and I agreed it best to announce the signing of the deal after the election so that it would not get caught up in the last few frenzied months of the campaign, with all the risks that entailed.

The United Nations has been the source of continued criticism of Australia's border protection policies for many years, and so rather than duck the tough issues, I gave a speech there on 21 September that set out our position plainly.

I said, 'In order to secure and maintain public support for immigration, multiculturalism and a generous humanitarian program, the public need to know that it is their government which controls their borders.'

Without that control, we wouldn't have been able to maintain the world's third-largest permanent refugee resettlement program, nor to increase our broader humanitarian intake by 35 per cent, let alone take an additional 12,000 refugees from the Syrian conflict zone.

I was proud to talk about Aliir Aliir, who played football for the Sydney Swans. He'd come to Australia with his family, refugees from the bloody civil wars in Sudan.

> There are thousands of migrant stories like Aliir's – leaders of government, of business, of science, of the arts. Australia wouldn't be the country it is today without their contribution. Their stories are our stories, their successes are our successes …
>
> Another fact we must recognise is that while it would be desirable for more nations to increase their humanitarian intake, as Australia is doing, the truth is, the scale of the refugee and internally displaced persons problem is so great – 65 million – that resettlement in other countries can never come close to being near enough.[7]

I had one other big international trip in 2016 – to Lima, Peru, for the APEC meeting. This was a noticeably unsettled conference. Trump had won a few weeks before, and the shock was still sinking in. All the concerns about populism expressed in Hangzhou were now in sharp relief.

Back in Australia, over several weeks in December, ASIO and the AFP working with Victoria Police had detected and monitored a sophisticated plot to attack Federation Square in Melbourne on Christmas Day – right across the street from St Paul's Cathedral. The assault was going to involve vehicles and bombs, which were being manufactured by the conspirators all in the name of ISIL.

The conspirators had been arrested overnight when I stood up at the press conference on 23 December with Justice Minister Michael Keenan and AFP Commissioner Andrew Colvin. We were able to confirm the threat was eliminated and all the conspirators and their explosive materials were in custody.

It was a reminder that terrorism had no borders.

'We see around the world the global threat of terrorism,' I said. 'The truck attack in Berlin earlier this week and similar terrorist attacks in the last few weeks including Nigeria, Yemen, Turkey, Somalia, Egypt and Jordan. Islamist terror is a global challenge that affects us all. These criminals seek to kill, but they also seek to frighten us. They want to frighten Australians and divide Australians. They want us to turn on each other. We will not let them succeed.'[8]

'What sort of year has it been?' I asked in my diary on the last day of 2016.

Turbulent I guess, successful in the sense we got re-elected and once back managed to get a lot of legislation through the Senate people said we wouldn't, including the two double dissolution bills. The narrower than expected election win has been blamed on me naturally and the poor campaign (viewed by the result) as well. As PM you take responsibility for everything.

Generally I think we have performed well since the election and to some extent the narrow majority in the House provides some discipline, but the general unsettlement in the political scene driven by Trump, Brexit, growing anxiety about change, jobs, slower growth is all causing uneasiness on the right and of course opportunists like Tony Abbott and Cory Bernardi will seek to take advantage of it. The Qld Nats are terrified of Hanson and One Nation, but it has to be said her vote at the last election was pretty close to what Palmer got in 2013.

What have I done wrong? I think probably I haven't been seen as being decisive or dynamic enough? That's the perception. People ask what do we stand for? Well we stand for our platform which we are implementing. The Australian *the other day said we didn't have a coherent economic plan – so what does that mean? Is it incoherent to reform superannuation (tick done), cut middle income taxes (tick done), reform VET FEE-HELP (tick done), restore the ABCC and establish the Registered Organisations Commission (tick, tick done), get on with the defence investment plan and establishing a sovereign defence industry in Australia etc etc. The only major element of our economic policy not yet done is the company tax cuts.*

Still the polls are not good, we are behind 52:48 or thereabouts and while I am consistently at least 10 points ahead of Shorten as preferred PM my net favourability is down. On the other hand there is no obvious alternative to me and certainly nobody whom you could say would do better at the polls. So there is some security in that. Frydenberg, Porter and Morrison are the three from whom the next leader will come. Dutton is too limited. Abbott is finished and Julie is over it, in my view. Barnaby is convinced she is plotting to do me in, but I doubt it … this isn't to say she wouldn't run for leader if I

fell under a bus, but would she push me under one? I can't see it. She didn't
move on Abbott and he treated her like dirt.

We held a New Year's Eve party at Kirribilli House (at my own expense) and watched the fireworks from the governor-general's lawn – apart from a tirade of drunken abuse from one of Murdoch's editors, it was a congenial evening.

Kirribilli House, a 19th-century sandstone cottage, is the official residence of the prime minister in Sydney. It's next to and effectively in the grounds of the substantial Admiralty House, which belongs to the NSW government and is provided for use by the Commonwealth on condition that it is the Sydney residence of the governor-general. The location – on Sydney Harbour across from the Opera House – is extraordinary.

Kirribilli House had been acquired by the Commonwealth in 1920 – essentially to protect the amenity of Admiralty House – and was used for various purposes over the years, including as accommodation for Admiralty House staff and for visiting dignitaries.

The first prime minister to live there for substantial periods was Bob Hawke. Then Paul Keating lived there as well as at The Lodge. But it was John Howard who made it his primary residence, rather than The Lodge, justifying it on the basis that his young children were all at school in Sydney. From then on, every prime minister, apart from myself, made it their Sydney base, and in some cases their home base, as Tony Abbott and Scott Morrison have done.

Lucy and I decided not to move into Kirribilli House when I became PM. It was claimed that this put the AFP to additional expense because they had to place guards around our home in Point Piper. However, if that argument was to be sustained it would mean that a future PM who didn't come from Sydney would have to move to Sydney to save expense. Rudd, of course, maintained his Brisbane home and was suitably protected.

Naturally, we preferred to stay in our own home and it was, most importantly, close to our Sydney grandchildren. But there was another deeper reason for not making the move as well. Having sunk into the darkest depression when I lost my job as opposition leader, I was determined not to do the same when, inevitably, my time as prime minister came to an end. Having that continuity of our own home, before, during and after the PM role, was going to be important to maintain peace of mind.

As to Kirribilli House itself, it isn't fit for purpose. It can comfortably sit for dinner no more than 10, and is too small for official meetings other than very intimate ones. It has magnificent views up the harbour, which is its strong suit, but because it has very little level lawn around the house, any large reception requires the construction of a marquee and a platform to provide enough space for the guests to gather together.

The Lodge isn't fit for purpose either. The official residence of the Australian prime minister, located a few kilometres from Parliament House, was built as a *temporary* residence for the PM in 1926. The work of a Melbourne architect, it was designed, like most posh Melbourne houses of that era, as though it was in England. It's dark and pays no respect to the Australian climate at all, with no verandahs or breezeways. It would be more at home in the stockbroker-belt suburbs outside of London.

It isn't a grand house by any means but is larger, for example, than most of the bungalows in the Canberra suburbs that surround it. Its reception rooms aren't big enough for large functions and so several times a year a marquee has to be erected next to the house to cater for Australia Day receptions and the like.

It does have a beautiful garden, but its amenity is rather diminished by the fact that in 1969 a freeway was built next to The Lodge, on the site of an old orchard that had been part of the original Lodge grounds. Loud traffic noise is ever-present, to the extent that the main 'Menzies bedroom' has to have double-glazed windows so that the occupants can sleep.

At the time I became PM, I was living in a flat I owned in Kingston overlooking the lake and was therefore far from disappointed that The Lodge was not ready for occupation as its renovation, begun under Gillard and continued under Abbott, was not quite complete. I would have dearly liked to stay in my flat, but I felt that as Lucy and I had decided not to move into Kirribilli House (for which I was criticised in some quarters), not moving into The Lodge would be a bridge too far.

Lucy, who has built several large houses and knows a lot about planning and design, went down to inspect the progress. She called me in a state of high anxiety.

'Darling, this is a huge scandal,' she whispered. 'Somebody has stolen millions. I can't believe it.'

Startled, I asked her what was going on.

'I've just gone through the house. It's a complete mess. No planning. They didn't even think of wifi, so there are all these little white boxes lying around the place, and the kitchen is unworkable – no bench space and no island. That makes it almost impossible to cater for a large function. But you know what's worse?' Her voice lowered. 'They have spent $7 million – and I just can't see where it has gone.'

I was astonished too. For that kind of money you could have built an entirely new house of that size and had plenty of change left over. A few minutes later she rang back. 'It's worse. They've spent $9 million!'

Well, as it finally turned out, the government had spent over $11 million on what must have been one of the worst renovations I'd ever seen. It turned out it had been overseen by Peta Credlin, but not even that explains the fiasco. There was no fixed-price contract entered into with the builder, no agreed design, the requirements and plans kept changing, and the architect, as he later told me himself, had limited experience in domestic architecture and had won the job because the Department of Finance esteemed his firm's work on designing the AFP headquarters!

In anywhere but the craziness of Canberra, presented with the challenge of renovating a 1920s house with important heritage considerations, any rational person would get a shortlist of the top three or four architects who specialise in that field and choose one of them. But not in Canberra, where the renovation of The Lodge sums up everything that's wrong with the unworldly culture of the public service.

Lucy was so shocked by the amount of money that had been wasted on the renovation, she herself paid for much of the soft furnishings, such as curtains and upholstery. To help with the interior decoration, she recruited Angela Marshall, who'd lived in The Lodge as a child with her parents, Malcolm and Tamie Fraser. Together they went out to a warehouse in Canberra where they found some of The Lodge's original furniture. They recovered the couch and armchairs for the morning room and were thrilled to find a photograph of Dame Enid Lyons (wife of PM Joe Lyons) sitting on the couch nursing one of her numerous children in the early 1930s.

Lucy also ensured that much of the soft furnishings were Australian, including some spectacular curtains with designs inspired by Australian flora. She also selected a largely contemporary collection of Australian paintings for the house, including some important Indigenous works. She was doing the best she could to make this very English-looking house look Australian.

We made one structural change to The Lodge. The house is very dark, and one of the few rooms with some natural light is, naturally, on the north-eastern corner. For some reason – in Malcolm Fraser's day, we think – a glass-panelled door on the northern side had been bricked up, and then in the Credlin renovation the room had been destined to be filled with noisy fridges and office equipment. A complete waste. We reinstated the door and set up the room as a sunny breakfast room suitable for smaller meetings.

The door gave me another insight into the parallel universe of Canberra. Once we had determined that there had indeed been a door and that reinstating it would not offend the heritage mafia, the next step was making the door. Quite by accident I learned that my department was proposing to spend up to $10,000 on an architect to design the door. Now, all of the doors at The Lodge are the same design. So I pointed out we simply needed a joiner to make a copy of one of the existing doors. Money was saved, the door was made – very handsome it was too and, naturally, a perfect facsimile of the other dozen or more doors.

I arranged for an audit to be done of the work on the renovation, which is now a public document. David O'Donnell, a very experienced construction lawyer, oversaw it and the conclusions were essentially as I have described – a clueless client who failed to give clear and consistent direction to the various contractors and consultants. Needless to say, the departments of Finance and of the Prime Minister and Cabinet did everything within their power to resist taking responsibility.

In the wake of this, I established an Official Residences Advisory Committee to oversee future work on The Lodge and Kirribilli House and to make recommendations for their future. It was made up of people with real experience in architecture and construction and would serve, I hoped, to ensure that there was no repeat of the $11 million fiasco I've described. If the current Lodge is to be retained as an historic home and if the prime minister should have an official residence in Canberra, then a new Lodge should be built. A site on Attunga Point on Lake Burley Griffin has been reserved for this purpose for many years. The new Lodge should be a modern, Australian-designed official residence. Like a modern embassy it would have public rooms for official entertaining and a private apartment suitable for the PM and his or her family to live in, if and when they are in Canberra.

Also, Kirribilli House should cease to be an official Sydney residence for the PM. If there's to be such a place in Sydney, why not one in every other state capital? Nobody would be prepared to pay for that! Likewise, I don't see any need for the governor-general to have a Sydney residence in addition to the Canberra one.

The best use for both Admiralty House and Kirribilli House would be as an integrated Commonwealth conference facility (a term I hate but can't think of a better one). With the kind consent of the governor-general, we did that on several occasions. A visiting head of state, such as President Widodo, can be received with an honour guard on the lawn in front of Admiralty House with the picture-postcard view of the Opera House and Harbour Bridge. The state rooms at Admiralty House are large enough for bilateral meetings and official lunches or dinners. Smaller one-on-one meetings and a press conference can be held at Kirribilli House.

The steeply sloping lawns of Kirribilli, while unsuitable for garden parties, are, however, excellent for rolling down. And when we had official receptions at Kirribilli, we always made sure there was plenty of cardboard on which kids could slide down the hill. This became so popular that after one of Peter Dutton's sons crashed into a large flowerpot (without complaint or apparent ill effect) I arranged for it to be wrapped in foam cladding whenever grassy slaloms were held.

On one occasion Lucy took off her shoes and demonstrated to young Jack and some other children how to roll down the slope. I was delighted and said, 'Hooray, Lucy, you are now the first prime minister's wife to roll down the hill.'

I heard a rather dry and thoroughly tongue-in-cheek comment from one of the longstanding staff. 'Certainly the first to do it sober, PM.'

CHAPTER 34

China and the region

'There are three types of carp in the West Lake,' President Xi Jinping told me. 'Do you know what type it was?'

We were sitting at the long leaders' table at the gala dinner of APEC in Lima on 19 November 2016. We'd discussed Donald Trump's pending presidency, the South China Sea, the prospects of political change in North Korea and many other weighty subjects, but we'd got on to Hangzhou, the beautiful Chinese city where earlier in the year Xi had hosted the G20 meeting.

I'd noticed Xi was drinking his own green tea and I asked him if it was Long Jing tea. It was my favourite too.

'Yes it is,' he said. 'From Hangzhou.'

I'd recalled the ferry ride across the West Lake in Hangzhou to the entertainment – a spectacular demonstration of Chinese culture, ancient and modern. Together with the governor of Zhejiang province, I was chatting at the front of our little ferry with Theresa May, Shinzo Abe and the prime minister of Italy, Matteo Renzi. We were about halfway across the lake when an enormous carp leaped over the side of the boat onto the deck. Shinzo and Theresa sidestepped the magnificent fish, and it was Matteo Renzi who deftly kicked it out through a scupper and back into the lake.

The governor was delighted. 'It took us three weeks to train that fish,' he'd said.

'I assumed he was joking,' I said to the president, who sipped some more of his tea before replying, 'He is a very good governor, but not known for his sense of humour.'

Training a fish to jump into a boat full of world leaders would be quite a challenge, but nothing to match the extraordinary achievements of China over the last 40 years. Never in all of human history have so many people, 850 million, been so quickly lifted out of poverty.

As I've often said, we live in a time of change unprecedented both in scale and pace, and nowhere more so than in China.

I first started travelling to China in the early 1990s, scouting out mining opportunities. In those days, there wasn't a lot of finance available for resources projects within China and the local technology was backward. The geological bureaus in each province were still operating under the same Russian principles on which they'd been set up – identifying and proving up many deposits without much, if any, regard being given to how they might be exploited.

So, assisted by Li Jing, a lawyer trained in Beijing and Melbourne, and geologist Zhou Bo, who'd also trained in Australia, together with Christian Turner, who worked with me at Turnbull Doyle Resources, and our senior geologist, Ralph Stagg, we set out to investigate many different opportunities in gold and other minerals. In the process, I came to know Bo Xilai, then the mayor of Dalian – he struck me as the most Western of Chinese political leaders, not at all the stern, formal demeanour of the Communist Party cadre.

Eventually, in 1994, we settled on developing a big zinc deposit at a place called Caijiaying, north of Zhangjiakou in Hebei Province. Zhangjiakou was originally a fortress city built to defend one of the gates on the Great Wall. We stayed in an old hotel built by the Japanese during their occupation of Northern China in the 1930s and it seemed nothing had been changed since the Japanese had left, except the bedsheets. It was the best hotel in town. And most of the places we stayed in were like that, old and run-down hotels or state guesthouses – all gone today in a modern China of steel and glass.

The Chinese parties we negotiated with were as keen to get our mining expertise as they were our capital, and the mine was one of the very few Sino-Western mining projects agreed and developed. Today, Chinese engineering companies are building mines and railways, bridges, tunnels and whole cities around the world.

Those encounters in China showed me a world that has now vanished. Instead of negotiating deals in spotless modern offices, we were out in the countryside, bumping along dirt roads, negotiating with officials in old rooms lined with worn-out armchairs, being plied with endless thermoses of tea. Every person I met – from governors and ministers to local geologists and engineers, regardless of their seniority or sophistication – was filled with an enthusiastic pride in their country's achievements and an enormous ambition for what it would achieve in the future. Again and again we talked about Chinese history, going back thousands of years.

It was while sitting at a dinner table in Zhangjiakou that I first heard about Deng Xiaoping's southern tour in 1984, when he'd announced that China must open itself up to the world. He'd noted that it was when China had turned its back on the world that it became weak and then was exploited and invaded by foreign powers. Of course Deng only made that speech after he'd seen the success of the Shenzhen special economic zone – an experiment designed and led by Xi Zhongxun, who's received too little credit for it. A point not lost on his son, Xi Jinping, who understands that, in China especially, history is written by the victors.

From my hosts' perspective all those years ago, China's rise was, as Deng had foretold it, simply a matter of restoring China to its place in the first rank of nations – a return to the natural order of things. And the only obstacle to achieving this economic progress was lack of order. Wise and stable leadership of a hardworking and disciplined nation was the way to get ahead.

We often discussed the merits of democracy and it was clear my Chinese companions were sceptics. 'After all,' the governor of Liaoning remarked thoughtfully one evening, 'just because the majority of the people want to do something doesn't mean it's right.'

They were fascinated by my leadership of the Australian Republican Movement, and amazed that the Queen of England was still Australia's head of state. One of our friends, in Shandong as I recall, joked, 'In 1949 Mao said, "The Chinese people have stood up." So you should say, "The Australian people stand up!"'

It was a joke, but there was a serious point there. Modern China was founded by Mao with that line, and it summed up a sense of extraordinary pride that the Chinese people have in their own sovereignty. Theirs was very hard-won, battling centuries of foreign oppression and occupation particularly from the Japanese, whose occupation of much of China in the 1930s and '40s was especially brutal. And that's not to mention the 19th-century Opium Wars, when the British went to war with China to enforce the right of their merchants to sell opium when Chinese officials were trying to stamp out drug addiction. It was, as I said years later, 'as if the Medellin Cartel sent gunboats up the Potomac to shell the Capitol until the Americans disbanded the Drug Enforcement Agency'.[1]

Not long after we'd done the deal on the zinc project, I joined Goldman Sachs and sold my share in it to Mladen Ninkov's Griffin Mining, which went on to build the mine. Bo Zhou stayed with the project and is in large part responsible for its success.

But while my business career took me away from China, I remained a keenly interested observer. Our son, Alex, left high school in 2000 and, before going to Harvard College, travelled to Shanghai and spent nine months studying Chinese, giving him the basis for continuing with his Chinese at Harvard.

Once in parliament, I often spoke about foreign policy, particularly when I was leader of the opposition, but the most considered speech I gave about China was in 2011 at the London School of Economics (LSE). With the help of my long-term economic adviser, Stephen Ellis, I put together a nuanced view of China's rise which rejected the 'new Cold War' attempts of many in the West to frame China as the modern equivalent of the Soviet Union – an enduring threat to the United States and its allies, and one which therefore must be contained.

I described the anxiety felt in the USA particularly, about the way in which China was forging ahead of America in science, technology and infrastructure – summed up in Tom Friedman's book with Michael Mandelbaum, *That Used to Be Us*.[2] But I rejected the proposition that China's economic growth meant it was inevitably going to become a military threat and quoted with approval Henry Kissinger, who'd recently argued that 'China's developed and historic sense of its central place will make it a less outwardly assertive leading power than the US'. He contrasted missionary US exceptionalism based on 'an obligation to spread its values to every part of the world' with China's disinterest in claiming its institutions are relevant outside China.[3]

I went on to say:

And indeed it is important to note that China's growth in power, both economic and military, has not been matched by any expansionist tendencies beyond reuniting Taiwan. Indeed very large territories in the North East of China taken by Russia under duress following the unequal treaties of Aigun (1858) and Beijing (1860) have not been left unresolved as a possible casus belli in years to come, but instead have been legitimised in new treaties signed only a few years ago.

China's government, I argued, was the Communist Party, whose dominance 'depends on a social contract – you the people let us run the country, and we the party will deliver rising living standards'.

This meant the consequences of a prolonged economic downturn in China would likely be a challenge to the Communist Party's leadership. In the USA or Australia, on the other hand, the legitimacy of government comes through the ballot box. If a severe recession hits, the crew will throw the officers to the sharks and elect new ones, but the ship of state will sail on. That isn't assured in China.

So, my thesis was that China had even more to lose from the economic woes a major conflict would bring. All of which led me to conclude that China wasn't another Soviet Union seeking to disrupt Western democracies, nor was it likely to seek to use its growing military power to provoke a conflict with the United States.

> It makes no sense for America, or its allies, to base long-term strategic policy on the contentious proposition that we are on an inevitable collision course with a militarily aggressive China ... This is no counsel for complacency – but our strategic response should be to hedge against adverse and unlikely future contingencies as opposed to seeking to contain (futilely in all likelihood) a rising power.

This earned furious condemnation from *The Australian*'s resident China hawk, Greg Sheridan, and for some years I was regularly framed as a 'panda hugging' China appeaser. This, of course, was precisely the kind of Cold War thinking I was criticising.

But there were some clues in the speech that pointed, for those who took the time to read it, to the approach I took while prime minister. While acknowledging China's achievements and the way in which the Chinese people have indeed 'stood up' after centuries of foreign domination, I said, 'China should respect the right of the Australian people to stand up for our sovereignty too.'

And I recognised that we needed a clear-eyed appraisal of the changing strategic balance in East Asia:

> As China rises to become the world's largest economy and in time a military rival, if not an equal, of the United States, we are presented with a nation whose institutions and culture are very different to ours. Yet China is, as I have noted, our largest trading partner and in large measure responsible for our current and prospective prosperity.

We have every reason, and indeed every prospect, of remaining close and becoming closer friends of those giants. But in doing so, and as Australia becomes accustomed to a multi-polar world, we have much to do to draw closer to the other countries in our region, including India, as we deepen our relations and trust with our neighbours.

Not just the Chinese people, but people right across East and South Asia have once again stood up. And so indeed should we.[4]

By the time I became prime minister, Xi Jinping had become president and a new, much more assertive foreign policy was emerging. As opposed to settling border disputes in a pragmatic manner, as it had with Russia in 2004, China started to press its claim to vast territorial waters in the South China Sea. Then, in 2013, it started to erect artificial islands and bases out of coral reefs, most of which had no visible features at high tide.

This created real tensions with its neighbours, and especially Vietnam and the Philippines. At the same time in 2013, Xi commenced his program of international infrastructure development along China's key sea and land trading routes – what is now called the Belt and Road Initiative (BRI).

China, like the USA, Australia and most other nations, engages in foreign intelligence-gathering operations. There was a time when countries used to deny they did – it was only after the *Spycatcher* trial that the UK, for example, admitted the existence of MI6, their Secret (foreign) Intelligence Service. I recall the Chinese ambassador visiting my office in Sydney back when I was opposition leader and him gravely assuring me, 'China does not engage in espionage anywhere in the world.' We struggled to keep a straight face because one of his delegation was the principal Chinese intelligence officer in Canberra.

All that aside, being shocked about Chinese spying is a bit like the scene in *Casablanca* where Captain Renault walks into Rick's Café and says, 'I'm shocked – shocked – to find that gambling is going on in here!'

However, what's become increasingly apparent over the last decade is the industrial scale, scope and effectiveness of Chinese intelligence gathering and in particular cyberespionage. They do more of it than anyone else, by far, and apply more resources to it than anyone else. They target commercial secrets, especially in technology, even where they have no connection with national security. And, finally, they're very good at it.

A last point, which speaks to the growing confidence of China, is that they're not embarrassed by being caught.

But beyond those points, by the time I became PM in September 2015, I felt that my approach to China and the region, as far as Australia was concerned, remained correct. And a key element in that was to recognise that we were living in a multi-polar world and that, in particular, we needed to do more to engage with our neighbours in South East Asia and India, neglected by Australia as we were mesmerised by the rise of China.

In the past, Australians had too often looked at the world as one of hubs and spokes, with our main hub being Washington. But we needed to see our region as more like a mesh and deepen the engagement and trust between us and our neighbours. All of these countries are smaller economies relative to China or Japan, but they're growing rapidly. Indonesia, already at 270 million people, will be the fourth-largest national economy in the world by 2050.

As described in chapter 26, I moved quickly to cement our relationship with Indonesia, but I didn't neglect the rest of the members of the Association of South East Asian Nations (ASEAN). I forged closer ties with our good friends in Singapore through a new and expanded free trade agreement and comprehensive strategic partnership, which covered, among other things, an expansion of the training facilities we provide in Australia for Singapore's armed forces. Prime Minister Lee Hsien Loong is one of the wisest and most civilised of people, as is his brilliant wife, Ho Ching, who heads up Singapore's $400 billion sovereign wealth fund, Temasek Holdings.

Julie Bishop and I were of the same mind on foreign policy, and to advance our ASEAN engagement we agreed to hold a special ASEAN summit in Australia in March 2018. In the Philippines, our intelligence support had been 'the game changer' in retaking Marawi from ISIL-backed insurgents – according to General Guerrero[5] – which had improved our standing with the Philippines government. And we'd developed much closer links with Vietnam, including a new strategic partnership announced at the summit, assisted by the good personal rapport I'd developed with Prime Minister Phuc. There was a lot more to be done, but by the time I left office our relations with most other countries in ASEAN were much further advanced.

After coming to office in September 2015, I had a formal meeting with President Xi at the G20 meeting on 16 November in Antalya, and with Premier Li Keqiang at the East Asia Summit in Kuala Lumpur five days later. Even more valuably, as I was later to do in Lima at the end of 2016, I spent a quiet hour speaking with President Xi at a lunch at the APEC meeting in Manila.

The discussions were all warm. Our China–Australia Free Trade Agreement had just come into force and both sides anticipated (as proved to be the case) considerable growth in trade, tourism and student numbers, including of Australians going to study in China. We shared a passion for innovation and science and discussed a wide range of issues from water scarcity in North China to the integration of mass transit and development in cities. Both President Xi and Premier Li are, above all, thoughtful technocrats, professional and pragmatic managers, who are focused on outcomes.

Which, of course, is why they and many Chinese (indeed many Westerners, if polls are to be believed) are sceptical about democracy. The Chinese system, since Mao, has produced one well-qualified and experienced manager after another as their leader, people who've demonstrated their capacity running cities, provinces or big institutions.

They point to the United States and ask what was the qualifying experience of presidents as unalike as Obama and Trump: the former a community organiser who hadn't run anything in the private or public sector before becoming president, the latter a real estate developer and reality TV host with no experience in government at all.

So there in a nutshell is an example of the difference: the Chinese system's legitimacy comes from the good government and strong economy it delivers (when it does); the US system's legitimacy comes from the fact the people voted for it (for good or ill).

In those days the only somewhat scratchy moments in meetings were when we discussed our concerns about the rising tensions in the South China Sea caused by China's island-building. Xi had actually raised the topic of the South China Sea himself, expressing the hope that Australia would uphold an objective and just position and not take actions which might undermine national sovereignty and international law. What he meant was: it's a long way from Australia, stay out of it.

Xi had previously referred to the need to avoid the 'Thucydides trap',[6] so I picked up on that and said that the way for a rising power to avoid creating anxieties among others was to work hard to build mutual confidence. While Australia had no claims in the South China Sea, nonetheless we had an interest in encouraging all claimants to work in a manner that builds trust and confidence.

We discussed North Korea at all our meetings. Xi's perspective was that Kim Jong Un was intractable, and the more you pushed him, the more he'd dig in. He lamented that North Korea hadn't followed the Chinese development model, as he and his father before him had been urged to do. But Xi was confident the regime wouldn't collapse – a combination of slowly improving living standards, albeit from an incredibly low base, and added to that an immensely efficient security apparatus, would work to suppress dissent.

As Angela Merkel and I had discussed only a few weeks before in Berlin, Xi saw himself as a man of destiny, a leader who was going to restore China to its previous greatness. He wasn't alone: the world has plenty of leaders who want to 'Make [insert name of country] Great Again'. We didn't have Trump in 2015, but Modi, Putin and of course Erdoğan, among others, all fitted that description. I suppose one could add Boris Johnson to that list today.

Xi and I met again on 15 April 2016 when I made a state visit to China for our annual bilateral talks. Lucy accompanied me and we had a pleasant dinner at the Diaoyutai State Guesthouse with President Xi and his wife, Peng Liyuan, who spoke flawless English. Lucy, as she always did, made an eloquent contribution to the discussion especially when the subject turned, as it always did, to issues of urbanisation and planning.

However, the tensions over the South China Sea increased markedly throughout 2016. China's claims to sovereignty over reefs and islands were based on an historically questionable claim by the nationalist government recorded on a map marked with 11, later nine, dashed lines that covered almost all of the South China Sea and traversed well into the exclusive economic zones (EEZs) of almost all the littoral states, including Vietnam, Malaysia, Indonesia and, especially, the Philippines.

The Philippines under President Benigno Aquino had brought a claim against China's island-building in the Permanent Court of Arbitration in The Hague and its judgement, delivered in July 2016, rejected China's claims. In particular it rejected the 'nine dash line' as a basis for sovereignty and upheld the rights of the littoral states, including the Philippines, to waters within their EEZ. It also confirmed that a country cannot by artificial means turn a reef into an island, occupy it and then claim the territorial waters a pre-existing, occupied island would have had. In other words, the legality of China's efforts to create facts on the ground, or above the water, was rejected.

Our position, and that of most other nations, was that the ruling should be respected and that the parties should settle their disputes peacefully and refrain from unilateral actions and especially the construction and militarisation of artificial islands. Xi had promised Obama the year before that China wouldn't militarise any of its new South China Sea islands. Yet he was doing precisely that. He said to me in Beijing that he was simply responding to the reactions of others.

China was irked by our attitude and told us so, repeatedly. Their view was that if only outsiders, and especially the Americans, would stay out of the issue, China could peacefully settle all the disputes. Which was another way of saying they wanted to quietly pick each of the littoral states off one by one.

Now, it was manifestly in our interests to maintain respect for the rule of law in our region because that was the only way we, and other smaller states, could be sure of preserving our own freedom and sovereignty. The key to that was the maintenance of a strong US presence in our region. Around a third of all global shipping passes through the South China Sea: the upholding of international law is of the utmost, vital importance.

I travelled to Vientiane, the capital of Laos, in September 2016 for the East Asia Summit, where the newly elected Philippines president, Rodrigo Duterte, made his first international appearance. It was quite a debut. At the plenary session, he described how as a young man he'd worked as a prosecutor but couldn't get convictions because the drug traffickers had bribed the judges. He said that he had then decided to run for mayor and won. 'And you know what I did to the drug traffickers?' he said. 'I killed them all!'

You could have heard a pin drop. Li Keqiang, who was sitting next to me, looked around as though something had gone wrong with the translation.

Duterte repeated, 'I killed them all!'

This unequivocal belligerence, however, wasn't matched with a consistent approach to the Permanent Court of Arbitration decision. Duterte seemed to flip between wanting to do a deal with China in return for billions for infrastructure and truculently defending Philippines sovereignty. Charitably, I guess you could say he likes to keep everyone guessing.

The point I made repeatedly to Chinese leaders – and Obama said he made the same point – was that their whole South China Sea strategy seemed quite counterproductive. Was the tenuous advantage given by establishing these forward operating bases worth the tensions that it was creating?

Everyone, including the leadership in Beijing, was surprised when Donald Trump was elected president. When President Xi and I discussed the prospect of a Trump presidency and a trade war with China in Lima, Xi was confident he could do business with Trump, believing that as a businessman he would be pragmatic and transactional. However, he also believed, as everyone else did I might add, that Trump's bellicose campaign rhetoric about China wouldn't be followed through in office. We were all wrong there.

While Australia wasn't about to back away from our defence of the rule of law in our region and our criticism, Xi and I did see eye to eye on the need to stand up to the rising tide of protectionism, which I described at the 2016 G20 in Hangzhou as being far from a ladder to get us out of the low-growth trap, instead a shovel to dig it deeper.

By the time Premier Li and his wife, Cheng Hong, a professor of English literature, came to dinner at our home in Sydney in March 2017, Trump was in office and showing every sign of carrying out his election promises, including exiting the TPP and demanding a better trade deal with China. He was also publicly complaining about allies getting a free ride under the US security umbrella and suggesting South Korea and Japan in particular should contribute more to the US military presence in the region.

In these circumstances, which China could see as one of opportunity, why the sharp elbows in the South China Sea?

'If China's aim is to replace, or at least balance, the United States as a pre-eminent naval power in the Western Pacific, surely the goal should be to win the trust and confidence of your neighbours?' I asked Li.

Li didn't argue with that, and pointed to the billions of dollars of trade flowing between China and all the countries in the region, not to speak of the billions in infrastructure investment.

'Sure, that's true,' I replied. 'But it doesn't create trust or confidence, let alone affection. Surely China should want to be seen as more of a cuddly panda than a scary dragon? Your growing strength makes people anxious.'

'Aha, the Thucydides trap again,' he laughed; there was a running joke that President Xi and I had a common passion for the history of the war between Athens and Sparta.

'Well, yes, but perhaps a different chapter. What really worries your neighbours is the dialogue in Book 5 between the Athenian ambassadors and the citizens of Melos, a much smaller city that wanted to remain neutral and independent. Impatient with their pleas for justice, the Athenians simply said, "Justice is found only between equals in power, as to the rest the strong do as they will and the weak suffer as they must."'

Li's visit to Australia was a great success, both substantively and politically. There was also some football diplomacy when the premier came with me to an Australian Rules football match between my team, the Sydney Swans, and Port Adelaide, whose principal backer was a Chinese property developer, Shanghai CRED. Port Adelaide was building a following in China and some official endorsement would be invaluable. In a picture for the folks back home in China, Li wore both the Port Adelaide scarf and the Swans scarf. It was, I suppose, a practical example of Chinese even-handedness! Li was disappointed we didn't sign up to the Belt and Road Initiative. I told him that we would be delighted to work on specific projects, but we would not sign up to a slogan when we had no control over its content or substance. While this created some heartache on the Chinese side, and earned me a ferocious rebuke from Andrew Robb, it was the right call. The BRI has become highly controversial in many countries. In Sri Lanka, a large Chinese loan was taken out to build a port at Hambantota. When it couldn't be repaid, the Chinese took over the port itself – presumably the strategic value offsets the questionable commercial economics of the deal.

Li was also disappointed that we could not secure Senate ratification of an extradition treaty with China that had been entered into in 2007 by the Howard government. Since that time, under Labor, reviews of extradition generally and human rights concerns had seen ratification put on hold. However, as prime minister, Abbott had not given the Chinese any reason to believe ratification would not proceed. This did not prevent him, after he ceased to be PM, from loudly opposing ratification.

Julie Bishop, reflecting DFAT's advice, supported ratification, as did the Attorney-General's Department. Although it never came up at leaders' discussions, we had every reason to believe that a failure to ratify the extradition treaty would make it harder for us to ensure that China did not impose the death penalty on Australian citizens convicted of capital offences.

While we had obvious concerns about the Chinese criminal justice system, we were satisfied there were enough protections in the extradition treaty and our own legislation to ensure that the treaty could not be used for political cases, and in all cases, we would make extradition subject to an undertaking that no death penalty would be imposed.

Both Premier Li and Politburo member Meng Jianzhu, who visited Australia in April 2017, were very understanding and recognised it was better for us to withdraw the ratification motion than have it defeated. In hindsight, it was probably the best outcome; the government and I were seen to keep our word as we did our best to secure ratification. Given the deteriorating state of human rights in China, it will be a long time, I expect, before the issue will be revisited.

A few months later I gave the keynote address at the Shangri-La Dialogue in Singapore – the leading security conference in the Asia Pacific region. Our host was our friend Prime Minister Lee Hsien Loong and so it was appropriate to cite his father, Singapore's founder, Lee Kuan Yew. Back in 1966, when Singapore was just a year old, he'd quoted an old Chinese saying, 'Big fish eat little fish and little fish eat shrimps.'

> Lee Kuan Yew discussed how the shrimp, as he modestly described his new nation, would survive. It could make itself unpalatable to the larger fish – by being self-reliant and strong. And it could make friends with other larger fish – strong alliances and collective security.
>
> He recognised then ... that we all have a vested interest in each other's security – that it is peace and stability which have formed the essential foundation for the remarkable advances in prosperity and freedom in our region above all.
>
> Lee Kuan Yew's message was not confined to the binary categories of stability and military conquest. He was speaking at a time of insurgency and foreign sponsored subversion – not a world away from the challenges of our time.[7]

And then I laid out Australia's agenda: a neighbourhood defined by open markets and the free flow of goods, services, capital and ideas, where freedom of navigation went unchallenged and the rights of small states were protected under a rules-based structure. In other words, a world where big fish neither eat nor intimidate the small. I said, 'This means cooperation not unilateral actions to seize or create territory or militarise disputed areas.'

I said baldly that 'China will play a larger role in shaping the region. It is natural that Beijing will seek strategic influence to match its economic weight. But we want to see China fill the leadership role it desires in a way which strengthens the regional order that has served us all so well.'

The rapid rise of a new power, be it modern China or ancient Athens, creates anxiety, and a coercive China would undoubtedly lead to resentment on the part of its neighbours. Twenty-first-century China will best succeed by respecting the sovereignty of others, and in so doing build a reservoir of trust and cooperation with its neighbours.

The feedback on the speech we had from Beijing wasn't positive. We were being pressured to say less about the South China Sea and the geopolitics of the region.

By the end of 2017, China had largely achieved its goals in the South China Sea. Not only had it constructed a series of islands and established them as fully militarised forward operating bases but it had normalised a strong naval, coastguard and maritime militia presence based on these islands and was using them to intimidate rivals who came near them. ADF planes and ships continued to fly and sail through the South China Sea and while China insisted it was no threat to freedom of navigation or overflight, those transits were regularly challenged by Chinese aircraft or ships even when they were well beyond 12 nautical miles from the recently constructed islands.

By constructing these artificial islands, China hadn't simply claimed territory that was within the territorial waters of other countries. It was also then claiming territorial waters around these new islands, which was also contrary to international law.

While we didn't recognise the legitimacy of this island-building – creating facts on the water – unlike the US Navy, our ships didn't transit within 12 nautical miles of the new islands. My judgement was that we could easily play into China's hands if we did. The People's Liberation Army Navy knows that if it conflicts with a US ship, it runs the risk of a rapid escalation into full-blown conflict. But an Australian ship is a different proposition altogether. If one of our ships were to be rammed and disabled within the 12-mile limit by a Chinese vessel, we don't have the capacity to escalate. If the Americans backed us in, then the Chinese would back off. But if Washington hesitated or, for whatever reasons, decided not to or was unable immediately to intervene, then China would have achieved an enormous propaganda win, exposing the USA as a paper tiger not to be relied on by its allies. My judgement was that given the volatile geopolitical climate at the time, especially between the USA and China, it wasn't a risk worth taking.

The US Navy continued to sail through the disputed areas in its freedom of navigation operations but there was no prospect that they'd cause the Chinese to back away from their gains. Negotiations with ASEAN over a 'code of conduct' has been going on for years and will likely continue for many more.

While we were surrounded by a blizzard of often hysterical and frenzied commentary on the China relationship, both in Australia and in China, I ensured the NSC had the expert intelligence and time to consider our approach thoughtfully and shrewdly.

We recognised that China's goal was to supplant the United States as the leading power in the region, and that was plainly not in our interests. We also knew, from first-hand experience, that China's policy towards other countries was thoroughly integrated. If a foreign nation disappointed China – for instance by criticising its conduct in some manner – then it could expect both criticism and economic consequences. Ministerial visits would be stopped or curtailed, trade deals would be frozen or not followed through, Chinese tourism would drop off, foreign businesses in China would be boycotted.

These bullying tactics were designed to force the foreign critic to become compliant. And they work, and not just with governments in Australia. Take the current situation in Xinjiang, where about a million ethnic Uyghurs, all Muslims, have been locked up in 're-education camps' and are subject to many other types of surveillance and oppression. Has the Muslim world protested? Hardly a word – the Saudi king was feted in Beijing, and the new prime minister of Pakistan professed to be barely aware of the issue when asked about it last year.

A threat is a combination of capability and intent. Capability can take years or decades to put in place, where it can be done at all. But intent can change in a heartbeat. In the six years between my speech at the LSE in 2011 and my Shangri-La address in 2017, China's capabilities, in every respect, had continued to grow; but what had really changed was its intent. Under Xi, it became more assertive, more confident and more prepared to not just reach out to the world, as Deng had done, or to command respect as a responsible international actor, as Hu Jintao and Jiang Zemin had done, but to demand compliance.

Most observers had expected that as China became wealthier, as its middle class grew, it would become more democratic. Twenty-five years ago, I'd thought it would develop into more of a federal system, with much greater autonomy in decision-making at the provincial and city level. In fact, under Xi, central authority has been enhanced, aided by all of the technologies of the internet and artificial intelligence to impose what's becoming a surveillance state. Even the old post-Mao paradigm of collective leadership has been challenged: the law has changed to allow Xi to remain president indefinitely, instead of there being a limit of two five-year terms. Contrary to historical experience and contemporary expectations, China is combining political authoritarianism with rapid economic and technological progress.

However, while Australia seeks to defend human rights everywhere, we have to recognise that our ability to influence Chinese domestic policy is extremely limited. Our efforts to do so will always be resented and, indeed, can be counterproductive in specific cases.

On the other hand, we have to stand up for our sovereignty and ensure that we don't allow foreign actors, including foreign nations, to covertly or corruptly influence our political affairs. The management, or mismanagement, of Australia's democracy must be solely in the hands of Australians.

When I became prime minister in 2015, I was briefed extensively on foreign espionage activities in Australia by the tall, austere director general of ASIO, Duncan Lewis. He was very level-headed and showed no signs of the paranoia that often besets those who spend too long in the realm of secret intelligence.

While many nations sought to spy on Australia, China represented by far the bulk of detected activity. It was mostly cyberespionage, generally managed by intelligence agencies in Shanghai. Their appetite for information seemed limitless, ranging from businesses, to universities to government departments and much else besides. It was on an industrial scale.

Concurrently, the United Front Work Department (UFWD), a wing of the Communist Party of China (CPC), worked to advance support for China's objectives in the Australian community generally and in the Australian Chinese community in particular. A number of prominent Chinese businessmen were working closely with the UFWD and their agenda included coopting Australian politicians and opinion leaders.

The road to doing this was, of course, money: political donations for both major parties and commercial opportunities as well. There was so much financial incentive to get on well with China; it was, as they say in the classics, 'win win'.

And while China was by far the biggest player in Australia, we were aware of Russia's efforts to meddle with the United States', and other nations', elections. We hadn't seen much evidence of Russian involvement in our 2016 election, but there was no reason it couldn't happen in the future or that other governments wouldn't follow their lead.

As I discussed all these issues with Duncan and with senior ministers, including George Brandis, it became obvious that Australian governments had simply not been paying attention to the changing circumstances around them. Our espionage laws were out of date, last revised during the Cold War, and we had no legislation to regulate, let alone prohibit, foreign political donations. With so much foreign, mostly Chinese, money flowing in and around politics, we also lacked any transparency legislation. We required lobbyists to put their names on a public register, but surely if somebody was seeking to influence Australian political affairs on behalf of a foreign government, we should know about it.

I asked Duncan to brief the leaders of the major political parties as well as ministers about the risks of foreign interference in their own political affairs. And I also asked George Brandis to come back to cabinet with a report on foreign interference in Australia and how we could counter it both with new espionage laws and a transparency regime. At the same time, China scholar John Garnaut, who'd been working in my office as a policy adviser, took time out to prepare within my department a detailed report on China's influence operations in Australia.

This would work in well with Australia's Cybersecurity strategy, which I'd launched in early 2016, and changes we made to our telecommunications security legislation, which gave the government the authority to intervene in telecom networks to stop or forestall foreign interference.

At a practical level, in 2017, I agreed with Premier Li that Australia and China should enter into an agreement not to engage in commercial cyberespionage. I was frank with Li – a large part of the Chinese cyberespionage in Australia was targeting the commercial sector, especially mining and resources, energy, agriculture and technology. As China had also done with the UK and the USA, we agreed that commercial cyberespionage was out of bounds. How effective that has been, again only time will tell.

Around that time, we'd identified the lack of a coherent approach to assessing the national security risks associated with foreign acquisitions of critical infrastructure. Indeed, there wasn't even agreement on what was critical infrastructure, let alone a list or register. A case in point was the previously mentioned 2015 sale of the Port of Darwin to a Chinese company, Landbridge. Even though it had been scrutinised by Defence, the whole process had seemed pretty ad hoc to me.

In August 2016, a far more serious snafu arose relating to the NSW government's proposed sale of a majority stake in Ausgrid to two Chinese companies, one of which was State Grid. Owned by the Chinese government, State Grid Corporation is the world's largest utility company; it owns almost all of the electricity transmission assets in China. State Grid had previously been approved, both by the Gillard and Abbott governments, to buy controlling stakes in gas and electricity utilities across Australia.

The negotiations had been going on since 2015 and no objection had been raised by anyone in Canberra. But at the 11th hour, as the final treasurer's approval was required, we became aware of certain national security concerns related to Ausgrid. As a result, the treasurer did not grant foreign investment approval. Scott Morrison and I shared NSW Premier Gladys Berejiklian's disappointment that these issues had not been flagged the previous year, before the sales process got underway. There had clearly been a breakdown in communications within our national security agencies. As a result, a big deal was stymied at the last minute.

We quickly moved to establish a Critical Infrastructure Centre (CIC) that would identify those infrastructure assets where a foreign acquisition could pose risks to national security – and why. This would, hopefully, ensure vital facts wouldn't be overlooked as they were with Ausgrid. Crucially, both would-be vendors and buyers could get an indication early in the process whether potential foreign buyers would be likely to get approval from the treasurer. The CIC monitors several hundred assets, mostly in telecommunications, ports, energy and water.

• • •

Managing the China relationship is a very delicate balancing exercise.

I knew, from years of experience of dealing with bullies, that if you take a strong position on something and then back down under pressure, you'll be mightily diminished. You'll lose respect and leverage. So, if you're going to draw a line in the sand, it must be one you're prepared to stand by and not flinch.

An Australian prime minister who ends up in conflict with China cannot expect any support or solidarity from the Australian business community. Overwhelmingly, they're totally invested in the economic benefits of the relationship and, as I saw many times, they'll always blame their own government if problems arise – even if the problems have nothing to do with government policy. Sometimes, when a Chinese Customs official says an Australian exporter's papers 'are not in order', they are, in fact, not in order. Nonetheless, if an Australian government quite reasonably stands its ground and China quite unreasonably over-reacts negatively (as it often does), Australian businesses will invariably blame their own government.

During my time the loudest critics of our China policies were some of the university heads. One of the most disappointing was Michael Spence, the vice chancellor of Sydney University. Of his full-fee-paying foreign students, 65 per cent are Chinese. At a particularly tense time, when we were endeavouring to pass foreign interference legislation, he publicly accused me and my government of 'Sinophobic blatherings'.[8]

Added to the list of regular critics are former politicians like Paul Keating, Bob Carr and our own Andrew Robb, and former diplomats like Geoff Raby. While they would disavow that it has any influence, all nonetheless have commercial interests in remaining on the very best terms with Beijing. And, of course, many politicians and their parties rely on generous donations from Chinese business figures.

Nobody wants to have a row with China, but far too many Australians aren't particularly fussed how high a price we pay to avoid one.

Finally, the most sensitive factor is the one and a quarter million Australians of Chinese heritage. The People's Republic of China is ostensibly a secular multicultural society celebrating the ethnic and cultural diversity across its vast landmass. However, the reality is that it's one of the most racially and culturally homogenous nations in the world: 92 per cent of its population is Han Chinese and there's one written language and one national spoken language – Mandarin, or *putonghua*.

(India, by comparison, is religiously, linguistically and ethnically diverse with 22 officially recognised languages alone.)

The Chinese government seeks to mobilise overseas Chinese, and especially Chinese students, to support Chinese government policy; this is one of the functions of the UFWD. The Chinese-language media in Australia is overwhelmingly controlled by, or completely beholden to, Beijing, and takes its line from the official media outlets in China.

As a consequence, it's important not to allow differences with the Chinese government to be portrayed as being 'anti-Chinese'. I went to great lengths to reject that perception, pointing out two of our own grandchildren were Australians with Chinese heritage. And of course, there are many, perhaps increasingly many, Australian Chinese who, while proud of China's achievements over the last 70 years, have deep reservations about the lack of freedom there.

By the end of 2017, George Brandis had completed the drafting of the new foreign interference and foreign influence laws. Ordinarily, this wouldn't have commanded a huge amount of attention, not least because we'd just succeeded in legalising same-sex marriage and that was the big story for the end of 2017; however, Senator Sam Dastyari had put paid to that.

Sam was an ALP senator and former secretary of the NSW Labor Party. He was a dyed-in-the-wool party apparatchik and a close adviser and confidant of Bill Shorten. He'd been in hot water the previous year for receiving money from a Chinese property developer, Huang Xiangmo, who'd been extremely generous to both political parties as well as establishing the Australia-China Relations Institute, which was chaired by former NSW Labor Premier Bob Carr. Huang was prominent in local Chinese community organisations, especially the Australian Council for the Promotion of the Peaceful Reunification of China, which was backed by the UFWD.

In 2016, Dastyari had given a press conference with Huang calling for Australia to support China's position on the South China Sea. He survived the fallout from this but on 29 November 2017, another incident was exposed. It was revealed on learning that Huang might be under ASIO surveillance (a fact the Labor leadership would have been advised of by Duncan Lewis), Dastyari had gone to Huang's house and tipped him off.

The Dastyari scandal undoubtedly damaged Labor, deservedly. Shorten finally had to drop him from his frontbench and on 25 January 2018 – by now thoroughly disgraced – Dastyari resigned from the Senate.

Yet in the heat of the political debate and name-calling, amped up to the max by the media, which loves nothing more than a spy scandal (that's if a sex scandal isn't available), Labor was able to represent us as being 'anti-Chinese', courtesy of our proposed foreign interference laws.

I thought about postponing their introduction until the new year, but it was important to get the committee process underway over the summer holidays so we could be sure of passing the laws in the first half of 2018.

On 7 December 2017, when I introduced the new laws into the House, it would have been ludicrous to make no reference to the storm about Dastyari and Chinese influence generally, and so I did, in measured terms. 'Media reports have suggested that the Chinese Communist Party has been working to covertly interfere with our media, our universities and even the decisions of elected representatives right here in this building.'[9]

I spoke about the question of foreign interference going beyond China, to Russia and other nations, including Iran and North Korea, and quoted the recently retired US director of national intelligence, James Clapper, in his testimony to the US Congress in May: 'If there has ever been a clarion call for vigilance and action against a threat to the very foundation of our democratic political system, this episode is it.'[10]

I emphasised the principles of the new laws: they were focused on the activities of foreign states and their agents in Australia, not the loyalties of Australians who happened to be from a foreign country. We're a nation in which most of us come from migrant families, and there's no place for racism or xenophobia in our country. But we wouldn't tolerate foreign influence activities that were in any way covert, coercive or corrupt.

The foreign influence transparency scheme was designed to ensure that people who were seeking to influence Australian political affairs on behalf of foreign governments and political parties placed their name on a register. The espionage legislation was amended to criminalise covert, deceptive and threatening actions by persons acting on behalf of a foreign principal that are aimed at influencing our political processes or otherwise prejudice our national security. Added to this was new legislation to prohibit foreign donations to political parties and organisations.

Chinese state-owned media denounced the new foreign interference and foreign influence legislation, angrily rejecting the suggestion that there'd been any CPC efforts to influence Australian politics. Andrew Robb – employed by Landbridge, the Chinese owners of the Port of

Darwin – lashed out at the foreign influence register. He claimed he'd been lumped in with Sam Dastyari – something I had certainly not done and hadn't observed others doing.

Immediately, the Labor Party started to frame both the new laws and our attacks on Dastyari as racist and 'anti-Chinese'. Kristina Keneally, Labor's candidate in the Bennelong by-election (John Alexander had resigned because of dual citizenship concerns), accused me of 'China phobia' and suggested I was channelling Pauline Hanson![11] The Chinese-language media followed Beijing's line and started attacking me and the government in the same terms.

This was a full-court press to intimidate the government with the goal of getting us to back away from the new foreign interference laws, and the more intense it became, the more resolved I was to make sure they were passed into law. I was confronted with this criticism on Saturday 9 December campaigning with John Alexander in Bennelong. I responded as forcefully and clearly as I could. This wasn't a time for slippery ambiguity.

> Modern China was founded in 1949 with these words: *'Zhōngguó ren men zhànqi lai'*, 'The Chinese people have stood up.' It was an assertion of sovereignty, it was an assertion of pride. And we stand up, and so we say: *'Aodàlya ren men zhànqi lai'*, 'The Australian people stand up.'
>
> Chinese people stand up for their sovereignty, and they expect Australian people and particularly Australian leaders to stand up for theirs. That is why we respect each other and that is why they respect me and my government.[12]

The following Monday, I was confronted with this again on *Q&A* and responded firmly:

> The suggestion that I or my government or Australia generally is anti-Chinese is absolutely outrageous. Every country is entitled to defend its national interest, and Australians, whether they are of Chinese background or not, expect their leaders to stand up for Australia. There are a million Australians of Chinese ancestry – a million. You could not imagine modern Australia, the most successful multicultural society in the world, without them, and among those one million Australians with Chinese ancestry is our granddaughter. So, the proposition that someone whose granddaughter calls him 'Yeye' is anti-Chinese is absurd.

Completely absurd. This is a question about our national interest and ensuring that our leaders, our senators, our members of the House, put Australia first. And Bill Shorten has failed that test by not standing up for Australia and chucking Dastyari out of the Labor Party and out of the Senate.[13]

Dastyari announced he'd resign the next day; both he and Shorten had bowed to the inevitable, but not soon enough to prevent the scandal materially assisting us in the Bennelong by-election, which we won. There wasn't much evidence that the 'Turnbull is anti-Chinese' campaign had any adverse effect, despite over 20 per cent of the electorate being of Chinese ancestry, mostly born in mainland China. Few Australian politicians had been more consistently and vocally supportive of multi-culturalism than me, and John Alexander himself was well liked and respected by the Chinese, Korean and other Asian communities in his seat.

Meanwhile, the fury in Beijing continued. Ministerial visits were put on hold, and our diplomats received regular scoldings. There was con-fected indignation about my quoting Mao and saying, 'The Australian people have stood up.' I could understand people being disappointed about my poor Mandarin pronunciation, but the idea that it was some-how offensive for me to quote Mao was unhinged. And what was worse, many Australians joined in the Chinese criticism.

Imagine if Americans were to express indignation about foreigners quoting Ben Franklin or Thomas Jefferson. Or arguing that the same patriotic sentiments those founders made for the United States could not be echoed by others on behalf of their own nations.

The Chinese ambassador in Australia, Cheng Jingye, gave an extensive interview in April 2018 complaining about the unjust criticism of China in the Australian media and threatened 'trading ties could be damaged if the situation is not repaired'.[14]

There were some trade interruptions designed to send us a mes-sage – delays in approving meat exporters, for example. But it wasn't substantial. Some wine exports were held up on the Shanghai docks and while the exporter, Treasury Wine Estates, complained this was a political decision, our trade officials in Shanghai weren't convinced. The wine was eventually cleared. Some Australian coal exports were turned away, but again both the Chinese and Australian sides affirmed it was for environmental reasons. Overall China–Australian trade has continued to grow substantially and in both directions.

Australians anxious about their place in the world shouldn't forget that China and Australia are dependent on each other in economic terms. China doesn't buy our iron ore or coal or gas, or send their kids to universities here, because they want to do us a favour.

However, Beijing would have been satisfied that their public indignation had been met with so much panic in the Australian business community and that the Labor opposition had been so quick to join in the criticism. There was little in the way of Australian solidarity – a reminder that China's biggest weapons aren't fleets and armies but RMB and dollars.

An important step in my firm, respectful and consistent approach to China was a letter I wrote to Xi Jinping on 22 May 2018, which Julie Bishop personally delivered to her Chinese counterpart, Wang Yi, at a G20 meeting in Buenos Aires. It was to address the criticism of my quoting Mao, which the ambassador to Australia had advised me had some currency within the Chinese government.

'Last year,' I wrote, 'I noted that modern China had been founded by Mao Zedong with the words "The Chinese people have stood up" and that this was a statement of national sovereignty.' I explained how I'd gone on to say that China respected other countries that likewise asserted their sovereignty and said that Australians stand up – albeit rendering both phrases in my very poor Chinese.

I reminded Xi of my longstanding interest in Chinese history and culture and that I had used those lines many times in the past in public speeches. The purpose had been to show that I understood the assertion of the Chinese people's right to chart their own course and stand up for their own sovereignty. It was intended to convey respect.

China and Australia are good friends. We share a region and our futures are inextricably linked. It goes well beyond our economic relationship. We are family with, as I noted earlier, well over a million Australians, including two of my own grandchildren, of Chinese heritage.

In these times of increased global uncertainty, we both seek the lasting prosperity and stability of our region. In taking steps to protect our national sovereignty and promote regional prosperity and security, we do not seek to undermine the interests of others.

It took a while to get the foreign interference and influence bills through the Parliamentary Joint Committee on Intelligence and Security – Labor was in no hurry to pass them. I made it clear to Shorten that if they didn't emerge from the committee promptly, with a bipartisan recommendation, I'd relist them for debate in the House. Following that, and assisted by some redrafting I did with Attorney-General Christian Porter, the bills were both passed into law on 28 June 2018 without a partisan debate. As I'd expected, the tensions with Beijing immediately calmed considerably. Had we dropped or delayed the laws' passage, we'd have won no thanks from – and lost much respect in – China.

The final step in the reconciliation process was a speech I gave at UNSW on 7 August in which I spoke positively about our China relationship, extolled free trade and noted the highly productive scientific collaboration especially in the field of photovoltaics.

While there was considerable back and forth with DFAT on the speech, I realised nobody had checked what Xi had said to the Australian parliament in 2014. In his speech I found a perfect quote to complement a restatement of our unwavering position. Overriding the reservations inside our bureaucracy – I wasn't prepared to take a backward step on matters of principle – I incorporated it in the following section:

> So in the midst of this rapid change, Australia continues to address its own interests by pursuing a relationship with China based on mutual respect and understanding. For our part we act to advance Australia's prosperity, ensure the independence of our decision-making and secure the safety and freedom of our people. And in doing so, we support an international order based on the rule of law, where might is not right and the sovereignty of all nations is respected by others; a principle President Xi endorsed when he addressed a joint sitting of the Australian Parliament in November 2014 and said:
>
> 'The United Nations Charter and the basic norms governing international relations should apply to all countries. With that, countries big or small, strong or weak, rich or poor, are all equal. This means not only equal rights and interests for all countries, but also equality of all countries before international rules.'[15]

The speech's content was consistent with everything I'd said before about the China relationship, but it was an effective reset because of its context and its warmth. Together with the letter, it gave the Chinese side an opportunity to dismount from what was looking like an increasingly shrill and, with the laws now passed, ineffective effort in megaphone diplomacy.

One of the thorniest problems we faced was how to manage the presence of telecommunications equipment from what are called 'high-risk vendors' in Australian networks. The most prominent, but not the only, high-risk vendors came from China.

5G is the latest evolution of wireless technology and offers greatly increased data rates and much reduced latency. But 5G is more than just faster wireless broadband. It's designed to connect in due course billions of devices, from the mundanely domestic fridges and toasters to our electricity grids, water supply, communication and data storage platforms.

5G networks will differ from 4G and 3G networks in several important ways that can increase vulnerability to external interference.

Our existing networks are divided into core and edge segments. On the edge is the radio access network, the mobile phone towers and antennae that connect directly with user devices like smartphones. They send signals to the computers at the core that deal with call and data routing, billing, authentication, identity management and lawful interception, among other things.

In a 5G network, these core functions will be largely virtualised; that is, rather than working on proprietary hardware, they will be software running on standard processors and moved to the edge of the network in order to improve latency and increase network capacity and speed. In other words, the core is no more: the intelligence it used to contain will be distributed throughout the network.

In the past, we've kept high-risk vendors from providing core equipment or capabilities, leaving them with the still lucrative market of edge equipment (of which there is, obviously, a great deal). Now that the core–edge distinction no longer exists, any full-service 5G vendor must meet stringent security requirements.

Right now a mobile network operator, like Telstra or AT&T, has just four full-service vendors from which to choose for its 5G network equipment. Two are from China (Huawei and ZTE) and two are from Scandinavia (Nokia and Ericsson).

Ferocious competition from the Chinese vendors on price and an absence of mind in Washington and other Five Eyes (the USA, Australia, the UK, Canada and NZ) capitals has got us to the position where, when network security is more important than ever, there's not one 5G vendor from our traditional allies. Indeed, there isn't one from Japan either, and the closest new prospect is Samsung of South Korea.

Throughout 2018, I'd been working closely with Mike Burgess at the ASD on how we should respond. I pressed Mike to do all he could to find a solution that would enable Huawei to play a role in our 5G networks and we discussed a number of techniques to mitigate the potential for interference.

We considered whether end-to-end encryption would reduce the risk of malicious interception because what is exfiltrated cannot be read. There is some validity in that, but it doesn't address what we regarded as the major risk. An adversary with a permanent beachhead in an economy's most important enabling platform technology would have the ability to make all or parts of the network – or devices and institutions within it – unavailable or unresponsive. In other words, there's a lot more to this than simply confidentiality of data.

After intense investigation and discussions with counterparts in other Five Eyes countries, the unequivocal advice was that the risks couldn't be mitigated.

That didn't mean we thought Huawei was currently being used to interfere with our telecommunication networks. Our approach was a hedge against a future threat: not the identification of a smoking gun but a loaded one.

As the ASD advised at the time:

If a state-sponsored adversary has enduring access to staff, software or hardware deployed into a target telecommunication network, then they only require the intent to act in order to conduct operations within the network. This greatly reduces the cost of operating within the network, and by extension this increases the effective likelihood of their doing so.[16]

Adding to these concerns was China's 2017 National Intelligence Law, which required companies and individuals to 'support, cooperate and collaborate' with the Chinese intelligence and security agencies.

We announced this decision on 23 August 2018, in the middle of what was to be my last week as prime minister. It was the subject of my last phone call with Donald Trump, who was both impressed and a little surprised that we'd taken this position.

I'd been speaking with Trump, as well as Mike Pence and others, about 5G for some time. It concerned me that over many years, the United States and its top allies had allowed leadership in wireless technology to shift to China and to Europe. This is arguably the most important enabling technology of our time; it seemed absurd that the United States and its closest allies like Australia weren't leading players.

Trump has subsequently said the right things about the United States becoming a leading player but he hasn't yet followed through with the action to make it happen. The United States doesn't have the same legal authority to ban one company or another from its telecom networks and Trump's efforts to keep Chinese vendors out are being challenged in the courts.

Our decision on 5G was the first formal ban of Huawei and ZTE in the world. We were careful in announcing it in as low-key a fashion as possible, but it has nonetheless been bitterly resented in Beijing, which has put enormous pressure on other countries – especially the United Kingdom – not to follow suit.

But you cannot compromise national security in the face of bullying, and the worst thing you can do is give a bully a big stick and hope that they won't use it against you. Maybe they never will, but if they do, you will only have yourself to blame.

Ultimately, the key to a healthy relationship between China and Australia is respect. Where we differ, we should do so civilly. When we're bullied or abused, we should respond in a considered and dignified manner, but never take a backward step.

Above all, we should never get sucked into the false premise that any criticism of or concern about China and its ruling Communist Party is 'anti-Chinese' or racist. There are millions of Chinese people in China, in Hong Kong, in Taiwan and around the world who are concerned about the increasing authoritarianism of Xi Jinping. Are the millions of demonstrators in Hong Kong racists? Of course not: they're no more 'anti-Chinese' than are Australians who seek to defend their own sovereignty and freedom from foreign interference.

CHAPTER 35

Matters of trust: reforming intelligence and Home Affairs

Nowadays, more than ever, intelligence is the key to national security. Whatever the context – terrorism, state-on-state conflict, cybercrime, foreign interference – good intelligence enables you to stay one step ahead of your opponents and pre-empt their plans.

As PM I received a flood of intelligence material from half-a-dozen intelligence agencies, principally the Office of National Assessments (ONA), the Australian Secret Intelligence Service (ASIS) and ASIO. Initially all of it was hand-delivered in hardcopy and only regularly available to me in Canberra. This had always been the practice, I was told. Never mind that the PM is not in Canberra often outside of parliamentary sitting weeks and as a result much of the information was weeks out of date by the time I saw it.

Finally, I managed to persuade the intelligence agencies to share the reports on a secure iPad, which could be delivered to me wherever I was in Australia!

That momentous reform aside, it was clear to me that there was a lot more to do in this area. The structure of our intelligence agencies had grown in an ad hoc way and hadn't been thoroughly reviewed for many years. Furthermore, the domestic security agencies – Australian Border Force, ASIO and the AFP, and the Office of Transport Security – were spread between different departments (Immigration, Attorney-General's and Transport respectively). The counter-terrorism and cybersecurity fronts were coordinated from yet another department: the Prime Minister and Cabinet.

For many years, there had been a proposal to bring all the domestic national security agencies together in one super-department, modelled on the UK's Home Office. Scott Morrison had championed this not long after the 2013 election, and while Abbott was initially supportive he then backed away from it, perhaps not wanting to give Morrison a bigger platform than he already had.

I found Scott's arguments persuasive. I had never believed the attorney-general should be responsible for the AFP or ASIO. In my view, the attorney-general's role is as the minister for integrity: the source of objective legal advice to the government, someone who ensures the security agencies obey the law and who is not compromised by being responsible for their day-to-day operations.

My own department of Prime Minister and Cabinet was also supportive of the Home Office model and encouraged me to pursue it after the 2016 election. The idea was to ensure all the key elements of domestic national security worked closely together, reporting ultimately to one cabinet minister: the minister for Home Affairs. At the same time, the agencies that oversaw intelligence services, such as the Inspector-General of Intelligence and Security and the Independent National Security Legislation Monitor, would move from PM&C into the Attorney-General's Department, which would also be the home of the planned federal ICAC.

While a machinery of government change like this was a decision for me as the prime minister, I discussed it at length with cabinet colleagues and in particular Peter Dutton, who was naturally very enthusiastic, and George Brandis, who was not.

George was planning to retire at the end of 2017 and become our high commissioner to the UK, so his concerns did not relate to hanging on to his existing turf – much as he enjoyed it. Rather he, like Julie Bishop, was very apprehensive of giving more power to Dutton.

A number of other cabinet members, including Morrison, had doubts about whether Dutton had the capacity to do the bigger job. On balance I was satisfied he could, and if he didn't, I could always replace him with someone else.

George, Julie and Christopher Pyne warned me that Dutton was after my job and was in league with Greg Hunt as his running mate. Back in March 2017, Pyne had copied me on a message to Morrison:

> The Right, including people you all think are 100 per cent for Malcolm are openly canvassing views on Dutton and Hunt as leader and deputy.

They are even suggesting me as deputy when people laugh at Hunt. As if I would serve under Dutton when I'm like a pig in mud doing what I'm doing. But please, don't believe Dutton that he's all Malcolm. He is not.[1]

This turned out to be right, of course, but I had credited Dutton with enough common sense and self-awareness to realise that whatever our problems were, he was certainly not the solution. I was quite wrong there – not the only time I made the mistake of assuming colleagues were more rational than they turned out to be.

But equally, if I had taken to heart every warning I received about the untrustworthiness of my senior team, I would not have been able to work with any of them. Cormann and Dutton told me not to trust Julie and George. Julie, George and Christopher told me not to trust Cormann and Dutton. Barnaby told me not to trust any of them, and everybody told me not to trust Morrison. I trusted them all, some more warily than others. I knew I was taking a risk but if I descended into a paranoid fog, as Abbott had done, I wouldn't be able to achieve anything.

Dutton's weakness, from my perspective at that time, was that he regularly did interviews with right-wing shock jocks, like Ray Hadley or Andrew Bolt, in which he would echo their extreme views on social issues like asylum seekers or so-called African gangs in Melbourne. He always apologised for going too far, and I generally gave him the benefit of the doubt. One of the problems, I would tell him, with appearing with right-wing shock jocks was getting carried away with their right-wing craziness – Abbott used to do this all the time too.

However, if my colleagues were apprehensive about Dutton, the various agencies involved in the restructure were horrified by the thought of working with Michael Pezzullo, the secretary of the Department of Immigration and Border Protection. Pezzullo is one of the most brilliant civil servants in Canberra. He has a long background working with Labor ministers, including Kim Beazley, and made his name in Defence writing the 2009 white paper. He is a tough-minded intellectual with hard-line views on border protection and security issues that could be easily categorised as 'right wing'.

Pezzullo desperately wanted to be secretary of Defence when Dennis Richardson resigned in April 2017, and he would have been a good choice except that the uniformed side of Defence were unanimously opposed to him. Indeed, I have never known anyone in the Australian Public Service who is more disliked by his senior colleagues than Pezzullo; and yet, in the same breath, his critics acknowledge that he is hard working and gets things done. I found him to give well-considered professional advice.

So with Pezzullo I was presented with an invidious choice. He was definitely well equipped to bring the new super department together and he believed in the concept. On the other hand, his poor interpersonal skills were a big obstacle to bringing together the agencies, all of which were led by very capable people and, moreover, had statutory independence.

I announced the Home Affairs reform on 18 July 2017, shortly after returning from the G20. In doing so, I placed Peter Dutton in a position of enormous responsibility. Views may differ as to whether I overestimated his competence, but certainly I misjudged his character.

As to Pezzullo, time will tell. I had counselled Mike, as have others, about improving his interpersonal skills and treating people with respect. Almost all of the subsequent grief associated with the creation of the new department has been caused by his, and to some extent Dutton's, authoritarian management style. Most of the top talent in the Home Affairs Department and its agencies, as with the Australian Signals Directorate, could take their cyber skills and earn more money else-where, and a disrespectful work culture will only encourage more of them to leave.

At the same time I announced the Home Affairs reforms – the biggest reform ever made in the structure of our domestic security arrangements – I also set out comprehensive reforms to the structure of our intelligence services themselves. These were the result of the Independent Intelligence Review I'd established in 2016, which was headed by Michael L'Estrange, a former secretary of DFAT, and Stephen Merchant, a former director of the ASD, assisted by Sir Iain Lobban, the recently retired head of GCHQ.

I created a new Office of National Intelligence (ONI), whose director would take over the work of the ONA and ensure the priorities and targets of our entire intelligence community were coordinated. The ONI would be the prime minister's principal adviser on intelligence matters and would make sure that the PM had access to the collective wisdom and insights of our 7000-person-strong intelligence community. I appointed Nick Warner as the first director of National Intelligence and Paul Taloni and Andrew Shearer as his deputies.

Nick had been head of ASIS for eight years and is a very experienced Australian diplomat and intelligence officer. One of the things I miss from my days as PM is Nick's regular reporting on his visits to intelligence services around the world. I exaggerate, slightly: 'My Dear Foreign Minister, I have just returned from a clandestine meeting with the Chief Assassin of the Ruritanian Intelligence Service. We met in an ancient cellar, underneath the Casbah in Tangiers …' When he finally retires from active spying, I hope Nick follows Stella Rimington into a second career as a novelist!

As earlier described, I had released Australia's first Cybersecurity strategy in 2016 and enhanced our cyber defences. As part of the 2017 restructure, I brought Mike Burgess, formerly deputy head of the Australian Signals Directorate, back from the private sector to become the new director general of the ASD, which was established as an executive agency with greater independence within the Defence Department and another direct line to the prime minister.

The object of the intelligence reforms was similar to that in the creation of the Home Affairs Department: greater coordination of national security agencies. There is always a tendency in bureaucracies for agencies to hang on to information – that is their currency, after all, and nowhere more so than in the world of secret intelligence. However, unless there is a culture of confident cooperation, things will get lost in the cracks, sometimes with deadly consequences, as the Americans found with 9/11.

Both the Home Affairs and intelligence reforms were historic and, together with the foreign interference and influence legislation, represented the biggest overhaul of our intelligence legislation since the 1970s.

But public sector reforms are a bit like business plans – the mediocre business plan well executed will always beat the brilliant business plan poorly executed. Their success depends entirely on the character and calibre of the people who are placed and retained in the key leadership positions.

CHAPTER 36

Trump

'Don't worry, Malcolm. The American people will never elect a lunatic to sit in this office.'

So Barack Obama had enigmatically assured me in the Oval Office in January 2016, when I asked him about the presidential race.

Well, it was now November and the unthinkable had happened. And lunatic or not, Trump had won.

It wasn't only Americans who were stunned. Nobody had expected a Trump victory and truthfully few were prepared for it.

He'd run a bombastic campaign, much of which seemed to us to be designed to ensure he wouldn't win. What sort of candidate would refer to his opponent, a distinguished former first lady and secretary of state, with a nickname like 'Crooked Hillary' and beam as his supporters chanted 'Lock her up'? How could you get elected in (by Australian standards) prudish America when you have talked about 'grabbing' women 'by the pussy'?

We knew what he'd said in the campaign, but did he mean it? After all, everyone seemed to accept he didn't expect to win. Was the whole campaign just an enormous exercise in self-promotion?

Every country and every leader tried to work out how to deal with Trump. Elaborate psychological analyses were written in foreign capitals – including our own. The general conclusion was that Trump was a narcissist who'd respond well to flattery. 'Lay it on with a trowel' was the consensus, echoing former British PM Benjamin Disraeli's advice on how to deal with royalty.

I felt this approach was quite mistaken. I'd never met Trump or dealt with him but knew plenty of people who had. He was typical of more than a few of the billionaires I've known – Kerry Packer, Conrad Black,

Jimmy Goldsmith and Bob Maxwell, just to name a few. And the one thing I'd learned with bullies is that sucking up to them is precisely the wrong way to go.

Just as imperial powers regard deference as their due, so do bullies – especially powerful ones – expect to be flattered. It doesn't win respect, nor does it earn gratitude. And if the bully in question is a particularly manipulative one, the flattery will be used against you. Personalities like that often appear utterly lacking in emotional intelligence, devoid of empathy. But that's not the whole picture: in my experience, the successful narcissistic bully is able to manipulate others effectively because he has a keen sense of others' vulnerabilities. Like any predator, he can sense fear and weakness from miles away.

So, the best way to deal with someone like Trump is to be frank and forthright. Be yourself, always be courteous – there's nothing to be gained from rudeness or scratchiness. But stand your ground. That suited me.

There was a scramble to contact Trump once the election result was known. He had no transition team in place, but, thanks to Joe Hockey, I got a number from US-based Australian golfing great Greg Norman and I was able to call Trump on 10 November and pass on my congratulations.

However, a major storm awaited us.

I'd agreed the refugee deal with Obama, in principle, at the White House in January 2016. It took some time to settle the terms of the deal and it was signed when I was in New York for the UN's leaders' week in September. As previously mentioned, both sides recognised we were better off not announcing it during the campaign lest Trump seize on it and make an issue of it.

So, the deal was announced on 13 November and the Department of Homeland Security got straight to work; 14 US officials arrived in Nauru in early December and started interviews. Naturally, we were anxious to ensure that the right-wing media in the USA, especially Fox News, didn't latch on to the deal and make it an issue, so we were careful to say as little as possible.

I spoke with Trump's incoming chief of staff, Reince Priebus, on 7 December and he gave me every impression they'd stick with the deal, recognising the importance of the US–Australian relationship.

In late January, we learned that Trump was proposing a new executive order to put a ban on refugees from Muslim countries – and it was immediately reported on as scuttling the refugee deal. After a very helpful introduction from Australian-born Dow Chemicals CEO Andrew Liveris, I called Trump's son-in-law and senior adviser, Jared Kushner, who conferenced in Trump's immigration adviser, Stephen Miller, and pressed on them the importance of sticking with the bargain I'd made with Obama. They were sympathetic and assured me the new executive order wouldn't prevent the refugee deal going ahead.

Over the days that followed, we reached out to everyone we could in the new administration. In a discussion with Julie Bishop, Vice President Pence assured her that the Trump administration would honour the deal. National Security Advisor Mike Flynn gave a similar assurance to Justin Bassi, his counterpart in my office. We felt our frantic lobbying had worked.

Our optimism was reinforced on 27 January when the executive order came out with language that expressly enabled the administration to admit refugees otherwise prohibited by the order if 'admitting the person would enable the United States to conform its conduct to a preexisting international agreement'.[1] Thanks, Jared!

Immediately, a call with Trump was set up for 9 am Sunday, Sydney time. We'd been assured the refugee deal was agreed, so we worked on the other topics to discuss.

Then the sky fell in. Just as I got to the office, Mike Flynn called Justin Bassi and Pence called Julie Bishop – both with the message that the president had changed his mind. He wouldn't, under any circumstances, honour the deal and would I please not even mention it.

We were in the prime minister's office in Sydney, looking down over the harbour with all of its benign tranquillity. I feared the call was going to be a rough ride. And it was.

Trump sounded tired. He was friendly enough at the outset but his mood quickly changed. As soon as I raised the refugee deal he became angry, repeating again and again that honouring the Obama deal would 'kill him' and 'embarrass him'. He said, 'I will be seen as a weak and ineffective leader in my first week by these people. This is a killer.'

I described how the deal was fair, benefiting the USA too. And the people on Manus and Nauru were not a security risk. But if you come by boat, you can't get into Australia. 'Even if you were a Nobel Prize winner,' I said. So you're a new CEO: you inherit some deals you don't like; you honour them, take a writedown and blame your predecessor.

Trump argued that, as a businessman, I must have torn up deals. I told him I hadn't. I believed promises should be kept, whether by companies or countries. I didn't make commitments lightly, and kept them when I did.

As his anger rose, Trump kept talking over the top of me, with more intensity; it was as though at times he was talking to himself or perhaps the people in the room, which of course included Steve Bannon, one of the deal's fiercest opponents.

At one point, I looked up from the phone across my desk at David Bold – his face was white with horror – so I turned to look out the window instead. I had to get Trump to commit to the deal. Not only was it vital for our whole plan to resettle the refugees without getting the people smugglers back in business, an early rejection by Trump would be a political catastrophe in Australia.

So, I reasoned with Trump and finally won him over.

> PM: You can certainly say that it is not a deal you would ever have done. You can say it is a deal you are sticking with because of the strong alliance …
>
> POTUS: That's the only thing I have a choice to say.
>
> PM: But you can also say …
>
> POTUS: I have no choice but to honour a deal made by my predecessor, I totally disagree with the deal, it's a horrible deal, a disgusting deal, and I would never have made the deal but I will honour the deal made by my predecessor. It's an embarrassment to the United States of America. And you can say that just the way I said it and as far as I'm concerned that's it. Okay? Malcolm, look, I've just had it.
>
> PM: Okay.
>
> POTUS: I've been making these calls all day long and this is the most unpleasant call I've had today. Putin was a pleasant call.[2]

At the end of it all, I still wasn't sure that Trump would stick to the deal. It was starting to dawn on us, and everybody else, that the Oval Office wasn't going to change Trump. He would be as capricious as president as he had been in business. This was going to be a presidency like no other.

The tone and the content of the call had been dynamite. We'd had nobody from my department or from the Department of Foreign Affairs present. We kept the transcript of the call secure and didn't release it to the bureaucracy in the usual way. Not that we didn't trust them, but at times you can't be too careful.

Mike Flynn and Justin Bassi reached an understanding that the White House would confirm they'd agreed to honour the deal, even though it was a bad one and they'd never have done it. For our part, our embassy and my office confirmed that the deal was going ahead.

Our plan had been to keep the whole thing very low-key. The deal was going ahead; Trump didn't like it but he was a man of his word and he was sticking with it. It wasn't a bad story; in fact, it reflected well on him. The Australian media, and in particular the ABC, badgered the White House for more detail, doing everything they could to turn it into a US news story, including by raising the issue in the White House briefing room. I wasn't surprised they relished the prospect of embarrassing Trump and, if the deal fell over, my government as well. But I wonder if the ABC's Zoe Daniel ever considered the refugees who stood to benefit from the arrangement.

In any event, as the media interest grew, it appeared Trump was having cold feet as on 2 February he tweeted, 'Do you believe it? The Obama Administration agreed to take thousands of illegal immigrants from Australia. Why? I will study this dumb deal!'

Later that day someone, presumably in the White House, briefed *The Washington Post* about the call; it described Trump 'blasting me', quoted him telling me this was his worst call so far, and that the deal I'd struck with Obama was the worst deal ever; it described his accusing me of planning to send him the 'next Boston bombers' – although it omitted to mention my riposte that the refugees on Nauru and Manus, unlike the Boston bombers, weren't from Chechnya.

The *Post* noted that the US embassy in Canberra had stated the White House had confirmed the refugee deal was going ahead 'one hour and forty minutes before Trump suggested in a tweet that it might not go ahead'.[3]

We assumed the leak had come from Bannon; his motive would have been either to produce enough heat to force Trump to renege on his commitment to me or, at the very least, to demonstrate to Trump's base that he'd agreed to the deal only through the most gritted of teeth.

Back in Australia, I declined to comment on media reports about the call, simply restating that Trump had agreed to honour the deal and that the conversation had been frank and courteous. I expressly rejected the claim that he'd hung up on me – as the transcript shows he did not.

The leaking of the details and later the transcript of the call had the opposite of its intended effect. The refugee deal had never been a big news story in the USA, despite the Australian media's attempts to make it so. However, berating one of America's closest allies *was* a big story and both fans of Australia and critics of Trump lined up to express their solidarity with us.

Our ambassador, Joe Hockey, was in heaven – fielding calls from dozens of senators and congressmen with assurances of support for Australia. Motions supporting the Australian alliance were tabled in both houses; one editorial after another deplored Trump's rudeness and praised Australia.

Amid all of this, Trump gave an interview in which he lavished praise on Vladimir Putin – the contrast was all too obvious and surreal. Berating allies, flattering tyrannical rivals.

For our part, it was working out well. Trump and/or Bannon had over-reached and now we had the upper hand. More importantly, unlike my counterparts leading other countries, I'd got off on the right foot with Trump. We'd had a row, that's true, but I'd stood my ground on a point of principle and he'd conceded. Joe was worried he might nurse this grievance and want to pay me back and, at one point, our diplomats were suggesting I offer Trump a concession on a tax treaty as consideration for his agreeing to honour the deal.

I rejected that approach, and the fact that it was proposed at all perhaps underlines the struggle of the traditional diplomatic establishment to understand a man like Trump. Where would the end to the concessions come?

However, we needed to ensure the personal relationship was as warm and positive as possible and so considerable effort was made to arrange a suitable visit for me to the United States to meet Trump for the first time.

The Australian American Association (AAA) had been planning a dinner on the 75th anniversary of the Battle of the Coral Sea, to be held in New York on 4 May. The timing was less than ideal for me, just before the budget, but the setting on the USS *Intrepid* – where Australian and US veterans of the battle would also attend – and the occasion were both ideal. The Battle of the Coral Sea was a major turning point in the Pacific War, when a combined US and Australian fleet turned back a Japanese armada heading to seize Port Moresby and cut off Australia from its US ally.

Jared Kushner told me on 1 May that Trump was still hurt about the refugee deal. 'He hadn't expected you'd come on so strong, although we knew that was your reputation.' I told him I didn't think the call was so bad. 'Malcolm, it was bad.' He told me Rupert Murdoch, whose father had founded the AAA, had persuaded Trump to go to the function on the *Intrepid*, and he urged me to be low-key and deferential.

In my diary that day I concluded, 'It sounds like Trump felt he had been bested in the negotiation and was furious with himself and with me. Well, WTF was I meant to do? Anyway sounds like we have to play it by ear and the goal of the meeting is simply not to have a row or a diplomatic debacle like so many of his other international meetings.'

Trump called me in the afternoon before the dinner to say he was running late: he had a big vote in the House of Representatives to repeal the Affordable Care Act and wanted to stay close to the phone until the votes were counted and then, of course, claim the victory. I perfectly understood – I'd have done the same – but the Australian media predictably tried to present it as a snub.

When Trump arrived, he was accompanied by Rudy Giuliani and Rupert Murdoch. His deference to Murdoch was greater than I've ever seen from any Australian politician and was in marked contrast to the high-handed way Trump treats most people. When he asked me if Rupert could join us for our bilateral discussion between leaders, I told him that wasn't a good idea, adding, 'The rest of the media will kill us; let's catch up with him later.'

For a first meeting, we covered a lot of ground. He talked about Kerry Packer a lot; he knew I'd been Kerry's lawyer and 'kept him out of jail', something Donald mentioned every time we met. Most billionaires keep an eye out for a good lawyer in a tight corner.

He is a big fan of Greg Norman and described in detail several tournaments he felt Greg had unfairly lost.

Trump is a natural isolationist. Everything he had learned about the history of East Asia from Xi and Abe only fleshed out what he believed about the bitter historical enmities between China, Japan and Korea. Xi in particular had left a big impression with his account of China's century of humiliation by foreigners, and Trump absolutely understood where Xi was coming from: Make China Great Again.

China, he believed had taken advantage of American complacency. He would have done the same if he were China's president. Nothing personal, it was business, and now he wanted to get ahead.

Whether it was East Asia or the Middle East, Trump's perspective was thoroughly dystopian. Everyone hated each other, had done for centuries and wasn't going to change. So the less the USA had to do with them the better.

After we'd had our one-on-one discussion and the media had left us, Donald suggested we ask Lucy and Melania to join us. Melania was found first and Donald described the refugee deal. By now he knew, just as I had told him, there were no security risks among the refugees.

'Melania, do you know, Malcolm has two thousand of the worst terrorists in the world locked up on a desert island and that fool Obama agreed to take them. Can you believe that? And now Malcolm has talked me into taking them too! He got me to do something I promised never to do! He is a tough negotiator!'

Melania smiled, faintly and mischievously. 'Just like you, Donald,' she said.[4]

The subject of an incandescent row a few months before was now something to make light of. It was just another deal. So, Donald could have been saying, 'Do you know, Malcolm has this really crappy property, and he persuaded me to pay ten million dollars more than it's worth.' Surreal or not, it meant that people, rigorously vetted by Homeland Security, would soon start to leave those islands and resettle in the USA.

But still I was worried that at some point he would try to even up. Trump had recently approved the dropping of the big bomb called the MOAB[5] in Afghanistan. He made a point of saying he didn't share the generals' excitement when they told him, 'We are locked and loaded,' just before he gave the order to drop the bomb.

I assumed this was Donald's way of assuring me that, despite his bellicose public language, he himself was far from being a warmonger. At that time he was filling his administration with generals. But he had opposed the invasion of Iraq and didn't, by any means, share the neo-conservatives' fantasy that the USA should use its military muscle to remake the world.

The Australian–American relationship is an especially close one, and while it helps for presidents and prime ministers to get on well, normally it isn't that important. The two systems, whether it be at the national security or the business level, are closely integrated.

In our own ways, Lucy and I were good examples. We owned an apartment in New York; had owned businesses in the USA; floated companies on the NASDAQ; my mother had lived for years in Philadelphia; and, for a time, I was not only a partner of Goldman Sachs but also a US taxpayer. Our son, Alex, studied at Harvard.

But with Trump, we faced a president who was supremely confident of his own judgement, obviously didn't pay much – if any – attention to officials and, in a manner I'd never seen anywhere before, played politics on an hour-to-hour media cycle, creating a crisis, then – if it went sour – creating another.

He was, as Joe Hockey used to say, a master at using weapons of mass distraction.

The other significant problem we faced was trade. It has to be remembered that Trump didn't expect to win the election and when he made one promise after another, he did so confident he'd never be called upon to deliver. So, many people hoped he'd abandon his populist promises and return to being a more conventional Republican president.

Trump set tremendous store on keeping his election promises, and for that you have to give him credit. But what many observers overlooked was that most of his economic views, especially on trade, were of long standing. He'd always been a protectionist: from the '80s he'd been accusing first Japan and then China and Europe of stealing American jobs. For those reasons, when he promised to pull out of the TPP, that was hardly surprising.

In our first call, I told him I recognised he was committed to doing this, but urged him to reconsider because of the strategic importance of the TPP. Interestingly, he said nobody had ever put that argument to him before.

The precautionary discussions that had taken place at the Lima APEC paid off and I became busy saving the TPP and ensuring it would continue without the USA, as the TPP-11. Meanwhile, Donald had more dramatic plans for trade. Not only was he planning to bully Mexico and Canada into concessions on the North American Free

Trade Agreement (NAFTA) and extract as-yet unspecified concessions from China, he was also planning to impose big tariffs on imported steel and aluminium.

American presidents, most recently George W. Bush, had done this before as a temporary measure, but Trump wanted a major reset, to throw up a wall of protection for the American steelmakers.

Now, economically this was nuts. By all means take action (as we have done in Australia) against dumping foreign steel below cost, but whacking a 25 per cent tariff on all imported steel coming into the United States will only put up the cost of steel by that amount, with adverse consequences for every other part of the US economy.

There's no doubt that the steel workers with their hard hats, tats and big biceps make for good photo opportunities, but it's a commodity industry and doesn't directly employ nearly as many Americans as people think. So I suggested to him it would make more sense to focus on the technology sector, where the jobs of the future are to be found and where the United States has been increasingly falling behind

In November 2017 the East Asia Summit was held in Manila. Shinzo Abe, Trump and I held a trilateral meeting and spoke frankly both in front of the cameras and privately about trade and North Korea.

Generally, I felt Trump was pretty tough on Abe. Shinzo had chosen to flatter him, which was no doubt a considered strategy. It may be that was what the Japanese public expected. But it wasn't the right approach in my view.

Trump repeatedly came back to historic issues from the Second World War that seemed calculated to make Shinzo uncomfortable. It was as though he wanted to keep him off-balance, his standard negotiating tactic. It didn't work; Shinzo was always cool and calm, never showing any sign of irritation.

Trump kept going on and on about the US trade deficit with Japan and at one point suggested he had a trade deficit with Australia. I corrected him, publicly, pointing out that he had a big surplus with us, and we didn't complain, and we had a big surplus with Japan and Shinzo didn't complain.

Trump's problem with trade was that he simply didn't understand that it wasn't a zero-sum game and believed that if you had a surplus with another country you were a 'winner' and if you had a deficit you were 'a loser'.

We talked about America's trade deficit with China on many occasions; it was almost an obsession with him. I urged him to stop trying to get the Chinese 'to buy more of our stuff' and instead focus on fair and reciprocal trade, a level playing field: if that were achieved, then the trade balance would be whatever it was, but would probably improve from his point of view.

When we met privately in Manila in November at the East Asia Summit, he asked me what I thought would happen if he banned all Chinese imports into the United States. 'A global depression,' I said, as quietly as I could. He was clearly straining with frustration, and returned again and again to the '$350 billion trade deficit, but it's really more like $500 billion, Malcolm'.

From my point of view, I could only do so much in trying to talk Trump around on trade generally – it was pretty clear that he had longstanding protectionist views he wasn't going to change. This was an important point: a lot of people saw Trump as an economic lightweight who'd come to the White House clueless and simply needed to be properly briefed and tutored on the right approach. The reality was quite different. He'd thought about these issues for many years, for decades in fact, and his mind was made up. Moreover, he had advisers and supporters who shared his views.

When Trump started threatening, early in his presidency, to take action to protect US industry by imposing tariffs on imported steel and aluminium, he was strongly encouraged by Commerce Secretary Wilbur Ross as well as his trade advisers Peter Navarro and Robert Lighthizer, who as far as I could tell simply wanted to use American muscle to extract better trade terms with other countries.

My singular objective was to protect Australia's interests. If Trump was going to play havoc with global trade, I had to do my very best to protect Australia, to differentiate us so that we weren't just another ally who was going to get run over by the Trump bulldozer.

So, after a lot of toing and froing between our embassy and the White House and between the various ministers and officials, it all came down – as it always does with Trump – to the great man himself.

After the love-in on the *Intrepid*, our next encounter had been in July at the G20 in Hamburg, hosted by Angela Merkel. She was a very courteous host, but it was obvious she couldn't stand Trump, and the feeling was mutual.

The challenge was finding a time to pin him down on the issue. He was certainly full of good cheer, inviting Lucy and me to ride in his car – 'The Beast' – with him and Melania, and generally radiating bonhomie.

Trump was even good-natured about my supposedly 'off the record' remarks at the press gallery ball in Canberra three weeks before. I'd given a rather Trumpian speech which brought the house down and, when it was leaked, went viral in the USA. 'So, you've been having a little fun at my expense, Malcolm?' Donald asked.

'Very affectionately,' I replied.

'It's not bad.' He shrugged. 'Lots of people think you are better than Alec Baldwin.'

Still, he knew I wanted a commitment on steel and he wasn't going to make it easy.

Finally, we agreed to catch up after one of the plenary sessions and so we headed off to find a meeting room. On the way, Emmanuel Macron joined us, as did Theresa May. In vain, I did everything short of tripping them both to get them out of the way – whatever they wanted to talk about, I knew it wasn't Australian steel or aluminium and I needed to get Trump by himself and extract a firm commitment.

On the way, Donald stopped and asked me if I'd ever seen his 'skiff' – or that's what it sounded like – and I could only say I hadn't as I wondered why on earth he was talking about a sailing boat. 'Oh, you gotta see it. It is so cool. Nobody, not even the Chinese or the Russians, can hear us in there. It is so secret!' Next thing, we took a right turn and found ourselves being led into a steel box the size of a container; all the while, Donald was explaining how utterly impenetrable it was to even the best bugs.

Of course, for the SCIF (Secure Communications Information Facility) to work, you have to have the door closed. Even though it probably wasn't a good idea to have a dozen or more people jammed into it, our trailing entourage piled in. With me were Finance Minister Mathias Cormann and our G20 sherpa – the senior Australian official guiding the G20 policy process – David Gruen. For Trump, there was at least Wilbur Ross, Steve Mnuchin and Gary Cohn. Emmanuel was there, as was Theresa, the German G20 sherpa and sundry other officials and diplomats.

Donald, Emmanuel and I were down one end of the SCIF and while I wanted to talk about steel, the president of France wanted to talk about the wording of the communiqué.

Donald wanted to talk about neither. 'Emmanuel,' he said, 'do you know Malcolm is the best lawyer in the world? The best. He kept my friend Kerry Packer out of jail. Nobody else could have done that.'

I was thinking, is this going to be a routine? So, on cue, I said, 'Oh, Donald, it wasn't that hard. He was innocent.'

Quick as a flash, Donald says with a big grin, 'No, he was so guilty, so guilty. Deserved to go to jail forever!'

To say that Macron was astonished by this is an understatement, but the routine continued.

'Emmanuel,' Donald continued, 'Malcolm has two thousand of the worst terrorists in the world – the worst in the world – locked up on a desert island.'

'They aren't terrorists, Donald,' I wearily replied.

'Oh, yes they are. They are the worst, and that fool Obama – the *worst* president *EVER* – agreed to take them to America. Can you believe that? Would you take them, Emmanuel?'

Macron opened his mouth but didn't say anything; his eyes just got wider.

'But you know what's worse? Now I have to take them! Malcolm, why do I have to take them?'

'Donald,' I said, 'they're yours. And they are very nice people. You will get on fine.' This was definitely becoming a routine.

To get to steel, I had to help resolve the wording issue with Macron. Trump quite sensibly didn't really care what was in the communiqué as not only was he never going to read it, neither was anyone else. So that done, before Emmanuel left I thought I'd see if I could chance my arm on one little word of my own.

A huge Organisation for Economic Co-operation and Development (OECD) report on environmental issues had been delivered to the G20 at the last minute and the diplomats wanted to say we 'adopted it' in the communiqué. Now, I thoroughly disapprove of this kind of lazy drafting – you take a report nobody has read and then incorporate it by reference into the communiqué to create the impression that everyone agrees to it. I wanted the communiqué to say we 'noted the report' but Angela Merkel said the best she could say was 'acknowledge'. I thought she was being pretty unreasonable, to be honest, and was surprised – when I raised it with her directly – that she wouldn't budge.

Maybe not a big deal, but as Donald was there and the German sherpa was there, I quickly described the issue.

Donald was on board. 'I think "note" is good. Malcolm's right,' he said.

The German sherpa didn't blink, just nodded and said, '"Note" it will be.'

It sure helps to be the superpower, I couldn't help thinking.

Resolving the wording issues got Macron and May out of the SCIF so we Australians were able to get down to the purpose of the meeting, which was to extract a commitment from Trump that he wouldn't impose tariffs on our steel or aluminium. I was particularly concerned about steel because the tariff was higher (25 per cent versus 10 per cent for aluminium) and because our steel industry had been struggling in the face of aggressive import competition from China. Add to that, the second steelmaker, Arrium, based in Whyalla, had gone into bankruptcy. The setting of the SCIF may have been bizarre, but I had to fight for those Australian jobs.

I explained to Trump that almost all of the Australian steel exports to the USA were of rolled coil made in Port Kembla shipped by BlueScope to Steelscape, its subsidiary in California. Steelscape turned the steel into roofing materials – mostly Colorbond. Trump's eyes lit up. 'Colorbond, comes in bright colours, right?' – it turned out that he was familiar with it. 'We used the gold-coloured one in some of our own projects. They really loved it in Brooklyn.'

Why did California need Australian steel? Well, as I described to Trump, the cost of shipping steel across the Pacific was about $40 a tonne versus $100 a tonne from the Midwest or East Coast steelmakers. So, I argued, if he put a tariff on Australian steel, all that would happen is that the cost of roofing steel on the West Coast would go up by about 12.5 per cent with no benefit to US steelmakers – the only winners would be the US Treasury and people who sold competitive non-steel roofing products. And the big loser would be the construction sector and American jobs.

'Donald,' I argued, 'you have a great trade deal with us – no tariffs, no quotas and a huge trade surplus. So why would you want to hit us, just because you can?'

Wilbur Ross was there and plainly didn't like the way the argument was going – he was a classic protectionist, didn't believe in free trade at all and saw no problem in the USA using its muscle to advantage its own steel sector at the expense of its allies'. But even Wilbur could see the point I was making about freight – Australian steel would still be cheaper than East Coast US steel in California after the tariff – so there was no bonanza for US steelmakers out of taxing Australian steel. And, in any event, we were tiny exporters to the USA – only about 300,000 tonnes out of an annual total of over 30 million.

Gary Cohn and Steve Mnuchin were more sympathetic participants in the discussion – they were opposed to the whole idea of steel and aluminium tariffs and had been fighting a rearguard action to restrain Trump from his trade war agenda (trade wars are easy to win, he had tweeted).

Well, we came out of the SCIF with a commitment from Trump that there would be no tariffs on Australian steel. Ross argued that only the Colorbond product should be exempted and we discussed the practicality of that, but to both Trump and me that sounded like Wilbur trying to white-ant the deal before it was concluded, so from my point of view, the president had given me a commitment – no tariffs on Australian steel or aluminium, full stop.

This battle went on within the administration between the free traders like Mnuchin and Cohn and the protectionists, Ross, Navarro and Lighthizer, but of course the protectionist in chief, the self-styled 'Tariff Man', was the president himself.

Trump was shaking up everyone else, but by the end of 2017 I felt we had reached a good and stable understanding – he was beating up America's allies around the world, but seemed to be leaving us alone. And then *The New York Times* rang our embassy in Washington: they had a question about our high commissioner in London, and former Foreign minister, Alexander Downer, and how he had set off the Federal Bureau of Investigation (FBI) inquiry into the Trump campaign's alleged links with Russia.

It all went back to 10 May 2016 when Downer had a few gin and tonics with George Papadopoulos, an American businessman who was working on the Trump campaign as a foreign policy adviser. Amid a wide-ranging chat about Trump's likely foreign policy, Papadopoulos told Downer that the Russians had indicated they would prefer Trump to win, rather than Clinton, and were prepared to assist him, including by anonymously releasing information during the campaign damaging to Hillary.

Alexander duly reported on this a few days later by cable to Canberra. It wasn't brought to my attention and as far as I can recall no action was taken on it. Trump was endorsed as the Republican candidate on 19 July, and that prompted Alexander to call on the US chargé d'affaires (standing in for their ambassador) and tell him all about the Papadopoulos discussion.

He had no authority from Canberra to do this, and the first we heard of it in Australia was when the FBI turned up in London and wanted to interview Downer. We were very reluctant to get dragged into the middle of the US presidential election, but agreed to Downer being interviewed on the basis it was kept confidential and any information he provided was not circulated beyond the FBI.

That all went well until December the following year, by which time Trump had been president for nearly 12 months, and *The New York Times* called.

Hockey did a good job trying to hose it down and ensure that Trump did not conclude Downer's action had been officially authorised or, as Papadopoulos later argued, was part of some kind of anti-Trump conspiracy. Fortunately sanity and the facts prevailed, but it provided an interesting frisson to our meetings at the White House in February 2018, the first one since Manila in November 2017.

Together with Lucy, I travelled to Washington and we were warmly received at the White House by Donald and Melania. The meetings went well; even the joint press conference proceeded without incident.

I didn't revisit the steel tariff issue in depth because I didn't want to give him an opportunity to change his mind, so simply noted that we appreciated his commitment that we'd be exempt, holding my breath that he wouldn't disavow the commitment in Hamburg. He didn't, instead reminiscing fondly about Colorbond, and once we moved on from trade to regional security, we were pretty much in agreement on most issues.

Back in Australia, a week later, we learned that Trump was about to make his decision on steel tariffs. So I called him again on 10 March.

We covered a lot of ground: regional security, China and North Korea as well as my concerns about how the United States and its allies had lost – and should work together to regain – leadership in wireless technology and especially 5G.

But my focus remained persuading him from imposing tariffs on our steel or aluminium. So I went through the big surpluses America had with Australia and how their trade deal with Australia should be their ideal.

I sensed, as I had before, that he didn't want to get pinned down to make a commitment, but I pressed on.

'Donald,' I said, 'you can use Australia as an argument because you can say we have a level playing field, we have a surplus, so we aren't going to impose steel tariffs.' He could, I argued, say to other countries, 'If you want to have no tariffs, give us a level playing field like the Australians do. Fair and reciprocal trade.'

Trump liked the term 'fair and reciprocal' a lot. That was very promising; that was a better theme for his trade policy than the American 'might is right' message, which might go down well in the Midwest but was so corrosive of American goodwill everywhere else in the world.

So in hands-on chief executive style, he started dictating a tweet, with me commenting on it as he went. How many years had we been an ally? Two hundred? 'No, just one hundred to 4 July this year,' I said. And at one point we nearly had 'the great state of Australia' in the message – 'Perhaps nation,' I suggested.

It was a practical and good-humoured collaboration. We even compared our Twitter followers (he had 158 million, I had only one), and finally settled on a very plain announcement saying that because of our fair and reciprocal military and trading relationship, the US would not impose steel or aluminium tariffs on the great nation of Australia.

And aluminium only just made it. I was so fixated on steel, it was only at the last moment I reminded him to include aluminium. No problems, steel and aluminium it was.

Trump's tweet, when it came out, was slightly different: 'Spoke to PM @TurnbullMalcolm of Australia. He is committed to having a very fair and reciprocal military and trade relationship. Working very quickly on a security agreement so we don't have to impose steel or aluminum tariffs on our ally, the great nation of Australia!'

We were taken aback by the reference to a security agreement – it hadn't been mentioned in the call with Trump – but we were assured both directly and via our embassy that this was inserted by the White House lawyers, and that it didn't detract from the president's unequivocal commitment.

Negotiations on what I should say went back and forth. I told my team I couldn't dissemble about the call. So I tweeted this: 'Great discussion today on security and trade. Australia/US trade is fair & reciprocal and each of our nations has no closer ally. Thank you for confirming new tariffs won't have to be imposed on Australian steel and aluminium – good for jobs in Australia and in US!'

On 22 March, Trump's proclamation on steel imposed tariffs on all countries with the exception of Australia, Argentina, South Korea, Brazil and the EU – pending further negotiations. It wasn't the unequivocal exemption we'd agreed, but it was a step forward. The challenge now was, in the midst of all of the Washington chaos, to hang on to it.

About a week later, Treasury Secretary Steve Mnuchin asked to speak with me – the topic was described as 'tariffs and time sensitive'. Straightaway, we were concerned the protectionists were pushing back and were trying to unwind Trump's unconditional commitment to no tariffs.

I spoke with Mnuchin on 31 March, our time, and summarised it this way in my diary:

Okay so a good call, Mnuchin has been sent by Lighthizer to speak to me about a quota – I don't think this has been to Trump however. His pitch is that they want to impose quotas on everyone else and so can we help them out with a quota on our steel. My counter argument went like this:

1. We do have an unconditional deal – he agrees with that.

2. It is important that the US has a moral basis for its efforts on trade, not just 'we are big so we will get what we want'. The President's use of fair and reciprocal is very powerful – it's hard to argue with a level playing field. Steve agrees with that.

3. So if the exercise is to level the playing field then the guys with the most level playing field (Australia) should get the best deal.

He said, 'It would be very helpful to us if we could agree on a quota, I am almost indifferent as to what the number is, but this is really more form over substance, helping us to negotiate other things, you guys are the perfect example. Look, we are not looking to you to reduce or anything else, or to stop you increasing, it would be helpful for us if you would agree to a quota.'

My response was that if they treat Australia like everyone else, even with a quota that is so large it has no practical economic impact, the US gives up a powerful argument for fair and reciprocal trade. So, I said, 'If the Europeans say "Why do the Aussies not have a quota?" the answer can be "Because our exports go into Australia tariff free and if you want to be treated the same, drop your tariffs on our exports to Europe."'

Mnuchin understood these arguments, described them as compelling, said he would go back to Lighthizer and if he had no success there go back to the president.

Mnuchin did come back and requested a call, which we held on 11 April, my time. At home I was being encouraged to give in on the request for a quota, on the basis we should try to land on large quotas for steel and aluminium (500,000 and 120,000 tonnes respectively). Trump would have a win, but our exports would be unlikely to rise to meet them.

I didn't agree. I wanted to hold Trump to the unconditional exemption which I believed was in both Australia and America's best interests.

I summarised the discussion in this message to Mnuchin right after the call.

Steve we remain concerned that any quota even if it has little or no economic impact will be counterproductive and be perceived badly here. Counterproductive in the sense that the US has the ultimate fair trade deal with Australia – no tariffs and no quotas. So what is the justification for a quota? Surely better to hold Australia up as an example of the kind of deal others should offer? In terms of perception the announcement the President and I made based on the discussion we had was not a conditional one. But always happy to discuss.

Of course very happy to provide assurance that all steel and aluminium going from Australia which is exempt is made in Australia. Transhipment not an issue for us.

The proposal you made on steel was Bluescope is exempted and there be a large enough 'other' quota to ensure no impact. If the other non Bluescope quota was say 100,000 tonnes it would never get even remotely close to being filled so would not have an economic impact. But the political and principle question is why impose any quota on the guy with whom you already have the best possible trade deal?

Perhaps the President and I should discuss again – you are far better off holding the Australian free trade agreement up as the ideal trade deal – you can't get better than no tariffs no quotas – complete market access for US exporters.[6]

The argument went on and on within the administration and by the end of April, our embassy in Washington was pretty pessimistic about our prospects of maintaining our exemption, so I wrote to Trump directly. Like Kerry Packer, he is more of a listener than a reader, so to be effective a letter has to be short and punchy and written not just to be read, but to be read aloud – more like a script. This one turned out to be very effective.

When we last spoke about steel and aluminium you confirmed that Australia would be exempt from any tariffs. This was in recognition of the fact that American trade with Australia is on the best possible terms.

No tariffs and no quotas. In fact it cannot get any better.

And a massive US$25 billion surplus in your favour!

How good is that?

Truth be told you have the best possible trade deal ever with Australia.

Other countries, including good friends and allies, do not offer the United States the complete and free market access which we do. And so you do have reason to complain that in many cases your trade with them is not fair or reciprocal.

That is not the case with Australia – if every country offered the United States the deal we deliver, you would not have much to complain about.

Since then, Treasury Secretary Steven Mnuchin has said to me that your Trade Representative Mr Lighthizer wants to impose a quota on Australian steel but on terms that do not have any economic impact. His proposal has been that for steel all exports from Bluescope (about 98% of our exports to the US) be tariff and quota free and for other steel exporters the tariff-free quota be high enough not to represent any practical limitation; we discussed a figure of 100,000 tonnes for the non-Bluescope exporters.

Steven and I did not discuss aluminium in any detail, but the same principle was to apply.

He said Mr Lighthizer's argument was that it was hard to impose quotas on other countries without imposing one on Australia.

I am writing to seek to persuade you that it is very much in your interest not to impose any quota on Australian steel or aluminium.

First, it would not be consistent with the deal we agreed on 9 March and subsequently tweeted about.

Second, it helps your argument for 'fair and reciprocal' trade if no quota is applied to Australia. You are able to say *'The Aussies impose no tariffs and no quotas on our exports to Australia – it is a fair, reciprocal deal. A level playing field. That's the kind of deal I like, so that's why they are not getting a quota.'*

On the other hand if you do impose a quota (leaving aside its inconsistency with our Free Trade Agreement), people will be able to say *'So the Aussies give you the best possible deal, and they still get a quota – so this is not about fair and reciprocal trade at all.'*

Finally in practical terms the lack of a quota offers no threat. We do not tranship steel from other countries (transport costs would preclude that) and would in any event guarantee any steel or aluminium free of tariff was made in Australia. And our steel and aluminium industries are very small, especially steel, and not in a position to make much if any additional impact in the US market.

So in summary, Donald, there is nothing for you to lose and a lot to gain by not imposing a quota on Australia, even the very benign quotas Steven discussed with me.

You will be seen as sticking to your commitment of 9 March (in which there was no mention of a quota), you will be seen to be acting consistently with the principle of supporting fair and reciprocal trade and you will have the Australian trade deal as a benchmark which others should aspire to.[7]

The letter persuaded a lot of people in the administration, and when I spoke again to Mnuchin on 6 May, I felt I was making real headway. Steve said to me, 'Surplus or deficit is an output – the key issue is whether the playing field is level.'

When the protectionists advising Trump continued to push for a quota on Australia, I had another call with the president on 22 May to try to turn him around.

Trump started determined that we would have a quota, and his concern was that if Australia was exempted, it would create a precedent. So my job was to persuade him that the singular position of Australia meant that it was in his interest to exempt us.

I said, 'When we last spoke we agreed there would be no tariffs on Australian steel and aluminium, we actually tweeted it and said that to the world, that was the agreement … This is really a political issue of principle, it's not really an economic issue … People will say, why have you got no tariffs on Australia? Is it because of the military alliance? And you can say, no, it's because it is fair and reciprocal, that's my principle, I want a level playing field. The Aussies have no tariffs and no quotas on us.'

Once again Trump saw the logic in our case and agreed that not only would there be no tariffs on our steel or aluminium but no quotas either. However, there was one important proviso. If we transhipped one piece of steel from China, or anywhere else, he said, the deal would be off.

'Donald,' I said, 'that's done and agreed. We will not tranship one kilogram.'

Ever since he was elected Trump has dominated the headlines in a way no other president has before. While many self-styled conservatives support him, he is not one of them. Conservatives defend and support established institutions. Radical, populist, Trump, the authoritarian iconoclast, takes them all on.

The economy, so far, has boomed under Trump. He has certainly delivered 'jobs and growth'. However, looked at from afar, America seems more divided, angry and polarised than I can remember. Libraries are being filled with analyses of Trump's wilful and intemperate nature, his 'chaotic' administration, scandals and conspiracies, real and imagined. Traditional political issues have been overwhelmed. The political debate has been distilled into one issue: Trump's giant personality.

He says America is more respected than ever. It depends what you mean by respect. Strength is respected when it is matched with values consistently advanced. Around the world, Trump's deliberate unpredictability generates fear rather than respect, anxiety rather than certainty. His view of the world is much closer to the 'don't tread on me' isolationists of centuries past than it is the neo-conservatives who, after the fall of the Soviet Union, sought to remake the world in America's image.

In our own region he has started, but not yet settled, a trade war with China. The COVID-19 crisis will no doubt further encourage protectionism. It seems impossibly far off at the moment, but at some point an expanded and enhanced TPP that includes China and the United States should be the goal.

At summits in Singapore and Hanoi, he has feted and flattered Kim Jong Un, who hasn't de-nuclearised and continues to test his missiles. So far, at least, the leader of the most powerful nation in the world appears to have been outmanoeuvred by the tyrant leader of a bankrupt slave state.

As he indicated when we first met, Trump is not a warmonger. And as he promised in his campaign, he is working to disentangle America from its engagement in the Middle East and Afghanistan, learning, as he has often said, that it is easier to get into these wars than to get out of them.

America may be stronger in economic and military terms, but its influence is diminished. In fact, under Trump, America seeks less influence, not least by rejecting many of the global institutions created by the USA after the Second World War.

Most consequential of all, I fear, will be his withdrawal from the Paris Agreement. The world will struggle to meet the challenge of global warming without American leadership.

And wherever Trump creates a leadership vacuum, others will fill it, often with values very different to our own.

But as the prime minister of Australia, my job was to protect our own particular interests and, as far as I could, influence him to act in a way that advanced our wider interests, in particular the continued commitment of the United States to our region. And in that regard, dramatic flourishes aside, he has not let us down. The 'indispensable nation' is nowhere more so than in our hemisphere.

We had a row over the refugee deal, but it is being implemented. A large number have been safely resettled in the USA after very careful security assessments. And we are fulfilling our side of the bargain too. He wouldn't have done the deal, that's true, but it was a fair one nonetheless.

Our only other contentious issue was the steel and aluminium tariffs. There, defying the stereotypes, he was both thoughtful and good-humoured. He started off with a different point of view, but listened to my arguments carefully.

I didn't solely base my case on our hundred years of mateship, or the ANZUS[8] alliance. A century of solidarity does matter a lot, and especially in Washington. But the USA has a lot of allies. My arguments persuaded him because I correctly couched them as being in his interest. If the Australian trade relationship is your ideal – fair and reciprocal, no tariffs, no quotas and, as it happens, a big surplus – then you should treat us differently to others where the playing field is far from level.

For all of Trump's so-called madness, in my own dealings with him I found him no less rational than many other billionaires I have dealt with over the years. For all of our differences, as two businessmen, we spoke the same language.

CHAPTER 37

The Pacific Step-Up

In 2016, the government resolved to step up our engagement with our Pacific island neighbours. I announced it at the Pacific Islands Forum (PIF) in September 2016 and it was laid out as a key foreign policy objective in the 2017 Foreign Affairs white paper, which I described at the time as a permanent and irreversible policy shift.

Australian leaders have often called the Pacific 'our backyard'. That's not the right term: it suggests we own it and take it for granted. The Pacific rather is our neighbourhood, and while vast, it's one in which we have special responsibilities and opportunities.

The PIF nations range from PNG, population 8.6 million, to Tuvalu and Nauru with populations of around 12,000, and tiny Niue and Tokelau with about a thousand residents each. All have been territories of former colonial powers, such as PNG was of Australia, Fiji and many others were of Britain and the Marshall Islands and Micronesia were of the United States. New Caledonia and French Polynesia are self-governing parts of France today, and are likely to remain so.

Their combined exclusive economic zones represent a quarter of the Pacific Ocean – and yet their population, excluding Australia and New Zealand, is about 10 million. More than 95 per cent of that is in PNG, Fiji (900,000) and the Solomon Islands (600,000) alone.

The economic and social development challenges are immense. Some of the world's most disadvantaged communities are in the Pacific. Further, climate change and rising sea levels are posing an existential threat to the low-lying island states like Kiribati and Tuvalu.

Over the years, Australia hasn't neglected the Pacific: we are by far the largest aid donor and their most trusted security partner, as had been demonstrated during the 2003–17 Regional Assistance Mission to Solomon Islands (RAMSI) intervention, when an Australian-led security force of police and military from several nations supported the Solomon Islands government in restoring order after a period of ethnic violence. The largest single recipient of Australian aid was PNG: over $500 million a year. During my government, Julie Bishop especially put in an enormous effort to visit the Pacific island states, clocking up dozens of visits.

I made sure to attend the PIFs in Micronesia in 2016 and Samoa in 2017 as well as visiting PNG and hosting many visits from Pacific island leaders. Politics is personal, and nowhere more so than in the Pacific. Not only did I make friends with the Pacific leaders, I took the time to understand their complex challenges.

And I was always prepared to get out a laptop and help draft the communiqué myself, which didn't go unnoticed. Samoan PM Tuilaepa Sailele said at the PIF he hosted, 'You must have been a good lawyer when you were young.'

Initially, we focused on increasing the level of economic integration with the Australian economy, especially with the smaller island states. We concluded in 2017 a new, expanded free trade and economic cooperation agreement called the Pacific Agreement on Closer Economic Relations (PACER) Plus and established the Pacific Labour Scheme. This enables citizens from most of the Pacific island states and Timor-Leste to take up low- and semi-skilled work in rural and regional Australia for up to three years. The scheme enables participants to acquire work skills in a range of occupations – typically in agriculture, hospitality, tourism, health care and aged care.

This decision institutionalised previous seasonal worker schemes that had helped improve the skills of Pacific island workers, which they can take home. The valuable remittances being sent home also supported their local economies.

I was concerned that our aid program be used effectively. Some of the small island states are simply not capable of generating enough income to provide the essential government services they need and rely on our backing to cover basics like security, health and education.

Whether big or small, all of the Pacific nations have vast exclusive economic zones over millions of square kilometres of ocean, which they lack the means to police. So a big part of our support is providing them with *Guardian* class patrol boats and the training to ensure they can be maintained. Totalling 21 and made by Austal in Perth, they're among the 54 naval vessels to be built in Australia under my government's naval shipbuilding plan.

But progress in the Pacific, as everywhere else, requires good governance, eliminating corruption and making sure investment reaches projects and places where it can genuinely generate an economic or social return and not simply line the pockets of one politician or another.

During my time as PM, we saw increasing levels of investment from China in the Pacific. Some countries, like Tonga, became heavily indebted to Beijing with loans that should never have been made – the borrower had no realistic prospect of being able to pay the interest let alone repay the principal.

In 2017, the Solomon Islands government, under Prime Minister Manasseh Sogavare, abandoned an Asian Development Bank–backed project to build a fibre-optic cable from Honiara to Sydney and announced it was planning to take up an offer from China's Huawei to build one instead. There was a flurry of allegations about corruption motivating the decision.

Leaving aside the issue of bribes, the move to Huawei sparked serious concerns. Our security agencies advised we shouldn't under any circumstances allow the Huawei cable to land in Sydney, the point from which most of Australia's international cables connect to the rest of the world. Huawei's counter-proposal was to take the cable from Honiara to Indonesia.

Around then, PNG was considering a similar Huawei offer.

Both countries needed to upgrade their telecommunications capacity – the Solomon Islands didn't have any cable connections and was relying on expensive satellite connections, and PNG's existing cable links were becoming heavily congested.

I concluded that it wasn't good enough for us to tell the Solomon Islands the Huawei cable couldn't land in Sydney without providing an alternative solution. And, consistent with our Pacific Step-Up policy, the alternative should be funded with aid money, not a loan. An Australian-funded cable network across the Pacific linking the Solomon Islands and PNG to the internet via Australia would constitute transformative economic infrastructure but also mean a Chinese company didn't become the dominant telecoms partner for our Pacific neighbours.

In June 2018, we signed a contract with the Australian company Vocus to build a cable network from Sydney to Honiara and Port Moresby. The bulk of the cost, $136 million, will be paid for out of our foreign aid budget. In addition we agreed that the cable will link the major islands in the Solomon Islands. We also agreed to fund a cable network around PNG.

The Coral Sea Cable project embodied the new approach my government had taken to the Pacific. While including social, education and health objectives, our aid also extends to the construction of transformative economic infrastructure, especially energy and telecommunications, that the Pacific leaders were telling me they needed. At the same time, we'd seek to ensure that critical communications infrastructure didn't fall under the control of China or any other country whose interests may not always be aligned with our own, let alone the values of Pacific island nations who've thrown off colonial rule in the last century, and are determined to protect their sovereignty in this one.

In recent years, China has been reported as taking an interest in establishing a naval base in variously PNG, Vanuatu and the Solomon Islands. In response to a request from PNG, I agreed to start work on the establishment of a joint Australian and PNG facility at their Lombrum naval base on Manus Island. The additional local jobs generated would be especially welcome when the last asylum seekers from the Australian-funded facilities on Manus were finally resettled.

In the same spirit, I also agreed with Fijian Prime Minister Frank Bainimarama in 2018, a few days before I was deposed, that Australia would fund the upgrade of their Blackrock police and peacekeeper training facility.

The alternative would likely have been a Chinese-funded development. Given the long association of the Australian and Fijian militaries in warfighting and in peacekeeping, it made perfect sense for us to ensure it continued.

Both projects supported my government's goal of ensuring Australia remains the preferred security partner for our Pacific neighbours.

It's good to see that Prime Minister Morrison has continued with the Pacific Step-Up I began in 2016. It isn't something in which we can afford to lose interest. Australia's response to climate change will, however, continue to be a sensitive issue in the Pacific. Several of the island nations are at risk of being wiped out by rising sea levels in the years to come, and all of the region faces enormous costs from climate change. The increased aid for climate change adaptation that we've provided as part of the Pacific Step-Up is welcome, but the Pacific expects us to move faster on reducing our greenhouse gas emissions as well.

They haven't forgotten the time Peter Dutton mocked the Pacific islanders' concerns about 'water lapping at your door'. To many on the right of Australian politics, climate change is a political or ideological issue. To those in the Pacific, it's a matter of survival.

CHAPTER 38

A very wild year: 2017

From the beginning of 2017, we were fully in the business of delivery. Despite a one-seat majority in the House, only 30 votes out of 76 in the Senate, catastrophes like section 44 flying at us from left field (about which, more later), not to speak of continuing internal destabilisation run by Abbott and his friends, we managed to achieve an extraordinary amount.

The internal dynamics of the leadership group had now settled down.

The most important relationships, in a policy sense, are between the PM, treasurer and Finance minister – at this time myself, Scott Morrison and Mathias Cormann – because between them they control the budget process through which everything has to be funded. The three of us worked effectively together. Scott and I got on well. Cormann, who was consistently delivering outcomes in the Senate, had also become a good and trusted friend to both me and Lucy and went to considerable lengths to burnish that friendship. But there were ongoing tensions with Morrison. Both Mathias and I struggled to manage his persistent indiscretion, as previously described.

Scott, for his part, didn't entirely trust Mathias, not because he saw Mathias as a rival for the leadership one day, but because he knew Mathias was close to Peter Dutton. Scott didn't trust Dutton at all and regarded him as deficient in all respects – character, intellect and political nous.

Within that troika it would be fair to say that each of them trusted me more than they trusted the other. For my own part I trusted Mathias implicitly. I was constantly warned about his supposed lack of integrity by his political rivals, especially George Brandis and Julie Bishop, but found him completely reliable – until of course he wasn't.

I didn't regard Scott as working against me in a rivalrous way, and reposed great trust in him, but he needed to be managed carefully and always counselled intensely about the need for confidentiality.

Barnaby Joyce was a turbulent partner as deputy prime minister, but we got on pretty well, in fact better than most Liberal and National leaders had in the past. He had bitter antagonisms but they were mostly within his own party. There was a gulf between those – like Canavan and Christensen – who loved Barnaby and others – like McCormack and Chester – who couldn't stand him.

The deepest animosity, which needed my constant management, was between Cormann and Dutton on the one hand and Julie Bishop and George Brandis on the other. I couldn't understand, ever, the depth of antagonism between them, but Dutton in particular never missed an opportunity to have a shot at Bishop or Brandis, and Cormann wasn't far behind him.

Julie was, of course, my oldest friend in the parliament. We'd known each other long before we went into politics. Unlike Abbott, I treated her with respect and deference and we were a highly effective foreign policy partnership. However, not least because of the gruelling travel schedule, the Foreign minister is always somewhat removed from the domestic political issues upon which the fate of every government turns.

Brandis, too, was a good friend – and a good lawyer. We worked closely together and I didn't pressure him to give me the legal advice I wanted, as Abbott used to do. He wasn't, however, as effective in wrangling deals through the Senate as was Mathias.

Christopher Pyne was a moderate and thus factionally aligned with Julie and George as well as Marise Payne and Education Minister Simon Birmingham. But he was able to get along with just about everyone – even those who loathed him couldn't entirely resist his wicked charm. He was a superb raconteur and, while a very efficient minister, his circumspection had its limits. When it came to gossip he was the soul of indiscretion, especially if it was amusing or salacious.

I'd appointed Pyne manager of opposition business in 2009. He'd held that position under Abbott and then became leader of the House when we went into government in 2013. He loved the complexity and intrigue of managing the House, especially cutting deals with his opposite number behind the speaker's chair. Both Anthony Albanese and Tony Burke on the Labor side had utterly confidential relations with Christopher – rare examples of constructive bipartisanship.

It has to be said that 2017 got off to a dreadful start. My friend Sussan Ley, the Health minister, was accused of arranging her ministerial travel so as to spend a lot of time in the Gold Coast – where she'd been looking for and finally bought an apartment.

It was a classic hit job. It appeared a disgruntled ex-staffer had initially made the claims to Annika Smethurst of the *Courier-Mail* and then further research through her travel claims did the rest. Sussan's initial explanation that the apartment purchase was unplanned and 'spur of the moment' wasn't credible and was quickly discredited. I begged her not to say any more to the media until she'd done all her homework.

But day after day there were bad headlines calling for her to resign or be sacked. Her colleagues rallied around to put the boot in – anonymously, of course. Various claims of expenses abuse were levied at other ministers, including Industry, Innovation and Science Minister Greg Hunt, who'd used the 'family reunion' entitlement to take his family on a trip to Noosa while he was notionally at least working on the Sunshine Coast.

Finally, on 13 January, Sussan resigned from the cabinet. I appointed Greg Hunt Health minister to replace Ley. Arthur Sinodinos had restored the cabinet process, so I appointed him minister for Industry, Innovation and Science and returned the cabinet secretary to a public service position in the shape of the very efficient Simon Atkinson. I also appointed Ken Wyatt minister for Aged Care and Indigenous Health – the first Indigenous Australian to be a federal minister.

The *Herald Sun* were delighted they'd got a scalp and reprised their front-page stories featuring Bronwyn Bishop's helicopter trip to Geelong in 2015 and Stuart Robert's failure to disclose a shareholding in a mining company controlled by a Liberal donor he'd been assisting in China.

I was sorry to lose Sussan. She was a friend as well as a good colleague who shared my liberal values. Sadly, however, she became bitter about having had to resign. By August 2018, frustrated because she hadn't yet been reinstated to cabinet, she threw her lot in with Peter Dutton on the basis that he'd promote her.

But I didn't waste the crisis. I announced the government would establish an Independent Parliamentary Expenses Authority (IPEA) to monitor these travel and other entitlements for MPs and senators. As I observed, the term 'entitlement' is part of the problem. 'These are not entitlements. They are no different to the business expenses that people have when they are travelling on behalf of their employer in the private sector. And they have to be justified.'[1] The IPEA was a big reform and has ensured transparency and accountability in a way we'd never had before.

The bright spot in January was the visit of Shinzo Abe and his wife, Aki, to Sydney. Happily, I persuaded him we should go ahead with the TPP without the USA. He was also the first head of government to join Lucy and me for dinner at our home. Our formal meetings were held at Kirribilli House then we travelled across the harbour on the Admiral's Barge[2] to our jetty at Point Piper.

In my first big speech of the year – on 1 February at the National Press Club – I set out to frame the government's agenda around our economic plan. I talked about our commitment to free trade and the TPP in particular.

> Political opportunists want us to turn inward, and revert to higher barriers to trade and investment.
>
> But they are doing nothing more than playing on the fears and hardships of those in the community who feel they have not shared in the benefits of globalisation and technological change. They offer the false promise that subsidies and trade barriers, under the banner of Australian first, are the answer to protecting jobs.
>
> But we have seen that film before. And it's not a pretty one. Whatever other countries may think, it is very clear that for Australia, more trade means more exports, which means more jobs and more opportunity. Those who oppose our export deals are really calling for less opportunity, diminished prosperity and fewer jobs.

My economic message was the same one we'd taken to the election. It was that our government was driving economic growth with lower business taxes, trade deals, affordable and reliable energy and economic infrastructure. This enabled us to provide the funds for schools, hospitals and infrastructure. And all of it was enabled by maintaining our national security, whether it was re-equipping our navy or keeping our borders secure against people smugglers.

The speech was especially important because it was the first time I'd spoken about the urgent need for pumped hydro and storage. Energy storage, long neglected in Australia, was also to be a priority in 2017.

> Last week at my request, ARENA [the Australian Renewable Energy Agency] and the Clean Energy Finance Corporation, agreed to work together on a new funding round for large-scale storage and other flexible capacity projects including pumped hydro. I've also written to Alan Finkel [Australia's chief scientist], asking him to advise on the role of storage and pumped hydro in stabilising the grid.

Large-scale storage will support variable renewables like wind and solar. It will get more value out of existing baseload generation and it will enhance grid stability. We're going to get on with it.[3]

As I said in response to a question, it was an indictment of governments, both state and federal, that for years they'd been pushing more renewables into the grid without planning for the storage to back them up.

That speech led to Snowy Hydro 2.0, Tasmania's 'battery of the nation' plan and a host of other pumped hydro and storage projects. All of these will ultimately make renewables reliable and achieve the zero-emissions energy sector we need.

The economic ministers and I were determined to maintain a credible return to surplus in 2020–21 as set out in the budget earlier in 2016. Scott's first presentation to the cabinet after the election had been pretty grim as he observed that our budget bottom line assumed a net $18 billion of savings, which had not been, and were unlikely to be, legislated. Added to that we had another $10 billion in new spending pressures we couldn't avoid, like defence operations and new listings on the PBS.

He presented several bleak scenarios, none of which saw us getting back into the black in 2020–21. If we slipped up on the path back to surplus, our credit would be downgraded by the ratings agencies and our economic credibility would be shot.

I hadn't minced words with the cabinet. 'So, what this means is that if we cannot get our savings through the Senate, we will have to find new revenue from increasing old taxes or imposing new ones. I know some of you don't think surpluses and deficits matter so much' – I was thinking of Barnaby and Dutton in particular – 'but, believe me, the only things people believe we do better than Labor are national security and economic management. And we can't afford to drop the ball on either.'

The team had been up to the challenge. Mathias had worked his negotiating magic again with Labor and the crossbench to secure the passage of a bipartisan Omnibus Savings Bill, which saved us over $6 billion over the forward estimates. Also we'd managed to get our hike in tobacco taxes passed, which gave us another $4.7 billion. All up, in the second half of 2016, we legislated or implemented $22 billion of budget repair measures.

Our success on all these fronts, however, wasn't matched by our Enterprise Tax Plan (ETP). It cut company tax to 25 per cent over 10 years and prioritised cuts to small and medium companies. Of all of our economic measures, the ETP was the one that had the surest return in terms of additional investment and economic growth. The election of Donald Trump with his promise to reduce US corporate tax from 35 per cent to 21 per cent only made the uncompetitiveness of our company tax regime even more apparent.

Scott Morrison was keen to drop the ETP as soon as it appeared that we wouldn't get it through the Senate. By then, we were in the lead-up to the 2017 budget and were considering dropping from the budget several proposed spending cuts that had no hope of getting passed – known as 'zombies'. Scott's argument was, why keep on the books a company tax cut plan if we couldn't get it passed?

The press gallery started to speculate that the government would abandon the company tax cuts or modify them. It was as though any discussion about contingency planning that Scott was party to would find its way into the media.

Meanwhile we were working on the 2017 budget and Scott wanted to find some new measures to promote housing affordability. These were the subject of intense discussion around the ERC table but once again, bits and pieces were finding their way into the media.

For this to happen in early 2017, when we were thinking about how we could get the company tax cuts through the Senate, was shocking. It came to a head – on a Newspoll weekend – when I was in Queenstown in New Zealand, with Scott, for the annual leaders' meeting. I was meeting with the new prime minister, Bill English, whom I knew well as he'd been Key's Finance minister for eight years – and, further back, leader of the opposition. *The Australian* was running a front-page story by Simon Benson, David Crowe and Sarah Martin claiming that Coalition MPs were in a push to deny the banks a share in the company tax cut. Tony Pasin and Luke Howarth were both quoted directly in support of this 'push', which was being linked to the recent appointment of former Queensland Labor Premier Anna Bligh as chief executive of the Australian Banking Association (ABA).[4]

Scott, when asked, replied to me, 'I had never heard of the proposal – we had a call about it late yesterday in relation to what Pasin had said and I dismissed it. I think it's a crazy idea, as does my office.'[5]

Supporting Country Fire Authority volunteers at a rally at Treasury Gardens in Melbourne, 5 June 2016, and below, at Sydney Children's Hospital on 3 November.

Sahlan Hayes, official photographer to PM Turnbull

Meeting little Lulu at the Sydney Children's Hospital, where we announced our Zero Childhood Cancer Initiative, 31 May 2016. *Carly Earl / Newspix*

On a streetwalk in Homebush with Craig Laundy on 14 May, I met and comforted Serge Oreshkin, whose son died on board MH17. *Andrew Meares / SMH*

Our grandchildren made regular appearances throughout the campaign. Daisy's son, Jack, got behind the wheel at a trucker's rally at Smeaton Grange on 19 June 2016. *Sahlan Hayes, official photographer to PM Turnbull*

Enjoying yum cha with Alex and granddaughter Isla during a campaign visit to Barton on 29 June. *Andrew Meares / SMH*

With the family backstage preparing for the official campaign launch on 26 June. *Sahlan Hayes, official photographer to PM Turnbull*

Announcing Snowy Hydro 2.0 on 16 March 2017 with Snowy CEO Paul Broad.
Alex Ellinghausen / SMH

With David Gonski and Simon Birmingham announcing our reforms to schools funding on 2 May 2017.
Sahlan Hayes, official photographer to PM Turnbull

Marking International Women's Day with Australian Defence Force Academy cadets, 8 March 2017.
Andrew Meares / SMH

Bringing the TPP back from the brink with Shinzo Abe during a walk along South Head on 14 January 2017.
David Foote / Auspic / DPS

A quiet chat with India's PM Narendra Modi on the steps of the Akshardham temple in Delhi on 11 April 2017.
Sahlan Hayes, official photographer to PM Turnbull

With French President Emmanuel Macron and his wife, Brigitte, at the Élysée Palace in Paris on 8 July 2017.
Sahlan Hayes, official photographer to PM Turnbull

At last! The House of Representatives votes to legalise same-sex marriage on 7 December 2017.
Kym Smith / Newspix

Arriving at Tennant Creek, NT, 22 July 2018. *Sahlan Hayes, official photographer to PM Turnbull*

Reconciled: with President Trump on board the USS *Intrepid* in New York on the 75th anniversary of the Battle of the Coral Sea, 4 May 2017, and below, with Lucy and Melania at the White House in February 2018.

Sahlan Hayes, official photographer to PM Turnbull

In London for CHOGM with Canadian PM Trudeau, UK PM May and NZ PM Ardern before a counter-terrorism meeting in April 2018.
Sahlan Hayes, official photographer to PM Turnbull

Meeting with Chancellor Angela Merkel at the Chancellery in Berlin on 13 November 2015.
Odd Anderson / AFP / Getty Images

Taking a walk in Sydney with Chinese Premier Li Keqiang during his visit to Australia on 25 March 2017.
Sahlan Hayes, official photographer to PM Turnbull

I uploaded this photo of me with granddaughter Alice at a Sydney Swans game to my Facebook page with the caption, 'Multitasking at the footy. #goswans', in September 2017. This provoked a social media outrage that I was having a beer while holding baby Alice. Mark Knight from the *Herald Sun* defended me with the cartoon below!

Below: Mark Knight

Talking TPP tactics with Mexican President Enrique Peña Nieto and his Trade minister, Ildefonso Guajardo, at the APEC meeting in Da Nang, Vietnam, November 2017.

A selfie with Donald Trump and Xi Jinping at the conclusion of the 2017 APEC meeting.

With other leaders at the 2017 APEC meeting.
Alex Ellinghausen / AAP Image

My assessment of Bill Shorten has at least amused Barnaby Joyce, 8 February 2017.
Lukas Coch / AAP Image

With Israeli PM Bibi Netanyahu visiting Moriah College in my electorate of Wentworth
in February 2017. *Sahlan Hayes, official photographer to PM Turnbull*

With Lucy and Emmanuel Macron at the Sydney Opera House, 1 May 2018. *Sahlan Hayes, official photographer to PM Turnbull*

Kayaking on Sydney Harbour with John Key on 20 February 2016.

A quick selfie with Lucy and staff before my press conference with President Trump at the White House in February 2018 (L–R: Mark Simkin, Clive Mathieson, Justin Bassi, Alex Robson, Philippa King, Sally Cray and Emily Zatschler).

Surveying the devastation left by the Tathra bushfire in NSW, March 2018.
Alex Ellinghausen / SMH

With Lucy, arriving at Buckingham Palace for CHOGM, 19 April 2018.
Commonwealth Heads of Government Meeting

Meeting with the Tickell family at Rylstone Farm in drought-stricken Charleville, Queensland, 5 June 2018.
Sahlan Hayes, official photographer to PM Turnbull

Serving Christmas lunch at the Wayside Chapel, Potts Point, in 2016.

A selfie with Year 6 students from St Catherine's in Sydney visiting Parliament House, Canberra, 31 May 2017.

At my final press conference as PM on 24 August 2018 in the prime minister's courtyard at Parliament House.
Alex Ellingausen / SMH

Right, Jack wasn't happy, and below, with Lucy, Daisy and Alice.
Left: Sean Davey / The Australian; below: Alex Ellingausen / SMH

The story of us: from the early days working together on the *Spycatcher* trial in 1986, to putting the finishing touches on my speech ahead of the Midwinter Ball in 2017.
Left: Peter Barnes / Newspix; right: Sahlan Hayes, official photographer to PM Turnbull

With the grandkids – Jack, Alice, Ronan and Isla – at Christmas 2018.

After the meetings in Queenstown, I flew on to Darwin and on the way I tried to get to the bottom of the Benson story. To my surprise I did. When I asked Luke Howarth how he came to be quoted, he said Michael Sukkar, Scott's assistant minister, had called him and said, 'The Treasurer and himself were annoyed about Anna Bligh's appointment … and that we should suggest we won't pass on company tax cuts to the banks.'[6]

Michael Sukkar confirmed this in writing and said he'd done this at Sasha Grebe's request: 'He explained that the Treasurer was very unhappy with the ABA and this was a way of sending them a message.'[7]

Sasha Grebe was Scott's trusted friend and senior media adviser. If he said something had the treasurer's imprimatur, nobody would doubt him for a moment. Sukkar said that Grebe had asked him to get a Queensland and a rural MP to talk to Benson and that was why he'd chosen Howarth and Pasin.

When I'd completed my enquiries I went back to Scott, also from the plane to Darwin. Scott denied Grebe was acting on his instructions and said he was devastated by his conduct. Grebe had no option but to resign or be terminated.[8] Scott and I had another very tough discussion. I told him that whether Grebe was acting on a frolic of his own (as Scott insisted) or at Scott's direction, as everybody had assumed, was beside the point. Scott and his office were simply not trusted to be discreet by colleagues who believed he would independently enlist his friends in the media to advance his own agenda. If Grebe was acting on his own, he did his boss, and the government, a lot of damage.

As we got down to the short strokes in negotiation with the senators on the ETP company tax cuts, Scott once again started sharing with the press gallery his desire to drop them. This time, no one could blame it on Sasha being out on a frolic of his own.

Mathias and I were at our wits' end as to how to manage Scott. As Mathias said, 'We have a Treasurer problem.' And the problem was one of trust.

> **Mathias Cormann:** People are looking for direction, they want to know that we have a plan and that we are committed to implement it … As I said yesterday on company tax cuts – having put them at the heart of our budget 8–9 weeks before an election – we can't put up the white flag less than a year after that election.

Malcolm Turnbull: No worries. He operates completely differently from us. We prefer to stay absolutely resolute on course until we decide to change. He wants to flag possible changes way in advance (why?) which reduces optionality and makes us look undecided. I can't work it out because it's so counter productive.[9]

A week later, despite Scott's briefing that we'd drop the tax cuts, we managed to get the first three years passed by the Senate. This meant that companies with turnover up to $50 million a year – fully half of the Australian private sector workforce is employed by this category of company – would see their tax come down first to 27.5 per cent and then by 2026–27 to 25 per cent. As usual, we had to do some deals with the crossbench to win their support – mostly committing to things we were planning to do anyway – but that was how to make the Senate work.

Mathias Cormann: Thank you Malcolm. For months I have been very focused on this particular fortnight and I'm so pleased that we got what we got. To lock in the first three years of our enterprise tax plan with a commitment to keep fighting for the remainder is just so good! Thank you so much for your Leadership. I have said it before I love working with you and your team! It is such a great privilege!!!

Malcolm Turnbull: It's a great privilege to work with you Mathias. To get this done with Scomo not helping and in fact undermining your effort and our objective was remarkable.[10]

I had no problem whatsoever with Scott's political pragmatism – he was, after all, a former state director of the party and looked at issues almost exclusively through a political prism. But working with him was difficult; so much of what we discussed or were thinking about found its way into the media. Many of my colleagues encouraged me, without success, to mistrust Scott and to see his briefings as malign, the calculated undermining and manoeuvring of a Machiavellian plotter.

And yet we enjoyed a close working relationship. Despite Mathias's begging me to be selective in what I told him, I continued to be open with Scott. He seemed to me to be my most likely successor, and as far as I could I preferred to work with him as a trusted partner.

Scott, like many politicians, wanted to keep himself constantly in the centre of things. That was the purpose, Mathias maintained, of Scott's constant stream of briefings, mostly to Simon Benson at News Corporation. Mathias thought this explained the bizarre episode on

Thursday 9 February 2017, when Scott appeared in the House waving a lump of coal around and urging members not to be 'afraid of coal'.

In the moment I was stunned and I thought it was a crazy stunt, although the look of horror on Pyne's face almost made it worthwhile. But while it damaged the government and Scott in the electorate at large, did it win him some kudos with the coal huggers on the right? It may have been more calculated than I thought at the time.

Mathias and I agreed we had to make sure Scott was a success. We had to recognise he was brittle emotionally and easily offended. At a practical level we both sought to ensure, as tactfully as possible, that he stayed out of negotiations with the Senate. He had a blustering manner that could easily be mistaken for bullying and was often counterproductive.

Having said that, most MPs were ineffective Senate negotiators. Over the 45th parliament, I gradually persuaded the ministers from the House to leave the Senate negotiations to the senators, and principally Mathias.

Labor's efforts to go after me because of my wealth hadn't been effective for them in 2015, but in the 2016 election they'd ramped it up. Now, given they'd won a lot of seats, they continued with it. Their object was to present the government as a bunch of hard-hearted capitalists led by 'Mr Harbourside Mansion' himself, utterly out of touch with the concerns of ordinary Australians. And so, whether it was pursuing free trade deals or cutting company tax, everything we did was put in that frame.

In return, I used to say that Shorten was so incompetent he couldn't even run a class war effectively, and there was a fair bit of truth in that. Take negative gearing. Shorten used to get worked up in question time and on occasion would lean across the table and say, 'Your mates in Wunulla Road won't be happy when we abolish negative gearing!'

There was a very respectable argument to abolish negative gearing and other countries had – including the United States. I have described how we considered abolishing it or dramatically curtailing it ourselves, in the lead-up to both the 2016 and 2017 budgets.

But as I delighted in pointing out, Labor's plan was hardly going to trouble my 'rich mates'. Labor's policy was to abolish net losses from rental property or business investments being offset against salaries or professional income. That would certainly prevent a wealthy barrister from negative gearing a rental property – as it would a police officer or a teacher. But it wouldn't prevent a wealthy person from offsetting their net rental losses against their substantial investment income from interest, dividends and rents.

It was always exceedingly personal, as on 8 February, when Shorten launched into me over the termination of some outdated welfare supplements to help fund our Child Care Benefit reforms, the most extensive in a generation, which substantially increased childcare support to over a million families. It was a reform any government could be proud of, not least because it was strictly means-tested – so much so that many families in my electorate of Wentworth on household incomes of over $350,000 lost the benefits they'd been previously receiving. I was no friend of middle-class welfare as I had demonstrated with my superannuation reforms the previous year.

'Mr Harbourside Mansion,' Shorten said, 'is seriously the most out-of-touch personality ever to hold this great office of prime minister: tough on pensioners, soft on banks, tax cuts for millionaires and payment cuts for Australian families,' and so on.

This transformation of Shorten – the right-wing, business-friendly, dealmaker, union leader – into an Antipodean version of Jeremy Corbyn was quite a sight and so I took the opportunity to give him some of his own back.

> We have just heard from that great sycophant of billionaires, the Leader of the Opposition. All the lectures he is trying to run are politics of envy. When he was a regular dinner guest at Raheen – always there with Dick Pratt, sucking up to Dick Pratt – did he knock back the Cristal? I do not think so. There was never a union leader in Melbourne that tucked his knees under more billionaires' tables than the Leader of the Opposition. He lapped it up – oh yes, he lapped it up! He was a social-climbing sycophant if ever there was one. There has never been a more sycophantic leader of the Labor Party than this one, and he comes here and poses as a tribune of the people. Harbourside mansions – he is yearning for one. He is yearning to get into Kirribilli House. Do you know why? Because somebody else pays for it: just like he loved Dick Pratt's Cristal ... Blowing hard in the House of Representatives, sucking hard in the living rooms of Melbourne.[11]

And so on for 10 minutes.

The backbench and our party members loved it – they would have liked me to rip into Shorten like that every day, but I knew that the aggression and theatrics that played well in the chamber during question time looked nasty, shouty and bad-mannered outside. Which is why I always tried to leaven the aggression with a touch of humour.

It was easy to see the line and length of Labor's attacks on me. First they said I was a rich bastard, gratefully appropriating the soubriquet of 'Mr Harbourside Mansion', actually given to me by Peta Credlin, and this plutocratic elitism of course led me to protect my rich mates. The media by and large enjoyed that too, and none more so than the Murdoch press which, of course, was owned by a family whose wealth exceeded mine by a hundredfold, at least. Second, they said that I was 'a disappointment' who had failed to deliver a republic, an emissions trading scheme and same-sex marriage because I was captured by the right wing of my party. At every opportunity, Labor would endeavour to wedge me against the right wing – Labor's opposition to a public vote on same-sex marriage being a good example. Of course, these attacks from the Labor Party were complemented by a contradictory line of attack from the right-wing media that I was in fact a Labor prime minister in disguise and a leftist. These critics pointed to my support for same-sex marriage and action on climate change, but in particular highlighted the 2016 reforms to superannuation and, indeed, the increase in the part pensions assets test – notwithstanding it had been one of Abbott's policies I'd inherited.

All of that was pretty obvious and, as a political script, largely wrote itself.

Shorten, however, was something of an enigma. He was always widely distrusted and disliked by many, if not most, Australians. He had been ahead of Abbott as preferred prime minister, but Abbott was toxically unpopular and seemed crazy and dangerous to many people. But even when my government was at its lowest ebb – tearing itself apart over same-sex marriage and energy policy, and with section 44 knocking over one minister after another – even then, I was always well ahead of Shorten as preferred prime minister.

But why? What was wrong with Shorten? Was it his track record as a union leader cutting deals with business, trading away members' penalty rates as he had? Was it his role in dispatching Kevin Rudd and then Julia Gillard? Those were the points we raised against him, and yet I don't believe that's the whole answer at all.

Sitting opposite Shorten for nearly three years, I came to the conclusion that he was unable to speak with conviction on anything. Often we'd both read prepared speeches on set-piece occasions. I'd go first and then

I'd listen to Bill. Many a time I felt his speech was better than mine, but he never did it justice. Occasionally, I wanted to jump up and say, 'Give me your speech and let me read it for you.' I used to feel sorry for his speechwriter, whom I imagined weeping in the office as Shorten mangled their sublime prose.

His critics would say he had no convictions. But I don't agree with that. He's a professional politician and very pragmatic. But he has showed great compassion during his career, whether it was representing the Beaconsfield miners or championing the NDIS. Somehow, perhaps, in his anxiety not to make a mistake he became so self-consciously contrived that he lost his authentic voice and so appeared to be 'shifty', as so many people said. Sometimes lifelong politicians spend so much time playing a role that they're not able to be themselves, to be authentic. Shorten, I concluded, was a better person than he appeared to be.

For our part, while particular policies and issues waxed and waned in their political salience, throughout my time in office, the Coalition's biggest liability was internal disunity. My internal enemies like Abbott and others could dial that up and down as they wished – supported by their friends in the right-wing media. On the other hand, Labor's big liability was Bill Shorten himself, and the closer we got to an election and the more likely he looked like winning, the bigger that liability would become.

Abbott was ramping up his internal opposition, producing an alternative election manifesto in February which naturally involved abolishing the RET and abandoning our Paris commitments as well as a long list of complaints, ranging from the decision to build the submarines in Adelaide (rather than Japan as he'd planned) to my decision not to live in Kirribilli House.

And at the same time the same-sex marriage issue was tearing up the party room.

I reflected on the state of play in my diary.

The media is very negative at the moment about me – lots of talk about the government being terminal, gleeful talk. Had a long chat with Paul Kelly about it and we agreed that what has happened is that the mainstream media has become disaggregated and marginalised by social media and an infinite range of additional channels on the internet. These new channels are invariably hysterical, extreme, often fact free and in order to maintain attention the main stream media has gone the same way, so that now even a broadsheet like The Australian *is full of prejudiced, extreme opinion because*

that is what drives traffic – clickbait – Fairfax and even the ABC have been
equally infected. So the media 'discourse' is now extreme and destructive –
everywhere and we see the consequence – Trump, Le Pen, Brexit etc. Kelly
observed that at News and especially on Sky the view is that I have to be
destroyed because I am too left wing – no better than Shorten – despite all the
evidence to the contrary. Indeed he says that on Sky they have lost all interest
in Australian politics as a struggle between Labor and the Coalition, rather
their fascination is between Turnbull the soft centrist and Tony Abbott the
muscular conservative (who let them down again and again). Crazy times.[12]

They were indeed. David Crowe gave me a similar account in October
2017 when he told me he was going to leave *The Australian*. I noted:

He says the culture there is so negative, so destructive he can't take it any more.
Says Boris [the editor, Paul Whittaker] is fixated on destroying the government
and me in particular, doesn't understand why, thinks it's because they believe
they have a following who click a lot and comment a lot on anything which
attacks me and praises Abbott. He sounded very depressed and despairing.[13]

It's worth pausing for a moment to reflect on my relationship with the
media in general and the Murdochs in particular.

Our media culture today is more debased than ever. Traditional curated
media has seen its business model smashed by the internet; Google and
Facebook in particular. And the crazy, fact-free rage of social media has
now infested what's left of the traditional, but still very influential, media.

I have dealt with all the leading media proprietors over many years –
current and departed, fathers and (almost invariably) sons. And the one
thing they prize above all else is power, and power over politicians. And so
they have always been ambivalent about me. My business background
and free market philosophy are appealing at one level, but my lack of
deference, and personal and financial independence are not. Media barons
and many other billionaires like politicians who are dependent on them.
Being a broke who cannot pay household bills does not necessarily endear
you to the electorate, but it does endear you to a wealthy individual who
wants to control you. Every time I heard a politician complain to wealthy
supporters how hard it was to get by on a parliamentary salary, I started to
wonder whether a federal ICAC maybe wasn't such a bad idea.

So, while it's easy to say that the Murdochs thought I was too liberal,
at the heart of it was the fact that they knew I was my own man, and had
seen that up close many times over 40 years. With Abbott they had a

deferential prime minister they thought they controlled. He and Credlin made cabinet decisions available to them before they were confirmed; they and their editors could rightly feel they had a hand in running the country. If more journalists who've worked at News Corporation were prepared publicly to tell the truth about the extent of their control and influence, even the most cynical Australians would be appalled. They leave their investigative courage at the office door and even after they've left, very few will talk.

I wasn't going to run my government in partnership with Rupert or Lachlan Murdoch or their editors, and I knew they'd resent that. The privileged access they'd had under Abbott wasn't going to continue under my leadership. Of course, their right-wing columnists needed little encouragement to attack me and my government, but employing Peta Credlin at Sky News and as a News Corp columnist was consciously giving a powerful platform to a vindictive, vengeful enemy of my government.

A similar assessment can be made of Alan Jones, Ray Hadley and their colleagues at 2GB – in their vanity and megalomania, Jones and Hadley berate and bully politicians who don't kowtow to them. They don't work for Murdoch, of course, but their agenda is the same – they want to have politicians in their pocket. And in too many cases they do.

My assumption with these characters was that in the final analysis they'd rather have me as PM than a Labor government and that more or less worked out in the 2016 election, although Credlin and her colleagues on Sky News were among our most relentless critics. But after that election, they increasingly bought into the Abbott madness of destroying the government to bring about its defeat so that Tony could come back as leader in opposition before returning to government in 2022.

I discussed this with Rupert and Lachlan on many occasions. Each time they tried to minimise the issue by saying Sky didn't have many viewers or *The Australian* many readers. True, but they had a lot of influence with Liberal branch members, as they knew. Jones became a lost cause, so much so that as we were to see at the end of 2017 and then in August 2018, he was actively trying to engineer the collapse of the government. News Corporation operates now like a political party. It attacks its enemies and protects its friends, as it did Abbott and as it is today protecting Morrison to the point of ignoring big issues of accountability. In the United States, Murdoch's Fox News' relationship with Trump is like that of the state-owned media of an authoritarian government.

With the rest of the media, I had few complaints other than about poor journalism. I had no issues with the ABC for bias (as so many of my colleagues did), but I did complain about their failure on occasion to check facts in the most rudimentary way. Their news department needs an editor.

It was Churchill, or perhaps Enoch Powell, who said the politician who complains about the media is like a sailor who complains about the sea. But the vicious personal partisanship of much of the media today is baffling to me. Why the Murdochs were so keen to see me gone, even at the risk of a Labor government, will remain a mystery to many. The most regular question I have had over the years from News Corp editors, executives and senior journalists is, 'Why do the Murdochs hate you?'

But then again, as we reflect on Rupert Murdoch's achievements, we have to ask, what good has he done apart from making himself and his family rich? His media have championed climate change denial relentlessly, and played a very influential role in the lack of climate action in our country and in the United States especially. So, over this last summer of 2019–20, his newspapers were filled with pages on the worst bushfires in our history facing pages mocking Greta Thunberg or anyone else concerned about climate change.

Murdoch's media are the fiercest defenders of Trump. And across the Atlantic, the keenest promoters of Brexit. They routinely exploit and encourage intolerance and racial and religious animosities. If America is a more divided, inward-turning nation today, Murdoch can claim plenty of the credit for making it so. What a legacy.

But returning to the events of 2017, at the heart of these crazy times was an element in the Coalition, both inside the parliament and in the party membership, that would rather Shorten was prime minister than me. They wanted to recapture the leadership of the Liberal Party for the right wing and thought the best way to do this was to go into opposition. They styled themselves conservatives but were more populist reactionaries in their politics, and like terrorists they were prepared to keep up their destructive destabilisation until they got what they wanted.

I wrote in my diary on 4 March:

I do have a sense of impending doom, but that is partly due to extreme exhaustion and not being well ... I wonder whether I shouldn't go to the GG and ask for a dissolution of the House of Reps? If the disunity in the party room continues, if Christensen moves to the cross bench as he keeps threatening to do and if Abbott continues his wrecking, should we not go to the polls and present the people with a clear choice – Turnbull or Shorten – and seek an outcome.

In the midst of this turbulent domestic environment, international issues were a welcome relief.

In February, Bibi Netanyahu visited Australia. It was the first time an Israeli prime minister had come to Australia. While Bibi was a polarising figure in his own country, he was well received in Sydney, and especially in my electorate of Wentworth. It has a large Jewish community to which, for all my life, I have been very close.

Bibi and I had first met in 2004 in Israel, but we had many good friends in common and an especially good connection in the former Israeli ambassador to Australia, Yuval Rotem, whose charm and political nous gave him an influence in Canberra way out of proportion to the size of the country he represented.

I'd always enjoyed Bibi's company. He's a tough, Machiavellian politician – he couldn't have survived as long as he has without being so. People criticise him for not having a long-term plan for peace, of just wanting to get from 'shabbat to shabbat'. But in fact he has a very clear-eyed view of the Middle East. His only goal is for Israel to survive and to prosper. And he'll do whatever deals, take whatever twists and turns that he needs, to achieve that.

We talked once about those in Europe and the USA who said the removal of Assad must be a condition of any settlement in Syria because he'd killed so many thousands of his own people.

Bibi replied, 'Malcolm, this is a tough neighbourhood. Killing your own is like buying the ticket to the ball game if you want to be a leader. Israel is the only country that's different. We have to be very pragmatic.'

His overwhelming focus was on Iran and its nuclear capability. We spoke many times while he was in Sydney, formally and informally, but consistently he described the Joint Comprehensive Plan of Action (JCPOA) as being a case of 'No bombs today, 100 bombs tomorrow'. Bibi had known Trump well for years, back from the days when Bibi was Israel's ambassador to the UN in the '80s, and his singular goal was to persuade Trump to pull out of the JCPOA. He succeeded in 2018 and, as well, Trump moved the US embassy to Jerusalem. From Bibi's point of view, Trump delivered.

From an economic perspective, there isn't a lot of trade between Australia and Israel, although it is growing. I'd drawn from Israel's example and experience when I launched our National Innovation and Science Agenda in 2015 and even appointed Saul Singer, the co-author of *Start-up Nation*, to the board of Innovation Australia. We'd also established one of our innovation landing pads in Tel Aviv as we sought to enhance the collaboration between Australian and Israeli entrepreneurs and technologists.

There was, however, a great deal more we could do together in the area of national security and intelligence. Bibi's ambition has always been to be a 'sixth eye' and he gave me a solemn undertaking that there'd never be any more Israeli espionage in Australia.

Naturally, I took this undertaking – given at the Bennelong restaurant, at dinner with Bibi's wife, Sara, and Lucy – with a grain of salt. Only time will tell. But we both instructed our intelligence agencies to increase their collaboration and some high-level visits followed. And it was thanks to a tip-off from the Israelis that in July 2017 our security agencies thwarted the plan to blow up an airliner, as previously mentioned.

While the intense discussions about Iran, Syria and Islamist terrorism were enthralling and consequential, the best part of Bibi's visit was when we went together to Central Synagogue and Moriah College, both in the heart of my own electorate. That day, Lucy and I were among friends – some, like David Gonski and David Lowy, whom I'd known for more than 50 years. There were my former business partners, like Russel Pillemer and his brothers, Gary Weiss and so many others. It was, as Frank Lowy would say, a very *heimisch* event. And to add to that, without the support of many of the people in the *shul* who joined the Liberal Party during the 2004 Wentworth preselection, I may never have got into parliament, let alone become prime minister.

For most Australians, the travails of Israel and the Middle East are as distant as they are confusing. But for so many in the Jewish community, Israel's struggle is their own and intimately tied to their own identity. At Moriah College, I talked about Australia as a multicultural nation and the contribution of Jewish Australians. I cited John Monash, our greatest general. The son of Jewish immigrants from Poland who went on to become an Australian general in the First World War, Monash was described by Montgomery himself as 'the best general on the Western Front'.

As I went to sit down, Bibi said to me on his way to the lectern, 'Monash: that's it. I'll work with that.'

He proceeded to speak about how Monash, the Jewish soldier, was the exception in modern times because, driven away from their land, Jews were stripped of the power to defend themselves. Calamity followed calamity, culminating in the greatest tragedy of all, the Holocaust.

But then returning to the land of Israel, Netanyahu explained, the Jewish people could once again fight to defend themselves.

'And the world wonders and they say, "What is this Israeli Army? Where did it come from?" It's been here all along but we had to come back to our state and rekindle that spirit … Be proud Jews. Stand up and be proud. Stand with Israel. Do this in Sydney and do it in Jerusalem and come this year to Jerusalem.'

It may be that this was a speech he'd given a thousand times, but the passion with which he delivered it registered with every student in the room and not one of them will forget it as long as they live.

The following night, President Joko Widodo and his wife, Iriana, joined us for dinner at our home. It was a busy week for international visits! The four of us had become good friends since our first meeting in Jakarta in 2015. We'd met at all the regular international conferences and spoke on the phone from time to time. My earlier conviction that Jokowi was one of the most important leaders in the world had only strengthened.

Our friendship was helped by several of Jokowi's colleagues – Tom Lembong, a key economic minister, and Retno Marsudi, his dynamic Foreign minister. Over the course of my prime ministership, Indonesia–Australia relations reached their closest level of understanding and cooperation. During dinner at our house on 25 February, Jokowi and I agreed on reducing Indonesia's tariff on Australian sugar as well as our reducing the tariff on Indonesian pesticides and we confirmed our commitment to an Indonesia–Australia free trade agreement – known as the IA-CEPA.[14] The Indonesian business community and government were very fond of regulation and protection, and only the president's leadership could push a deal through a thicket of vested interest.

Jokowi and I got to know each other well enough to talk frankly about the political currents in both Indonesia and Australia that were sceptical of the other. This was particularly prominent in Indonesia, where our 1999 military intervention at the request of the UN to support East Timor's independence was readily interpreted as part of a grand plan to break up Indonesia, with West Papua the next province to be split off. Jokowi knew this was paranoid stuff, but nonetheless wherever I could, I repeated our support for the territorial integrity of Indonesia, and frankly, we had no interest in any more bankrupt, let alone failed, states in our region.

The goodwill we built up together enabled us not only to get the IA-CEPA and a comprehensive strategic partnership agreed, but also considerable enhancements in our security cooperation. After all, our whole border protection tactic of turning back boats depended on the willingness of the Indonesians to cooperate.

As two couples enjoying each other's company, our shared interests – from business, to leading cities and countries, to life on the world stage – made for easy conversation. Infrastructure was a frequent topic, especially urban planning and mass transit. Our get-togethers were always relaxed and recorded in many selfies taken on our terrace in Sydney.

The second-last week of March 2017 saw the passage of our childcare reforms – steered through the Senate by Simon Birmingham. It wasn't popular with the more affluent members of the community, but it enabled us to ensure more parents were able to stay in the workforce after their children were born. A family on an average household income of $107,000 with two children in long-daycare three days a week would be nearly $2000 a year better off.

Labor (for reasons I couldn't fathom) opposed these reforms, but on any view they represented an increased investment in childcare that was better targeted at the low- and middle-income families who most needed government assistance. Given that increasing female participation in the workforce was an important part of our 'jobs and growth' economic plan, this was a much-needed reform.

I had a hectic international agenda in the first five months of 2017. Not only did we have visits from Indonesia, China, Sri Lanka, Afghanistan and Israel, I also visited PNG, New Zealand, Jakarta, Singapore, India, Iraq, the UAE, Afghanistan and the United States. At the same I was trying to wrangle the budget into shape, keep the party from splintering over same-sex marriage and, of course, fend off the continued guerilla warfare from Abbott and his supporters.

My diary entry of 9 April recorded the intense pace and pressure of the week just gone:

> *On Monday I was in a helicopter visiting Lismore, Murwillumbah and Eagleby flood victims, that evening had the Afghan President for a dinner and meeting, the next day the 4th was Cabinet and then a meeting with the Indigenous Advisory Council and the Digital Transformation committee of cabinet – then on Wednesday flew down to Devonport first thing to make an announcement about the Mersey hospital – a crazy idea of Abbott and Howard from 2007 that is costing us $730 million to get out of,[15] then an Anglicare Dinner that night in Sydney with a business visit to Gladesville and lots of meetings in between. Thursday saw me in Sydney for a meeting with the President of Nauru and then a long ERC and finally an address to 900 people for the Sydney Institute dinner, I thought the speech was a bit dry and economic but I guess you have to back in the tax cuts, in the course of that day managed Tony Nutt's resignation as federal director and had the Liberal Party Federal Executive the next morning with a dreary presentation from Andrew Robb of his election report – part of which involved saying much of our campaign had been boring (unlike him), on Friday Trump responded to the chemical attack Assad had made on the 4th with a strike on a Syrian airfield – I supported it strongly. Then off to PNG. Saturday finds us up on the Kokoda Track at Isurava meetings with [Prime Minister Peter] O'Neill in Port Moresby and now Sunday I am on my way to India having spent a pleasant hour with Alex, Yvonne and Isla in Singapore – and in the midst of all this sorting out the Budget, trying to rein in Scomo's ill-discipline and sort out a commitment to a solar alliance with Modi.*

'You have done business all over the world,' Narendra Modi asked me in Delhi, 'but not in India, why is that?'

I explained to Modi that I had always found doing business in India too hard – too much protection, too much regulation. 'The irony is that your business community speak English, your laws are in the common law tradition and you are a democracy, but still, authoritarian, communist China has to date been more open to foreign investment.'

Modi is acutely aware that 40 years ago China and India had a similar GDP per capita – now China's is five times larger. There are many explanations, but one stand-out is that China opened up to the world and India did not.

The two countries are profoundly different, but apart from their size they share a bitter experience of colonialism. Modi looks back to a golden age of Hindu India, before the Muslim invasion and domination, beginning in the 12th century and succeeded by the British in the 19th century; their Raj only ended with India's independence in 1947.

Modi and I rode the subway together to visit the Akshardham temple, where Modi took me on a Disneyland-like boat ride past one exhibit after another demonstrating how almost all of human civilisation's greatest advances, scientific and spiritual, had come from Hindu India.

So Modi is an economic reformer and moderniser, trying to drag his nation into the 21st century while navigating all the complexities of a vast democracy. At the same time he is a Hindu nationalist, and has been accused throughout his career of discriminating and inciting violence against India's 200 million Muslims. He is at once reaching into a future of advanced technology and science, and harking back to before the Muslim and then British invaders.

Australia's relationship with India has been underdone. Partly that is our fault, as we have been mesmerised by the rise and opportunity of China. But equally, India's protectionism has rebuffed our efforts to conclude a free trade agreement. When I went to India in April 2017, I had hopes that Modi could break the resistance we were meeting with the Indian trade bureaucracy. He was warm and encouraging, but the negotiations ultimately went nowhere. More recently India declined to participate in the Regional Comprehensive Economic Partnership (RCEP), a trade deal between ASEAN and other countries including China, Japan and Australia. RCEP is a more traditional and low-ambition trade deal compared, say, to the TPP. But even that was too much for India.

Modi and I had more success on the strategic front and regular strategic discussions are now being held by officials from Australia, India, Japan and the United States. This revival of the 'Quadrilateral' has not been welcomed in China, which was delighted when, in 2008, Kevin Rudd pulled out of it. India, as a consequence, has been cautious about rejoining, but with the re-election of the Coalition in 2019 I am confident that strategic cooperation will continue.

My visit to India was all too short and crowded with events. Wherever we went we were surrounded by reminders of empire and none more so than being escorted by mounted lancers as we drove into the Rashtrapati Bhavan, formerly the Viceroy's House. There, surrounded by a monument to British India, I was received by Modi, the charismatic leader of modern India. And as the bands played and we inspected the honour guard, across the front of the palace ran two monkeys. The larger one, as big as a boy, stopped and looked down at the spectacle for a moment, and then grabbing one of the potted fruit trees shook it vigorously in what I imagined was a protest at our human vanity.

While contemplating the fate of empires, ancient and modern, I was also trying to stay on top of the budget preparation and had brought Katrina di Marco to India with us to ensure that. Back home, and despite the departure of Sasha Grebe and the experience of 2016, when Scott's front-running of budget policies had cost us dearly, he was at it again. In 2017, Scott was determined to make housing affordability the centre of the budget. He wanted, once again, to abolish or severely restrict negative gearing and reduce the amount of the capital gains discount available to investors in residential property. He was also keen to allow first-home buyers to use their superannuation savings for a home deposit – an idea I'd sharply criticised back in 2015 as undermining the object of superannuation and only likely to fuel demand. My very strong view had always been that the unaffordability of housing was essentially a supply-side problem – because of planning restrictions, we weren't building enough dwellings.

Scott didn't fundamentally disagree with me on that, but he was convinced that politically we should be cracking down on negative gearing, for the same reasons he'd advocated in the lead-up to the 2016 budget.

We were planning to abandon some of the so-called zombie savings measures from Abbott's 2014 budget – some because we couldn't get them through the Senate; others, like the Medicare indexation freeze, because they were political poison.

Mathias Cormann, on the other hand, was adamantly opposed to any change to negative gearing, capital gains tax or allowing super contributions to be used for first-home owners' deposits. To some extent, his perspective was affected by the fact that the Perth property market had been in a slump since the end of the mining construction boom a few years before.

Between the three of us, there was a very robust argument. Scott claimed that the rising levels of housing debt were a threat to our

AAA rating and we needed to curb negative gearing to protect it. Mathias was shocked that we'd consider abolishing negative gearing less than a year after we'd won an election promising not to do so. He also thought the 'super for housing' idea was plain crazy: 'Scomo has wanted to bully us into a position on this for a very long time. He wanted to do it last year and irrespective of what we argued in the lead-up to the election he immediately revisited it after the election.'[16]

Scott's bullying started to rattle Cormann. The relationship between the two was becoming tense. Reasoning with Mathias, I reminded him of the history.

> So the threshold question is: do we have a political problem [with housing]? If you agree (I think it is clear we do) then what is the credible response? Bear in mind btw that the original motivation for looking at negative gearing was to raise revenue because Scomo had raised expectations about personal income tax cuts to be funded by GST – as we recall, me more than most, bringing us back to 50-50 ... Well there's the problem – why can't he have a calm discussion like you and I are able to have. Anyway think about the solution to the political problem.[17]

Scott's budget plans were finding their way into the press, just as they had in 2016, culminating in one of the more ludicrous *Daily Telegraph* front pages. On Good Friday, 14 April, Scott was portrayed pleading, 'Give me back my budget,' and there was a claim that I was 'emasculating' the treasurer by asking him to reach consensus with Mathias Cormann and Peter Dutton.[18] Scott was quoted dismissing the claims as 'complete rubbish' but few would imagine he, or someone close to him, hadn't had a hand in it.

That day, I messaged him. We needed to settle this appearance of division:

> The public briefing and discussion has to stop – I assume somebody was trying to 'defend' you with today's article but it is completely counter-productive for all concerned. And needless to say, we have a complex list of proposals on housing, the full detail of which we have only had for a few days and we should be able to discuss them and debate them in private without it being turned into a personality contest by the media. This latest outburst began with Benson's front page on Monday and rolled on from there, distracting from all the good things we are doing not least of which was my visit to India.[19] Anyway let's have a further

discussion about it, and frankly agree on how we move forward to the budget without further blow-ups like we have had this week.[20]

Nothing is more corrosive of good government than policy consideration being front-run in the media. I found it completely incomprehensible and couldn't see how anyone's interest or agenda was assisted. Scott adamantly denied any responsibility, but regrettably nobody believed him, especially after the Sasha Grebe incident in February.

He settled down after the media outbursts in April and we brought the budget together. We agreed not to touch negative gearing or capital gains tax – for essentially the same reasons we hadn't 12 months before. As previously mentioned, we did remove some deductions for property investors – like travel costs. And while Scott fought hard for it, I wouldn't agree to allow superannuation to be tapped for a housing deposit. I did agree to a new scheme to allow people to save up to $30,000 in a new First Home Super Saver Scheme that would have the tax advantages of super but would be additional to it.

The housing package in the budget also contained additional support for affordable housing and incentives for older Australians to downsize.

By the end of the process, I – and then Scott – had become persuaded that we needed to approach housing demand with a scalpel, not an axe. After discussions with the Reserve Bank and APRA, we concluded that the best way to cool down demand was with macroprudential controls that the regulators could calibrate depending on the circumstances and the locality. These controls included limiting the amount of interest-only loans that could be used for investment properties or the amount of the loan relative to valuation and so on. As it turned out, this was the right call – the tightening of credit did dampen investor demand and by 2018 that became a credit squeeze with the banking Royal Commission.

The two most controversial parts of the budget were an additional tax on the big banks of 0.06 per cent of their liabilities to raise about $1.5 billion a year, and adding 0.5 per cent to the Medicare levy for the purpose of fully funding the NDIS.

The bank tax was well received, except by the banks. When Scott responded to their concerns by saying, 'Cry me a river,'[21] he wasn't being very statesmanlike but he did speak for millions of Australians.

The increase in the Medicare levy was effectively an increase in income tax, but it too was well received – better than I'd expected. Coupled with our lifting the indexation freeze on the Medicare schedule (which meant doctors had less reason not to bulk-bill) and the Medicare Guarantee Fund, it demonstrated a commitment to ensuring vital government services were paid for. As it turned out, we couldn't get the increase in the levy through the Senate, and by 2018, thanks to record jobs growth and the tax revenues that followed, we concluded we didn't need it to fully fund the NDIS. But the fact that we'd proposed it showed how seriously we were committed to supporting people with disabilities. And in doing so it helped restore the public confidence in the government that had been so shaken in the 2014 budget.

We stuck with the company tax cut policy, for all the right reasons, and matched it with additional anti-avoidance legislation – as I said at the time, we believe in lower taxes but paying tax is compulsory. We also ensured that the overseas digital giants paid GST, whether it was Netflix subscriptions, Facebook and Google advertisements, or Amazon on the goods they sold in Australia.

Budgets are a time for reset, and we could have coupled it with the establishment of a Royal Commission into the banks, but decided, again for the best of reasons, not to do so.

Calls for a banking Royal Commission had been around for a long time and generally followed each new example of banks mistreating their customers. In my speech at the Westpac anniversary in 2016, I'd been critical of the banks' failures to put their customers first, and this had led to Shorten calling for a Royal Commission. This was seen as overreach in the media, but he'd tapped into a vein of populist anger. Having been involved in several Royal Commissions over the years, I believed they should only be called where there's a problem or an event that isn't well enough understood and needs to be investigated.

With the banks, we knew what the problem was. Essentially, there'd been a governance or cultural failure to act as fiduciaries for their customers – to put them first and in doing so apply the golden rule: do unto others as you would have them do unto you.

My judgement was that a Royal Commission would be unlikely to discover anything new – the regulators, including ASIC, had been very active. I was concerned that we needed to take action immediately – and we had done so from early 2016 – and if we called a Royal Commission many, including the banks, would say that we should wait until it had reported.

The first thing we did was institutionalise regular accountability of the banks to the parliament by requesting the House Economics Committee – very well chaired by David Coleman – to inquire into the banks on a regular basis. The new member for Chisholm, Julia Banks, first made her parliamentary name on that committee and deployed all of her business and legal experience to great effect. There's no substitute for bank chief executives having to front up to a parliamentary committee twice a year – as they now do and, I imagine, will do forever. As I said then, Royal Commissions come and go, but the oversight provided by the parliament will continue.

We also established a new Banking Executive Accountability Regime, of which Scott was very proud and which enabled APRA to oversight the behaviour of senior bank executives to ensure that they upheld high standards of integrity in the management of their banks. Shortly after my Westpac anniversary speech, we'd asked Professor Ian Ramsay to examine the avenues for Australians to resolve disputes with banks, and as a consequence Kelly O'Dwyer delivered a new one-stop shop for consumers, an Australian Financial Complaints Authority, that would deliver swift, affordable justice.

ASIC's resources and powers were strengthened with additional funding, and we introduced protections for corporate whistleblowers, including those in accounting firms who called out tax offences. And, of course, we imposed the Major Bank Levy in the 2017 budget.

In other words, rather than establishing a Royal Commission and waiting several years for it to recommend reforms like this, we got on with them. The calculus concerning a banking Royal Commission was solely a political one. At my request PM&C had prepared a draft terms of reference for a Royal Commission in early 2017, just in case. While Kelly O'Dwyer was an early internal advocate, Scott was the last to be persuaded. He seemed to feel a Royal Commission would be seen as a humiliating backdown for himself.

However, by November the political pressure to establish a Royal Commission had become even more intense. It had become a means of punishing the banks, of delivering them a cathartic flogging. Once we had lost our majority on the floor of the House with both Barnaby Joyce and John Alexander facing by-elections because of section 44 ineligibility, we were unable to resist those on the backbench who were proposing to cross the floor and establish a parliamentary inquiry. It was looking chaotic.

Scott and Kelly had done a lot of work with the banks to get their agreement to a compensation scheme for those who'd been mistreated by their banks but couldn't afford to bring action through the courts. Those plans, however, had to be shelved when we finally decided to let our arms be twisted and establish the Royal Commission.

Under former High Court Judge Ken Hayne, it ran for the year that it was allotted, found not much new other than more examples of misconduct that were well known to the regulators like ASIC, and made recommendations which either confirmed or built upon the reforms we'd already put in place. It did, however, provide 12 months of headlines about bankers being bad, about regulators being complacent, and about private wealth advisers neglecting their clients' best interests.

Several, like NAB chairman Ken Henry, performed poorly in the witness box, which resulted in savage attacks in the media. The lawyers did well out of it. On the other hand the commission did succeed in raising the profile of the banks' failures and the scale of their problems. Whether it worked as a forensic exercise is questionable, but as a show trial it certainly did. The general consensus would be that the Royal Commission has been 'a good thing' and 'an overdue wake-up call'. But we can't deny that among the big losers have been the Australian public, because one of the consequences of the commission was that the banks became even more risk averse and lending terms for consumers, investors and small business became tighter than ever. If banks feel that they'll be blamed if their borrowers' businesses fail, then they'll naturally lend less.

As I acknowledged at the time, I made a political mistake in not calling the Royal Commission earlier. Frankly, I should have thrown the banks to the wolves in April 2016. Shorten, the cynical populist, had been right on the politics but my principled, overly legal approach was politically wrong. The other thing I overlooked was the strength of the frenzied, public desire for a cathartic show trial and flogging of bankers and the impact of that driving home in the minds of banks and their customers of the need for change.

But as we will see in the chapters that follow, despite all the political dramas and fighting on two fronts against enemies external and internal, we managed to achieve so much: reducing company tax for most firms, reforming personal income tax, legalising same-sex marriage, and securing the TPP trade deal without the USA, not to speak of standing up to our great and powerful friends in Washington and Beijing.

CHAPTER 39

Same-sex marriage

I have always been an advocate for marriage.

If you ask Lucy, perhaps a little too enthusiastically: I first asked her to marry me on our second date. It wasn't long after we'd met in January 1978; she was 19 and I was 23. I'd met Lucy in her father's chambers. I was writing a profile of him for *The Bulletin* and just as well the great man kept me waiting, chatting to his beautiful daughter, who was noting up his law reports during the holidays.

Struck by the young Miss Hughes, I sent her some flowers, but when they arrived at the QC's chambers she'd gone.

'That Malcolm Turnbull is a very charming young man,' Tom announced as he came home that evening. Lucy's parents had not long before divorced and she was living with her dad in a terrace house in Darlinghurst. 'He so appreciated my giving him an interview he sent me these flowers.'

Sceptical, Lucy inspected the flowers. The news that the flowers were for her, not for him, was a rocky start to my relationship with my future father-in-law.

Lucy and I were married two years later.

Now, we both had divorced parents, and about half of all marriages nowadays do end in divorce. Still, the two of us were determined back in 1980 to stick together and we have. And we're firmly of the view that ours would be a happier, stronger society if more people were married and fewer divorced. Humans are social animals and we are best when we're with people we love and who love us.

And so both of us have always believed that gay and lesbian couples deserve the same support and recognition as we've received.

The journey from only a few decades ago of society criminalising homosexual conduct and now legally recognising same-sex marriages in so many countries has been as swift as it has been overdue.

The same-sex marriage issue progressed in Australia rather differently than it did in other countries. Here the focus was initially on practical reforms to remove discrimination against gay and lesbian couples. In the last days of Howard's government there was quite a stormy cabinet debate about treating same-sex couples equally in terms of their rights under Commonwealth superannuation schemes.

I was in favour. Joe Hockey backed me up. Abbott, Andrews and Minchin were all strongly against. Finally I told them a story.

> My friend Tony Doherty often conducts the six pm Sunday Mass at St Mary's. Recently, a rather frail old lady was leaving the cathedral and as he bade her good night she asked, 'Father, is it true that the Archbishop [George Pell] said, "God made Adam and Eve, not Adam and Steve?"' Tony wearily confirmed that he had, indeed, said that. 'Very well,' the old lady continued. 'Will you ask him for me, if God didn't make Adam and Steve, who did?' And with that question hanging in the air she tottered off into the dusk.

There was a moment's silence. Howard put his palms down on the table. 'That's it. Discussion is over. Malcolm, you come with me and we will settle it.' And so we did; the proposal was adopted.

Later when Rudd became PM, I was pleased, as opposition leader in 2009, to support the removal of a long list of discriminations against same-sex couples. But the issue of marriage remained.

Same-sex marriage, and homosexuality generally, had been a divisive issue within the Liberal Party for quite some time. John Howard had chosen – in 2004 and before I entered the parliament – to amend the Marriage Act to state specifically that marriage was only between a man and a woman. This was purportedly in order to avoid having to recognise same-sex marriages contracted overseas, but the truth was Howard saw it as a wedge because it split the Labor Party's socially conservative working-class voters from their socially liberal inner-city voters. Right-wing unions, most notably the Shop, Distributive and Allied Employees Association (SDA), were vehemently opposed whereas most of the other unions were supportive.

However, when the law was changed in 2004, while there wasn't yet strong enough support in the community or the parliament to legalise same-sex marriage, Howard's move to amend the Marriage Act and make opposition to same-sex marriage party policy offended a longstanding tradition of the Liberal Party.

From its inception, the Liberal Party has recognised the right of a backbencher to cross the floor on any issue without the automatic expulsion a Labor member would face if they did the same thing. Equally, the Liberal Party has always treated issues around marriage and private morality as 'free votes', which means that even ministers can vote as their conscience suits. And, of course, from time to time prime ministers have chosen to declare a particular issue is such a conscience issue, as Howard did with the republic, where it is easier to manage the party room.

The 2004 amendment to the Marriage Act should have been a free vote as almost all previous marriage law legislation had been, but it wasn't. That had created a very unhappy precedent.

By 2011, a private members' bill was on the order paper to legalise same-sex marriage. Prime Minister Gillard, most implausibly, said she believed marriage should only be between men and women. I used to say at the time that both Gillard and Abbott were wrong on this issue, but at least he was sincerely wrong.

Labor said that their members would be allowed a free vote on the bill and so the question was: what would we do? At a shadow cabinet meeting on 12 December 2011, we discussed the matter at some length. Abbott, who was opposition leader, insisted there should be no change to our policy and no free vote, pointing out we'd gone to the 2010 election with support for traditional marriage only as our policy. As the debate progressed, only a handful of us – myself, Brandis, Hockey and Pyne – supported a free vote on the bill. Joe and I had been unable to get to Canberra for the meeting – our plane was cancelled – and so participated by telephone. Towards the end of the discussion, when it was obvious our cause was lost, I repeated the argument for a free vote, saying, 'Gay marriage isn't a threat to any of our marriages. If you want to campaign against threats to marriage, campaign against adultery.'

There was a long silence, interrupted by Joe who said, 'I think the line's dropped out.'

Abbott replied, 'No, Joe, we're still here. Just examining our consciences.'[1]

Without a free vote on our side, the bill couldn't muster a majority in the House and, to be honest, may not have done so anyway. There weren't a large number on our side who'd vote for same-sex marriage at that time, even if given every opportunity to do so. And there was a solid contingent on the Labor side who opposed it.

The issue wasn't going away and I decided to consider it in a detailed and thoughtful way in a speech I gave the following year – an annual lecture at Southern Cross University in honour of Michael Kirby. Instead of arguing for legalisation of same-sex marriage on the ground of equality (which was self-evident) I looked at the arguments against it. It was clear that they were all grounded in hatred, or at least condemnation, of homosexuality.

> I am utterly unpersuaded by the proposition that my marriage to Lucy is undermined by two gay men or two lesbians setting up house down the road, whether it is called a marriage or not.
>
> Regrettably this aspect of the debate is dripping with the worst sort of hypocrisy and the deepest pools are found at the feet of the most sanctimonious.
>
> Let us be honest with each other. The threat to marriage is not the gays. It is a lack of loving commitment – whether it is found in the form of neglect, indifference, cruelty or adultery, to name just a few manifestations of the loveless desert in which too many marriages come to grief.[2]

Early in 2013, I spoke to Abbott again about the issue and why we should go to the election this year with a commitment to have a free vote.

> *He said to me that at the appropriate time he would say that without changing his personal position he would allow the decision of a conscience vote to be determined by the party room following the election. He said that in his view if 20 per cent of the party room wanted a conscience vote then he wouldn't stand in its way. Well let's see if he sticks with that. I reminded him of Wyatt Roy's wise remark that for people under 30 your position on this issue essentially determines if you are a civilised person or not.[3]*

By the time of the 2013 election, Rudd was back and was promising to allow a free vote on same-sex marriage in the first hundred days of the new parliament. I pressed Abbott to agree to the same timeline, but he simply didn't want to talk about or canvass the issue in any way, and scoffed at Rudd even thinking same-sex marriage was an important issue.

I wrote back to Abbott:

It's his research that drives his interest. It is a big vote motivator among the u40s and especially among u30s. My point is that by allowing a free vote the timing is in the hands of the parliament. The politics of this has dramatically changed given the developments in UK and NZ [where it had been legalised] – and already more than 1/3 of Americans live in states where ssm is legal.[4]

Following our election win in 2013, my expectation was that one way or the other we'd have a free vote on same-sex marriage; it seemed the only way to deal with the matter. While the religious right, including Abbott, wanted to keep kicking the issue off into the long grass, it was plain that its resolution couldn't be postponed indefinitely.

However, as the Abbott government's electoral prospects rapidly declined, especially after the disastrous 2014 budget, Abbott had even less interest in having the marriage issue resolved. The issue was poisonously divisive. And it was, as I had said, dripping with hypocrisy. Many of the staunchest advocates of 'traditional marriage' were the keenest practitioners of traditional adultery. And the same moralisers who'd scathingly denounce homosexuals and rage about how same-sex marriage would destroy the Australian family, would never dream of denouncing adultery or desertion, let alone address the underlying causes of family breakdown.

Much of the opposition to same-sex marriage was simply political. Many on the right knew that the issue galvanised their base. Churches were good recruiting grounds for branch stackers and one of the best lines to get a congregation to sign up was 'ensure the Liberals don't legalise gay marriage'. Michael Sukkar, Kevin Andrews and Alan Tudge, among others, were assiduous branch stackers in Victoria, famously recruiting Mormons to eventually shift control of the Liberal Party in Australia's most liberal state to the hard right.[5]

But in the wider community, opinion had been changing. Between 2005 and 2015, according to data from the Household, Income and Labour Dynamics in Australia (HILDA) survey, the percentage of Australians who strongly supported same-sex marriage rose from 19.2 per cent to 46.3 per cent. That percentage continued to rise in 2016 to 62 per cent, according to an Essential poll.[6]

Shortly after the Irish conducted their May 2015 referendum in which a majority had voted for same-sex marriage, Abbott had been asked whether he'd favour a public vote on the issue in Australia. To my relief, he'd rejected that idea (correctly) as being inconsistent with our parliamentary traditions. So, when I went to see him on 7 July 2015, I was trying to persuade him to allow a free vote in the parliament and I didn't expect that we'd be discussing the merits of a public vote.

> *Tony is very anxious about [same-sex marriage], much more than I thought he was. He says he fears that if there is a free vote he will be seen by the right, his base, to have betrayed them. I pointed out that the best political outcome was for the issue to be resolved following a free vote and that it would be very damaging for us to go to the next election with Labor being able to say if you want SSM you have to kick the Libs out. He agrees with that but goes back to worrying about his betrayal of the right. He hates the idea of gay marriage and speaks about it with an intensity and bitterness that I think his sister would find very confronting. He raised the idea of a plebiscite, I said that it was a bad idea, but it could only work if it was absolutely locked in that if the people voted Yes, the law would change. He agreed with that and we discussed passing a bill which provided for SSM but wouldn't go into force until there had been a national Yes vote in a plebiscite. He thought voting on it could only be voluntary and we discussed attendance versus postal/electronic ballots. I told him that I thought compulsory would have more legitimacy but would favour the No vote. He still seemed to prefer voluntary, which is odd. I pointed out that a plebiscite would likely be popular – everyone likes to have a say – but it was at odds with all our parliamentary traditions. I told him that if he offered the public a vote, it would be near impossible not to proceed with it. We should, I said, deal with this issue as we have indicated we would, with a free vote in the Parliament.[7]*

Dozens of private members' bills to legalise same-sex marriage had been presented to the parliament over the years.[8] The one Warren Entsch – with cross-party support – had been getting ready in 2015 assumed there'd be a free vote on the matter.

As described in chapter 24, after the chaotic party room discussion about same-sex marriage on 11 August 2015, Abbott decreed that there'd be no free vote in this parliament but that in the next parliament the issue would be put to the people in a popular vote.

Abbott was convinced the views of the conservatives mirrored mainstream Australia. He and his backers, like Kevin Andrews, Eric Abetz and the younger generation such as Michael Sukkar and Zed Seselja, saw a same-sex marriage vote as the opportunity to demonstrate they understood the public mood better than the moderates; they firmly believed middle Australia was like them and would vote down same-sex marriage, and perhaps most importantly it would show moderates like me, Christopher Pyne, Marise Payne, Simon Birmingham, George Brandis and Kelly O'Dwyer that we were out of touch with the views of regular Australians.

More strategically, those on the right of the party saw a public vote as an ideal opportunity to motivate and recruit as members people with strong anti-same-sex-marriage views. A number of more moderate Liberals – especially from Victoria, such as Scott Ryan and Tim Wilson – were keenly aware of this. Tim Wilson wrote to me later in the year after I'd become prime minister:

> Australia has always been denied a grassroots opportunity to organize on a social conservative cause. By going to a plebiscite we are gifting the perfect environment for the lunar right to develop the entire infrastructure for an ongoing campaign on deeply conservative causes into the future ... they'll be able to build lists of potentially tens (if not hundreds) of thousands of self-identified people who oppose a change in the law. That of course means lists for people who can then be pushed to join political parties into the future. That has a potentially very concerning impact on the direction of the Liberal Party and for your Prime Ministership if it is harnessed.[9]

It was that shambolic meeting of 11 August, precipitated by the same-sex marriage debate, that had led to the spill and my becoming prime minister. And on the very day I was sworn in, I'd pledged in a written agreement with the Nationals – the Coalition Agreement – to hold a public vote on marriage equality.

As I'd said to Abbott back in July, once you've committed to give the public a say on an issue, it's very hard to take it back. And moreover, the plebiscite policy had, however chaotic its origin, gone through cabinet and party room and had been announced as government policy. We couldn't afford any more broken promises.

At this stage, Labor was keeping their options open on a plebiscite. Only two years before, Shorten had told the Australian Christian Lobby

(ACL), 'I would rather that the people of Australia could make their view clear on this than leaving this issue to 150 people.'[10]

Most of my colleagues in favour of marriage equality wanted to get it done before the election. Pyne eloquently summed up the reason for moving quickly:

> My hunch is we get it off the agenda. At the next election it will wreck the election. Every [ultraconservative] Christian group will be going crazy causing trouble. Since I have stated my position I have had four emails from my seat complaining. The thing is no one but mad people cares … If you do it after you have the same problem as doing it during the election. And you have the prospect of Scomo smelling the leadership chair again. We should get it out of the way in December when the political year is over anyway.[11]

In the final event, we didn't have time before the election to legislate for a plebiscite and hold it, so in the course of the 2016 election campaign I simply committed to give every Australian their say on the issue and to campaign for a 'yes' vote.

Interestingly, quite a few of my colleagues who supported same-sex marriage also grew to find they quite liked the idea of a plebiscite. Pyne explained to me that he had a large and very conservative Greek community in his electorate of Sturt. They were vehemently opposed to same-sex marriage, so the plebiscite policy allowed him to argue that he'd have no more say on the issue than any other Australian – therefore no reason to vote against him at the election!

Nevertheless, the same-sex marriage issue dogged us during the 2016 campaign and was used against us both by the progressives on the left and the social conservatives on the right. Pauline Hanson, for example, campaigned strongly against it and used Wyatt Roy's support for same-sex marriage to justify preferencing against him in Longman, an electorate that was both much older and more conservative than Wyatt. He lost the seat.

After we won the election, I hoped Bill Shorten would support the plebiscite and we could get on with it.

However, Shorten knew that the longer the issue dragged on, the more it would divide my side of politics. It was a thorn in my side and he was determined to keep it there as long as he could and give it a thorough twist for good measure.

In an effort to answer the criticism that a plebiscite would cost too much money, Warren Entsch had raised with Nick Xenophon the idea of a postal vote as a means of containing the cost. As it happened, the cost savings weren't material. Moreover, the Senate crossbench wasn't of a mind to support a public vote of any kind.

I introduced the legislation to enable the plebiscite on 14 September 2016, making it very clear that Lucy and I would be voting 'yes'.

> We do not believe that if same-sex couples are allowed to have their union recognised as marriage that will undermine our relationship of long standing … If there was something we could do to make families happier it would be a wonderful thing. We know that the breakdown of the family unit is one of the great causes of hardship, of poverty, of so many of our social ills. So we are a government – and I am sure the opposition joins with us on this – we are a parliament committed to marriage, and we are committed to people supporting each other and sticking together, working hard, supporting their children and their families and enabling their dreams. And that is why I support same-sex marriage.

I pointed out that we had a clear election mandate to hold the plebiscite and we were determined to keep our promise. Then I turned to the arguments against us.

> Firstly, [a plebiscite] is not part of our traditional parliamentary process. That is certainly true, and that is why many conservatives would say it is too much of a novelty – it is too much of an innovation, if you like. Of course, we are in the age of innovation, as I have said before, so that should not be a disqualification. The other one is the cost – and that is substantial – but then you have to ask yourself: what price democracy? So those are two arguments that are valid. We have dealt with them, we have considered them and we have decided to proceed to the plebiscite.

Another argument put forward was that the plebiscite would lead to an upsurge in anti-gay sentiment. It would give the anti-same-sex-marriage movement the opportunity to mobilise, which could (as Tim Wilson believed) not only change the face of the Liberal Party, but also lead to divisive and hurtful views about homosexuality being given mainstream attention and re-normalised.

I recognised this was a possibility, and it was one I was keen to avoid at almost any cost. Yet the party had committed to the plebiscite – we'd taken it to the previous election – and while the opponents of marriage equality believed there was a deeply conservative silent majority waiting to rise up and stop the homosexuals tying the knot, I had no doubt that the nation would vote 'yes'. Every national poll on the issue supported me in this belief.

Fundamentally, I believed the Australian people could be trusted to have a civil conversation on the topic. We'd taken the plebiscite as a commitment to the election and, as a party, we'd honour that by respecting the intelligence, civility and will of the Australian people. I said:

> If ever there was an issue to be put to a plebiscite, this is one that can be and should be, because it is a very straightforward question. It does not have the same kind of implications – far-reaching, often unknowable implications – of, for example, voting on Brexit, as the British did recently.
>
> The real reason, I think, many people oppose the plebiscite is because they believe that if there were to be a free vote in the parliament same-sex marriage would be supported, and so they do not want to run the risk of the Australian people giving them the wrong answer. For our part, we put our faith in the Australian people and we know that their answer, whether it is yes or no, will be the right answer, because it is theirs.[12]

Once passed by the House, the bill went to the Senate, where it was defeated on 7 November, 33 votes to 29. Labor, the Greens, NXT and Derryn Hinch all voted to block the bill.

Shorten was delighted. He hoped that now the internal pressure from supporters of marriage equality to allow a free vote would blow up my party room and bring an end to my leadership. And of course my internal opponents on the right were also keenly anticipating the opportunity.

While Labor's motives for opposing the plebiscite were entirely political, they adopted the argument expressed by many in the LGBTIQ community (which I'd addressed in the House): that the debate around a plebiscite would bring out so much angry and uncivil language that it would be psychologically damaging to gay and lesbian people.

Since 2015, the Liberal Party room had become more supportive of same-sex marriage, although it was still a long way from a majority.

But we now had in the House of Representatives three openly gay men: Trent Zimmerman, elected to replace Joe Hockey in December 2015, as well as Tim Wilson and Trevor Evans. Added to them from the Senate was Dean Smith, a WA senator who'd always run with the right in a factional sense but felt that he could now safely support same-sex marriage.

If ever there was an example of the Liberal Party being a broad church, this was it. On one end of the pew we had out and proud gay men who wanted to marry their partners. On the other end we had the religious right, who believed homosexuality was a satanic abomination, some of them claiming legalising same-sex marriage would lead inexorably to polygamy and, indeed, people being able to marry animals.

I'd learned from my first time as leader that my primary responsibility was to keep the party together and that meant I needed to have strong allies from the conservative wing. The two leading figures on the right were Peter Dutton and Mathias Cormann. Each of them was widely distrusted by their colleagues, many of whom warned me constantly against trusting them. But if I took to heart every warning I received of a colleague being untrustworthy I wouldn't be able to work with any of them.

Cormann and Dutton had come to the view, as indeed had Barnaby Joyce, that the legalisation of same-sex marriage was inevitable. The pair was also confident a plebiscite would record a strong 'yes' vote. They didn't share the optimism of the religious right campaigners like Lyle Shelton from the ACL who believed Australians would vote 'no'.

But if we couldn't get a plebiscite agreed to by parliament, what could we do? The best option was to persuade the party room that since the plebiscite had been blocked, we should now get on and have a free vote.

In order to prepare for a free vote, Mathias worked quietly with Penny Wong, the Labor Senate leader. They established a select committee to consider the draft amendment bill George Brandis had earlier circulated, and thereby give the various religious groups and other conservatives the ability to register their concerns about protecting religious freedom. In particular, churches and church schools didn't want to be obliged by anti-discrimination legislation to make church halls available for same-sex wedding receptions. They also wanted it to be clear that ministers of religion shouldn't be obliged to solemnise a marriage that was inconsistent with their faith.

Working together on what Mathias described as a 'black op', our goal was to secure a high degree of consensus between right and left on the language of a marriage amendment bill. After all, the more rational, and sincere, opponents of same-sex marriage had to consider the risk that same-sex marriage would be legalised. It was in their interests to keep any amendments as least bad as possible from their point of view.

It startled Mathias to learn George Brandis was proposing to make Eric Abetz the chairman of the committee. Abetz was a die-in-the-ditch opponent of same-sex marriage, a fully paid-up Turnbull hater and Abbott's staunchest ally, together with Kevin Andrews. Mathias was panicked.

> I don't know what George is thinking I'm sorry. But I have no reason to raise this with him. I believe you must tell him no to Eric and instruct that it must be [David] Fawcett … Does this make sense? As part of my very secret consultations [with Labor] I said that I would make sure it would be Fawcett and not someone like Eric [Abetz] or [Cory] Bernardi. I would have thought this is a no brainer if we want this to work.[13]

I ensured Fawcett was the chair, and the committee did a good job. It didn't finally settle on a new amendment bill but it enabled us to flush out most of the concerns from the religious right and ensure that they were all heard. And it made a number of suggestions to improve the amendment bill including, most importantly, a provision that established a new category of marriage celebrant: a religious marriage celebrant who would, unlike other celebrants, be able to decline to solemnise a marriage if it conflicted with their religious beliefs.

My own view was that this was a price well worth paying. In principle, I couldn't see why we wouldn't simply provide that any celebrant could decline to solemnise a marriage for any reason; after all, it's hard to see why a couple would want a celebrant who disapproved of their marriage.

However, while Mathias and I were keeping our own counsel, the more enthusiastic supporters of same-sex marriage within our party were less discreet. On 4 February 2017 the Fairfax press reported that a group of them opposed the plebiscite and were planning to press ahead for a free vote as soon as the Senate select committee's report was tabled.

One of the more depressing aspects of parliament is that almost everybody wants to write themselves into the story, and many leaks are merely an effort in self-promotion. On this occasion, all it did was alert our internal opponents. They then counter-briefed, promising to blow the government up if we backed away from our commitment to a public vote.

It was becoming increasingly obvious that the party room wouldn't support a free vote. There began to develop support for what Mathias described as a 'controlled explosion', where enough Liberals crossed the floor in (a deniably authorised) defiance of government policy to vote for and pass a marriage amendment bill. It would be an embarrassing defeat for the government but at least the issue would be resolved.

I didn't like that idea – 'controlled' and 'explosion' didn't seem to go together in this volatile context. Among the moderates, Pyne and Brandis were proposing we get 30 or more signatures to petition a reconsideration of the policy, take it to the party room and have a secret ballot. Pyne thought we might get the result we wanted but wasn't sure, and nobody was doing the numbers.

There was one possible solution – a postal ballot. At the time of the plebiscite legislation being debated in the Senate and recognising the concerns some people had about how nasty a same-sex marriage plebiscite could be, I'd canvassed this option with Nick Xenophon and other crossbenchers. The big problem with a postal vote of course is that it couldn't be compulsory; younger people might be the least likely to vote, so it could result in a low turnout and hence low legitimacy or – from my point of view, worse still – a 'no' vote because, so it was contended, the most motivated and likely to vote were the opponents.

I needed to keep Barnaby and the Nats close to me on this issue and so I worked through it with Barnaby over dinner on 19 March. I wrote up a joint assessment of the issue while I was with him, mostly in his words. While we hadn't agreed yet on a solution, he was definitely focused on a constructive approach. And that was progress.

While we hope to keep Labor out of office for a long time – they will win an election one day. And when they do, they will pass a gay marriage law in what – the first, second or third week? And assuming we can stay in office for a long time, how long do we think we can stop our own people crossing the floor? Let's get real. Labor has 69 votes in the house, they can count on 4 cross benchers so they would need three of our people to cross the floor. We have three openly gay men on our side not to speak of a number of others who are strongly supportive – we have kept them from crossing the floor to support a Labor bill, but for how much longer?

So a fundamental question is this: if we accept gay marriage is going to happen, do we want it to be on our terms or Labor's? A gay marriage law passed during our government would provide extensive protections for religious ministers, celebrants and others. Labor's would not. Would we rather simply own up and say 'Our side of politics is so divided on this, this is one issue with which we can't deal.' Now Barnaby and I would vote differently in a plebiscite – but we are both agreed this is a long way from being a high priority issue. In fact every minute we talk about it, we are going backwards. We want to talk about energy, about jobs, about investment in infrastructure, about trade, about creating the economic growth Australians need. So what do we do about the plebiscite?

There is not one cabinet minister with whom we have discussed this who doesn't think we need to get the matter resolved before the election. Apparently nobody wants to have the plebiscite at the time of the next election – the easiest solution – let alone go to the next election with our existing policy. So now is the time to have a frank discussion. We don't need positioning. We need clear solutions and we need to settle on one which the whole cabinet can publicly support.[14]

As was so often the case, just when we were starting to get things lined up on this issue, we were derailed by an indiscretion. And it was a big one. We'd had a federal council meeting in Sydney on 23 June, ending with a big dinner at which David Petraeus was the guest speaker. Afterwards, as is tradition, both the moderate and right factions of the Liberal Party repair to a comfortable bar or restaurant. The moderate faction event is known as the Black Hand dinner – for reasons I've never discovered.

I didn't attend any of these events and sensibly went home to bed. Christopher Pyne kicked on and, presumably well lubricated, gave a speech in which he rejoiced that the moderates were now firmly in charge of the government. 'Friends, we are in the winner's circle but we have to deliver a couple of things and of those we've got to deliver before too long is marriage equality in this country. We're going to get it. I think it might even be sooner than everyone thinks. And your friends in Canberra are working on that outcome.'

Somebody recorded the remarks – in the era of the smartphone, you have to assume that will always happen – and they found their way into the News Corp tabloids the following Monday. Leaving aside the stupidity of rubbing salt into the wounds of the right, Christopher was understood to be hinting at a move away from the plebiscite policy and towards a free vote, which of course many, if not most, of the moderates supported.

Andrew Bolt, another fully paid-up Turnbull hater, wrote, 'Pyne's prediction could detonate an explosion that destroys the party and Turnbull's leadership.'[15]

Christopher Pyne is so clever and amusing, it's hard to be cross with him for long, but he had tried my patience this time.

> Christopher this issue of you and Abbott and SSM has dominated the news today. I can't describe how damaging it has been. One thing you need to do in addition to hosing it down is to stress that I run a very consultative government; all members of the cabinet and the party from all wings of the party are involved and contribute. You have to eat every word you uttered basically – elegantly of course. The triumphalism you expressed is so corrosive and of course so wrong.[16]

Christopher proceeded to ring virtually every colleague and offer an apology and over some time the uproar subsided. But as he conceded the following day, he had, unwittingly, killed the prospect of moving away from the plebiscite.[17]

In early 2017, Dutton and Cormann had both come around to the idea of holding a postal ballot and it began to gather some currency in right-wing circles. I was careful not to give it any public support at all, indeed to gently pour cold water on it whenever I could and at the same time allow the supporters of same-sex marriage to continue to raise the prospect of crossing the floor. This began to convince the conservatives that a postal ballot was better than an Entsch-led floor crossing and, if Turnbull didn't like a postal ballot, maybe it was a good idea. Pyne's indiscretion at the Black Hand, while thoroughly welcome to the right, had increased their paranoia that there could be a moderate floor crossing being planned to deliver marriage equality without a popular vote.

This reasoning worked to swing around Lyle Shelton, the head of the ACL. Dutton said to me on 16 July: 'I've spoken with Lyle.

Their preference is a full plebiscite, but essentially their view is Entsch et al will cross the floor so that makes the postal plebiscite the best option in the circumstances.'[18]

In July the LNP state council actually passed a motion calling for a postal ballot. It was developing very good conservative credentials.

Peter's job was to present a credible, conservative face for the postal ballot solution. My job was to remain sceptical and stick with the existing policy, even though it carried with it the risk of Mathias's 'controlled explosion' occurring.

Both Cormann and Dutton remained in regular contact with me and even more regular contact with my closest advisers, Sally Cray and David Bold. Sally had built up a particularly strong relationship with both Mathias and Peter – they'd speak almost every day, as would I, to gauge the mood of the right as we worked through the same-sex marriage issues and others too.

There were a number of attempts to find a compromise on the issue. Tim Wilson worked with religious groups and conservative colleagues on a bill that provided for two classes of marriage: civil and religious. It was well intentioned but too complex; we had to find a way to make the straightforward stand for equality, for fairness, that I knew was not only right but that a majority of Australians wanted.

By July and the LNP state council resolution, we had enough conservative support for a postal ballot locked in to mean that if we could hold it, we'd be able to resolve the issue. But how do you do that without legislation?

George Brandis was strongly opposed to a plebiscite; he felt it was legally risky to do it without legislation and had advice from the solicitor-general to that effect. In fact, Stephen Donaghue had advised that there was a 'high risk' that the High Court would find that legislative authority was needed before the government could spend funds to conduct the plebiscite. At a cabinet meeting in Perth on 1 August, George argued with great feeling that we should go back to the party room and insist on a free vote.

We were all moved by George's stirring address to the cabinet. Legalising same-sex marriage was of enormous importance to him. But at that particular moment his passion for the reform and his almost equally passionate opposition to a public vote was becoming an obstacle for me in achieving our goal.

Privately, I was growing in confidence that we could make a postal plebiscite work. There was promise, I believed, in using the ABS. Moreover, I had to do everything I could to keep the party together, and the only way to do that was to try to deliver a popular vote.

If we were blocked by the High Court, that would be the time to have the hard conversation about a free vote because only the most destructive part of the right seriously wanted to go to the election without this being resolved. Or so I thought. As subsequent events showed, I consistently underestimated the self-destructive agenda of my internal opponents.

Daniel Ward was the smart lawyer in George's office who picked up a clue in an earlier advice on plebiscites that suggested that a voluntary postal survey asking people their views on same-sex marriage could be constitutional under the parliament's census and statistics power in the constitution and thus be conducted by the ABS. I seized on that and, working closely with Mathias on the one hand and George on the other, I at least became satisfied that we had a reasonable chance of surviving the inevitable High Court challenge.

With some encouragement, the solicitor-general looked more carefully at the ABS option and concluded, with many reservations, on 3 August that 'there are reasonable arguments that it would be valid for the Government to proceed'. That was about as enthusiastic an endorsement as we were likely to get from our very measured and cautious law officer.

Scott Ryan, the special minister of state and responsible for electoral matters, was strongly opposed. Scott, now the president of the Senate, is a constitutional conservative and he deplored the whole plebiscite idea. To him, changing the Marriage Act was a job for parliament, not some experiment in direct democracy. He was quite right of course, but our operating environment was an imperfect one.

As fate would have it, Ryan fell ill and had to take some time away from his ministerial duties. I made Mathias acting special minister of state, and he now took over the process.

In the first week of August in 2017, George and Mathias presented a joint submission to cabinet for a postal survey. It was approved by cabinet and was ready to go to a special Liberal party room meeting that I called for 4 pm on 7 August 2017. The press gallery were salivating at this prospect as they remembered the infamous six-hour meeting chaired by Abbott, which contributed to his demise. I was determined my government would be different.

Sally and I spent the weekend of 5–6 August talking to colleagues and at length with Peter and Mathias about the various views of MPs. Sally was putting a spreadsheet together so we knew exactly where each MP sat on the issue and which conservative MPs Peter and Mathias had to work on. Together we made dozens and dozens of calls. In some ways, I conducted my own party room meeting one on one with colleagues that weekend so they'd vented before getting into the party room proper.

At 4 pm on Sunday 6 August, Sally and David Bold came to my home and we discussed where we were at and what I would say.

My message to the party room on the Monday morning was simple. As my speaking notes recall:

> We are not the party to break promises – as the Australian people would rightly punish us for that. We made this promise and we intend to honour it. It is a matter of trust. Australians are sick of people saying one thing before an election and doing the opposite after. Everyone remembers Julia Gillard – 'there will be no carbon tax under a government that I lead.' And what happened? Labor broke that promise, they broke the trust of the Australian people. We are better than that. We keep our promises. How else can we expect Australians to have faith in us or the democratic process? Now the Parliament will not back the plebiscite that we promised. But we promised to give Australians a say in this issue and that is what we will deliver.

I was confident this message would resonate because colleagues had been so critical about Abbott breaking promises when they urged me to take over as prime minister.

Dean Smith was scathing about the postal vote. He described plebiscites as 'corrosive', as 'a stain on our democracy'. Together with Trent Zimmerman and Tim Wilson, he wanted us to drop the plebiscite policy altogether. Hardly anyone else in the party room agreed with them, however.

The plan I proposed was to put our plebiscite bill back into the Senate, so if Labor didn't like a voluntary postal ballot they could vote for our original compulsory attendance ballot. If it failed in the Senate, as we knew it would, then we'd proceed with the postal ballot.

Almost all the speakers agreed with the plan. Abbott was opposed of course, saying a postal ballot would be seen as 'Mickey Mouse' and arguing we had no need to deal with the issue swiftly, but rather fairly and that would take more time. Like Shorten, he wanted the issue to continue to destabilise the party, the government and my leadership.

A number of strong supporters of marriage equality, like David Coleman, Sarah Henderson and Julia Banks, spoke in favour of the postal ballot pointing out they had gone to an election promising to give people a say and we should honour our promise.

After just two hours, the party room overwhelmingly agreed to adopt a postal plebiscite, 'an ABS statistical analysis', and Mathias and I made the announcement after the joint party room the next day. It would be a voluntary postal survey. The survey would be posted out on 12 September and papers had to be returned by 7 November for a result to be announced a week later, on 15 November. That would give parliament the final sitting fortnight of 2017 to amend the legislation.

The 16 million postal surveys would contain the simple question: Should the law be changed to allow same-sex couples to marry?

It was a painless and methodical meeting and said a lot for the consultative approach I had with colleagues and the way Sally coordinated my consultation with the party room. The most divisive issue in the Coalition party room had sailed through painlessly, in contrast with Abbott's approach. But I wasn't naive enough to expect that would be the end of it.

Andrew Wilkie, the independent MP from Hobart, together with several marriage equality groups, opposed the postal vote and had challenged the constitutional validity of the survey.[19] I recalled the solicitor-general's rather tepid endorsement of our plan and shuddered a little. We couldn't afford for this to fail. But on 7 September the court upheld the survey 7–0.

The decision was handed down during question time.

'The Leader of the Opposition must be relieved that the promise he gave to the Australian Christian Lobby in 2013 is now being delivered by the Coalition,' I said, gently mocking Shorten's earlier promise of a public vote.

I reminded the House that Lucy and I would be voting 'yes' and encouraging others to vote 'yes', but my critics on the left – appalled that the Liberal Party was on the verge of delivering marriage equality –

now tried to make an issue of how much campaigning I would do for the 'yes' vote.

I did all the campaigning I thought would help the 'yes' vote, which didn't involve going to the often rowdy vote 'yes' rallies being held around the country. I didn't think they helped the cause; indeed some were counterproductive – we wanted middle Australia to be reassured that voting 'yes' wasn't just fair but safe. Consulting closely with the Yes campaigners, and in particular Tom Snow and Andrew Bragg, it was clear that there were two messages – it was fair; we ought to get on with it. So, Lucy and I did a 20-second video together in which we delivered those messages and then walked to a postbox and posted our ballots! It went viral and was exactly the right tone and message.

I should observe here that many people who were scathing about the postal survey said that young people don't write letters and don't know what a letterbox is. Our daughter, Daisy, droll schoolteacher of teenagers, observed, 'Really? Young people have very good eyesight and letterboxes are red and generally on street corners. I think the young people will find them!'

And they not only found the letterboxes, a record number of young people enrolled to vote in the lead-up to the ballot.

In order to get the vote 'yes' message across, my office had devised a plan to dramatically increase FM radio appearances, knowing that those stations only wanted to talk to me about same-sex marriage. It gave me the opportunity to campaign on a daily basis.

The media made that the focus of numerous stories. Then Fairfax journalist Amy Remeikis wrote: 'A shift in Prime Minister Malcolm Turnbull's media strategy has seen him participate in almost as many FM radio station interviews in the past month as he has the whole year, giving the Coalition leader a chance to drop in a little of the "Malcolm" along with the stuffier "Prime Minister".'[20]

Phil Coorey even lowered the tone of the *Australian Financial Review* to run a column on my FM radio appearances. He pointed out that, to non-political listeners, the fact I supported same-sex marriage was actually news to them. 'In an interview with 2Day FM, presenters Em Rusciano and Harley Breen were stoked when Turnbull said he and wife Lucy would be voting yes. "Oh, wow," said Rusciano. "That's great to hear, Malcolm," said Breen. Subsequently, the radio station reported the "revelation" as news that day.'[21]

And so it was. Most mornings and afternoons of the 'campaign', I'd appear on a different FM radio station urging Australians of all ages to vote a resounding 'yes!' for marriage equality. Most of the conservatives, glued to 2GB and Sky News, were oblivious to my daily campaigning.

More publicly, I did launch the NSW Liberals and Nationals for Yes campaign with Daisy and gave a strong speech backing the move. Some in the party weren't happy I did this, particularly Dutton and Cormann, but they understood how important the issue was to me personally.

The conservatives in the cabinet who were notionally voting 'no' by and large didn't campaign at all. Dutton, Cormann and Morrison all took plenty of criticism for doing that. From a political point of view, the main 'no' advocates were Matt Canavan (who was temporarily out of cabinet because of the citizenship eligibility crisis), Connie Fierravanti-Wells, Zed Seselja, Michael Sukkar and of course Tony Abbott.

The Yes campaign were thrilled by Abbott's efforts. Every time he was in the news urging people to vote 'no', the 'yes' vote went up on their nightly track. Even so, he had a moment of sympathy when one unruly critic hit him in Tasmania, a political assault that was condemned as thoroughly un-Australian. Canavan was particularly shrill in his efforts for the 'no' case, channelling Abbott's rhetoric from the republican debates of the '90s and saying politicians couldn't be trusted. I gently encouraged him to drop that line – he was after all a politician himself.[22] Sadly, for many LGBTIQ people the campaign proved to be a very painful experience. One young friend of our family had just come out as a lesbian to the friends she'd made from a conservative church community. The political was personal and she felt anyone who was voting 'no' was disrespecting her.

We felt for her and supported her during the anxious weeks while the postal vote was returned. And I deplored some of the hateful language used by the 'no' case. One benefit of the vote being a postal one, of course, was that there were no polling stations so no particular locations where conflicts could occur, as they may well have in a conventional attendance ballot.

My commitment, and the government's commitment, was that if there was a majority 'yes' vote, we'd have a free vote on a private members' bill to legalise same-sex marriage. I'd never set a threshold for the participation. If three people vote, I used to say – me, Lucy and Tony Abbott – we were still going to legalise same-sex marriage! But nobody knew what percentage would vote. This was a completely voluntary vote and people could just throw the ballot paper in the bin together with their junk mail.

As the ballots were returned Mathias kept me updated and, to our delight, the response rate exceeded all our hopes. After 10 days nearly 50 per cent of the ballots had been returned and at the end of the process, nearly 13 million ballots came back, 79.5 per cent – it was incredible. I was so proud of our country: so many people cared so much that they'd voted. All those claims about Australians being apathetic and only interested in 'bread and butter' issues were wrong: 80 per cent wasn't far short of the participation rate in a federal election, where voting is compulsory. It was way ahead of voting rates in countries where voting is voluntary.

But the best news was yet to come and it was, like the High Court decision, on a sitting day, 15 November. Mathias and I watched the announcement from my office.

The ABS chief statistician, David Kalisch, took his time delivering the big number. He knew that everyone would listen to everything he said before he announced the result, and nothing he said afterwards.

At live sites across the nation, thousands of Australians collectively held their breath as Kalisch said, 'For the national result: yes responses 7,817,247, representing 61.6 per cent of clear responses ... No responses 4,873,987, representing 38.4 per cent of clear responses.'

Yes! Finally, Australia had said 'yes' to marriage equality!

I immediately logged on to the website to look at how my electorate of Wentworth voted. I was confident we'd have had one of the strongest 'yes' votes. And we did, with 80.8 per cent of residents who voted in Wentworth voting 'yes'. In fact, no state or territory voted 'no' and 133 out of 150 electorates voted 'yes', with the only large 'no' votes in the Western suburbs of Sydney.

I messaged Mathias:

Malcolm Turnbull: My dear friend, the postal survey is one of the most remarkable political events we will ever see. Nobody could have ever imagined such a high participation.

Mathias Cormann: And 75% Yes in Warringah. Not that you should ever point that out. Let people find that for themselves.

> **Malcolm Turnbull:** And so much for the proposition that 'they all hate gay marriage in Queensland'.
>
> **Mathias Cormann:** Ha! Yes.[23]

Mathias's joy was not because gays could marry. He claimed to be opposed to it, although I think that was largely a pose for his conservative supporters. For him, it was just a barnacle we had to get off the ship of state. Dutton took much the same view, as indeed Barnaby had when we discussed it back in March.

But whatever my collaborators' motivation, the good news was we had got it done. Well not quite, we now had to legislate and I was determined to act on the will of the nation – as quickly as possible. Same-sex couples had waited long enough!

It was a week in which only the Senate was sitting and we all agreed the bill be put straight to the Senate to deal with it.

In the media, the bill was known as the Dean Smith bill (Dean Smith made sure the media called it this) although many internally referred to it as the Fawcett bill as Fawcett was the chair of the committee. And of course George's team called it the Brandis bill. Success has many fathers! We knew it should have been called the Cormann–Wong bill, because its origin was the Senate committee they quietly collaborated to set up earlier in the year with precisely this purpose.

The opponents of same-sex marriage were shocked by the result. After the announcement I flew back to Sydney with Lucy and Scott Morrison. Scott was utterly deflated; he couldn't believe his own electorate had voted 'yes'. 'I don't feel this is the country I grew up in any more,' he complained.

A lot of them felt like that, and now started to try to frustrate the quick passage of the legislation by proposing additional and elaborate protections for 'religious freedom', which ranged from allowing religious schools to discriminate against gay teachers and students, to ensuring bakers could refuse to bake cakes for gay weddings. The longer we left it, the more this type of opposition would flare up and there was a powerful constituency in the party and in the churches trying to hold us up.

Senator James Paterson, a Liberal from Victoria, was persuaded by the 'no' campaign to propose his own bill to legalise same-sex marriage, with a whole range of provisions to entrench continued discrimination against gays. There were plenty of other outbreaks from the right along the way. Many amendments were proposed, most were defeated, and with strong discipline on our side, the bill passed the Senate on 29 November by 43 votes to 12 and moved to the House of Representatives.

It was also a free vote in the House of Representatives and it sailed through; just four MPs voted 'no'. Even Dutton voted 'yes' on the floor because the nation and his electorate had said 'yes' and he respected their views. Abbott and Morrison, such staunch opponents of same-sex marriage, didn't vote in the chamber – although both their electorates had voted 'yes', Abbott's with a big majority of 75 per cent.

And so it was, on 7 December 2017, a few minutes before 6 pm, the Australian parliament finally gave same-sex couples the legal right to marry.

I was so happy; this was a great and long-overdue reform. 'We've voted today for equality, for love, it's time for more marriages, more commitment, more love, more respect. This is Australia: fair, diverse, loving and filled with respect.'[24]

What a moment for our parliament and the nation. Almost all MPs standing on one side of the House to vote 'yes'! MPs from every party embracing each other and saying 'yes' to love and 'yes' to marriage.

Love and mutual respect. The very foundation of our society. Tim Wilson even proposed to his partner, Ryan Bolger, on the floor of parliament!

With the benefit of hindsight, I'm convinced the postal ballot turned out for the best. It wasn't my first choice, not by a long way, but for those who felt alienated or unloved because of their sexual orientation this was an overwhelming vote of confidence. Undoubtedly, it was painful for many people, but the truth is that we can't avoid debates of this kind – as we have seen in 2019 over Israel Folau's social media post that homosexuals will go to hell. What was important about the 2017 marriage equality vote was that the result was such an overwhelming and emphatic assurance for LGBTIQ Australians. The nation wrapped its arms around same-sex couples and said, 'We love you and we respect you.'

The next day, 8 December 2017, together with George Brandis, I went out to Government House, where together with Governor-General Sir Peter Cosgrove, we met as the Executive Council for His Excellency to give the royal assent. We were joined by Ben Bartlett from my office and Liam Brennan from George's – two of our long-term staffers who'd worked tirelessly for many years advocating this reform.

Same-sex marriage was now legal, overseas same-sex marriages were recognised in Australia from midnight that day and the first same-sex marriages could be held in Australia within 30 days.

This was a great reform, for equality and fairness but also for love over hate. We'd faced formidable obstacles within my own party from those vehemently opposed to same-sex marriage but also from Labor, which saw the issue as one which they could use to split my party and bring down the government. But dodging and ducking past all these obstacles, we managed to get it done. And amidst all of the other reforms and achievements of my government it will be the most enduring.

Thirty-nine years after I first asked Lucy to marry me, 38 years after a sceptical vicar agreed to marry us, all couples – no matter their sexuality – now had the chance to marry just like Lucy and I had done.

CHAPTER 40

Giving a Gonski

There was nothing special about the press conference advertised for 2 May 2017 at the Commonwealth Parliament Offices in Sydney. The prime minister and the Education minister – the Labor MPs and journalists would have shrugged: some pre-budget announcement or another, more of the background noise leading into the budget.

But who was that third guy with Turnbull and Birmingham? Jeez … It's David Gonski!

David Gonski is my old school friend, debating partner and neighbour. We've known each other, literally, for more than 50 years. When we were at school, we used to joke about our respective destinies; David asked me to appoint him chief justice when I became prime minister. But among the many grandiose visions we had for ourselves, they didn't include David becoming a secular saint and political icon of the education unions and the left of the Labor Party.

This would have all seemed most improbable, especially as David, like me, gave up the law after a decade or so and went into investment banking. By 2011, he was one of Australia's leading capitalists and a director of banks and many other blue chip companies.

In 2010, Julia Gillard had recruited David to chair a review of federal school funding, and his report at the end of 2011 had observed that school funding was inconsistent and often inequitable. He recommended that schools should be funded, by the federal and state governments, consistently and on the basis of need.

Gillard used this report as intellectual ballast for her campaign to get more financial resources into schools. She said that Labor would deliver

'Gonski'; her supporters proclaimed that they 'gave a Gonski' and, of course, that my side of politics did not.

I found this mildly entertaining, as I observed in the House during the debate on Labor's Australian Education Bill in 2013: 'It is a matter of some concern to me that my old friend David Gonski has become not simply a leading business figure and a great lawyer, but also now a proper noun. Indeed on occasions he has become a verb. It is a very disturbing development for a gentleman of his standing. Whether he is going to be decapitalised as the next step in his grammatical progression is yet to be seen.'[1]

While Abbott, reflexively, and Shadow Education Minister Pyne, inexplicably, were highly critical of Gonski's recommendations, I thought they were perfectly sensible – a penetrating glimpse of the obvious, really, and consistent with my own values. Of course funding should be needs-based. That's why I supported means-tested scholarships at my – and David's – old school, Sydney Grammar. More than 30 years ago, when I first made some serious money, I endowed an additional means-tested scholarship in memory of my father, who'd struggled to send me there.

While getting funding right was of vital importance, equally so was the need to ensure that we improved the educational outcomes from our schools. As I said in the same debate: 'In Australia, educational spending per student has already risen, in real terms, over 40 per cent in the past decade; yet according to the OECD PISA [Programme for International Student Assessment] rankings, our outcomes have declined from among the strongest in the world in 2000 to still fairly good in 2009 but well behind a leading group of five school systems, four of them in East Asia.' The most recent PISA scores in 2019 show that deterioration in relative performance has continued.

The position we should have taken was to welcome the Gonski principle but critique Labor for its failure to follow up with education reforms, such as paying teachers on performance not just seniority, which research demonstrated would improve student outcomes.

But no – Gonski became synonymous with 'caring more for and spending more on schools'. And as far as the public were concerned, Labor gave a Gonski and we didn't.

Labor, knowing they were going to lose the 2013 election, had inflated school funding in their final budget to a point no government could reasonably afford. Why? Because it would give them a free attack when we had to rein in the spending projections. Abbott had recklessly promised 'no cuts to health, no cuts to education', despite knowing Labor's spending commitments were unaffordable.

And in Abbott's 2014 budget, the Labor Gonski funding was continued only until the end of 2017, after which it would revert to Consumer Price Index (CPI) increases that were, in fact, less than the annual increase in teachers' salaries alone. It simply added to the political catastrophe of that budget.

The political hardheads will always say that the Liberals can never win on education or on health. The best we can do is neutralise the issue, and more realistically mitigate the damage and offset with our strengths of economic management and national security.

In the frantic months after I became prime minister, we didn't have the time to find a long-term resolution to the Gonski issue. So, in the 2016 budget, we simply increased the indexation from CPI (about 2 per cent) to 3.56 per cent (based on the growth in teachers' wages) for 2018 and subsequent years. This reduced the fury of our critics somewhat but wasn't the long-term solution we needed.

In October 2016, Simon Birmingham presented the government with a characteristically keen analysis of the problem. We were in a real jam: the problem of spending more but getting worse student outcomes remained. If we were to continue with Labor's funding plans, we'd need an additional, unaffordable, $8.2 billion over the next four years. Without passing new legislation we could, by administrative decisions, save $5.9 billion of that, but almost all of that cut would come out of government schools – the ones who needed the money the most.

Worse still, the Labor model wasn't just unaffordable from a budgetary point of view, it was also inequitable. In the frenzy of the Gillard government, both Julia and, as it happened, Bill Shorten had been running around the country cutting deals with one school system after another – be they government, Catholic or independent. The result was 27 different deals. There was no consistency. The same sort of school with the same needs would get dramatically different federal funding per student depending on which state it was in, whether it was Catholic or independent.

Gonski's Schooling Resource Standard (SRS) – an estimate of how much total public funding a school needed to meet the educational needs of its students – was then $9951 for a primary student and $13,087 for a secondary student. Additional loadings applied for low socioeconomic circumstances, disability, Indigeneity, remote location and lack of English skills.

Historically, the states and territories had funded their own schools, but over many years the Commonwealth had provided a growing, but minority, share of the costs. On the other hand, for non-government schools (mostly in the Catholic system), the federal government picked up most of the costs and the states and territories made much smaller contributions. The Commonwealth payments in respect of non-government schools were meant to be discounted from the SRS to account for the capacity of the school community to pay – so a posh private school in my electorate of Wentworth would get less government funding than a poor Catholic school with a largely migrant student body on the outskirts of Sydney or Melbourne.

However, intimidated especially by the Catholic schools lobby, the Labor Party in 2012 guaranteed no school would see funding (or its historic growth in funding) reduced. This meant that in the case of some of the more affluent Catholic schools, it would take 150 years of slow transition before their funding was genuinely, equitably needs-based.

We were caught. We couldn't reduce the spending on schools education without legislation other than by penalising the schools that needed the funding the most. And to get legislation passed, we'd need the support of the Senate crossbench, which meant that we'd need a compelling and genuinely fair new deal for school funding.

So, when I stood up with David Gonski to announce our new school funding policy, I hadn't just won David's endorsement, I'd ensured that all of those 'I give a Gonski' posters, banners, corflutes, T-shirts and hats were heading to the recycling bin. Because we didn't just 'give a Gonski', we had his support: he was standing right next to me as we announced our new school funding policy. And, for the first time, it was genuinely national, consistent and needs-based.

What's more, David had agreed to head a new review, Gonski 2.0, to examine the big question of how we'd ensure the increasing funding would actually result in better student outcomes. How could we get Australian kids back where they belonged, at the front of the pack?

Labor no longer had the exclusive rights to 'Gonski'. Most importantly, Labor couldn't credibly criticise any of the work he completed because, after all, they'd made him the voice of education policy beyond reproach and he was backing our plan.

The day after the announcement, Lucy and I were flying to New York to meet with Trump so I had the time to write about it in my diary.

So for more than six months now, a year more likely, I have been talking to David Gonski about what we would need to do to get his endorsement. After all the Labor 'Gonski spending' was not what he had recommended, they had done 27 different deals many of them sweetheart deals and there was no consistency. The classic was the deal done with the ACT Catholic schools where the Schooling Resource Standard agreed was not based on Canberra (an affluent area) but the average of the Catholic system across Australia.

Anyway over many ERCs and Cabinets we have worked on a new plan which would involve spending more money – but how much more? Nothing could equal the lavish promises, unfunded, of Labor of course. In any event in the last few weeks I managed to get to the point with David where he agreed he would endorse our policy if we spent an extra $2 billion in the first four years, which we agreed to do. The upshot was that over the decade we would spend another $18.6 billion.

Labor and the Greens have invested millions in their 'I give a Gonski' campaigns and so when we announced our new policy yesterday with David the shock was seismic. The reception was overwhelmingly positive, although the Catholics are starting to stir up concern – largely I think because they feel that the way we are allocating money per school will reduce their ability to move money around within their system. That's not true of course, but it will make it more obvious when they are doing so.

How do I feel about it? I think, I hope, that we are doing some good here. That we are getting another toxic, rancid Abbott monkey off our back and of course the second part of the exercise, Gonski 2.0, is to examine how the money should best be spent in order to maximise the educational value from our investment.

Generally it would be fair to say however that I left Sydney completely shattered and utterly exhausted, head spinning. Part of the problem is that almost every day now Abbott pops up in the media to attack the government either directly or indirectly, the opposition to him of course in the party gets stronger and stronger as he is seen to be more destructive and he is now calling publicly to be made a cabinet minister, although I would say that the view within the cabinet is more resistant to that than ever. After all, he would just leak and undermine. He did that to his own cabinet and one of the things I have demonstrated in my cabinet is that we can operate in confidence, with the exception of some frontrunning by colleagues – especially Scomo – or actual mistakes, like the guy in Porter's office who yesterday mistakenly emailed to SBS the Social Services budget measures!!! [Mark] Simkin managed to buy them off into not publishing it by giving them an exclusive interview with me on the Trump visit before I left.[2]

I'd always felt that the focus of the education debate should be on outcomes, which came from quality teaching, rather than simply funding. So much of our education policy was catering to the industrial objectives of the teachers' unions rather than the needs of the students.

The unions had successfully pressed for smaller class sizes which naturally meant more teachers. But all the evidence showed that additional resources were better used to increase teachers' pay and, in particular, ensure they improved their qualifications and training through their careers. Beyond that, and more controversially, many argued that teachers' pay should be based on teaching outcomes (as it is in most occupations), although others said that would undermine the team-based support systems in most schools. Either way, my own experience had confirmed teacher quality was the key. Brilliant, charismatic teachers had set me up for the rest of my life. We needed more of them.

I was reminded of an experience some years before when a new school, Reddam House, was established in my electorate by a private company from South Africa. A headmistress of one of the old established schools in the area was incensed. These South Africans, she told me with indignation, were actually talking to students at her school, finding out who the best teachers were and then offering them a job. 'And at a higher salary! What will I do?'

'Pay them more to keep them,' I suggested.

'That's not how we do it here,' she told me firmly.

I gently suggested that she'd have to get used to competition if she wanted to retain her best teachers.

The truth is we don't pay teachers enough and we don't value their work enough. But that means we need to invest more in their training and be prepared to pay classroom teachers more to improve their qualifications, collaborate with their colleagues and above all keep teaching, so that they don't have to move out into administration or another profession altogether in order to get a better salary. And if you want a reality check, if you're standing at the school gate for afternoon pick-up, the intricacies of school funding are of much less interest in the parents' discussion than who's teaching their kids and who are the best teachers.

Madonna Morton, who was my education adviser when I first became prime minister, had been part of Gonski's team when he'd prepared his report for Gillard. It was Madonna who first suggested we get David to do another review, not about funding but about how we could get better outcomes from the funding. This second stage had, in fact, been recommended by Gonski in his first report but never acted on.

In the course of our discussions about school funding and other areas of economic reform, I asked David if he would undertake a second review. 'Malcolm,' David replied, 'as you know I love you dearly. But' – I could sense this was going to be expensive – 'if you want to get people behind a new approach that delivers the better results we all want, you'll have to put more money on the table.'

And so began a negotiation between David, myself and Simon Birmingham. While Simon was initially sceptical about the value of Gonski 2.0, I became increasingly convinced that if we were going to break out of this 'You don't give a Gonski' paradigm we found ourselves framed in, we'd have to craft a new deal, true to David's original vision, and show our good faith by investing more in it. If we did that, we might be able to get the political momentum we needed to get a major reform through the Senate.

Remarkably, our discussions with David never leaked. It says a great deal about Birmo's discretion and that of his staff. The deal could only work if it was a complete surprise.

And it did. As I walked in first for the press conference, I could hear someone saying, 'Who's the third lectern for?'

Gonski's endorsement put Labor in a difficult position. In the end, they struggled to attack us on school education funding. It was barely a passing issue in the 2019 campaign. And as I reminded my colleagues at the time, particularly Dutton and Morrison, it showed what you could do if you conferred in private, made a decision and then announced it at a time and in a manner of your own choosing.

When Birmo, Gonski and I announced our plan on 2 May 2017, I confirmed we'd increase funding from $17.5 billion in 2017 every year, reaching $30.6 billion in 2027. I also announced that Gonski would chair an independent panel of education experts on what we'd call the 'Review to Achieve Educational Excellence in Australian Schools'.[3] It would provide an evidence base that would lead to the development of a new national schooling agreement between the Commonwealth and the states on how the extra funding could be used to improve outcomes. We were reforming the system. Tony Crook, who was a deputy secretary in the Department of Education, did all the formulas and numbers to ensure it was a genuine needs-based funding model. It was time to bring the school funding wars to an end, to put aside the patchwork of special deals that had been implemented under Labor.

The Quality Schools initiative would see Commonwealth funding rise from 17 per cent to 20 per cent of the school resourcing standard for state schools, and from 77 per cent to 80 per cent for non-government schools. Not only would it be needs-based and equitable, so that students with greater needs would receive a higher level of funding, but it would finally deliver on Gonski's vision. As I said at the time, 'Every parent wants the best for their child. Our children deserve schools that are properly and fairly funded, which encourage the highest academic standards, teachers who encourage and inspire and facilities in which children can excel, laying the foundation for a lifetime of achievement.'

With increased and fair funding, the initiative would also help to turn around Australian students' performance in maths, science and reading. I truly believe, as I said that day, that 'the most valuable resource we have in our nation is not under the ground, it's walking around on top of it. By investing in our children's education, by ensuring that we take responsibility for them having the quality education, the great learning, the great skills that they deserve, we will be building the human capital, the most valuable capital of our nation.'[4]

The announcement was well received by the public and, importantly, in our party room. Marginal seat holders are always nervous about Labor scare campaigns about schools and hospitals so were happy to sell the message about the funding boost and to have the backing of the Gonski brand behind them. It gave them a strong foundation to argue in their local streets.

There were obviously some in the party room who didn't like spending more money but I was confident our plan was the right one: for the first time, consistent, fair, needs-based funding. And from a political point of view, it would be one less scare campaign Labor could run against us at election time.

Others had concerns about Catholic schools not receiving enough funding, particularly Victorian MPs like Michael Sukkar, Alan Tudge and Kevin Andrews. My internal opponents on the right largely saw Gonski 2.0 as an opportunity to attack me, and the usual suspects like Tony Abbott, Andrew Hastie and Tony Pasin joined in.

Despite public concerns being expressed, largely through *The Australian* newspaper, the reforms passed through the party room without a great deal of controversy. We had no issues with any of the MPs wanting to cross the floor.

The concerns of the Catholics came as a real shock to us. In the past the Catholic schools system in each state had been funded on what was called a 'system weighted average' that reflected the average socioeconomic circumstances across the whole school system, as opposed to assessing each school and funding it accordingly.

In order to demonstrate the fairness of our system, we proposed to end special deals like this and so we put the amounts each school would receive on the department's website.

Over the years Catholic bishops, like George Pell, had always insisted the virtue of funding the Catholic schools in one lump sum, as a system, was so that they could cross-subsidise the poorer schools at the expense of those in the wealthier suburbs. And this claim seemed so plausible, given the Church's mission, that none of us gullible politicians questioned it.

As it turned out, quite the reverse was the case. Anthony Fisher, the archbishop of Sydney, was the one tasked to speak to me and he explained that 'the problem' with our needs-based model was that more funding would go to schools in 'the poorer outer suburbs of Sydney and country New South Wales'.

I was astonished. 'But don't you do that now?'

There was a long pause. 'Malcolm, if your reforms go through, it would mean the fees at St Francis's school in Paddington would have to go up.' St Francis is a not-at-all-posh little primary school in Oxford Street, Paddington, with a history of achieving great academic results. As Fisher knew, it's about 500 metres from where our grandchildren live.

'But, Anthony,' I replied, 'surely you're not suggesting that fees in a school in my affluent electorate should be lower at the expense of a school in North St Mary's? The parents of St Francis would be horrified to learn you were doing that.'

The archbishop sighed. 'I am afraid to say, on this occasion, the politician has a more idealised view of human nature than the archbishop.'

I pressed my case and explained that while the funding was assessed on a school-by-school basis, and transparently so, it would still all come to the Church in one cheque and they could then distribute it as they saw fit. If they wanted to subsidise fees in posh areas at the expense of schools in poor areas, they were free to do that.

'Oh, come on, Malcolm,' said Fisher. 'You know, once you tell people how the government has assessed need and shown how much each school would get, we could never get away with it. People would say we were short-changing poor schools to benefit rich ones.'

This was the fundamental issue: he was objecting to transparency and accountability and wasn't prepared publicly to defend how they moved government money around their school system.

I told him that in my view this wasn't an argument he could successfully sustain. In 2017 people wanted to know the truth about the government's use of their taxes and if he wanted to shift money around schools, he'd have to make that case to the parents, not rely on keeping them in the dark.[5]

The conversations and written exchanges with Fisher were some of the most unedifying and disappointing I'd ever undertaken with a Church leader. It all became very clear. We'd been misled, perhaps by our own naiveté, into thinking the Church would allocate funding strictly according to need. I'd always assumed some of the parents' fees paid to a Catholic school in my electorate went to subsidise a school in a poorer area. But not so. I could only assume that the objective of the Catholic system was to maintain enrolments in middle-class areas. And the way they did it was by keeping fees lower than equity, as we'd understand it, would dictate. At one point, for example, Fisher argued schools in my electorate were needier than our estimates because the parents had bigger mortgages.

Fisher, however, wasn't speaking for all the Catholic school systems. In the final result, most of the Catholic schools around the country, including some of the most advantaged, like the big Jesuit schools of

Riverview in Sydney and Xavier in Melbourne, recognised that what we were doing was fair. Nevertheless, we faced continued resistance from the Catholic school system in Victoria, where a particularly vicious campaign was waged by their chief executive, Stephen Elder, who tried to mobilise Catholic school parents in Liberal seats to protest and, when the time came, vote against us.

Fisher's objections to transparency and the accountability which came with it underlined the heart of the problem with so much of the Catholic hierarchy, tragically chronicled by the Royal Commission on Institutional Responses to Child Sexual Abuse. Like many Catholics, my relationship with the Church has been shaken by the shameful revelations of child sexual abuse and its cover-up by Church authorities. But in a different, less shocking way, the opposition to our school funding reforms appalled me just as much. I felt too many of the Church leaders were more interested in defending their system and resisting accountability than in fulfilling Jesus's mission to the poor.

While all this was happening, we had to move fast to get the legislation through the Senate before the rearguard action from our Catholic critics (shamefully and opportunistically supported by Labor) got more momentum. Birmo did a magnificent job in negotiating with the Senate crossbench. He sold to the right-leaning crossbench members that this was a cheaper option than what Labor had proposed. Cory Bernardi and David Leyonhjelm always liked options that would save the budget money and as such we had little trouble securing their support. The NXT people liked the policy. They agreed it was genuine needs-based funding and, being from South Australia, knew Birmo well and held him in high regard.

In fact, we almost got the Greens to support the policy. Sarah Hanson-Young in particular was a strong supporter of the plan because she could see it was fairer than Labor's existing arrangements. Had it not been for Lee Rhiannon, who threatened to blow up the Greens party over this issue, we'd have had the entire Senate, minus Labor, support it, such was the fairness of what we were proposing. It was another example of how treating the crossbench with respect and going about our job courteously delivered outcomes.

I vividly remember the late-night sitting to pass the legislation, on the evening of 22 June 2017. The House of Representatives was the last House to pass the Gonski reforms, after the Senate moved amendments.

What a night it was.

As the moment approached, Tanya Plibersek yelled at me across the chamber. 'Gonski thinks you're a fraud!' she said. 'You're cutting funding!' Of course, we were spending less overall than Labor had promised – without them having any means of paying for it. But what we were spending was both a substantial increase on the status quo and, above all, it was fair.

The loopiness of the Labor attack included the complaint that we were going to pay 20 per cent of the SRS for state schools and up to 80 per cent for (the neediest) non-government schools. This ignored the fact that the 20 per cent was a significant increase on the federal government's support for those public schools – which are, after all, the responsibility of the states and territories.

Indeed, one of the most valuable elements in our reform was that it required the states to agree to maintain their own funding of their own schools to at least 75 per cent of the SRS; Victoria particularly objected to this requirement. Otherwise – melancholy experience tells us – as the additional federal dollars roll in, state government dollars will roll out, with the school and the students no better off in net terms.

It was not only a very long night but a nervous one. The numbers were extremely tight in parliament and the debates continued until well after midnight. At different points, some MPs retired to their offices for a few drinks, and you always worry that one or two will fall asleep. Or might just go home. There was speculation Tony Abbott wouldn't vote. Nola Marino, the chief government whip, was on her toes all evening making sure our MPs turned up for the final division.

Labor were playing games. They deliberately had next to nobody vote on a couple of amendments early on, creating the perception a few of their people had gone home, to try and lure us into a false sense of security and allow some of our team to go home. But like clockwork, for the final vote all of Labor's MPs turned up. Thankfully, so did ours! We won the vote 71–64, at 2.01 am on Friday 23 June. Gonski 2.0 had become a reality.

As soon as the vote passed, I went back to my office and congratulated my staff, particularly David Bold, who'd worked so closely with Birmo in shaping the policy and ensuring we had Senate support. Birmo and I had our photo taken together at just on 3 am. It had been months in the making but together we'd reformed education funding in Australia.

About four hours later Birmo was on breakfast television. I'm not certain he even slept before going on air.

It was worth it. We'd instituted the genuine needs-based funding that David Gonski first proposed in 2011. And in doing so, proved we not only gave a Gonski, but had a Gonski! It's amazing what can be achieved from a friendship that started in the playground of Sydney Grammar School.

As a postscript, there remained a fierce debate about the accuracy of the way in which socioeconomic status was determined. A review we set up chaired by Michael Chaney recommended improving it by using, as we can today, parents' specific income tax data to get a fairer assessment of the school community's capacity to pay. I was very supportive of this. Frankly, in an ideal world I'd prefer that funding was directed to the student on a means-tested basis and not the school at all.

As a consequence of the Chaney Review, we were planning to contribute an additional $3 billion of support over 10 years for Catholic and independent schools. After the coup in August 2018, Scott Morrison agreed to give the Catholics and independent schools that amount plus an additional $1.6 billion over 10 years, without any particular rationale, other than as a way of buying some peace.

We saw to it that there's now no shortage of money for school education in Australia. The challenge is to make sure it's spent on hiring, retaining and supporting the people upon whose knowledge and charisma all depends – our teachers.

Great teachers changed my life. With our reforms we ensured that in the years to come, more great teachers will keep teaching and, as they do, change the lives of millions of Australians.

CHAPTER 41

The Trans-Pacific Partnership

John Key and I were reflecting on global affairs over a nightcap on the top
floor of the Belmond Hotel in Lima.

It was 19 November 2016 and our first evening in Peru for the APEC
summit. The 48-hour flight time to and from the summit was only an
hour or two less than the entire time we were to spend on the ground in
Lima. Those hours, though, have defined the global trade landscape for
generations to come.

Less than two weeks earlier, Donald Trump had won the US election.
Barack Obama still had two months of his presidency to run and so
continued to represent the United States at these global conferences.
John and I both admired Barack Obama, and like everyone else at the
APEC meeting, were apprehensive about Trump. However, my focus –
Australia's focus at APEC – was on the Trans-Pacific Partnership, the
huge free trade deal between 12 Asia Pacific nations: Australia, Brunei
Darussalam, Canada, Chile, Japan, Malaysia, Mexico, Peru, New Zealand,
Singapore, the USA and Vietnam. It had promised to open Australian
exports to more markets than ever before, cutting 98 per cent of tariffs.

But all that was now in jeopardy. Trump's pledge to withdraw from
the TPP was a core election promise and there was nothing to suggest he
wouldn't follow through. Obama's hope that the TPP would be approved
by Congress during the 'lame duck' period between the November
election and when the new congress assembled in the New Year had
assumed Hillary Clinton winning the election. All in all, by the time we
assembled in Lima, while a few of the leaders were hoping Trump would
change his mind, most were predicting the TPP was dead.

Earlier in the day, I'd met with the Peruvian president, Pedro Pablo
Kuczynski. A 78-year-old economist and former banker, he'd lived in the

USA for so long that he was called 'El gringo'. When we discussed the possibility of a TPP without the USA, to my surprise he was positive about the idea.

John also liked the idea of going ahead with the TPP even if the Americans pulled out. Both our countries already had good access to the US market, so most of the benefit of the TPP came from the additional access we secured to the other economies. We decided to talk to all the APEC leaders and find out who was up for a TPP-11, without the USA.

Our respective bureaucrats thought it was impossible. The TPP had been US-led and they couldn't conceive of such a big deal being done without its sponsor. It would be like 'unscrambling an omelette' one said to me.

The next day, 20 November, I met with Obama in the Lima Convention Centre. Among other issues, we discussed the TPP. Obama strongly supported the USA being in the TPP, not so much from an economic and trade perspective, but more from a strategic and national security perspective. He felt joining the TPP sent a strong message to China that the USA wouldn't be vacating the region into which China was so aggressively seeking to expand its influence.

I raised with Obama the prospect of a TPP-11. He liked it, said it was vital for the region that the partnership carried on and encouraged me to continue down that path. He added, 'Don't write that down, as you never know who is listening.'

I replied, 'But we do know who's listening,' which he found amusing.

There'd been speculation that Trump might reconsider once he became president and was properly briefed by the US agencies. Obama felt that was unlikely but said if the nations were of a mind to continue as a TPP-11, it would put pressure on Trump to reconsider.

Despite the impending demise of the TPP-12, Obama kept a planned function for the TPP-12 nations in Lima. There was a real sadness as we said farewell to him and anxiety that the TPP wasn't going to be realised because of Trump's election. Obama was publicly emphasising the possibility that Trump could be persuaded to change his mind on TPP and might be different in office. A lot of us, more in hope than expectation, repeated Mario Cuomo's line that 'We campaign in poetry, govern in prose' – to which President Michelle Bachelet of Chile dryly interjected, 'I didn't notice a lot of poetry in that election.'

• • •

I raised the TPP-11 concept with a number of the other nations. Trudeau and his Trade minister, Chrystia Freeland, were both positive – Chrystia more than Justin. Of course, as long as NAFTA stayed in force, there was nothing for them to gain in terms of access to the US market. But they welcomed greater access to the Asian markets and especially Japan.

Our host, President Kuczynski, became more enthusiastic as we continued to discuss the prospect. He saw the rising tide of protectionism as one of the biggest threats to the global economy, and keeping the TPP alive, even without the USA, would be an important way of standing up for free trade and open markets. We got on very well in fact, and one of the outcomes of that meeting was an Australia–Peru Free Trade Agreement.

In Lima, Shinzo Abe said that like me he had emphasised the TPP's strategic importance to Trump. He still hoped that Trump could be persuaded not to withdraw from the deal and was concerned that if we moved without the USA it could alienate the president-elect and make it even less likely that he would stay in.

In truth most leaders were simply hoping Trump would change his mind, something both John Key and I thought was unlikely.

'What are you going to say when people say you're flogging a dead horse?' John genially asked over a beer in Lima.

I thought for a minute. 'Well, I suppose I'd just have to say that if the horse is dead, it won't mind the flogging.'

We drank to that, being animal lovers from way back.

To make this work, I had to persuade Shinzo Abe. Japan was the third-largest national economy in the world and so the second-biggest market in the TPP after the United States. As long as Japan was on board, a TPP-11 was a chance.

Abe was due to come to Sydney for a bilateral visit in January 2017, a week before Trump's inauguration. By then it would be pretty clear if Trump was for turning or not.

We began 14 January walking along the cliffs at South Head and then reconvened at Kirribilli House for meetings, after which, together with Lucy and Shinzo's wife, Akie, we went across the harbour on the Admiral's Barge to dinner at our home.

After Lima, Trump had restated his commitment to pull out of the TPP and Shinzo's hopes of persuading him to stay in were fading. It would be harder to sell the deal in Japan without the USA. And how would the other countries react to a TPP-11? Nations like Malaysia and

Vietnam had only entered into the TPP because of the trade access it provided to the United States.

I could tell Shinzo's only reservation, understandably, was whether a TPP-11 would upset Trump. Shinzo had made a huge investment in courting Trump and, especially with the North Korean threat becoming more acute all the time, he didn't want to fall out with his new golfing buddy.

'Shinzo,' I said over dinner at our home that night, 'if we don't do the TPP-11, the whole project will die, never to be resurrected – a pile of papers in a lawyers' office. We have this one moment while there are still people around the region committed to the deal, to get on with it. And if we do, it's not a rejection of Donald; we are doing him a favour. It's a free option for him. We keep the deal alive and at some point in the future, he could rejoin, or if not him a future president.'

Shinzo saw the logic in that. By the time he left Sydney the next morning, 15 January, he'd agreed to join me in taking the lead on TPP negotiations over the coming months and that we'd work together to conclude a TPP-11 if, as we expected, Trump did pull out. Shinzo said he would speak to Vietnam about the issue and try to get a firm answer out of Trump, whom he was due to meet in March.

Domestically, Bill Shorten mocked me for trying to revive the TPP. He told the National Press Club on 31 January, 10 days after Trump's inauguration, 'Attempting CPR on the TPP is a waste of time. It's worse than a vanity project – it shows he puts his own ego ahead of Australia's national interest.'

I took Shorten to task over that. No matter how long a shot it may have seemed, why would you give up on opening more markets for Australian exports, and more jobs for Australians in export industries?

Dad had always told me, 'Never take a backward step,' which meant, stay on the front foot, stay positive, moving ahead. And that seemed more right than ever. We couldn't give up on free trade just because America had acquired a protectionist president.

Shinzo played golf with Trump in the United States in March. He told me Trump asked him for his views on trade and Shinzo had explained why he believed the TPP was a good idea. Trump didn't give a clear indication then whether he was open to the US remaining in the TPP or leaving. But realistically, I couldn't see how Trump could stay in – his election pledge had been utterly unequivocal.

I got the sense Shinzo was cautious about being overly bold with Trump, given the worsening crisis with North Korea, which was acutely complex for Japan. Not only were North Korean missiles flying over Japan but Shinzo was under a lot of pressure from his own people to secure the return of the Japanese citizens that the North Koreans had abducted over the years.

Shinzo and I kept talking to the other leaders – comparing notes as we did. We both spoke with Vietnam's prime minister, Nguyen Xuan Phuc. He was initially hesitant about proceeding without the United States, but as the reality of Trump's very different administration sank in, it became obvious that if we didn't get the TPP-11 done, there'd be no deal at all.

Prime Minister Phuc and I got on very well. His enthusiasm for Vietnam's future was almost contagious. He could see there was a real upside for him in the TPP-11 and there was always the chance the USA could rejoin in the future.

I knew we couldn't let the momentum stall. We pressed the cause of the TPP-11 everywhere, always in partnership with Japan. By April, the Japanese were openly supportive of proceeding without the USA. I got the feeling that they, and other countries, were feeling a little liberated that we could do it ourselves: the United States wasn't as essential as everyone had thought.

Our goal was to sign off the TPP agreement at the November 2017 APEC meeting in Da Nang, Vietnam. The signing was to be the highlight of the whole summit. The Trade ministers of the TPP-11 nations had met and agreed to proceed. All that was left for the national leaders was to sign, smile and shake hands.

The Vietnamese PM, my friend Mr Phuc, had assembled all the leaders around a large table. Flags everywhere, cameras everywhere. This was set to be a great diplomatic triumph for Vietnam.

We waited a while and then we noticed Shinzo Abe wasn't there and neither was Justin Trudeau. What was going on?

Then a very flustered looking Shinzo appeared, apologised for the delay and said we couldn't proceed to sign today.

I asked him what had happened.

'Justin won't sign. He's pulling out.'

'What?' I replied. 'His Trade minister said it was all done last night. Is he trying to scuttle the deal?'

Shinzo looked devastated. 'I think so.'

I was extremely disappointed with Justin and felt really bad for Shinzo Abe. He'd put so much into the TPP-11 and this was a very public humiliation. Likewise for Prime Minister Phuc of Vietnam. He had dozens of cameras waiting to record the historic moment, and then it hadn't happened. Everyone was perplexed.

And it wasn't as though we hadn't bent over backwards for Justin, even agreeing to rename it the 'Comprehensive and Progressive Trans-Pacific Partnership'.

I felt let down by Trudeau too. Like any young, good-looking leader, he was always liable to be described by his critics as a lightweight. But I'd found him more thoughtful than some of his reviews suggested. This last-minute backflip looked flaky. Had I misjudged him?

As fate would have it, we had a bilateral scheduled with Canada immediately after this detonation of the TPP-11. Justin always wore perfectly tailored suits that fitted like a glove, bright socks and on this occasion two-tone shoes.

'What do you think of the socks?' he asked, crossing his legs as he sat down.

'Justin,' I said, 'we're not here to talk about your socks.'

I didn't waste any time. 'What, Justin, is going on? You have just humiliated our friend Shinzo, who happens to be the leader of the third-largest national economy in the world. And, if that wasn't enough, you have humiliated our host, Prime Minister Phuc.'

Justin didn't give me any explanation for his conduct, just insisting that nothing was agreed until it was agreed and it wasn't agreed and … just words. I could only assume it was domestic politics back in Ottawa. But, if that was the case, why did his Trade minister say the deal was on the night before? And why didn't Justin give us a heads-up months before?

I felt like a grumpy old man scolding Justin about it, but I had to be frank. I told him this flakiness was going to do a lot of damage to Canada's standing with Japan. Even some of the non-TPP leaders had been shocked. It wasn't respectful and it certainly wasn't the way you do business in ASEAN.

'So,' I asked him, 'does this mean you're out for good? What are we meant to say?'

Justin agreed he'd say, 'Discussions will continue,' which was better than nothing, but not much better.

Shinzo and I met shortly afterwards and agreed we'd keep going. However, Shinzo pointed out that Canada's withdrawal would create a major problem with Mexico, which – like Canada – was part of NAFTA, which Trump was threatening to renegotiate or cancel.

So, the following day, 11 November, I met with President Enrique Peña Nieto and his Trade minister, Ildefonso Guajardo. They couldn't understand Justin's conduct either and were pessimistic about the prospects of his changing his mind. They felt he'd lacked the strength to say 'no' months ago and now lacked the strength to say 'yes'.

Enrique suspected Justin may have been worried about offending Trump. I said to him that might be so, but the best way to deal with Donald was to be up-front, frank and stand your ground; there was no other way to win his respect.

By the end of the meeting, they'd agreed we should press ahead with the TPP-11; they would try to talk the Canadians around but made no promises. As Ildefonso pointed out, they especially liked the deal because it gave them much better access to the Japanese market than they currently had – so the deal was worthwhile.

But there was a timing problem. There were national elections in July in Mexico and any deal would need to be signed well before then.

'But you understand, Malcolm,' Enrique concluded, 'our big priority is NAFTA. So we can help, but you and Shinzo will have to do the heavy lifting.'

Chile was in a similar position. Michelle Bachelet was leaving office in March 2018 and said that had to be the deadline otherwise Chile was likely to withdraw.

I lobbied all leaders to continue progressing and negotiating to complete the deal as planned.

As the weeks went on, Canada began to say their concerns centred around protecting their television and music industries. It was still largely unclear what those concerns were, but we continued to negotiate in good faith to meet their needs.

All negotiators remained at the table.

I met with Abe again on 18 January 2018 in his office in Tokyo. I said to him that we needed to get the deal concluded with or without Canada. 'We have to keep the train moving, we can't stop. If Canada won't come, make it a TPP-10; if Mexico does the same, a TPP-9. We can always add other carriages along the way, but we have to get started.'

Shinzo agreed. With elections and political changes imminent in Mexico and Chile, he knew we needed a quick close. He thanked me and said how much he appreciated my support in reaching agreement on the TPP the previous year, recalling it all began during his visit to Sydney in January. We agreed we would maintain momentum and get it signed no later than March 2018.

He told me that Trudeau's special envoy was coming to Japan the following day and would meet with Japan's minister for Trade. Shinzo indicated that he wasn't sure what Canada's intentions were. He felt Canada might have a sense of guilt about their behaviour in Da Nang. Either way, it was important to ensure there was no repeat of what happened at Da Nang.

Shortly afterwards we were told the Japanese Trade minister had left no doubt in the mind of his Canadian visitor. With the encouragement of our trade negotiators, the Japanese showed two draft press releases to the Canadian. One was for a TPP-11, the other for a TPP-10. 'Right now, we are pretty indifferent as to which one we issue.' It worked.

The next day, after a quick consultation with Ottawa, the Canadian envoy said he believed agreement could be reached and so the 'TPP-10' announcement never had to be made.

On 23 January 2018, Trudeau told the World Economic Forum that Canada was back in the TPP-11.

A month later, on 21 February, the text for the TPP was released.

True to our word in Shinzo Abe's office on 18 January, where we pledged we'd make it a reality by early March, the TPP was signed on 8 March 2018.

And on 30 December 2018 after Japan and five other nations had ratified the treaty, it came into force. I tweeted a photograph of myself and Shinzo Abe from the day we discussed the TPP-11 in Sydney.

Nearly 2 years ago in Sydney @AbeShinzo and I determined to keep the #TPP alive after US under @realDonaldTrump had pulled out. Thank you @AbeShinzo @leehsienloong @jacindaardern & other TPP-11 leaders for defying the dead end of protectionism! More trade means more jobs.

What a win for Australia!

The TPP-11 ended up being one of the most comprehensive trade deals ever concluded. It eliminated 98 per cent of tariffs in the trade zone with a combined GDP worth $13.7 trillion.

Australian farmers, manufacturers and businesses small and large now have much greater access to some of the largest and fastest-growing markets in the region.

And it's an enduring achievement. In the years to come, I have little doubt a future US administration will sign up to it, assuming President Trump doesn't change his mind. And there are many other countries that will seek to join. The United Kingdom has already started discussions to do so, and in our region South Korea, Thailand and Indonesia have all expressed interest in joining as well.

There are a lot of things you do in politics that would have likely happened anyway. This was not one of them.

Had Bill Shorten been prime minister, there'd have been no Trans-Pacific Partnership. He thought the deal was dead and urged me to walk away. And to be fair to Bill, I'm not sure that another Liberal PM would have been as persistent as me. The conventional wisdom from the diplomats, business and commentariat was that the TPP was utterly doomed once Trump pulled out.

The TPP-11 story shows how Australia can achieve great outcomes if we work collaboratively with the countries in our region and not be mesmerised, let alone intimidated, by the imperial powers in Washington and Beijing.

CHAPTER 42

And another one bites the dust: the citizenship crisis

'Hi, PM. It's Matt Canavan. Are you sitting down?'

It was 24 July 2017 at midday, and unknown to Matt (or anyone else in politics) I wasn't simply sitting down, but lying down. And just coming out of an anaesthetic. I was thoroughly chilled. A few hours before, my surgeon, Mark Winder, had drilled into my back to remove part of a bulging disk that had been giving me excruciating sciatic pain for several months. The sciatic pain had gone but a different sort of pain was coming my way.

Matt blurted out, 'I'm an Italian citizen. My mum rang me and told me she'd made me an Italian citizen. I checked with the Italian embassy and they say I've been registered as an Italian citizen. So, I think I have to resign from the Senate.'

He was very emotional, which was typical of Matt. He was the youngest member of the cabinet and one of the most numerate, and extremely conservative. He was as furious and passionate an opponent of same-sex marriage as he was a supporter of the coal industry and the Adani project in particular. He was also notoriously indiscreet – currying favour with journalists, particularly Renee Viellaris at the *Courier-Mail*. Matt had been Barnaby's CoS and was as fiercely loyal to his old boss as he was critical of his internal rivals like Michael McCormack.

'Okay, Matt,' I said, suddenly wide-awake. 'So, whether you're an Italian citizen or not is a matter of Italian law. Why are you so sure your mum is right?'

Matt told me how his mother, whose father was born in Italy, had been entitled to Italian citizenship and had applied, without his knowledge, for him to have Italian citizenship as well. Which was granted, although he hadn't been aware either about the application or its being granted. In fact he said he had told his mother when she was getting an Italian passport that he didn't want one.

This shouldn't have been a big deal. After all, millions of Australians have dual citizenship and millions more would be entitled to become citizens of another country.

But then there was section 44 of our constitution, which sets out five grounds on which a person is 'incapable of being chosen or of sitting as a senator or a member of the House of Representatives'.

The first was the one of concern here – disqualifying anyone who: 'Is under any acknowledgement of allegiance, obedience or adherence to a foreign power, or is a subject or a citizen or entitled to the rights or privileges of a subject or citizen of a foreign power.'

In the weeks before this phone call not one but two Greens senators had had to resign as they were in breach of section 44. Scott Ludlam was born in New Zealand and Larissa Waters was born in Canada, and neither had renounced their citizenship of those countries before running for parliament.

But what about the Australian-born children of foreign citizens? What if the foreign law decrees that they're citizens of the foreign country, and what if, like Matt, they know nothing about it?

Thinking quickly I said to Matt, 'There are two legal questions here, Matt. First are you in fact a citizen of Italy under Italian law? Then, assuming you are, will the High Court of Australia regard that as disqualifying you, if, for example, you weren't aware of it?'

Matt told me he'd earlier called Barnaby, so I patched Joyce in with Attorney-General Brandis. Canavan said his mother had sent him some citizenship forms to fill in back in 2006, but he hadn't done so. He was adamant he hadn't given any consent to taking up Italian citizenship. We agreed we'd get the advice of an Italian lawyer in Rome on the first question of Italian law and then take that to the solicitor-general for advice on the Australian law implications.

'Now, Matt,' I said, 'the most important thing is, say nothing to anybody else until we know what the law is on this.'

Within an hour of us speaking, the story about his predicament was on the *Courier-Mail* website. It emerged that not only had he told his staff about it (who promptly started calling staff in other offices), he'd also spoken to the LNP president, Gary Spence, and other members of the state executive.

George and Matt did a press conference in Brisbane; Matt told his (rather implausible) story and announced he'd step down as a minister pending the resolution of the matter in the courts.

That afternoon I noted in my diary, 'The clearest fact is that at no time did [Matt] provide any consent to the embassy or his mother for him to be registered as an Italian citizen so it seems impossible for this to have been done lawfully. It raises some very puzzling questions if it is possible.'[1]

Well, that was an understatement. It appeared that since 1912, Italian law had decreed that Italian citizenship flowed through the male line from one Italian male citizen to his children forever. In other words, if a man was a citizen of the Italian Republic in 1870 and then immigrated to Australia, then each and every male descendant would also be an Italian citizen unless one of them had renounced that citizenship.

Now, this global, time-travelling reach of the Italian citizenship law didn't impact on Matt Canavan when he was born in Southport in 1980 to Maria, his Australian-born mother, because Maria's Italian-born father had renounced his Italian citizenship a month before her birth in October 1955. However, Matt's maternal grandmother, also born in Italy, didn't renounce her Italian citizenship until September 1959.

Matt was born in 1980, and so he was an Australian citizen only. But then three years later, in deference to modern notions of gender equality, the Italian Constitutional Court declared, retrospectively, that Italian citizenship should pass to any child whose parent – male or female – was an Italian citizen at the time of their birth. This meant that Mrs Canavan became retrospectively an Italian citizen, courtesy of her mother, at birth in 1955 ... as was Matt at his birth in 1980.

Brandis was busy getting the Italian legal advice together and there was one glimmer of hope – could Matt Canavan really be said to have become an Italian citizen until he was registered as a citizen? And how could somebody be registered without their consent?

But the big question was: what was the Australian High Court going to say about it? How was it consistent with our sovereignty that a foreign country could change its law, render an Australian citizen also a citizen of their country and, by so doing, make them ineligible to sit in the Australian parliament? What if the UK parliament changed the law to decree that the foreign-born grandchildren (as opposed to just the children) of UK citizens were also UK citizens? Then I would be ineligible to sit in the parliament, as would dozens of others. After all, more than half of Australians have at least one parent born overseas, and if it's hard enough to keep up to speed with Australian law, what hope does anyone have of keeping track of foreign citizenship laws?

All of this was in some respects an intellectual distraction from the more gritty business of wrangling my turbulent party room over divisive issues like same-sex marriage and energy policy. By the end of July Australia had four senators with citizenship problems: the two Greens, Ludlam and Waters, who'd both resigned from the Senate; Canavan, who'd resigned as a minister; and the One Nation senator and arch climate change denier Malcolm Roberts, who'd been born in the UK but was claiming he was no longer a UK citizen. All of their cases were headed to the High Court.

But then it got a whole lot worse.

The 10th of August was a busy Thursday, the last day of sittings for that week. Also on my schedule were security briefings with AFP Commissioner Colvin and ASIO Director Duncan Lewis followed by a call with Vice President Mike Pence to discuss the latest sanctions on North Korea.

In between meetings, Barnaby stuck his head through the door.

'We need to talk. I've got bad news.' I could see that he was redder than usual.

He paused.

'No, it's not *that* bad news.'

I didn't have time to think what the bad news he wasn't going to tell me was before he continued, 'I'm a Kiwi, a New Zealand citizen. The high commission has just confirmed it. It's my father: he was born in New Zealand. He's lived here ever since he left university; he didn't even have a New Zealand passport when he came. He was a British subject!'

Determined that Barnaby wouldn't make the same mistake as Canavan, I quickly established that the deputy PM had kept his citizenship problems to himself. But journalists were sniffing around, he told me, and the NZ Labour opposition were onto it with a question on the matter listed in the House in Wellington for next week.

'Okay, Barnaby, let's do this. First, not a word to a soul until we know for certain what the New Zealand law is. We'll get Peter Woolcott [our high commissioner in Wellington] to get a top silk to give us some advice. And then we need to get the advice from the solicitor-general on the Australian law implications. But for God's sake, don't talk about it to anyone.'

Barnaby hurried off and I phoned Christopher Pyne, the leader of the House and our chief tactician.

If Barnaby resigned and went to a by-election, we'd not only lose the deputy prime minister – never a good look – but we'd lose our majority. At the time, with Tony Smith as the speaker, we had 75 votes on the floor. Labor had 69 and the crossbench five, to make 74. But with Barnaby out, we'd be tied on 74 votes: we wouldn't be able to carry any motion Labor opposed unless we had at least one crossbench MP voting with us. And I knew there were a number of our own backbench, especially among the Nationals, who were quite prepared to vote against the government. George Christensen, for instance, was always threatening to cross the floor.

Christopher and I considered proroguing parliament for long enough to hold the by-election or getting a deal with Cathy McGowan to pair Barnaby so that we'd have, at worst, 74 votes to 73. Then again, why would Cathy help us out?

By the next morning Christopher had spoken with the clerk and confirmed that in previous disqualification cases no pair had been given, so we didn't have a precedent. We'd concluded prorogation was going to be a very bad look and that the best course of action from a political point of view was to try to manage the House without a majority for the course of the by-election, trusting that the crossbench would continue to give us support on confidence and supply.

For much of that morning I was out of touch with the lawyers and tacticians; I was locked up in a bunker at the Defence Department getting a briefing on the latest intelligence on the North Korean nuclear threat. It felt like the theme of the day should be 'Impending Annihilation'.

If we had Canavan in strife and now Joyce, how many others were there? Sally Cray checked with Andrew Hirst, the federal director of the Liberal Party, and his counterpart, Ben Hindmarsh, at the Nats. As expected, nobody knew. All candidates had to assert they were eligible under section 44 but there'd been no systematic checking of whether people had parents who were foreign citizens. Those who'd been born overseas generally renounced their foreign citizenship – like Abbott,

Cormann, Keenan and Fletcher, among others. But this citizenship by descent issue had been overlooked – at least by the Coalition parties.

How did we know there weren't others who – like Barnaby – might have to go to a by-election? We could soldier on for five weeks down one vote, but if we lost more to section 44, we'd be toast. And while I was confident Barnaby would win a by-election in his safe National Party seat, what if the next member with a problem was in a marginal seat?

I could see the government unravelling, and fast.

Lucy and I were both attracted to some comments by Justice Deane in a previous citizenship case from the early '90s called Sykes v Cleary, where Deane had suggested that in order for a foreign citizenship to be disqualifying, the Australian person affected would have had to have acknowledged or acquiesced to it. This wasn't a precedent, rather an argument, but it made sense to me. As I messaged George Brandis on Saturday the 12th:

> We think Matt will be okay because he was an Aussie citizen and then at 3 had Italian citizenship purportedly imposed on him by a foreign law. So if that's right why does it make a difference that the imposition occurred at the time of a person's birth ie simultaneously with his becoming an Australian citizen?
>
> This distinguishes the case from Malcolm Roberts who did know he was a UK citizen, and potentially from Ludlam and Waters who arguably ought to have known [as they had been born overseas]. This could be a big opportunity for the Court to inject some sanity into the application of section 44(i) which is overdue.[2]

When the New Zealand advice came through, it was unequivocal. Barnaby was and remained a New Zealand citizen by descent. Barnaby's father had renounced his New Zealand citizenship in 1978, when he took up Australian citizenship, but this didn't change Barnaby's situation. He was a Kiwi.

But what did it mean for Australian law? We spent some hours on the phone with Stephen Donaghue, the solicitor-general, and with George. And his advice was what we'd hoped for.

> In my opinion the High Court is more likely than not to find that s.44(i) of the Constitution does not prevent a person who was born in Australia, and who became an Australian citizen by reason of that birth, from being chosen as a Senator or Member of the House of

Representatives, by reason only of the fact that the person is also a citizen of a foreign country by descent … the better view is that s.44(i) should be held to apply … only if the person has taken some step to establish, assert, accept or acquiesce in the conferral of foreign citizenship.

I called a meeting of the governance committee of the cabinet, which consisted of myself, the deputy PM, Julie Bishop and the attorney-general. Barnaby recused himself of course. We considered the advice from the solicitor-general and agreed that Barnaby should stay in the cabinet but, in order to address any remaining doubts, refer the matter to the High Court so that it could be considered together with the Canavan case.

In the meantime, we were trying to find out how many other potential problems we had. At least we were buying ourselves some time.

Barnaby referred himself to the High Court on the Monday morning, explaining that the solicitor-general had advised he was eligible to sit, but to avoid any doubt the High Court should consider the matter. At the same time I wrote to Shorten suggesting that he identify any of his members who had similar problems so we could refer them all to the High Court as a job lot. Bill replied, rather smugly, that the Labor Party had a very thorough vetting process and they had no citizenship by descent problems.

As often happens in the heat of the question time bear pit, I went too far in expressing my confidence that the High Court would rule in our favour, at one point saying, in words that came back to haunt me, 'The Deputy Prime Minister is qualified to sit in this House, and the High Court will so hold.'[3] Better to have stuck to the form of words I'd used earlier in the debate about being 'very confident' the court would find Barnaby wasn't disqualified.

In the meantime, more and more potential problems were arising. Nola Marino had an Italian father and an Italian husband. A number of our members had Greek parents – Michael McCormack, Julia Banks and Alex Hawke. Josh Frydenberg's mother was born in Hungary and Jason Falinski's father was born in the Soviet Union. Now we had lawyers working overtime to get us some answers.

But at least we'd survived and so by 7.30 when the parliamentary day was finally winding down, I was sitting in Sally Cray's office with my media team trying to persuade ourselves that the media coverage of our misfortunes could have been worse.

And then Senator Fiona Nash put her head around the door. 'Hi, Malcolm. Sorry to intrude, but' – she hesitated and then quickly said – 'I am a UK citizen.'

'Ha, Fiona, very funny,' I replied.

'No, I'm serious.'

Sally Cray put her head in her hands. This had to be a bad dream.

Within the space of a week, we'd potentially lost to section 44 the deputy prime minister and leader of the Nationals, the Nationals deputy leader and a Nationals cabinet minister.

The whole episode was dripping with irony. Initially, everyone was focused on the members and senators with European (as opposed to British) heritage, but it turned out that the bulk of the problem wasn't with would-be Greeks or Italians but rather with those, like Barnaby or Fiona, who had fathers born in the UK or other Commonwealth countries.

As the *AFR*'s Phil Coorey (himself of Lebanese heritage) observed, 'You can blame the Poms, not the wogs, for this citizenship crisis.'[4]

When the constitution was drafted, Australians were – like their British or New Zealand cousins – all British subjects. Australian citizenship didn't exist, as such, until 1948 and indeed it wasn't until 1999 that the High Court decided that for the purposes of section 44(i) the United Kingdom was a foreign power and thus a person holding UK citizenship couldn't validly sit in the Australian parliament.[5]

The decision to tough it out made for some rough months in the House, but it gave us time to work out where we stood with the rest of our members. One by one we secured legal advice that all of our members with foreign ancestry were not dual citizens, although that didn't stop the Labor Party alleging that many of them were disqualified.

The High Court gave their decision on 27 October 2017. We all expected the court would seek to draw a 'bright line' – to give an interpretation of section 44 that was practical.

Our submission was that foreign citizenship by descent shouldn't disqualify unless the Australian citizen had adopted it or acquiesced to it; for example, by taking out a foreign passport or, after being alerted to the foreign citizenship, failing to take steps to renounce it.

While this certainly passed the common sense test and was consistent with what Justice Deane had said some years before in Sykes v Cleary, it didn't impress the seven judges of the High Court.

They had their own bright line in mind which was as harsh as it was unforgiving: if you were a foreign citizen, regardless of whether you knew about it or not, you were out. 'Proof of a candidate's knowledge of his or her foreign citizenship status (or of facts that might put a candidate on inquiry as to the possibility that he or she is a foreign citizen) is not necessary to bring about the disqualifying operation of s.44(i).'[6]

In one stroke we lost Barnaby and Fiona – and the National Party its two leaders – and we lost our majority in the House of Representatives. We now had only 74 seats on the floor out of 148, so long as Tony Smith, one of ours, remained in the speaker's chair. Barnaby resigned, and the speaker immediately called a by-election for Barnaby's seat of New England to be held on Saturday 2 December.

There was one consolation: Matt Canavan was found not to be an Italian citizen – based on the court's assessment of the advice from Rome on Italian law. Their conclusion was that Matt's Italian citizenship wasn't activated until he'd been registered as an Italian citizen and he couldn't validly be registered without his consent, which he'd never given.

This was of immense importance because it meant our other would-be Italian, Nola Marino, should be in the clear. So too should be our would-be Greeks: in addition to similar Greek legal advice, we also had statements from the Greek embassy that they weren't Greek citizens.

With such a resounding defeat in the High Court, my critics enjoyed reminding me of my ebullient confidence about our prospects.

I made the best of it. Only a few weeks before, we'd successfully beaten the High Court challenge to the same-sex marriage postal vote and plenty of people had said we'd lose that too. With my 50 per cent success rate on High Court predictions, I declared I'd retired from judicial forecasting!

In the wake of Barnaby's resignation I took over his portfolios of Agriculture and Water Resources. Then I swore Matt Canavan back in as minister for Resources and Northern Australia. I passed Fiona Nash's former portfolios for the time being to Darren Chester and Mitch Fifield. Senator Nigel Scullion, the minister for Indigenous Affairs, had been appointed by the Nats as their interim leader pending the outcome of the by-election.

It all looked pretty ragged, but it was the best I could do in the circumstances, especially as I had a long-committed visit to Israel scheduled to commemorate the 100th anniversary of the Light Horse's charge at Beersheba.

Fiona Nash's departure was a loss. Because her vacancy was filled by a countback of the Senate vote in 2016 rather than a by-election, unlike Barnaby, she had no opportunity to make a swift return at a by-election. Fiona had been a steadying influence within the Nationals, particularly with her often unruly leader, and had often been a source of encouragement to me when political perils were abundant – as they all too often were.

On 31 October I was in Israel when the Liberal senator from Tasmania, Stephen Parry, announced that his father had been born in the United Kingdom. As president of the Senate, he'd been in the chair when one senator after another had been referred to the High Court in precisely the same circumstances. But he hadn't said a word about his own position, hoping the High Court would rule Barnaby and Fiona weren't disqualified.

Parry didn't help matters by saying that he'd discussed his situation some time before with Mitch Fifield, a fellow senator and minister for Communications. After going through the motions of checking with the UK Home Office, he resigned from the Senate on 2 November.

The government was under enormous stress now. Not only were we one seat down in the House, our earlier protests that we didn't have any other dual citizens rang very hollow in the wake of Parry's revelation. Abbott and his supporters were cranking up internal criticism, which was being well amplified by the right-wing commentators such as Jones, Bolt and Credlin.

So the opposition, sensing there was a chance to push the government over and into an early election, went into overdrive calling for a full 'audit' of every member's citizenship status. The frenzy was intense: members were being bombarded with questions about their ancestry and deluged with dubious legal opinions about one foreign citizenship law after another.

On the way back from Israel on 2 November, I was contacted by a distraught Josh Frydenberg. He told me *The Australian* newspaper was planning to claim that he was a Hungarian citizen because his mother had been born in Budapest in 1943.

We worked through the problem over WhatsApp – Josh in Melbourne while I was flying over the Indian Ocean.

Joshua Frydenberg: My mum is very upset after fleeing Hungary under threat of extermination there is the ridiculous claim we are all still considered citizens.

Malcolm Turnbull: This whole saga is ridiculous.

Malcolm Turnbull: I find the Australian's pursuit of you sickening. The Hungarians did their best to deprive your mother of her LIFE for God's sake!

By the time I landed late that evening, I was confident we had all the facts and the law we needed.

Malcolm Turnbull: Brilliant – you see what a team we are! I research Hungarian citizenship law from the plane and you get the goods from the archives.

Malcolm Turnbull: I couldn't have gone through Yad Vashem with you, we would have been crying the whole time. It is a shattering experience and even more so the second time.

Joshua Frydenberg: Yep so good of you to go. How should we handle this in the morning? Maybe you should go out and smash them.

Malcolm Turnbull: I might just do that.

And so I did the next morning.

Josh Frydenberg's mother Erica Strauss was born in 1943 in the Budapest ghetto. That's where the fascists had pushed all of the Jews in together as a prelude to sending them to the gas chamber. She wasn't a Hungarian citizen when she was born and neither were her parents.

You know why? The Hungarian fascist Government, allied with Hitler, stripped the Jews of all of their rights. The right to citizenship and the right to life.

Her family fled Hungary at the end of the war. It's a miracle they weren't killed, as so many of their relatives were. Three quarters of all the Jews in Hungary were murdered in the Holocaust and the prelude to murdering them was depriving them of their citizenship, rendering them subhumans in the eyes of the fascists and the Nazis.

I wish that those who make these allegations about Josh Frydenberg could think a little deeper about the history of the Holocaust. So, Erica Strauss came to Australia as a stateless person.

She had no citizenship.

She came to Australia, she became an Australian citizen and she is Josh's mother.

Has this witch-hunt become so absurd that people are seriously claiming that Josh Frydenberg is the citizen of a country that stripped his mother and her family of their citizenship and would have pushed them into the gas chambers, had it not been that the War was ended before they had time to do so?

It's time we returned to the land of common sense and the rule of law.[7]

While I was in Perth, my chief of staff, Peter Woolcott, told me that the governor-general, Sir Peter Cosgrove, had spoken to Martin Parkinson about the citizenship saga and that he wanted to see me. I called Sir Peter at 11.15 am from my car and made these notes afterwards:

He kept saying to me that 'people' were urging him 'to do something', I asked who were the people and he nominated Alan Jones and Andrew Bolt. He said they were urging him to undertake an audit, take charge etc. I said to him that the Government's position was very clear. There was only one institution that could determine an MP's eligibility to sit, and that was the High Court, the Parliament has the means to refer people to the High Court for determination of eligibility and has recently done so in seven instances. And will do so again with Parry. (Remember he told me when we last met he would not agree to prorogation if I asked for it, I didn't comment on that.) I told him that until such time as the House passed a motion of no confidence in the Government he had no cause for concern, if the House did do that I would give him advice as to what to do – to commission somebody else to form a government or, more likely, call an election. Referencing his apparent anxiety (or so it seemed to me) I said that leaders had to lead, and not allow themselves to be bullied by rowdy populists like Jones and Bolt. 'But they have a big audience, lots of people listen to them,' he said. I repeated that our duty was to do the correct thing, uphold the law and the Constitution and not be pushed around.[8]

I wasn't sure what to make of the conversation. As I noted in my diary, when I'd last seen Sir Peter Cosgrove, he'd volunteered that I shouldn't expect him to agree to proroguing the parliament if I asked him to do so pending the resolution of the citizenship cases or by-elections that followed. It wasn't an unconsidered remark as he'd made the same point to the attorney-general, George Brandis. I hadn't commented at the time.

In the call in November, I didn't enquire whether Sir Peter had spoken directly to Jones or Bolt or was simply watching them on television. Certainly they were, as usual, furiously campaigning against me. His Excellency seemed more assured at the end of the call, but it was an unsettling one at a very unsettled time.

Back in Canberra, the following Monday, 6 November, I held a cabinet meeting and agreed to reject the audit proposal backed both by Labor and Abbott's supporters inside and outside the parliament. It seemed to me that it would resolve nothing. An auditor, no matter how well qualified, couldn't give an MP a clean bill of health. The only people who could do that were the High Court and, as we'd just learned, you couldn't presume what views they might hold.

Instead I proposed that members and senators make a full disclosure of their citizenship status, including details of where their parents were born, whether they'd ever had a foreign citizenship and, if so, how it had been renounced. Later, after negotiations with the Labor Party, we expanded the disclosure to the form it has now to include the same details about grandparents. As I said at the time, only racehorses and stud cattle will have more of their bloodlines in the public domain than Australian politicians.

It all felt completely absurd and it was.

But then, within hours of the cabinet meeting, it got worse. John Alexander, the former tennis champion and now member for Bennelong, revealed that his father too had been born in the United Kingdom, but that he'd always assumed that he wasn't a UK citizen.

I spoke to John and he was sincere in his belief; he didn't have any documents – it was at best family legend. Now he too went through the rigmarole of checking with the UK Home Office to see if his father had renounced his UK citizenship at some time before John was born.

By Friday 11 November, it was obvious John couldn't establish he wasn't a UK citizen and so he resigned from parliament. There was just enough time to schedule a by-election in Bennelong on 16 December, the last feasible date before the summer holiday season.

While we were confident of winning New England on 2 December, Bennelong was another matter. John was sitting on a 10 per cent margin, but it was a by-election. The government wasn't travelling well in the polls and Labor fielded former NSW Premier Kristina Keneally as their star candidate and put in a huge effort to win the seat.

The loss of John Alexander really exposed us in the House. We were now down to 73 votes on the floor of the House, with Labor on 69 and the crossbench on five.

The week of 14 November was a momentous one. On Tuesday 15 November, we received the results of the marriage equality postal ballot – an historic victory both in terms of the size of the 'yes' vote (62 per cent) and the size of the participation (80 per cent). Absolute, unqualified triumph. How sweet it was!

Still, disaster was looming. The House was due to sit again for two weeks beginning on 27 November. The New England by-election was to be held on the Saturday, 2 December, between the two sitting weeks.

Christopher and I went back and forth trying to work out what to do. We had to minimise the time we sat without a majority on the floor of the House. Not only were we at risk from Labor and the crossbench, but Credlin and Bolt were saying that an unnamed Coalition MP was going to cross the floor and vote to bring down the government unless I was replaced. We suspected, and it was later confirmed, that this was the far-right LNP member for Mackay, George Christensen.

In the background, I'd been under pressure from the Nationals and some of our own backbench to call a Royal Commission into the banks. It was mounting and I had little doubt that enough of them would take advantage of our temporary minority to cross the floor and vote to establish a parliamentary commission of inquiry into the banking sector. Eventually, I headed that off by calling the Royal Commission into the banks myself on 30 November.

Still determined to find a way through, Christopher and I looked at the power of the speaker to change the dates for when the House sits. Should we cancel the last two sitting weeks altogether? But then we wouldn't be able to legislate for marriage equality before the year's end. Should we try to sit even later into December when we were sure Barnaby would be back?

Finally, I decided we should cancel the sitting week of 27 November and then sit for the following week, beginning 4 December. Assuming Barnaby had a resounding win, we could get him back into the parliament before the end of that sitting week. And once he'd been re-elected, hopefully his imminent return would discourage Christensen and any other would-be government wreckers from doing their worst.

The cancellation of the first of the two sitting weeks was met with widespread condemnation from the media, the Labor opposition and, of course, Tony Abbott. From a practical point of view, nothing was lost. The only big urgent legislative task for the parliament at the end of the year was the marriage equality amendments and we'd agreed to put them through the Senate first. That way, the senators could spend the first week debating same-sex marriage, pass the bill and the House could deal with it when it resumed in the second week.

Fortunately, Barnaby had a thumping win on 2 December with two-thirds of the primary vote. The poll was declared a few days later and he returned triumphant to the House of Representatives to be sworn in shortly before question time on the 6th.

This was as well because it meant we had just enough members to defeat, in a tied vote, a resolution put up by the Labor Party and supported by the crossbench seeking to refer to the High Court a number of members with possible eligibility issues. As well as some Labor people who'd been UK citizens at the time of nomination, from our side there was Julia Banks, Alex Hawke, Nola Marino, and also Jason Falinski who – like Josh Frydenberg – had a complicated ancestry lost in the upheavals of the Second World War. Josh wasn't on Labor's list, no doubt because of the strong defence I'd made of him in Perth. Frankly, Falinski's position wasn't materially different. All of our people had legal advice that they weren't dual citizens and Labor presented no evidence to the contrary.

The debate had its especially absurd moments. As I pointed out to the House, Hawke and Banks both had letters signed by the Greek Ministry of the Interior confirming they weren't Greek citizens. I asked whether Labor 'was seriously contending that the House should make such a fool of itself as to send off to the High Court somebody that the Greek Government says is not a Greek citizen'.[9]

I asked Christopher to see whether we could persuade the crossbench to refer the Labor members and Bek Sharkie who, like Labor senator Katy Gallagher, were UK citizens at the time they nominated. Each of them had argued they weren't disqualified because they'd sent in their notice of renunciation before nominating and thus had taken 'all reasonable steps' to renounce their UK citizenship.

Christopher came back to me at the table to report.

'Well, they say they won't refer the Labor people unless we refer at least one of ours.'

'Do they care who it is?' I asked.

'No, not at all. Anyone will do,' said Christopher.

'So, we could throw Julie in? Or the speaker?' I helpfully suggested.

'Sure,' said Pyne. 'I can fix it up right now if you like.'

Julie was laughing, almost in tears, at the absurdity of it all.

'No,' I concluded. 'There are limits to this farce. We won't refer anyone where there isn't a genuine question about their eligibility. The High Court will think we've all gone mad otherwise.'

'Well, everyone thinks we're mad anyway. Can't imagine why the judges would be any different,' Christopher shrugged.

The upshot was that only David Feeney was referred to the High Court. He had no evidence of even lodging an application to renounce his UK citizenship. He resigned a few months later, before his case was heard. A by-election was held in his seat of Batman in March 2018 which we didn't contest – it was a safe Labor seat.

The Katy Gallagher case was heard by the High Court early in the new year. Her argument was that she'd done all she could to get rid of her UK citizenship before she nominated and so shouldn't be disqualified.

The High Court gave its answer on 9 May 2018 and it was unequivocal: Gallagher was disqualified because she'd been a UK citizen at the time she nominated. The only exception could be when a foreign country presented an 'irremediable obstacle' to their citizenship being renounced, and that was certainly not the case with the UK Home Office. In other words, if you want to run for parliament and you're a dual citizen, it's your responsibility to get rid of the foreign citizenship before you nominate.

The Gallagher decision meant that three more Labor MPs – Justine Keay in Braddon, Susan Lamb in Longman and Josh Wilson in Fremantle – were all clearly disqualified, as was Bek Sharkie in Mayo. And so they resigned and by-elections were called in their seats.

By 2018, everyone was fed up with the eligibility crisis. The High Court, in their wisdom, had decided on the harshest possible construction of section 44. Ultimately, seven members of the 150-strong House of Representatives were either disqualified by the High Court or resigned and – apart from David Feeney, who didn't recontest – were all re-elected at by-elections.

Out of 76 senators, eight were held to have been disqualified by the High Court over dual citizenship; only two – Canavan and Nick Xenophon – survived a High Court review of their status.

In addition to that, two more senators – Bob Day and Rod Culleton – were disqualified under other provisions of section 44.

In an ideal world we'd be able to amend the section to provide that people were only disqualified by foreign citizenship by descent if they'd taken an active step to adopt it. That, as it happened, was the original formulation of the section in the constitutional debates in the 1890s.

But realistically, the chances of persuading the Australian people to change their constitution to allow people with foreign citizenship to sit in the parliament are exceedingly low. Accordingly, while it may be worth trying to amend the section, it would be most unwise to rely on that as a fix.

So, a big part of the answer has to be vigilance. We changed the Electoral Act to require those nominating for parliament to provide evidence that they're in compliance with section 44, including details of where their parents and grandparents were born and what citizenships they'd held. This will at least make the issue front of mind for those planning to run.

Most of the cases, as Phil Coorey memorably observed, have involved people with UK parents and renouncing that citizenship is straight-forward. But there are many others, in our multicultural society, who'll find it much harder to prove they're not dual citizens because it's far from clear what the foreign law is or because the foreign country isn't amenable to their citizenship being renounced.

And this is particularly problematic with countries, like Italy, that purport to pass citizenship down in an unbroken line over many generations. The UK at least only confers citizenship by descent from fathers and (since 1983) mothers.

It means the composition of our parliament is hostage to the laws of other countries. These can change and – as we saw with Matt Canavan – appear to make someone a citizen retrospectively.

Political parties, whose vetting processes have been far from perfect, will err on the side of caution and where someone's background is complex, knock them back as candidates. In a preselection contest, a powerful argument against a rival would be, 'They may have a section 44 problem.'

We may all regret that the High Court wasn't more creatively practical in 2017.

CHAPTER 43

Culture, opportunity and respect

'*Yanggu gulanyin ngalawiri, dhunayi, Ngunawal dhawra. Wanggarra lijinyin mariny bulan bugarabang.* Today, Mr Speaker, we are meeting together on Ngunawal Country and we acknowledge and pay our respects to their Elders.'[1] When I spoke those words on 10 February 2016, acknowledging we were on Ngunawal land, it was the first time an Australian prime minister had spoken an Aboriginal language in our parliament.

The chamber has heard plenty of words, but these seemed to fill the space, hanging heavily in the air long after I'd moved back to speaking in English. Were the words reproaching us for our silence, our neglect?

When the British arrived in 1788, the First Australians spoke more than 250 distinctly different languages and 800 dialects. Only a handful are being passed on to children today. Another 100 or so are spoken only by old people. This is one tangible aspect of the losses Indigenous Australians have sustained, and that successive governments have been struggling to address. The lost languages of Australia's Aboriginal and Torres Strait Islander peoples are part of an interrupted Dreaming, the disconnection of too many Indigenous Australians from their land.

The reality all Australians have to confront is that the Europeans who settled in Australia from the late 18th century, including my ancestors, were invaders. They seized this land with blood and iron as conquerors do. And even in their triumph, they didn't treat our First Australians with the magnanimity, let alone the respect, they deserved.

As a nation we still have a long way to go to reconcile those historic injustices. The suffering imposed on Aboriginal people by the forced removal of their children and degradation of their culture has left families traumatised and broken.

As I said when I was opposition leader, responding to the first Closing the Gap report in 2009, 'There is no shortage of goodwill in Australia to promote an end to Indigenous disadvantage.'[2] The challenge is finding agreement on what to do.

Not long after I became prime minister, I spoke to Dr Chris Sarra, a charismatic schoolteacher, professor, Aboriginal leader and now director general of Queensland's Department of Aboriginal and Torres Strait Islander Partnerships. I asked him what were three things we could do to improve Indigenous policy in Australia.

He said it was important to embrace and celebrate the humanity of Indigenous Australians. Look at aspirational and optimistic policy approaches that instil hope rather than despair and, finally, do things *with* Indigenous Australians, not *to* Indigenous Australians. That advice formed the core of my approach. It reflected respect for and confidence in Indigenous Australians.

Speaking in an Indigenous language in parliament in 2016 was as historic as it was overdue. It paid respect to the culture and the people of the land on which we were deliberating. But, perhaps more importantly, it spoke to resilience and renewal.

We celebrate many languages in Australia: our multicultural nation rejoices in all the languages of the world. Except for those that are uniquely Australian.

All my life I've loved language and the mysteries of poetry, the best definition of which is 'that which cannot be translated'. But oral cultures are fragile, lacking the permanence of writing and recording. As I moved around Australia engaging with different communities, I was always curious to learn words and phrases from other Indigenous languages. In Arnhem Land, I was able to learn some words of Yolngu matha, and will never forget the 'fire words' Galarrwuy Yunupingu shared with us at the Garma Festival of Traditional Cultures in 2017. In Broome, I learned about the Yawuru language and the phrase *mabu liyan*, a concept of well-being, positivity, responsibility and love. Utterly untranslatable – it is poetry – but you know it when you see it, or rather feel it, among the proud Yawuru mob.

When the time came for me to give my first Closing the Gap report, in February 2016, I asked my Indigenous Affairs adviser, Kerry Pinkstone, whether I could make the traditional acknowledgement of country in the language of the local people.

We reached out to Doug Marmion at the Australian Institute of Aboriginal and Torres Strait Islander Studies. AIATSIS is one of Canberra's least known treasures, a place where so much of the culture and language of our ancient continent has been saved and, more importantly, revived.

Incredibly, in February 2018 I was the first prime minister to visit AIATSIS[3] and, in addition to providing extra funding, moved the institute into the Department of the Prime Minister and Cabinet, which would bring it closer to the core of Indigenous Affairs policy.

Doug introduced me to Tyronne Bell and Glen Freeman, who were part of the Ngaiyuriija Ngunawal language group. It has been far too long since the Ngunawal people spoke their own language. Their civilisation was smashed by European settlement. But the members of the Ngunawal language group have worked to bring together the pieces of their language, recorded in old books and records, even some early sound recordings. Like people carefully walking along a rocky shore gathering together the remnants of a ship wrecked in a storm, they have been able to recover and revive their own language. And as they've done so, drawing back into the present an ancient language almost lost, they've felt again the cruel stories of heartbreak and loss.

One of those remnants of their language was a lullaby an old Aboriginal woman remembered more than a hundred years ago. '*Midu wuli burin gabul nurl*' – the mother's lullaby for her baby.

This is some of what the old lady remembered:

'*Nudula nindi wurula bulu i bulu gun wurula bulu nura dula … nuru wurula guni.*'

'I am rocking you slowly skyward … swinging.'

It's heartbreaking to read those words, to speak them, knowing that a tiny baby was rocked to sleep by a mother, who wanted no more than that her baby should be safe. But that baby was far from safe, as was her mother, and the language in which she sang.

The words I learned filled me with complex and competing emotions: joy that they had been saved but a deep sadness for all the other words that were lost. Sitting in the prime minister's office, dominated by the anxious challenges of the present, I felt transported to a different time and place as we spoke words that were tens of thousands of years old.

• • •

Tony Abbott had made a practice of spending a week each year in a remote Aboriginal community and he was critical of me when I didn't continue it. However, while I respect Tony's work in that area, and agree that the challenges of remote Aboriginal communities are real and raw, I dispute the impression – readily reinforced by the media – that isolation and social disadvantage is the entirety of Aboriginal experience. And in that respect I felt his sincere and well-intentioned visits were counterproductive. They contributed to a narrative of deficit, despair and disadvantage whereas I wanted all Australians, and particularly young Indigenous Australians, to understand that to be Aboriginal is to be successful, to be a winner, to be capable of realising your dreams and to be your best. After all, the vast majority of Indigenous Australians live in cities, like the rest of us, and are getting on with their lives, raising families, working, learning and investing.

In January 2016, I visited La Perouse on the northern edge of Botany Bay – incidentally, the first prime minister to officially do so, even though it's about 20 minutes' drive from the centre of Sydney. Chris Ingrey, the CEO of the local land council, welcomed me. The ancestors of the community at La Perouse had fished in Botany Bay for 60,000 years. They'd seen Captain Cook in 1770 and Captain Phillip in 1788, and today they watch the A380s fly in and out of Sydney's airport.

Of course, I visited many remote communities, including the most remote in the Anangu Pitjantjatjara Yankunytjatjara (APY) lands of South Australia and the Northern Territory. Andrea Mason was the CEO of the Ngaanyatjarra Pitjantjatjara Yankunytjatjara Women's Council and, with Chris Sarra, was co-chair of my Indigenous Advisory Council (IAC). Andrea's life's work spans the tiny communities of her birth and the capitals and boardrooms of our biggest cities. She and Chris were two of my wisest guides.

Chris Sarra's advice was my mantra – we must stop doing things *to* Indigenous people and start doing things *with* them. A good example of that was rolling out the cashless debit card, which quarantined 80 per cent of a recipient's welfare payments so the funds couldn't be withdrawn as cash or used on booze, tobacco or gambling. The Labor Party and the welfare lobby generally opposed the card, but I was more interested in what local people wanted for their communities.

In 2017, we visited Kalgoorlie, where the local shire councils had all resolved to support the trial of the cashless debit card. I was very moved by the passionate words of Betty Logan and her daughter as they talked about the misery of drug and alcohol addiction and how they saw the card as offering a chance of change. They were Aboriginal women, but most of the people who would use the card in Kalgoorlie would be non-Indigenous. As I said at the time, 'If you looked into the eyes of the children who are suffering from foetal alcohol syndrome, who are suffering from violence because their parents are on the grog all the time, you wouldn't hesitate to say this card is an act of love.'[4]

The Indigenous Affairs portfolio had undergone significant change under the Abbott government. The signature reform was to create the Indigenous Advancement Strategy by removing all Indigenous programs from departments and combining them into one single funding pool in the Department of the Prime Minister and Cabinet. After such a significant change, which was still being implemented when I became PM, it didn't seem wise to undertake further major reforms and so I retained Nigel Scullion, an energetic senator for the Northern Territory and fierce advocate for Aboriginal and Torres Strait Islander peoples, to continue as the minister for Indigenous Affairs.

When I was opposition leader, I'd said, 'Ending Indigenous disadvantage must be a constant call on every minister and every portfolio.'[5] That remained my conviction in 2015, and I was concerned that the new super-department created under Abbott could lead to other ministers assuming Indigenous issues were someone else's responsibility. Equally, it was obvious that most of the spending on Indigenous Australians was in the mainstream departments of Health, Education and Social Services – as it was for all Australians.

So, my response was to create the Indigenous Policy Committee (IPC) as a subcommittee of cabinet, where the ministers would be responsible for ensuring their portfolios were still working in the interests of all Australians, including our First Australians, rather than relying on the one agency to do all the heavy lifting.

This proved a more effective forum when we integrated the advice of the IAC. Each meeting of the IPC began with a presentation by and discussion with Chris Sarra and Andrea Mason, the co-chairs of the IAC. This regular and direct access to cabinet was, I was told, a first and didn't even happen in all the time the Aboriginal and Torres Strait Islander Commission (ATSIC) existed.

There are vastly differing views within Indigenous communities about how to achieve better social outcomes, just as there are in any other community. As Chris Sarra had said, 'There have been a lot of well-meaning policies and well-meaning people whose well-meant objectives have not been met and whose policies on all too many occasions have been counterproductive.'[6]

Economic empowerment was the key, which is why policies such as the Indigenous Procurement Policy (IPP) became so critical. The IPP was the brainchild of Andrew Forrest, who'd undertaken a review of Indigenous employment following the 2013 election. It requires federal government departments to ensure at least 3 per cent of government contracts go to Indigenous-owned businesses.

The IPP began in July 2015 and four years later, over 1500 Indigenous-owned businesses have been awarded more than 12,000 contracts worth more than $2 billion. In 2012–13, by contrast, only $6.2 million of Commonwealth contracts were awarded to just 30 Indigenous-owned businesses. The IPP has now been expanded so that by 2027 the target will be 3 per cent of Commonwealth contracts by value. And I was able to use the COAG meetings to encourage the states and territories to adopt similar programs.

The IPP wouldn't have been possible without the energy of Nigel Scullion and the work of Supply Nation, led by Laura Berry, who was born and raised on Ngunawal land in Canberra. Supply Nation has not only ensured the integrity of the process but also mentored many young Indigenous entrepreneurs as they've started in business.

I highlighted the achievements of Indigenous entrepreneurs like Ray Pratt, who has built a large electrical contracting company; doctors like Marilyn and Marlene Kong; and scientists like Dr Cass Hunter and Mibu Fischer at the CSIRO – and many others.

One way of doing that was at Indigenous business receptions, like the one I spoke at on 14 February 2017, when I delivered the Closing the Gap report.

And last night the Prime Minister's courtyard was abuzz with enthusiasm, with positivity, and the hope of leaders challenging us to again think past the statistics.

Bright, determined women and men stood tall, as successful people in their fields of work, proud of their heritage, anchored in their culture.

While we must accelerate progress and close the gap, we must also tell the broader story of Indigenous Australia – not of despondency and deficit but of a relentless and determined optimism.

That being Aboriginal and Torres Strait Islander Australian means to succeed, to achieve, to have big dreams and high hopes, and to draw strength from your identity as an Indigenous person in this country.

As Prime Minister, Mr Speaker, I will continue to tell those stories – to talk about the strengths of our First Australians.

We have among us five Indigenous Members of Parliament, who bring this same pride, this same strength here to the heart of our democracy.

Ken Wyatt, the first Indigenous Member of the House of Representatives, and now the first Indigenous Minister to be appointed in a Commonwealth Government. As well as Linda Burney, Senator Pat Dodson, Senator Malarndirri McCarthy and Senator Jacqui Lambie.[7]

Throughout my time as prime minister, whether it was in big cities like Sydney or Brisbane, or with the Wirangu people in Ceduna, South Australia, the Yolngu people in Arnhem Land, the Larrakia in Darwin or the Yawuru in Broome, everyone wanted to have greater opportunities to get ahead, to get a better job, to start a business, to have a bigger say in how their community is run and in particular how government funding directed to support their community is spent.

It always amused me how white politicians would emerge from the raucous, fractured disagreements of Canberra only to complain that Indigenous communities couldn't agree on what to do. My experience was that it was often easier to identify a sense of common purpose among First Australians than it was among the members of the Coalition party room!

Noel Pearson is an inspiring Aboriginal leader. He grew up in Cape York in Far North Queensland, trained as a lawyer and has argued that Aboriginal communities have to take responsibility for their people and directly address their social problems. We'd first met years before when I visited Weipa with other business leaders in the 1990s and we'd had common cause in the republic campaign. Noel had won support from both Labor and the Coalition for his concept of Empowered Communities, and after the 2013 election, Tony Abbott funded the preparation of an Empowered Communities report by Pearson's Cape York Institute, which was received in March 2015.

After I became prime minister, we set about implementing the recommendations to establish Empowered Communities in eight locations: the Central Coast of New South Wales, the APY Lands, East and West Kimberley, Goulburn Murray, La Perouse, Cape York and Arnhem Land.

Each of the Empowered Communities established its own representative Indigenous council and executive, which was designed to ensure all of the government funding for Indigenous programs was coordinated, creating real transparency around what particular local organisations were being funded to do and what the result of their work was.

The concept was designed for additional regions to opt in as reforms were tried, tested and refined, allowing other regions to become Empowered Communities, as Murray Bridge in South Australia did in early 2019.

The concept was similar to the City Deals I'd established as the basis of our Cities policy. The goal was to get all the relevant players around the same table so that they could agree on what they wanted to achieve and then coordinate their efforts. The government funded the additional administrative resources to make this happen – we called it the glue money because it helped tie a lot of otherwise loose ends together.

Generally, the Empowered Communities have done well, and none better than La Perouse. New policy approaches take time, and this one is still in its infancy, having only been out on the ground in regions since 2016. There have been problems getting state government agencies effectively involved, which is one of the reasons in 2018 I invited the state and territory leaders down to Canberra for the release of the Closing the Gap report and secured their agreement to refresh the Closing the Gap agenda so that it would set goals and monitor results for state and territory governments, as it did with the Commonwealth.

In 2018, I visited Tennant Creek with the Northern Territory chief minister, Michael Gunner, at the invitation of the local Barkly Regional Council. There had been a number of shocking cases of child abuse in Tennant Creek. Meeting with the local welfare agencies, police and Aboriginal leaders, it was all too obvious that people hadn't been talking to each other and, in particular, hadn't been sharing information about the situation of vulnerable children who were victims and at risk of domestic violence.

It was one young woman police officer who, on her own initiative, started to bring all the information about these kids together in one database – that was the kind of coordination that needed to be strengthened. So, I committed to establish a regional version of a City Deal in the Barkly region which would involve all the Commonwealth, territory and local government agencies as well as the Cultural Authority Group and other leaders of the Warumungu people.

It said something that I was the first prime minister to formally visit Tennant Creek. It's a remote community of 3000 – a third of the population of the Barkly region. Most of the region's people are Aboriginal. The high levels of crime, alcoholism, domestic violence, child abuse and neglect have resulted in a large number of government agencies and NGOs seeking to help.

And yet despite the fact that most of the region's people are Aboriginal, the local leaders felt they'd been shut out of the conversation. In other words, well-meaning people were trying to do things *to* Aboriginal people, not *with* them.

I spent the evening with the local police who told me of young children wandering the streets neglected, and all too often looking after each other and the adults who should have been caring for them. But there was no shortage of entrepreneurship to encourage. I was delighted to buy a few of local artist Dion Beasley's 'Cheekydog' T-shirts for the grandchildren.

The regional deal at least went some way to providing a framework to assist local leaders to have a voice, local services to be better coordinated, and to maximise investment of public sector funds. I hope the deal can grow and achieve great things in the region.

But there remains a deep concern that not just families but institutions and governments are failing to protect children. In July 2016, ABC's *Four Corners* program showed scenes of appalling and brutal mistreatment of young people, mostly Aboriginal, in the Don Dale Youth Detention Centre in Darwin. What was even worse was that this effectively institutionalised abuse had been known to the Northern Territory authorities for some time and yet official inquiries into the centre hadn't revealed the full extent of what was going on.

Normally, a scandal like this would be dealt with solely by the responsible state or territory government, but it was obvious that there were systemic failings in the Territory government itself, then led by Country Liberal Party Chief Minister Adam Giles. Speaking with George Brandis, the attorney-general, and Nigel Scullion, the Indigenous

Affairs minister, we agreed that we had to get to the bottom of this as quickly as possible and so resolved to establish a Royal Commission to expose what had occurred and the culture that allowed it to occur and remain unrevealed for so long.[8]

Justice Margaret White and Human Rights Commissioner Mick Gooda conducted the inquiry, which reported in November 2017. Successive Territory governments had deprived Aboriginal people of autonomy – over their lives and those of their children. A terrible cycle ensued – disempowerment followed by neglect followed by more intervention – and all accompanied by the grim trappings of modernity: alcohol and drugs, among many others.

Michael Gunner has been implementing the recommendations. The chief minister told me the number of kids in detention has been drastically reduced, with alternatives to detention showing a 75 per cent success rate in terms of kids not reoffending, whereas with detention almost all kids reoffended, and out-of-home care for Aboriginal kids is, as far as possible, with relatives.[9] So progress, but still so much to be done.

The most controversial issue during my time as prime minister was undoubtedly that of constitutional recognition and in particular the proposal for a 'Voice' to parliament. The Australian constitution makes no acknowledgement of the First Australians other than to discount them. Prior to the 1967 referendum,[10] under the constitution Aboriginal people weren't counted in determining a state's entitlement to seats in the House of Representatives or per capita grants from the Commonwealth. Moreover, the Commonwealth parliament was expressly prohibited from making laws with respect to Aboriginal people. Since 1967 Aboriginal and Torres Strait Islander Australians have been counted and the Commonwealth parliament does have the power to legislate with respect to them. The 1967 referendum was a watershed and seen as granting political equality to Aboriginal and Torres Strait Islander Australians but the legacy of dispossession and disadvantage left a lot to be done.

There had been a reference to the First Australians in the new constitutional preamble proposed in 1999 at the same time as the republican amendments – but both failed to carry a majority in the referendum. Howard had promised to revisit the Indigenous recognition issue in

2007. Not much progress was made in the Labor years, but in 2014 Tony Abbott had promised to 'sweat blood' to achieve it.

When I became prime minister, I formally appointed the members of the Referendum Council, already chosen by Tony Abbott. There were equal numbers of eminent Indigenous and non-Indigenous Australians and their task was to develop and propose a set of constitutional amendments.

A huge amount of work had been done by many groups and committees, not least of which was Reconciliation Australia, and the reform agenda was focused on recognition of the Aboriginal history of Australia in the preamble, the removal of archaic racist provisions (like section 25), and the insertion of some language to require the Commonwealth parliament to exercise its power to legislate for the advancement or benefit of Aboriginal and Torres Strait Islander Australians.

I was fully committed to delivering this constitutional recognition and, while I'd inherited the process and the personnel from Abbott, I worked closely with the council, as I did with Bill Shorten, to seek a proposal that was both acceptable to Indigenous Australians and would succeed at a referendum.

The Referendum Council planned to conduct a series of consultations in the course of 2017 to culminate in a conference at Uluru on 23–26 May 2017. There was a meeting of the council in the cabinet room on 25 November 2016. Bill Shorten and I both attended, as did the Aboriginal members of parliament – Ken Wyatt, Linda Burney, and senators Malarndirri McCarthy and Pat Dodson.

Referendum Council member Noel Pearson said that he was expecting the Uluru conference to recommend that there be a change to the constitution to establish 'a Voice', which would be a national advisory assembly composed of and elected by Aboriginal and Torres Strait Islander peoples. He said the parliament would be obliged to seek the advice of this assembly on any legislation affecting Aboriginal people. He had no more detail to offer – his theory was that the constitution should contain a generally worded requirement, with the parliament to be responsible for the detailed design. The object of the constitutional amendment was so that the Voice couldn't be abolished, as ATSIC had been in 2005. Few lamented the loss of the Canberra-based peak body, which had been discredited by poor governance. However, there was and remains regret that the local regional councils had been abolished as well.

A general discussion followed and there wasn't a lot of support for the Voice around the room. Shorten and I both expressed the same view: we weren't comfortable with the constitution establishing a national assembly open only to the members of one race, and moreover we both said we thought it would have no prospect of success in a referendum. 'A snowball's hope in hell,' as Bill had previously said to me.

I pointed out to Noel that surely the objective should be to have more Indigenous Australians elected to the parliament – we were after all in the presence of Ken Wyatt and Linda Burney, the first Indigenous man and woman to be elected to the House of Representatives.

Noel said, 'So, you're saying we can't recommend a Voice!' I responded they could recommend what they liked; it was just that I didn't think it was a good idea, let alone one that would be carried in a referendum.

After the meeting was over, I returned across the corridor to my office and Pearson followed me. He then became very angry, stood very close and started to swear at me because I hadn't agreed with him. I didn't respond in kind. 'Noel, you can recommend whatever you wish – you're entitled to my honest opinion, not my acquiescence.'

Pearson abused Ken Wyatt and Pat Dodson when they spoke to him later that afternoon. He seemed furiously indignant that everyone hadn't agreed with him.

Both Shorten and I were presented with the final report of the Referendum Council on 30 June 2017. It contained the 'Uluru Statement from the Heart', which recommended the Voice to parliament as Pearson had proposed. The council also said that the Voice was the only constitutional amendment they recommended. In other words, all the other proposals and options were rejected. It was the Voice or nothing.

The 'Uluru Statement from the Heart' left me deeply conflicted. It was a beautiful piece of poetry, a cry for a say, for agency, for respect. But it contained no detail at all about how such a Voice would be designed.

And how could there be any real limits on what it advised on? After all, every piece of legislation affects Indigenous people. It was unrealistic to say that parliament could, or would, simply ignore the Voice's advice, or decline to give it time to consider that advice.

In practical terms, such a Voice would effectively evolve into a third chamber.

And where would its legitimacy come from? Who would define the franchise, the eligibility of someone to vote for the Voice? How would small, remote communities get represented at all, given that the vast majority of Indigenous Australians live in cities?

And how would the Voice relate to or advise state and territory parliaments, who are primarily responsible for most of the policy areas that impact on the day-to-day lives of Indigenous Australians – such as health, education, justice and child protection to name a few?

Pearson's idea was that some general language establishing the Voice would be put in the constitution as 'a hook' to enable the assembly to be established. But given the near impossibility of persuading the Australian people to vote for any contentious change to the constitution, what hope would you have with a proposed change that lacked any of the detail?

Lucy and I attended the Garma Festival at Gulkula in Arnhem Land in August 2017 and the night before the main events, we sat around a campfire with Bill Shorten and Labor MP Linda Burney, among others. Bill announced that he was going to say he'd support the Voice. I asked him why he'd changed his mind. 'Well,' he said, 'you decided to come here, and so I had to come too. And we can't come here and say we don't agree with it.'

When I spoke at Garma on Saturday 5 August, I did so honestly and respectfully. I said that the cabinet was giving the Voice careful consideration and described some of the problems of the proposal, both practical and principled:

> What would the practical expression of the Voice look like? What would the voice look like here for the Yolngu people? What would it look like for the people of Western Sydney, who are the largest population of Aboriginal peoples in Australia?
>
> Is our highest aspiration to have Indigenous people outside the parliament, providing advice to the parliament? Or is it to have as many Indigenous voices, elected, within our parliament? What impact would the Voice have on issues like child protection and justice, where the legislation and responsibility largely rest with state and territory governments?

My cabinet were overwhelmingly supportive of my view that we shouldn't establish a Voice to parliament in the constitution. On 26 October 2017 we formally rejected the proposal.

Here is part of my joint statement with Attorney-General George Brandis and Indigenous Affairs Minister Nigel Scullion.

The Government does not believe such an addition to our national representative institutions is either desirable or capable of winning acceptance in a referendum.

Our democracy is built on the foundation of all Australian citizens having equal civic rights – all being able to vote for, stand for and serve in either of the two chambers of our national Parliament – the House of Representatives and the Senate.

A constitutionally enshrined additional representative assembly for which only Indigenous Australians could vote for or serve in is inconsistent with this fundamental principle.

It would inevitably become seen as a third chamber of Parliament. The Referendum Council noted the concerns that the proposed body would have insufficient power if its constitutional function was advisory only.

The Referendum Council provided no guidance as to how this new representative assembly would be elected or how the diversity of Indigenous circumstance and experience could be fairly or democratically represented.

Moreover, the Government does not believe such a radical change to our constitution's representative institutions has any realistic prospect of being supported by a majority of Australians in a majority of States.

I finally agreed with Bill Shorten on the terms of reference for a Joint Select Committee on Constitutional Recognition relating to Aboriginal and Torres Strait Islander Peoples and the committee was formally established in March 2018 – chaired by Labor's Senator Pat Dodson and the Coalition's Julian Leeser.

The committee sensibly concluded that much more work needed to be done on the detailed design of a Voice before parliament could decide whether, and if so how, to establish it. It lamented the way in which all of the other recognition proposals had been rejected. And most significantly it concluded the strongest support was for local and regional voices, the design of which should reflect the varying practices of different Indigenous communities.[11]

I agree with that conclusion. Throughout all my discussions with Indigenous communities, whether they're in the cities or in remote areas, there's been strong support for greater agency, greater voice but at a local level, where they can achieve better outcomes on the ground – as the Empowered Communities are doing.

I do regret that the focus on the Voice has drawn attention away from developing and expanding the Empowered Communities initiative. Every Indigenous community should be an empowered one.

Prime ministers often appear to have more power than they do. Social problems centuries in the making cannot be resolved in any one government. But I believe I was able to raise the profile of Indigenous languages, interest in and respect for which is growing around Australia. Also I believe my support for Aboriginal enterprise and entrepreneurship has enabled real economic advancement, and the Indigenous leaders I encouraged will continue to lead the way both in their own endeavours and as role models for others.

CHAPTER 44

Barnaby and the bonk ban

A moment's calm and concentration. There aren't many in a prime minister's life and they're cherished. Thursday 11 May 2017 found me alone in my office quietly reviewing the reception of that year's budget.

Budget week is always the most exhausting of the parliamentary year. From the moment the budget is announced at 7.30 pm on the Tuesday, the prime minister and the treasurer are working in a frenetic tandem of speeches and media interviews, all trying to sell the budget in that narrow window of attention before the Australian public (and their faithful servants in the press gallery) lose interest.

The parliamentary week always ends with the opposition leader's budget in reply speech at 7.30 pm on the Thursday. Parliament is adjourned at 5 pm as attention gets ready to shift to what the opposition has to say.

Just as the opposition had politely listened to Scott Morrison on Tuesday night, so we would now with, I hoped, equal decorum listen to Bill Shorten describe how our budget was heartless, reckless and financially illiterate, demonstrating our complete and utter unfitness to occupy the Treasury benches ... and so on.

But the good news was that once it was over, I'd be rushing out to the airport – to fly back to Sydney and Lucy. It'd be only a brief reunion. I'd leave home at 6.30 the next morning to go into the Seven Network studios for more budget salesmanship on *Sunrise*.

But the tranquillity of the moment was short-lived.

Sally Cray and senior media adviser Daniel Meers appeared, more worried than usual.

The Daily Telegraph's political editor, Sharri Markson, had rung Meers to say she'd learned that Barnaby Joyce and his press secretary,

Vikki Campion, had been spotted together at a Canberra doctor's surgery. She'd insinuated that Vikki was having a pregnancy test. A 'please explain', she told Daniel, had been given to Barnaby's office but no response had been forthcoming.

Barnaby is a complex, intense, furious personality. Red-faced, in full flight he gives the impression he's about to explode. He's highly intelligent, often good-humoured but also has a dark and almost menacing side – not unlike Abbott – that seems to indicate he wrestles with inner troubles and torments.

Barnaby had been a dramatic change from Warren Truss. Where Warren was dour and deliberate, Barnaby was wild and unpredictable and generally shot from the hip. He had no interest in detail but often showed the capacity to distil issues down to their essence and in language people in the bush would relate to.

Prior to coming to see me, Sally and Daniel had spoken at length with Barnaby's senior staff. They'd been doing their best to keep a dysfunctional office on the rails.

The gossip was clearly becoming an issue so I asked Barnaby to come round to see me. At the time he and I had a strong level of trust. We were very different people – the media liked to describe us as 'yin and yang' – but the partnership was working.

Barnaby had become aware of what Markson was chasing so I asked him what was going on. He gave me an unequivocal assurance he wasn't in a sexual relationship with Vikki.

We then moved on to how he was going to handle the Markson enquiries. He told me Vikki was lonely, didn't have family to support her and was concerned about her health, so to provide moral support he'd accompanied her to the doctor for some check-ups.

Without questioning his assurance, I reminded him, just for the record, that it was simply not defensible for him, as deputy prime minister, to be having an affair with one of his staff. It could only end badly, I told him, and he agreed.

We left the meeting on good terms. Barnaby's office didn't comment to Markson but advised her on background and off the record what had occurred and she decided not to run with the story.

It wouldn't be true to say that I had no doubt he was lying to me as there've been examples of very intense relationships between ministers and staff that aren't sexual in nature. That said, over the years I've been accused by colleagues of being too trusting on matters of this kind. In any event, he was the deputy prime minister of Australia; he'd been around long enough to know that as the leader of a conservative political party, being a champion of traditional marriage while practising traditional adultery – and especially with one of his own staff – was dynamite.

Following that particular fire drill, things seemed to be settling down. Barnaby and his wife, Natalie, appeared together at the Midwinter Ball and she accompanied him on a ministerial visit to Europe. I'd given that trip my approval, encouraged by the signs of harmony in the Joyce household.

Later in the year, Vikki Campion moved out of Barnaby's office to work for Matt Canavan. I was only dimly aware of these moves. While staff assignments were formally approved by my office, the Nats controlled their own staffing arrangements.

Around the same time, of course, Barnaby came under enormous pressure from the citizenship saga, the ruling against him in the High Court and then having to go through a by-election in New England. Then whispers about his affair started to circulate, which Barnaby shut down with denials. He started to complain to me and others that his rivals were spreading the rumours. It was hard to know what was true.

However, the clouds of ambiguity were swept aside by a photograph of a very pregnant Vikki Campion on the front page of *The Daily Telegraph* on 7 February 2018. The dogged Sharri Markson had finally got her story. It was too bad for Vikki of course, not to speak of Natalie Joyce and her daughters.

Up until then, the government had been having a promising start to the year. We'd had an immediate boost in the first Newspoll of the year, published on 4 February. Our primary vote was up two points, my standing as preferred prime minister was up four points and my satisfaction rating had increased five points.

The Australian's Simon Benson wrote:

While Liberal leadership tensions are likely to be put to rest, with Coalition voters overwhelmingly backing Mr Turnbull as leader, Bill Shorten's pursuit of a radical left-wing economic agenda is set to be tested.

With the first Newspoll of 2018 showing the Coalition lifting its primary vote two points in the past two months, pressure is likely to intensify on the Opposition Leader, with Newspoll also revealing that almost half of all voters prefer either Anthony Albanese or Tanya Plibersek to Mr Shorten as federal Labor leader.[1]

The party room was buoyant and the media had begun to talk up our electoral fortunes again. The momentum was very much with us.

The Barnaby Joyce scandal derailed all of that.

It put me in a very difficult position. The media wanted to know the obvious – had I raised the rumours with the deputy prime minister?

Of course I had. But I was mindful of Barnaby's family and his own state of mind. So, I elected not to confirm that publicly at the time. How could I confirm the deputy prime minister of Australia had lied to the prime minister?

The overwhelming public view, 65 per cent according to Newspoll, was that Barnaby should resign as deputy prime minister. Would I sack him, I was asked. Well, I had no authority to sack him. He was the leader of the Nationals and only the parliamentary members of the National Party had the power to do so.

Inevitably, a frenzy of finger-pointing followed. Every time a Labor person sought to exploit Barnaby's predicament there were mutterings from our side about similar behaviour on their side.

It didn't take a huge amount of empathy to realise that in the real world, where our voters lived, all of this stank. 'So that's what the politicians do when they're in Canberra? Spend our money boozing and screwing the staff!'

Then again, when you look at it from the politicians' point of view, you'd think parliament is almost designed for this kind of thing. Hundreds of people away from home, long hours, too much drinking and what had been for many years a tacit agreement with the press gallery that dalliances wouldn't be reported on. (Well, with one or two massively high-profile exceptions.) Because they're private matters, or so it was said.

It wasn't the infidelities that surprised me but the extraordinary lack of discretion. Isn't it obvious that in a small ministerial office of, say, a dozen people, it will become a problem if the minister is sleeping with one of the staff? And given the high recognition of anyone in politics, isn't it obvious that hanging out in bars and restaurants with, generally, much younger women is going to draw attention? And not just of journalists: Canberra, after all, is full of spies and quite a lot of them don't work for us.

I'd already had to speak to several ministers about this kind of thing. But the reality is that too many of them regarded it as acceptable to sleep with their staff. Conduct that would today get you sacked in the private sector was, apparently, perfectly okay in Canberra. What was worse was that all too often the keenest practitioners of traditional adultery were also passionate defenders of traditional marriage. The same-sex marriage debate was dripping with such hypocrisy and, yet again, the pools were deepest at the feet of the sanctimonious.

On 11 February, I started drafting some changes to the Ministerial Code of Conduct to expressly prohibit sexual relations between ministers and their staff. This wasn't about adultery. It was about power. Among far too many politicians there is an ugly blokey culture of disrespecting women, which is no longer acceptable in contemporary Australia, let alone corporate workplaces, and should have no place in our parliament. How easy is it for the invariably younger female junior staff member to resist the advances of her older male boss? And when it goes sour, who is the one that has to change jobs? And to just add to the hypocrisy, if you weren't allowed to employ your spouse in your office, how could it be acceptable to employ your lover?

So I was surprised to find such strong opposition from the leadership group when I raised the ban on Monday 12 February. Only Pyne and Morrison supported the proposal. Barnaby, to his credit, said he wasn't opposed in principle but wanted the change to be delayed 'until the dust settles' so that it would not be seen as criticism of him.

As the week wore on, the scandal only got worse. Questions arose about when Vikki was moved to Canavan's office and then subsequently to the National Party whip's office. How much did the PMO know about it? And what about other ministerial Casanovas? Barnaby's own public reactions showed no contrition or empathy for his family, let alone his girlfriend.

I was due to be overseas for three days the following week. Was Barnaby going to be acting PM in my absence? If so, he wouldn't be able to go to ground: every day he'd be grilled about Vikki Campion. So, he agreed to take a week's leave, which he certainly needed to try to sort out his own domestic arrangements, not least with his wife, Natalie.

I mulled over the decision for most of the week until I brought it to a head on the Thursday afternoon, 15 February, after the final question time of the week. Scott and Christopher both came back to my office at the conclusion of parliament.

I was due to fly to Tasmania later that evening. Publicly, I was under mounting pressure to force Barnaby to resign as deputy prime minister. I couldn't help being angry with him. How could he have been so stupid, so recklessly selfish, as to do so much damage to our government. I couldn't sack him as he was the leader of the National Party and yet as every day wore on and we all lined up to defend him, we appeared to be condoning his conduct.

Christopher and Scott strongly supported the changes and my getting out to announce them there and then. As Christopher said, 'If you don't make this change now, we'll all get sucked into Barnaby's sordid mess. We can't let it drag on.'

He was right, I had to speak from the heart and Australians had to know what I was going to do to change the standards in their parliament. When I spoke to the press, I told them that we knew 'the real issue is the terrible hurt and humiliation that Barnaby by his conduct has visited on his wife, Natalie, and their daughters and indeed his new partner'.

I said that Barnaby had made a shocking error of judgement and would be taking leave next week. But this incident had raised serious issues about the culture of parliament and the Ministerial Code of Conduct, an outdated document that didn't speak strongly enough for the values that we all should live – 'values of respect, respectful workplaces, of workplaces where women are respected'.

I planned to make changes to the ministerial standards – specifically, that 'Ministers, regardless of whether they are married or single, must not engage in sexual relations with their staff. Doing so will constitute a breach of the standards.'[2]

I wasn't there to moralise but to recognise that whatever may have been acceptable, or to which a blind eye was turned in the past, in 2018 it wasn't acceptable for a minister to have a sexual relationship with somebody who worked for them. And with that, the ministerial standards changed.

Barnaby was furious with me and said so. We met a few days later and agreed on a way my department could audit his expenses and put to rest, one way or the other, the claims that he'd manipulated his travel so as to maximise the time he could spend on the road with Vikki, all at government expense. Then we put out a statement in which we confirmed we were working together to deliver good government and which added, 'Barnaby's concern was less about the sentiments Malcolm had expressed but the forcefulness with which he did, and the timing.' In short he wished I'd been less emphatic and had waited to make the rule change until after the 'dust had settled'.[3]

And that is essentially a question of judgement. Without a strong statement from me, I didn't believe the dust could settle and so I had to move when I did. Was my language too strong? Or perhaps it was my tone that made it so obvious how appalled I was by the mess he had created.

Barnaby was later to resign on 26 February, after Catherine Marriott, a prominent Western Australian cattle industry leader, made a complaint that Barnaby had behaved inappropriately towards her. Knowing Barnaby as well as I did, I had no doubt that the first person he'd blame for his troubles was me, and the last one was himself.

Not long before he resigned, he said to some cabinet colleagues, 'You know, if I resign, I could make a lot of trouble for Malcolm, working with Tony on the backbench.'

Shortly after the 15 February media conference, the press pack left, C1 rolled in, and we went out to the airport to fly to Tasmania.

That evening I looked at the front pages of the following day's newspapers. The media team always got them early. The tabloids had a field day. 'THE JOY-CE OF NO SEX' screamed the *Herald Sun*. 'NO MINISTER – PM BANS SEX' was *The Daily Telegraph*'s front page.

The ban had created a circuit breaker that pulled us out of the sordid spiral Barnaby was dragging us into.

Senior figures in the media, like Peter Hartcher, were scathing about it. And there was plenty of grumbling, mostly private, from colleagues. I had to reassure everyone that the rule change wasn't retrospective!

Changing culture and behaviour like this is very hard. But this was one case where I could make a hard and fast rule that set a clear standard.

There were then plenty of jokes about the ban, but it won't be changed. The office romances of ministers are the fairest of fair game for the media. Hopefully, this measure will over time help to make parliament a safer and more respectful place to work.

CHAPTER 45

Diplomacy, disloyalty and turning the corner on debt

2017 had ended uneasily. There was real satisfaction in finally legalising same-sex marriage but the citizenship crisis had generated much uncertainty. While Joyce and Alexander were out of the parliament pending their by-elections, there was a week where we had only 73 votes on the floor of the House and Labor and the crossbench had 74. We'd been very vulnerable – including to attacks from within the Coalition. The major attack – launched on 20 November – was when Andrew Bolt and Peta Credlin announced that an 'unnamed Coalition MP' would quit the government if I was still prime minister by the end of the parliamentary sittings.[1] When their would-be saboteur, George Christensen, changed his mind at the last minute and didn't go through with it, this enraged Credlin and Bolt. The latter wrote on 3 December, 'He told me that he meant his threat and explicitly told me I should report it without fear that he'd back down and make me look like a party to mischief.'[2]

Christensen's conduct was especially sickening – not simply because he was taking advantage of the temporary absence of his close friend, Barnaby Joyce, but because it was his misconduct that had resulted in one of my worst moments as prime minister.

There is plenty of bad news in a prime minister's life. Often it's tragedy, innocent lives lost in a natural disaster or a terrorist attack. But 15 September 2017 was uniquely awkward.

Federal Police Commissioner Andrew Colvin had asked to see me alone. We sat down at 12.30 and he told me that some months earlier the AFP had been given a tip that Christensen was involved in questionable activity in the Philippines. Sceptical at first, they'd made some enquiries and learned that since 2014 he'd been spending about 100 days a year away mostly in the Philippines as well as Thailand. Colvin described how Christensen had an unusually complex online presence and had been spending substantial sums in Manila bars and nightclubs as well as making many small payments to women there. Against the advice of our embassy in the Philippines, he had been staying in seedy hotels in Angeles City, which was not only recklessly unsafe but made him vulnerable to being compromised.

Colvin said he was telling me because Christensen was about to go to Manila on an official visit. They expected he'd stay on there after the official business was over. The Philippines police were aware of their concerns and it was possible, if his conduct did involve a breach of the law, that there could be an arrest. He said if the conclusion was that there was nothing illegal going on – in other words, he wasn't involved in sex with minors – then they'd simply counsel him on his imprudent behaviour.

Christensen is a young man, grossly obese and at that time single. He manifested a familiar collection of right-wing views: he denies climate change, denounces Muslim immigration and presents as a devoutly religious person. Not only is there a statue of the Virgin Mary in his office, he has a tattoo of her on his right shoulder!

Regardless of whether his conduct in the Philippines broke the law or not, for a member in a marginal seat to be spending nearly a third of the year overseas, on full pay as an MP, staying in a seedy part of Manila and hanging out in bars and nightclubs beggared belief. The hypocrisy made me sick.

I was also staggered that the National Party whip had either not known about Christensen's long absences or not cared. He should have been pulled into line a long time ago. His National Party colleagues knew he spent a lot of time in the Philippines – nobody apparently was aware how much.

Whether I should have been briefed at this point or not is a good question, but having been told, I was now in a position where I couldn't under any circumstances let Christensen know about the police interest in his conduct or let on that I knew about it, lest he cover his tracks.

The AFP continued their investigations over the months that followed and eventually concluded, by June 2018, that they couldn't find any evidence of illegal conduct. In the lead-up to the May 2019 election, Christensen announced he had a girlfriend in the Philippines, whom he subsequently married. Despite his Manila escapades being public knowledge by the time of the election, he was returned with an increased majority. It says something about our times, that conduct which in years past would have finished the career of any politician has been so readily forgiven by his electorate.

Credlin and Bolt insisted that Christensen had used and misled them, but the idea that that pair was being manipulated – innocent dupes in the hands of big George – strains credulity. A more objective assessment would say the three of them were in it together right from the jump and then, at the last minute, Christensen lost his nerve.

Kerry Stokes later revealed to me that around this time, before Christmas 2017, he was invited to a meeting with Alan Jones. Tony Abbott was also there and the pair asked him to help them in bringing down my government. He said to me that he told them they were mad and left.

However, Jones wasn't put off. According to Angus Taylor, Jones asked him to publicly call for my resignation. Taylor knocked him back, as others unknown to me may have done. But Jones was more successful with John Barilaro, the National Party deputy premier of New South Wales, who on 1 December called for me to resign. It was a pretty feeble attempt to get momentum for a coup underway, but as Taylor wrote to me at the time, 'Jones' only mode of operation right now is "destroy the joint".'[3]

From a policy point of view, we were scraping the bigger barnacles off the boat. School funding had been addressed with Gonski 2.0, the citizenship mess seemed to be over at least for our side, same-sex marriage was legal. The big wicked problem remaining was energy. Not wanting to repeat the events of 2009, I was very careful with the National Energy Guarantee (NEG), as I will relate elsewhere, to make sure it had the support of the cabinet and the party room. Nobody could say I wasn't being assiduously inclusive and consultative.

Barnaby's baby and the 'bonk ban' were a massive distraction in February 2018. I happened to be in the exquisite Dillon Drawing Room of Blair House in Washington on 22 February when Mathias Cormann abruptly interrupted my contemplation of its 1770 green Chinese-painted wallpaper. Mathias, ever glued to his smartphone, told me that Joyce had resigned as leader of the Nationals and deputy PM. It didn't cause much of a stir in DC; the president was sympathetic.

The first few months of 2018 were busy on the diplomatic front. In Japan at our annual leaders' meeting, Shinzo Abe and I resolved to press on with the TPP even if the Canadians pulled out again. That worked, and the TPP-11 was agreed and signed in March.

My February US trip had included the National Governors Association Winter Meeting in Washington. Australia was the guest nation and with me was a large business delegation and most of the state premiers. I had an opportunity to speak not just to the president and federal officials but almost all the state governors as well. One of them was my old friend and partner from Goldman Sachs days, Phil Murphy, the governor of New Jersey. Phil and Tammy Murphy are a formidable political team, and Phil has all of the blarney of a Boston Irishman, which is why I'd urged him to run for president when we first met, 21 years before.

The almost universal feedback from the governors was that we'd done the right thing by sticking with the TPP. They envied the preferred access our farmers had to the Japanese market.

Lucy accompanied me on this visit, which included a reception and lunch at the White House. The Trumps were charming and hospitable, and I succeeded in confirming yet again that there would be no tariffs on Australian steel or aluminium. 'You backed the President into a corner,' Gary Cohn, his national economic adviser, later remonstrated. I thought that was a bit rich coming from another former Goldman Sachs partner.

The ASEAN–Australia Special Summit in Sydney in March 2018 was very successful, deepening cooperation on security, including counter-terrorism, trade, resisting the protectionism coming from the USA, and on smart cities and connectivity, a particular passion of both PM Lee of Singapore and myself. Stronger ties with ASEAN – and particularly its biggest member, Indonesia – continued to be a key objective of my government's foreign policy.

It was in April that the first real sign of troubles with Dutton emerged. During his time first as minister for Border Protection and Immigration and then Home Affairs we had worked together very well. I felt we broadly shared the same objectives under the belief that immigration is a recruiting exercise managed in Australia's national interest: ensuring that the system supported our economy with the skilled migrants we needed, and generally upholding our integrated multicultural society. So, with strong support from other ministers, including Scott, we reformed the 457 temporary visa system and also proposed increasing the English-language requirements for new citizens.

There had been for many years a budget assumption that annual permanent migration would be 190,000 people. This was about two-thirds skilled visas and a third family reunion, almost all foreign spouses of Australian citizens. The Immigration Department had treated this as a target, and in the 2016 budget, consistent with my philosophy on immigration, the cabinet had resolved that it was a ceiling; in other words, we should not take more permanent immigrants than our economy required and if that was less than 190,000, so be it.

On 10 April, *The Australian* claimed that Dutton had sought to reduce the 190,000 figure to 170,000 but had been rolled by me and by Morrison.[4] The clear purpose of the briefing was to position Dutton as taking a harder line on immigration than me or Morrison. As Dutton confirmed to me at the time, he had made no such proposal to cabinet or to any committee of cabinet, but the briefing to *The Australian* continued and coincided with the government losing 30 Newspolls in a row – a benchmark my enemies in the media and in the party hoped to exploit.

Scott began then to be concerned that Dutton was positioning himself to be drafted. I was less suspicious, but concerned about the hamfistedness of it all. If Dutton had wanted to reduce the permanent migration figure he could have readily presented it to ERC or cabinet, but had not done so. Scott confirmed Pezzullo, Dutton's secretary, did not want to change the figure – as a ceiling, it gave us flexibility. Moreover, the real growth in migration was not in the permanent migration stream but in the growing number of temporary visas and especially foreign students, of which there were now around half a million in Australia. Scott summed it up well: 'Whatever Dutts may have wanted had nothing to do with policy, just crass politics, and he wasn't prepared to bowl it up.'[5]

Dutton for his own part tried to persuade me the troublemaker was Barnaby Joyce and that the whole exercise was part of a News Corporation 'mini campaign during the 30 [Newspolls] mark'.[6]

The whole episode left me very disappointed with Dutton, as I wrote in my diary at the time: 'He is very loose and imprecise, he lacks the intellect and discipline that he needs to perform at the highest level, very wooly – not a detail guy and its showing. I am going to take a much closer role with respect to his portfolio as a result. A pity, I thought he was better.'[7]

April also took me to London for the Commonwealth Heads of Government Meeting. The UK's diplomatic objective was to ensure that the Commonwealth nations agreed that after the Queen's death, Prince Charles would succeed as head of the Commonwealth. This was far from assured. India had real reservations.

We'd given the UK and Buckingham Palace our assurance of support. While I'm a republican in the Australian context, I couldn't see any better option than Charles and, at a personal level, I've always found him to be a thoroughly decent man with sensible and progressive views on the environment in particular.

But nothing was to be left to chance and to demonstrate the awesome convening power of the British monarchy, the royal family turned out in force for a state dinner at Buckingham Palace and the conference itself at Windsor Castle.

The charm offensive worked and the Commonwealth leaders agreed that Charles would be the next head of the Commonwealth. Pointedly, this was a personal appointment and was expressed as being based on an assessment of his qualities and commitment to the Commonwealth. In other words, the leaders didn't accept the British royal family possessed an hereditary right to the office.

After CHOGM, Lucy and I travelled to France for one of the most moving ceremonial visits of my time as prime minister. It was also the backdrop for one of the funniest moments.

Anzac Day 2018 was the culmination of our commemoration of the sacrifice of 60,000 Australian dead in the First World War. One of them was Lucy's great-uncle Roger, whose grave we visited at Heilly Station in Flanders. Roger was a doctor who'd been in France for only a few weeks when he was fatally wounded. His brother, Geoffrey Hughes, Lucy's grandfather, was an ace fighter pilot serving in the Royal Flying Corps nearby and rushed to his brother, who died in his arms.

On 24 April, I'd opened the Sir John Monash Centre, a modern museum and memorial to both Australia's greatest general and the troops he led in the First World War. The new Monash Centre was next to the Australian Memorial at Villers-Bretonneux, the site of the battle when, on 25 April 1918, Australian troops – supported by British and French Moroccan brigades – recaptured the town in what became a final turning point in the war. The Monash Centre was Tony Abbott's idea and I was glad that he was there, together with the French prime minister, Édouard Philippe.

However, the most solemn moment came in the hours before dawn in front of the Australian Memorial, an austere stone tower flanked by walls showing the names of over 10,000 Australians who died on the Western Front and for whom there is no grave.

As I sat in the dark waiting for the dawn, Lucy and I reflected on the visible damage to the monument inflicted in the Second World War – only a few years after it had been officially opened in 1938. A monument to commemorate the war to end all wars, completed just in time for another.

The speeches were sombre and dignified and the music and pageantry likewise. It was bitterly cold and it rained. A bleak setting to contemplate so many young lives thrown away in the folly of war.

I spoke of the dead. 'We honour their bravery, their sacrifice and their loyalty. We show they are not forgotten.' But I added, as I always did, 'For the best way to honour the courage and sacrifice of the diggers of World War One is to support the servicemen and women, the veterans and the families of today.'

But then, amidst the grim solemnity, came a very special Australian moment.

We were sitting with Prince Charles and the French PM on the left-hand side of the huge audience. The serried ranks of ministers, generals, admirals and air-marshals were all around us.

The Australian flag was in front of us, at half-mast. Across the other side of the memorial, France's *tricoleur* was also at half-mast. The bugler had played 'The Last Post', and now he began to play the 'Reveille'. All in white, an Australian sailor was manning the lanyards on the Australian flagpole; a French soldier was doing the honours on his side. Each looking straight ahead.

I noticed something was amiss. The Australian flag wasn't slowly rising; it was coming down. Lucy poked me. She'd seen the same. I expected a warrant officer would swiftly rectify the misdirection. But nothing happened. As the French flag rose, ours continued to sink.

So, I got up and walked over to the sailor. 'Our flag is falling; it's meant to be rising,' I whispered in his ear. He looked up and then, entirely in accordance with naval tradition, swore emphatically. Our flag reversed direction and shot up the flagpole, beating the French one to the top.

Nobody seemed to have noticed. They must have been frozen. Charles was droll. 'Very decisive action, Prime Minister,' he said.

After the dawn service, we headed into Villers-Bretonneux itself, walked down Rue de Melbourne, and visited the Victoria School, whose hall bears the inscription, '*Nous n'oublions jamais l'Australie*' – we never forget Australia. Surrounded by Australian and French veterans and the descendants of those who'd fought so bravely a century ago, the more relaxed ceremony in V-B was in its own way as moving as the dawn service.

If my brief word to the sailor avoided one disaster, Lucy's suggestion of a round of coffees with brandy at the bar served to thaw us out. Édouard regaled us with stories of how much brandy he'd had to drink in his campaign to be elected mayor of the tough port city of Le Havre.

Once we were back in Australia, President Emmanuel Macron visited us, the first French president to do so. The submarine contract constitutes a multi-generational partnership between Australia and France and already we had a team of naval architects and engineers working in Cherbourg whom I visited at the Naval Group HQ.

With New Caledonia and French Polynesia, France is a Pacific nation and part of our strategy was to encourage France to be more engaged in our region. We supported the admission of New Caledonia as a member of the Pacific Islands Forum.

Macron and I had got on well from the first time we met at the Hamburg G20 in 2017 and then dined in the garden of the Élysée Palace. We shared a similar political outlook and values, just as we shared a concern about the rise in right-wing authoritarian populism around the world and the protectionism and xenophobia that has come with it.

But the best moment of the visit was unplanned. Emmanuel speaks excellent English (so much better than my now woeful French), but at the end of our joint press conference on 2 May, ever gallant, he said, 'Thank you, Malcolm, and your delicious wife for your warm welcome ...'

Of course in French *délicieuse* means delightful, but far from offended, Lucy was thrilled. 'If the handsome forty-year-old president of France wants to call me delicious, I will certainly not complain!' she said.

The international agenda didn't distract me from the business of getting the 2018 budget together. In both 2016 and 2017, we'd produced good budgets that had been well received. We'd progressively dropped the zombies from the disastrous 2014 budget and had maintained our trajectory to a budget surplus in 2020–21. Because of the record jobs growth during my time as PM, tax receipts grew above estimations and so revenue was higher than expected.

On our third budget, in 2018, Scott and I had learned a lot about working with each other and the process was by far the smoothest. There was no front-running of budget measures and our deliberations were held, as they should be, in confidence.

In addition to the Western Sydney City Deal, in the lead-up to the budget I announced the Commonwealth's commitment of $5 billion to building the new rail line from Melbourne to Tullamarine Airport in partnership with the Victorian government. Just like the North South Rail Line that is part of the Western Sydney City Deal, this was an investment rather than a grant, with the project to be jointly owned.

Victorian Premier Daniel Andrews and I sat down together in the PM's office in Melbourne and agreed on a route through Sunshine that we'd concluded offered the best outcome both in terms of cost and city shaping. As well, we agreed Victoria would provide new tram services to the new urban renewal project we were planning on the 128-hectare Maribyrnong defence site.

Our strong revenues enabled us to drop the proposed increase in the Medicare levy from the 2017 budget. We were now confident we had enough revenue to fund the NDIS into the future. We were able to forecast a tiny surplus of $2 billion in 2019–20, a year early, but we were careful to call it 'a balance' and maintain our plan to have a surplus budget in 2020–21.

We were also able to turn the corner on debt. Net debt would peak as a percentage of GDP in 2017–18 at 18.6 per cent and then fall every year thereafter. This reduction in net debt was enabled by the usual factors – revenues steadily growing faster than spending – but was assisted by the way in which I'd shifted as much of our spending on infrastructure from grants to the states, which showed up as an expense, to investments in assets that we owned.

But most importantly, in 2018 we achieved a major reform to personal income tax – a part realisation of my tax reform plans of 2005. I'd promised in late 2017 that in 2018 we'd deliver tax relief for middle-income Australians and the budget did. Over 10 million Australians got a tax rebate of up to $530 and about half received the full amount. So, that was useful cash in the hand in the here and now.

But a series of changes to tax rates and thresholds followed, to culminate in 2024–25 with the elimination of the 37 cent tax bracket – with the consequence that from that tax year, 94 per cent of Australians wouldn't pay a marginal rate of more than 32.5 cents in the dollar. Specifically, the 32.5 cent bracket would cut in at $41,000 up to $200,000, from where the 45 cent rate would apply.

Inexplicably, the Labor Party furiously attacked this reform despite the fact that the principal beneficiaries were people on middle incomes and that the top 20 per cent of income earners would continue to pay the same share of total income tax – around 61 per cent. Suggesting that people on $150,000 or $200,000 a year are 'the big end of town' and 'Malcolm's rich mates', as Shorten did, was part of Labor's disastrous class war strategy that ultimately contributed to their surprise election loss in 2019.

The popularity of the reform assisted its quick passage through the Senate. In the 2019 budget, Treasurer Josh Frydenberg built on this by reducing the 32.5 cent bracket to 30 cents.

A few months before the budget, Labor had announced it would no longer allow investors who received franked dividends to get a cash refund from the ATO if they couldn't use the credit to offset their other tax liabilities. This would have overwhelmingly impacted on self-funded retirees on relatively low incomes and superannuation funds.

The cash refund was costing about $5 billion a year. But Labor utterly failed to recognise the hardship this change would impose on retired Australians, most on low incomes. We weighed into the 'retiree tax' with gusto while Labor equally trumpeted it as an example of their attack on 'the top end of town'. The problem was, as I often pointed out, that anyone with substantial assets would be able to use their franking credits to offset tax liabilities elsewhere in the portfolio. We'd considered dropping the unlegislated part of the company tax cuts – those applying to companies with revenues over $50 million a year. By the time of the budget, Scott supported sticking with them. In doing so, I relied heavily on Mathias's assurance that he was close to stitching together the numbers on the crossbench to pass them. I relied on the same assurance when we decided not to drop them before the July by-elections.

The twists and turns of the negotiations with the crossbench, especially with Pauline Hanson, could fill a book of their own. We looked at every possible angle: increasing the threshold to $100 million a year, extending it to all companies except the banks – and other variations. But we couldn't get there, and so in what turned out to be the week of the coup, we put the full company tax cuts up in the Senate for one last time. When they were rejected on 22 August, Mathias, Scott and I formally announced they were abandoned and we wouldn't take them to the next election.

I don't think, as others have suggested, Mathias was setting me up, and I accept he did come close to obtaining agreement. He had a proven track record of getting legislation through the Senate. But, all that said, while I had no doubt that it was the right policy, with the benefit of hindsight we probably would have been better off dropping the tax cuts for bigger companies at the 2018 budget or shortly thereafter.

By July 2018, our focus had turned to one of the most complex barnacles – the Western Australian share of the GST. Few things are more arcane than the way in which the Commonwealth Grants Commission divides among the states and territories what is now around $70 billion being received from the GST. I'd be surprised if more than a dozen Australians at any time understood how the model worked.

The big idea behind horizontal fiscal equalisation is to ensure that the smaller states are able to afford their citizens the same level of public services as the larger states. The benchmark had been, for many years, that the GST shares should be adjusted so that overall those smaller states and territories had revenues comparable to the state with the strongest fiscal capacity, and for many decades the system had worked fairly well. New South Wales and Victoria received less than 100 cents in the dollar of GST collected in their states. The big beneficiaries were Tasmania, the Northern Territory, South Australia and, in years past, Western Australia.

However, the mining boom after 2007 saw Western Australia's state minerals royalties more than treble.[8] It became the strongest state and, as a result, started to receive around 30 cents in the dollar.

This unfair GST share had become the biggest issue in Western Australia. But at the same time every other state, especially Tasmania, was on the alert for any change that would result in their receiving less money. So, the Commonwealth proceeded to top up WA with additional payments, which were gladly received but didn't represent a long-term fix. The system had lost all credibility in Western Australia and was too complex to explain.

We'd commissioned a Productivity Commission review of the GST split in May 2017 which reported a year later and recommended that the shares be equalised to the average of the states' fiscal capacity.

The political challenge was how to deliver a GST share to Western Australia that would be seen as fair in Perth without any of the other states being worse off. I was very lucky to have three good friends as Liberal premiers in key states – Will Hodgman in Tasmania, Steven Marshall in South Australia and Gladys Berejiklian in New South Wales. The deal nearly ran off the rails when Scott had a colourful row with the Tasmanian treasurer, Peter Gutwein. I heard about it from Will Hodgman, so I called Scott. He said he had been rude and had apologised. 'Did you use the "f" word?' I asked him.

'Oh yes,' he said. 'But … also the "m" word.'

What was that, I asked, genuinely mystified. 'Mendicant,' said Scott. Oh dear, I thought, that's a fighting word to a Tasmanian!

But Will was unruffled and so, carefully, we put together a deal in which a 75 cents in the dollar floor was set and none of the smaller states was worse off. As usual, a substantial additional Commonwealth contribution to the GST pool – this time of around $1 billion a year – made it all work.

The resolution was absolutely critical to our prospects in Western Australia. We'd have lost almost every seat in that state without it. Delivering durable GST reform was, and will remain, a long-term asset for the Coalition in WA. And to have done this without making enemies everywhere else was remarkable.

But there remained enormous anxiety around the cabinet table and especially from Peter Dutton. I wrote this in my diary on 4 July just before we announced the new arrangements:

Dutton basically never wants to do anything risky, he is not a leader, lacks courage or conviction, other than when he can revert to some hard line measures he thinks will go down well on 2GB. This is not to say he is a bad guy, but rather that he doesn't have the courage to make a call – always preferring to be hanging back, muttering about risks without offering an alternative. Happy to push on open doors only.

I was feeling pretty good about our position in early July. On 8 July I wrote:

> *Generally the sense is that things are going better for us, the LNP were happy yesterday (when I spoke at their State Convention), Abbott and Joyce are trying to ramp up an internal war on energy/Paris etc supported by The Australian and Sky News – wreckers all of them. But as David Speers had to acknowledge this morning, the Reachtel poll on the question showed a mere 68% against leaving Paris – so that's precisely the type of policy we should adopt!*

As described in chapter 42, on 9 May, the High Court decided that a Labor senator from the ACT, Katy Gallagher, was ineligible under section 44. Three Labor members of the House were in the same situation. So too was Bek Sharkie of the Centre Alliance party, formerly known as NXT. All resigned. Accordingly, we faced by-elections in Longman in Queensland, Mayo in South Australia, Braddon in Tasmania, and Perth and Fremantle in Western Australia.

Wisely, we didn't run in the two Western Australian seats, both safe Labor. Georgina Downer did run for Mayo, her father's old seat, but the prospects of unseating Bek Sharkie were never good and despite an energetic and well-resourced campaign she was unsuccessful.

The two marginal Labor seats of Braddon and Longman were different and we decided to contest them, even though by-elections normally swing against the government; it was nearly a century since a government had won a seat from the opposition. In the Bennelong by-election, I'd been able to argue that if Labor won the seat, Shorten would be almost in The Lodge. However, whether Labor won or lost Braddon and Longman, the Coalition would still have a majority. So, the by-elections were an opportunity for voters to have a free kick at the government without any risk of changing it, or so it seemed.

Despite this, and my frequent reminders of that history, expectations developed that we might win one or both of these seats. Several public polls indicated we were ahead, although the only minister who suggested we'd win Longman was Peter Dutton. His seat of Dickson was adjacent to it. Our own polling, however, as Dutton knew, was never that confident. In May our poll in Longman showed us losing 58:42 to Labor, which was about where we finished on 28 July when the by-elections were held. Our primary vote was down by about 9 per cent with most of that going to

One Nation. However, on a two-party preferred basis the swing to Labor was less than 4 per cent and so, in fact, below the average for by-elections.

The LNP had struggled to find a candidate in Longman. 'Big Trev' Ruthenberg wasn't well known in the electorate until it appeared he'd claimed he had a Defence Force Service Medal, to which he wasn't entitled. It was an innocent mistake, he said, but in the heat of a campaign very damaging. For many voters, it was about the only thing they knew about him, and that in an electorate with a lot of veterans. By contrast, the Labor member, Susan Lamb, was well liked and, as had been the case with Joyce and Alexander, voters didn't seem to blame her for her ineligibility. The LNP never believed it could win Longman and limited its spending on the by-election whereas Labor spent a fortune on television, radio and social media.

In Tasmania, our candidate for Braddon, the former Liberal member Brett Whitely, was a good campaigner but had many detractors in the electorate. The Tasmanian division, however, couldn't find an attractive cleanskin candidate. Whitely was also running against a popular independent, Craig Garland, a local fisherman. Eric Abetz didn't help by savagely attacking Garland, who went on to win more than 10 per cent of the primary vote and preferenced Labor. The final result in Braddon was very close, a tiny swing against us and one readily explained by local factors.

Without those local factors, we'd almost certainly have won Braddon, but Longman, realistically, wasn't winnable. My internal enemies, including Dutton and Abbott and their friends in the right-wing media, sought to create a panic within the LNP – never hard to achieve. They pointed to the swing to One Nation as evidence the Liberal Party under my leadership was too left-wing. Once again they were arguing we needed to be more like Pauline Hanson.

The timing of the by-elections couldn't have been worse. We were bringing the NEG negotiations with the states to a head. Abbott and co were ramping up the campaign against the NEG and calling on us to pull out of the Paris Agreement, as Trump had done.

Ironically, just as the right wing were denying climate change, Australian farmers were suffering its worsening consequences. Much of Queensland had been in drought for several years, but by winter 2018 it had extended into most of New South Wales and Victoria as well. Lucy and my properties weren't exempt.

Over the years of running the farm since Dad's death on 11 November 1982, we'd seen several droughts and the invidious choices that face graziers. If you destock your property and the drought breaks, prices go up and you struggle to restock. If you buy hay and hand-feed your stock and it doesn't rain, you'll take a big financial hit and have to destock anyway. In this current drought, I wished I'd destocked sooner.

There was then, and still is, a lot of uninformed hysteria about drought. People in the cities, especially in the media, get carried away with the emotion of it all. Crazy ideas are proposed – like using the army to cart water to farms whose dams are dry. Politicians talk about building dams – as though that is going to help the thousands of farmers, like us, whose properties aren't connected to any irrigation scheme.

I spent a lot of time listening to farmers, some wise and well informed – like NFF President Fiona Simpson, whose property is on the Liverpool Plains – others completely overwhelmed by the natural disaster and feeling helpless and devastated. For too many farmers, helplessness in the face of nature's ruin has led to deep depression and death.

The cabinet agreed to provide additional welfare assistance both in terms of payments to families and support for continuing employment in local communities. It all helps, but we couldn't deliver what's really needed: rain.

And as I listened to one farmer after another, the message was consistent. As they pored over their rainfall records, some going back well over a century, it was obvious that the climate had changed. It was getting hotter and it was getting drier – just like the scientists said it would. Rainfall was becoming more erratic and 'hundred-year droughts' were coming around every 10 years, it seemed. And of course, hotter and drier means more fires.

The irony was sickening. Climate change was devastating rural Australia at the same time as many of its political representatives in the Liberal and National parties were calling for more coal-fired power stations and wanting to withdraw from the Paris Agreement.

I used to phone farmers so I could get a first-hand sense of what they were facing. One night at The Lodge, as I finished my last call, I wondered: will there ever be a reckoning between the farmers of Australia, battered by the reality of climate change, and the politicians who denied it was occurring at all?

CHAPTER 46

Climate denial and the National Energy Guarantee

Of all of the toxic time bombs ticking away in the prime minister's desk drawer, none was more dangerous than energy policy, and nobody was politically more at risk from it than me.

So, as I noted down the wicked problems I had to resolve, right at the top of the list was energy policy.

I was certain about our objectives. We needed to evolve our energy system to a point where all, or almost all, of our energy came from zero- or near-zero-emission sources. And on the way, meet our Paris Agreement obligations to cut our emissions by 26–28 per cent by 2030.[1] Where we had to use fossil fuels, we needed to be able to offset those emissions in some way. This transition had to be achieved in a manner that enabled us to keep energy affordable and reliable – in other words, we had to keep the lights on and be able to afford to pay for it.

I was confident we could reach this trifecta of low emissions, affordability and reliability with renewables, plus storage. Assisted by the electrification of the economy, including electric cars and trucks and electric (rather than gas) heating, huge cuts in emissions are very achievable, but we needed a plan.

Most Australians would agree with all of that, but in the microcosm of the Liberal and National party rooms we faced a different reality. Many of my colleagues simply didn't believe climate change was real and wanted to pull out of the Paris Agreement.

A number of them, and especially Abbott, wanted to use energy once again as the means by which to bring down my leadership, as they'd done in 2009. And I had to recognise that around my cabinet table were people who, while they supported my leadership for the time being, had been prominent in the anti-ETS insurgency in 2009, including Mathias Cormann and Barnaby Joyce.

A few weeks before I became PM, the Abbott cabinet had resolved to agree to the Paris Agreement (to be signed in December 2015) and to commit to those emissions reductions targets. We also had a longstanding pledge to review all our climate policies by 2017 which meant that during the 2016 election campaign I was able to keep the climate issue fairly low-key.

Since then, knowing they couldn't credibly accuse me of being a climate change denier, Labor had instead tried to portray my failure to abandon Abbott's toothless climate policies as evidence of my lacking conviction on what had been core political values.

It was precisely the same attack they'd made about same-sex marriage and my failure to abandon the plebiscite policy – all of which seemed very hollow when I actually legalised same-sex marriage. And these attacks from the left had one goal: to wedge me against my own party room and bring my leadership to an end. It was the one goal Shorten and Abbott had in common.

Nevertheless, results matter. On energy I knew I had to navigate not just a tricky technical policy area but also this extremely dangerous political environment. As usual, the so-called conservative voices in the media whose climate denialist views were shared by a large percentage, maybe a majority, of Liberal and National Party members were helping to weaponise the issue.

But it wasn't just the politics that were tricky. Following Abbott's review of the RET, the target had been reduced, not unreasonably, but there had been considerable and justified anxiety that his real agenda was to scrap it altogether. There was a chill on investment followed by a rush to invest both in large-scale renewables and rooftop solar once the new target was confirmed. Both wind and solar generate at zero marginal cost. In other words, no matter what the capital cost of the wind or solar farm, there's no additional cost to produce another megawatt hour (MWh) of electricity, and that of course is because there's no fuel cost. This means that wind and solar will always bid at the lowest prices into the National Electricity Market (NEM).[2]

This additional variable renewable energy (VRE) was coming into the NEM in large quantities and undermining the business model of coal-fired generation. Coal-fired generators need to run continuously, but with high levels of VRE they can only sell their output at a satisfactory price some of the time. This impact on their business was occurring at the same time as a number of those old coal-fired power stations were getting to the end of their useful lives. Without any bipartisan integration of climate and energy policy and with a growing awareness in the business world about the urgent need to decarbonise, there was simply no prospect of new private sector investment into coal-fired generation.

The RET imposed no restriction on where new renewable capacity should be built and certainly didn't require assurances of back-up for when the wind didn't blow and the sun didn't shine.

South Australia attracted nearly half of all the wind farms built in Australia and a good deal of the solar as well. Not only did it have a great wind resource but it traditionally had high power prices. And its Labor government was an enthusiastic supporter of renewables.

By 2016 the wind farms in South Australia alone could produce more than 100 per cent of the state's demand, but then when the wind dropped, zero. Solar panels worked more predictably and also at times of high demand: a hot summer's day would see both air-conditioners and solar panels working overtime, at least until the sun went down. But wind wasn't at all aligned with demand. For much of the year the windiest hours were at night, and heatwaves often coincided with still, windless days.

This additional energy supply ultimately caused the state's 520 MW coal-fired Northern Power Station to close in May 2016 and some of the state's gas-fired electricity-generating capacity was mothballed as well. Increasingly, South Australia relied for back-up on an interconnector with Victoria when the renewables weren't generating.

On 28 September 2016, a violent storm knocked out a series of transmission lines and simultaneously caused a number of wind farms to switch off, triggering a blackout across South Australia. While power was restored to Adelaide within hours, some of the state's industrial heartland including BHP's Olympic Dam and the steelworks at Whyalla (which the Northern Power Station used to serve) were without power for weeks. The furious political debate that followed was dumbed down into a debate about whether it was caused by too much renewables and not enough coal (as Barnaby Joyce often said) or whether it was simply a freak storm.

But one thing was becoming obvious to me, as I said at the time: we clearly hadn't recognised that a grid increasingly based on VRE was entirely different to what we were used to and had to be carefully planned.

Part of the problem had been the breezy assumption that we'd always have cheap gas available to run peaking plants that could be quickly switched on or off to meet variations in renewable energy.

The COAG Energy ministers met immediately after the blackout and on 7 October 2016 commissioned the chief scientist, Alan Finkel, to lead an independent review into the security of the NEM.

Previously, I mentioned my determination to integrate climate and energy policy, which is why I'd appointed one of my most capable younger ministers, Josh Frydenberg, minister for the Environment and Energy. In late November, the cabinet had agreed on the terms of reference for the review of our climate policy – back in 2013, we'd promised it would be conducted in 2017. Now that the Finkel review was the main show in town, I asked Josh to put the terms of reference on the department's website but to say nothing about it. Let it speak for itself; don't discuss it or speculate about it and above all don't canvass what it might or might not cover.

The terms of reference were posted on Monday 5 December. To our horror, Josh went out on ABC Radio and said the review would include consideration of having an emissions intensity scheme (EIS) for the energy sector; this wasn't even referred to in the terms of reference. This of course set off Abbott, Bernardi and other climate change deniers in the Coalition, who quickly started to frame a new round of the climate wars within the party.

If we were ever to move to an EIS, as I told Frydenberg the following afternoon in my office, it would have to be as the result of a carefully considered analysis by Finkel, with widespread industry support and proof that it would lower prices. Now he, and therefore we, had to beat a retreat and rule out an EIS rather than spend the summer fighting about a policy we didn't know whether we'd support.

It was, in a smaller and less consequential way, the same mistake Morrison had made in front-running the idea of raising the GST – you invite a debate on a policy you haven't yet adopted, aren't in a position to powerfully defend, and then, when you disavow it, you're seen to have retreated. I reminded Josh that, as I'd learned from bitter experience, it's only the things you say that get you into trouble. Silence or circumspection rarely create a problem.

· · ·

The South Australian blackout had confirmed that we were facing a real energy crisis. And it seemed that the biggest oversight was introducing so much VRE into the system without making provision for it to be stored or backed up.

As generation became more intermittent as coal-fired generators closed down, the need for gas peakers increased. But to make matters worse, gas prices on the east coast were going through the roof. Gas peakers were setting the price, and as a result electricity prices were growing at a compound rate of 8 per cent.

This ugly combination meant the wholesale cost of generation went up by about 18 per cent in 2016–17 and was only going to go higher following the imminent closure of Victoria's Hazelwood Power Station, a 50-year-old burner of brown coal – the dirtiest and highest-emission fuel of all. In the next year, following the closure of Hazelwood, wholesale costs of generation were expected to increase a further 42 per cent.[3]

At my request, on 20 December 2016 Oliver Yates, the head of the Clean Energy Finance Corporation (CEFC), gave me a detailed brief on pumped hydroelectric energy storage (PHES) – pumping water uphill when electricity is cheap and running it downhill to generate electricity when prices are high.

January 2017 was a time of intense research for me, and I consulted widely. Jeff Connolly from Siemens was very helpful, as was Grant King, the former CEO of Origin Energy, which operated a pumped storage system on the Shoalhaven River.

The most interesting work was that of Andrew Blakers at the ANU, whom the Australian Renewable Energy Agency had funded to do a national atlas of potential off-river pumped hydro sites. Blakers's thesis was that there were thousands of sites for relatively small (say 10-hectare) dams to be built, not connected to a river system, but with sufficient difference in elevation to make pumped hydro viable. Like most people, I'd always assumed that as a flat, dry continent with not much in the way of water or mountains, Australia wasn't a promising environment for new hydro. Besides, who would want to build a new dam with the inevitable environmental disputes?

After speaking to Blakers, I read deeply on energy-storage technologies in general and pumped hydro in particular. As a frustrated engineer I love this kind of research. It took me back to my time as Water minister and my research into Roman aqueducts. Before long, I was convinced that we needed to make the construction of new pumped hydro a national priority. And the need was urgent because while it was possible to build a new solar farm or wind farm in a year or two, the planning and construction of new hydro systems would take far longer. If we didn't get moving, we'd see more old coal-fired clunkers exit the system without anything reliable to replace them, other than increasingly unaffordable gas peakers.

My first big political speech in 2017 was on 1 February at the National Press Club. I said that 'Energy storage, long neglected in Australia, will also be a priority this year' and announced that the previous week I'd asked ARENA and the CEFC to establish a new funding round for large-scale storage projects, including pumped hydro, and asked Alan Finkel to specifically address the role of pumped hydro in stabilising the grid.

As soon as the speech was over, I asked my chief of staff, Drew Clarke, to contact Snowy Hydro and Hydro Tasmania to request a briefing on the potential for pumped hydro in their schemes. Snowy had a small pumped hydro system; Hydro Tasmania had an even smaller one – but they weren't often used. As I pored over the maps of the two schemes over the summer, it had seemed to me there must be the potential to link some existing dams at different elevations to produce the circular pumped hydro system we needed.

Paul Broad, Snowy Hydro's ebullient chief executive, was almost jumping out of my phone he was so excited. 'Heard your speech, PM. Great stuff. We've blown the dust and cobwebs off some old filing cabinets and have we got a pumped hydro scheme for you! Four options in fact, but one of them's a cracker – Tantangara to Talbingo, seven hundred metres difference in elevation. Only problem is twenty kilometres of mountain in between. But back in the seventies, they designed every bit of it, and we've got all the plans.'

And he wasn't kidding. Tantangara to Talbingo sounded a bit of a mouthful so I named the project Snowy 2.0 and on 15 March announced we'd fund the feasibility study for the project. Snowy initially estimated the construction cost would be around $2 billion, and although this later was revised to $3.5 to $4.5 billion, the economics of the project were still very compelling.

Snowy 2.0 was a practical way to make renewables reliable, to buy wind and solar energy when it was cheap, pump water uphill to Tantangara and then, when the wind dropped and the sun went down, generate electricity by running the water back down into Talbingo. Snowy 2.0 would also support renewables by being a buyer of renewable energy at times when there was oversupply – a windy weekend or evening, or the middle of a hot summer's day.

Snowy 2.0 would also iron out some of the increasing volatility in electricity prices. And most importantly, because the two dams are so big, Snowy 2.0 would be able to generate 2000 MW for seven and a half days without repumping. Situated right in the heart of the National Electricity Market between Sydney and Melbourne, it was the ideal battery.

The coal lobby were appalled by the Snowy 2.0 announcement and their friends in the parliament, including Tony Abbott, were quickly calling on the government to fund a new coal-fired power station. I explained that the reason the government, as opposed to the private sector, had to fund Snowy 2.0 was because Snowy Hydro was government-owned – by the Commonwealth, New South Wales and Victoria in fact – and efforts to privatise it back in 2006 had met with furious public opposition.

I invited the two states to share in the investment in Snowy 2.0 but offered to buy their shares as an alternative. They took me up on that and we announced on 2 March 2018 that we'd reached an agreement to pay New South Wales and Victoria more than $6.2 billion to become the 100 per cent shareholder of Snowy Hydro.

Josh Frydenberg and Scott Morrison were both enthusiastic supporters of Snowy 2.0, although this didn't stop Scott notoriously bringing a lump of coal to wave around in the chamber at question time a few weeks later. It wasn't his finest hour (as I'm sure he'd privately admit).

Considerable engineering, geological and financial analysis were done in 2017 and 2018 and by the time I ceased to be PM, the economics of the Snowy 2.0 project were confirmed. It was estimated to have an internal rate of return of over 8 per cent, very good for a big infrastructure project, and Snowy Hydro said they could fund it without any additional government equity, so long as they could retain all their earnings, and not pay dividends, for five years. The Morrison government decided to keep the dividends and invest some additional capital (this made the budget outcomes look better but made no difference in cash terms) and the project was given the green light in late 2018.

Snowy 2.0 was the single most important and enduring decision of the many I made on energy. It provided exactly what the evolving energy market needed: flexible, zero-emission, dispatchable, on-demand energy. And, because of the size of the two dams, it has the capacity to be expanded from 2000 MW to, ultimately, 8000 MW.

There are a lot of things you do in government that are worthy but, frankly, are fairly obvious responses to the circumstances of the time. Snowy 2.0 was a project that wouldn't have been resurrected by anyone else. It was, in its initial idiosyncrasy, very much my own idea, as was its Tasmanian counterpart.

The only other big hydro scheme in Australia is Hydro Tasmania, or 'the Hydro', which is in fact larger than Snowy Hydro but more conventional in design. It has less of the heroic tunnelling and engineering that had made the Snowy so famous.

Hydro's reaction to my storage vision was less eager, but I managed to enthuse Premier Will Hodgman, writing to him on 9 February 2017, a week after my Press Club speech. 'This is a time to think big. Imagine if Tasmania became Australia's battery! You have the best wind resource and while I haven't mapped it, the pumped hydro potential must be enormous.'[4]

As a state-owned utility, Hydro Tasmania had been run very conservatively and to maximise dividends for a long time, but by 20 April Will Hodgman was enthused with my 'battery of the nation' vision and we agreed that ARENA and Hydro Tasmania should start scoping out additional pumped hydro scheme opportunities. At the same time, we'd proceed with proving up the business case for a second interconnector across Bass Strait, now known as the Marinus Link.

'Battery of the nation' isn't as far advanced as Snowy 2.0, but these two hydro schemes offer the best opportunities in Australia for very large-scale pumped hydro storage that will ensure Australia makes an affordable transition to zero-emission energy as the old coal-fired power stations close over the next few decades.

The pumped hydro projects would be years in construction. They were an example of doing what governments all too rarely do – identify a looming problem and plan well ahead to meet it. And both began in my boatshed over the summer of 2016–17 as I puzzled over energy storage.

A more immediate energy problem, however, was gas. For many decades, the gas market in the eastern states had been supplied from large conventional gas fields onshore in South Australia and Queensland and offshore in Bass Strait off Victoria. Unlike the gas development on Western Australia's North West Shelf, it hadn't been exported. It was an entirely domestic market. Prices were around $4 a gigajoule (GJ) – a measure of the energy component of gas equivalent to about 17 per cent of a barrel of oil.

However, by the 2000s, horizontal drilling and fracking had opened up the possibility of extracting gas from coal seams and exploration began – mostly in New South Wales and Queensland. A gas boom developed in Queensland and in the enthusiasm six 'trains' (essentially huge refrigerators) to make liquefied natural gas for export were built on Curtis Island near Gladstone in Queensland. Despite warnings from both gas customers and the federal Energy department about what this would do to gas prices, the Labor governments in Canberra and Brisbane forged ahead with the approvals. No objection was made by their political opponents in the Coalition, who were just as keen to please the gas industry. In a shocking neglect of the national interest, nothing was done to reserve or ring-fence enough gas for the domestic market.

It should always have been expected that the consequence of opening up the eastern Australian gas market to exports would result in Australian customers paying a global price, around $8 per GJ, which was about twice as high as they'd been used to paying. However, there was worse news in store, because the big LNG trains had been built on very optimistic assumptions about both the quantity of coal seam gas that would be extracted and the cost of doing so.

By early 2017, we were facing a serious crisis. The shortage in east coast gas coupled with the export commitments of the owners of the three LNG trains meant that Australian wholesale customers were paying prices of $15 to $20 a GJ – in other words, three to four times what they'd been paying only a few years before and around twice the global price. Manufacturers with operations in the USA in particular were starting to move production out of Australia because of the uncompetitively high cost of gas and electricity.

Gas is a vital input for many manufacturing businesses, either as feedstock or as a source of thermal heat. Over 60,000 jobs were at risk. And to further complicate matters, the price of wholesale electricity is set by the highest bid accepted in any five-minute period. As coal closed down and as more VRE entered the market, gas peaking plants were called on more often and thus set the price – 9 per cent of the time in 2014, rising to 24 per cent of the time in May 2017.[5]

With all that demand, surely there'd be more supply? Not at all. Community concern about fracking and its impact on ground water had resulted in ferocious opposition to further exploration and development. The climate-change-denying shock jock Alan Jones was especially vocal. Gas exploration and fracking in particular was being opposed by both the Green left and natural supporters of the National Party in the bush.

The Labor government in Victoria had effectively banned onshore gas development of any kind and in practical terms the Liberal–National government in New South Wales had done the same.

Finally, if that wasn't enough bad news on gas, the Australian Energy Market Operator (AEMO) reported in March that there was likely to be a shortage of gas in 2018–19 that would result in a shortage of electricity supply in the National Energy Market.[6] AEMO questioned whether other energy sources could make up the gap.

I held a number of meetings with the big gas producers in March 2017 and they undertook to ensure there was enough gas for the electricity sector, but I wasn't able to get an assurance that there'd be sufficient gas supply for manufacturing at affordable prices.

It was completely unacceptable that Australia, the second-largest exporter of LNG, could have a gas shortage at home. So by 27 April, I found myself, a Liberal prime minister and free-trade advocate, in the unlikely position of announcing export controls on gas.[7]

John Howard was not impressed. 'The more I hear you talk about gas, the more you sound like Malcolm Fraser, not Malcolm Turnbull.'

He had a point, but we didn't have any choice. We needed to be able to override the contractual commitments of the exporters who'd agreed to export more gas than they were producing and were drawing gas for export out of what had previously been available for the domestic market.

It was heavy-handed, and I hated doing it, but the threat of regulation worked. Wholesale prices, which had been as high as $20 per GJ, came back to export parity prices, around $8–$10. That relieved the pressure in 2017 and 2018, but the long-term problem remains. We're seeing the absurd situation of energy companies planning to build LNG import terminals in New South Wales and Victoria – two states where there are enormous gas reserves under the ground, untapped because of political opposition.

The upshot of course is that gas in eastern Australia is at best about twice as expensive as it is in the United States and that isn't going to change. This underlines the vital importance of building more storage in the form of pumped hydro to be able to affordably firm the variable renewable energy from wind and solar as we decarbonise our energy sector.

Alan Finkel's review was delivered in June 2017 with 50 recommendations aimed at ensuring the stability of the grid and an orderly transition to a low-emissions energy future. Alan canvassed an EIS but recommended a Clean Energy Target (CET) that would provide incentives for generators to produce power with emissions below a baseline. All of his recommendations were immediately adopted by governments, including the Commonwealth, apart from that relating to the CET.

The debate that followed underscored the profound problems the Liberal and National parties have in dealing with energy and climate policy. Whereas Morrison, Frydenberg and I, in particular, were looking at the CET from the perspective of what it would mean for energy prices, others – like Barnaby Joyce and Matt Canavan – were exclusively concerned about what it would mean for coal. Above all, they wanted to be assured that by introducing the CET we wouldn't have less coal-fired generation in 2030 than we would otherwise. Their concerns were mirrored by people like Craig Kelly, George Christensen, Keith Pitt and of course Tony Abbott, who regarded coal-fired energy as good in and of itself. They waged war against Finkel, the CET, indeed any effort to reduce emissions. Abbott, who had after all agreed to sign up to the Paris Agreement, was now calling for us to pull out of it and follow Trump.

He claimed the Paris targets had only ever been 'aspirational', overlooking not just the fact that it was his government that made the commitment but that he'd said at the time, 'We have pledged a 26 to 28 per cent cut by 2030. Unlike some other countries which make these pledges and don't deliver, Australia does deliver when it makes a pledge.'[8]

Abbott's determination to block the adoption of Finkel's recommendations knew no limits. We'd had strong support from Paul O'Malley, the CEO of BlueScope, the large steelmaker. Abbott phoned him and said he was being used by me and Frydenberg and he should dissociate himself from the Finkel review. To his credit, Paul pushed back, writing back to Abbott saying the Finkel review 'addresses energy security and reliability better than any review I have yet seen. This is really good for the country. Getting the detail right is now the critical next step'.[9]

The flakiness of some members of the government started to be an issue with business. On 22 June 2017, Matt Canavan, the Natural Resources minister, told Catherine Tanna, CEO of EnergyAustralia, that he wanted the government to build four new high-efficiency, low-emission (HELE) coal-fired power stations. A startled Cath Tanna later told me and Josh the meeting with Canavan was 'terrifying' and described the HELE proposition as 'batshit crazy'.[10]

When Audrey Zibelman, the new head of AEMO, gave her support to the Finkel review, Alan Jones flew into her, saying, 'This woman is a global warming advocate and a promoter of wind turbines … That woman, watch for her, she should be run out of town.'[11] Jones was relentless in his attacks, licking his lips as he inveighed against 'Frydenberg, Finkel, Zibelman' for doing my misguided bidding.

Part of this love of coal was based on a desire to promote investment in Queensland, such as the giant Adani project; part of it was based on a completely fact-free assertion that coal-fired energy was cheaper than any alternative; part of it was based on climate denialism and a rejection of the science on global warming. And, of course, there were always those who simply wanted to use the issue to blow up my government.

This point of view in the party room was difficult to counter. Trying to get them to focus at least on the hip pocket, I often said to the cabinet, 'We want to be, and can be, the cheap and clean energy party, not the coal-fired energy or indeed renewable energy party.' And reminded them that we should be guided by 'engineering and economics, not ideology and idiocy'.

I recall a meeting in 2018 in my office with a number of the more conservative members: Keith Pitt, George Christensen, Barnaby Joyce, Tony Pasin, Andrew Gee and a few others. They were arguing we should build a new coal-fired power station. Why, I asked. Because it would deliver cheaper power. Okay, I asked, what coal price are you assuming? They didn't know. How much coal will the new plant use for each megawatt hour? Again, they didn't know. How much do you think the new plant will cost? No idea. I was patient and polite as I explained the economics of a new coal-fired power station and how it was no longer competitive with renewables plus storage to deliver dispatchable power. They weren't convinced.

The deputy leader of the Nationals, Bridget McKenzie, had also been there listening carefully. She hung back as the men filed out. 'You can't reason with them, PM,' she said. 'It's religion. They don't care about the numbers.'

The real-world political context to this was simple: retail energy prices had doubled over 10 years.

The biggest single contributor to that was excessive regulated returns on the equally excessive historic investment in energy infrastructure – poles and wires. We couldn't undo the gold plating of years past, but by abolishing limited merits reviews of rulings by the energy regulator, we scaled back the ability of the network companies to jack up their prices.

We also ensured the big retailers alerted their customers to take advantage of the best deals on offer and that had the effect of saving many households hundreds of dollars a year.

The immediate problem, however, was that wholesale energy prices – about 40 per cent of a typical retail bill – had on average more than doubled over the past three years. The spike in gas prices, which my draconian gas export regulation addressed, had been a big part of that.

We found ourselves going around in circles because, above all, the biggest long-term contributor to the rising wholesale prices was that the only new investment in generation was in wind and solar supported by the RET. The lack of certainty in energy and climate regulation meant nobody was investing in anything else. Despite the obvious implications for grid stability of more and more VRE in the system, little or nothing had been done to promote storage or the provision of the services that maintain a stable frequency across the network.

As Finkel and every other review and report said, as the peak industry bodies pleaded, Australia needed a consistent, settled investment frame-work for energy that took into account the need to ensure affordability, reliability and a steady reduction in emissions in line with our interna-tional commitments. The failure to deliver that has meant higher energy prices, higher emissions and weaker economic growth.

Put another way, we were paying a high price for the failure to recognise the huge implications of moving from an electricity network dominated by large centralised synchronous spinning turbines powered by burning coal to a patchwork of solar and wind generation, the rate of which was varying by the minute. Plus the patchwork was all spread out – not just at hundreds of large-scale sites, many in regional Australia far from the centres of demand, but on millions of homes.

Within the government we discussed Alan Finkel's proposed CET for months during 2017. Joyce and Canavan's singular focus was to structure the CET to permit the construction of new HELE power stations, in particular in North Queensland.

In 2017, it could still, just, be argued, in a way it can't today, that a new HELE plant be considered as a part of the future energy mix to provide dispatchability as many more old coal-fired clunkers closed down and emissions reduced overall.

We were pressed by Barnaby and Matt to fund a feasibility study into a new HELE power station in North Queensland. Scott and I both felt, as did Josh, that a few million dollars for a study may be a price worth paying if it kept the Nats in the tent long enough to settle our overall energy policy. No study was undertaken during my time, and of course they didn't stay in the tent.

However, I pointed out three fundamental problems with their ambitions. The first was demand for a new power station was political not economic. There was plenty of energy available in North Queensland from existing plants and a huge amount of additional renewables being built, including pumped hydro for reliability.

The second was that the banks would simply not finance new coal-fired generation.

Third and most importantly, it was increasingly obvious new coal-fired generation was more expensive to build and operate than an equivalent amount of renewables firmed by storage and/or gas peakers – a conclusion the industry had already reached and the feasibility study would inevitably conclude. And the trend was not coal's friend: the cost of renewables and storage were continuing to fall.

But as Bridget McKenzie had said, none of this mattered to them: it was religion. And if the government could invest in Snowy 2.0 why not, as Abbott often said, Hazelwood 2.0? The idea that anyone, let alone the government, would build a new power station burning the dirtiest, highest-emission fuel of all – brown coal – beggared belief.

And as for Snowy, the only reason the government was investing in Snowy was because it belonged to the government and given its iconic status could never be privatised. This is much lamented in business circles because the return on Snowy 2.0 will be very good.

Abbott, supported by a small group in the party room but a large group of commentators in the Murdoch and other right-wing media, continued to campaign against the CET – indeed any energy policy that sought to reduce our emissions.

They ramped this up in March 2018 as a group of about 20 Nationals and right-wing Liberal MPs formed the 'Monash Forum' to promote the construction by the government of new coal-fired power stations.

The energy sector, however, was firmly in support of the CET. Indeed, the industry was in favour of any policy that could end the climate wars and produce some policy certainty that would allow them to invest with confidence.

While the press gallery and most of my colleagues were enthralled with the politics of emissions reduction and Abbott's continuing war on the government, I was focused on a bigger problem. Alan Finkel's CET, were it to be adopted, would certainly address the problem of reducing emissions across the energy sector. And if it were adopted and won cross-party political support, it would encourage continued investment. All good.

However, the CET didn't address the growing problem of maintaining reliability in the electricity network. We had, with the RET, force-fed variable renewables into the system and particularly into South Australia. How were we going to ensure that there was sufficient storage and firming capacity to keep the lights on when the wind didn't blow and the sun didn't shine? Snowy 2.0 and projects like that were of vital importance but they'd take years to build and wouldn't be enough in and of themselves.

Alan Finkel had tried to address this by proposing a generator reliability obligation requiring new large-scale renewable projects to be able to firm a certain amount of their generation capacity. So a 100 MW wind farm may have to be able to provide an amount of firmed power to keep dispatching for several hours when the wind wasn't blowing. It might be a battery or a gas peaker or a contract with a hydro operator.

This made sense at first glance, but it had several deficiencies. It didn't apply to existing renewables where we already had a problem, especially in South Australia. Neither did it differentiate between regions where there was plenty of fast-starting, on-demand firming power, such as in Queensland and Tasmania from gas and hydro respectively on the one hand, and regions where there was a big shortage such as South Australia on the other.

The CET had been designed to deliver investment certainty in respect of emissions, and was widely welcomed, but it wasn't doing enough on reliability. And it shared a defect with the RET: it operated outside and on the energy market, rather than being part of it.

As household energy prices continued to rise, I got all the big retailers together in my office on 9 August 2017. We had a frank and productive discussion and they agreed to contact all their customers who were on standing offers and encourage them to move to a plan that would enable them to save, in many cases, hundreds of dollars a year. As Scott Morrison often observed, inertia and complexity are the best friends of an energy retailer.

The August meeting was notable because in the course of it we discussed the growing concern of AEMO that there'd be a shortfall of dispatchable electricity in New South Wales when the old Liddell power station was closed, as planned by its owner AGL, in 2022. Andy Vesey was AGL's CEO and at the meeting he said AGL wouldn't keep it going past 2022 but would consider reasonable offers from responsible parties who might acquire it and keep it running until at least 2025, when Snowy 2.0 was expected to be in operation.

Subsequently, Vesey backed away from his offer to sell Liddell but the stoush with him had one benefit: it focused AGL's attention keenly on the need to provide alternative dispatchable power to make up for what will be lost when Liddell closes. It also highlighted the urgency of designing a change to the energy market rules that prioritised reliable supply.

One of Finkel's recommendations had been to establish an Energy Security Board (ESB) to oversee the implementation of his report and the energy security and reliability of electricity supply across the NEM, to ensure better outcomes for consumers. It was to have an independent chair and deputy chair as well as the heads of the various energy market agencies: John Pierce, chairman of the Australian Energy Market Commission; Audrey Zibelman, CEO of AEMO; Paula Conboy, chair of the Australian Energy Regulator. We recommended Kerry Schott be the chair and Clare Savage her deputy.

By now, I'd known Kerry for at least three decades. Over the years she'd restructured a series of government-owned businesses as well as being CEO of Sydney Water. She'd become one of the most respected advisers to governments of both complexions and combined in a fairly unique way an understanding of business, economics, utilities, government and politics.

It was in a meeting with Kerry and Audrey that we first discussed why we couldn't combine the reliability and emissions reduction requirements in one mechanism. They both concurred, as did the other members of the board, including John Pierce. Starting in August, they began to work on another approach, which we later dubbed the National Energy Guarantee.

The cabinet considered and agreed to proceed with it on 16 October 2017 and, together with the ESB members, we announced it on 17 October. It was designed as a market rule that obliged retailers to have a mix of generation that was reliable and always available as well as meeting an emissions intensity that matched our Paris obligations. The reliability requirement would trigger contract requirements for retailers in regions where there was a shortage of firming generation. The trigger was more likely to be needed in South Australia than in Queensland, for example.

But the emissions intensity across the NEM would match our Paris commitments. In those states whose governments set more aggressive emissions targets (such as South Australia and Victoria), their retailer reliability obligation was more likely to be triggered as the need for firming generation rose with their increases in VRE.

The reliability requirement would provide a real incentive for more dispatchable generation to be built; indeed, the ESB's own modelling found that under the NEG an additional 1086 MW of dispatchable capacity would be built over and above the 2000 MW of Snowy 2.0. The NEG, however, was technology-agnostic and the reliability requirement didn't discriminate between coal, gas, hydro or even batteries. All could provide firm, reliable, on-demand power and it was up to the market to get the right mix. Obviously, given the need to reduce emissions over time, a combination of renewables plus storage was an attractive, and the most likely, way of providing new dispatchable capacity.

The ESB also found the NEG would result in a reduction in wholesale electricity prices by 23 per cent between 2020 and 2030. Together with our other policies, that would mean household bills would be about $400 a year less compared to bills in 2017. For business, it meant a lot. A supermarket would save about $400,000 a year on its electricity bill.

Over the months that followed, the NEG won support from the business community, the energy sector, the trade union movement and, most importantly, the state governments, who are members of the COAG Energy Council. Even the Labor ones responded positively. Business, above all, was relieved that at last there appeared to be a durable energy policy that dealt with emission reductions and reliability in the energy sector. It was a framework that would enable firms to invest with confidence.

There's never been an energy policy with a broader base of support than the NEG. The only source of opposition remained within the Liberal and National parties. When Josh presented the NEG to the party room, despite some opposition, predominantly from Tony Abbott, it had majority support. However, by mid-2018, the question remained whether we could get enough support to be able to get the NEG passed through the House of Representatives. How many of our colleagues would be prepared to vote against the government, as Abbott had said he would?

Josh had taken the NEG to the August meeting of the COAG Energy Council and the states had agreed to proceed. Almost all of the legislation required to make it happen was, in fact, state legislation, which would be passed by the South Australian parliament and then adopted by the other state and territory jurisdictions in the NEM. The only role for the Commonwealth parliament was to set out the emissions reduction trajectory – calculated in order to meet the 26–28 per cent emissions reduction target.

I was in Perth over the weekend of 11 and 12 August speaking at the WA state conference. With our recent reset of the GST share to benefit Western Australia, I was well received.

I asked Mathias how he thought the party room would be on the NEG. He wrote back: 'I feel good about it too. Inevitably there will be some discussion, but we will end up with strong support. It will be a massive signature achievement to add further to a remarkable record of reform in this Parliament in the face of constant knocking and naysayers.'[12]

We brought the NEG back for the third time to the party room on Tuesday 14 August – formally to get approval to introduce the bill that set out the emissions reduction trajectory. There was a long debate and a substantial majority was in favour of proceeding.

Abbott, however, was ramping up his opposition and was now in open rebellion, describing the policy as 'a crock' and claiming that by legislating in the way we proposed, we'd be putting the 'voluntary targets' of the Paris Agreement into law.

Phil Coorey wrote in the *AFR*, 'Tony Abbott is so keen to destroy the National Energy Guarantee and, by extension, Malcolm Turnbull, that he is prepared to throw himself under a bus.'[13]

At the meeting, a few more members reserved their right to not support the bill, and I could sense the ground was shifting and not to our advantage. By the Thursday of that week, eight MPs had reserved the right to cross the floor, including Keith Pitt, a National Party assistant minister, Kevin Andrews, Tony Abbott, Craig Kelly (of course), Andrew Hastie, Andrew Gee, Tony Pasin and George Christensen.

I held a series of meetings with the members with concerns and did so in good faith, seeking to reassure them that the NEG would indeed see a reduction in electricity prices. Some of them were simply concerned that there should be new coal-fired generation constructed and a number of the Nationals, including Keith Pitt and George Christensen, demanded the government commit $5 billion to support new coal-fired power stations. They had no interest in whether that was economic or a worthwhile use of government funds.

Josh was having similar discussions. During the course of Friday he told me that some of the members, notably Michael Sukkar and Andrew Hastie, had said they didn't want to legislate the emissions reduction target because it was legislating the Paris Agreement, which many of the conservatives wanted us to pull out of – as Trump had done. Josh, Scott and I agreed we'd look at different ways of setting the target for the purpose of the NEG. From a legal perspective it actually didn't matter; the issue at this point was entirely political.

On Friday, at Josh's request, I spoke to Sukkar about it and also to Hastie. I didn't agree to make any change to our approach but, again in good faith, I discussed the possibility of setting the target by regulation. That was an approach Hastie had said would settle his concerns.

Within half an hour of my discussion with Hastie and Sukkar, the substance of the call had been briefed to *The Australian* and we were being accused of having backed away from our Paris commitment. It was becoming obvious that Josh and I weren't dealing in good faith with any of these people and that far from wanting to resolve a problem, they were seeking to make it worse.

The next morning, Saturday 18 August, *The Australian* ran 'Retreat on Paris emissions target may not save Malcolm Turnbull' across the front page. The story quoted Abbott and Andrews condemning any change of approach as being 'even worse' and also included some commentary from Barnaby Joyce urging me to consider resigning before the next election.[14]

Plainly, this dispute was about a lot more than energy policy.

By the Sunday, Morrison, Frydenberg and I had agreed that we shouldn't try to set the target by regulation – that was clearly a trap being set by our internal opponents. And we drafted amendments to the NEG legislation to provide that any changes to the target would need independent assurance from the Australian Competition and Consumer Commission (ACCC) that it wouldn't increase electricity prices.

Lucy and I had spent the Sunday visiting drought-affected communities in New South Wales with the National Party leader, Michael McCormack, and his wife, Catherine. They'd joined us at The Lodge for dinner the previous night. Michael was anxious that Barnaby was going to make a run for the Nationals leadership in the coming week. He also said he didn't think he could hold the Nationals to vote for the NEG in the House.

I'd invited the cabinet to dinner at The Lodge on the Sunday night to discuss the growing crisis around the NEG. The media were alerted to this and so we moved the dinner to the dining room in the PMO to avoid ministers being doorstopped as they arrived. There was a growing sense of alarm. Dutton and Hunt both advised they couldn't make the dinner. Given the speculation about a Dutton leadership challenge, I was determined he attend and sent a VIP plane to Brisbane to pick him up so he had no excuse but to join us.

At the dinner, we canvassed our options. We had received in June the final report of the ACCC's inquiry into retail electricity prices that Scott had commissioned back in March 2017. We considered the report's recommendations and confirmed an earlier decision to adopt them all. This meant establishing a simple default price to replace the confusing 'standing offers' that resulted in many consumers paying too much for their energy. And we also agreed to the recommendation to underwrite new dispatchable power on a technology-agnostic basis. I'd flagged both of these in a Facebook video I'd worked up with Scott Morrison earlier in the day.

But at the dinner Josh told us he no longer had any confidence we could pass the NEG without Labor's support. He said that as many as a dozen MPs would cross the floor. The rest of the ministers confirmed this assessment. My initial instinct was to introduce the bill and stare the wreckers down – let them cross the floor and be seen to do so. But the cabinet was vehemently opposed to this. And not just those on the right. Pyne and Frydenberg were as opposed as Morrison and Dutton. They argued there was a group that wanted to use this to bring down our own government. McCormack said the Nationals wouldn't sit with Labor to vote for the NEG. I concluded I had to keep my cabinet colleagues as close as I could, and so, with deep reservations, I agreed.

So, the first fateful decision of that fateful week was made – we resolved that we wouldn't introduce the NEG legislation until we were confident we could pass it without Labor support. The cabinet both on Sunday night and at the formal meeting 24 hours later reaffirmed our commitment to the emissions reduction part of the NEG; it was a question of practical politics and timing. We needed the dust to settle enough to see a way through what was apparently developing into the beginnings of a leadership challenge.

The press was full of speculation that Dutton was being encouraged to make a challenge. He and Hunt, reputedly his running mate, had tried to avoid the Sunday dinner. I knew they were both ambitious, but there was simply no rational basis to conclude a change of leadership would improve our prospects, and certainly not to Dutton. As I looked around the table, I wondered whether a self-destructive madness was descending on us.

The members who were planning to cross the floor on the NEG knew that they were threatening the very existence of the government. The NEG was our key energy policy and not one cabinet minister, including Dutton, had uttered a word against it during our many discussions. It had the support of a clear majority in the party room. Whether it was better to put it on hold, as the cabinet decided, or be defeated on the floor of the House was an interesting question. Either way, it would be a big setback. I had to conclude that there was a growing group in the party room who either wanted to bring down the government, as Abbott did, or were utterly reckless about the consequences of their actions.

CHAPTER 47

The coup

Over the weekend of 18–19 August I tried to persuade myself that the leadership speculation in the media was, as Scott Morrison described it, 'just another 2GB Sky News conspiracy'[1] – like the attempted coup at the end of 2017 that Alan Jones had tried to foment with Abbott.

Throughout all my time as prime minister, Abbott had been working hard to bring down my government with consistent support from a number of so-called conservative voices in the media – Alan Jones and Ray Hadley on 2GB, as well as Peta Credlin, Andrew Bolt, Piers Akerman and many others at News Corporation.

While the News Corporation newspapers were always supportive of Abbott, the intensity of their efforts to damage my government varied from time to time. The exception was *The Australian*, which was as consistently destructive as it could afford to be without losing all of its diminishing credibility as a serious newspaper. Similarly, Sky News 'after dark' was relentless.

These outlets didn't have big audiences, but they did reach a large percentage of the older, more conservative Liberal and National party members. Ted O'Brien, the member for Fairfax in Queensland, was an old friend and fellow republican. But he said it was 'Like Alan Jones and Peta Credlin are having a branch meeting with my members every night', when he explained why he was supporting Dutton.

There wasn't a lot I could do to appease these insurgents – after all, they wanted my head. Abbott's plan, we knew, was to ensure we lost in 2019, then he would return as opposition leader after the loss and lead the Coalition back to victory in 2022, an insane agenda which, as Rupert Murdoch later admitted to me, had strong support within News Corp.

The worst possible outcome for Abbott would be for me to win the 2019 election. He knew that he wouldn't be elected leader again before the election, so his strategy was to continue damaging my government so that I couldn't win. We were all aware that our biggest weakness was disunity and internal instability and that whenever it blew up, our numbers went down. So, Abbott knew – just as Rudd had with Gillard – that he could dial the Newspoll numbers up and down.

I'd been urged to put Abbott into the cabinet by John Howard and, of course, by Abbott himself. However, knowing Abbott as well as I did, I was certain that a portfolio wouldn't distract him from his central mission of revenge and destruction. While I was happy years before to get on with sorting out the NBN, my assessment of Abbott is that – like his friend Credlin – he's almost entirely driven by hatred and negativity. It's what gets him out of bed in the morning. And the rest of the cabinet realised that. Apart from Barnaby on a few occasions, nobody supported Abbott making a return to the cabinet. As Julie said, 'If Abbott was back in this room, we could never have a frank discussion on anything.'

So, my strategy with Abbott was simply to ignore him, and hope that each eruption would have less impact than the previous one.

And this worked relatively well until August 2018. What changed was that, for the first time, a senior cabinet minister, Peter Dutton, decided that he'd make a run for it. I was slow to believe that he was doing so, although several colleagues, including Christopher and Julie, had warned me that he was.

I've always assumed people have a reasonable amount of self-awareness and Dutton had never struck me as being so self-delusional and narcissistic as to imagine that he could successfully lead the Liberal Party. More relevantly, it had never occurred to me that others would think he could either.

Dutton had given an ambiguous answer to 2GB's Ray Hadley on Thursday 16 August when pressed on why he hadn't resigned from the cabinet over the NEG. In fact, Dutton had never stated any opposition to the NEG. Then, as rumours started to mount in the media, he'd been slow to make a statement showing his support for the government, despite my asking him to do so.

I learned from several Queensland MPs that Gary Spence, the LNP president, was urging them to support Dutton in a challenge and that over the weekend Abbott had given a speech to a Young Liberals event saying he looked forward to serving in 'a Dutton government'.[2] Then there was Dutton's reluctance to attend the cabinet dinner to discuss the NEG on the Sunday night. The Monday papers were full of speculation about a Dutton challenge. A few minutes before the Monday morning leadership meeting Dutton had texted me: 'Malcolm I fully understand if you would prefer I didn't come to leadership this morning. Let me know what your preference. Thanks.' I phoned him and asked what he'd meant but he had nothing to say, so I said to come to the meeting and I'd assume he was a loyal member of the executive.

By Tuesday morning, 21 August, I'd reluctantly concluded not only that Dutton was planning a challenge but that it was being coordinated with supporters in the media. And not just the usual list of Turnbull-hating delcons on 2GB and Sky News. *The Australian* was clearly on the move, as were the News Corporation tabloids, in particular the Sydney *Daily Telegraph* and Brisbane's *Courier-Mail*. It was on.

Having been involved in many leadership challenges, it was all horribly familiar. I knew that Dutton would want to keep his hands clean as long as he could. In much the same way as Morrison orchestrated the empty chair spill against Abbott in February 2015, Dutton would ensure that backbenchers demanded I resign so the insurrection appeared to come from the backbench. This would enable Dutton to claim that he was reluctantly drafted.

Subsequent events and revelations confirm that my suspicions were well founded. As we know now (but I didn't know at the time) Dutton had told Steve Ciobo on the Sunday night that he was going to challenge, that he had the numbers and knew so because his friend Mathias Cormann was doing them for him. I learned subsequently that on the Monday, Ciobo had visited Julie Bishop to discuss the pending Dutton challenge and in his artless way asked her if she'd want to stay deputy after the change of leadership.

So, I could see that I was in dire straits, as I had been before. Once the conspiracy and destabilisation has developed this far it's very hard to survive. Even if I saw it off, our polls would crash, which would in turn set off another round of destabilisation. The simple fact is that I was faced with a growing group of people who wanted to destroy the government. And they were led by Peter Dutton, the minister for Home Affairs, whose duty it was to defend Australia's national security. He was conspiring with

News Corporation – a foreign-owned media company. And we worry about the Chinese Communist Party's foreign influence operations!

I didn't have time to reflect on the ironies of the moment. Emotionally, for me and Lucy, this was all bringing back the terrible memories of 2009. I'd seen this horror film before.

The insurgents' move would be to gather momentum and at some point, possibly as early as the 9 am Tuesday party meeting, ensure that some backbenchers demanded a spill and called on me to resign. While I was prepared to accept Morrison's assurances of continued loyalty, I knew that some of his supporters were starting to urge him to make a move himself. I was told by Scott Briggs that Alex Hawke was trying to restrain them, but that a number of ambitious people in that small Morrison group, including Stuart Robert – who desperately wanted to get back in the ministry – and Ben Morton, were starting to agitate.

If a motion to declare the leadership vacant was moved, it would potentially attract the votes of both Dutton and Morrison supporters. Each camp was likely, in my experience, to have an inflated view of their prospects and believe they could beat the other in a ballot.

Craig Laundy had reported to me early on the Tuesday morning: 'I reckon they're still short – but am worried about Scomo's minions especially Hawke, Robert, [Lucy] Wicks and [Bert] van Manen. I think they've shifted – and not sure whether Scomo's lost control or he's shifted.'[3]

So, my assessment as at Tuesday morning was that if not that morning but very shortly thereafter, I'd face a call for a spill, which I could only avoid holding by declaring my position as leader vacant and inviting a challenge. Scomo's supporters were less likely, I calculated, to vote for Dutton in a contest against me, than to vote for a motion to declare the leadership vacant – opening the way for Morrison to run.

Right then, time wasn't on my side. My opponents had momentum, their friends in the media were reporting they had the numbers, and I didn't have the means to disprove them without having a ballot.

The leadership group met as usual, at 8.30 am, in my office. Dutton was present but obviously on edge, as were the others. I motioned Julie to stay after the meeting ended and told her I was planning to spill my position and flush Dutton out. Julie agreed it was the best way to break the insurgents' momentum. 'You should spill my position too,' she said.

Once I called the party meeting to order, I addressed the issue of unity and reminded everyone of what we knew all too well: Labor's biggest liability was Shorten; ours was disunity. When there was a reasonable amount of discipline, our numbers improved; when there wasn't, they went down. In other words, our biggest enemy was ourselves. I told them that we couldn't allow this leadership speculation to go on, and accordingly I was going to declare the position of leader and deputy leader vacant and call for nominations.

As I began talking about leadership, and before I called the spill, a close friend of Dutton's, Luke Howarth, had leapt to his feet and said, 'You should resign; so should Abbott. We need a new leader.' But in the hubbub that followed my announcement, he was drowned out.

I nominated and so did Dutton. It was a long wait while the ballot papers were handed out. How many times had I been through this, I asked myself. About six times in fact. I looked around the room: did they realise the gravity of the occasion?

Morrison sent me a note while the ballots were being distributed: 'I don't know why we didn't discuss this. But that's your call. Turnbull is on my ballot.'

I replied, 'Thanks! It's the right call. The room has to make up its mind.'[4]

The numbers were 48 for me, 35 for Dutton. I wondered whether some of Morrison's supporters had taken the chance and voted for Dutton, hoping they didn't accidentally deliver him a win. Subsequent accounts of these events indicate that Stuart Robert and Alex Hawke had organised about half-a-dozen of them to vote for Dutton – enough to lift his numbers up to a level that damaged me but didn't get Dutton over the line. If Morrison's friends had voted the way he said he did, the Dutton insurgency would have been utterly dead that morning.

When the deputy's position was spilled, nobody stood against Julie. Morrison reminded me to offer Dutton the chance to stay in the ministry, which I did, but he declined. We then moved on to the joint party room meeting, when the Nats joined us and mostly talked about our position on energy. The adoption of the ACCC reforms was welcomed and the decision not to present the legislation relating to the emissions reduction part of the NEG was acknowledged. The majority of the room knew full well that a militant and reckless minority was holding them and the government hostage.

Shortly afterwards, I met with Mathias Cormann and Peter Dutton in my office. At this stage, Cormann appeared anxious to patch things up and asked whether Julie could be persuaded to step aside so that Peter could be deputy leader. I asked them why we'd want to lose our most popular colleague. 'Because people think she's Malcolm Turnbull in a skirt,' Dutton replied.

Julie's slender, elegant profile flashed through my mind. 'I can't think of anyone less like me in a skirt than Julie, Peter,' I replied. 'But, seriously, if you want to be the deputy leader of the Liberal Party, then you could have challenged her today.'

Dutton scowled. 'You know I could never beat her in a ballot: she's a woman.'

Mathias asked me whether she was going to run again. Was she interested in being governor-general? I told them that while I thought Julie would make a magnificent governor-general, I knew she had no interest whatsoever in another government job after she left politics. And would she run again? I had no doubt she'd run in 2019, I told them.

'And, Peter, in any event,' I added, 'even if Julie were to resign or fall under the proverbial bus, why are you so sure you would win the ballot?'

Dutton has subsequently claimed I offered him the deputy leadership of the Liberal Party. That is a lie. And a nonsense. Because I could no more deliver the deputy leadership of the Liberal Party to someone than I could deliver the leadership of the National Party.

I told Dutton that even if he didn't want to serve in the ministry, we should put this behind us. The vote had been held and the matter was settled. We had to unite and stabilise the government.

Dutton was unmoved. 'I'm going to keep going until I get the numbers. I'm not stopping,' he told me.

We managed to get through question time, but shortly afterwards several ministers and assistant ministers admitted they'd voted for Dutton and offered to resign. They were my own assistant minister, James McGrath; the assistant minister for Science, Jobs and Innovation, Zed Seselja; Morrison's assistant minister, Michael Sukkar; the minister for International Development and the Pacific, Concetta Fierravanti-Wells; the minister for Law Enforcement and Cyber Security, Angus Taylor; the minister for Citizenship, Alan Tudge; and from the cabinet, the minister for Health, Greg Hunt and also Steve Ciobo and Michael Keenan.

So, including Dutton and assuming no others, 10 members of my own executive, including four cabinet members, had voted for Peter Dutton.

All of them represented betrayals to some degree, but probably the worst were James McGrath and Connie Fierravanti-Wells. McGrath was assistant minister to the prime minister – a position which, in his warped view of the world, apparently carried with it no obligation of loyalty. The thing was, I'd brought James back to Australia in 2009 to be deputy director of the Liberal Party after Boris Johnson had sacked him for some remarks offensive to people of Caribbean heritage. He'd been part of the very close group who'd assisted with the numbers prior to my challenging Abbott. When I'd given him additional responsibilities in Immigration, he'd screamed at me that I was making him 'waste his time doing shit work for shit people'. By that he meant considering applications by people to have visa conditions waived so they could stay in Australia. I realised then that he should have stayed a political operative in the party machine. He had no interest in the hard work of government.

But Fierravanti-Wells is an interesting case study in treachery, ingratitude and bitterness. In the lead-up to the 2016 election, the NSW division's preselectors had placed her in a spot on the Senate ticket that would ensure she wasn't elected. A hardworking party official, Hollie Hughes, had been placed in the higher, winnable spot.

Connie, however, was one of my ministers and so I prevailed upon Hollie to step down from that winnable spot and ensure Connie instead kept her seat in the Senate. Without my personal intervention, Connie wouldn't have been elected. Hollie was a supporter of mine, as were those who'd voted for her. So, I was placing my loyalty to my ministers ahead of factional loyalties.

To give Morrison credit, he urged me to drop Fierravanti-Wells, as did Julie Bishop. Connie was Julie's junior minister and was consistently disloyal to her. She had an exaggerated assessment of her own abilities and despite my support for her, resented me for not making her attorney-general. I should have taken their advice.

In the course of the Tuesday afternoon and evening I spoke to all those who'd offered their resignations.

Steven Ciobo – one of Dutton's closest friends – told me he didn't want me to accept his resignation, that the insurgency was complete and utter madness and that he'd tried to urge Dutton to pull back. He said that Cormann had been doing Dutton's numbers and had voted for him in the Tuesday ballot. (Ciobo later publicly confirmed that Dutton had told him, as he told his other close friend Michael Keenan, on the Sunday evening flying down to Canberra that Cormann was doing his numbers.[5])

He added that if Dutton were deputy leader, he'd be settled. Could I engineer Julie's retirement, he asked, as Dutton didn't want to challenge her because she was a woman. Ciobo also gave me an undertaking he wouldn't support any future spill or challenge against me.

Alan Tudge had a mix of complaints about policy and people. He claimed, without any particulars, that Sally Cray had 'briefed against him'. I reminded him of how Sally had helpfully and discreetly managed a rather awkward situation he had got himself into. 'If she'd wanted to brief against you, wouldn't that have found its way into the public domain, Alan?' I asked. He went a little pale but conceded the point.

At the end of the discussion, he agreed we should draw a line under this challenge and instability and needed to be united under my leadership to the next election. 'You can count on my support in any spill or challenge in the future,' he added. 'And I'll do my best to prevent one occurring.'

By the morning of Wednesday the 22nd, I had unequivocal assurances of support from the cabinet ministers Hunt, Keenan and Ciobo, as well as from Tudge. Taylor was unequivocal on the Tuesday night, but hedged on Wednesday morning, only to give a less-than-convincing assurance of support by Wednesday afternoon. I'd accepted the resignations of Dutton and Fierravanti-Wells – they were lost causes.

Dutton was in the media first thing on the Wednesday morning talking up his credentials and freelancing some new policy ideas, including taking the GST off energy – overlooking the fact that the GST goes to the states, who'd demand compensation if such a change were made.

Ray Hadley on 2GB, like his colleague Alan Jones, was demanding a switch to Dutton and even read a supportive text message from 'a Liberal MP', who turned out, it was reported, to be none other than Dutton himself.[6] In the corridors of parliament, Dutton's supporters were busy trying to build up their numbers – promising unlimited backing from Rupert Murdoch's News Corporation if there was a change. The Murdoch tabloids were ferociously supporting Dutton with headlines like 'The Pete is on' and predicting, and encouraging, a second challenge. The Fairfax papers urged me to call an election. Outside of the media, the consensus was that the insurgency was insane. Darren Chester, one of the moderate National Party members, was adamant that he and others would go to the crossbench if there was a switch to Dutton.

At 9.40 am on the Wednesday, I spoke on the phone with Rupert Murdoch. He was in Australia and we'd been trying to line up a time to meet or speak. Clive Mathieson, my chief of staff, a former editor of *The Australian*, was present during the call.

I explained to Rupert that unless the insurgency was brought to an end we'd be heading for an election. Dutton wouldn't be able to command a majority in the House. Three Nationals – Chester and two others – would go to the crossbench, and some Liberals as well. I told him that Sharkie and McGowan wouldn't guarantee supply and confidence. 'Rupert, if you look at your own Newspoll you can see we will be going from being very competitive, as we are now, to giving Labor the biggest electoral gift they could ever have.'

He asked about Longman, and I pointed out that the swing in that seat was only 3.6 per cent, less than the average by-election swing, and in Braddon there was virtually no swing against us at all.

'News is seen to be driving this, Rupert. Your papers and Sky appear to have signed up to the Credlin–Abbott "we have to burn the village to save the village" strategy. As you know, Abbott wants us to be wiped out in 2019, so that he returns as leader after the election, leading us to a glorious victory in 2022.'

Murdoch replied, 'That's only if Tony keeps his own seat.'

I said I thought he likely would hold it. 'Rupert, this insurgency has been going on for a long time. We've talked about it many times. It's being fired up in your papers and on Sky at night.'

Murdoch interrupted to say (as he often had before), 'There aren't many viewers at that time of night.'

I replied, 'True, but it is being watched by our supporters and party members. This whole exercise is seen as being written and directed by your company. Credlin and Abbott's fingerprints are all over it. This has been a whole process of destabilisation, and Bill Shorten, the most left-wing Labor leader since Whitlam, will be the beneficiary. Do you seriously want us to lose, so that Abbott can come back in opposition? It's crazy.'

Murdoch said, 'I think Boris [Paul Whittaker, editor of *The Australian*] is the only one who wants to do that. But Abbott would say that's what you did to him.'

'Rupert, it's not the same. I went to Abbott, told him that I was going to challenge him and won the ballot. If I'd lost I would have gone, and I told him that. This has been a News Corp–backed guerilla campaign against me. Paul Kelly would agree with everything I have said to you; it's madness.'

Murdoch said, 'We can't have an election now, and Fairfax haven't been helpful either. Let me talk to Lachlan. I'm retired. I'll talk to Lachlan.'

Later that day I spoke with Kerry Stokes, who'd been texting and calling me with messages of support. He'd earlier written to say he'd spoken directly to Mathias and believed he'd stick with me. Dutton, he said, would be a disaster.

Kerry told me that during Murdoch's current visit to Australia he'd caught up with him and Murdoch had said, 'We have to get rid of Malcolm.' Stokes, taken aback, asked him why. Murdoch said, 'He can't win, he can't beat Shorten.'

Stokes responded by saying that was clearly not true: I was way ahead of Shorten as preferred PM, the polls were very close and the government was very competitive. And there was nobody who could do better. Stokes said that Murdoch took all that in and then declared, 'Three years of Labor wouldn't be too bad.'

Horrified, Stokes tried to talk him round; Murdoch shrugged it off.

Stokes subsequently gave an account of that to several others and while the details of what was said differed, the substance was the same. So, I have no doubt he was telling me the truth. The disturbing part of it was that in acknowledging a coup to remove me would likely put Shorten into power, Murdoch was clearly signing up to the lunatic Abbott agenda.

Around midday on the Wednesday, not long before question time at 2 pm, Mathias Cormann came to my office. He told me that Peter Dutton now had the support of a substantial majority of the party room. 'I know personally of ten people who didn't vote in the ballot yesterday who are now supporting him,' he told me. I asked him who they were, and apart from himself, he didn't nominate anyone.

I responded by saying that I now had assurances of support, in writing, from all of the ministers who'd voted for Dutton, apart from Dutton himself and Fierravanti-Wells. 'So, Mathias, as far as I can see, Dutton's numbers are dwindling.'

I'd reposed enormous trust in Mathias, so I asked him whether he thought this insurgency was wise. 'No, it's complete madness,' he said.

'Well, then, Mathias, why are you supporting it? This is just terrorism.'

Mathias agreed. 'I know it is terrorism, but they won't stop. You must resign now, before question time, and make an orderly handover of power to Peter Dutton.'

I pointed out to Cormann, as Sally Cray had done earlier that morning, that if he supported the destruction of my government, there was no assurance Dutton would emerge as my successor. 'Mathias, right now the coup has run out of steam. People are walking away from Dutton. Why are you trying to save the insurgency? Can't you see that if you wreck my government – our government – Morrison is more likely to be my successor than Dutton? Is that what you're trying to achieve?'

Mathias would have none of that. 'The only viable successor is Dutton. Anyway, you know what I think of Morrison.'

Nobody worked more closely with Scott than Mathias and I did. Mathias regarded Scott as emotional, narcissistic and untrustworthy and told me so regularly. From my own point of view, by this stage, Scott and I were working extremely well together. My only problem with him had been his thinking aloud in the media and that had been much less frequent of late. Of course, if Mathias had a poor opinion of Scott, Dutton's dislike of him was even stronger.

I assured Mathias that I did know what he thought about Scott but that he should think very carefully about the course of action he was embarking on. 'Mathias, I am not falling on my sword for Peter Dutton or anyone else. If you want to blow up the government, you have to take responsibility for it and be seen to do so. I am a great believer that if you want to be an assassin you have to be prepared to have blood on your hands.'

He left me and, not long afterwards, a rumour started to circulate that I was going to resign before question time. It appeared to have come from the office of Christian Porter, another close associate of Dutton and Cormann.

We'd made one last attempt to get the Senate to agree to extend the company tax cuts that morning, and failed. Mathias had come tantalisingly close to having the numbers, or so he said, on many occasions over the last few months, which was why we hadn't formally abandoned the tax cuts for larger companies. Sticking with the company tax cuts no doubt hurt us electorally, especially in the by-elections, and some believed Mathias had kept them on the agenda in order to undermine the leadership. I'd give him the benefit of the doubt on that score. He did think he could get them passed. But close isn't good enough. And even he admitted it was a lost cause, so at about 1 pm I held a press conference with Morrison and Cormann to formally announce it.

This was the famous press conference where Morrison pledged his loyalty to me, putting his arm around me and saying, 'This is my leader, and I'm ambitious for him.'

To which I replied, 'Good on you. Thanks, ScoMo.'

Mathias Cormann was also asked about his loyalty, and said, 'I support Malcolm Turnbull as Prime Minister.' And again, 'I was very grateful when Malcolm invited me to serve in his cabinet in September 2015. I have served Malcolm loyally ever since. I will continue to serve him loyally into the future.'[7]

The ministers who'd voted for Dutton all pledged their loyalty to me and the government in Wednesday's question time. Alan Tudge was particularly effusive, even though it was well known he'd been intimately involved in Dutton's plans, as had been Greg Hunt, who was planning to be Dutton's deputy so that he could realise his lifelong ambition of being Foreign minister.

Not long after question time, around 4 pm, Cormann returned to my office with Mitch Fifield, the Communications minister, and Michaelia Cash, the minister for Jobs and Innovation. Cash was sobbing – that showed some humanity I thought and perhaps a recognition that I had stuck with her over the AWU raid fiasco. They sat down at the table in my office; I remained behind my desk. Cormann went through the same argument he'd made in the morning.

I said, 'Mathias, this is madness. And you are here, the leader of the government in the Senate, and you are asking me, the Prime Minister, to give in to terrorists.'

Mathias agreed, 'It is madness, and it is terrorism, but you have to give in to it.' He claimed that he, Mitch and Michaelia were only some of the people who were switching to Dutton. 'You should resign now, make it easier for yourself, so that Peter can become prime minister.'

Fifield didn't utter a word throughout the meeting, just opening his mouth occasionally as if to say something. But no words came out. He looked shell-shocked. Cash kept quietly sobbing, occasionally whispering, 'Yes,' as if to agree with things Mathias had said.

I urged them to reflect on what they were proposing to do. 'Mathias, Mitch, Michaelia – we have been good friends for a long time. This has been a good government.' They all nodded. 'This coup attempt has failed. Now Dutton and his supporters are like terrorists saying they will continue wrecking until the majority gives in to them. We cannot give in to this terrorism.'

Cormann interrupted me, saying again, 'You have to give in to the terrorists.'

The meeting ended without any resolution. I hoped that Mathias would change his mind, but I wasn't optimistic. I knew that if he and the others resigned and called on me to quit, it would be very hard for my government to survive. And he knew that too. So, why did he move against me?

Over time, I have with immense sadness come to the conclusion that Cormann was well aware of Dutton's plans and had given Dutton every expectation that he supported them. They were very close friends who walked up to the top of Red Hill before dawn every sitting day and dined together all the time. It's utterly inconceivable that Cormann wouldn't have been in the loop and so when Dutton told Ciobo that Cormann was doing his numbers for him, he was probably telling Ciobo the truth.

You have to develop a thick skin in politics, but Mathias's betrayal hurt me. Over the years, I'd come to trust him and rely on him to get things done in the Senate and manage the complicated personalities in the right of the party.

He'd won the confidence of the staff in my office, including Sally, and he'd gone out of his way to win Lucy's confidence as well. Scott didn't have much interest in international conferences and so Mathias would accompany me to the G20 and other meetings that Finance ministers attended. His fluency in German and French meant he was particularly effective in Europe.

Mathias had demonstrated his skill at getting one difficult piece of legislation through the Senate after another, and had been a very skilful collaborator in getting the same-sex marriage postal vote accepted by the right in the party room and approved in the High Court.

He often joined me for a meal at The Lodge and talked openly about his future, how he missed his wife and daughters. 'I can't do this forever,' he'd say. 'When you leave, so will I. Perhaps we should go into business together.'

But by Wednesday 22 August, despite all the frenzied commentary in the media, the steam was, as I've said, coming out of the coup. Most of the ministers who'd voted for Dutton had pledged their loyalty to me and repeated that publicly. Others who'd voted for Dutton, like Queensland MP Andrew Wallace, had had second thoughts and assured me of their support in any future ballot.

In other words, the purpose of the spill on Tuesday had been achieved. Dutton had been shown up not to have the numbers he'd claimed.

The public reaction to the coup attempt was one of furious condemnation. Everyone outside the right-wing media echo chamber was agreed: this was lunacy and calculated to hand government to the Labor Party.

It was in the midst of all this that Mathias decided to throw his friend Dutton a lifeline by breathing life back into the coup. As I would say to him nearly three weeks later, at a time when he needed to be strong and loyal, he proved to be weak and treacherous.

Apart from Julie, the other big figure in the government was Scott Morrison and we were in constant contact over the weekend. Initially, he'd said to me the insurgency was a 2GB/News/Sky News conspiracy that lacked real support and discouraged me from calling a spill. But by the Monday, like me, he'd have known the insurgents planned to do that themselves anyway. After I'd won the ballot on the Tuesday, he urged me not to have another meeting that week. 'They want to speed it up,' he said. 'We want to slow it down.' He advised me to send everybody home at the end of the week so that after two weeks of getting their ears boxed by their furious constituents they'd return to Canberra in a better, saner frame of mind.

I agreed with all of that. However, by the Wednesday I was hearing that Scott's supporters were making calls on his behalf. Scott spoke to his close friend Simon Benson, who confirmed in *The Australian* at 10.22 am that Scott's close allies Alex Hawke and Ben Morton were openly doing the numbers for him.[8]

· · ·

Another issue had found its way into the crazy mix. On the Monday night there'd been a report on the Ten Network by Hugh Riminton that Dutton could be ineligible to sit in the parliament because of his interests in a childcare centre in Queensland.[9] Section 44(v) states that a person is not eligible to sit in the parliament if they have a direct or indirect pecuniary interest in a contract with the public service of the Commonwealth. I had no forewarning of this story or of the issue related to Dutton and it was largely overlooked in the madness of the week until, on Wednesday, the Labor Party asked me in question time if I'd sought the solicitor-general's advice on the matter. I said that the government hadn't and, after checking with Dutton, confirmed he had legal advice to say he wasn't in breach.

Later on the Wednesday, the Labor Party produced an opinion, written in April, from leading constitutional lawyer Bret Walker, stating that Dutton was ineligible. It was a detailed and thorough piece of work and, after I spoke with Christian Porter, the attorney-general, he agreed to get the advice of the solicitor-general.

This was the standard procedure, which we'd followed in section 44 cases.

I was troubled by the Walker advice. As soon as the section 44 citizenship issues arose with Canavan, Joyce and Nash, and before the ruling of the High Court, we'd obtained advice about the consequences of their potentially being in breach of section 44. The solicitor-general had advised that their dual citizenship meant they'd never been eligible to be a minister beyond 90 days after they were first sworn in in 2013. Every act they'd undertaken since then was invalid. There was an argument, which the solicitor-general rejected, that the invalidity only applied to actions they'd taken after they'd become aware of their potential ineligibility. The only way to validate those invalid decisions was with legislation.

Canavan had resigned from the ministry, but Joyce and Nash stayed in place until the court gave its decision. In that interim period, where a decision had to be taken by them, we made sure it was taken by another minister sworn to the same portfolio, thereby reducing the number of potentially invalid decisions. Of course, we couldn't do anything about the decisions made before the ineligibility issue blew up.

I'd been keeping the governor-general informed about the unfolding crisis throughout the week of the coup. He was extremely anxious and would have welcomed my calling an election. The government, and the parliament, was looking like a chaotic rabble, and the argument for letting the people sort it out was compelling.

But the Dutton ineligibility issue raised an even darker prospect. If there was any doubt about Dutton's eligibility, how could he possibly be sworn in as prime minister? Every single act of his – from recommending the appointment of ministers, to appointing senior public servants, to sending our troops into conflict – everything would be under a cloud of questionable legitimacy. It was unthinkable.

I discussed this with Porter, calmly and professionally. I told him that this issue of Dutton's eligibility was one in which the governor-general took the keenest interest. Porter suggested that perhaps Dutton could take advantage of the provision in section 64 that says a person can be a minister without being an MP for three months. But that had been dealt with by the solicitor-general in his advice in 2017. If Dutton was ineligible today, he'd been ineligible for years – he couldn't revive the three-month exemption period by resigning and being reappointed.

Porter was, I knew, a good friend of Dutton and a close political ally. I had no illusions where his loyalties lay. But I expected him to fulfil his duties as attorney-general professionally and one obvious requirement was that we obtained the solicitor-general's advice as urgently as possible. It obviously needed to be available before any potential spill meeting was held.

Initially, Porter was proposing that it couldn't be completed until the following week, but at my insistence we committed to have the advice by the Friday morning.

Porter also argued that the governor-general had no business inquiring into the eligibility of a person being sworn in as prime minister. He contended that the governor-general's only concern was whether the would-be prime minister commanded the confidence of the House of Representatives. And by the Friday morning he produced some advice from the Australian government solicitor in support of this proposition.

I had no doubt whatsoever that if the governor-general believed Dutton was ineligible, he wouldn't appoint him, regardless of what the House of Representatives said. Any suggestion to the contrary, no matter how distinguished its advocate, is nonsense. The constitution vests the executive power of the Commonwealth in the governor-general, which he or she has to administer in accordance with the constitution, a provision of which requires ministers, and thus prime ministers, to be lawfully elected members of parliament or senators.

However, the more relevant question was what would the governor-general do if the solicitor-general's advice was supportive of Dutton's eligibility, but acknowledged there was substantial doubt about the issue. In other words, like the advice the solicitor-general gave about Barnaby Joyce, the better view is that he's okay, but real doubts remain. Our practice in the past had been that where there was doubt the matter would go to the High Court. Could the governor-general conscientiously swear somebody in as prime minister knowing that their constitutional eligibility was the subject of proceedings in the High Court? After all, the solicitor-general hadn't had a good track record predicting what the High Court would say on section 44 in the past.

Porter has subsequently given a self-serving and inaccurate account of our discussions. He didn't at any time urge me to resign, nor did he make any threats to contradict me publicly if I were to say I didn't believe the governor-general would accept Dutton as prime minister. The only emotional part of our discussion was when, utterly unprompted, Porter started to tear up at the other side of my desk as he bemoaned the narrow, 2 per cent, margin by which he held his seat and how he was now inevitably going to lose it. 'I didn't come here to do this, I came here to sit in your chair, and now I'm going to lose it all,' he moaned.

I did my best to console him. 'Christian, it's not all about you, remember. And if you do lose your seat, you won't have to come to Canberra and you can spend more time with your family.'

On the Thursday, Labor moved in the House to refer Dutton to the High Court. I could have finished him off by voting for it or ensuring some of our side did. But I stuck to the principled approach we'd taken in the past – obtain the solicitor-general's advice and then, should there remain a doubt about eligibility, refer it to the High Court.

When the solicitor-general's advice appeared on the Friday morning, it was in the same terms as the advice we had for Joyce. His 'better view' was that Dutton was eligible but 'it is impossible to state the position with certainty ... I consider there to be some risk ... that the High Court might conclude that there is a conflict between Mr Dutton's duty as a parliamentarian and his private interests.'

The solicitor-general's advice had been written in haste and, as I read it, I was certain that at least one part of it wasn't just questionable but plainly wrong. The bulk of the advice was about the nature of the Commonwealth Child Care Benefits that the Duttons' centre received and whether a general statutory scheme like that really amounted to 'an agreement' with the Commonwealth.

However, in the previous 24 hours, another matter had arisen. The Duttons' childcare centre did have a specific agreement with the Commonwealth to subsidise the salary of an 'additional educator' to support the inclusion of children with special needs. The solicitor-general, however, concluded Dutton didn't have an indirect pecuniary interest in the agreement because the amount of the subsidy would have been entirely consumed in paying the salary of the additional educator. This couldn't be correct, and my own legal team agreed. If the Commonwealth paid the salary of one of the Duttons' staff, that relieved them of part of their expenses – it was plainly a pecuniary benefit.

Happily, the party room didn't elect Dutton as leader. If they'd done so, I'd have advised the governor-general not to swear him in as prime minister unless and until the High Court had concluded he was eligible to sit in the parliament. In the meantime, the deputy prime minister could have served as acting prime minister. The governor-general may not have taken my advice, but in my view the risk of having a constitutionally ineligible person in the office of prime minister is utterly unacceptable.

The discussions with Porter were a reasonably calm and civil distraction from the madness that was going on elsewhere in the building.

After discussing the crisis with the governor-general at some length, I'd gone to bed on Wednesday night resolved to call an election the next morning. I'd made an appointment with the governor-general for 8 am. The necessary correspondence was drafted and ready for me to sign.

The *Herald* and *Age* editorials were right: the Liberal Party room had demonstrated it lacked the discipline to manage government and the right-wing wreckers around Abbott and Dutton – both within and without the parliament – weren't going to stop. Should we be giving in to the terrorists, as Cormann had urged?

Sally Cray, David Bold and Lucy all counselled against an election. They pointed out that I'd have to run an entirely personal campaign, not just against Labor but against the right of my own party. I couldn't possibly win. 'And you'd end up having to pay for it, again,' they added.

I felt that I was caught up in a degrading and corrupt parody of democracy. There were no genuine differences on policy, nor was there any expectation that a change of leadership would improve our prospects – quite the reverse. It was pretty obvious, as Morrison and so many other colleagues were saying, the Dutton camp wanted to get rid of me because they feared I'd win the election, not because they thought I'd lose it.

By Thursday morning, I knew that unless Cormann thought better of his defection, my prospects of survival were very slight indeed. If I could get to the end of the week, the next set of polls would be catastrophic. I'd need to replace close to half the Liberal ministers in the cabinet and realistically would almost certainly be forced to an early election.

So, once again, as I had in 2009, I was contemplating my own political demise. How was I going to die? In 2009, convinced I had no support left at all, I stood as a candidate after the spill motion was carried. I'd said I'd do so, and expected to get half-a-dozen votes, if that. As it happened, I ran second to Abbott; Hockey, who ran third, was eliminated. In the final ballot, Abbott beat me by one vote. Some people, including Hockey, believe that if the ballot had been between Hockey and Abbott, we'd have been spared Abbott. I don't know if that's true or not, but ever since that day I've worried that by running I helped deliver Tony Abbott the leadership of the Liberal Party with all of the disastrous consequences for Australia that followed.

Morrison was clearly getting ready to run. Should I make way for him? At the time, I wasn't persuaded that Morrison had been working against me, as many later suggested. Scott's dream sequence, it seemed to me, was for us to have an election on 2 March 2019 as we'd agreed, win it, and then he'd have expected me to retire sometime in the course of that term. We had no agreement to that effect, but he knew me and Lucy well enough to know that I wouldn't be seeking re-election in 2022 at the age of 68.

On the other hand, there's no doubt at least half-a-dozen of Scott's closest allies (and he didn't have a large number) voted for Dutton in the ballot on the Tuesday. The idea that they did that without his knowledge is fanciful. Scott is a control freak and I'd seen before in the ballots in 2015 how he'd publicly vote one way while ensuring his supporters voted the other way.

So, regrettably, while it's never possible to be 100 per cent certain about these things, I have come to conclude Scott was playing a double game: professing public loyalty to me while at the same time allowing his supporters to undermine me. It was, of course, precisely what he'd done in 2015 when he said he'd voted for Abbott in the leadership ballot but worked closely with me to ensure his supporters voted against Abbott.

Morrison was my natural, most likely and best qualified successor and, while more conservative than me on social issues, was, I believed, a responsible, safe pair of hands. But Dutton, were he to become prime minister, would run off to the right with a divisive, dog-whistling, anti-immigration agenda, written and directed by Sky News and 2GB, designed to 'throw red meat to the base'. With no constraints, Dutton would do enormous damage to the social fabric of Australia. It's one thing having the tough cop handling border protection and counter-terrorism, but not at the head of our multicultural society.

I considered my next step. Should a spill motion be carried, I'd treat that as a vote of no confidence and not contest the leadership ballot. That would result in a contest between Dutton and Morrison. But would Morrison win? That was the question.

Events moved quickly. The Thursday morning papers were full of 'D-Day' headlines predicting another spill and a Dutton win. Cormann came round to my office again with Michaelia and Fifield. I was meeting with what was left of my leadership group and so they were asked to wait in the prime minister's sitting room. When I got up to go and see them, Morrison came with me. 'You need a witness,' he told me.

Their message was the same as the previous day and soon afterwards the trio resigned from the cabinet and made their defection public at a press conference. Within a short space of time, all the ministers who'd pledged their support to me the day before resigned as well. Their pledges of loyalty didn't last 24 hours.

By midday on the Thursday, seven of the 16 Liberal members of my cabinet had resigned, as well as three ministers outside of cabinet and three assistant ministers. Thirteen in total.

I told Scott, Julie and the rest of the leadership group that if I received a petition for another meeting signed by a majority of the party room, 43 names, then I'd hold one this week. Otherwise, we'd meet again in two weeks. I said I'd invite a motion for a spill of the leadership at the opening of the meeting and if it was carried I'd treat it as a motion of no confidence and wouldn't run in the ballot for leadership. 'That will mean it's between you and Dutton,' I said to Scott. 'And you as well, Julie, if you decide to run.'

She replied, 'I think I should run.'

From that point on, I knew my leadership was over. The sadness would hit me soon enough, I knew, but in the moment I had to play the game right down to the finish. And above all I had to make sure Dutton did not win, not for my sake or the party's, but for Australia's.

Christopher Pyne begged me not to put the spill motion to a ballot but to just step aside. He said he was worried the vote in favour of the spill would be humiliatingly high. I told him everyone in the party room had to take responsibility for their own actions and if they wanted to play their part in destroying their own government, then they should do so, and be seen to do so. 'I take responsibility and accountability very seriously,' I told him.

Scott was concerned he didn't have enough time to get the numbers to beat Dutton, and begged me under no circumstances to have the meeting on the Thursday, as did his closest supporters like Stuart Robert. I had no doubt Dutton would struggle to get the 43 signatures if the names were to be published; that was going to give Morrison time.

Pyne told me Dutton had asked if we could adjourn the House early on Thursday afternoon to avoid question time and arrange for a meeting to be held. Although it was a bad look, having a question time with much of the ministry resigned would have been worse, so I went along with it. As for the meeting, Scott's idea of postponing it for two weeks was simply not viable any longer. The mass resignations following Cormann's betrayal meant the leadership had to be resolved.

Determined to share Dutton's eligibility problem with as many people as I could, I stressed its significance when I held a press conference at about 1.30 pm.

> I cannot underline too much how important it is that anyone who seeks to be prime minister of Australia is eligible to be a member of parliament. Because a minister, let alone a prime minister, who is not eligible to sit in the House is not capable of validly being a minister or exercising any of the powers of a minister.

I laid out the sheer insanity of the insurgency.

> The government that I have led has been a very effective one. We have achieved an enormous amount in economic and social reform in this

parliament, despite the fact that we have had a one-seat majority in the House and a minority in the Senate. The cabinet has worked very, very cohesively and confidentially. It's been a very good cabinet. I want to thank all the cabinet ministers.

The reality is that a minority in the party room supported by others outside the parliament have sought to bully, intimidate others into making this change of leadership that they're seeking.

It's been described by many people, including those who feel they cannot resist it, as a form of madness.

It is remarkable that we are at this point, when only a month ago we were – as you all know being avid readers of polls – just a little bit behind Labor in the public polls and on our own polls, a little bit ahead. But on any view thoroughly competitive.

And I described what everybody knew to be true. 'What began as a minority has, by a process of intimidation, persuaded people that the only way to stop the insurgency is to give in to it.'[10]

Later it would emerge that, in some cases, the bullying and intimidation was matched with offers of advancement and not just into the ministry. Jane Hume was a Liberal senator for Victoria, very much out of favour with the hard-right group controlled by Michael Sukkar and Michael Kroger, who ran the party in Victoria. She was almost certainly going to lose her preselection to be replaced by Karina Okotel, a party vice-president and member of the religious right. Jane had told me and Lucy on the Wednesday evening, 'You don't have to worry about my support; I'm rock-solid.'

But when Kroger and Sukkar told her that if she supported Dutton she'd get her preselection confirmed – and another six years in the Senate – she switched and signed the petition for the meeting. Jane's singular focus was to secure her preselection and, like many others, personal loyalties or political commitments wouldn't stand in her way.

Sarah Henderson, on the other hand, was offered a ministry by Dutton's henchmen but knocked it back.

Michael Kroger was the president of the Victorian division. Swapping me for Dutton would guarantee electoral disaster in Victoria's upcoming state election, but Kroger supported it nonetheless. Gary Spence, the president of the LNP, was campaigning hard for Dutton among the Queenslanders, as were a number of their major donors.

That evening, Nick Greiner, the federal president of the Liberal Party, held a dinner for the federal executive. He told me that of the 14 officials present, 10 wanted Dutton to lead the party. It demonstrated, he said, how far the party had swung to the right. Nick supported me throughout the week.

Later, on 5 October, I noted a chat with Nola Marino, the shrewd chief whip, who was still very bruised and bitter about the coup.

> *She thinks the move against me was inspired by Abbott and his group and based solely on hatred of me, she thinks they were solely focused on ensuring I couldn't get clear air and they were concerned I would win, not that I would lose. She said a number of the colleagues had said to her they only voted for the spill because they felt as long as I was leader the insurgents would not stop their destabilisation. So in a nutshell they gave in to the terrorists.*

Crosby Textor had been running monthly surveys, or tracks, for the Liberal Party. Since the budget in May, we'd been ahead of Labor on a two-party preferred basis: 51:49 in May after the budget, 54:46 in June and 52:48 in July. The last three Newspolls showed us just behind Labor at 49:51. I was well ahead of Shorten as preferred PM on all the polls. On our July track, for example, I was ahead of him 56:27, and among soft voters 53:21. We were, in short, in our most favourable position in the polls since the 2016 election. Both Scott Morrison and I were quietly confident we'd win in 2019. As I'd said to the party room on the Tuesday, our biggest liability – and greatest threat – was our own disunity.

Sally and Lucy organised a party at The Lodge that Thursday night for my staff. I hadn't given up, but everyone knew it was likely to be my last night as prime minister. With so many ministers resigning, it seemed scarcely possible that the spill motion wouldn't be carried. But the insurgents hadn't produced their petition yet. At my press conference, I'd said we could hold the meeting at noon on Friday – now less than 24 hours away. But if they couldn't get the signatures by then there'd be no meeting this week.

I'd been very fortunate to have a great team in my office throughout my time as PM, indeed throughout my time in politics. Some, like Sally Cray and David Bold, had worked with me for years – dating back to the days of the Howard government. They'd helped me achieve so much in the 45th parliament, wrangling with crossbenchers, negotiating with other ministers, placating unhappy colleagues and together handling the flood of information, issues and decisions that sweep across the PM's desk every day. It was a happy office. None of my chiefs of staff or Sally, my principal private secretary, were tyrants or control freaks. It was also a respectful office; the blokey Canberra culture disrespecting women had no place in it.

So, it was a sad evening. I tried to cheer them up. All was not lost, I said. I don't think I persuaded many people. They knew Dutton and Cormann and the rest of the plotters had wrecked the government.

Daisy and James were there too with their kids. Lucy was barely holding it all together. What a ghastly business it is being married to a politician. Now, for the second time, she was watching her husband being overthrown by the same gang of right-wing thugs.

As I looked around the room that night I saw so many dear friends whose political careers would now, like mine, come to an end. Had I let them down, I asked myself. So many of their faces showed they were wondering the same thing.

I had taken great care not to repeat the mistakes of 2009. The NEG had been consulted and workshopped over many months – the antithesis of a captain's call. I had stuck with the cabinet and done everything I could to hold them together. The public weren't demanding I go, as they had Abbott or even Gillard. But still, the wreckers did their work. And for what? If you listened to Dutton and Abbott's friends in the media, I was a leftist, demonstrated by taking climate change seriously. So, through that crazed right-wing prism, virtually a communist.

The next morning started with calm. Morrison was busy gathering his numbers and my supporters were with him. Julie was resolved to run, but the moderates who'd supported me were being urged to vote for Morrison in the first ballot. They feared that if Julie went into the second ballot, Dutton would beat her. Regrettably, I think that analysis was probably correct. There are too many people in the party room who wouldn't vote for Julie simply because she's a woman. An ugly reality.

Lucy was with me in the office. Craig Laundy dropped in and out, but compared to the usual busy hum of the prime minister's office, it was deathly quiet. Arthur Sinodinos had been on leave and terribly sick with cancer for nearly a year. We had missed his wise counsel in cabinet. The drugs had made him very vulnerable to any infection but he bravely came down to vote for me one last time. Rowan Ramsey sent me a message to pledge his support and ask if I could approve a grant that was on my desk to fund 50 per cent of an overpass in his electorate. I wrote back, 'Okay will chase it up. And many thanks for your support. Assuming these guys actually get the 43 signatures – don't vote for the spill!' and a few minutes later, 'Signed the letter to McVeigh re the Overpass.'

Rowan messaged back, 'Thank you. You do not deserve today.'[11] Ever the gentleman. That was 8.17 in the morning.

Nola Marino, the chief whip, came round to see me at about 10 am and asked if I insisted on seeing the signatures. Would it be okay if she simply confirmed there were 43? My answer was that I needed to see them all and I would publish the lot. Everybody had to be accountable for what they were going to do. Finally, the petition arrived from Dutton, and once the signatures had been confirmed as genuine, the meeting started soon after midday.

The first motion was to spill the leadership. I commended my continued leadership to the party room. The votes came back 45 for the spill, 40 against. There was visible surprise that so many voted to keep me. Three votes the other way and I would have remained leader.

Then the ballot was held for the leadership. Dutton, Morrison and Julie nominated. On the first ballot Dutton received 38, Morrison 36, Bishop 11 and was eliminated.

Julie was devastated by her low vote. Apart from her and me, only nine of her colleagues had voted for her. And not one from Western Australia. Most of them, under Cormann's influence, were for Dutton.

On the second ballot, Morrison won against Dutton 45:40.

Julie didn't run for deputy leader; she'd had enough. Frydenberg, Hunt and Ciobo nominated. If looks could have killed, Hunt would have fallen over dead. He'd been Dutton's wannabe deputy and had been working towards this day for months. Never liked, he'd never been more despised than he was at that moment. And with good cause. He was a strong supporter of the NEG, and of Frydenberg who was his closest friend. But he conspired to blow up the government for no reason other than his own advancement. The votes came back and Frydenberg had won an absolute majority on the first ballot. So, that was the new team – Morrison and Frydenberg. I wished them well. It was almost over.

All I had to do now was say goodbye. There'd be a final press conference in the prime minister's courtyard, then a drive out to Government House to resign and recommend Morrison be sworn in as prime minister, a last drink with my staff and then I'd walk out the doors never to return. That was it.

Morrison rushed around to my office to try to persuade me not to resign from parliament. Sally sent Daisy to shoo him away so I could compose my thoughts before I addressed the assembled media.

I'm always at my calmest at the worst times: my mind clears, my heart seems to slow, objectivity prevails over passion. And so I was that afternoon. This is what I said:

> It may surprise you on a day like this but I remain very optimistic and positive about our nation's future.
>
> I want to thank the Australian people for the support they've given me and my government over the last nearly three years. We've been able to achieve, as a progressive government, as a progressive Liberal Coalition government, enormous reforms and very, very substantial achievements.
>
> You know, the foundation of everything you do in government is a strong economy and we have delivered – as we promised – jobs and growth. You may have heard that before. We've got record jobs growth in Australia last year. We have strong economic growth, 3.1 per cent – as you know, higher than any of the G7 economies.
>
> That has enabled us to do so much more. Despite the minority position in the Senate and the one-seat majority in the House of Representatives, we've been able to deliver substantial taxation reforms. Much more than many of you – probably any of you – thought possible.

I described some of our achievements: the biggest personal income tax reforms in more than 20 years; reductions in company tax for small and medium businesses; legalising same-sex marriage; commencing the construction of the biggest renewables project in Australia, Snowy Hydro 2.0; committing to a rail link to Melbourne Airport; building Western Sydney Airport; keeping the TPP alive when Trump pulled out; and maintaining the refugee resettlement deal in the face of Trump's fury. I described our reforms to childcare and to school funding, our massive investment in the capabilities of the ADF and so many other achievements.

> So, I'm very proud of my government and my ministers' record in achievement. I want to thank them. I want to thank all my colleagues.

I want to thank my staff, but above all I want to thank my wife, Lucy, for her love and support. I want to thank our children – Alex and his wife, Yvonne, and our daughter, Daisy, and her husband, James.

It isn't easy being either married to or the child of a politician, let alone a prime minister. Often children get attention from the media and others that they frankly don't deserve, in terms of people wanting to have a crack at their father by going after them. So, it's been tough on them at times, but I want to thank them for their solidarity and loyalty and love. Our grandchildren, of course, are a great joy. I look forward to spending some more time with them and with Lucy.

But, finally, I want to thank the Australian people for everything they have done for me. It has been such a privilege to be the leader of this great nation.

I love Australia. I love Australians. We are the most successful multicultural society in the world and I have always defended that and advanced that as one of our greatest assets. We must never allow the politics of race or division or of setting Australians against each other to become part of our political culture.

We have so much going for us in this country. We have to be proud of it and cherish it.

Now, I suppose I should say something about the events of the last week or so. Look, I think you all know what's happened. There was a determined insurgency from a number of people – both in the party room and backed by voices, powerful voices, in the media – really to, if not bring down the government, certainly bring down my prime ministership. It was extraordinary. It was described as madness by many and I think it's difficult to describe it in any other way.

In the party room meeting today, I was impressed by how many of my colleagues spoke or voted for loyalty above disloyalty. How the insurgents were not rewarded by electing Mr Dutton, for example, but instead my successor – whom I wish the very best, of course – Scott Morrison, a very loyal and effective treasurer. I want to thank him, of course, for his great work, but above all I want to thank Julie Bishop. She is a very dear friend. We've been friends for over 30 years. She's been an extraordinary Foreign minister; I would say our finest. She has been a loyal deputy and just a great colleague and friend. So, I thank Julie very much. As you know, she's stood down as the deputy and she's succeeded by Josh Frydenberg.

Again, I wish Josh all the best. He's been a very loyal and capable minister.

Laura Tingle asked me about climate policy and the Coalition.

In terms of energy policy and climate policy, I think the truth is that the Coalition finds it very hard to get agreement on anything to do with emissions ... climate policy issues have the same problem within the Coalition of bitterly entrenched views that are actually more ideological views than views based, as I say, in engineering and economics. It's a bit like same-sex marriage used to be. Almost an insoluble problem.

... Australians will be just dumbstruck and so appalled by the conduct of the last week. You know, to imagine that a government would be rocked by this sort of disloyalty and deliberate – you know, insurgency is the best way to describe it – deliberate, destructive action, at a time when ... there are differences on policy, but frankly, all of them were resolvable, able to be resolved with a little bit of goodwill. Of course, a month ago, as I said yesterday, we were a little behind in the national polls and a little bit ahead in our own polls. So, I think many Australians will just be shaking their heads in disbelief at what's been done.

I concluded as positively as I could.

Look, I came into politics at the very mature age of 50. I've had a very good time here in the parliament. I've always been focused on what I can deliver for the Australian people.

Again, the critical thing is with politics, it's not about the politicians. That's why this week has been so dispiriting, because it just appears to be, you know, vengeance, personal ambition, factional feuding, or however you'd describe it. It hasn't had anything to do with 25 million Australians. And the Australia we should be focused on, above all else, are these little ones. You know, it is the next generation that we are working for here in this place. And we have achieved a great deal.

There are some things that I would have liked to have completed or done more on. But to be really honest with you, we have got so much more done in this government, and particularly in this parliament, than I expected and certainly a lot more than any of you expected – sceptics that you all are.

So look, thank you all very much and I wish you all the best.

Above all, I wish the new Prime Minister-elect the very best, and his team.

Thank you.[12]

By then I'd been joined by Daisy and Lucy and two of our grandchildren, Alice and Jack. As we all prepared to go back inside, Jack made his own memorable contribution to the press conference. He'd just spent two hours staying as quiet as a four-year-old can in an office of shocked and sad staffers. Now he ran in front of the lectern and, noting the media pack weren't forlorn, started hooting and booing them. As so many people wrote to me later, 'Jack spoke for all Australians.'

One of the questions I'd been asked, as I had been the day before, was whether I'd resign from the parliament and I confirmed I would. There was no secret about my intentions there – I'd made them very clear for some time. There was no way I was going to be like Abbott or Rudd, a miserable ghost hanging around to overthrow my successor.

And more importantly, I knew that right now my duty to the nation was discharged. I'd run my race as prime minister and achieved much more than I'd thought possible. I'd ensured Dutton didn't succeed me. But with the government's future in the hands of others, my obligations now were to myself and my family.

Daisy and James had arrived with Jack and Alice on Thursday the 23rd. We had longstanding plans to mark Alice's second birthday, which was on the following Sunday.

The last weekend at The Lodge was surreal. Daisy and James did their best to be good-humoured. The children were puzzled that their usually doting grandparents were so distracted but otherwise were unmoved by the drama surrounding us. We celebrated Alice's birthday with a beautiful cake The Lodge staff made for her. And we had her little party in the morning room, where Lucy and I had reinstated the door that had been bricked up in Malcolm Fraser's time.

I didn't want to fall into the abyss of despair that I had in 2010. And I knew that to have any hope of avoiding that darkness, I had to get out of parliament and away from politics as quickly as possible.

We left Canberra that Sunday, for the last time. The new prime minister had the big plane so one of the Challengers was waiting to take us back to Sydney. As we drove out to the RAAF base, the police in our car were told we wouldn't be allowed to drive onto the tarmac and up to the plane. A nice touch, I thought. We'd have to carry our bags across the tarmac, a perfectly forlorn sight for the cameras to record from their positions on the other side of the airfield fence. I rang the Defence minister, Marise Payne, and got the order countermanded.

Looking back at that crazy week, what would I have done differently? The biggest question is whether I should have spilled the leadership on the Tuesday. In my view, had I not done so, there would have been a call for a spill anyway and the insurgents at that point had momentum. As Scott said at the time, they were trying to 'fake it 'til they make it' and the only way to show they were fake was to call them out.

Knowing what we know today, I think, on balance, it was the right call. And if Cormann hadn't swung behind Dutton as his insurgency faltered, I'd have seen off Dutton and his challenge. Equally, if Morrison's friends hadn't tactically supported Dutton, the coup would have utterly failed. But these things are hard to assess; you're dealing with imperfect information and often very emotional and irrational people.

Once the vote on Tuesday had been had, I could have said there'd be no more meetings that week, as Scott Morrison suggested. On balance, that would have been worth doing. Yet it may not have worked. If Cormann had still betrayed me the way he did, the pressure to hold the meeting wouldn't have abated, especially given the furious support for the insurgency from the Murdoch media.

Requesting the 43 signatures, making people accountable, was definitely the right thing to do. It slowed Dutton's momentum. If I couldn't keep myself in the PM's office, the next priority had to be to keep Dutton out of it. And that worked.

Should I have called an election on the Thursday morning? The governor-general would have welcomed it, that's for sure. As would many Australians. Having to run a personal campaign seeking a mandate for my leadership against both Shorten on the left and Dutton and Abbott on the right held some appeal to me. But I made the right call not to do it: it's hard to see how it wouldn't have resulted in a Labor victory.

Should I have contested the leadership once the spill was carried? My concern here was that if I ran against Dutton, and Morrison or

Bishop chose not to contest – a rerun of Tuesday – I might have lost. I knew the party room well enough to be sure that the terrorist tactics would be starting to work: some would vote for Dutton just to end the insurgency – as Nola later confirmed. It's neither courageous nor honourable. It's weak, but that's human nature.

Had I run in a ballot with Morrison and Bishop, there was the real risk we'd repeat the experience of 2009: the other two would get knocked out early and I'd end up in a final ballot against Dutton and lose.

In either of the last two scenarios, the risk of Dutton winning was too high. So, essentially, I sacrificed my own chances, such as they were, in order to make sure Morrison prevailed.

Some last words:

As Morrison was sworn in on Friday evening, I messaged him. 'Congratulations Prime Minister, and good luck!'

He replied the next morning.

> Only you can know how I feel today, but I cannot begin to know how you feel. I loved working for and with you. I'm really proud of what we did. And that is always how I will always feel and speak of it. I want you to know I am thinking about you a great deal and you know I pray for you. That doesn't change now. I don't know why all this happened, but now it has come upon me, you know I will be relying on my faith, friends and values to overcome and conquer what is ahead … Thank you for all you've done for me. But above all as one PM to another, thank you for everything you did for our country. No one knows that contribution better than me. Love you mate.

I replied, 'You too Scomo!'[13]

It wasn't until 11 September that I heard from Mathias Cormann, who sent me a long self-serving note in which he professed his loyalty:

> I was not part of any planned conspiracy or insurgency.
>
> I genuinely backed you until events developed, sadly, which in my judgement made our position irretrievable. I immediately and honestly advised you directly.
>
> I was genuinely blindsided by the leadership ballot on the Tuesday and events developed rapidly from there.
>
> All this has been very painful – yes I know first and foremost for you and for that I'm very sorry. But also for me. My wife was genuinely traumatised by it all.

In the end, the reason for my judgement on the Wednesday, for better or for worse, was that I felt there was no way back, that the ultimate conclusion was inevitable, and that the only question was how long and how painful the transition would be and what that would ultimately mean for our cause. I tried to do the right thing for the right reasons in the right way in incredibly difficult circumstances.

I replied:

Mathias, at a time when strength and loyalty were called for, you were weak and treacherous. You should be ashamed of yourself, and I can well understand how disappointed your wife is in your conduct. She probably thought, like most of us, that you were a better man than you turned out to be.[14]

Cormann's treachery was the worst and the most hurtful. He'd become a trusted friend of mine, and of Lucy as I've described above. He used to send me pictures of his children and on occasion asked me to pose for photos with his daughter when she visited him in Canberra. On 10 July, he sent one of those pictures to Lucy with the message, 'Lucy had to share this with you too. Great catch up for my five year old with Malcolm today. Will be very meaningful to her as she gets older …' Indeed it will be.

I'd always trusted Cormann, ignoring constant warnings that he was an untrustworthy Machiavellian schemer. Julie Bishop, who knew him well from Perth, was especially suspicious – and of course the feeling was mutual. So, his treachery didn't surprise others as it did me. But his innumeracy surprised everyone. Dutton didn't have the numbers at any stage – as the ballots demonstrated. If Cormann, Fifield and Cash had voted against the spill on the Friday, it wouldn't have been carried: there'd have been 43 votes against and 42 for.

The coup of August 2018 brought my prime ministership to an end. But the people responsible for it inside and outside the parliament didn't get the outcome they wanted. Dutton, Abbott and Cormann and most of the insurgents despised Morrison. Abbott and Credlin, in particular, hated him for his two-faced behaviour in 2015. On the other hand, Morrison was at least a social conservative – the days of a liberal leader of the Liberal Party were over, perhaps forever.

George Brandis wrote me a very warm and wise letter a few days after the coup. He correctly characterised the terrorist tactics of the right wing of the party. 'The thuggish events of last week showed the new leaders of the Right are not prepared to accommodate more moderate voices at all. They have repudiated the approach of John Howard – indeed they have repudiated Robert Menzies, for a Liberal Party from which liberalism is expunged is not the party Menzies founded.'

But then he had a word of criticism for me.

> Your fatal mistake was, of course, to trust Dutton. If I may say so, I, and others, warned you many times that he was stalking you, and that his 'support' for you would be rescinded the moment he saw the opportunity to seize the leadership … Malcolm, you trusted the wrong people. You mistook a cordial working relationship for political loyalty. When it counts, the only people who were ever going to be loyal to you were your loyalists. You are not the first political leader to have been cut down by their Praetorian Guard, but you made it so much easier for them by recruiting your Praetorian Guard from among your natural enemies and inevitable rivals. Politics, at least at times of crisis, isn't a transactional business. It is a tribal one and in the end the tribes always revert to type.[15]

George's criticism has considerable merit although I don't recall his warning me about Dutton 'many times'. It never occurred to me that Dutton, let alone anyone else, would seriously consider himself a viable candidate for leader or that we'd do better with him at the helm. I was equally astonished that otherwise rational people like Cormann would support him. But in the final analysis, for so many of them the only thing that mattered was their tribal connection.

Every advancement Steve Ciobo had enjoyed in politics had been under my leadership. Abbott hadn't rated him, and neither did Morrison. But, a friend of Dutton, he still turned on me, as did so many others I'd promoted.

Now, of course you cannot simply promote your own loyalists, but George was right – there is a profound lesson for leaders here. You cannot treat politicians as rational actors, especially those like Dutton, Cormann, Ciobo and numerous others who'd been in the game all their lives. Having come into politics at 50 from the rational world of business, I always assumed people would, more or less, act in their rational best interest. But that assumption is wrong, at least in the Liberal Party and especially with its right wing.

On the other hand, had I not trusted Cormann and Dutton and worked closely with conservatives and moderates alike, my government would not have achieved as much as it did. And if I had spent all my time fretting about who was plotting what, as other leaders have done, I would have achieved even less.

Meanwhile, the brand damage to the Liberal Party was immense. Following the coup, the party's vote collapsed and stayed collapsed for months. In 2015, I'd replaced a leader whom the public wanted gone and our numbers shot up. In 2018, nobody could explain why the coup had occurred – least of all Morrison. In the Victorian state election in November 2018, there was a 6.8 per cent swing against the Liberal Party and nine Liberal seats were lost in the Legislative Assembly. Some were formerly very safe seats like Hawthorn, with swings of close to 10 per cent. Thirty per cent of voters in seats lost to Labor said they couldn't vote Liberal because of the coup and that included 17 per cent of traditional Liberal voters.[16]

The sheer brutality of the week's events, and in particular the way in which so many members were bullied by Dutton's supporters, shattered several political careers. Ciobo and Keenan, both young men who'd supported Dutton, didn't run again at the 2019 election; Julie Bishop wouldn't accept a ministry in Morrison's government and also retired in 2019. Julia Banks, the hero of Chisholm in the 2016 election, resigned from the Liberal Party in protest and went to the crossbench, running as an independent against Greg Hunt in Flinders in 2019. She was unsuccessful but her courage and principled stand against the bullies won her a lot of admiration.

In Warringah, Abbott knew he was likely to lose at the 2019 election but insisted on running. A grassroots citizens movement sprang up to 'Vote Tony Out'. They selected as their candidate Zali Steggall, an Olympic skier and barrister, and she trounced him, winning with a 57 per cent majority. Narcissist to the end, Abbott said he'd rather lose than quit. Of course, it was always all about him. A drover's dog with a Liberal handle would have won that seat.

In Wentworth, for the by-election of October 2018, the Liberal Party endorsed former diplomat Dave Sharma as their candidate. He was on track to win until, in the last week, Morrison had a brain snap and announced plans to move Australia's embassy in Israel to Jerusalem, as Trump had done. This was, and looked like, a cheap attempt to buy

Jewish votes. But in any event the more observant Jews, who were most likely to care about the issue, would have already voted by post or pre-poll: they don't vote on polling day, which is a Saturday and the Jewish Sabbath. Added to that, Barnaby Joyce decided to threaten a new challenge for the Nationals leadership and for good measure called for Snowy Hydro 2.0 to be abandoned and replaced with a new coal-fired power station. That went down like a lead balloon in climate-conscious Wentworth.

Dr Kerryn Phelps was running as an independent and she narrowly won the by-election – which was quite an achievement, given I'd held the seat with a 67 per cent majority. Dave Sharma then narrowly won the seat back for the Liberal Party in May 2019 at the general election. He wisely by and large kept Morrison and other ministers, apart from Josh, out of the electorate and ran as a 'Modern Liberal' to try to differentiate himself from what was seen as the swing to the right since the August coup. I stayed out of the general election as well, but gave Dave some good campaigning advice, which he used to his advantage.

Lucy and I were in New York during the by-election. I'd written a letter of farewell and thanks to my constituents, resigned a week after the coup and then left. I had concluded the best thing I could do for Morrison was to stay well away. He asked me to write a letter to the Wentworth constituents urging them to vote for Dave, but the text they proposed was so disingenuous I concluded it was better I say nothing.

Morrison's promise about Jerusalem created enormous resentment in the Muslim world, and especially in Indonesia, whose president was about to sign the free trade agreement and comprehensive strategic partnership we'd agreed earlier in the year. I went to great lengths to reassure my friend Jokowi that Morrison was a good man with good intentions, and that the Jerusalem announcement was a rookie's error. I sought to persuade Morrison of the damage he was doing to our relations with our closest neighbour and he thankfully crab-walked back from his decision, announcing that while Australia recognised West Jerusalem as Israel's capital (a position taken only by Russia and certainly not consistent with Israel's policy), the embassy wouldn't be moved until there was a final peace agreement with the Palestinians. Calm was restored, and the IA-CEPA was signed in March 2019.

The months leading up to the election in May 2019 were very difficult. It's awkward, to say the least, to be an election issue without being a candidate in the election. So, I kept a low profile, working on my book and managing my own affairs. Beyond an appearance on *Q&A*, I made few public statements after the coup, even when provoked by the occasional vicious personal attacks from Peter Dutton and his supporters. Several private conversations were reported to the media, which made me realise that in the crazy political climate of the time I couldn't afford to talk candidly to anyone in politics.

To the surprise of everyone, including himself, Morrison won the 2019 election and for much of the same reasons as I would have done. Labor's class warfare and promise of higher taxes, especially targeted at self-funded retirees, were extremely unpopular. Added to that, Shorten remained unliked and untrusted – he still couldn't speak with conviction and it showed.

Scott benefited from the fact that we'd neutralised both health and education as issues. Mediscare couldn't work a second time – hospital funding was at record highs – and we were clearly giving a Gonski on school funding. Scott also benefited from ferociously partisan support from the Murdoch media. Plus Clive Palmer spent over $80 million purportedly promoting his own party but in reality attacking Labor and Shorten.

Climate change, or the Coalition's inability to deal with it, would have been a bigger issue in the campaign had it not been for Shorten's inexplicable handling of it. When asked what his higher emission reduction targets would cost, he said it wasn't possible to quantify. This was an absurd answer. The cost of variable renewables, especially solar, was falling rapidly just as the maintenance costs of the old coal-fired power stations were increasing. There were many economic analyses of the electricity market. With a few plausibly reasonable changes to their assumptions about the cost of renewables and the retirement timetable of existing coal generators, Shorten would have been able to say that his policy would either add to or make very little difference to GDP. It was as though the certainty of victory had made him reckless.

Shorten's bizarre non-answer gave Scott and Josh Frydenberg (the only other minister who got much attention in Morrison's largely one-man campaign) the licence to conjure up enormous costs and risks. Even Labor's policy to support electric vehicles was going to 'kill the Australian weekend', presumably because the EV's battery would run out on the way home from a country drive.

Morrison too ran a strong, tight campaign. He's a professional politician who understands marketing and messaging better than most. His cringe-worthy 'daggy dad' persona is more exaggerated than entirely contrived, but in net terms it probably helped. All that aside, however, the truth is that Labor lost the election that the Coalition, after the August coup, didn't deserve to win.

Conclusion

I started to write this conclusion on Daisy's 35th birthday, 5 January 2020. Over 8 million hectares have been burnt out in New South Wales and Victoria and more in all the other states and territories. Sydney is ringed by fire. Hundreds of holidaymakers are huddling on beaches to shelter from the flames. They are shrouded in smoke – in some places so thick it's pitch dark in the middle of the day; in other places the sky is blood red. Yesterday Penrith, in Sydney's west, was the hottest place on earth, registering just under 50 degrees Celsius. Canberra, Burley Griffin's garden city, has the worst air quality on the planet. Apocalyptic sums it up.

It looks like the end of the world, people are saying. But what if it doesn't just look like it, but is?

Regrets – I've had a few, but none greater than our failure, the world's failure, to effectively address global warming. I gave it my best shot – in government, opposition and government. What could I have done differently? In opposition, I stared down the climate deniers and fought tooth and nail to get the CPRS legislation passed. If I'd succeeded then, I have no doubt, we'd have an emissions trading scheme today. It would be about as controversial as the ETS in New Zealand – in other words, not at all.

But I was defeated in 2009, and by just one vote, and we ended up with Abbott. Would I have been better ducking and weaving and temporising? Living to fight another day? People always complain politicians don't stand up for what they believe in; but what if the consequence of doing so means an even worse politician with even worse policies takes charge?

Then in government, as PM, I took the greatest care to ensure the NEG had the widest possible support. I kept the cabinet together and consulted thoroughly with the party room. When a backbench revolt threatened to defeat the government in the House, the cabinet resolved to beat a tactical and temporary retreat, not abandoning the policy but trying to avoid a potentially fatal confrontation. That didn't stop the wreckers, as you've just read.

Morrison professed to be as committed to the NEG as I was. He and I were equally insistent it was, and should remain, our policy. But then, once he was PM, he dumped it. So now, while the reliability element has been legislated by the states and territories, in the absence of the emissions reduction element we have no coherent national policy to integrate energy and climate. The consequence is that we will have higher emissions, higher prices and less investment in new generation than we would have had with the NEG.

And worse still, at UN COP25 – the 2019 Madrid Climate Change Conference – our Energy minister was working with Brazil and Saudi Arabia among others to undermine an effective global effort to cut emissions.

The tragedy of our politics is that in 2020, as the evidence of global warming is more apparent than ever, with the longest drought and the worst fires in my lifetime, our climate policy is more politicised and divorced from reality than ever. The Coalition is held hostage by a toxic alliance of the political right within the Liberal and National parties, the Murdoch and other right-wing media and the fossil-fuel lobby itself, with its big donors, including Gina Rinehart and Clive Palmer.

Of course, the picture in the United States is, if anything, worse and much more consequential. Obama's attempt to lead on climate action was always being undermined by the Congress, but now we have President Trump, who leads on climate inaction, denounces global warming as a fraud, promotes coal and mocks renewables.

And as he and his admirers elsewhere do so, temperature records are being broken, coral reefs are being bleached, sea levels are rising and … Australia is on fire. What the political tacticians and commentators forget is that you cannot negotiate with physics.

For me, the most frustrating part of all this is that we now have the means to drastically reduce our CO_2 emissions without undue economic cost. It is very clear that the cheapest new generation is a combination of renewables and storage. This transition will involve careful planning and design but we no longer have to wear an economic hair shirt to save the planet. Abundant, cheap, zero-emission electricity is within our grasp.

Back in 2009, surveying the devastation of the Black Saturday bushfires in Victoria, I wondered when the physical consequences of climate change would be so stark that the climate denialists would realise they are wrong and we could respond with the common purpose that the climate crisis demands. If the fires of this summer just past don't wake up the Australian public to demand a swift and substantial cut in emissions, then what will?

Much of what governments and politicians do is business as usual: administration. That shouldn't be belittled. A new road, a new hospital, a new tax law may be obviously needed, but it makes a big difference if they're well designed and built on time and budget.

But there are also instances when a leader can make something happen that otherwise wouldn't have occurred.

So, looking back, I ask, what were some of the things I did in public life that others wouldn't have done? Most of them are from my time as prime minister, but certainly they include the federal takeover of interstate water in 2007.

However, as prime minister, you have the opportunity to do so much more. I couldn't rely on a long term in office; I had to do as much as I could while I had the opportunity. And I didn't waste it.

The National Innovation and Science Agenda reflected my values and my priorities, as did the Cities Agenda. Both were radical, transformative economic policies. Snowy Hydro 2.0 and the Tasmanian 'battery of the nation' pumped hydro projects were equally my own vision. As was the Commonwealth government itself building Western Sydney Airport, a key element of the Western Sydney City Deal.

In some cases, my personal stamp is on the way I went about achieving outcomes, such as enlisting the support of David Gonski to reform school funding. Or my capacity to withstand the displeasure of many Coalition supporters, such as by winding back excessive tax breaks for the rich in 2016 in the course of reforming superannuation. And while establishing the ABCC and the Registered Organisations Commission were policies I inherited from Tony Abbott, I don't think many others would have taken the gamble of the double dissolution which enabled us to get them passed into law.

The biggest social reform in my time was legalising same-sex marriage. It was long overdue. But had either my predecessor or successor been PM, each passionately opposed to marriage equality, I doubt we would have seen that reform under a Coalition government.

Planning to re-equip our defence forces was certainly underway when I became PM, but the decision to build so much in Australia and create a sovereign, sustainable and continuous Australian naval shipbuilding industry was my own, as was the commitment to develop an Australian cybersecurity industry. More than most, I could see how an Australian defence industry would support my vision of an innovative, technologically advanced nation.

All of these domestic reforms, no matter how idiosyncratically mine in their conception, were team efforts and couldn't have been delivered without the support of enthusiastic colleagues, both political and in the public service.

In the international arena, while I always had support from my ministers, especially Julie Bishop, my advisers and diplomats, the outcomes I secured were very personal, none more so than with Trump. There is only one decision-maker in the White House today, and the blandishments of diplomats and other officials count for less now than in any previous administration. Not many, if any, Australian politicians would have gone toe to toe with the American president and changed his mind in the way I did.

In keeping the TPP alive I worked closely with Steve Ciobo and chief negotiator Justin Brown. But had I not persisted and been able to win over other leaders, particularly Shinzo Abe, the TPP would be dead today. Instead, it is alive and well, and will be generating jobs for Australians for many years to come.

While a closer relationship with Indonesia is of vital and obvious importance, it has often proved elusive. We wouldn't be where we are today – with a free trade agreement and a comprehensive strategic partnership – without the close rapport Jokowi, myself and our wives established from the time of our first meetings in 2015.

The Pacific Step-Up was both overdue and a team effort but the Australian government itself building what is now called the Coral Sea Cable System to the Solomon Islands and PNG was my initiative.

So, I have done the state some service.

Of course, I left the prime minister's office with many things undone – settling a coherent energy and climate policy foremost among them. And there was more to be done. I was only weeks away from presenting a plan for a federal integrity commission to the cabinet, and it's remarkable that nearly 18 months since I lost office it has still not seen the light of day.

And while there was not one successful people-smuggling expedition to Australia during my time, I wasn't able to realise my goal of resettling all the asylum seekers in PNG and Nauru.

But my overwhelming sense is gratitude that I was able to get so much done in the difficult circumstances and time I had. My government's list of reforms, in just under three years, is a formidable one. And, importantly, those reforms show every sign of enduring, not least because most of them have bipartisan support.

I certainly made mistakes, and said I would at the time. Not all our policies will work, I used to say, but when one doesn't, we'll dump it or amend it and, better informed, try something else. There is no place for set and forget, not in the 21st century. But looking back, I'm relieved that I didn't make one of those political mistakes the consequences of which are almost impossible to reverse – like invading Iraq in 2003, or holding the Brexit referendum, or allowing a million Syrian refugees to walk into Germany.

What have I learned? Well, this big book contains the lessons of a lifetime, but in politics more than anywhere else I learned that nothing is so important as character. There is no other line of work in which so little store is put on telling the truth. A company director who misleads his shareholders could end up in jail or ruined by litigation. Politicians routinely dissemble; the press gallery seldom calls them out, often connives in the deceit and, when they get away with it, praises them for their political skills.

A person of good character, who can be relied upon to tell the truth, and take care to do so, is too rare in politics. Some of the most intellectually talented people are let down by their lack of character and integrity. In business, you can generally pick and choose with whom you deal. In politics, the cast is supplied by the electorate and that inevitably means you have to work with people who could, at any moment, betray you.

It would be fair to say that I was too trusting, but if I had only trusted my closest colleagues, my government would have achieved very little.

Our nation, our Australian project, is a remarkable one. But we cannot take its endurance or its success for granted. We will have to work hard to maintain Australia as a prosperous high-wage economy with a generous social welfare safety net. And innovation, free trade and open markets will be the key to doing this.

We cannot assume that our security will be perpetually, or unconditionally, underwritten by the United States. We need to look to our own defences both in military terms and, above all, in building closer ties across our region. That will require constant attention.

One of the bitter paradoxes of the modern world is that in so many places, despite all our advanced technology, we are less respectful and tolerant of difference than we were in past centuries. Australia is an exception – the most successful multicultural society in the world. But we cannot be complacent about that success and Australians must continue to reject those who try to divide us, whether it is angry voices in the media or in politics.

And we have far more to do as we work with First Australians to achieve justice and reconciliation. In doing so, we must not let the setbacks and frustrations along the way blind us to the very real progress that has been made.

So, what's next? More adventures with Lucy, I hope, and if our lives to date are any guide, quite a few will be unexpected. But we both look forward to supporting and investing in Australian innovation. That lifelong passion is undimmed and the prospects for Australian technology and entrepreneurship are greater than ever.

And while I was determined to leave parliament when my time as PM was over, I haven't lost interest in politics and public affairs. In particular, I remain committed to an Australian republic and, above all, to seeing effective Australian and global action to cut our emissions and address global warming.

Now that the 2019 election is over, I am free to play a more active role in public life. I have surrendered the title of prime minister, but I retain the most important title in our democracy: an Australian citizen, with all of the responsibility and opportunity that entails.

Notes

Chapter 1   Coral and Bruce
1   William Shakespeare, *The Tragedy of Coriolanus*, act 3, scene iii

Chapter 2   Books, bananas and Jack Lang: school and university
1   Malcolm Turnbull, 'Lang: a man who knew how to hate', *Nation Review*, 3–9 October 1975
2   One of the centre-right predecessors of the modern Liberal Party
3   Malcolm Turnbull, 'At home in Stonehouse country', *Nation Review*, 28 February – 6 March 1975

Chapter 4   Packer: defending the Goanna
1   Kerry Packer, '"Each and every one of the allegations made against me ... are false, and demonstrably false"', public statement, *Sydney Morning Herald*, 29 September 1984
2   John Lyons, 'Raging Turnbull', *Sydney Morning Herald, Good Weekend*, 13 April 1991
3   Paul Barry, *The Rise and Rise of Kerry Packer*, Bantam Books, Sydney, 1993, p. 268
4   As recorded in Richard Ackland, 'A sureness that weakens Turnbull's case', *Sydney Morning Herald*, 17 October 2003
5   Andrew Fowler, 'The Turnbull files', *The Monthly*, 7 October 2015

Chapter 5   Spycatcher: taking on Number 10
1   Lionel Bowen, 'Mr Kerry Packer', news release, 26 March 1987
2   Malcolm Turnbull, *The Spycatcher Trial*, William Heinemann Australia, Richmond, 1988, p. 63
3   Ibid., p. 44
4   Ibid., p. 184
5   Ibid., p. 124
6   Ibid., pp. 114–15
7   Charles Moore, *Margaret Thatcher: The Authorized Biography*, vol. 3, *Herself Alone*, Allen Lane, London, 2019, p. 241
8   Turnbull, *The Spycatcher Trial*, p. 184
9   Ibid.
10 Ibid., p. 135
11 United Kingdom, House of Commons, *Debates*, 6th series, vol. 106, 27 November 1986, col. 427 (Neil Kinnock and Margaret Thatcher)
12 A (disputed) comment from Rt Hon. Michael Alison MP, quoted in most London papers on 2 December 1986; for example, '"Wally" joke fuels row', *The Times*, 2 December 1986
13 Turnbull, *The Spycatcher Trial*, p. 195
14 Ibid., p. 199

Chapter 6   Moguls, madness and the media
1   Lucy Hughes Turnbull, *Sydney: Biography of a City*, Random House, Sydney, 1999
2   Turnbull & Partners Pty Ltd, 'Confidential report to Fairfax bondholders', 16 October 1990

Chapter 7   From Siberia to Silicon Valley
1   OzEmail registration statement, 28 May 1996

Chapter 8   An Australian republic

1   Thomas Keneally, *Our Republic*, Harcourt Education, Port Melbourne, 1993, p. 77
2   Judith Brett, *Robert Menzies' Forgotten People*, Melbourne University Press, Melbourne, 2007, p. 146
3   Australia, House of Representatives, *Debates*, 18 February 1953, p. 57 (Robert Menzies)
4   Malcolm Turnbull, *The Reluctant Republic*, William Heinemann Australia, Port Melbourne, 1993, p. 251
5   Now merged with the Union Club
6   Turnbull, *The Reluctant Republic*, p. 166
7   Malcolm Turnbull, *Fighting for the Republic: The Ultimate Insider's Account*, Hardie Grant, South Yarra, 1999, pp. 15–16
8   Michael Millett, 'Royalists wage personal war on Turnbull', *Sydney Morning Herald*, 13 September 1997

Chapter 9   Second time lucky: member for Wentworth

1   Wendy Spry, preselection reference, 2004
2   Malcolm Turnbull and Max Raine, conversation, 11 February 2004
3   Joe Hildebrand, 'Turnbull is headed for back bench', *The Daily Telegraph*, 1 March 2004

Chapter 10   On the backbench

1   Australia, House of Representatives, *Debates*, 29 November 2004, pp. 63–8 (Malcolm Turnbull, maiden speech)
2   Malcolm Turnbull, Connections WJ Craig Lecture, Melbourne, 24 November 2005
3   Malcolm Turnbull and Jeromey Temple, 'Taxation reform in Australia: some alternatives and indicative costings', 1 August 2005

Chapter 11   First rung on the ladder: parliamentary secretary

1   Malcolm Turnbull, speech at Press Club, Adelaide, 22 November 2006
2   Later to become the director of the Australian Christian Lobby and campaigner against same-sex marriage
3   John Howard, *Lazarus Rising*, HarperCollins, Sydney, 2010, p. 617

Chapter 12   Water is for fighting over

1   Australia, House of Representatives, *Debates*, 8 August 2007, pp. 4–9 (Malcolm Turnbull, second reading speech)

Chapter 13   Surviving 2007

1   Australia, House of Representatives, *Debates*, 29 March 2007, pp. 100–4 (Malcolm Turnbull, ministerial statement)
2   Australia, House of Representatives, *Debates*, 15 August 2007, pp. 2–5 (Malcolm Turnbull, second reading speech)
3   Phillip Coorey, 'Back off, Turnbull warned, as the arguments begin', *Sydney Morning Herald*, 13 September 2008

Chapter 14   Leader of the opposition

1   Malcolm Turnbull, speech at National Press Club of Australia, Canberra, 24 November 2008
2   Australia, House of Representatives, *Debates*, 3 February 2009, pp. 15–18 (Malcolm Turnbull, second reading speech)
3   Malcolm Turnbull, Sir Robert Menzies Lecture, Melbourne, 8 October 2009
4   Australia, House of Representatives, *Debates*, 12 February 2009, pp. 1269–70 (Malcolm Turnbull)
5   Australia, House of Representatives, *Debates*, 14 May 2009, pp. 3973–80 (Malcolm Turnbull, second reading speech)

6 Australia, House of Representatives, *Debates*, 9 February 2009, p. 686–9 (Malcolm Turnbull)
7 Peter Costello and Malcolm Turnbull, conversation, 2009

Chapter 15   Climate, denial and downfall
1 John Howard, speech at AIG annual dinner, Canberra, 13 August 2007
2 Rupert Murdoch, speech at forum, Tokyo, 7 November 2006
3 Australia, Prime Ministerial Task Group on Emissions Trading, *Report of the Task Group on Emissions Trading*, Department of Prime Minister and Cabinet, Barton, June 2007
4 Paul Kelly, 'Howard's policy change without the real passion', *The Australian*, 6 June 2007
5 'Malcolm and the malcontents', *Four Corners*, ABC TV, 9 November 2009
6 Malcolm Turnbull, 'Statement regarding an emissions trading scheme', media statement, 24 July 2009
7 Dennis Shanahan, 'We must vote for ETS: Abbott', *The Australian*, 24 July 2009
8 Malcolm Turnbull, speech at Hunter Business Chamber luncheon, Hunter Valley, 1 September 2009
9 'Turnbull still best to lead Coalition', *Courier-Mail*, 26 November 2009
10 'Turnbull's chance to rebuild', *Sydney Morning Herald*, 26 November 2009
11 Laurie Oakes, interview with Malcolm Turnbull, *Today on Sunday*, Nine Network, 29 November 2009
12 '"We're close friends," Turnbull reminds Hockey', *The Australian*, 1 December 2009

Chapter 16   A dark aftermath
1 Australia, House of Representatives, *Debates*, 8 February 2010, pp. 578–82 (Malcolm Turnbull, second reading speech)
2 Australia, Prime Ministerial Task Group on Emissions Trading, *Report of the Task Group on Emissions Trading*, Department of Prime Minister and Cabinet, Barton, June 2007, p. 6
3 Phillip Coorey, 'Turnbull to quit politics', *Sydney Morning Herald*, 6 April 2010
4 Malcolm Turnbull, 'Unlike politicians, the threat of global warming is here to stay', *Sydney Morning Herald*, 7 April 2010
5 Malcolm Turnbull, private diary, 26 April 2010
6 Ibid., 29 April 2010
7 'Turnbull confirms he'll stay in politics', ABC News, 1 May 2010, www.abc.net.au/news/2010-05-01/turnbull-confirms-hell-stay-in-politics/417554
8 Stephanie Peatling and Heath Aston, 'Climate's right for the return of the man who would be PM', *The Sun-Herald*, 2 May 2010

Chapter 17   Back from the edge and back on the frontbench
1 'Kevin Rudd's polling since 2006', *Australian Financial Review*, 24 June 2010
2 Julia Gillard and Wayne Swan, joint press conference, Parliament House, Canberra, 24 June 2010
3 Malcolm Turnbull, 'Axed and humiliated: someone should give this poor bastard a hug', *Sydney Morning Herald*, 30 June 2010
4 Peter Hartcher, 'Gillard rocked by leaks', *Sydney Morning Herald*, 28 July 2010
5 Phillip Hudson, 'A new fight: Gillard ditches campaign script for the "real" Julia', *Courier-Mail*, 2 August 2010
6 *Channel Ten News*, Channel Ten, 16 August 2010

Chapter 18   The NBN
1 Data over cable service interface specification
2 Hybrid-fibre coaxial
3 Paul Fletcher, *Wired Brown Land*, NewSouth Books, Sydney, 2009

4 Figure collated from NBN Co, *Annual Report 2013–14*, NBN Co Ltd, Sydney, 30 June 2014, p. 21; NBN Co, *Annual Report 2018*, NBN Co Ltd, Sydney, 30 June 2018, p. 25
5 NBN Co, 'National Broadband Network: rollout information', 17 January 2020; 30 June 2013
6 Information provided to author by NBN Co, January 2020

Chapter 19   The 43rd parliament
1   Malcolm Turnbull, private diary, 20 November 2012
2   Ibid., 28 February 2011
3   Ibid., 31 May 2011
4   Ibid., 20 July 2011
5   Malcolm Turnbull, Inaugural Virginia Chadwick Memorial Foundation Lecture, Sydney, 21 July 2011
6   'Respect science in great climate divide', *Australian Financial Review*, 23 July 2011
7   Turnbull, private diary, 6 September 2011
8   Ibid., 17 September 2012
9   Ibid., 9 October 2012
10 Ibid., 21 June 2012
11 Ibid., 29 June 2012
12 Ibid., 13 and 20 November 2012
13 United Nations High Commissioner for Refugees
14 Turnbull, private diary, 19 September 2011
15 Ibid., 19 June 2012
16 Ibid., 22 June 2012; see also 'GMG and the Scott Trust: key questions answered', *The Guardian*, 23 July 2015
17 Turnbull, private diary, 22 January 2012
18 Australia, House of Representatives, *Debates*, 14 August 2012, pp. 8493–6 (Malcolm Turnbull, statement on indulgence)
19 *Q&A*, ABC TV, 19 March 2012
20 Australia, House of Representatives, *Debates*, 9 October 2012, pp. 11581–5 (Julia Gillard)
21 Turnbull, private diary, 9 January 2013
22 Ibid., 5 December 2012
23 Ibid., 4 February 2013; see also Tony Abbott and Russell Matheson, joint doorstop interview, Campbelltown, 2 March 2013
24 Turnbull, private diary, 21 March 2013
25 Ibid., 26 March 2013
26 Ibid., 27 March 2013
27 Ibid., 14 April 2013
28 Phillip Coorey, 'Turnbull preferred to lead Liberals', *Australian Financial Review*, 17 June 2013
29 Turnbull, private diary, 18 June 2013
30 Dennis Shanahan, 'Labor out of the doldrums as Rudd picks up where he left off', *The Australian*, 1 July 2013
31 Turnbull, private diary, 15 July 2013
32 Ibid., 28 and 29 July 2013. For example, a poll from 19 July 2013, by ReachTEL for the Seven Network, showed the Coalition leading Labor 58 to 42 per cent on a two-party preferred basis with Turnbull as the leader, as opposed to 51 to 49 with Abbott as leader. Heath Aston, 'Opinion polls now turn around to threaten Abbott', *Sydney Morning Herald*, 20 July 2013
33 Turnbull, private diary, 4 August 2013
34 Ibid., 7 September 2013

Chapter 20 Tony and Peta

1 Malcolm Turnbull, private diary, 25 January 2014
2 Malcolm Turnbull, letter to George Brandis, 24 March 2014
3 Turnbull, private diary, 24 March 2014
4 Ibid., 31 March 2014
5 Ibid., 5 April 2014
6 Ibid., 30 September 2014
7 Ibid., 24 February 2014
8 Crosby Textor, 'Federal qualitative research strategic memo', 7 May 2015

Chapter 21 'Not like you do, Alan'

1 Malcolm Turnbull, private diary, 28 May 2014
2 Latika Bourke and Mark Simkin, 'PM Tony Abbott declares support for Malcolm Turnbull after Bolt's leadership speculation branded "crazy, unhinged"', ABC News, 2 June 2014, www.abc.net.au/news/2014-06-02/turnbull-rebukes-unhinged-bolt-over-leadership-speculation/5493684
3 Phillip Hudson, 'Abbott pinned down by budget', *The Australian*, 3 June 2014
4 Alan Jones, interview with Malcolm Turnbull, *The Alan Jones Breakfast Show*, Radio 2GB, 5 June 2014
5 Turnbull, private diary, 5 June 2014
6 'The ambitious minister for miscommunications', *The Australian*, 3 June 2014; 'Malcolm's excellent adventure', *The Australian*, 6 June 2014
7 'Nation needs to hear true message on fixing budget', *Weekend Australian*, 7 June 2014
8 *Insiders*, ABC TV, 8 June 2014; 'Best leader of the Liberal Party', Essential Report, 3 June 2014, essentialvision.com.au/best-leader-of-the-liberal-party-4
9 Turnbull, private diary, 30 June 2014
10 James Massola and Lisa Cox, 'Tony Abbott vows to "shirtfront" Vladimir Putin over MH17 tragedy', *Sydney Morning Herald*, 13 October 2014
11 James Massola and Ben Grubb, 'Data retention hokey pokey', *Sydney Morning Herald*, 9 August 2014
12 Turnbull, private diary, 7 August 2014
13 Ibid., 24 September 2014
14 Mark Kenny, 'Gough Whitlam's lesson for today's politicians: Stand for something and get stuff done', *Sydney Morning Herald*, 24 October 2014

Chapter 22 Arise, Sir Phil the Greek

1 Malcolm Turnbull, private diary, 14 November 2014
2 Ibid., 5 December 2014
3 Samantha Maiden, 'Joe Blow: Turnbull tops Hockey as preferred treasurer', *Sunday Herald Sun*, 7 December 2014
4 Turnbull, private diary, 9 December 2014
5 Ibid., 14 December 2014
6 Matthew Knott, 'A determined love: Malcolm Turnbull calls for Australians to stay united following Martin Place tragedy', *Sydney Morning Herald*, 16 December 2014
7 Turnbull, private diary, 21 December 2014
8 Ibid., 30 December 2014
9 Ibid., 31 December 2014
10 Ibid., 16 January 2015
11 Ibid., 22 January 2015
12 Jessica Marszalek, 'The wrong tone', *Courier-Mail*, 28 January 2015
13 Turnbull, private diary, 28 January 2015
14 Ibid., 31 January 2015
15 Ibid.

16 Ibid., 2 February 2015
17 Leigh Sales, interview with Scott Morrison, *7.30*, ABC TV, 2 February 2015
18 Samantha Maiden and Simon Benson, 'Plan to appoint Turnbull treasurer', *The Sunday Telegraph*, 8 February 2015

Chapter 23   A very dangerous prime minister
1 John Lyons, 'Tony Abbott in command, but is Peta Credlin in control?', *The Australian*, 21 February 2015
2 Tony Abbott, national security statement, Australian Federal Police Headquarters, Canberra, 23 February 2015
3 In 2014, Australia's GDP at market exchange rates was US$1.5 trillion. World Economic Outlook Database, International Monetary Fund, October 2014
4 Malcolm Turnbull, private diary, 20 March 2015
5 Ibid., 12 April 2015
6 Phillip Hudson, 'Budget win for voters, economy … and PM', *The Australian*, 18 May 2015
7 Turnbull, private diary, 24 May 2015
8 Ibid., 25 May 2015
9 Simon Benson and Neil Doorley, 'Pledge against grip of jihadis', *The Daily Telegraph*, 26 May 2015
10 Simon Benson, 'Coalition backbench turns on Malcolm Turnbull and Julie Bishop for opposing laws to strip citizenship from terrorists', *The Daily Telegraph*, 1 June 2015
11 Malcolm Turnbull, Paul Fletcher and Peter Hendy, joint doorstop interview, Queanbeyan, 3 June 2015
12 Turnbull, private diary, 5 June 2015
13 Ibid., 11 June 2015

Chapter 24   'It was all a bit of a shock': leader again
1 Malcolm Turnbull, private diary, 14 July 2015
2 Ibid., 15 July 2015
3 Ibid., 30 July 2015
4 Ibid., 31 July 2015
5 Michael Brissenden, interview with Malcolm Turnbull, *AM*, ABC Radio, 3 August 2015
6 Turnbull, private diary, 17 August 2015
7 Ibid., 20 August 2015
8 Liberal opposition leader in Victoria
9 Liberal opposition leader in South Australia
10 Turnbull, private diary, 22 August 2015
11 Samantha Maiden, 'Stop the karma bus: Joe Hockey, this is where you get off', *The Sunday Telegraph*, 30 August 2015
12 Turnbull, private diary, 1 September 2015
13 Ibid., 3 September 2015
14 Ibid., 5 September 2015
15 Ibid., 10 September 2015
16 Ibid., 14 September 2015
17 Malcolm Turnbull, press conference, Parliament House, Canberra, 14 September 2015
18 For example, Phillip Coorey, 'Ruddslide: polls show Labor increasing its lead', *Sydney Morning Herald*, 12 March 2007
19 According to Crosby Textor, 'Federal track', 14 August 2015, Labor led in the marginal seats by 56 to 44 and on the basis of self-nominated preference allocation by 61 to 39. The Liberal primary vote was at 33 per cent, with Labor at 38 per cent and the Greens at 18 per cent. Shorten was ahead of Abbott as preferred PM by 46 per cent to 33 per cent, and Abbott's net favourability was –38. By contrast, mine was +32, and Julie Bishop's +25
20 Turnbull, private diary, 14 September 2015

Chapter 25 'We did it, Baba!': prime minister

1 Malcolm Turnbull, doorstop interview, Canberra, 20 September 2015
2 Lisa Cox, 'There will be no wrecking, no undermining, and no sniping: Abbott's final statement as prime minister', *Sydney Morning Herald*, 15 September 2015
3 Malcolm Turnbull and Tony Abbott, telephone conversation, 23 December 2015
4 Malcolm Turnbull, Mathias Cormann, Christopher Pyne and Scott Morrison, group conversation, WhatsApp, 1 November 2016
5 Malcolm Turnbull and Michaelia Cash, joint press conference, Melbourne, 14 September 2015
6 Malcolm Turnbull, speech at Melbourne Institute / Australian 2015 Economic and Social Outlook Conference, Melbourne, 5 November 2015

Chapter 26 Innovation, trade and a *blusukan* with Jokowi

1 16 October 2015
2 Malcolm Turnbull, speech at launch of National Innovation and Science Agenda, CSIRO, Canberra, 7 December 2015
3 William Buck Australia, '2019 venture capital report', William Buck Australia, 8 February 2019, www.williambuck.com/2019-venture-capital-report/
4 As recorded in Damon Kitney, 'BCA chief dispels myths on innovation', *The Australian*, 6 November 2015
5 Malcolm Turnbull and Annastacia Palaszczuk, joint press conference, Southport, 11 October 2015
6 Ash Carter, 'Remarks on the next phase of the US rebalance to the Asia-Pacific', speech at McCain Institute, Arizona State University, Tempe, 6 April 2015
7 Malcolm Turnbull, private diary, 3 October 2015
8 Ibid., 6 October 2015
9 Australia, House of Representatives, *Debates*, 15 October 2015, p. 11398 (Malcolm Turnbull)
10 Turnbull, private diary, 12 November 2015

Chapter 27 'Can you say that again in English, PM?'

1 Malcolm Turnbull, 'Final statement to G20 members', Antalya, 17 November 2015
2 Malcolm Turnbull, speech at United Nations Climate Change Conference, Paris, 30 November 2015
3 Australia, House of Representatives, *Debates*, 24 November 2015, pp. 13483–7 (Malcolm Turnbull, ministerial statement)
4 Greg Sheridan, 'ASIO chief Duncan Lewis "is playing politics" on Islam', *The Australian*, 17 December 2015
5 Samantha Maiden, 'Terror alert', *The Sunday Telegraph*, 13 December 2015
6 For example, Malcolm Turnbull, Karen Andrews and Luke Simpkins, joint doorstop interview, Landsdale, 9 December 2015; Malcolm Turnbull, press conference, Tokyo, 18 December 2015
7 Greg Sheridan, *The Australian*, 17 December 2015
8 David Wroe, 'ASIO briefings', *Sydney Morning Herald*, 17 December 2015
9 Malcolm Turnbull, private diary, 31 December 2015
10 Malcolm Mackerras, 'Turnbull a safe bet to win election in 2016 and 2019', *Canberra Times*, 28 October 2015
11 Andrew Burnes, report on Liberal Party funding, 31 August 2016

Chapter 28 Tax reform and other indiscretions

1 'End to appalling behaviour is at PM's discretion', *Sydney Morning Herald*, 5 January 2016
2 Georgina Mitchell, 'Peter Dutton left red-faced after texting mishap', *Sydney Morning Herald*, 3 January 2016

3   NAB monthly business survey data showed a surge in business confidence immediately after the 2013 election, but these gains slowly eroded over time, and the index declined rapidly from +8 to +1 from June 2015 to August 2015. See NAB Group Economics, 'Monthly business survey: September 2013', NAB, 8 October 2013, business.nab.com.au/monthly-business-survey-september-2013-4761/; NAB Group Economics, 'NAB monthly business survey', NAB, August 2015, business.nab.com.au/wp-content/uploads/2015/09/2015m08-NAB-business-survey.pdf

4   Malcolm Turnbull and Jeromey Temple, 'Taxation reform in Australia: some alternatives and indicative costings', 1 August 2005

5   OECD, 'Personal income tax: top statutory and marginal tax rates for employees', OECD Tax Statistics, accessed 15 December 2019, doi.org/10.1787/data-00806-en

6   Malcolm Turnbull, speech at Australian Chamber Business Leaders' annual dinner, Canberra, 25 November 2015

7   For example, Samantha Maiden, 'PM's plan to cut the debt', *Sunday Herald Sun*, 1 November 2015

8   Treasury brief, 21 January 2016

9   For example, Samantha Maiden, 'Super payday', *The Sunday Telegraph*, 21 February 2016; Samantha Maiden, 'PM aims at top negative gearers', *The Sunday Telegraph*, 21 February 2016

10 Australia, House of Representatives, *Debates*, 23 August 2011, pp. 9058–60 (Bill Shorten)

11 Australia, House of Representatives, *Debates*, 14 March 2012, p. 2857 (Julia Gillard)

12 Chris Bowen, *Hearts and Minds*, Melbourne University Press, Melbourne, 2013, pp. 65–6

13 Australia, Budget Paper No. 3, 'Federal Financial Relations 2019–20', 2 April 2019

14 Australia, Budget Paper No. 1, 'Budget Strategy and Outlook 2019–20', 2 April 2019

Chapter 29   Keeping Australia safe

1   Malcolm Turnbull, press conference, Commonwealth Parliamentary Offices, Sydney, 9 October 2015

2   Duncan Lewis, SMS to Malcolm Turnbull, 9 October 2015

3   James Brown, *Anzac's Long Shadows*, Redback, Melbourne, 2014

4   'Election 2016: Malcolm Turnbull, Bill Shorten honour RSL 100-year anniversary', ABC News, 5 June 2016, www.abc.net.au/news/2016-06-05/turnbull-shorten-honour-rsl-100-year-anniversary/7479436

5   Malcolm Turnbull, speech at launch of Defence white paper, Australian Defence Force Academy, Canberra, 25 February 2016

6   Greg Sheridan, 'PM pushed back Abbott subs date', *The Australian*, 2 March 2016

7   See inter alia Australia, Senate Economics Reference Committee, 'Future of Australia's naval shipbuilding industry (part II): Future submarines', Canberra, November 2014

8   Sam Weir and Malcolm Turnbull, conversation, 2016

9   *Environment Protection & Biodiversity Conservation Act 1999*, s. 140A

10 Australia, Uranium Mining, Processing and Nuclear Energy Review Taskforce, *Uranium Mining, Processing and Nuclear Energy: Opportunities for Australia?*, report to prime minister, Department of Prime Minister and Cabinet, Barton, 2006

11 Derek Woolner and David Glynne Jones, 'Future-proofing the Attack class (part 1): propulsion and endurance', *The Strategist*, Australian Strategic Policy Institute, 14 June 2019, www.aspistrategist.org.au/future-proofing-the-attack-class-part-1-propulsion-and-endurance/

Chapter 30   The element of surprise: proroguing the parliament

1   The quota for elections is $1 / V + 1$, where V is the number of vacancies. See also Damon Muller, '(Almost) everything you need to know about double dissolution elections', Parliament of Australia, 29 April 2016, www.aph.gov.au/About_Parliament/Parliamentary_Departments/Parliamentary_Library/ FlagPost/2016/April/Double_Dissolutions

2   Australia, House of Representatives, *Debates*, 4 November 1992, p. 2549 (Paul Keating)
3   In the 46th parliament, elected in 2019, the seats in the House were increased from 150 to 151
4   Niki Savva, *The Road to Ruin*, Scribe, Melbourne, 2016
5   'Questions on notice: what is prorogation?', Parliament of Australia, 3 September 2019, www.aph.gov.au/About_Parliament/House_of_Representatives/About_the_House_News/News/QoN_Prorogue
6   Peter Hartcher, 'Hopeless ditherer to decisive leader in masterful move', *Sydney Morning Herald*, 21 March 2016

Chapter 31   Cities, Kevin and the budget

1   'City Deals', Australia, Department of Infrastructure, Transport, Cities and Regional Development, last updated 11 October 2019, www.infrastructure.gov.au/cities/city-deals/
2   Peter Mitchell, 'US: Kevin "Ruddovich" avoids Bishop comment', AAP General News Wire, 18 April 2016
3   Malcolm Turnbull, private diary, 2 May 2016
4   Ibid., 16 August 2016
5   Malcolm Turnbull, speech at Westpac 199th anniversary, Sydney, 6 April 2016
6   Turnbull, private diary, 9 May 2016

Chapter 32   The 2016 election

1   Leaders' debate, Windsor, Sydney, 13 May 2016
2   Malcolm Turnbull, private diary, 15 May 2016
3   Bernard Lagan, 'Australian minister says refugees are illiterate and a drain on welfare', *The Times*, 18 May 2016
4   Malcolm Turnbull and Steve Ciobo, doorstop interview, Josef Chromy Wines, Tasmania, 20 May 2016
5   Malcolm Turnbull, 'Refugee comments are a necessary reminder', *The Age*, 20 May 2016
6   An Italian restaurant in Melbourne
7   Member for Stirling, minister for Justice
8   Member for Latrobe, former Victorian police officer
9   Senator for Tasmania, minister for Tourism
10   Member for Deakin
11   Member for Casey, speaker of the House
12   Member for Aston
13   Turnbull, private diary, 25 May 2016
14   Tom McIlroy, 'Election 2016: Bill Shorten's "spend-o-meter" comment explained', *Sydney Morning Herald*, 24 May 2016
15   Andrew Probyn, 'Private Medicare', *The West Australian*, 9 February 2016
16   Australia, House of Representatives, *Debates*, 9 February 2016, pp. 1032–3
17   'Bill Shorten well wide of the mark with Medicare scare campaign', *Australian Financial Review*, 10 February 2016
18   'Medicare payment reforms worth exploring', *Sydney Morning Herald*, 15 February 2016
19   'Tony Abbott has spoken to SBS in the final hours of the 2013 election and promised that there will be no cuts to public broadcasters', SBS News, updated 30 January 2014, www.sbs.com.au/news/no-cuts-to-the-abc-or-sbs-abbott
20   Malcolm Turnbull, speech at federal campaign rally, Sydney, 26 June 2016
21   Malcolm Turnbull, speech at Kirribilli House, Sydney, 16 June 2016
22   Turnbull, speech at federal campaign rally
23   Sexton Marketing Group, 'A 400 sample poll in the federal seat of Warringah', 24 June 2016
24   Estimate provided to the author from network executives
25   2016 Campaign Track Report T3, Day 39, 24 May 2016
26   2016 Campaign Track Report T10, Day 26, 7 June 2016
27   2016 Campaign Track Report T24, Day 4, 28 June 2016

28 2016 Campaign Track Report T25, Day 3, 29 June 2016
29 'Turnbull says he can still form government', ABC News / YouTube, 2 July 2016, youtu.be/K3m3fnU5JgA

Chapter 33   Back in government

1 For a thorough Liberal analysis of the campaign, see Tony Nutt, speech at National Press Club, Canberra, 22 September 2016
2 Malcolm Turnbull, press conference, Parliament House, Canberra, 18 July 2016
3 Louise Yaxley and Lucy Sweeney, 'Greg Hunt admits Katherine mayor Fay Miller not the only recipient of his strong language', ABC News, first posted 31 May 2018, updated 1 June 2018, www.abc.net.au/news/2018-05-31/greg-hunt-says-sorry-to-katherine-mayor/9818938
4 Malcolm Turnbull, private diary, 2 October 2016
5 This was on 22 December 2016
6 Malcolm Turnbull, message to Martin Parkinson, WhatsApp, 19 August 2016
7 Malcolm Turnbull, 'Australia's national statement in the general debate of the 71st session', speech at United Nations General Assembly, New York, 21 September 2016
8 Malcolm Turnbull, Michael Keenan and Andrew Colvin, joint press conference, Sydney, 23 December 2016

Chapter 34   China and the region

1 Malcolm Turnbull, 'Same bed different dreams', speech at London School of Economics, London, 5 October 2011
2 Thomas L. Friedman and Michael Mandelbaum, *That Used to Be Us: How America Fell Behind in the World It Invented and How We Can Come Back*, Picador, New York, 2011
3 Turnbull, 'Same bed different dreams'; see also Henry Kissinger, *On China*, Allen Lane, London, 2011
4 Turnbull, 'Same bed different dreams'
5 Malcolm Turnbull, doorstop interview, Manila, 14 November 2017
6 A theory of Graham Allison set out in his 2017 book, *Destined for War* (Scribe, Melbourne), to the effect that when one great power threatens to displace another, war almost always follows. This is derived from the first chapter of Thucydides's *History of the Peloponnesian War* (431 BCE), in which he wrote, 'What made war inevitable was the growth of Athenian power and the fear which this caused in Sparta.'
7 Malcolm Turnbull, speech at 16th IISS Asia Security Summit, Shangri-La Dialogue, Singapore, 2 June 2017
8 Andrew Clark, 'Sydney Uni's Michael Spence lashes government over "Sinophobic blatherings"', *Australian Financial Review*, 28 January 2018
9 Australia, House of Representatives, *Debates*, 7 December 2017, pp. 13145–9 (Malcolm Turnbull, second reading speech)
10 James R. Clapper, statement concerning Russian interference in the 2016 United States election, before Committee on the Judiciary, Subcommittee on Crime and Terrorism, United States Senate, Washington, DC, 8 May 2017
11 Rachel Baxendale, 'Kristina Keneally accuses Turnbull of "fuelling suspicion of Asians"', *The Australian*, 13 December 2017
12 Caitlyn Gribben, 'Malcolm Turnbull declares he will "stand up" for Australia in response to China's criticism', ABC News, 9 December 2017, www.abc.net.au/news/2017-12-09/malcolm-turnbull-says-he-will-stand-up-for-australia/9243274
13 *Q&A*, ABC TV, 11 December 2017
14 Glenda Korporaal, 'China delivers trade warning amid strain on ties', *The Australian*, 30 April 2018
15 Malcolm Turnbull, speech at University of New South Wales, Sydney, 7 August 2018; Australia, House of Representatives, *Debates*, 17 November 2014, pp. 12720–6 (Xi Jinping)
16 Unclassified statement from the Australian Signals Directorate

Chapter 35   Matters of trust: reforming intelligence and Home Affairs
1   Christopher Pyne, message to Scott Morrison, WhatsApp, 7 March 2017

Chapter 36   Trump
1   'Executive order protecting the nation from foreign terrorist entry into the United States', White House, Washington, DC, 27 January 2017
2   Greg Miller, Julie Vitkovskaya and Reuben Fischer-Baum, '"This deal will make me look terrible": full transcripts of Trump's calls with Mexico and Australia', *The Washington Post*, 3 August 2017
3   Greg Miller and Philip Rucker, '"This was the worst call by far": Trump badgered, bragged and abruptly ended phone call with Australian leader', *The Washington Post*, 2 February 2017
4   Malcolm Turnbull, private diary, 6 May 2017
5   Mother of all bombs
6   Malcolm Turnbull, message to Steven Mnuchin, WhatsApp, 16 April 2018
7   Malcolm Turnbull, letter to Donald Trump, 27 April 2018
8   Australia, New Zealand, United States Security Treaty

Chapter 38   A very wild year: 2017
1   Malcolm Turnbull, 'Statement on parliamentarians' expenses', press release, 14 January 2017
2   A 12-metre-long launch with three crew, designed for ceremonial occasions
3   Malcolm Turnbull, speech at National Press Club, Canberra, 1 February 2017
4   David Crowe, Sarah Martin and Simon Benson, 'Malcolm Turnbull rejects calls to deny banks tax cut', *The Australian*, 18 February 2017
5   Scott Morrison, message to Malcolm Turnbull, WhatsApp, 18 February 2017
6   Luke Howarth, message to Malcolm Turnbull, WhatsApp, 18 February 2017
7   Michael Sukkar, message to Malcolm Turnbull, WhatsApp, 18 February 2017
8   Scott Morrison, message to Malcolm Turnbull, WhatsApp, 18 February 2017
9   Matthias Corman and Malcolm Turnbull, conversation, WhatsApp, 21 March 2017
10   Ibid.
11   Australia, House of Representatives, *Debates*, 8 February 2017, p. 294 (Malcolm Turnbull)
12   Malcolm Turnbull, private diary, 4 March 2017
13   Ibid., 16 October 2017
14   Indonesia-Australia Comprehensive Economic Partnership Agreement
15   In a desperate effort to hold on to the seat of Bass in the 2007 election, Prime Minister Howard and Health Minister Abbott had agreed to take over and operate the Mersey hospital, which the Tasmanian government was proposing to close; it was a very expensive gesture and did not save the seat
16   Mathias Cormann, message to Malcolm Turnbull, WhatsApp, 7 April 2017
17   Malcolm Turnbull, message to Mathias Cormann, WhatsApp, 7 April 2017
18   Sharri Markson, 'Treasurer Scott Morrison 'emasculated' by colleagues', *The Daily Telegraph*, 14 April 2017
19   From which I had returned the day before, 13 April 2017
20   Malcolm Turnbull, message to Scott Morrison, WhatsApp, 14 April 2017
21   Simon Benson, 'Treasurer takes his revenge on the banks: "cry me a river"', *The Australian*, 10 May 2017

Chapter 39   Same-sex marriage
1   Malcolm Turnbull, private diary, 12 December 2011
2   Malcolm Turnbull, 'Reflections on gay marriage', Michael Kirby Lecture, Gold Coast, 7 July 2012
3   Turnbull, private diary, 11 February 2013
4   Ibid., 12 August 2013

5 Ben Schneiders and Farrah Tomazin, 'The religious minority seizing power in the Liberal Party', *The Age*, 3 June 2018

6 Francisco Perales and Alice Campbell, 'Who supports same-sex marriage in Australia? And who doesn't?', ABC News, 31 August 2017, www.abc.net.au/news/2017-08-31/same-sex-marriage-who-supports-it-and-who-doesnt-hilda-data/8856884

7 Turnbull, private diary, 7 July 2015

8 Deidre McKeown, *Chronology of Same-Sex Marriage Bills Introduced into the Federal Parliament: A Quick Guide*, Research Paper Series 2017–18, Parliamentary Library, Canberra, 2018

9 Turnbull, private diary, 12 November 2015

10 Originally reported in Dennis Shanahan, 'Federal election 2016: Bill Shorten flips on gay marriage plebiscite', *The Australian*, 29 June 2016

11 Turnbull, private diary, 3 September 2015

12 Australia, House of Representatives, *Debates*, 14 September 2016, pp. 845–8 (Malcolm Turnbull, second reading speech)

13 Mathias Cormann, message to Malcolm Turnbull, WhatsApp, 1 December 2016

14 Turnbull, private diary, 19 March 2017

15 Andrew Bolt, 'Pyne cheers as PM trashes Libs', *Herald Sun*, 26 June 2017

16 Malcolm Turnbull, message to Christopher Pyne, WhatsApp, 26 June 2017

17 Christopher Pyne, message to Malcolm Turnbull, WhatsApp, 27 June 2017

18 Peter Dutton, message to Malcolm Turnbull, WhatsApp, 16 July 2017

19 Paul Karp, 'Marriage equality postal vote to be challenged in High Court by Andrew Wilkie and advocates', *The Guardian*, 9 August 2017

20 Amy Remeikis, 'Malcolm Turnbull, FM radio star: inside the PM's rejigged radio strategy', *Sydney Morning Herald*, 5 September 2017

21 Phillip Coorey, 'Fran and Leigh, Fitzy and Wippa: they all get a vote', *Australian Financial Review*, 8 September 2017

22 Turnbull, private diary, 10 October 2017

23 Malcolm Turnbull and Mathias Cormann, conversation, WhatsApp, 15 November 2017

24 Australia, House of Representatives, *Debates*, 7 December 2017, p. 13144 (Malcolm Turnbull, third reading speech)

Chapter 40   Giving a Gonski

1 Australia, House of Representatives, *Debates*, 3 June 2013, pp. 4772–3 (Malcolm Turnbull)

2 Malcolm Turnbull, private diary, 3 May 2017

3 Australia, Department of Education and Training, *Through Growth to Achievement: Report of the Review to Achieve Educational Excellence in Australian Schools*, Canberra, 2018

4 Malcolm Turnbull, Simon Birmingham and David Gonski, press conference, Sydney, 2 May 2017

5 Malcolm Turnbull and Anthony Fisher, telephone conversation, 8 May 2017

Chapter 42   And another one bites the dust: the citizenship crisis

1 Malcolm Turnbull, private diary, 24 July 2017

2 Malcolm Turnbull, message to George Brandis, WhatsApp, 12 August 2017

3 Australia, House of Representatives, Debates, 14 August 2017, p. 8265 (Malcolm Turnbull)

4 Phillip Coorey, 'You can blame the Poms, not the wogs, for this citizenship crisis', *Australian Financial Review*, 10 November 2017

5 *Sue v Hill* (1999) 199 CLR 462

6 *Re Canavan; Re Ludlam; Re Waters; Re Roberts [No 2]; Re Joyce; Re Nash; Re Xenophon* [2017] HCA 45 (27 October 2017) [71]

7 Malcolm Turnbull, press conference, Perth, 3 November 2017

8 Turnbull, private diary, 3 November 2017

9 Australia, House of Representatives, *Debates*, 6 December 2017, pp. 12875–7 (Malcolm Turnbull)

Chapter 43   Culture, opportunity and respect
1 Australia, House of Representatives, *Debates*, 10 February 2016, pp. 1171–5 (Malcolm Turnbull, ministerial statement)
2 Australia, House of Representatives, *Debates*, 26 February 2009, pp. 2034–8 (Malcolm Turnbull)
3 Craig Ritchie, letter to Malcolm Turnbull, 5 September 2018
4 Malcolm Turnbull, Alan Tudge and Rick Wilson, doorstop interview, Kalgoorlie, 1 September 2017
5 Ritchie to Turnbull, 5 September 2018
6 Ibid.
7 Australia, House of Representatives, *Debates*, 14 February 2017, pp. 895–900 (Malcolm Turnbull, ministerial statement)
8 Michael Brissenden, 'PM announces Royal Commission into abuse at NT youth detention centre', interview with Malcolm Turnbull, *AM*, ABC Radio, 26 July 2016
9 Michael Gunner and Malcolm Turnbull, conversation, 9 December 2019
10 Australians voted on the question 'Do you approve the proposed law for the alteration of the Constitution entitled "An Act to alter the Constitution so as to omit certain words relating to the people of the Aboriginal race in any state so that Aboriginals are to be counted in reckoning the population"?'
11 Australia, Joint Select Committee on Constitutional Recognition of Aboriginal and Torres Strait Islander Peoples, *Final Report*, Parliament, Canberra, 2015, pp. viii, 10

Chapter 44   Barnaby and the bonk ban
1 Simon Benson, 'Newspoll: PM surges as pressure increases on Shorten', *The Australian*, 5 February 2018
2 Malcolm Turnbull, press conference, Parliament House, Canberra, 15 February 2017
3 Malcolm Turnbull, private diary, 17 February 2018

Chapter 45   Diplomacy, disloyalty and turning the corner on debt
1 Andrew Bolt, 'Coalition MP: Turnbull must be sacked or I'll quit', *Herald Sun*, 20 November 2017
2 Andrew Bolt, 'George Christensen wimps it', *Herald Sun*, 3 December 2017
3 Angus Taylor, message to Malcolm Turnbull, WhatsApp, 1 December 2017
4 Andrew Clennell, 'Secret plan to cut back on migrants', *The Australian*, 10 April 2018
5 Scott Morrison, message to Malcolm Turnbull, WhatsApp, 15 April 2018
6 Peter Dutton, message to Malcolm Turnbull, WhatsApp, 14 April 2018
7 Malcolm Turnbull, private diary, 10 April 2018
8 Australia, Productivity Commission, *Horizontal Fiscal Equalisation: Inquiry Report*, no. 88, Canberra, 2018, p. 11

Chapter 46   Climate denial and the National Energy Guarantee
1 United Nations Climate Change, 'What is the Paris Agreement?', United Nations Framework Convention on Climate Change, 2020, unfccc.int/process-and-meetings/the-paris-agreement/what-is-the-paris-agreement
2 Note that the NEM operates on the east coast only. Australian Energy Market Operator, 'National Electricity Market', 2020, www.aemo.com.au/Electricity/National-Electricity-Market-NEM
3 Australian Competition and Consumer Commission, *Restoring Electricity Affordability and Australia's Competitive Advantage: Retail Electricity Pricing Inquiry; Final Report*, Canberra, June 2018, p. 49
4 Malcolm Turnbull, message to Will Hodgman, WhatsApp, 9 February 2017
5 Expert Panel, *Blueprint for the Future: Independent Review into the Future Security of the National Electricity Market*, Australia, Department of the Environment and Energy, Canberra, June 2017

6 Australian Energy Market Operator, *Gas Statement of Opportunities: For Eastern and South-Eastern Australia*, Melbourne, March 2017
7 Malcolm Turnbull, Arthur Sinodinos and Matt Canavan, doorstop interview, Incitec Pivot, Gibson Island, 27 April 2017
8 Tony Abbott, doorstop interview, Port Moresby, 10 September 2015
9 As recorded in Josh Frydenberg, message to Malcolm Turnbull, WhatsApp, 14 June 2017
10 Ibid., 22 June 2017
11 Alan Jones, *The Alan Jones Breakfast Show*, Radio 2GB, 12 July 2017
12 Mathias Cormann, message to Malcolm Turnbull, WhatsApp, 11 August 2018
13 Phillip Coorey, 'The next energy war will be over emissions all the way to the election', *Australian Financial Review*, 15 August 2018
14 Simon Benson and Joe Kelly, 'Retreat on Paris emissions target may not save Malcolm Turnbull', *The Australian*, 18 August 2018

Chapter 47   The coup
1 Scott Morrison, message to Malcolm Turnbull, WhatsApp, 18 August 2018
2 Simon Benson, Dennis Shanahan and Joe Kelly, 'PM's leadership on knife edge', *The Australian*, 20 August 2018
3 Craig Laundy, message to Malcolm Turnbull, WhatsApp, 21 August 2018
4 Malcolm Turnbull and Scott Morrison, conversation, WhatsApp, 21 August 2018
5 Nikki Savva, 'Daggers drawn on eve of downfall', *Weekend Australian*, 29 June 2019
6 David Crowe, 'Radio host Ray Hadley in storm over Peter Dutton text message', *Sydney Morning Herald*, 22 August 2018
7 Malcolm Turnbull, Mathias Cormann and Scott Morrison, press conference, Parliament House, Canberra, 22 August 2018
8 Simon Benson, 'Morrison backers doing the numbers', in 'PoliticsNow: MPs calling for party room meeting to be held tonight', *The Australian*, 22 August 2018, www.theaustralian. com.au/nation/politics/politicsnow-malcolm-turnbull-faces-uphill-struggle-to-stay-pm/ news-story/2f25eab196bbe3e1c74225e687ae8e89
9 Hugh Riminton, 'Constitutional cloud emerges over Peter Dutton's business interests', 10 Daily, 20 August 2018, 10daily.com.au/news/politics/a180820xwi/constitutional-cloud-emerges-over-peter-duttons-business-interests-20180820
10 Malcolm Turnbull, press conference, Parliament House, Canberra, 23 August 2018
11 Rowan Ramsey and Malcolm Turnbull, conversation, WhatsApp, 24 August 2018
12 Malcolm Turnbull, press conference, Parliament House, Canberra, 24 August 2018
13 Malcolm Turnbull and Scott Morrison, conversation, WhatsApp, 24 and 25 August 2018
14 Mathias Cormann and Malcolm Turnbull, conversation, WhatsApp, 11 September 2018
15 George Brandis, letter to Malcolm Turnbull, 29 August 2018
16 Tony Nutt, *2018 Victorian State Election Review: Report to the Administrative Committee*, Liberal Party of Australia (Victorian Division), Melbourne, October 2019, p. 75

Index

Acknowledgements

One of the most dangerous parts of any politician's speech is the acknowledgements; the list of the various dignitaries that are present. A mention is rewarded with at best a mild purr, more often an indifferent nod. But an omission may never be forgiven.

It is impossible to acknowledge all those to whom I owe so much.

So with great apprehension I begin.

In some ways this book is a love story because most of it, like most of my life, has been the story of Lucy and me. Meeting and marrying her was my greatest good fortune. We have been together for more than 40 years. I have a better sense of Lucy and me than I do of me. My greatest debt, my deepest thanks, will always be to Lucy.

As an only child I don't have a large family but as you have read I was very fortunate to have a great father and my mother, while not a consistently maternal role model, instilled in me values of scholarship and literature that stayed with me all my life. Bruce's second wife, Judy, became and remained a dear friend.

Our children, Alex and Daisy, and their spouses, Yvonne and James, have given us love, support and such joy, not least of which are their children, Jack, Isla, Alice and Ronan, all of whom at one time or another, like their parents, have been roped into political duties.

Lucy has a much larger family than me, and the Hughes clan over the years have always been good friends and supporters – especially Lucy's father, who taught me so much about advocacy, her mum, Joanna, and her stepmother, Chrissie. Her brothers, Tom and Mike, and their families have been more than relatives, but good friends and political, legal and commercial allies as well.

So many great friends and mentors. Among those not already mentioned are, in journalism Trevor Sykes, and in law, Tony Mason and Aleco Vrisakis. And so many good friends, too many to name and more than I deserve, but including Bruce and Nicky McWilliam, Andrew and Amanda Love, and Michael and Judy McMahon. From Goldman Sachs, Tim Dattels, Carlos Cordeiro and James del Favero. And the North Bondi Surf Club, including Peter Moscatt, John Cahill and Peter Switzer from my youth, and from today, Grant McMah and Mark Cotter.

I have worked with many wonderful colleagues and partners about all of whom I could have written colourful chapters. Many of them are mentioned in this book, but too many are not, such as my learned friends and rivals at the Bar and the journalists at *The Sunday Times*, *The Bulletin* and Channel Nine.

I have been very lucky in my business partners, especially Lucy! I have stayed friends with almost all of them including Bruce McWilliam, Theo Onisforou,

Gary Weiss, Kerry Schott, David Spence, Sean Howard, Trevor Kennedy, and Russell and the wider Pillemer clan. It's wonderful to be working again with Nick van der Ploeg as I return to venture capital. On the farming side of our business, Libby McIntyre managed East Rossgole for about five years after Bruce was killed, and since 1992 our farms in the Hunter have been managed by Guy Thomas and his wife, Tricia. In these dry times especially, thank you.

If you need a small platoon of supporters in business, in politics you need an army. Whether it was the republican campaign of the 1990s or my parliamentary political career I have had the backing of so many Australians.

The great Wentworth preselection battle alone required thousands of supporters. There are too many to list, but I couldn't have done it without the help of Jason Falinski, Alex Calvo and Adam Schofield, who controlled the Point Piper branch which swelled to be the party's biggest. Since those days the branch has been led for many years by our dear friend Judy Crawford, as the Wentworth conference has been by John O'Sullivan.

Rounding up new members needed a big team which included Scott Briggs, Russell Pillemer, Gary Perlstein, John O'Sullivan, Michael Taouk, Michael Carr, Danni Roche, Deborah Hutton, Mark Coppleson, Fiona and Mark Playfair, Trevor and Judy Atherton, Bev Martin, Mary-Lou Jarvis, Tony Marano, Robin Crawford and dozens of others. No friend was left unrecruited, and without exception they swung in behind me.

I couldn't have got there without great political guides and mentors including Andrew and Penne Peacock, Shane Stone, Lynton Crosby, Mark Textor, Bill Heffernan, Susan Atwill, Nancy Gorton, Nick Greiner, Michael Yabsley and of course John Howard.

All politics is local and the first duty of any MP is to look after their own electorate. I had a great team in my Wentworth office, many of whom went on to work for me in my ministerial and leadership roles. The Wentworth team included mayor of Waverley and Liberal Party stalwart Sally Betts, Anthony Orkin, Tommy Tudehope (who later ran social media in the PMO), Jack Pinczewski, Aneta Vasilevska, Bruce Notley-Smith and in more recent years Jacqui Munro, Jaimi Primrose-Levi, Kathryn McFarlane, Alice Collins-Gallagher, Whitney Brennan and Tanya Doyle. Darel Hughes made sure the Wentworth conference's finances were always in order.

Speaking of finances, throughout my time in politics Sue Collins and for the last decade or so Laura Jacobsen have looked after our family finances and crucially ensured that my members' interest disclosures have been accurate and up to date. Glenys Hess has handled our tax affairs and while I was PM Josephine Linden managed our financial investments. Anything to do with a prime minister's finances is nerve-racking work, so thank you.

Throughout my career as a minister, shadow minister, leader of the opposition and as prime minister, I had talented and loyal teams. Our offices were always respectful places to work.

Sally Cray has worked with me almost continually since 2006 and in the process became an honorary daughter and one of Daisy's best friends. She was my principal private secretary when I was prime minister. In that role she ran the political side of our office, managing some of the most complex relationships in the parliament and in the party. Most importantly she oversaw my schedule, ensuring that the office did not, in its enthusiasm, 'kill the candidate'. Sally's good humour was legendary and her laugh, like Lucy's and Daisy's, could be heard from one end of the building to the other.

Sally was supported by our close friend, the calmly determined David Bold. Much of our success in getting legislation through the Senate was due to David's ability to work with a fractious crossbench, not to speak of our own Coalition colleagues and the opposition. He was skilfully aided by Ben Bartlett, another Senate whisperer. Sam Harma, Sarah Wood, Jocelen Griffiths, Luke Nayna, Annabell Shaw and Ebony Richards helped manage the office's liaison with the backbench.

I thank the federal directors of the Liberal Party during my time, Lynton Crosby, Brian Loughnane, Andrew Hirst, and especially the incomparable Tony Nutt, whose dedication to the party is unrivalled. He always gave wise and considered advice, generally laced with historical analogies both ancient and modern.

The worst job in politics, worse even than being opposition leader, is being honorary treasurer of the Liberal Party. I know. Andrew Burnes held that poisoned chalice during my time. Thank you!

Melissa Chan and Jacqui Kempler were both brilliant advisers and programme managers, and it's great to be working again with Melissa today, as I am with Emily Zatschler.

My chiefs of staff as PM were Drew Clarke, Greg Moriarty, Peter Woolcott and Clive Mathieson. They all ensured the office worked harmoniously and policy was developed and delivered.

As Drew used to say, the scarcest resource in the Commonwealth government is the prime minister's time. I had very capable executive assistants managing my diary including Sue Cox, Jenny Brennan, Sam Cusack and Di Honan. Manning the phones in the PMO is dangerous work – often the calls are very frank and not always polite. Shannon Armstrong and Monica Vasileska were among the many patient and courteous receptionists in the front line.

I have had many brilliant economic advisers including, in the PMO, Kat Di Marco, Alex Robson, Elise Little, Peter Hendy, and as opposition leader, Paul Lindwall. Stephen Ellis and Jon Dart made an immense contribution in every way, above all in helping put together our plan to restructure the NBN. In the PMO, Mark Brudenell and Ali McDonald (both of whom were also with me in Communications) made vital contributions to delivering the National Innovation and Science Agenda.

It is hard to describe what Alistair Campbell did other than to say his brilliant mind contributed to every aspect of our work. Whether it was statistics, data scraping social media, political and public service gossip, budget modelling – nothing seemed beyond him. He was supported by crack researcher Andrew Hallam.

Foreign policy and national security are at the heart of every prime minister's work and I had a great team. My principal international advisers were Frances Adamson, Greg Moriarty and Philippa King. Justin Bassi handled national security and was supported by Pete Anstee and for a period John Garnaut.

Madonna Morton was an excellent education adviser – her fingerprints are all over Gonski 2.0. Cindy 'Matron' Barry was deft in helping craft the new hospital deals in 2016. She was succeeded by Cath Patterson, who advised on health and education from 2018.

Bruce Male advised me on environment and water, both when I was Environment minister in Howard's government and when I was PM. Sid Marris shrewdly advised me on energy. Other senior policy advisers included Nigel Everingham (industry), Mark Wood (health and ageing) and Chris Daffey (infrastructure). Michael Napthali and Alix Collins (arts), Alison Green (corporate and government). Hellen Georgopoulos was my CoS in Environment. Richard Windeyer was my CoS in Communications, aided by Jenelle Frewen.

After Arthur Sinodinos had restored order to the cabinet office, he was succeeded by the very efficient Simon Atkinson as cabinet secretary, assisted by Sue Kruse, David Hughes, Jodie Doodt and Sarah Gall among others.

Communications and the media, both mainstream and social, are right at the heart of every political office and I was very well supported throughout my time as PM. In addition to those already mentioned, our media team included Brad Burke, Tony Parkinson, Mark Simkin, Hayden Cooper, Daniel Meers, Chloe Younan, Gemma Daley, James Murphy, Amy Keenan, Matt Moran, Liam O'Neil, Caitlin Keage, Tom Adolph, Chelsea Lahav and David Allender as well as the indestructible veteran Tony O'Leary.

Sahlan Hayes was a wonderful friend and photographer. Together with videographer Tony Walters and social media wizards Tommy Tudehope and Larissa Moore we were able to maintain an engaging social media stream that bypassed the mainstream media.

The advancers who ensured my outings did not result in disaster were indefatigable. They were led by Janelle Walker and included Emily Zatschler, Alice Hermes, James Hart and Vincent Woolcock, who had advanced for every Liberal leader since Malcolm Fraser.

Thank you too to the staff at The Lodge and Kirribilli House led by house managers Trina Barry and Adam Thomas. They always made us feel at home, whether it was a formal dinner for a visiting president or a very casual evening with the grandchildren.

The Australian Federal Police did a superb job keeping me safe wherever I was and provided the static guards around our house. They were often supported by the state police, especially the NSW water police who followed me around the harbour when I was out kayaking. Most importantly they kept as low a profile as possible so I didn't feel stifled by the security bubble. And they appeared to enjoy my frequent trips on public transport which I always preferred to the armour-plated C1.

There aren't many roles more difficult than writing speeches for me. All my team made a contribution, but especially Tony Parkinson, John Garnaut and most recently Rebecca Rose. However, only Sally Cray helped write a speech in real time, amending the Google Doc to add a new paragraph while I was at the lectern!

There is no shortage of lawyers in Canberra, but there are few as talented as legal advisers Daniel Ward and Amy Dobbin.

I owe a great debt, as does our nation, to the Australian Public Service, led for most of my time as PM by Martin Parkinson, and equally to all our defence, security and intelligence services. Their professionalism and dedication are examples, indeed reproaches, to the politicians whose agendas are all too often self-interested.

There are dozens of MPs and senators referred to in my book, and many more I worked with who are not. But while I have had happy and unhappy experiences with many colleagues (often the same), I could not have achieved anything in politics and government without them.

Likewise with the Liberal Party itself. It is always a turbulent, and often a troubled, institution. But it remains the largest grassroots political organisation in Australia, and without the support of its members, especially in Wentworth, I could not have been elected to parliament, let alone have been a minister or prime minister. And for that support, much thanks.

My appreciation is due to Hardie Grant Books. Their director Sandy Grant has published all my books and was the managing director of Heinemann during the *Spycatcher* trial. His team on this book included publisher Arwen Summers, editor Anne Reilly, project editor Emily Hart, marketing and publicity manager Kasi Collins and managing director Roxy Ryan.

This book covers so many years and events; the research has been enormous. I couldn't have written it without the help of many of my old team including Daniel Meers, James Hart, Alice Collins-Gallagher, Emily Zatschler and Melissa Chan. Thanks, too, to the Parliamentary Library. Kerry Pinkstone helped with the chapter on First Australians; Philippa King, Justin Bassi, Pete Anstee and John Garnaut helped with the foreign policy and national security chapters. Jon Dart, JB Rousselot and Bill Morrow reviewed the NBN chapter.

Lucy, Daisy, Sally Cray, David Bold and Ben Bartlett also helped recall and confirm events and read the chapters as I wrote them, making many editorial suggestions. Daisy brought to my book the same forthright attention to detail she shares with her students. Clive Mathieson, returning to his former editorial avocation, was kind enough to read the whole draft and provide comments.

I couldn't have finished the book without their help. Thank you.